EVERYMAN'S LIBRARY

EVERYMAN,
I WILL GO WITH THEE,
AND BE THY GUIDE,
IN THY MOST NEED
TO GO BY THY SIDE

WILLIAM SHAKESPEARE

Romances

with an Introduction by Tony Tanner
General Editor – Sylvan Barnet

—

EVERYMAN'S LIBRARY

229

First included in Everyman's Library, 1906

These plays are published by arrangement with New American
Library, a division of Penguin Books USA, Inc.

Pericles: Copyright © 1965 by Ernest Schanzer. Copyright © 1963, 1988 by
Sylvan Barnet.
Cymbeline: Copyright © 1968, 1988 by Richard Hosley. Copyright © 1963,
1988 by Sylvan Barnet.
The Winter's Tale: Copyright © 1963, 1988 by Frank Kermode. Copyright ©
1963, 1988 by Sylvan Barnet.
The Tempest: Copyright © 1964, 1987 by Robert Langbaum. Copyright ©
1964, 1987 by Sylvan Barnet.

Introduction © Tony Tanner, 1996
Bibliography and Chronology © David Campbell Publishers Ltd.,
1996
Typography by Peter B. Willberg

ISBN 1-85715-229-8

A CIP catalogue record for this book is available from the
British Library

Published by David Campbell Publishers Ltd., 79 Berwick Street,
London W1V 3PF

Distributed by Random House (UK) Ltd.,
20 Vauxhall Bridge Road, London SW1V 2SA

Typeset by Acc Computing, Castle Cary, Somerset
Printed and bound in Germany
by Graphischer Grossbetrieb Pössneck GmbH

ROMANCES

CONTENTS

_____

Introduction

Romance	xiii
Pericles	xxix
Cymbeline	lvi
The Winter's Tale	xci
The Tempest	cxxviii
Select Bibliography	clxiii
Chronology	clxxii
PERICLES	1
CYMBELINE	113
THE WINTER'S TALE	257
THE TEMPEST	375

something rare
Even then will rush to knowledge.
                    (*The Winter's Tale* III, i, 20–21)

INTRODUCTION

ROMANCE

> feigned nowhere acts
>
> (Thomas Nashe)

> Did you ever dream of such a thing?
>
> (*Pericles* IV, v, 5)

> The dream's here still. Even when I wake it is
> Without me, as within me; not imagined, felt.
>
> (*Cymbeline* IV, ii, 306–7)

> Your actions are my dreams.
>
> (*The Winter's Tale* III, ii, 80)

> And rather like a dream than an assurance
>
> (*The Tempest* I, ii, 45)

> The imagination may be compared to Adam's dream – he awoke
> and found it truth.
>
> (John Keats, *Letters*)

Trying to differentiate and distinguish the characteristic features of 'romance' and 'realism', Henry James came up with a characteristically surprising image:

The real represents to my perception the things we cannot possibly *not* know, sooner or later, one way or another; it being but one of the accidents of our hampered state ... that particular instances have not come our way. The romantic stands, on the other hand, for the things that, with all the facilities in the world, all the wealth and all the courage and all the wit and all the adventure, we never *can* directly know; the things that can reach us only through the beautiful circuit and subterfuge of our thought and our desire ... The only *general* attribute of projected romance that I can see, the only one that fits all its cases, is the fact of the kind of experience with which it deals – experience liberated, so to speak; experience disengaged, disembroiled, disencumbered, exempt from the conditions that we usually know attach to it ... The balloon of experience is in fact of course tied to the earth, and under that necessity we swing, thanks to a rope of remarkable length, in the more or less commodious car of the imagination; but it is by the rope that we know where we are, and from the moment that cable is cut we are at large and unrelated: we only swing apart from the globe – though remaining as exhilarated, naturally, as we like, especially when all goes well. The art of the romancer is 'for the fun of it' insidiously to cut the cable.

Attempting to work out the implications of the extended metaphor, we might offer something like this – the imagination can travel a long way from the surface of reality, i.e. the earth. In a 'romance', sometimes we feel we are still in touch, however remotely, with the earth, and sometimes we sense we no longer are. That 'rope' would seem to be something like our sense of relative plausibility – 'our general sense of the way things happen' in James's own words. But it may be a very tenuous rope, and, still following the image, it may prove difficult to say whether the rope is cut or not. As James recognized with another image. 'It is as difficult ... to trace the dividing-line between the real and the romantic as to plant a milestone between north and south ...' It is, of course, not difficult to plant that milestone between north and south; it is impossible. Or rather such an act of demarcation is arbitrary, and decreed and controlled by convention; either imposed by authority, or agreed by consensus. To be *really* real, James discovers, the novel must incorporate 'romance'.

James was writing as a late nineteenth-century novelist. Not so very many years before this, in the 1870s, another Victorian, Edward Dowden, was the first to designate Shakespeare's Last Plays as 'Romances'*. By then the word had acquired a lot of semantically blurred luggage since the time it simply meant a tale in a vernacular Romanic language – 'Isn't it romantic?' is not the sort of question worth going into here. The Elizabethans and Jacobeans used the word of stories but not of dramas. Shakespeare never used the word at all – not of plays,

---

*The first person to use 'romantic' in connection with Shakespeare seems to have been Coleridge. '*The Tempest*, I repeat, has been selected as a specimen of the romantic drama; i.e. of a drama, the interests of which are independent of all historical facts and associations, and arise from their fitness to that faculty of our nature, the imagination I mean, which owes no allegiance to time and place – a species of drama, therefore, in which errors of chronology and geography, no mortal sins in any species, are venial, or count for nothing.'

not of anything. Yet, bearing in mind the contemporary
Jacobean uses of the word, Dowden's classification is an astute
and helpful one. And James's tentative definition of generic
romance as dealing with experience 'liberated ... disengaged,
disembroiled, disencumbered, exempt from the conditions
that we *usually* know attach to it' (my italics) is appropriate to
bear in mind as we approach these last plays by Shakespeare,
dealing as they do with the *un*usual and extraordinary – even
the seemingly 'miraculous' – in human experience. But we
should also bear in mind James's recognition that you cannot
finally demarcate 'romance' from 'the literally true' – and
perhaps also Mervyn Peake's brave affirmation from the depths
of great suffering that 'to live at all is miracle enough'.
'Wonders will never cease' is a popular saying; and that's
literally true in Shakespeare's Romances, in which an almost
unceasing wonder comes to prevail. It may be that the rope
to that Jamesian balloon is both always cut and never permanently severed.

But, eschewing further paradox, let us be more, relatively
speaking, mundane. Here is Dr Johnson to keep our feet, and
our balloons, on the ground. 'In romance, when the wide field
of possibility lies open to invention, the incidents may easily
be more numerous.' In other words – anything can happen,
endlessly. The romance tale permitted, or rather encouraged,
a copious abundance of incident, with little or no concern for
verisimilitude, plausible links of cause and effect, or clear
continuity. A romance invariably concerns the course of true
love running very rough indeed. It comes out all right *in the
end* – poetic justice is always, satisfactorily, done and seen to
be done. But before that, *anything* can happen – distressed
damsels in danger and heroic knights in armour, losings in
the forest and findings in the court, shipwrecks and pirates,

---

And this is Edward Dowden in his *Shakespeare* (1877): 'He seems to have
learned the secret of life, and while taking his share in it, to be yet disengaged
from it ... In these "Romances" ... a supernatural element is present ...
Shakespeare's faith seems to have been that there is something without and
around our human lives, of which we know little, yet which we know to be
beneficent and divine.' I owe this footnote to Ian Donaldson.

traps and escapes, evil queens and beneficent magicians, death and resuscitation, danger and rescue, desolation and comfort, disguise and recognition, enigmas from oracles and salvation by gods. And, as Nabokov would say, much, much more.

The Elizabethans did not employ the word 'romance' much, though the noun had been around since the thirteenth century (the adjective 'romantic' arrives in the seventeenth century). Yet there were at least two incalculably influential Elizabethan romances – Sidney's *Arcadia* (of which more in a moment), and Spenser's *The Faerie Queene*. And, crucially for our present interest (and Shakespeare's plays), there had been a series of translations of early Greek romances from the middle of the sixteenth century onwards. These romances date from the second and third centuries AD. They are episodic, processional 'quest' stories, involving perilous journeys and final recognitions and reunions. We find in them the origin of the heroine figure, such as she appears in Shakespeare's Last Plays. Too much detail would distract us unnecessarily here and I will allow a scholar in the field to summarize. Here is Carol Gesner:

In Greek romance the 'quest' usually is begun when a pair of youthful lovers – frequently married – are separated. Their desire for reunion usually motivates the journey. The minor episodic adventures frequently include storm and shipwreck, followed by various combinations of brigands, pirates, brothel keepers, poisoners, and kidnappers. Usually the hero and heroine experience imprisonment, slavery, and attempted seduction. The great crisis frequently comes to the heroine rather than to the hero: as a result of some misfortune she falls into an unconsciousness so deep that it is mistaken for death. Eventually she is restored to the hero, most often at the conclusion of the romance in a trial-like recognition scene in which all mysteries and mistakes are explained and all loose threads are knitted up again.

The most important of them are – the *Babylonica* of Iamblichus (the motif of apparent death occurs four times); *Chaereas and Callirrhoe* of Chariton of Aphrodisia (in which the resourceful heroine is so beautiful she is mistaken for a goddess – like Pastorella in *The Faerie Queene*, the prototype for some of Shakespeare's heroines); *Apollonius of Tyre*, known to us only through a sixth-century Latin translation (this provides almost the entire plot of *Pericles*); the *Aethiopica* of Heliodorus of Emesa (which has a wicked stepmother, oracular dreams, grief over a dead body mistakenly thought to be that of a beloved, insistence on the heroine's virginity – immemorially associated with magic power and central for Shakespeare); *Daphnis and Chloe* by Longus (crucial for its pastoral setting); *Leucippe and Cleitophon* by Achilles Tatius (apparent death and resurrection, oracular dreams, emphasis on the heroine's virginity, and so on). It can be seen at once how many of the themes and motifs of these early prose romances turn up in Shakespeare's Last Plays either through direct appropriation or by refraction through the work of others – though some of them are, of course, as old as folk tale itself. And what Shakespeare makes of them is itself a wonder.

The romance world is one of extremes – the good are very good, the evil very evil; the noble are beautiful, the bad are ugly. Frank Kermode aptly describes this as 'an extension of platonic realities into the phenomenal world'. There is small concern for psychological and narrative plausibility – the attention is turned, rather, to the mysterious more-than-human forces and powers which seem to shape and determine human fates, rough hew them how we will. These may be Chance, Fortune, an inscrutable Providence, or even Divinity itself, and there is often a tendency towards theodicy, even theophany whereby the gods not only look down but come down (note that Shakespeare's deities appear *in dreams* – which I suppose you could call hedging his bets). This should not be regarded as showing an inclination to illustrate and reinforce an orthodox religion (which would produce allegory, at best,*) but rather a desire to grasp and display those times

---

*I will just note here that until quite recently, there was a persistent drive to 'explain' the Last Plays in terms of – or perhaps co-opt them for – anthropology or religion. I quote some wise words of John Danby. 'The first of these has been based on *The Golden Bough* and the fertility cycle and rebirth. The second has been similarly based on the Christian conception of regeneration and resurrection. Neither, I think, is as satisfactory as the contemporary and conventional scheme which Shakespeare used. Anthropology does not take us far enough. By its insidious precipitations it tends to silt over the clear and sharp contours of the Renaissance moral world. The second explaining system errs in the opposite direction. It carries us too far and too fast. It particularizes in a field of meaning beyond Shakespeare's

continued on next page

and events in life when it *seems* that something transcendent gleams through the usually less radiant texture of sublunary human doings and affairs. But it *is* important to bear in mind that the English humanist romancers were all Protestants, and for Protestants, as Howard Felperin pointed out, life itself was a matter of continuous trial and tribulation, so that the tests and trials in, say, *The Faerie Queene* and *Arcadia* inevitably have some relation to, and flavour of, the tests and trials of an exemplary Christian life. (As Felperin remarks, the Christian epic itself – paradise, the fall, expulsion, the wanderings and buffetings of history, salvation, paradise regained or heaven – was the canonical romance of both medieval and Renaissance culture, so there was bound to be a strong pull for secular romances to adopt something of its ethical and eschatalogical system.) And here I must say a little about Sidney's *Arcadia*.

Deprecated today ('a monument of dullness' – T. S. Eliot, one of his less happy pronouncements), this was 'for a century and a half the best-loved book in the English language'(John Buxton). Between 1590 and 1638 there were seventeen issues. But although it contains just about every adjunct, accessory and feature of romance tales, down to marauding bears and revealing birthmarks, it is arguably more important for the philosophy and spirit which informs it. And this 'is something gravely moral, Christian, and Renaissance, in spite of its Greek names and pre-Christian terminology'. I quote John Danby. He has written very illuminatingly on the *Arcadia*, showing that it was Sidney's project to bring classical, romance and chivalric themes 'within the orbit of an instructed Renaissance Christianity'. Danby discerns four interlocking spheres in Sidney's romance world.

---

intention – though Shakespeare, I have no doubt, would know St Paul and the burial service, and accepted the New Testament. To theologize the Last Plays, however, is to distort them. Though patience as Shakespeare conceives it implies St Paul and the New Testament, patience as Shakespeare realizes it in the Last Plays is a familiar and well-walked parish in a wider diocese. Nor is the parish presided over by the Fisher King, and in it St Paul is taken for granted but not allegorized in every Whitsun pastoral.' And Philip Edwards: 'It is a disservice to Shakespeare to pretend that one is adding to his profundity by discovering that his plots are symbolic vehicles for ideas which are, for the most part, banal, trite and colourless.'

INTRODUCTION

There is first the sphere of virtue and attained perfection; then the sphere of human imperfection, political and passionate, surrounding and likely at any minute to threaten the first; around these again, the sphere of non-human accident, chance, or misfortune, the sphere of the sea and storms; and finally, enclosing all, the sphere of the transcendent, guaranteeing after the 'storm or other hard plights' that the ending will be a happy one – given patience.

'Patience' – the Christian virtue (Christus Patiens), not classical Stoic fist-clenched passivity – Danby sees as vital for Sidney (as it is to be for Shakespeare). He quotes Milton deploring the conventional notions of heroical poetry, indicating his loftier intention:

> Warrs, hitherto the onely Argument
> Heroic deem'd, chief maistric to dissect
> With long and tedious havoc fabled Knights
> In Battels feign'd; the better fortitude
> Of Patience and Heroic martyrdom
> Unsung.

> (*Paradise Lost* XI, 28–33)

Sidney himself, writing of the *Odyssey*, said: 'Well may you see Ulisses in a storme, and in other hard plights; but they are but exercises of patience and magnanimitie, to make them shine the more in the neere-following prosperitie.' The usual adversities which characterize the romance tale, for Sidney have a purpose. Danby: 'Fortune is the school of Patience. It leans on and demands the transcendent. It is the point at which the human discovers the divine.' In Sidney's work there is, of course, the external world of events – the realm of endangered heroines and heroic courage; but there is also the inner world of 'the passive and possibly unrewarded virtues – singleness, constancy, devotion, command over one's will and one's possible self-division'. Virtues are as important as fortunes. In line with this new importance of the inner world, it is important to note some of the literal components of romance moving into metaphor. Thus, for example, there is no more recurrent feature of the romance than danger at sea – for Sidney, and Shakespeare too. But, in the *Arcadia*, when Pyrocles leaves Musidorus, the latter exclaims: 'Pyrocles, what means this alteration? ... Heretofore I have accused the sea, condemned the pirates, and hated my evil fortune that deprived me of thee; but now thyself is the sea which drowns my comfort ...' Again, Sidney describes Antiphilus as being 'suddenly borne into an ocean of absolute power, he was swayed withal, he knew not how, as every wind of passion puffed him'. The terms of romance now apply to the inner environment as well; and in this topography the most important qualities are Christian patience allied with Aristotelian magnanimity. This is as true for Shakespeare as it is for Sidney.

'Nothing almost sees miracles/But misery' says Kent in the stocks (*King Lear* II, ii, 168–9). That tragedy stresses the *almost* – heart–breakingly. The Last Plays delete it. It is as if we, and the characters, *do* see miracles. There is a new mood of enhanced wonder and an intensified lyricism of reconciliation in Shakespeare's last four plays which sets them apart from the problem comedies and outright tragedies which preceded them; though we should remember that there are all sorts of adumbrations and foreshadowings – preparations for, gestures towards, tentative anticipations of – the materials and themes of these last romances throughout Shakespeare's work – from the beginning indeed, starting with *The Comedy of Errors*. We might briefly consider them as a group.

I start with a quotation from Philip Brockbank:

We may say of Shakespeare's Last Plays that each is about the renewal of creative life in an afflicted state of society. In each a miraculous providence works, through different agencies, to saving purpose. But in each an element of self-confessed artifice qualifies the auspicious outcome to remind us that the ultimately reassuring moral order that can be displayed to us in the theatre is indeed theatre; it cannot be transposed too promptly into 'fact' – the verity of it is under suspicion.

That 'element of self-confessed artifice' is crucial. Wilson Knight writes with customary thrilled eloquence of these plays as being 'myths of immortality' and one can see what he means. At the same time, we must recognize that they offer little or no reassurance of life after death, or survival in the life-ever-after to come. The miracles and resurrections are staged, sometimes doubly so, as when Paulina, in *The Winter's*

Tale, arranges a theatrical coup (a 'statue' starting to move), a performance which is itself Shakespeare's *coup de théâtre*. Which is not to deny that the plays are in themselves 'miracles' (literally – wonderful things, objects of wonder).

Brockbank's point may be reinforced in another way by John Danby:

Shakespeare during the last period is comparatively relaxed. He makes a toy of thought ... we might describe the plays of the final period as works in which formula, and schema, and intelligent manipulation, are the dominant things. Up to 1606 Shakespeare was growing. His works are an existential record of his growth. After that time all his work seems to be that of a man who has got things finally clear and is no longer worried. Not only are things clear, they are almost cut and dried. Shakespeare now can engage or disengage himself just as far as he wishes. He can be unanxious, he can even be careless. All the time, certainly, he can preserve that attitude which Sidney Greville called *ironia* ... I have myself no doubt that the last plays are less serious than those of the tragic period ... we are taken by beauty continually. The last plays are the fancies of a Lear dreaming of Cordelia refound. They exist at a remove from reality. They give us a schema for life rather than the life itself.

I will come back to 'dreaming'. Of course, in all this periodizing of Shakespeare's life, it behoves us to remember that it is quite undiscoverable whether Shakespeare himself knew that these *were* his 'last' plays: he might simply have been embarking on new experiments in the medium of which he was, by now, complete master. (The idea that he was trying to imitate the younger and successful Beaumont and Fletcher is both unverifiable and unconvincing – by this stage in his career Shakespeare had no need to copy anyone. Similarly, there is no evidence that he was adapting to new conditions obtaining in the indoor theatre, Blackfriars, taken over by Shakespeare's company in 1608.) But he does seem to have 'sailed into a calm' with the writing of these plays.

At the same time, there is much that is harsh and painful – anti-romantic – in these last plays; something more than the wind and the rain that were gathering in the later comedies. Jaques and Touchstone ironize and mock the Duke's benign vision of life in the Forest of Arden, but they do not threaten it in the way Antonio and Caliban do Prospero's island. It is good for Leontes and Hermione to be reunited and reconciled after sixteen years; but they have lost, irreparably, irrecoverably, perhaps the best years of their lives. There is always some residual bitterness in the sweetness. These last plays 'subsume tragedy in the process of transcending it', as Felperin puts it. The suffering and loss of Pericles remind us of Lear; in the insanely furious jealousy of Leontes we hear again Othello; the humiliation of Imogen and Hermione is only just less fatal than the treatment meted out to Desdemona and Cordelia. Felperin: 'side by side with the magical speech-music exist the harshest cacophonies of the tortured soul familiar from the great tragedies'. And there is a major difference from the comedies. There, the obstacles to felicity which have to be circumvented are erected by paternal interdiction, bad law, or some perverse individual. In the Romances, while there are certainly evil agents, one feels that there is something in the very nature of things which can work to obstruct, interrupt, and delay human happiness.

But also something which can work to restore it. The deep feeling that after winter comes the spring runs throughout these plays. The key mythic figure here is Proserpina, specifically invoked by Perdita who effectively becomes her. Marina is Proserpina from the sea, while Proserpina's mother, Ceres, is summoned to bless Miranda. We are back with Ovid. 'The Rape of Proserpine' is told in *Metamorphoses*, Book V. Prior to her abduction by Pluto, we are told that it is 'always spring', which means the Golden Age – 'Springtime it was, always, for ever spring'. The rape of Proserpina, and her return from Hades for six months of the year, effectively marks the start of the Silver Age which saw the coming of the seasons and agriculture:

> Then Jupiter
> Curtailed the pristine spring and led the year
> Through winter, summer, autumn's varying days
> . . .
> Then in long furrows first were set the seeds
> Of grain and oxen groaned beneath the yoke.

While we are with the Ages, we might note that in the last,

'hard' Age of Iron, when 'all evil straight broke out', for the first time 'men sailed the sea'. Given the importance of voyages, and shipwrecks – not to mention the very hard presence of evil – in the Last Plays, we might think of them as showing an Iron Age world finally blessed with a Silver Age restoration. Proserpina returns to earth.

Just as, in Jonathan Bate's words, 'Ovid returns to the surface of the drama.' He points out that one of the effects of Perdita on the winter court was – 'Who was most marble there changed color' (*The Winter's Tale* V, ii, 96–7), which alludes to what is perhaps Ovid's 'most celebrated story of artistic creation' – that of Pygmalion, who somehow coaxes and caresses his statue of a beautiful girl into life (Book X). As Bate points out, there are some dark aspects of the story which Shakespeare omits, concentrating instead 'on three positive aspects of the story: the power of the imagination or wish-fulfilment, the magic of the awakening, and, crucially, the art that outdoes nature'. Nature restoring nature, and art outdoing nature, are two potencies everywhere under consideration in the Last Plays: it would not be wrong to think of them as, in some way, presided over by the spirits of Proserpina and Pygmalion. And Diana, 'the tutelary goddess of the Last Plays' in Danby's view. Chastity – and virginity – play a vital role in these plays. Proserpina returning figures fertility, and fertility requires seedings and couplings. The Last Plays are, indeed, centrally concerned with love, and the triumphs of love. But it is a very chaste, chastened love – there is little trace of the erotic here (Venus is explicitly banished in the masque in *The Tempest*). For instance, the act by which Pericles begat Marina is occluded, or idealized, by choric Gower:

> Hymen hath brought the bride to bed,
> Where by the loss of maidenhead
> A babe is molded.

> (III, Gower 9-11)

The point was neatly made by Carol Neely, who also noted that, in the Romances, on the one hand raw male sexual power tends to be blunted or transmuted into benign forms, while, on the other hand, 'mothers are not merely absent but are explicitly dead or else die or apparently die in the course of the play'. This allows female sexuality to be represented by the chaste innocence of younger daughters, with a resultant shift of emotional and dramatic emphasis to father–daughter bonds. With the exception of Imogen, already a wife (albeit a very chaste one), the heroines, aged between fourteen and sixteen, are noticeably younger than Shakespeare's other heroines, apart from Juliet. In comparison with Marina, Perdita and Miranda, Portia, Beatrice, Rosalind, Viola and Helena, while chaste enough, seem positively worldly-wise, and quite capable of engaging in a certain amount of controlled sexual banter and innuendo unthinkable in their innocent young successors. These totally virtuous, idealized, even conventionalized, beautiful young figures, more universal than individual, merit Sidney's description of his Arcadian Philoclea. Adversity, and indeed anything else, 'could no more imperfect her perfections than a die any way cast could lose its squareness'.

Shakespeare was never one to concern himself over-much with the unities of time and place, and he was certainly never concerned, as a neo-classical dramatist like Ben Jonson was, to make time passing on the stage the same as time passing for the audience. But in the Last Plays (with the curious exception of *The Tempest*), he plays fast and loose with time and place as never before: the action in *Pericles* takes place 'dispersedly in various Countries', and there are scenes in six different cities; while we have a fourteen-year gap here, a sixteen-year interval there – in these plays, Time, as they say, *flies*. And even appears on stage, to let us know it.

Enter Time, the Chorus.

I that please some, try all, both joy and terror
Of good and bad; that makes and unfolds error,
Now take upon me, in the name of Time,
To use my wings. Impute it not a crime
To me, or my swift passage, that I slide
O'er sixteen years, and leave the growth untried
Of that wide gap, since it is in my pow'r
To o'erthrow law, and in one self-born hour
To plant, and o'erwhelm custom. Let me pass;

INTRODUCTION

The same I am, ere ancient'st order was
Or what is now received.
. . .
Your patience this allowing,
I turn my glass, and give my scene such growing
As you had slept between.

(The Winter's Tale IV, i, 1–17)

We have had devouring time, injurious time, 'envious and calumniating time'; and we have seen how the 'unfolding' power of time became increasingly important for Shakespeare, a mysterious, invisible, inexorable process by which 'error' and evil were finally exposed. Now, with Time standing on the stage, chatting to the audience while amiably turning his glass, he is beginning to look suspiciously like Shakespeare himself, saying to the spectators: with your permission, I can do anything. Time has become wax in his hands. He can even make us feel we have been asleep.

A recurrent feature of the Last Plays is characters experiencing what Brockbank called 'a rapture of recognition'. Northrop Frye remarked that this 'spirit of reconciliation ... is not to be ascribed to some personal attitude of his own, but to his impersonal concentration on the laws of comic form'; quoting this, Kermode comments: 'In the Romances, this act of concentration was focused on the recognition, which was to be studied with a new intensity and thoroughness in relation to romance-plots; for it has a special force in these extensive tales of sundered families, wandering kings, and lost princesses.' In a not very helpful way it could be said that simply to read a book is to enact a recognition scene of one kind or another (the Greek words are close: 'anagnostes' = reader, 'anagnorisis' = recognition). But given the special importance of 'recognition' in the Romances, it might be worth saying a little about its more general centrality for literature (here I must recommend Terence Cave's fine book *Recognitions*, from which I am taking some material). Early recognition scenes invariably involved the revelation of true identity and the re-establishment of kin. The Ur figures, or paradigms, are Oedipus and Odysseus. Odysseus knows who he is and who are his, and becomes a witting imposter to regain his own; while

Oedipus is an unwitting imposter who has to find out who he is and who his own really are. Odysseus occults his identity until he can be safely recognized by his wife; Oedipus is after the occulted facts about his parents. Either way, the recognition – felicitous or tragic – is of kin. There were always possible extensions to these motifs. For instance in New Comedy, which is dependent on disguises, secrets and confusions, as well as false identities, the recognition is a disclosure to all of 'what has been done', and is not limited to the emergence of unforeseen or hidden kinship relations. (We have seen Shakespeare making use of these devices in his early comedies.) Clearly the notion of 'recognition' may be extended, or attenuated, so that the object recognized may be a relation, a state of affairs, a fact, a higher order, a hidden law, a truth about Being, a truth about self, or something so elusive that you lose it in the act of trying to find and speak it.

But Cave points to a potentially more complicated and disturbing aspect of 'recognition'. He calls recognition a 'scandal', not only because recognition plots are often about a scandal (incest, murder, adultery), but also because they represent 'a shift into the implausible'. What emerges is 'a sense of a means of knowing which is different from rational cognition. It operates surreptitiously, randomly, elliptically and often perversely, seizing on precisely those details that from a rational point of view seem trivial.' From Aristotle on there has been an attempt to differentiate a 'low' sort of recognition plot, involving birthmarks and scars and rings and what-not, and a 'high' kind, registering the discovery of order, causality, harmony, truth. And, as Cave brilliantly shows, it can't be done. The higher recognition seems to celebrate an order and offers a sense of security, while the lower suggests that we are laughably, worryingly, appallingly, at the mercy of randomness and contingency, bits of matter which happen to turn up, or fail to. But the distinction will not hold and the higher is always infected with traces or hints of the lower. For no evidence is absolutely conclusive, no proof is total. Can Penelope be *absolutely* sure that the man she goes to bed with is Odysseus? A recognition scene thus affords a not-quite-complete reassurance.

The recognition scene shows that the beast can be caught – or at least that *a* beast can be caught: but the magic has to be constantly repeated to exorcize all the times it hasn't worked and *we haven't noticed*: the hanging of the innocent man, the survival of the impostor, the adultery or incest that continues concealed and unchecked, the bastard brought up as the rightful heir.

Thus, Cave suggests, a residual unease and anxiety can be traced in even the most triumphant and satisfying recognition scenes.

I want to make one more general point about the Last Plays. The epigraphs I used for this section indicate that all these plays in some way participate in the 'nowhere' realm of dreaming. In this connection Allardyce Nicoll has an interesting point to make concerning the Court Masque. Shakespeare knew about masques of course, and used them. However, Nicoll discounts claims sometimes made, that Shakespeare was directly, even heavily, influenced by the Jacobean masque as it was ushered in at Whitehall by Ben Jonson's *The Masque of Blackness* on 1 January 1605. The appeal of these masques was new, and Inigo Jones's dazzling contributions must have been part of the novel attraction. And, suggests Nicoll, there was one feature which very probably *did* influence Shakespeare – 'the fundamental novelty of Jones's method – the changeability of his scenes'. Palaces, temples, towers 'dissolve' suddenly into each other, and delicate cloud-work contributes to the sense of an 'insubstantial pageant'. Nicoll points us to Prospero's most famous speech, and, as an example, he cites *The Vision of the Twelve Goddesses* by Samuel Daniel (1604). This masque starts with Night waking up her son, sleeping, sleepy Somnus, and asking him to provide some 'pleasing novelties' for the expectant audience:

> And make their slumber to beget strange sights,
> Strange visions and unusual properties,
> Unseen of latter ages, wrapp'd up in mysteries.

Somnus complies:

> Dear mother Night, I your commandment
> Obey, and dreams t' interpret dreams will make
> As waking curiosity is wont
> ...

Be this a temple, there Sibylla stand,
Preparing reverent rites with holy hand,
And so, bright visions, go, and entertain
All round about whilst I'll go to sleep again.

Iris, 'the daughter of wonder' (note), appears in a 'fair Temple of Peace' and announces 'the coming of a celestial presence of Goddesses' to an amazed Sibylla. And as the goddesses duly appear (they include Ceres and Proserpina, and silvery Diana who will also appear in *Pericles* – the 'goddess argentine'), Sibylla's wonder-struck reaction could almost have come from one of Shakespeare's Last Plays:

What have I seen? where am I, or do I see at all? or am I anywhere? was this Iris ... or else but a phantasm or imagination? ... what perspective is this? or what shall I herein see? O admirable Powers! What sights are these?

'Dreams to interpret dreams' could be one, fruitful, way of thinking about Shakespeare's Last Plays. And the, apparently magically produced, changing fleeting spectacles of these later masques could well have contributed significantly to the atmosphere of Shakespeare's Last Plays, in which, says Nicoll, we often 'have the impression that we are floating away into a realm of the spirit and are coming very close to the world of the gods'. I myself think, rather, that we tend to feel 'wrapped up in mysteries' – as we do when we are at the mercy of our own dreams. Only here, Shakespeare is master of the dreams. As he was, of course, in the in some ways anticipatory *A Midsummer Night's Dream.*

The most memorable actual dream in Shakespeare is Clarence's dream in prison, in *Richard III.*

Methought that Gloucester stumbled, and in falling
Struck me (that thought to stay him) overboard
Into the tumbling billows of the main.
O Lord, methought what pain it was to drown!
What dreadful noise of water in mine ears!
What sights of ugly death within mine eyes!
Methought I saw a thousand fearful wracks;
A thousand men that fishes gnawed upon;
Wedges of gold, great anchors, heaps of pearl,

Inestimable stones, unvalued jewels,
All scatt'red in the bottom of the sea.
Some lay in dead men's skulls, and in the holes
Where eyes did once inhabit there were crept,
As 'twere in scorn of eyes, reflecting gems
That wooed the slimy bottom of the deep
And mocked the dead bones that lay scatt'red by.

(I, iv, 18–33)

All the time, his soul is trying to find 'the empty, vast, and wand'ring air' (I, iv, 39); but it is a bad dream and he is drowned, and passes over into 'the kingdom of perpetual night' (I, iv, 47). This strange, rich, undersea realm of wrecks and treasures, where drowned men seem to be being magically transmuted into priceless precious things, is an imaginative world away from the constricted arid land where Richard pursues his grim and gruesome political ends. But it is distinctly closer to the worlds of *Pericles* and *The Tempest*, and more generally to the sense of wonder out of wreckage which pervades the Last Plays. Those 'reflecting gems' which, marvellously, *woo* the bottom of the deep 'in scorn of eyes', *as 'twere*, anticipate 'Those are pearls that were his eyes'. But – *are*. The magic has become literal. The dream is the play.

PERICLES (1608)

What seas what shores what grey rocks and what islands
What water lapping the bow
And scent of pine and the woodthrush singing in the fog
What images return
O my daughter.

(T. S. Eliot, *Marina*)

Did you not name a tempest,
A birth and death?

(V, iii, 33–4)

Gentlemen,
This queen will live

(III, ii, 93–4)

The play opens with the appearance on stage of a single figure who announces that he is the fourteenth-century poet, John

Gower. There was a Chorus in *Henry V*, but to have a long-dead poet coming on to announce (and effectively to direct) the play is something entirely new in Shakespeare. Let's consider what he says:

> To sing a song that old was sung,
> From ashes ancient Gower is come,
> Assuming man's infirmities,
> To glad your ear, and please your eyes.
> It hath been sung at festivals,
> On ember-eves and holidays,
> And lords and ladies in their lives
> Have read it for restoratives.
> The purchase is to make men glorious;
> *Et bonum quo antiquius eo melius.*
> If you, born in those latter times,
> When wit's more ripe, accept my rhymes,
> And that to hear an old man sing
> May to your wishes pleasure bring,
> I life would wish, and that I might
> Waste it for you, like taper-light.
>
> (I, 1–16)

An *old* song, sung by an *ancient* poet – so, for the audience, it is doubly old. Gower has risen from ashes – a miraculous Phoenix-like *resurrection*. He is going to address the *ears* and the *eyes* – he will tell, and he will show. The song is habitually performed at festivals, pre-fasting evenings, and holidays – a customary part of public, communal celebrations. It has been read for its *restorative* power. The 'purchase' (gain or benefit) is to make men 'glorious' – a strange line, to which I will return: followed by the apparent *non sequitur* in Latin, meaning – the more ancient a good thing is the better. Then a final rather self-deprecating, indeed self-sacrificing (wasting), apologetic hope that these wittier 'latter times' will accept his inevitably rather old-fashioned presentations. We have heard this acknowledgment of generational difference before, with the sense that the smart young things no longer have time for the older pieties, as in the King of France's quoting of the late Count Rousillon's feeling of alienation from 'younger spirits, whose apprehensive senses /All but new things disdain' (*All's*

Well that Ends Well I, ii, 60–61). The fundamentals of the play's form and content are, in fact, adumbrated or pre-figured in these lines (my italics act as rather crude pointers), and what we are about to watch and listen to will be emphatically an *old* tale – 'like an old tale … like an old tale still', as the wondering Gentlemen in *The Winter's Tale* keep reiterating (V, ii, 30, 65).

Why this stress on the oldness of the tale (or 'song')? Why is 'ancient Gower' there at all? For a start, it *is* a very old tale, probably from an ancient Greek romance concerning Apollonius (= Shakespeare's Pericles) of Tyre. It survived in a Latin version of the sixth century AD, and it entered the *Gesta Romanorum* (a Latin collection of tales from the thirteenth century – this was the 153rd story), and was disseminated in versions all over Europe. It is the main story in Book VIII (which treats of 'Unlawful love') of John Gower's *Confessio Amantis* (1393), which was Shakespeare's main source – so Gower's appearance as the presiding impresario is very proper. There was also a prose version by Laurence Twine, *The Patterne of Painefull Adventures* (1576 and 1607), which Shakespeare undoubtedly drew on. The adventures of Pyrocles (*sic*) in Sidney's *Arcadia* (1590) might also have been in Shakespeare's mind – shipwrecks, chests from the sea, helping shepherds, found armour, pirates, and so on – though all this may simply argue a common older source. Also relevant are legends of Christian saints, particularly that of St Agnes (again known in many versions from the seventh century onwards). Among other features of her life, she was sent naked to a brothel where an angel protected her life, much to the consternation of the brothel regulars; she also revives an apparently dead Roman. So – yes; old, old, old. ('Some mouldy tale like *Pericles*' – Ben Jonson.)

Just why this particular story should have exerted such a hold on the European imagination (and be it said, going by contemporary evidence, *Pericles* was by some way the most popular of Shakespeare's plays before the theatres were closed in 1642), can only be a matter of speculation – conceivably, it has something to do with the worrying proximity, and the felicitous avoidance, of incest (of all taboos, apparently the most universal). An old tale, then, being again retold. (It may also be an old play rewritten. I will not address the unresolvable question of whether the first two acts are wholly, or partly, by Shakespeare; or not by him at all. The writing there is certainly not in Shakespeare's mature style – Geoffrey Bullough thinks it 'jejune and rigid' – but whether Shakespeare was building on the cruder efforts of a now unknown minor dramatist, or rather taking up one of his own earlier abandoned beginnings and seeing it through to a richer conclusion, is undecidable. But he had shown an interest in this old tale in his very first play and, having alerted readers to alternative theories, I shall treat the whole of *Pericles* as Shakespeare's play.) Shakespeare duly gives his play an 'atmosphere of the antique', as Bullough says, with Gower using obsolete words and forms and having recourse to old-fashioned devices – pageant, ceremonial scenes, *tableau*-like dumb shows, and so on. This makes it all seem curiously distant – violent deeds muffled by frames and long perspectives. But this archaic feel and flavour is hardly gratuitous or diversionary. The implication is, surely, that some old and abiding truths are best displayed in an avowedly archaic ('mouldy') mode, leaving the audience undistracted by innovational technical flair. Brockbank has a more general suggestion: 'It happened at the beginning of the seventeenth century, and would happen again at the end of the eighteenth, that a society with a highly complex and civilized literary culture looked back to old tales and to the Middle Ages in search of rich simplicities, expressed in innocent speech and show.' Shakespeare is de-sophisticating his audience.

'To make men glorious' – Gower's announced intention – was the aim of the medieval legends of the saints and of the miracle plays derived from them (these plays were called simply 'miracles', so if you saw one you could indeed say that you had 'seen a miracle' – relevant for Shakespeare's audience). It was F. D. Hoeniger who first persuasively argued that *Pericles* closely parallels the structure of certain miracle or saints' plays. Such plays (performed all over England from around 1100 to 1580) depicted events and stages in the lives of saints and martyrs, and were like holy romances, showing happiness (or triumph, beatification, salvation – some heavenly reward) after long suffering. You could see romance as a secularized 'miracle'. Here is Hoeniger:

All that was needed in *Pericles* was to carry one step further the process of secularization, already much in evidence in some of the later miracle plays: to replace God or Christ by Diana or Neptune, and the Christian saint or apocryphal character by a prince or princess; for there is no greater difference between the saints' legends and the romance of Apollonius of Tyre. They are both biographical romances. The fate of Pericles, like that of St Andrew or Mary Magdalene or Tobit, is governed by Providence. Like them, he undergoes manifold adventures, which bring upon him great suffering. Like them, he is lifted out of despair by a miraculous-seeming intervention of a god – a Christ or a Diana.

This, then, is the sort of thing that Gower is going to put on for us. By as it were handing over the presentation of the play to Gower, Shakespeare ensures that it is almost entirely undramatic. Gower habitually *tells* (narrates, reports, summarizes) and *then* shows (leaves 'to the judgement of your eye'); the acted scenes are more like illustrations or demonstrations than agonistic discoveries. This means that whatever else the audience experiences, it is seldom suspense, until the final act, when showing effectively overtakes, supplants, and relegates telling, and we are left to witness what T. S. Eliot called 'the finest of the "recognition scenes"'.

An old tale, then; but in fact a very new kind of play which involves evoking and invoking more archaic modes, both of thinking and depicting, of telling and showing. The tale itself is of a prince who leaves his city to seek a bride. A renowned beauty attracts him, but to gain her he must solve a riddle – or forfeit his life. He sees that the answer to the riddle is that the beautiful princess is committing incest with her father, the king. The Prince flees in horror and, after shipwreck, finds himself in a happier kingdom where he wins a fitting bride. Marriage is swiftly followed by pregnancy and, with auguries of felicity, the couple set sail for the Prince's own kingdom. There is another shipwreck, in which the mother apparently dies in childbirth and is buried at sea. The devastated Prince takes the baby girl to another country where seeming friends promise to bring her up alongside their own daughter. Some sixteen years later this traitorous couple plan the murder of the girl, because her many perfections are serving to eclipse their own daughter. The scheme is foiled, and the girl is abducted by pirates, who sell her to a brothel in another country. Just at this time, the Prince (now King) arrives to take his now grown-up daughter back, only to be told that, sadly, she has died. Prostrate with grief, the King enters what seems to be a terminal silence, refusing all human communication. The daughter meanwhile has miraculously chastened the brothel world, and become a renowned and accomplished teacher of the arts. Her father's ship unwittingly puts in at the very port city where she practises her skills. Told of the King's aphasic melancholy, the local ruler suggests that the amazing young girl should be allowed to try out her 'sacred physic' on him. The King initially rebuffs her (in Twine, he kicks her in the face and she falls bleeding; in Gower he punches her; Shakespeare, habitually more sparing of visible violence, has him simply push her away). She persists and recognition follows in due course. An oracular vision reveals that the mother is still alive, having in fact been saved after her sea burial. An ecstatically happy reunion ensues in the temple of Diana, and the profound, simple (archaic) romance pattern of love, loss, and restoration, is completed. Bonds thought severed are rejoined, and the wretchedly scattered and miserably separated family is finally reassembled and at one.

Even thus crudely summarized, the story shows itself to be totally unamenable to neat, tight plotting. There are so many cities; so many spaces and gaps; so much wind-driven hither-and-thithering; so much storm and 'tempest'; such blank stretches of time; such various magics; so much that is utterly, almost unutterably, extra-ordinary – and everywhere the sea, the sea. The climactic recognition scene takes place on board a ship riding at anchor off Mytilene; we actually see Pericles 'on shipboard' helplessly remonstrating with the fierce storm during which his wife (apparently) dies, while at the end he succumbs gratefully to 'this great sea of joys rushing upon me' (V, i, 195); and two key scenes take place on the seashore, that bottomlessly, endlessly suggestive liminal area where our

constitutive elements meet, and the firm gives way to the
flowing – with Pericles emerging from the sea, and Marina (so
named by Shakespeare because she was 'born at sea'), as it
were, returning to it. There is, indeed, a very 'elemental'
feeling to the play – where we come from, what we are
exposed to, to which we will return.

> The river is within us, the sea is all about us;
> The sea is the land's edge also, the granite
> Into which it reaches, the beaches where it tosses,
> Its hints of earlier and other creation
>
> ('The Dry Salvages')

T. S. Eliot's lines are particularly apt for this play.

The dislocated, apparent randomness of events; the prevailing feeling of man being adrift in floods and tides of
unchartable, unplottable contingency; the sense, indeed, of
human helplessness, is poignantly expressed in Marina's opening speech:

> Ay me, poor maid,
> Born in a tempest, when my mother died,
> This world to me is as a lasting storm,
> Whirring me from my friends.
>
> (IV, i, 17–20)

'Whir' is not, not properly, a transitive verb; but of course,
once Shakespeare has used it in this way – as he does only
this once – we are stunned by its rightness, and realize that
no other word would do. We have entered an actively
'whirring' world. It is a question whether there is any super-
vising, supervening power controlling or directing this fragmented, tempestuously unpredictable world. 'The gods' are
very frequently invoked, with Jove, Juno, Apollo, Aesculapius
and Priapus named, and Diana actually appearing, albeit in
a dream, in Shakespeare's first theophany, which takes place
during an annual celebration of Neptune – we are certainly
in a pagan world. But 'the gods' were invoked in *King Lear*,
and much help they were there. Are these all just helpless
gestures to an empty sky?

That is not quite the feeling here. Wilson Knight thinks these are more active and potent gods: 'there is a greater sense of their reality, beneficence, and intervention'. He senses an increasing 'religious reverence' and maintains that 'Shakespeare's drama is aspiring towards the eternal harmony and the eternal pattern'. More generally, Bullough thinks that the 'old tale' of Apollonius with its oracular vision and final temple scene 'helped to revive in Shakespeare the sense of an overriding benevolent Providence which he had rejected in *Lear* and ignored in *Coriolanus*, and to evoke the note of healing and forgiveness which he was to seek in the last three romances'. Many commentators agree that, while the play is undoubtedly secular in both content and intention, it has *some* Christian relevance – a classical world with biblical resonances (as one might see Pericles now as a pagan prince, now as Job or Everyman). The old tale itself, says Hoeniger, presents 'a pattern of the course of human life partly analogous to the biblical one', the basic similarity being that man has to suffer much before he will see and understand God's purposes. 'Shakespeare conceived the significance of the tragicomic pattern of the story of Apollonius of Tyre more deeply than did Gower or Twine ... he was led to a view of the place of suffering in a great man's life more like that of another profound view, the Christian one.' The stress should be on '*analogous*' – the play is in no way an adjunct to orthodox Christianity. But you could certainly say that in both the Bible and the play, God/gods move(s) in a mysterious way His/their wonders to perform. And wonders there certainly are, however brought about.

That being said, as Gower tells it, it is always Fortune that is responsible for events. 'Providence' is never mentioned (Shakespeare only used the word half a dozen times, and we have to wait until *The Tempest* for 'Providence divine'), while we hear of Fortune on some eighteen occasions. And a pretty rough-handed Fortune it is:

> Till fortune, tired with doing bad,
> Threw him ashore

(II, Gower 37–8)

> Let Pericles believe his daughter's dead
> And bear his courses to be ordered
> By Lady Fortune

(IV, iv, 46–8)

Marina is placed in a brothel ('this sty') by 'most ungentle fortune' (IV, vi, 102), and Gower's fortune is never less than 'fierce and keen' (V, iii, 87). So what brings about the miraculous dénouement – has the harsh old Wheel of Fortune ameliorated into a benign Wheel of Providence, as some suggest? Do the gods finally intervene as they so conspicuously did not in *King Lear*? Or is it all up to inscrutable Chance – miraculous luck *finally* balancing out atrocious luck, but don't bank on it? People will respond in different ways. Certainly we sense the presence of something mysterious and wonderful in the enraptured unfoldings of the last act. I think the prevailing feeling is that fortune has suddenly, inexplicably, begun to exercise a calming, self-rectifying influence on events – confusion yields to coherence, and the tempest gives way to music. But the experience is theatrical, not theological, and none the less valuable for that. '*Pericles* offers its reassurance, creating a world in which death is an illusion and the dream of immortality is appeased without the postulate of an afterlife' (Brockbank).

The only unity this whirring, scattering play has – apart from Gower standing there pointing, narrating, and moralizing – is the fact that all the incidents bear directly on the weal and woe of Pericles and his daughter, Marina. The minor characters are relatively undeveloped, often nearer to types than individuals. And Pericles is an unusual sort of hero in that he is completely passive. He initiates almost nothing on his own behalf (he brings relief to a starving city). He travels in search of a wife, and wins one in a medieval tournament rather fascinatingly being held in ancient Greece, but he is far from being a passion-driven lover. Mainly we see him escaping or departing. He does not, like many heroes, take things (or people) by the scruff of the neck, one way or another, and try to shape them to his desires or aspirations – rather, things happen *to* him. He simply endures the slings and arrows – and finally the gifts – of outrageous Fortune. He is not the maker, and certainly not the master, of his fate. We see no moral failings, no struggling with conflicting emotions – no mistakes or errors, in fact. He certainly does nothing to deserve or to bring down the calamitous suffering visited on him;

considerations of tragic flaws or hubris are irrelevant here. As put on by Gower, the man is wholly good (and thus, as a character, almost wholly uninteresting). The fact that he has no meaningful or revealing relation to his destiny increases the sense that accident rules all – call it Fortune, call it gods. In his next two romances, Shakespeare shows the hero initially guilty of wicked mistakes and thus to a large extent responsible for the events thereby set in train; in his last romance, the hero has been the victim of wickedness. Either way, the old tale of restoration and recognition is given an ethical meaning. This is accomplished, as Kenneth Muir succinctly puts it, 'by replacing the workings of an arbitrary providence by the operations of sin and forgiveness'. Meanwhile, Pericles simply suffers in self-imposed silence.

He is thereby sometimes held up to be demonstrating an exemplary Christian-type patience, even piety. It is pointed out that whereas Lear rages at the angry elements on the stormy heath, Pericles almost respectfully submits to them:

> Wind, rain, and thunder, remember, earthly man
> Is but a substance that must yield to you;
> And I, as fits my nature, do obey you.
>
> (II, i, 2–4)

Shortly thereafter, the elements, as he thinks, take his wife's life. He is often enjoined to 'Patience', yet he scarcely seems to need such exhortations. Again:

> We cannot but
> Obey the powers above us. Could I rage
> And roar as doth the sea she lies in, yet
> The end must be as 'tis.
>
> (III, iii, 9–12)

'O, sir, things must be as they may', as the First Fisherman says to him on the beach (II, i, 119). This sounds more like stoicism, or just fatalism, than Christian humility. It has been suggested that Shakespeare took the name 'Pericles' from Plutarch's life of an Athenian with that name and whose great patience is stressed; but I think Ernest Schanzer is right to discount this and point instead to the Pyrocles in Sidney's *Arcadia* with whom

Shakespeare's Pericles shares many qualities and accomplishments. Now, the only defect in Pyrocles' knightly perfection is a
lack of patience in adversity, which might seem to spoil the fit.
On the contrary, says Schanzer, it clinches it.

'He shuts himself away from all human society, and when
Marina visits him, he has not spoken to a living soul for three
months. Can Shakespeare really have thought that this is the
way in which exemplars of patience accept the blows of
fortune?' Schanzer finds support for this view in a prose
narrative by one George Wilkins, entitled *The Painfull Adventures of Pericles Prince of Tyre*, published in 1608 and almost
certainly based on viewings of Shakespeare's play. The Quarto
of the play, published in 1609, is a notoriously bad one, and
the reporter(s) who offered this reconstruction of the play
certainly got things wrong and possibly left things out. Be that
as it may, in Wilkins' version, Lysimachus comments on
Pericles' behaviour thus: 'though his misfortunes have beene
great, and by which he hath great cause for this sorrow, it is
great pity he should continue thus perverse and obstinate',
while Marina comments that 'it was most foule in him to
misgoverne himself'. Put it this way: if you are plunged into
near-unbearable grief by the death of a loved one, and if you
had a strong tendency to extreme reactions, you might try to
kill yourself by beating your head against the wall, as Sidney's
Pyrocles does when he thinks his beloved Philoclea is dead; or
you might simply die to the world, petrifying yourself into a
sealed-up vessel of unassuagable cosmic fury – which is perhaps
what Pericles does when he thinks his beloved Marina is dead.
Perhaps he is warned so often to be patient because those who
know him are aware of a proclivity for the opposite. (There is
at least a hint of this in his first reaction to the loss of his wife
at sea: 'O you gods!/Why do you make us love your goodly
gifts,/And snatch them straight away? We here below/Recall
not what we give, and therein may/Vie honor with you' (III,
i, 22–6). As who should say – 'You *bastards*!') True patience *is*
extremely important in all these late romances, and I will come
back to this. Here we may just note that Marina *does* show
real, positive endurance and patience in her very extreme
adversity, not retreating into a helpless grief but entering and

engaging with the world as an admired teacher of artistic skills. Remember Milton's 'I cannot praise a fugitive and cloistered virtue', which seemed apposite for Isabella in *Measure for Measure*. Perhaps Shakespeare also deprecated a 'fugitive and cloistered' grief as well, no matter how understandable. Arguably, we are meant to see a *contrast* between the reactions and behaviour of the father and the daughter. In the last act, the man is manifestly psychically ill – he is indeed called 'a kingly patient' (V, i, 72), the noun *not* the adjective – and Marina has to engage him in a long session of therapy.

The play is very definitely about the father *and* the daughter, and their very different lives up to the time of their strange reunion in the last act. The title page of the first Quarto makes this very clear (it also makes it clear that it was staged primarily at the Globe and not Blackfriars):

THE LATE, and much admired Play, Called Pericles, Prince of Tyre. With the true Relation of the whole Historic, adventures, and fortunes of the said Prince: As also, The no lesse strange, and worthy accidents, in the Birth and Life, of his Daughter MARINA, As it hath been divers and sundry times acted by his Maiesties Servants, at the Globe on the Banck-side. By William Shakespeare.

This dual focus, or double plot, is something new in Shakespeare's plays, and it occurs in three of the last romances. The sort of love interest which drove most of the earlier comedies is reduced or vestigial. The emphasis and interest has moved to familial relationships, particularly that of father and daughter. In this play, the proposed marriage between Lysimachus and Marina is arranged in a peremptory three lines (V, i, 262–4), and Marina is never heard to assent to it – her last words are for her rediscovered mother. And the whole play moves, in its disjunctive, episodic way, from the bad incest between father and daughter of the opening act, to what we may call the good 'incest' of the last act.

Gower starts by telling us of the incest of Antiochus and his daughter, a relationship Antiochus protects with a riddle which his daughter's suitors never solve and thus pay the penalty of losing their lives – 'as yon grim looks do testify' says Gower, pointing to a row of heads displayed on the palace walls. ('Yon' is used frequently, as is the imperative 'see' or 'behold'. There is a lot of pointing in the play, as there is of moralizing – a sort of ethical pointing.) We then see the King and his daughter, with Pericles enthusiastically praising her virtues and beauty. He has recourse to a standard trope:

> See where she comes, appareled like the spring,
> ...
> Her face the book of praises, where is read
> Nothing but curious pleasures
>
> (I, i, 13–16)

She turns out to be a false spring (Marina will be the true one), and Pericles misreads the book ('curious' then meant 'exquisite', as any edition will tell you; but our more common meaning of strange or odd was emerging in the seventeenth century, and it turns out that her pleasures *are* 'curious' – curiouser and curiouser, as you might say). Willing to 'hazard' his life, Pericles asks for the riddle, which concludes:

> I sought a husband, in which labor
> I found that kindness in a father.
> He's father, son, and husband mild;
> I mother, wife, and yet his child.
> How they may be, and yet in two,
> As you will live, resolve it you.
>
> (I, i, 67–72)

We might note that the riddle is somewhat different in the sources, where the answer is Antiochus himself. Moreover, only Shakespeare has the daughter present while Pericles is reading the riddle in front of her father – he wants to foreground daughters – and of course here *she* is the answer. As in the sources, the daughter remains nameless. In Twine's version, confessing to her nurse that her father has 'violently forced her', the daughter laments 'O my beloved nurse ... even nowe two noble names were lost within this chamber ... Where is my father? For if you well undestoode the matter, the name of Father is lost in me, so that I can have no remedie now but death onely.' The dread of incest must have something to do with the threatened loss of distinct identity; for if, like Oedipus in the most famous incest legend, you can become at once son, husband, father, and brother (to your own children), then all generational differences and demarcated kinship roles have collapsed into each other and individuation is lost. Most societies stigmatize and taboo incestuous sexuality as perverse: perhaps, as used to be surmised, because it distinguishes us from animals who seem to be indifferent about the matter; perhaps because it destroys the family, and endangers the future – for a father 'forcing' his daughter is the past devouring the future. Daughters are to be exchanged, and given in marriage *out* of the family. Antiochus' daughter is right; she has lost her name – and her future.

Pericles has no trouble with *this* text, and it makes him 'pale to read it' (I, i, 76). His shocked realization – a constantly recurring one in Shakespeare – is that appearances cannot be trusted; the beautiful girl is a 'casket stored with ill' (I, i, 78). Realizing that if he answers the riddle correctly and thus reveals that he knows their guilty secret he will be killed, Pericles asks the King's permission to remain silent – and does so with an elaborate image which I find extraordinary but have never seen commented on:

> All love the womb that their first being bred;
> Then give my tongue like leave to love my head.
>
> (I, i, 108–9)

This conjoining – strong to the point of near identification – of the child in the womb and the tongue in the head, is somehow deeply suggestive in a play about a lost child and her dumb-struck father. More seriously, if loving the womb wherein your being is bred were to be translated into an adult activity, it would indeed be the ultimate Oedipal incest. With his image, Pericles – no doubt unconsciously – could be pleading for far more than the right to silence. Antiochus realizes that Pericles has discovered his secret, but feigns courtesy and friendship while planning murder. But Pericles has learned the lesson of deceptive Antioch – 'How courtesy would seem to cover sin' (I, i, 122), and duly makes his escape.

Back in Tyre, he worries lest the powerful Antiochus will have him pursued, and falls prey to a barely explicable 'dull-eyed melancholy' (I, ii, 3) – not the first Shakespearian hero to whom that happens. Setting out on his destinationless travels, he arrives at the famine-struck city of Tharsus. There we hear the Governor Cleon reveal that the people are close to cannibalism: 'mothers ... are ready now/To eat those little darlings whom they loved' (I, iv, 42–4). Part of the riddle of the daughter of Antiochus was 'I am no viper, yet I feed/On mother's flesh, which did me breed' (I, i, 65–6). Cannibalism is perhaps the most ancient taboo of all, and is curiously linked with incest as part of some primal confusion – 'chaos and old night' – out of which human society emerged. Saturn devouring his children looms in the misty antecedents to the first Greek tragedy, which indeed dramatized this emergence (the *Oresteia* of Aeschylus). Intra-familial – incestuous – cannibalism is the ultimate negation of the family and the transmissive separation of generations. Again, the future is ingested. This has not, in fact, yet happened in Tharsus when Pericles arrives with his timely aid of corn. But it is curious that the travels of Pericles should start with dangerous brushes with these two most ancient of dreads – curious, and perhaps part of the enduring and ubiquitous appeal of this 'old tale'. Setting sail again, he is shipwrecked, and thrown up on an unknown beach. It is as though his identity has been washed away in the storm – 'What I have been I have forgot to know' (II, i, 75); but with the help of local fishermen, and his 'rusty armor' which they have netted, he reassembles himself as a knight and duly wins a local tournament and the king's daughter who, unlike his previous choice, is a glorious casket stored with *good*. In another reversal, her father pretends to be angry, but is really pleased. Such bad/good inversions are characteristic of fairy tales and old romances, and such is the atmosphere of the first two acts.

Act III finds Pericles in the middle of a terrible storm at sea, and also finds Shakespeare beginning to write in his recognizably late style. Pericles gains a daughter in these impossible conditions:

> Now, mild may be thy life!
> For a more blusterous birth had never babe;
> Quiet and gentle thy conditions! For
> Thou art the rudeliest welcome to this world

That ever was prince's child. Happy what follows!
Thou hast as chiding a nativity
As fire, air, water, earth and heaven can make,
To herald thee from the womb.

(III, i, 27-34)

Having welcomed a daughter, he has (as he thinks) to bury a
wife – the close conjunction of things dying with things new-
born is a distinguishing feature of the atmosphere of the
Last Plays.

A terrible childbed hast thou had, my dear;
No light, no fire. Th' unfriendly elements
Forgot thee utterly; nor have I time
To give thee hallowed to thy grave, but straight
Must cast thee, scarcely coffined, in the ooze;
Where, for a monument upon thy bones,
And e'er-remaining lamps, the belching whale
And humming water must o'erwhelm thy corpse,
Lying with simple shells. O Lychorida,
Bid Nestor bring me spices, ink and paper,
My casket and my jewels

(III, i, 57-67)

It is a beautiful exequy – touchingly intimate and solicitous
('my dear'); awed, at the bleak indifference of the elements;
somehow tranquillizing, with the 'humming water'; and finally
mysteriously peaceful, with his wife at rest 'lying with simple
shells'. The undersea world seemingly has its own placating
processes – to which Pericles will despatch his wife, suitably
accompanied by spices and jewels. Disaster has been turned
into ritual.

We shortly see him leaving the new-born Marina with
Cleon and Dionyza at Tharsus (they owe him a favour since
he relieved their starving city) who promise to bring her up
like their own daughter. But before that, there is a strange
scene with Lord Cerimon which affords us perhaps the first
certain intimation that we have entered the world of Shakespeare's late romances. Cerimon is a master of 'secret art':

'Tis known, I ever
Have studied physic, through which secret art,

> By turning o'er authorities, I have,
> Together with my practice, made familiar
> To me and to my aid the blest infusions
> That dwells in vegetives, in metals, stones;
> And I can speak of the disturbances
> That nature works, and of her cures
>
> (III, ii, 31–8)

We have met herbalists and apothecaries before; and, seeking to allay the suffering of her father, Cordelia prays:

> All bless'd secrets,
> All you unpublished virtues of the earth,
> Spring with my tears! be aidant and remediate
> In the good man's distress!
>
> (*King Lear* IV, iv, 15–18)

Her 'blest secrets' are Cerimon's 'blest infusions', and his 'vegetives' are her 'virtues of the earth' (= medicinal plants). Shakespeare has already shown an interest in good or white magic, and mysterious remedies; you may recall Helena's dead father (in *All's Well*) 'whose skill was *almost* as great as his honesty; *had* it stretched so far, *would have* made nature immortal' (I, i, 20–22, my italics). But it didn't – though he handed on some powerful secret recipes to his daughter. Just what 'aidant and remediate' powers man's art may draw out of nature to cure 'disturbances' which nature herself 'works', is an increasing concern for Shakespeare. Marina is successfully 'aidant and remediate' to her father in this play in a way which is debarred to Cordelia in the intractably bleak world she moves through. And remember that, as Gower indicated at the start, the whole story is intended to serve as a 'restorative' – for all of us.

Cerimon values 'cunning' (skill) more than 'riches' because 'immortality attends the former,/Making a man a god' (III, ii, 30–31); and it does indeed come to seem that he has attained the skill that Helena's father just fell short of. When some gentlemen bring in the casket/coffin containing the 'corpse' of Thaisa, he calls for his 'boxes', a fire, and some 'still and woeful music', saying:

> Death may usurp on nature many hours,
> And yet the fire of life kindle again

The o'erpressed spirits. [I have read
Of some Egyptians, who after four hours' death
Have raised impoverished bodies, like to this,
Unto their former health.]

(III, ii, 82-7)

(The lines in brackets are hopelessly garbled in the Quarto, and the much clearer words from Wilkins' prose narrative have been inserted.) Cerimon, it seems, has learned the 'secret art' of resurrection. Thus his triumphant speech:

The music there! I pray you, give her air.
Gentlemen,
This queen will live: nature awakes; a warmth
Breathes out of her. She hath not been entranced
Above five hours. See how she 'gins to blow
Into life's flower again!

(III, ii, 92-7)

And Thaisa wakes – as if returned from the grave:

Where am I? Where's my lord? What world is this?

(III, ii, 107)

A resurrection! It is, as the amazed watching Gentlemen declare, 'most strange!', 'most rare!' Cerimon is, as Wilson Knight long ago pointed out, an early sketch for Prospero.

Right, says Gower, imagine Pericles back at Tyre, and Thaisa gone to Ephesus to be a votaress in Diana's temple. 'Now to Marina bend your mind'. She has, he tells us, 'gained/ Of education all the grace' which has made her 'the heart and place/Of general wonder' (IV Gower 5, 8–9, 10–11). To keep us fully informed in advance, he tells us we will see envious Dionyza planning her murder – which immediately we do. Marina then enters with flowers – exactly like Ovid's Proserpina – lamenting her dead nurse:

No, I will rob Tellus of her weed
To strew thy green with flowers; the yellows, blues,
The purple violets, and marigolds,
Shall as a carpet hang upon thy grave,
While summer days doth last.

(IV, i, 13-17)

'Tellus' is a female personification of the earth, and Marina 'robbing' Tellus is a gentle reminder that, in some important way, this play is concerned with the meeting-point, and inter-penetration, of sea and land. The scene takes place on the seashore. Taken down the beach by her appointed murderer, she is brusquely abducted by some pirates who suddenly appear. Like Proserpina she is taken off to an infernal under-world – in her case a brothel in Mytilene; of which, again like Proserpina, she will become effectively queen.

Moving to the brothel, we are back, briefly, in the world of *Measure for Measure*. (The Last Plays often contain echoes and short reprises of features of earlier plays. In this play, for example, the relation between the murderous Dionyza and appalled, weak Cleon is Goneril and Albany, in little, all over again.) With the brothel scenes, Shakespeare elaborates consid-erably on his story material for the first time. Pander, Bawd and Boult are all his own. Their low talk outside the brothel reflects the rankness and rottenness which comes with their trade. They sorely need a fresh wench, and to that end they buy Marina from the pirates. They gather gloatingly round her. Boult is told that, since he 'bargained for the joint', he will be allowed to 'cut a morsel off the spit' (IV, ii, 136–7). He in turn promises that he will inflame the lusts of the regular customers with his descrip-tions: 'I warrant you, mistress, thunder shall not so awake the beds of eels as my giving out her beauty stirs up the lewdly inclined' (IV, ii, 149–51). It is all nastily lubricious and concupis-cent. Marina calls on Diana to help her preserve her 'virgin knot' – but 'What have we to do with Diana?' says the old Bawd, as they lead Marina into the brothel. She seems doomed to be forced into whoredom.

Two intervening scenes show Pericles brought to the sup-posed tomb of Marina, erected by Cleon and Dionyza to conceal the fact she was, as they think, murdered. In dumb show '*Pericles makes lamentation, puts on sackcloth, and in a mighty passion departs.*' Then we are back in front of the brothel, and apparently something strange has been happening. Two regulars are hurrying away:

Did you ever hear the like?
No, nor never shall do in such a place as this, she being once gone.

But to have divinity preached there! Did you ever dream of such
  a thing?
No, no. Come, I am for no more bawdy houses. Shall's go hear the
  vestals sing?

(IV, v, 1-7)

However she did it (and it is interesting that Shakespeare
chooses *not* to show us *this* miracle), she has somehow talked
or preached the customers out of their lusts, and kept her
virginity intact. Inside the brothel, Pander, Bawd and Boult
are discussing their problem. 'Fie, fie upon her! She's able to
freeze the god Priapus, and undo a whole generation. We
must either get her ravished or be rid of her ... she would
make a puritan of the devil' (IV, vi, 3–5, 9). But it seems that
ravishing Marina is easier said than done – her 'virginal
fencing' seems undefeatable. Then there follows a rather
curious episode. Lysimachus, who is in fact the Governor of
Mytilene, comes in disguised, apparently bent on some of what
is usually on offer. 'How now! How a dozen of virginities?' (IV,
vi, 21). Left alone with Marina, he first addresses her as he
might a prostitute, then, when she explains that all she wants
is to be 'free from this unhallowed place' (IV, vi, 106), he says:

> *Had I brought hither a corrupted mind,*
> Thy speech had altered it. Hold, here's gold for thee:
> Persever in that clear way thou goest,
> And the gods strengthen thee!

(IV, vi, 110–13 – my italics)

And he leaves. But if he didn't come with 'a corrupted mind',
what on earth was he doing disguised in a brothel in the first
place? Here again, the reporter seems to have gone wrong. In
the Wilkins version, Lysimachus goes to the brothel for the
very reason you might expect a man to go to a brothel, and
is converted by Marina's passionate pleading and telling
reproaches ('virginal fencing' taken to a high art). He admits
as much: 'I hither came with thoughtes intemperate, foule
and deformed, the which your paines so well have laved, that
they are now white.' She has done it again – another one
'sent away as cold as a snowball' (IV, vi, 145). This is more
plausible than the weird version which stands in the (pirated)
Quarto.

Angrier than ever – 'She makes our profession as it were to stink afore the face of the gods' (IV, vi, 141–2) – Bawd and Boult determine to 'have your maidenhead taken off' and 'crack the glass of her virginity' – 'she shall be ploughed' (IV, vi, 133, 148, 151). But, left alone with Boult, she assails him with blistering reproaches about his occupation, until he says in self-defence:

What would you have me do? Go to the wars, would you? Where a man may serve seven years for the loss of a leg, and have not money enough in the end to buy him a wooden one?

(IV, vi, 175–8)

Danby says that Boult is the only person in the play to ask an awkward question, and suggests that it is out of place here. Certainly it sounds an odd note of realism which we might expect more readily in, say, one of the history plays. Marina soon conquers him with her eloquence, and persuades him that he will be better off if he promotes her as a teacher:

> If that thy master would gain by me,
> Proclaim that I can sing, weave, sew, and dance,
> With other virtues which I'll keep from boast;
> And I will undertake all these to teach.

(IV, vi, 187–90)

Marina – Mistress of the Arts.

This is what Gower emphasizes at the start of the last act. In her dancing, singing, learning, she is '*like* one immortal', 'goddess*like*' (my italics), and her needle composes:

> Nature's own shape of bud, bird, branch, or berry,
> That even her art sisters the natural roses

(V Gower 6-7)

where 'sisters' is used for the only time by Shakespeare as a verb. 'Absolute Marina' indeed (IV Gower 31). These last plays are much concerned with familial relations, and an art actively serving as a 'sister' to nature is as important as a daughter who can act like a mother to her father – as we are about to see. And for once, Gower does not tell us what is to happen, taking us back to Pericles, now on his ship, and leaving us with – 'what is done in action . . . Shall be discovered. Please

xlix

you, sit and hark' (V Gower 23–4). What follows will be 'discovery' rather than illustration – for the characters, but also for the audience. And indeed, after Gower has drawn the curtain for the act to begin, almost immediately we have a character drawing another curtain to reveal the prostrate, seemingly petrified Pericles – a spectacle within a spectacle. (There will be other curtains to be drawn, veils to be lifted.) It is almost as if Pericles is becoming an abstract exemplar of a condition, a fate. This feeling of characters becoming like figures in allegory – 'allegorized' as it were – is an important part of the atmosphere of the extraordinary scene to follow.

> Behold him. This was a goodly person
> Till the disaster that, one mortal night,
> Drove him to this.

(V, i, 35–7)

Helicanus is about to tell the story of Pericles to Lysimachus – the play is full of narrators, narratives, narration, when –

> Sit, sir I will recount it to you.
> But see, I am prevented.

(V, i, 63–4)

Marina enters. She will both stop, and come before, the spoken narrative, as though to give us the unmediated thing itself – 'better than reportingly'.

She is asked to draw on her 'sacred physic' to cure Pericles, and promises to 'use/My utmost skill in his recovery' (V, i, 76–7). But as she attempts to address Pericles, he rudely pushes her away. Her reaction starts the cure – and the magic.

> I am a maid,
> My lord, that ne'er before invited eyes,
> But have been gazed on like a comet. She speaks,
> My lord, that, may be, hath endured a grief
> Might equal yours, if both were justly weighed.
> Though wayward fortune did malign my state,
> My derivation was from ancestors
> Who stood equivalent with mighty kings:
> But time hath rooted out my parentage,
> And to the world and awkward casualties
> Bound me in servitude.

(V, i, 86–96)

1

The scene that ensues is peculiarly moving because we are all the time in possession of a knowledge towards which we watch the main characters falteringly, incredulously, and finally ecstatically move. Pericles is the main beneficiary; Marina, with her apparently scarce-credible stories, draws him back into speech, and brings him psychic healing. Her opening, gently reproachful, speech cracks his aphasia, and, as if awakening from a death (for this is another resurrection), he gropes disjointedly for words:

> My fortunes – parentage – good parentage –
> To equal mine – was it not thus? What say you?
>
> (V, i, 99–100)

Her answer, given what we know to be their actual relationship, is exquisitely poignant:

> I said, my lord, if you did know my parentage,
> You would not do me violence.
>
> (V, i, 101–2)

He starts to press her with questions – a dormant mind galvanized into activity – 'what countrywoman?/Here of these shores?' (V, i, 103–4). She answers with a riddle (like Helena in this, as in her healing gifts):

> No, nor of any shores.
> Yet I was mortally brought forth, and am
> No other than I appear.
>
> (V, i, 105–7)

Those last six words are of crucial importance both for the play, and for Shakespeare as a whole. Many more Shakespearian characters than Duncan have found that 'there's no art to find the mind's construction in the face' (*Macbeth* I, iv, 11–12), a discovery made to their pain, if not their horror (as when Pericles realizes that the 'glorious casket' of the daughter is 'stor'd with ill'). Evil people are not what they *seem* – the word which echoes and re-echoes throughout the whole of Shakespeare. It is one of the felicities afforded by romance that the good people *are* as they 'appear' (while the evil figures, here Antiochus and his daughter, Cleon and Dionyza, duly come to a bad end). If this play does act as a 'restorative', it is perhaps in part because it restores our faith in at least some appearances. Marina can make you want to trust the world again.

The mounting urgency of Pericles as he moves closer to what, for him, is an entirely impossible truth, communicates itself to us, even though we are 'in the know', and the wonder begins to rise. It is a seamless process, but two ways he addresses Marina deserve special note:

> Falseness cannot come from thee; for thou lookest
> Modest as Justice, and thou seemest a palace
> For the crowned Truth to dwell in.
>
> (V, i, 122–4)

and

> yet thou dost look
> Like Patience gazing on kings' graves, and smiling
> Extremity out of act.
>
> (V, i, 140–42)

He is seeing Marina, not yet as a daughter, but allegorically – almost abstractly – as Justice and Truth personified; and architecturally – a palace, and a funerary statue of Patience 'gazing', in effect, on *his* grave. For, lying there unwashed, hairy, and dumb, Pericles must resemble, at the start, an unburied corpse. And this is the Patience which really matters. We have encountered it before:

> She sat like Patience on a monument,
> Smiling at grief
>
> (*Twelfth Night* II, iv, 115–16)

> His face still combating with tears and smiles,
> The badges of his grief and patience
>
> (*Richard II* V, ii, 32–3)

> patience and sorrow strove
> Who should express her goodliest
>
> (*King Lear* IV, iii, 17–18)

Viola, Richard II, Cordelia – there is something of all of them in Marina. The figure of Patience is an image found in tomb sculpture and other art, as well as in emblem books. Claire

Preston has written admirably and enlighteningly about how 'the culture of emblems and their dialectic of word and figure' – emblems contained a picture and, underneath, an epigrammatic moral to be drawn from it – helps to explain some of the unusual and distinctive features of the play, its 'stasis, formality, and inaction'. In connection with Pericles' words to Marina, Preston comments: 'The exterior emblem motto implied by the play as a whole and by this scene especially is something like "*Patientia vincit omnia*".' 'Extremity' we may take to cover every sort of calamity (including the extreme act of suicide). Shakespeare uses the word quite frequently, but only here with a capital E, thus personifying it into an actual entity to be confronted and somehow bested. This play, like other Last Plays, certainly contains 'a sea of troubles' but, rather than taking arms against them, Marina–Patientia 'smiles' them away – a beautiful image which perfectly embodies the irenic, even beatific, atmosphere the Last Plays manage to distil.

As Pericles' memory begins to stir, he breaks out of his catatonic depression, and frozen feelings begin to flow again, finally bursting into full flood:

> O Helicanus, strike me, honored sir!
> Give me a gash, put me to present pain;
> Lest this great sea of joys rushing upon me
> O'erbear the shores of my mortality
>
> (V, i, 193–6)

The 'tempest' has turned 'kind', and metamorphosed into a metaphor for joy. The restoration of Pericles both to his daughter and to psychic sanity is accompanied by a request for 'fresh garments' and the playing of music (as in *King Lear*, but where the cure is short-lived). Only Pericles can hear the music – 'rarest sounds!' – and he declares it to be 'the music of the spheres' (V, i, 232). It puts him into 'thick slumber', during which he has his vision of Diana. While listening to Marina's seemingly impossible story, Pericles declared:

> This is the rarest dream that e'er dulled sleep
> Did mock sad fools withal. This cannot be ...
>
> (V, i, 164–5)

Now, he dreams a goddess, who finally instructs him – 'Awake, and tell thy dream' (V, i, 251). In this atmosphere, the dream to be told is true, and 'cannot be' gives way to 'has to be'. Accelerating unstoppably towards the total revelation and completed miracle of the conclusion, the play finally reunites father and daughter with the wife and mother, Thaisa, 'supposed dead and drowned' (V, iii, 35). Wonder on wonder.

The central restoration is that of the proper relationship between father and daughter, so monstrously inverted at the start of the play. When Pericles is finally convinced that Marina *is* his long-lost, thought-dead, daughter, he cries:

> O, come hither,
> Thou that beget'st him that did thee beget
>
> (V, i, 197–8)

Anthropologists tell us that incest and riddles are closely associated, perhaps the apparently impossible (the riddle) standing in for the actually unthinkable (incest). Here, with the image of his daughter giving him (new) life, as he once gave her life, Pericles is pointing to a metaphorically good 'incest' which puts the family to rights. And that is very satisfying and reassuring. Though there is possibly a shadow of the story *not* told, or avoided – the Oedipal story of a man who sets out on his travels to *avoid* incest, only to discover that that has been his destination. Widowed Pericles – another travelling man – might have married the gifted nurse in a foreign land who cured him, if the unimaginable truth had not emerged. It is, arguably, a close thing. Terence Cave calls this 'the hidden other face of recognition'. And there *is* just the faintest shadow of something else, which I think is an important part of the play's rich conclusion. At one point, as the weepingly incredulous Pericles is listening to her story, Marina, tentative and reticent throughout, says 'It may be/ You think me an impostor' (V, i, 180–81). It is a word Shakespeare seldom used, and, interestingly, the only other person who defends herself against the possible imputation is Helena, another daughter with miraculous-seeming healing powers – 'I am not an impostor' (*All's Well* II, i, 157). Of course Marina is the true Marina; *of course* she is. However, perhaps just a little bit more evidence:

> this is Marina!
> What was thy mother's name? Tell me but that,
> *For truth can never be confirmed enough,*
> Though doubts did ever sleep.
>
> (V, i, 202-5 – my italics)

She names Thaisa and he is convinced. But the italicized line cuts exactly two ways – you can never have too much confirmation; but on the other hand, you can never have *enough* confirmation. This is also just hinted in the reunion of Pericles and Thaisa. He is following the instructions of a goddess, and when Thaisa names herself he gratefully acknowledges 'Immortal Dian' (V, iii, 36). However, it's just that bit more reassuring when she recognizes his ring as a gift of her father. 'This, this! No more,' he cries out happily (V, iii, 39). Well, perhaps just a little more. This man coming in –

> Can you remember what I called the man?
> I have named him oft.
>
> (V, iii, 51-2)

She names him correctly – names have an almost talismanic quality in this play, and it is important to get them right – and Pericles is even more pleased – 'Still confirmation' (V, iii, 53). Shakespeare is certainly not suggesting in any way that Marina and Thaisa are impostors. He is just blinking once at the fact that they just, *just*, could be. In these matters there never can be perfect proof, complete 'confirmation', absolutely certain knowledge. And in this play there are so many 'gaps'. Indeed one of Gower's functions is to 'stand i' th' gaps to teach you/The stages of our story' (IV, iv, 8-9). Put another way (and I suppose this is Cave's point), a chancey recognition scene – and nothing more chancey-looking than the reunion of Pericles and Marina – might awaken in us a dim sense of all that we (they) might *not* have recognized: unexposed impostors, or undetected incest. Rather than decreasing our sense of wonder at the end of this play, such considerations, stirring only at the very periphery of thought, should enhance it. It might so easily have all been otherwise.

The theologian, Richard Hooker, writing in the 1590s, said of the celebration of the birth of Christ at Christmas: 'The

love and mercy of God towards man which this way are
become a spectacle as neither men nor angels can behold
without a kind of heavenly astonishment.' Intending no dis-
respect for Hooker's theology, I wish to borrow a phrase from
him for a more secular occasion; since I think we can hardly
do better than to say that we behold Shakespeare's spectacle,
too, with 'a kind of heavenly astonishment'.

CYMBELINE (1610)

> I see before me, man. Nor here, nor here,
> Nor what ensues, but have a fog in them
> That I cannot look through.
>
> (III, ii, 79-81)

> It is no act of common passage, but
> A strain of rareness
>
> (III, iv, 93-4)

> Fortune brings in some boats that are not steered.
>
> (IV, iii, 46)

'You do not meet a man but frowns.' So begins this extraordinary play, classifiable, if at all, rather helplessly as a tragical-
comical-historical-pastoral-political romance. There are more
frowns to come – frowns of worry, frowns of anger, but
mainly frowns of incomprehension as, increasingly, 'perplexity'
overcomes the participants in the myriad, mixed actions. The
'fog' which centrally engulfs the heroine, Imogen, settles
variously on them all, until they cannot see to see – to borrow
Emily Dickinson's powerful formulation. In no other play do
so many characters seem so blind. 'I am amazed with matter'
cries the bemused King (IV, iii, 28): 'I remain perplexed in
all' laments a bewildered servant. There is a bit of a war in
the play (there is a bit of everything in this play), during which:

> friends kill friends, and the disorder's such
> As War were hoodwinked.
>
> (V, ii, 15-16)

When War is blundering around blindfolded, and disorder
itself seems to be, as it were, losing its grip, then you have a

mess indeed. 'Confusion thick' – and thickening, seems to be the order–disorder of the day (V, iii, 41). 'How comes these staggers on me?' cries out Posthumus, near the end (V, v, 233), and by this time everyone, including the audience, is feeling dizzy. If ever a conclusion was calculated to affect all concerned with a thrilling vertigo, it is the astonishing last scene of this play – compositionally one of Shakespeare's greatest *tours de force* – during which (according to a critic with a head for numbers) no less than twenty-five plot complications are untied in less than five hundred lines. There is nothing else like it.

And so much the better, Dr Johnson would have said.

To remark the folly of the fiction, the absurdity of the conduct, the confusion of the names, and manners of different times, and the impossibility of the events in any system of life, were to waste criticism upon unresisting imbecility, upon faults too evident for detection, and too gross for aggravation.

There is the eighteenth century in full throat. But neo-classicism's geese are romance's swans, and the lamentable vices denounced with such juridical relish by the great Doctor can turn into radiant virtues when looked at with a – dare one say it – less blinkered eye. Certainly the play plunges ever more deeply into anarchy, and seems to court the risk of a collapse into chaos. With seemingly quite unrelated plots starting at different points and at different times in Roman Britain, Renaissance Italy and primitive Wales, and the fragmented events spinning centrifugally out of control, it becomes increasingly difficult to see how any of the agents involved might take over the direction of things, or impose some kind of order and inter-relatedness. There is no Duke Vincentio, no Prospero to hand; indeed there is no artificer or organizer (baleful or benign) in sight. Just thickening fog. And yet, in what seems like the last few minutes of this very long play, everything is resolved, clarified, unified, without a loose end left behind. Never was a more dazzling feat of tidying-up. Do we thank Jupiter, who puts in a rather bad-tempered, belated appearance; or rather marvel at Shakespeare, who by now clearly does know every trick in the theatrical book – and then some? But if he is pushing back the boundaries of his art – to what end?

The play is extremely rich in material, and some extravagant claims have been made, not unjustifiably, for the historical and religious significance manifestly attaching to some of its themes. Wilson Knight was right to point out that it exceeds any other play by Shakespeare in the fecundity of its classical and mythological reference – it is a work, he says, 'saturated with religious suggestion' – and right, too, to maintain that at least part of the purpose of the play is to emphasize the importance of ancient Rome in Britain's history. These are major matters and I will return to them. But I want to start by trying to suggest something of the distinctive atmosphere of this unique play. Shakespeare is by now a past master at exploiting what Bertrand Evans calls 'discrepant awareness', whereby the audience knows more than some or all of the characters for some or all of the time. We can thus watch them wading ever more deeply into error, or arriving, slowly or suddenly, at true knowledge, with the relevant attendant emotions of horror and joy, anxiety and relief. But in no play do the audience know more, and the participants less, than in *Cymbeline*. One way to make sure an audience is in the know is for a main plotter, through asides or soliloquies, to keep us informed of his (or her) devices and intentions. Whomsoever else Richard III and Iago trick and bamboozle, they have no surprises for us and, effectively, no secrets from us. For a wonder, this is exactly *not* the case with the one Iago*ish* plotter in this play, who gives us our one pure surprise – more of which later. For the rest, neither the play nor the people in it seem inclined to keep any secrets from *us*; from each other is a different matter. This results in some curious effects, of which I will give three examples.

The unnamed Queen – she is just a generic Bad Queen – asks her physician, Cornelius, to prepare a 'strange ling'ring poison' for experimental purposes. In a long aside, effectively to us, he says (I summarize): 'I can see through this wicked Queen, but I have tricked her. She thinks I have given her a deadly poison. Little does she know that it's a harmless sleeping draught. I've made a fool of her' (I, v, 33–44). Now this is the sort of stage effect most of us will have experienced in pantomime, and one result is to drain the figure of the Queen immediately of all real threat and menace. However nasty she is (very – torturing animals and so on), we know that ultimately she can do no lasting harm. You never feel that about Lady Macbeth. When the male-disguised Imogen is taken by the Romans, she gives the name of the corpse (which she thinks is Posthumus) as Richard du Champ, then offers this aside (I summarize): 'Actually, I'm lying a bit here, but it's harmless enough. I do hope the gods will understand – that is, if they are listening' (IV, ii, 377–9). Other Shakespearian heroines make no such apologetic asides about their resourceful inventiveness. Here, it slightly lowers the tension, and makes us a bit more aware of the theatricality of what we are watching. When Posthumus finds himself back in Britain, supposedly obliged to fight on the side of the Italians, he says in soliloquy: 'Therefore, good heavens,/Hear patiently my purpose' (V, i, 21–2). This is really for our benefit as he goes on to explain that he will take off his Italian clothes, dress up as a British peasant, and at least fight for Imogen's side. This is really rather back-stage stuff, and, again, it makes us aware that, in various little ways, Shakespeare keeps giving us glimpses of the reverse side of the tapestry.

But if we are, if anything, over-informed, the characters suffer from pitifully partial knowledge. True, everyone knows *something*, his or her little patch as it were; but nobody knows much. As the play progresses, we acquire more and more secrets, while watching the varying ignorance of the participants grow and grow. The character who suffers most from this process is Imogen, as we see from the first act. Firmly defying her blusteringly tyrannous father; coolly taking the measure of her treacherous stepmother ('Dissembling courtesy!'); treating Iachimo's insinuations and overtures with superb, well-bred contempt – Princess Imogen is not only by a long stretch the most intelligent (not to say the most attractive) character in the play; she shows herself well qualified to join the ranks of those masterful, independent spirits, Portia and Rosalind. But she isn't given a chance. Whereas they actively decided to assume male roles, both to give themselves access to areas of

experience usually debarred to women, and to work to revita-
lize and restore a social order which has gone wrong, the
Princess Imogen is advised *by her servant* to abandon her female
identity ('You must forget to be a woman', III, iv, 156), and
she never masters or makes much of her male role (in the
Welsh mountains, she is happiest singing and cooking). Leah
Scragg makes the relevant point succinctly: 'previously a
change of identity affords the opportunity to enter the play
world on a new footing. In *Cymbeline* by contrast the opposite
is the case, in that the heroine adopts a disguise in order to
leave her world rather then enter it.' Completely in control in
the opening scenes until the departure of banished Posthumus,
Imogen is thereafter never again fully the mistress of her
situation, nor is she a partner in our awareness. She seems to
get further and further from us as she enters deeper and
deeper into the fog. I might just add here that the phenomenon
of things passing out of sight into distances of *air* (key word) –
ships, birds – is another delicate motif, contributing to the
atmosphere of the play. As in Imogen's exquisite lines about
how she would have tried to 'after-eye' Posthumus's
departing vessel:

> I would have broke mine eyestrings, cracked them but
> To look upon him till the diminution
> Of space had pointed him sharp as a needle;
> Nay, followed him till he had melted from
> The smallness of a gnat to air

(I, iii, 17–21)

'Diminution of space' has an added resonance in a play which
brings ancient Britain, Renaissance Italy and wild Wales
together in the same spot. And I have a quite unjustifiable
sense that Shakespeare would like us to experience this play
as somehow taking place at the very periphery of vision, where
lands and times and events merge together – and the gnat
melts to air.

Imogen, then, is unique in her pitiable plight. Marina
experienced life as 'a lasting storm'; but she pretty quickly
masters the brothel, and what she knows she knows, as
Pynchon would say. Imogen, to all intents and purposes,

knows nothing; and, once she has fled from the hostile court, is entirely at the (honourable) mercy of Welsh outlaws and Roman invaders. 'No heroine in the comedies is cast in such a role,' writes Bertrand Evans, 'kept unaware so long, ignorant of so many secrets, abused by so many practices, endangered from so many quarters.' None of which, needless to say, reflects on the character or capacities of Imogen herself. It is just the nature of the world in which she, unhappily, finds herself. She has no one to guide her, as Vincentio looks out for Isabella (Portia and Rosalind simply take over the show). In this world, there don't seem to *be* any guides (Pisanio does a loyal servant's limited best; Philario is sensible, and ignored, in Rome). Finally it is only Imogen's own quick 'eyestrings' less than four hundred lines before the end – 'I see a thing/ Bitter to me as death' (V, v, 103–4), i.e. her ring on Iachimo's finger – which set in train the tumble of revelations and recognitions which so 'staggeringly' conclude the play. Of this final scene Evans writes: 'For us, the experience of the closing scene is that of witnessing the revelation of secrets that have been locked in our minds, and of observing the effects of their revelation upon the persons who have been ignorant of them and to whom they are of most concern ... The release of each secret accomplishes a welcome reduction, degree by degree, of the pressure that has been mounting in our minds since error first began to pile on error; one effect of the scene, thus, is the relief of overmuch understanding, painful because it has been unsharable.' This is part of the special experience of *Cymbeline.*

It is perhaps most helpful to identify three potentially quite separate stories which Shakespeare has most cannily interwoven. They involve, respectively, a newly married but separated couple (mainly romance); a disrupted dynasty (which involves both pastoral and something close to fairy tale); and an international dispute (history and pseudo-history). The marriage between Imogen and Posthumus must have been a 'handfast' (I, v, 78 – a word used only once again by Shakespeare; curiously in his very next play, *The Winter's Tale*). This was an old form of irregular or probationary marriage contracted by the parties joining hands and agreeing to live as man and wife – for a princess to agree to such an unceremonious bonding does indeed reveal 'a strain of rareness', as Imogen claims. It was a marriage but not yet a legal finality, which is presumably why, out of her innate 'pudency' (lovely word, and used only this once, for this rarest of heroines – II, v, 11), 'Me of my lawful pleasure she restrained' (II, v, 9), as Posthumus bitterly complains, insanely convinced that Imogen has afforded Iachimo what she refused him. That it was this sort of unsanctified marriage would seem to be born out by the simple fact that the boorish Cloten still thinks he can win her, denying the validity of her 'contract'; and she, while doing everything possible to repulse him, never simply says – you're wasting your time, I'm already married.

It is this recent, secret, away-from-court 'marriage' – to a commoner, at that – which so enrages her father, King Cymbeline (in this way the play starts rather like *Othello*), who instantly separates them by banishing Posthumus. In this, he plays the traditional role (in comedy) of the obstructing, prohibiting father who seeks to block young love. Here, he literally 'comes between' the lovers.

> or ere I could
> Give him that parting kiss which I had set
> Betwixt two charming words – comes in my father,
> And like the tyrannous breathing of the north
> Shakes all our buds from growing.

> (I, iii, 33–7)

Wrathful, foolish, '*imperceivant*' King Cymbeline (the italicized word only appears this once in Shakespeare – Cloten ludicrously misapplies it to Imogen, but it will do very nicely for Cymbeline, and indeed many others in this fog-bound play) has indeed sunk his court and realm into a 'winter's state' (II, 4, 5). He has disrupted the due processes of nature ('shakes all our buds from growing'); he has somehow lost his two sons (the legitimate heirs), alienated his one remaining true child (Imogen), and effectively handed power over to a poisonous, poisoning second queen and her monstrous son, so the feeling of sterility is strong in the air. It will require the enactment of an apparent 'death' and rebirth, or resurrection – as in some primitive fertility rite – to re-establish the proper cycle of the seasons, and bring the fruit back to the trees.

Cymbeline was a king of ancient Britain when the Romans still held sway over it, and I will return to this. But following the banished Posthumus, we find ourselves in Renaissance Rome – a curiously easy modulation – and here the romance story starts. It is based – closely – on a story in Boccaccio's *Decameron* (Day 2, Novella 9), which is, in turn, a relatively sophisticated version of a widespread folk tale involving the wager on a virtuous wife. The husband who bets on his wife's virtue is invariably tricked by false evidence into believing that she has betrayed him, and orders her death. She escapes, often in male disguise, and is finally enabled to reveal the truth. She is reunited with her contrite husband, and the villain is punished. Boccaccio's version, involving Italian merchants, is decidedly middle-class; Shakespeare prefers to set it at the level of the court, since that way he can make it intermesh with the historical–political material which will later come into prominence – but he retains much of the mercantile talk of coins, prices, values, weights, measures etc. Boccaccio has his wronged wife, Ginevra, escape, as a young man, into the Oriental and Moslem world of the eastern Mediterranean, where (s)he rises to high office under the Sultan of Alexandria. This was no use to Shakespeare, who needed to restrict his already sufficiently disparate material to Britain and Italy, so, in Bullough's words, 'he substituted the popular medieval theme by which the ill-used woman wanders in search of her man into a pastoral setting and there finds solace and help until she can be reinstated'. Thus, instead of the Orient – Wales. Also, in Boccaccio the convicted villain who faked the evidence is fiendishly tortured to death (impaled on a stake, covered in honey, devoured by flies, wasps, and hornets). Shakespeare, *Titus Andronicus* aside, the least ghoulish of writers, prefers to have him forgiven – though he may have a specific reason for this, as well.

The story involving dynastic disruption only starts to emerge in the first scene set in Wales (III, iii). Here we meet Belarius who combines two conventional roles in pastoral romance – the rusticated courtier, and the shepherd father. We learn that he was unjustly banished – Cymbeline's angry mistakes go a long way back – and that he abducted the two baby princes (fearing the corrupting influence of Cymbeline's disastrous court), so that the lost royal children (who don't know their true parentage) have grown up in the wild Welsh mountains. When the starving Imogen stumbles into their cave, it is the beginning of a process which will in time knit them into the swelling master-narrative accommodating them all. Shakespeare could have found material for the interlude in Wales in a number of Greek romances. (In this connection Carol Gesner makes an interesting observation: the motif of the hero striking the unrecognized heroine at a trial-like public occasion, as Posthumus does Imogen, is standard and recurrent in Greek romance. It never advances the plot, so it must be there for another reason. It is certainly the most *painful*, literally shocking, moment in Shakespeare's play.) Shakespeare also almost certainly borrowed from an anonymous play, *Love and Friendship* (acted 1582). This play contains, for instance, a fleeing heroine named Fidelia (cf. Imogen's pseudonym Fidele) who finds refuge with a hermit in a cave. Shakespeare added the folk-tale motif of the Wicked Stepmother, eager to advance her own, hideous child. But there was almost certainly a more substantial reason for choosing Wales as the setting for this part of the play. The summer of 1610 saw the investiture of Prince Henry as Prince of Wales, to great rejoicings and many entertainments – one of which may well have been *Cymbeline*. The use of Milford Haven as the landing place for Posthumus and the Romans would certainly resonate for the contemporary audience, since it was there that Henry, Earl of Richmond, landed when he came to save England from Richard III. He became Henry VII, the Tudor ancestor through whom the current James I could be connected with the Tudor mythology of the descent from the Trojan Brut. Wales plays a special part in the legends and myths concerned with the founding of England. And this looks towards the third, international story.

What exactly is the 'name and birth' of that Posthumus who has just married Imogen? asks the somewhat bemused Second Gentleman in the busy, frowning first scene of the play. First Gentleman:

> I cannot delve him to the root. His father
> Was called Sicilius, who did join his honor
> Against the Romans with Cassibelan,
> But had his titles by Tenantius, whom
> He served with glory and admired success,
> So gained the sur-addition Leonatus
>
> (I, i, 28–33)

Shakespeare and his contemporaries were interested in origins and in delving their nation 'to the root' – Troy? Rome? Lud? Brutan? Britain? – but if they strained their eyestrings to see where the gnat of early Tudor history melted into the air of the unseeably previous, they would find themselves in the, well, fog of ungraspable legend – Geoffrey of Monmouth's *History of the Kings of Britain*; Holinshed's early Chronicles. Shakespeare certainly turned again to Holinshed, not this time for the historically anchored Tudor material, but to glance at the insecurely drifting Brutan material (Brut was supposedly descended from 'Aeneas the Trojan', legendary founder of Rome, and was said to have founded Britain). There he would have found those British–Latin names – Sicilius, Tenantius, Cassibelan; not to mention Posthumus, Innogen (possibly what Shakespeare intended), Guiderius and Arviragus, Cloton and, of course, 'Kymbeline or Cimbeline'.

Kymbeline or Cimbeline the sonne of Theomantius was of the Britains made king after the deceasse of his father ... This man (as some write) was brought up at Rome, and there made knight by Augustus Caesar, under whome he served in the warres, and was in such favour with him, that he was at libertie to pay his tribute or not. Little other mention is made of his doings, except that during his reigne, the Saviour of the world our Lord Jesus Christ the onelie sonne of God was borne of a virgine, about the 23 yeare of the reigne of this Kymbeline ... some writers doo varie, but the best approoved affirme, that he reigned 35 years and then died, and was buried at Londonn, leaving behind him two sonnes, Guiderius and Arviragus.

Holinshed notes that there was some subsequent dispute between Britain and Rome over tribute money, with the Romans planning (at last) to invade. He thinks it was the son, Guiderius, who 'gave occasion to breach of peace betwixt the Britains and the Romans, denieing to pay them tribute':

But whether this controversie which appeareth to fall forth betwixt the Britains and Augustus was occasioned by Kymbeline, or some other prince of the Britains, I have not to avouch: for that by our writers it is reported that Kymbeline, being brought up in Rome, and knighted in the court of Augustus, ever shewed himselfe a friend to the Romans, and chieflie was loth to breake with them, because the youth of the Britaine nation should not be deprived of the benefit to be trained and brought up among the Romans, whereby they might learne both to behave themselves like civill men, and to atteine to the knowledge of feates of warre.

From these hints Shakespeare drew out the international theme of the play, the rising tension between Rome and Britain. This third action starts properly in III, i, with the arrival of the Roman ambassador, Lucius, though we have had preparatory hints concerning the paying of Roman tribute in II, iii and iv. Shakespeare, in fact, makes it Cymbeline who refuses to pay the tribute – not his son. He could have taken this idea from Spenser's *Faerie Queene* (which he certainly knew). This is from the 'chronicle of Briton kings' (Book II, Canto 10):

> Next him *Tenantius* raigned, then *Kimbeline*,
> What time th'eternall Lord in fleshly slime
> Enwombed was, from wretched *Adams* line
> To purge away the guilt of sinfull crime:
> O joyous memorie of happy time,
> That heavenly grace so plenteously displayd;
> (O too high ditty for my simple rime.)
> Soon after this the *Romanes* him warrayed;
> For that their tribute he refused to let be pay'd.

The most important feature of the remote and misty reign of Cymbeline was that it coincided with the reign of Caesar Augustus in Rome and the birth of Christ. This, understandably, has been used to suggest that there is a larger, more significant action going on here, a play we can't see behind the play we can. Thus Northrop Frye: 'The sense of a large change in human fortunes taking place off stage has to be read into *Cymbeline*.' And Francis Yates: 'The universal imperial *justitia* and *pax* was sanctified through that birth, and through the interpretation of the prophecy in Virgil's Fourth

Eclogue as applying both to the peace and justice of the Augustan golden age, and to the birth of Christ, the Prince of Peace, in that age.' Thus was the Empire Christianized. 'The interpretation of the reign of Cymbeline as contemporary with the reign of Augustus, in which Christ was born, gave it an atmosphere of the sacred; it approximated the British sacred reign to the sacred reign of Augustus Caesar; it drew together British imperial and Roman imperial sacred legend in some new fusion of Britain and Rome. This is exactly what happens in *Cymbeline* which is dominated by a vision of a Romano-British imperial eagle.' Shakespeare certainly knew all about the sacred importance of the Augustan Peace. The increasingly dominant Octavius Caesar confidently predicts, near the end of *Antony and Cleopatra*, 'The time of universal peace is near' (IV, vi, 5). There is, perhaps, a just comparable moment in this play, when the 'curiously oracular jailer' (Frye) says, after the freeing of Posthumus: 'I would we were all of one mind, and one mind good. O, there were desolation of jailers and gallowses' (V, iv, 175–6). But I hardly think that this, or indeed anything else in the play, points to what Felperin calls 'a momentous change for the better in the fortunes of the entire human community'.

Felperin offers what might be called an eschatalogical reading of the play. 'The incarnation represents a turning point within Christian history from the eras of nature and law to a new era of grace. The former are characterized by wrath and justice – motives associated with tragical history [= the first four acts of *Cymbeline*]; the latter by love and mercy, motives associated with romantic comedy [= Act V of *Cymbeline*].' He could hardly be more confident: 'Jupiter is a divine lame duck whose term of office is about to expire and the ending of the play has more to do with the doctrine of another deity whose reign is about to begin ... The Roman gives way to the Christian not only within the action as a whole but within each character, the tragical history gives way to romance.' (I imagine that this far from even-tempered Jupiter would be surprised to hear of his imminent redundancy, and might well feel inclined to pay Felperin one of his sulphurous visits – but I stray from the real world.) This is all very satisfyingly neat and cut-and-dried; and the evidence for such a reading is – just about – there, if you care to isolate it and, as I think, exaggerate it. But it risks turning the play into something of a tract, albeit of a high order (Felperin is a very subtle reader). Many intelligent people read the play along these lines, and it is only appropriate to place this version before readers of this introduction. But the play just doesn't *feel* like this to me. I think we need something with a bit more of a 'stagger' in it.

One other aspect of the Roman material in the play should be mentioned. Caius Lucius, the Roman ambassador and general, is 'honourable' and 'holy'; he is also courteous, gracious, kind and reasonable. All of which, the King of Britain – on the evidence we see – is notably *not*. Yet, we recall from Holinshed, Cymbeline was knighted in the court of Augustus Caesar, and wanted the youth of Britain to be brought up among Romans so that they would learn to behave 'like civill men' and acquire the martial virtues. In a word, for Britain, Rome – and this was felt to be historically true – was *the* civilizing influence. The strident, sneering nationalism of Cloten and the Queen when they refuse and reject Lucius (III, i) should be registered as a jarring and inappropriate isolationism – football-terrace stuff (admittedly, in a different kind of history play, it might pass for rough-tongued patriotism). Cymbeline's final, willing reconciliation with Rome signals his release from thraldom to the wicked Queen, and a return to the larger civilizing forces of the world.

But if Lucius is one (ancient) Roman, Iachimo is another (Renaissance) Italian, closer to Machiavelli than to Augustus Caesar. In him the civilized virtues have run to super-subtly smooth manners and a refined self-satisfying aestheticism (he certainly seems to appreciate Imogen's physical beauty more than Posthumus does). Posthumus, despite the hyperbolically good report we hear of him in the first scene, emerges as neither particularly refined, nor conspicuously elegant of manner. His first appearance in Italy shows him prickly and quarrelsome, while his subsequent behaviour, however we finally take it, is hardly that of a truly civilized man. There is a national point here, concerned with Britain's ancestral strengths and weaknesses, which certainly interested Shakespeare. Brockbank quotes a contemporary *Description of Britain* in which the dullness of the British – 'men of great strength and little policie, much courage and small shift' – is contrasted with the 'craftinesse, subtile practises, doubleness, and hollow behaviour' of the ingratiatingly polite Italians. As a straightforward, honest, literal-minded British lad, Posthumus is hopelessly out of his depth in Rome (there is a hint of the bull in the china shop). But, while Iachimo simply crumbles in battle, Posthumus's heroism turns the day for Britain, and there is no doubt that his basic virtues and strengths are vindicated – having been, though, not only sorely tried, but all too easily abused.

The enlarged inter-national (and thus, as it were, inter-spatial, inter-temporal) dimension is absolutely vital; but the core and main thread of the play is the romance story concerning the (recently married) lovers, just as Imogen is herself the linking 'strain of rareness' that runs through its more 'common passages'. The first two acts dramatize the testing of that love, with, as is invariably the case in Shakespeare, the man failing the test while the woman remains constant. Forced apart in the bustling, scattering first scene, Imogen and Posthumus barely have time to swear their love ('I did not take my leave of him, but had/Most pretty things to say' – Imogen's sweet words, I, iii, 25–6), and plight their troth with the exchange of a ring and a bracelet (and how important these little *things* prove to be; how deeply involved we are with our merely material adjuncts and accessories!). But she has, as it were, barely finished her incomplete farewell to her paragon and 'jewel', when we are in Rome in the company of assorted foreign gentlemen expressing degrees of scepticism about the growing reputation of this British Posthumus, who is about to arrive to spend his banishment with his friend Philario.

The leading sneerer is Iachimo – he clearly finds his pleasure in disparaging and belittling – and he reveals an important aspect of his mentality in his opening remarks. I think I saw the man once: 'But I could then have looked upon him without the help of admiration, though the catalogue of his endowments had been tabled by his side and I do peruse him

lxix

by items' (I, iv, 4–7). He will, in due course, peruse by items,
catalogue, and tabulate the sleeping body of Posthumus's
wife, though of course no one can know that yet – except
Shakespeare, who is giving us an early clue as to how Iachimo's
mind works. He thinks in inventories. As far as he is concerned,
a man – and a woman – is *exactly* the sum of his, or her,
isolatable and itemizable parts. What he can't peruse and
catalogue – as might be, devotion, loyalty – isn't there. A
sharp eye, but a hard eye – and a cold one. He is the last
person for the rather hot-headed young Briton, now *dépaysé*
(out of his country, thus disoriented), to tangle with; but that
is what Posthumus impetuously does.

He allows himself to get involved in a quite improper and
degrading wager about the physical virtue of his absent wife,
foolishly – and arguably offensively – boasting her to be more
chaste, more virtuous, more everything, than any other woman
of any country. Cunningly, Iachimo starts to play on the
comparable and relative values of the diamond ring on Posthumus's hand, and the wife who gave it to him – both no
doubt excellent, but you cannot be sure that either is the
absolute best. Posthumus maintains that he 'rates' them just
as he has said, maintaining a difference. The exchange which
follows is crucial:

The one may be sold or given, or if there were wealth enough for
the purchase or merit for the gift. The other is not a thing for sale,
and only the gift of the gods

Iachimo. Which the gods have given you?

Posthumus. Which by their graces I will keep.

Iachimo. You may wear her in title yours, but you know strange fowl
light upon neighboring ponds. Your ring may be stol'n too. So your
brace of unprizable estimations, the one is but frail and the other
casual. A cunning thief, or a that-way-accomplished courtier, would
hazard the winning of first and last.

(I, iv, 87–99)

Iachimo wants to bring Imogen down from the gods and
into the market – and to his great shame, Posthumus lets him.
He seems to have a grasp of the crucial difference between

the ring, which indeed must remain, at least theoretically, within the realm of the purchasable; and his wife, who is, as he correctly says, 'not for sale'. The ring is a symbol of their love; Imogen is love itself. But for Iachimo, a woman, any woman, *is* simply another 'ring' (the obscenity intended), so he can speak mockingly to Posthumus of his '*brace* of unprizable estimations', and refer indifferently to 'she your jewel, this your jewel' (I, iv, 159), as much as to say – six of one, half a dozen of the other. And notice how Iachimo draws seemingly casual traces of suggestive insinuation in front of the less urbane young Briton: 'you know strange fowl light upon neighboring ponds'. If he doesn't take the hint and make the application, Posthumus might well register this as a meaningless irrelevance. But when the grosser parts of his imagination have been stirred, it will be a different matter. (In the next play, Leontes will give himself the nightmare of imagining how any man may have 'his pond fished by his next neighbor' – *The Winter's Tale* I, ii, 195.) Iachimo wants matters of value and worth to be measured in ducats, and when Posthumus agrees to remove his ring (when she gave it him, Imogen abjured him to keep it on till 'Imogen is dead', I, i, 114 – she will, duly, 'die') to match the gold which has been staked on Imogen's seducibility, he effectively hands her over to Iachimo, who promises to bring him '*sufficient testimony* that I have enjoyed the dearest bodily part of your mistress' (I, iv, 155–6, my italics). Posthumus enters wholeheartedly into the business of 'articles', 'covenants', 'lawful counsel' whereby the disgraceful wager is given specious respectability. Only the sensible Philario 'will have it no lay' (I, iv, 153); 'Gentlemen, enough of this. It came in too suddenly; let it die as it was born ...' (I, iv, 126–7). Things coming in 'too suddenly' – eruptive violence – is often the mark of tragedy, and, at the moment, that's the way this play is tending. The wager, once 'born', will not 'die', and there will have to be other deaths before there are other births.

There follows a strange little scene, back in Britain, which looks rather pastoral – the Queen and her ladies gathering flowers – violets, cowslips, primroses. For distilling fragrances, you might think. But the Queen has graduated from perfumes to poisons, and she's after a real killer – only to be tricked by her virtuous physician, as we have seen. There is something pantomimic in this scene; but we might recall that a dumb-show of a sleeping king having literal poison poured into his ear was at the centre of Shakespeare's first tragedy; and while the Queen's efforts are rather fee-fi-fo-fum, there are always subtler poisons for the unsuspecting (or too suspicious) ear in Shakespeare. As loyal Pisanio instantly recognizes when he incredulously reads the letter from his master, describing Imogen's adultery and ordering her murder.

> Leonatus,
> O master, what a strange infection
> Is fall'n into thy ear! What false Italian,
> As poisonous-tongued as handed, hath prevailed
> On thy too ready hearing?
>
> (III, ii, 2–6)

Spot on – and, as so often in Shakespeare, it is a pity that a master can't see what is instantly clear to his servant. But that's the play. The poisonous-tongued *and* poisonous-handed (both – quite right, Pisanio) 'false Italian' is, of course, Iachimo; and after the wager scene we see him working his poison.

Or failing to. Obviously, his first destination is the court of King Cymbeline, where he can try out his assorted wiles on Princess Imogen. He arrives with flattering letters of introduction from Posthumus (part of the wager), but as soon as he sees her, he knows he has an impossible task.

> All of her that is out of door most rich!
> If she be furnished with a mind so rare,
> She is alone th' Arabian bird, and I
> Have lost the wager.
>
> (I, vi, 15–18)

The relationship between what a person looks like on the outside ('out of door') and his internal 'furnishing' – misleading discrepancy and contradiction, or honourable congruence and continuity – is a concern, and a dramatically exploitable resource, in almost all of Shakespeare's plays. Here, there are quite a number of references to 'without/within', but they are fairly relaxed – 'less without and more within' says Posthumus amiably enough, as he pulls on a peasant's smock prior to plunging into battle – and possible discrepancies do not seem to occasion much concern. Cymbeline is every inch a bloody fool, and shows it; Imogen is as virtuous as she is fair; Cloten is reliably boorish *all* the way down, and so on. Iachimo is quite a smooth ingratiator, but he is manifestly not a man to go on a tiger hunt with. If anyone, Posthumus is the big let-down: 'so fair an outward and such stuff within' says the eulogizing First Gentleman in the first scene (I, i, 23). But some of that 'stuff within' turns out to be rather nasty.

Recognizing that he will never win the wager in the sense in which it was made, Iachimo invokes 'boldness' and 'auda-city', and first he tries something he is good at – filthy sexual innuendo, murmured with courtly disgust as if in a half-aside. The line is – how could any man, with such a peerless woman, want to go after trash?

> Sluttery, to such neat excellence opposed,
> Should make desire vomit emptiness,
> Not so allured to feed ...
> ... The cloyed will –
> That satiate yet unsatisfied desire, that tub
> Both filled and running – ravening first the lamb,
> Longs after garbage.

(I, vi, 44–9)

These are very powerful speeches, and the very *idea* of uncon-trolled sexual lust (since that is all this is) seems always enough to call forth Shakespeare's strongest, indeed most *disgusted* language – that tub both filled and running seems to have stood permanently somewhere in the grounds of his imagina-tion. Sane Imogen simply thinks Iachimo is mad; so, aban-doning the oblique approach, he more straightforwardly describes Posthumus as living a wild, debauched life in Rome, in terms taken from the extreme reaches of lasciviousness and foulness. Clean Imogen simply hears it with sadness, and tells him to desist. 'My lord, I fear/Has forgot Britain ... Let me hear no more' (I, vi, 112, 117). Iachimo then makes a perhaps desparate, certainly disastrous, attempt to incite Imogen to take her revenge – with him:

Should he make me
Live like Diana's priest betwixt cold sheets,
Whiles he is vaulting variable ramps,
In your despite, upon your purse? Revenge it.
I dedicate myself to your sweet pleasure ...

(I, vi, 132–6)

at which point Imogen promptly calls for the police – or rather Pisanio and, by implication, the palace guards, telling him to report to the King that a 'saucy stranger' is using his court 'to expound his beastly mind to us' (I, vi, 151–3). Not, certainly, a good day for Iachimo. But, never without a stratagem, he recoups by congratulating Imogen on her performance, and felicitating Posthumus in having such a faithful wife – he was just *testing* her. By nature given to trust, Imogen believes and forgives him, and indeed offers hospitality. But no, he must leave on the morrow, only asking as a favour that she will afford a trunk full of precious gifts for the Emperor 'safe stowage'. Of course – 'I will keep them/In my bedchamber' (I, vi, 195–6). 'Send your trunk to me' – so she concludes the first act (I, vi, 209); how ominously, we have yet to learn.

This confrontation of Iachimo and Imogen is one of Shakespeare's great scenes – never more piquant adversaries, with such different resources to draw on! Never mind the looming war between Rome and Britain, *this* – however you care to name its contesting qualities or virtues or skills or powers – is the battle at the soul of the play, to be shortly followed by what must be a unique scene in Shakespeare. Imogen is in her bed, attended by a lady, about to go to sleep: she turns down the page of the book she has been reading, asks for her taper to be left burning, dismisses her lady, and prays to the gods to protect her from fairies and 'the tempters of the night' (II, ii, 9). She sleeps; all is peace: and then *Iachimo comes from the trunk* (which of course was there for safe-keeping). This is the one totally opaque deed in the play, and it should take us, the audience, *completely* by surprise. This is unusual, particularly in this play where people are given to announcing their intentions. Cunning, plotting villains in particular in Shakespeare, invariably let the audience know what they are planning, perhaps thus to involve us in the somewhat guilty complicit pleasure of enjoying the uninformed discomfiture of their victims. But Iachimo has not dropped us a word nor tipped us a wink. We should be as surprised as Imogen – except that Imogen is asleep, so now we know something she doesn't know. But that spectacle of the figure of Iachimo silently emerging from the trunk in the nocturnal bedroom may be sufficiently troubling; who knows *what* comes out at night, within us and without us? It is, at the same time, rather comic – not exactly Box-and-Cox, but that way inclined. We should bear this mixed tonality in mind – particularly, as it happens, in another scene involving another 'trunk'.

Iachimo's forty-line soliloquy over the sleeping Imogen is amazing. Everything about the setting and situation suggests and presages rape. Imogen has been reading about the rape of Philomel by Tereus in Ovid's *Metamorphoses* (Iachimo finds the book with the page at which she stopped turned down – Shakespeare showing one of the key sources for his own art on stage, another glimpse into the works, as it were); while Iachimo, in a moment of misplaced solidarity, invokes '*Our* Tarquin', whose rape of Lucrece Shakespeare himself had, of course, written about. These were two of the most violent rapes in mythology or history, and they set dire precedents. But Iachimo is gentleness itself, speaking with a hushed reverence and awed appreciation that bespeak a finer sensibility than – so the feeling sometimes goes – an oily little Italian seducer has any right to. He seems initially to be, as it were, stunned into poetry; his first dozen lines are exquisite, quite transcending his usual cynical manipulation of discourse. It seems another voice, from:

> The crickets sing, and man's o'erlabored sense
> Repairs itself by rest.

to:

> The flame o' th' taper
> Bows towards her and would underpeep her lids
> To see th' enclosèd lights, now canopied
> Under these windows, white and azure-laced
> With blue of heaven's own tinct.

> (II, ii, 11–12, 19–23)

But this sort of entirely non-prurient wonder won't get the job done – as he realizes. 'But my design'. And he sets about his 'inventory' – 'I will write all down' – proceeding to itemize the contents of the room and, as far as he can (a mole on the left breast), the details of Imogen's body. His penetrations and appropriations are entirely ocular. 'That I might touch!' he sighs at one point: but he can't-mustn't-won't. The Tarquin he invoked differed exactly here:

> His rage of lust by gazing qualified;
> Slacked, not suppressed; for, standing by her side
> . . .
> His drumming heart cheers up his burning eye,
> His eye commends the leading to his hand;
> His hand, as proud of such a dignity,
> Soaking with pride, marched on, to make his stand
> On her bare breast, the heart of all her land . . .
>
> (*The Rape of Lucrece*)

Iachimo can only use his hands to steal Imogen's bracelet – a symbolic violation of her chastity, if you will, but still a scopic one. Because, of course, he has come, not for direct sex, but for indirect 'evidence': the bracelet – 'this will *witness outwardly,*/As strongly as the conscience does *within,*/To th' madding of her lord'; the mole – 'Here's a *voucher*/Stronger than ever law could make' (II, ii, 35–7, 39–40 – my italics). With these, plus his 'inventory' – 'I have enough' (II, ii, 46) – he returns to the trunk, with the uncharacteristically unconfident lines – 'I lodge in fear./Though this a heavenly angel, hell is here' (II, ii, 49–50). Hell is where? In the bedroom? In the trunk? Perhaps in Iachimo himself? Not clear – but certainly, a sudden shiver. The whole astonishing, voyeuristic episode is one which it can be both gripping and unsettling to participate in – as we, fellow intruders in the bedroom, inevitably do.

After a short scene, allowing a break for his return to Italy, Iachimo is back in Rome, boasting to Posthumus of an easy triumph – 'the ring is won', and he means both of them (II, iv, 45). His demonstration that he has 'knowledge of your mistress' (II, iv, 51) – meaning carnal knowledge – falls into two parts. First, drawing no doubt on his 'inventory', he meticulously describes the decorations on the walls of her bedroom, on the chimney or fireplace, and on the ceiling. The main subjects – in tapestry and in sculpture – are Cleopatra meeting Antony on the swelling Nile, and 'Chaste Dian bathing' (throw in two silver andirons in the form of 'two winking Cupids') – as if the room is brimming with rising eroticism and an enticingly displayed and vulnerable chastity (the golden cherubims on the ceiling seem to come from somewhere else, though I suppose they would be fairly Cupid-like). The main feature, though, is the striking life-likeness of the art:

> a piece of work
> So bravely done, so rich, that it did strive
> In workmanship and value; which I wondered
> Could be so rarely and exactly wrought,
> Since the true life on't was

(II, iv, 72–6)

and

> Never saw I figures
> So likely to report themselves. The cutter
> Was as another Nature, dumb; outwent her,
> Motion and breath left out.

(II, iv, 82–5)

Forget the sex – look at the art-work. At the start of *Timon of Athens*, the Poet says to the Painter of one of his works:

> I will say of it,
> It tutors nature; artificial strife
> Lives in these touches, livelier than life.

(I, i, 37–9)

It was a common enough contemporary figure; here it is probably a piece of rank flattery, and thus absurdly exaggerated. But the idea of an art that, as it were, steals a march on nature, goes one better, outdoes or outskills it, clearly haunts or delights Shakespeare during the writing of these last plays, when he must have felt that he had more tricks up his sleeve than life itself. As it is his pleasure to demonstrate to us.

These details of the decorations are what Iachimo calls his 'circumstances' which, he says to Posthumus 'must first induce you to believe' (II, iv, 61, 63). The word means 'details' or 'particulars', but it is particularly appropriate since all this is what we would now call (merely) 'circumstantial evidence', *not* proof. Posthumus, rightly, sees it in this way, too. Iachimo could have found out these details in any number of ways without even coming near the person of Imogen, and as far as Posthumus is concerned, Iachimo has lost the wager. Then Iachimo produces the bracelet. Within ten lines Posthumus hands over the ring given to him by Imogen – completely assured, just like that, of Imogen's infidelity.

> The vows of women
> Of no more bondage be to where they are made
> Than they are to their virtues, which is nothing.
> O, above measure false!
>
> (II, iv, 110–13)

Philario again tries, vainly, to introduce a little sense – hang on man, bracelets can be lost or stolen. Posthumus pauses, but Iachimo only has to repeat that 'I had it from her arm' (as indeed he did) for Posthumus to revert – eagerly, as one feels – to his conviction of Imogen's 'incontinency':

> No, he hath enjoyed her.
> The cognizance of her incontinency
> Is this. She hath bought the name of whore thus dearly.
>
> (II, iv, 126–8)

Philario – 'this is not strong enough to be believed' (II, i, 131) – is wasting his time. 'Never talk on't./She hath been colted by him' (II, iv, 132–3). One feels Posthumus's perverse pleasure in using coarse language about his wife. Just to make sure – or just to turn the knife – Iachimo describes how much he enjoyed kissing the mole under Imogen's breast. That *really* does the trick.

> Spare your arithmetic; never count the turns.
> Once and a million!
>
> (II, iv, 142–3)

> O that I had her here, to tear her limb-meal!
>
> (II, iv, 147)

We have seen before in Shakespeare how men will explode

into the crudest, most deranged form of sexual jealousy on
the smallest amount of (obviously) manufactured 'evidence' –
which Posthumus will swear amounts to 'testimonies ... proof
as strong as grief' (III, iv, 22–4), while Iachimo later admits
it was just 'simular (simulated) proof' (V, v, 200) – and we are
to see it one more, shattering, time, in the next play. As a
phenomenon it clearly fascinated Shakespeare; and, as clearly,
he saw that there could be in men a deep, masochistic pleasure
in the self-torturing thought of infinite ('once and a million')
sexual betrayal. It is a deeply worrying male proclivity which
could have – Shakespeare is often at pains to show – endlessly
ramifying destructive consequences.

And now Posthumus is all over the place, having abandoned
his better self which was invested in his love for (and trust of)
Imogen. He is given a long, incoherent soliloquy, full of gross
sexual fantasizing:

> Perchance he spoke not, but,
> Like a full-acorned boar, a German one,
> Cried 'O!' and mounted
>
> (II, v, 15–17)

and spluttering, uncontrolled misogyny:

> For there's no motion
> That tends to vice in man but I affirm
> It is the woman's part ...
> All faults that have a name, nay, that hell knows,
> Why, hers, in part or all, but rather all.
> ... I'll write against them,
> Detest them, curse them.
>
> (II, v, 20–22, 27–8, 32–3)

That should settle their hash! This, of course, is all furious,
flailing foolishness – a tantrum. Posthumus has become stupid,
coarse, out of control. He has nowhere to go, and he disappears
from the play. Interestingly though, the next two acts will be
plagued by a man who is – stupid, coarse, out of control; and
I can assure you that something funny *is* going on here.

The third act sees the opening up of the action to the
growing row between Rome and Britain and its extension to
the new area of Wales, where we meet the long-banished

Belarius and the King's two lost sons, Guiderius and Arviragus. Imogen, following her 'longing' ('mine's beyond beyond', III, ii, 57), is deceived into setting out for Milford Haven (which is in Wales) by a letter from Posthumus, where he has ordered Pisanio to murder her. It is at this point that Imogen enters the fog. The scenes in the Welsh mountains allow Shakespeare to open up pastoral issues concerning the differing claims and gifts of nature and nurture, and the various dispositions of natural man – thus, Cloten is a born savage made worse by civilization, while Guiderius and Arviragus are brought up as *enfants sauvages* yet reveal innately royal blood:

> How hard it is to hide the sparks of nature!
> These boys know little they are sons to th' King
> ...
> I' th' cave wherein they bow, their thoughts do hit
> The roofs of palaces, and Nature prompts them
> In simple and low things to prince it much
> Beyond the trick of others.
>
> (III, iii, 79–80, 83–6)

Belarius, understandably perhaps, given his bad experiences at court, extols the superior nobility of their simple, primitive life in the wild nature of the mountains. But for the young boys it is 'a cell of ignorance ... a prison':

> Out of your proof you speak. We poor unfledged
> Have never winged from view o' th' nest, nor know not
> What air's from home ...
>   We have seen nothing,
> We are beastly: subtle as the fox for prey,
> Like warlike as the wolf for what we eat.
> Our valor is to chase what flies.
>
> (III, iii, 27–9, 39–42)

Now, this very aerial play – heights and distances, good and bad air to breathe – is full of birds, both mean and proud: puttock, crows (lots of them), jay, raven – most nobly, the eagle; and, supremely, the phoenix. Belarius reveals something about his cowed (not coward) state when he sends the boys racing up to the heights of the hills, telling them to look down on him with a bird's-eye view – 'I'll tread these flats' (III,

iii, 11). He thinks that they will thereby learn a lesson of caution, seeing:

> The sharded beetle in a safer hold
> Than is the full-winged eagle.
>
> (III, iii, 20-21)

A defeated and disappointed man, Belarius has become a convinced hugger of the earth. But princes will needs be airborne, and warrior eagles rather than creeping beetles will command the concluding spaces of the play. And the Welsh mountain retreat is a far from safe refuge – as becomes apparent when the war threatens to engulf them all. Pastoral dreams cannot withstand the rigours of history; and the play refuses to sentimentalize life in the mountain wastes.

When Imogen learns, from the letter to Pisanio, that Posthumus has convicted her of adultery and ordered her death, she perceives a terrible danger which, potentially, threatens society itself.

> All good seeming,
> By thy revolt, O husband, shall be thought
> Put on for villainy, not born where't grows,
> But worn a bait for ladies.
> . . .
> Goodly and gallant shall be false and perjured
> From thy great fail.
>
> (III, iv, 55-8, 64-5)

The world is full of bad seeming which takes in good people – Shakespeare has no more constant theme. But what happens when people will not believe in '*good* seeming' – then *nothing* and no one will be trusted, and goodbye all the virtues. It is, indeed, a 'great fail'. Somehow, the play will have to work to rehabilitate 'good seeming'. But not before there has been some more 'seeming' of, let's say, an indeterminate kind, not least in the form of two disguisings (Pisanio provides both sets of clothes – visibly, the wardrobe man). The first is nothing new in Shakespeare. Imogen, who is now 'dead to my husband' (III, iv, 132 – since Pisanio is supposed to have killed her), dresses up as a boy and sets out to seek service with the 'noble' Roman, Lucius, who is advancing towards Milford Haven.

She is thus the last, and it has to be said least high-spirited, of Shakespeare's epicene heroines. One little aspect of this disguising is worth noting. The wondrous whiteness of Imogen's skin has been noted, and Pisanio regrets that she must expose it to 'the greedy touch/Of common-kissing Titan' (III, iv, 164–5), i.e. get sun-burned ('Titan' is a name applied to the sun by both Virgil and Ovid). Belarius and the princes worship the sun and 'heaven' (the boys are referred to as 'hot summer's tanlings', IV, iv, 29, and you won't be surprised to learn that they are the only 'tanlings' – little tanned ones – in Shakespeare, or indeed anywhere else!), and when Imogen stumbles, as it were, into their territory, she has exchanged the court for life under the open sky – the larger point being that the play is overseen by Jupiter, ruler of the heavens.

I will come back to Imogen's Welsh interlude. But the other disguising – of Cloten – is something else again. I must go back to a short scene in the second act when Cloten was urging his exceedingly unpleasant and unwelcome attentions upon Imogen. She tries to remain courteous in her rebuffs, but when Cloten dismisses Posthumus as 'base slave', she flares out:

> His meanest garment
> That ever hath but clipped his body is dearer
> In my respect than all the hairs above thee,
> Were they all made such men.

(II, iii, 135–8)

All Cloten can do is to stand there repeating incredulously 'His meanest garment?' – four times! Some critics have wondered at this – Frank Kermode, for example, found it excessive. But surely the impression we should get is that of a record that has got stuck. I register Cloten as a kind of automaton – an assemblage of all the conventional stage properties used to identify the villain. He makes all the most horrible and obnoxious villain-like noises – that is what the machine is geared up to do. But he is never intended to come across as a *human* being. Bizarrely enough, in one of my very few appearances on the school stage, I played Guiderius, and when I walked on with Cloten's head, saying:

> This Cloten was a fool, an empty purse;
> There was no money in't. Not Hercules
> Could have knocked out his brains, for he had none
>
> (IV, ii, 113–15)

I was invariably met with gales of laughter. This was doubtless occasioned by my own inherent, undisguisable ridiculousness, but even then I dimly perceived that there was no known histrionic art which could render this entry anything but comic. Brockbank is surely right in suggesting that, with these lines, the 'clotpole' stage head would have been displayed as a hollow property. Very well, it might be said; but what is the point in confronting us with this noisy, hollow contrivance? This takes us to his disguising.

When Cloten hears that Imogen has fled from court, he is sure that she has gone to meet Posthumus, and he determines to follow. First, he bullies Pisanio into helping him, as now he has Posthumus's servant. He tells Pisanio to bring him a set of Posthumus's garments, and it so happens that Pisanio has 'the same suit he wore when he took leave of my lady' (III, v, 125–6). While waiting for the clothes, Cloten runs over his planned revenge.

> She said upon a time – the bitterness of it I now belch from my heart – that she held the very garment of Posthumus in more respect than my noble and natural person, together with the adornment of my qualities. With that suit upon my back will I ravish her; first kill him, and in her eyes. There shall she see my valor, which will then be a torment to her contempt. He on the ground, my speech of insultment ended on his dead body, and when my lust hath dined – which, as I say, to vex her I will execute in the clothes that she so praised – to the court I'll knock her back, foot her home again. She hath despised me rejoicingly, and I'll be merry in my revenge.
>
> (III, v, 134–47)

The brutality machine is turned up to full volume (automata which seem to be alive may look comic, but they can also be very frightening). Pisanio brings the clothes, and Cloten is off.

We next see him wandering around in Wales, well pleased with his disguise – 'How fit his garments serve me!' (IV, i, 2–3): they are suitable – and they fit. He is still relishing his coming revenge – 'Posthumus, thy head, which now is growing

upon thy shoulders, shall within this hour be off' (IV, i, 16–17).
As luck, and the play, would have it, it is *his* head which is off
within the hour, he having run into Guiderius and made the
mistake of treating him contemptuously as some sort of outlaw
mountain criminal. At which provocation, the rightful heir to
the throne quite fittingly despatches and then decapitates the
vile pretender. Which in turn leads to what must be the
strangest scene in Shakespeare. Imogen is thought dead (she
has taken Pisanio's potion which is, in fact, a safe sleeping
draught), and the two young princes lay her out for what
seems like some sort of Celtic, pre-Christian burial – the body
on the earth, strewn with herbs and flowers. At the instigation
of Belarius – 'He was a queen's son, boys' (IV, ii, 244) – they
bury the body of Cloten in the same way, laying it next to
Imogen. They leave – and, of course, Imogen soon wakes up,
understandably dazed, still half in a dream. But then she see
the body.

> A headless man? The garments of Posthumus?
> I know the shape of's leg; this is his hand,
> His foot Mercurial, his Martial thigh,
> The brawns of Hercules; but his Jovial face –
>
> (IV, ii, 308–11)

except, of course, there isn't a face. 'How? 'Tis gone.' Where's
the head? Where on earth is the head? – one imagines her
casting around. The killer might at least have left the head?
(Whatever else this is, it cannot entirely exclude the comical.)
Then, with more laments, and execrations for Pisanio and
Cloten who, Imogen is sure, have killed Posthumus, she falls
on the body, as for one last embrace – 'O my lord, my lord!'
(IV, ii, 332). The Romans approach, Lucius talking to his
Soothsayer, when the spectacle makes him stop – 'Soft, ho,
what trunk is here?/Without his top?' (IV, ii, 353–4). I think
this brings us close to one, at least, of the centres of this
strange play.

Let's go over the moment. A somewhat dazed, half-awake
Imogen finds herself lying next to a headless body wearing
Posthumus's clothes. She not only assumes that it is Posthumus,
but identifies the body, part by part, as that of her beloved –

yet it is the body of the figure she most abhorred, on which she proceeds to throw herself. What is this telling us? Is it the head alone (= quality of mind, refinement of intelligence and understanding) which differentiates man from man? (cf. Imogen just previously:

> But clay and clay differs in dignity,
> Whose dust is both alike.

(IV, ii, 4–5)

– *how* does living clay differ in dignity?) Take off the heads or 'tops', and is there then no difference between Posthumus and Cloten? *And* didn't we see Posthumus effectively 'lose his head' in Rome, succumbing figuratively to what has overtaken Cloten literally? This point was nicely made by Robert Hunter, who suggested that, since we see the insanely jealous Post-humus adopting the mindless savagery of Cloten, during Posthumus's two-act absence Cloten provides us with a present parody of him. Others have suggested that the execution of Cloten in Posthumus's clothes acts as a vicarious or symbolic (or substitute) death of Posthumus's bad self. However you take it, there is certainly an odd continuity between Posthumus and Cloten; and, despite what looks like their all too obvious oppositeness, a curious kind of heads-and-tails identity. They are never on stage together; and their only reported encounter is a very slight skirmish in which neither is hurt (they 'play' rather than 'fight'). The relationship is, I think, more than parodic – though it may well include the warning that if a man loses his grasp on his best self, he may easily relapse into a *parody* of a human being. Not so different as you might think. And Imogen has been unwittingly involved with an inappropriate 'trunk' before – the one containing Iachimo which she ordered to be brought to her bedroom. Thus the poor woman has, variously, spent the night with, and lovingly embraced, the two male 'trunks' which were most hateful to her. Can you ever be really sure who, what, you are embracing – what is in anyone's 'trunk'?

Imogen also has a potentially troubling relationship with the two young princes in the Welsh mountains. Of course, the exiles treat 'him' (she is now Fidele) with all the rural courtesy which displaced courtiers usually encounter – to their surprise – in their pastoral interludes:

> These are kind creatures. Gods, what lies I have heard!
> Our courtiers say all's savage but at court.
> Experience, O, thou disprov'st report!
>
> (IV, ii, 32–4)

So far, this is, conventionally, as it should be. Fidele acts, gratefully, as their 'housewife' (they are the *hunters*), sings to them like an 'angel', and turns out to be a wonderful cook (the point is emphasized – 'But his neat cookery!', IV, ii, 49 – Shakespeare had no need of the 'culinary triangle' of Levi-Strauss to appreciate the importance of cooking methods in signalling culture). This is all domestically harmonious. But the young princes find Fidele *very* attractive. Belarius reacts to him as 'an earthly paragon' – 'Behold divineness/No elder than a boy' (III, vi, 43–4) – not the first time a Shakespearian heroine is taken for a divinity. The boys react, as it were, more physically:

> Were you a woman, youth,
> I should woo hard but be your groom in honesty.
> I'ld bid for you as I do buy.
>
> I'll make't my comfort
> He is a man. I'll love him as my brother ...
>
> (III, vi, 68–71)

Just as their bearing is royal without their knowing they are princes, so here, their behaviour is fraternal without their knowing they are brothers – such are the pleasing ironies of romance. But the certain implication is, that *if* Fidele was a girl – as of course s/he *is* – their attentions would be a good deal closer. Once again, we have a light skirting, flirting with the possibility of incest. Not, I think, gratuitously, and certainly not pruriently – there is not a hint of any untoward behaviour; quite the reverse. But Shakespeare is clearly interested in the imponderable ways in which the sexual impulses are involved in those all important drives which make for family bonds and bondings. If you want to think of sublimation (though the concept seems too crude) – the transforming of the sexual drive into something finer – you may find it in the beautiful dirge the boys speak at Fidele's 'funeral':

> Fear no more more the heat o' th' sun
>   Nor the furious winter's rages
> ...
> Fear no more the frown o' th' great;
>   Thou are past the tyrant's stroke ...
>
> (IV, ii, 258–65 on to 281)

Though in fact there is more heat, and sun, and frowning still to come for the not-dead Fidele; and tyranny has not yet essayed its last stroke. This is not the Forest of Arden.

Indeed it is not; for soon the area is engulfed in the war between the newly-landed Romans and the Britons – 'the noise is round about us' (IV, iv, 1). Characteristically, Belarius wants to hide in the mountains; but Guiderius and Arviragus want to 'look on blood' and try themselves in battle – for royal blood is also knightly-warrior blood – and they all make towards the war. The fog now is at its thickest, and the next person to loom out of it is Posthumus (he has come over as part of the Italian contingent). The Cloten-part of his identity has, as it were, been ritually killed off, so it is not surprising that we see and hear his better self re-emerging. He now bitterly regrets the 'death' of Imogen (he has a bloody handkerchief – Pisanio's 'proof' that he carried out his fatal instructions), shows contrition, and blames himself. Evidence of recovered sanity comes in his remark:

> You married ones,
> If each of you should take this course, how many
> Must murder wives much better than themselves
> For wrying but a little!
>
> (V, i, 2–5)

'Wrying but a little' – just deviating a little from the straight and narrow – shows he has gained a sense of proportion; you don't kill a wife on account of a little loose sex. Note that Posthumus still believes that Iachimo *did* pleasure himself with Imogen. This is important, not only because it reveals that he has learned to forgive her; but also because, in the brief fragment of the war which next occurs in dumb-show, Posthumus, now dressed as a British peasant, actually encounters Iachimo (fighting for the Romans). And '*He vanquisheth and disarmeth Iachimo and then leaves him*' (V, ii, directions). As Hunter points out, this means that we actually *see* Posthumus effectively forgiving Iachimo, whom he would certainly recognize, and whom war would allow him legitimately to despatch. This briefly glimpsed moment adumbrates the mood at the end of the play when Posthumus will be able to say to an abjectly repentant Iachimo:

> The pow'r that I have on you is to spare you;
> The malice towards you to forgive you. Live,
> And deal with others better.

> (V, v, 418–20)

At the sight of which, the inanely choleric old Cymbeline, who goes on wildly trying to hand out death sentences up to the last moment, finally gets the point:

> We'll learn our freeness of a son-in-law:
> Pardon's the word to all.

> (V, v, 421–2)

These merciful gestures have been seen as constituting the specifically Christian turn to the otherwise pagan play; but while there is a deal of Christian terminology in the play (free play is made with the word 'election' in reference to lovers' choices, for example), it seems to me more in keeping with the mood of reconciliation, reunion, recognition (often necessitating contrition and forgiveness) which Shakespeare works to bring about at the conclusions of these last plays. And if Shakespeare has no trouble in putting Renaissance Italy and Celtic Wales in ancient Britain (or vice versa), he certainly won't think twice about having them all in Christendom – even with Jupiter still reigning under his 'radiant roof' (V, iv, 91). Shakespeare's theatre is much more capacious than theology. The atmosphere or mood at the end of the play is neither firmly pagan nor distinctly Christian – it is simply Shakespearian; neither very definitely here, nor unmistakably there: rather – 'beyond beyond'.

The last act recounts the brutal confusions of war ('lolling the tongue with slaught'ring' – as graphic as *Guernica*: V, iii, 8), the heroic exploits of Posthumus and the triumphant trio of Belarius, Guiderius and Arviragus. Britain and Cymbeline are saved by the virtues and efforts of those whom the King had so stupidly and blindly banished. Careless of life (still thinking he is guilty of Imogen's death), Posthumus allows himself to be wrongfully imprisoned and sentenced to death (well, 'fear no more – tavern bills' says the rather jocular Jailer – surely, as Brockbank suggested, a lightly comic echo of the earlier dirge: V, iv, 129–30), and it is in prison that his parents and Jupiter appear to him in a dream. Jupiter is given what is often taken to be a crucial speech (he is answering the family ghosts who are both reproaching him, as men have always reproached their gods, along the lines of – why do you let such atrociously unjust things happen? and asking his help – 'Peep through thy marble mansion', V, iv, 60):

> Be not with mortal accidents opprest.
>> No care of yours it is; you know 'tis ours.
> Whom best I love I cross; to make my gift,
>> The more delayed, delighted …

> (V, iv, 69–72)

This is more or less how gods have always answered men, when they deign to talk to them at all. God moves in a mysterious way – and don't ask questions. This is, as it were, the bottom line of religion. Jupiter's announcement of himself and his ways is little more than a theological platitude, and the idea that this manifestly stagey theophany is an electrifying revelation of godhead among mortals seems to me misconceived. Jupiter then makes what must have been a tricky theatrical exit – 'Mount, eagle, to my palace crystalline' (V, iv, 83).

Against this, we may put the relatively unillumined human perspective of Pisanio: 'Fortune brings in some boats that are not steered' (IV, iii, 46). There's the question – is there a god, any god, overseeing, directing, 'steering' all? Is there any kind of Providence 'shaping' our rough-hewn manglings? Does a divinity 'peep through' marble mansions, blankets of dark, whatever? ('Peep' is the perfect, modest word – for whatever the state of our unbelief, there are times when most of us have a sense, a glimpse, that something more than us might just have an eye for what is going on down here.) Is there a Jupiter – or is there just a Shakespeare, using the god's name to put his signature deifically on the play? Or should we defer to Fortune, more or less tidying things up? The questions manifestly cannot be resolved (unless we are sure we know the answers all along), and I'm not sure that it greatly matters when it comes to responding to the play. What Shakespeare *does*, having brought matters to an unholy state of utter confusion (he has thrown in an oracular text, found by Posthumus when he wakes in prison, to further confound matters and add to the growingly-felt need for explanations), is, effectively, to invite us to wonder at how quickly the fog can be burned off. As it does in the remaining scene, in an explosive series of revelations and recognitions which can hardly be kept pace with, so that the audience is dazzled while the characters stagger. The peak, and cracking point, comes when Posthumus strikes the as-yet-unrecognized Imogen to the ground. At this, it is as if, not only we, but the play itself cannot take any more, and it rushes unpausingly to a conclusion with a torrent of clarifications and recognitions. 'Does the world go round?' asks the dizzied King (V, v, 232). Yes it does; bringing in its changes and its restorations, time's revenges (Cloten and the Queen are dead) and the season's rebirths and renewals. The fruit is back on the tree, and the lovers are in one another's arms. 'Hang there like fruit, my soul,/Till the tree die' (V, v, 263–4) says Posthumus to Imogen as she embraces him – all error cleared – in a line that brought tears to Tennyson's eyes. The Phoenix has risen from its ashes (Imogen, 'th' Arabian bird'); the Roman eagle is 'on wing soaring aloft', united to the 'radiant Cymbeline'; the 'majestic cedar' of Britain has been 'revived'. And now – 'such a peace' (the last words). All clear. All settled. All over.

Shakespeare has taken an assortment of the most disparate, incongruous, intractable material imaginable, all concerning important matters – sexual, familial, dynastic, political, imperial; and proceeds to show with what a light touch it can be handled. He allows it to puddle and fog together to the point of hopeless chaos, and then – whoosh! it's all significantly related and cleared up. And suddenly the play seems to have been like Imogen's dream:

> 'Twas but a bolt of nothing, shot at nothing,
> Which the brain makes of fumes.

(IV, ii, 300–301)

Our pleasure should be tragical-historical-comical-pastoral-romantical; and also, theatrical-magical. *Cymbeline*, it seems to me, is the most *extra-ordinary* play that Shakespeare ever wrote. How does he do it? Staggering!

THE WINTER'S TALE (1611)

> Who was most marble there changed color

(V, ii, 96–7)

> warm life,
> As now it coldly stands

(V, iii, 35–6)

Thunder from a clear sky. For the ancient Greeks, it bespoke the gods – was the gods speaking. It is the sign given to Odysseus before he re-enters his home. Oedipus knows the gods are calling him to his mysterious death by 'harsh and constant thunder'. It is heard again in this play by Cleomenes and Dion on their visit to the oracle:

> the burst
> And the ear-deaf'ning voice o' th' oracle,
> Kin to Jove's thunder

(III, i, 8–10)

But there is thunder out of a clear sky among mortals, too. Leontes' sudden jealousy is not animated, motivated, precipitated by anything at all – not even the insinuations of a Iago or the goadings of a Iachimo. Nothing. It just erupts, explodes, bursts – thunder from a clear sky. E. M. W. Tillyard refers to the 'god-sent lunacies' of the Greeks – Ajax, Heracles. This is apt enough, but Shakespeare makes it clear that there is *no* influence working on Leontes outside his own sick mind

and 'pestered' senses. His destructive outburst is another 'great
fail' – perhaps the greatest one in Shakespeare. What might
be involved in effecting any kind of restoration after the
damage he has caused (not least to himself) occupies the rest
of the play.

As in *Pericles* we have three acts showing the destruction
and scattering of a royal family; a fourth act centring on the
long-lost daughter; and a final act dedicated to recognitions
and family reunion. But Pericles was quite blameless for what
befalls him and his family; whereas Leontes is the absolute
author of, and exclusively responsible for, the disasters that
destroy his house. Not that Shakespeare is offering a drama-
tization of the etiology of jealousy, a psychological tracing of
its inception and its workings. He simply starts with the final
explosion, and an incredible feeling of out-of-nowhere-ness. It
is instructive to compare this opening with that of his main
source for the play, the romance *Pandosto* by Robert Greene.
(In part, Shakespeare follows Greene very closely – there are
more echoes of his source than in any other play; but he
makes some absolutely crucial changes, to which I will come.)

Greene starts his tale with a long paragraph moralizing on
the dangers of jealousy: 'Among all the passions wherewith
human mindes are perplexed, there is none that so galleth
with restlesse despight, as the infectious soare of jealousy', and
so on. The story starts with a description of the growing
affectionate friendship between Bellaria (Hermione) and
Egistus (Polixenes), beloved friend of Pandosto (Leontes). Bellaria is very friendly indeed with Egistus, 'oftentimes comming
her selfe into his bed chamber, to see that nothing should be
amiss to dislike him'. There is never a hint that this is other
than chaste courtesy, though I suppose there are quite a few
husbands who might raise the shade of one eyebrow at such
demonstrative concern. Their intimacy develops – long walks
together, 'private and pleasant devices' – until 'a certaine
melancholy passion entring the minde of Pandosto, drave him
into sundry and doubtefull thoughts'.

First, he called to minde the beauty of his wife Bellaria, the comeliness
and braverie of his friend Egistus, thinking that Love was above all
Lawes, and therefore to be staied with no Law: that it was hard to

put fire and flaxe together without burning; that their open pleasures might breede his secrete displeasure. He considered with himselfe that Egistus was a man, and must needes love: that his wife was a woman, and therefore subject unto love, and that where fancy forced, friendship was of no force.

These and such like doubtfull thoughtes *a long time* smoothering in his stomacke, beganne *at last* to kindle in his minde a secret mistrust, which increased by suspition, grewe *at last* to be a flaming Jealousie, that so tormented him as he could take no rest. (my italics)

And now the story gets under way. Pandosto's jealousy is very reprehensible, no doubt, and he pays for it. But it is prepared for, explained if not excused, and given a relatively long incubation period before it grows at last to be a 'flaming Jealousie'. In Shakespeare's play there is none of this – we are confronted with spontaneous combustion.

There are two other major changes Shakespeare makes to his source which it is worth noting before we consider the play. When the oracle proclaiming Bellaria's (Hermione's) innocence is read out, Pandosto (unlike the more deranged Leontes) *instantly* accepts it, and is ashamed, repentant, apologetic – though it's too late, of course. His son dies, and then Bellaria dies, and dies in good earnest. Shakespeare, or rather Paulina, keeps Hermione alive in secret – *but*, and this is unique in Shakespeare in relation to such a key bit of information, the secret is kept from the audience, as well as from the King and court. The original audience of the play, many of whom would have read the popular *Pandosto*, would certainly have been sure that Hermione was truly dead at the end of Act III – and so, ideally (but now impossibly), should we.

In the concluding part of the story, when Dorastus (Florizel) arrives at Pandosto's court with Fawnia (Perdita), Pandosto is so taken with Fawnia's beauty that he feels a sudden overwhelming lust for her. He has Dorastus thrown into prison (and 'heavie Irons') to get him out of the way, and, 'broyling at the heat of unlawful lust', trys to persuade Fawnia to submit to his 'hot desire', threatening to use his 'power' to compel her 'by force' if necessary. When he is thwarted in his base intention, he says she will be put to death. He discovers that she is his daughter by the same plot moves that operate in

Shakespeare, but his reaction is very different from that of Leontes.

Pandosto (calling to mind how first he betraied his friend Egistus, how his jealousie was the cause of Bellaria's death, and that contrarie to the law of nature hee had lusted after his owne daughter) moved with these desperate thoughts, he fell into a melancholic fit, and to close up the Comedie with a Tragicall stratageme, he slewe himselfe ...

The incest possibility is only fleetingly glimpsed at in *The Winter's Tale*. Leontes expresses a momentary desire to have Perdita for himself; but, under correction from the ever vigilant Paulina, hastily says that all he meant was that she reminded him of his 'dead' wife – as indeed, well she might since she is her daughter. As in the previous two plays, Shakespeare allows the merest whiff of incest to linger briefly in the air. But he has other business in hand, and a quite other conclusion in mind. He will close up his almost-tragedy with a comic 'stratageme' which nobody else could have dreamed of.

The Winter's Tale opens in Sicilia, and this marks another, smaller, change which Shakespeare makes to his source. The play moves from Sicilia to Bohemia; in Greene, it is the other way round. (Though Shakespeare gives Bohemia a coast – probably because he wants a shipwreck: it doesn't matter, any more than it matters that in a play set in a pre-Christian era there are references to an Emperor of Russia, a Puritan, a Renaissance artist, Whitsun pastorals, the betrayal of Christ. This is romance.) Sicilian and Bohemian lords are discussing the very close relationship and amity that exists between their two kings:

Camillo. They were trained together in their childhoods; and there rooted betwixt them then such an affection, which cannot choose but branch now. Since their more mature dignities and royal necessities made separation of their society ... they have seemed to be together, though absent: shook hands, as over a vast; and embraced as it were from the ends of opposed winds. The heavens continue their loves!

Archidamus. I think there is not in the world either malice or matter to alter it.

(I, i, 23–35)

They conclude by emphasizing the importance of the child, Prince Mamillius, Leontes' son and heir. The emphasis is both on the two boys' closeness and near inseparability; and on the inevitable separation occasioned by their 'more mature dignities and royal necessities'. What these mature necessities amounted to is indicated by the consequent discussion of the child. Kings must marry and breed. The 'malice and matter' which will indeed 'alter' the two men's loving relationship is going to stem from that simple fact.

The second scene opens with Polixenes saying that 'Nine changes of the wat'ry star' have passed since his arrival. Here, he mentions the fact to lend force to his insistence that it is high time he returned to his own kingdom. It will soon take on much more importance, since a sojourn of nine months will afford Leontes some 'matter' to back up his paranoid insistence that Hermione's new-born child was fathered by Polixenes. This detail is not in Greene but it is in Ovid in a very different, but perhaps not unrelated context. *Metamorphoses* includes the story of one of Diana's nymphs, Callisto, who was raped by Jove. After 'nine times the crescent moon had filled her orb' she gives birth, and Diana – thinking Callisto was a willing partner to her unchaste act – is so furious she turns Callisto into a bear. 'She was a bear, but kept her woman's heart.' She is always having to flee from hunters, and is nearly killed by her own son out hunting – Jove intervenes and turns them into stars. It wouldn't do to make too much of this; but there *is* an important bear in Shakespeare's play (probably also being hunted when he kills Antigonus), and I think Bate has a point when he says that both Callisto and Hermione are wrongfully accused of conceiving a child out of their own wantonness and lust. Shakespeare uses the bear, but he turns Hermione into something else.

As if to emphasize the importance of breeding, Queen Hermione enters, visibly pregnant. There have been a few pregnant women in Shakespeare's previous plays: Tamora must be pregnant at one stage in *Titus Andronicus*; Jaquenetta is mentioned as pregnant in *Love's Labor's Lost*; we are told that a babe has been 'molded' in Thaisa, in *Pericles*; and it is the evidence of sexual activity 'grossly writ' on the almost completely silent Juliet that prompts Angelo to initiate his reign of terror in *Measure for Measure*. But there is nothing like the central focus that there is on the pregnant Hermione who, we soon hear, 'rounds apace' and 'is spread of late into a goodly bulk' (II, i, 16, 20). That growing, unborn babe is, and will provide, vital 'matter' – in every sense. 'Birth' is what Carol Neely calls 'the play's central miracle'. The word 'issue' occurs fourteen times, far more than in any other play; and, as it happens, seven times it refers more specifically to children, and seven times more generally to outcome – though, of course, it invariably glances at both. As Cleomenes and Dion return with the 'sealed up' oracle, they hope that when the contents come out –

> something rare
> Even then will rush to knowledge ...
> And gracious be the issue!

> (III, i, 20–22)

The 'something rare' will turn out to be the knowledge of Hermione's innocence, *and* the birth of her daughter Perdita – both come in a 'rush'; and the overall 'issue' will, *finally*, prove to be 'gracious'. 'Thou met'st with things dying, I with things new born' (III, iii, 112–13) is, rightly, a famous and memorable line, but the whole lexicon of pregnancy, birth, breeding, delivery – used literally and metaphorically – is pervasive. The birth of the baby, Perdita, is described in a way which, potentially, generalizes it enormously.

> This child was prisoner to the womb and is
> By law and process of great Nature thence
> Freed, and enfranchised

> (II, ii, 58–60)

The 'law and process of great Nature' will have to do a great deal of freeing and enfranchising, outside the nursery as well. The final 'enfranchisement' will be the liberation of Hermione from stone, a process which, Neely suggests, imitates labour and delivery. Neely writes well of the importance of the whole vocabulary of birth in the play. 'The metaphors emphasize the fundamental components of the process of reproduction;

union and fullness, labour and separation, creation and loss, risk and fulfilment, enclosure and enfranchisement.' Certainly, the reproductive repair of the damage caused by the two kings is entirely dependent on three women – Hermione, Paulina and Perdita.

The scene proceeds with courtly courtesy as the Queen is enlisted by Leontes to persuade Polixenes to defer his departure. Hermione takes Polixenes back to his childhood relationship with her husband – 'You were pretty lordlings then?'

> We were, fair Queen,
> Two lads that thought there was no more behind
> But such a day tomorrow as today,
> And to be boy eternal.
>
> (I, ii, 62–5)

Psychoanalysts – not that I'm eager to draw them in – recognize what they indeed call a '*puer eternus*' syndrome, the arrested mental and emotional condition of a man who wishes to remain 'boy eternal' and avoid growing up with its attendant responsibilities. Leontes and Polixenes clearly have some of that disposition. Polixenes looks longingly back to when 'we were as twinned lambs' and only changed 'innocence for innocence'; and if, he says, our spirits had 'ne'er been higher reared/With stronger blood' we would have remained untainted by original sin (I, ii, 67–74). Hermione is quick to see the implication – 'By this we gather/You have tripped since', 'tripped' being a nicely polite way of saying 'fallen'. The exchange which follows is conducted at the level of decorous banter – but, in retrospect it is heavily ominous.

> *Polixenes.*   O my most sacred lady,
> Temptations have since then been born to's, for
> In those unfledged days was my wife a girl;
> Your precious self had not then crossed the eyes
> Of my young playfellow.
>
> *Hermione.*   Grace to boot!
> Of this make no conclusion, lest you say
> Your queen and I are devils. Yet go on,
> Th' offenses we have made you do we'll answer ...
>
> (I, ii, 75–83)

By Eve man fell – so the Good Book says. Polixenes is blaming the irresistible temptations and compulsions of sex (that 'stronger blood' that comes with growth) for the loss of his and Leontes' 'innocence' and their consequent separation, eternal boys no longer. Hermione laughingly points out the damning implications for the two Queens in this line of thinking. This is all courtly playfulness – the sort of poised and witty courtesy appropriate in a regal group. But Hermione *is* about to be turned into a 'devil'; and both she and her daughter will be made to 'answer' for imaginary offences attributed to their sexuality, or rather their sex. For somewhere in these boy-kings, there is a fear of woman as such – a fear which can turn to loathing, as Leontes is about to demonstrate (Leontes is, of course, the guiltiest in this respect, but Polixenes is not exempt, as a later outburst to Perdita will reveal).

Hermione 'grace-fully' – and she is, and will prove to be a figure of 'Grace' – persuades Polixenes to stay, and Leontes is well pleased. And then, quite suddenly, he is something else.

> [*Aside*] Too hot, too hot!
> To mingle friendship far is mingling bloods.
> I have tremor cordis on me; my heart dances,
> But not for joy, not joy.

(I, ii, 108–11)

Just what his heart *is* dancing with is hard to define. His next three speeches, and then his soliloquy after Hermione and Polixenes have left to walk in the garden, are among the most extraordinary that Shakespeare ever wrote. I know nothing else in literature which so tellingly dramatizes a mind procuring its own unease. At times seeming to talk to his uncomprehending young son, but really talking semi-coherently to himself in what Tillyard called 'hot and twisted words', Leontes is diving into the unfathomable depths of self-generated jealousy, the perverse, male, masochistic relish of imagined sexual betrayal which Shakespeare has keenly eyed in previous plays. To Leontes' wilfully disordered perception, courteous and friendly exchanges become 'paddling palms and pinching fingers' (I, ii, 115). Having lodged the sick-sweet thought in his mind that his wife is betraying him, Leontes scratches the sore and tongues the wound.

> Inch-thick, knee-deep, o'er head and ears a forked one!
> Go play, boy, play: thy mother plays, and I
> Play too – but so disgraced a part, whose issue
> Will hiss me to my grave
>
> (I, ii, 186–9)

Children's play, sexual play, theatrical play – Leontes' over-heated and distempered imagination is melting everything into a scorchingly self-tormenting synthesis. Sexual nausea is fuelling the fire:

> And many a man there is, even at this present,
> Now, while I speak this, holds his wife by th'arm,
> That little thinks she has been sluiced in's absence,
> And his pond fished by his next neighbor, by
> Sir Smile, his neighbor ...
> Physic for't there's none;
> It is a bawdy planet ...
> Be it concluded,
> No barricado for a belly. Know't
> It will let in and out the enemy,
> With bag and baggage.
>
> (I, ii, 192–206)

Foul, unspeakably foul; but what a *pleasure* to spit out the words – sluiced, fished, belly, in and out, bag and baggage. Who can understand the mind's, and the mouth's, strange self-mortifying satisfactions? The larger, unspoken question is – what do we do about, how do we cope with, our inescapable sexuality? Shakespeare really is going for the big 'issues'.

As can happen in the broken and disjunctive self-picking mutterings of an erstwhile sane (majestic) mind, the murmured roving ravings of Leontes happen on an enigmatically and confusedly illuminating core.

> Can thy dam, may't be?
> Affection! Thy intention stabs the center.
> Thou dost make possible things not so held,
> Communicat'st with dreams – how can this be? –
> With what's unreal thou coactive art,
> And fellow'st nothing. Then 'tis very credent
> Thou mayst co-join with something, and thou dost,
> And that beyond commission, and I find it,

And that to the infection of my brains,
And hardening of my brows.

(I, ii, 138–46)

Starting by considering whether his son's mother could possibly
be unfaithful, he embarks on a semi-unintelligible yet curiously
revealing musing on the power of lustful passion ('affection'): it
'stabs the center' – of women, certainly; but also of a man's
heart; perhaps it goes to the heart of the world itself. It makes it
possible for people to dream of impossible (prohibited) things
(sexual acts), and then to make the dream seem real. So when
there *is* something (someone) real there, it is easy to believe that
lust will actually commit unthinkable things – as it is doing now,
and it's driving me mad as I feel myself becoming a cuckold.
That – filling in the lacunae left or jumped over by his incon-
sequent thinking – is one sort of sense. But if you hear it as
Leontes (unconsciously) saying that *my* passion is coactive with
unrealities, is communicating with dreams, and is peopling a
vacancy – he is revealing no less than the deep truth. His brain
is *self*-infected, and his head is hardening indeed.

Now determined beyond doubt that his wife is 'slippery', he
speaks of her in foul terms to Camillo, who bravely responds –
'You never spoke what did become you less/Than this' (I, ii,
282–3). But, for Leontes, the 'evidence' is now so obvious and
overwhelming – how fertile is a fixated mind! – that anyone who
cannot see it, or attempts to gainsay it, is a liar and an enemy.
Ordered to poison Polixenes, Camillo – seeing that Leontes is
now beyond reach in an insanely distorted world of his own
making – instead tells Polixenes of Leontes' grotesque delusion,
which occasions a telling exchange:

> *Polixenes.*   How should this grow?
> *Camillo.* I know not: but I am sure 'tis safer to
> Avoid what's grown than question how 'tis born.

(I, ii, 432–4)

This is, at present, the best wisdom at court. They make a
stealthy departure for Bohemia.

Their flight is proof on proof to Leontes: 'How blest am I/
In my just censure, in my true opinion' (II, i, 36–7). He then
develops at some length a surprisingly coherent image:

c

> There may be in the cup
> A spider steeped, and one may drink, depart,
> And yet partake no venom, for his knowledge
> Is not infected; but if one present
> Th' abhorred ingredient to his eye, make known
> How he hath drunk, he cracks his gorge, his sides,
> With violent hefts. I have drunk, and seen the spider.
>
> (II, i, 39–45)

So much was common superstition (that spiders were only venomous in food and drink if you saw them). For Leontes, the figure fits his case perfectly – you detect the self-pitying self-dramatization in the last line. What is becoming clearer, and more worrying, is that he *needs* to see the spider, he *likes* to see the spider, there *must be* a spider! Hence the following unbelievably gross speeches to his wife. He calls her, in front of the court, 'adult'ress', 'bed-swerver', 'traitor', and announces that Polixenes 'has made thee swell thus' (II, i, 61). With truly regal dignity and restraint, Hermione makes a memorable response:

> When you shall come to clearer knowledge ...
>   Gentle my lord,
> You scarce can right me throughly then to say
> You did mistake.
>
> (II, i, 97–100)

Leontes orders her son to be removed from her, and has her imprisoned. As often happens, subsidiary figures keep their sanity and still see clearly. Antigonus says:

> You are abused, and by some putter-on
> That will be damned for't. Would I knew the villain
>
> (II, i, 141–2)

Posthumus was 'abused' by 'putter-on' Iachimo. Here, of course, the 'villain' is Leontes abusing Leontes. It takes Shakespeare to show us how a man can be a 'putter-on' to himself.

Nobody can reach him, or, as we say, get through to him now. 'The matter, [that word again]/The loss, the gain, the ord'ring on't/Is all properly ours', he announces (II, i, 168–70). This is a true claim, though not in the sense he intends it. He

is asserting his royal 'prerogative'; but, in effect, he *is* ordering
– disordering – 'the matter', disposing of the material and
arranging the 'reality', to suit and fit his own determinations.
And, like jealous characters before him, he is absolutely certain
of his evidence. He refers again to the sexual relationship
between Hermione and Polixenes –

> Which was as gross as ever touched conjecture,
> That lacks sight only, naught for approbation
> But only seeing, all other circumstances
> Made up to th' deed

(II, i, 176–9)

'Approbation' is 'proof', and Leontes is sure he has all he
needs. He lacks what Othello asked for – '*ocular* proof'; but,
as Iago reasonably enough pointed out, it is in the nature of
the deed that this kind of proof is effectively unobtainable.
Instead, Iago proffers 'imputation and strong circumstances'
(*Othello* III, iii, 403); these are enough for Othello, and they
are enough for Leontes, though he has proferred them to
himself. He relies on 'circumstances' and 'conjectures' (in the
Induction to 2 *Henry IV* 15–16, 'Rumor is a pipe'/Blown by
surmises, jealousies, conjectures'). That all this is no evidence
at all but rather the reverse, hardly needs stressing. But
Leontes is King, and he has the power, and thus the ordering
of the matter – if he says that it is so, then, to all intents and
purposes, it *is* so. But only for a while. He reveals that he has
sent Cleomenes and Dion to the oracle of Apollo (which, like
Greene, Shakespeare mistakenly thought was at Delphos) 'for
a greater confirmation' and he is confident that 'from the
oracle/They will bring all' (II, i, 180, 185–6). Indeed they will.

Paulina (Shakespeare's creation) now enters the play. Hermione has given birth to a daughter in prison, and Paulina
determines to take the baby to the King, confidently breaking
through the lords who would prevent her unwanted approach
with the promise:

> I
>
> Do come with words as medicinal as true,
> Honest as either, to purge him of that humor
> That presses him from sleep.

(II, iii, 35–8)

Medicine and purgation the sick King certainly needs, but an outspokenly reproachful woman carrying what he takes to be the illegitimate child of his wife is the last thing he wants. It drives him into a mad fury. While Paulina resolutely points out the baby's likeness to the King (eye, nose, lip, forehead, chin, cheek – body parts are important in this play), thanking 'good goddess Nature, which hast made it/So like to him that got it' (II, iii, 102–3), Leontes is frantically ordering his men to 'take up the bastard', burn the bastard, dash the bastard's brains out – he says the word at least eight times, much as he kept calling Hermione 'adultress', as if mere reiteration provides some assuaging satisfaction, or perverse profaning pleasure. Of the many subsequent ironies prepared for in this abusive repetition of 'bastard', none extends further than this –

> Shall I live on to see this bastard kneel
> And call me father?
>
> (II, iii, 153–4)

Only if you are very lucky, very penitent, very blessed by 'great goddess Nature'. But, for now Leontes orders that this 'female bastard' should be taken to 'some remote and desert place' and abandoned (II, iii, 174).

The short opening scene of Act III is literally a breath of fresh air, reminding us how unpleasantly heated, fetid and claustrophobic the court has become. Out on the open road, Cleomenes and Dion are marvelling in retrospect at the atmosphere on the temple-island of the oracle – 'The climate's delicate, the air most sweet,/Fertile the isle' (III, i, 1–2) – bringing home to us the indelicacy, foulness, and sterility (children dead and thrown out) which have prevailed in the preceding scenes. Dion says:

> I shall report,
> For most it caught me, the *celestial* habits
> (Methinks I so should term them) and the *reverence*
> Of the *grave* wearers. O, the sacrifice,
> How *ceremonious, solemn, and unearthly*
> It was i' th' off'ring!
>
> (III, i, 3–8 – my italics)

The italicized words remind us of all the positive, civilized qualities and dignities which Leontes has abandoned or destroyed in his own court, where, truly, all the 'ceremonies of innocence' have been drowned. Oh for a cup of this island air – one might fairly yearn. But we are instantly plunged back into the inverted, deranged world that Leontes is creating around him. We are in what Leontes calls 'a court of justice'. It is, of course, quite monstrously the reverse.

We have, more than once in Shakespeare, seen ruthless characters appropriate the language and procedures of the law, and subvert, *per*vert, them to serve, and seemingly justify, their own wilful and dastardly purposes – Othello and Angelo come to mind, but the phenomenon is widespread. It is, of course, a standard practice of all tyrants; and in trying to clear himself of such a charge, Leontes simply draws attention to its truth and applicability.

> Let us be cleared
> Of being tyrannous, since we so openly
> Proceed in justice, which shall have due course,
> Even to the guilt or the purgation.
>
> (III, ii, 4–7)

Oh no it won't; or rather, in the end it *will*, but not through the agency of Leontes.

He continues with his unevidenced accusations, and Hermione's three long speeches in her own defence are models of dignity, decorum and poise. As she so accurately says:

> if I shall be condemned
> Upon surmises, all proofs sleeping else
> But what your jealousies awake, I tell you
> 'Tis rigor, and not law.
>
> (III, ii, 109–12)

Shakespeare often speaks of the 'rigor' *of* the law; Leontes has substituted it *for* the law. It seems a too moderate word for his behaviour. Hermione appeals to a higher court:

> if powers divine
> Behold our human actions – as they do –
> I doubt not then, but Innocence shall make
> False Accusation blush, and Tyranny
> Tremble at Patience.
>
> (III, ii, 27–31)

INTRODUCTION

The personifications bring in something of the atmosphere of a morality play – appropriately enough, since Leontes has become the embodiment of Tyranny, while Hermione will prove herself the quintessence of Patience – that indispensable virtue in these late plays. Hermione rests her case, as it were:

> Your honors all,
> I do refer me to the oracle:
> Apollo be my judge!
>
> (III, ii, 112–14)

Leontes gives the order – 'Break up the seals and read.' And now Apollo delivers some of *his* thunder:

'Hermione is chaste, Polixenes blameless, Camillo a true subject, Leontes a jealous tyrant, his innocent babe truly begotten, and the King shall live without an heir, if that which is lost be not found.'

> (III, ii, 130–33)

Leontes tries to dismiss it – a last hopeless madness:

> There is no truth i' th' oracle,
> The sessions shall proceed; this is mere falsehood.
>
> (III, ii, 137–8)

But then things start to happen quickly.

He is told his son has died, and Leontes realizes that the gods are angry:

> Apollo, pardon
> My great profaneness 'gainst thine oracle.
> I'll reconcile me to Polixenes,
> New woo my queen, recall the good Camillo
>
> (III, ii, 150–53)

– and everything will be fine again. But rectification, reparation and restoration are not so easily achieved or arrived at – not by a very long way. Paulina then enters with the news that the Queen is dead, and it is now that Paulina comes into her own and takes on a dominant role. She is the deliberately tactless and abrasive voice of accusation and reproach and even 'vengeance'. In modern parlance, she gives Leontes a tongue-lashing; she says all the things that the 'dead' Hermione would be all too justified in saying – indeed, Paulina effectively

stands in for the Queen during her long absence. She calls
Leontes a lot of unkingly names in a most uncourtly manner.
Think of all the tyrannous, damnable things you have done,
she tells him, 'And then run mad indeed, stark mad' (III, ii,
181). Leontes cowers before her, concedes the justice of what
she says, and agrees to follow the course of penitence and
repentance she lays down. Effectively, she becomes the custo-
dian of his conscience. One of her speeches is prophetic – and
not, I feel, without a degree of calculation. She insists that
Hermione is dead:

> I say she's dead; I'll swear it. If word nor oath
> Prevail not, go and see; if you can bring
> Tincture or luster in her lip, her eye,
> *Heat* outwardly or *breath* within, I'll serve you
> As I would do the gods. But, O thou tyrant
> Do not repent these things, for they are heavier
> Than all thy woes can *stir*; therefore betake thee
> To nothing but despair.

> (III, ii, 201–8 – my italics)

Now, not that anybody else knows it, including the audience,
but this is simply not true. Hermione is not dead. This is
artifice (or lying with a positive purpose); and I sense that
Paulina already has her long-term plot in mind, since this
speech anticipates the final scene in which 'heat', 'breath',
and 'stir' will prove to be the crucial, climactic words and
phenomena. But of course, everyone from the King down
believes Paulina; and as far as the audience is concerned the
action has come to a tragic conclusion. But it's only the end
of Act III. What will Shakespeare do now?

There is, in fact, one more scene to Act III, and it serves
as a bridge between the court of Sicilia and rural Bohemia.
Set on the famously non-existent sea-coast of Bohemia, it
shows Lord Antigonus depositing the dead Queen's rejected
child in a deserted spot, as ordered by the King. Antigonus is
convinced that Hermione is dead because he has had a
particularly vivid dream. He says to the babe that he is sure
he has seen her dead mother's spirit:

> thy mother
> Appeared to me last night; for ne'er was dream

So like awaking.

(III, iii, 16-18)

There is a greater 'awaking'-dream yet to come. In this one, Hermione has seemingly returned to instruct Antigonus:

> In pure white robes,
> Like very sanctity, she did approach
> My cabin where I lay; thrice bowed before me,
> And, gasping to begin some speech, her eyes
> Became two spouts; the fury spent, anon
> Did this break from her: 'Good Antigonus,
> Since fate, against thy better disposition,
> Hath made thy person for the thrower-out
> Of my poor babe, according to thy oath,
> Places remote enough are in Bohemia,
> There weep, and leave it crying; and for the babe
> Is counted lost forever, Perdita
> I prithee call't ...'

(III, iii, 21-33)

In this apparitional form, Hermione appears as something of a goddess (and something of a fury), rather like Diana ordering Pericles in a dream; she has taken on an unearthly, holy authority. Something, some power, seems to be intervening to direct things. (In *Pandosto* the baby is abandoned in a boat in the sea and arrives at the island of Sicilia by chance.)

Antigonus of course obeys; and here is laying Perdita down in a remote part of Bohemia. Stormy weather threatens; the day darkens ominously – 'A savage clamor' (III, iii, 55). He exits 'pursued by a bear'. Incontestably a comical stage direction looked at flat. But, in context, it is not funny. The bear, itself probably either starving or being hunted and frightened into attack (Callisto), like the storm at sea which wrecks the ship while the bear is tearing Antigonus to pieces, is part of the 'savage' side of nature which seems to have been activated and released in relation or response – in some obscure way – to the savage and unnatural acts of Leontes.

Then a shepherd enters – and we are in a different world. It is not just that he speaks in prose, which we have not heard since the gentlemanly chatting of the opening scene – though of course that does have the effect of slackening the tension.

The voice is also so down-to-earth, of-the-earth; in touch, as one feels, with what Whitman called the 'primal sanities of nature'. The Shepherd talks easily of 'country matters' – hunting and herding, stealing and fighting, browsing and wenching (he is notably relaxed about sex). Here, one feels, is a clear-sighted, sober-minded realist. After hearing Leontes raving round his Sicilian court, it makes a change. Finding little Perdita, the Shepherd instinctively takes her up – 'for pity'. Similarly, his son Clown (in the original sense of rustic), goes off to bury the remains of Antigonus – 'That's a good deed' says his father approvingly (III, iii, 132). Between them, they take care of 'things new born' *and* 'things dying'. This is not to idealize or sentimentalize our country cousins. Simply, they are people with sound instincts still in place – perhaps, indeed, partly because they have never had to negotiate the complex power relations, the hierarchical rituals and ceremonial deferences, the bribes and threats, of court. Shepherd and Clown remain nameless – they are generic, even telluric, and long may the earth continue to produce them.

At the start of Act IV, Time comes forward himself and whisks away sixteen years, inviting us to turn our attention to the children of the Kings: Prince Florizel, and Perdita 'now grown in grace/Equal with wond'ring' (IV, i, 24–5). This effortless 'sliding' over 'wide gaps' of time is entirely appropriate in a romance. But it must not be thought that the omitted time leaves no traces – just as it is the time which permits Perdita to grow to beauty, so it is the time which will bring wrinkles to her mother's face. As Time says, he is responsible for the bringing in of the 'freshest things'; but he will also 'make stale/The glistering of this present' (IV, i, 12–14). He allows 'errors' to be made; but ensures that matters will, in due course, be 'unfolded'. He ruins, and reveals; erases and renews. As Kermode has pointed out, Shakespeare's attitude to Time is comparable to Spenser's as expressed in the Mutabilitie Cantos:

> All things steadfastness do hate
> And changed be: yet being rightly weighed
> They are not changed from their first estate,
> But by their change their being do dilate,

And turning to themselves at length again,
Do work their own perfection so by fate.

The subtitle of *Pandosto* is: 'The Triumph of Time. Wherein is discovered by a pleasant Historie, that although by the meanes of sinister fortune, Truth may be concealed yet by Time in spight of fortune it is most manifestly revealed.' Shakespeare prefers more compact, pregnant formulations, but the feeling is shared.

Then a short scene which reveals Polixenes' concern that his son is spending a lot of time away from the court at the house of a shepherd who is reported to have 'a daughter of most rare note' (IV, ii, 45). Polixenes intends that he and Camillo should visit the place, in disguise. Then we meet another figure created by Shakespeare for this play (though drawing on Greene's *The Art of Conny-Catching* pamphlets – informed accounts of devices of thieving and gulling) – Autolycus. He announces his ancestry:

My father named me Autolycus, who being, as I am, littered under Mercury, was likewise a snapper-up of unconsidered trifles.

(IV, iii, 24–6)

In fact, he was sired by Ovid:

And to the wing-foot god [Mercury] a wily brat
Was born, Autolycus, adept at tricks
Of every kind, well used to make black white,
White black, a son who kept his father's skill.

His brother, born to Chione from Phoebus, was Philemon, 'famed alike for song and lyre'. In the play, Autolycus takes on both roles – he tricks and sings. Bate says that the appearance of Autolycus 'confirms that the play is shifting into the register of myth'. Yes and no. The rest of this act is full of contemporary rural realities, and as Wilson Knight suggested you can, as it were, find as much Hardy as Ovid in this world – it is the coalescence of the classical and folkloric which generates the quite special atmosphere.

Autolycus enters singing:

When daffodils begin to peer,
With heigh the doxy over the dale,

Why, then comes in the sweet o' the year,
For the red blood reigns in the winter's pale.

(IV, iii, 1–4)

The winter's pale(ness) is a reflection of the winter's tale
which, effectively, was told and dramatized in the first three
acts. Good red blood (not the bad hot blood of Leontes' sick
imagining) is rising to flush it out. The sourness of the court
is about to give way to the sweetness of the country. The
daffodils beginning to 'peer' anticipates the entry of Perdita
in the next scene, looking like 'Flora,/Peering in April's front'
(IV, iv, 2–3). The word 'peer' occurs quite frequently in
Shakespeare, invariably referring to what we would now call
members of the House of Lords. Its – infrequent – use as a
verb, as far as I can find, always denotes something positive:
the sun peers, honour peers, proud rivers peer, perhaps gods
peer, and life peers ('through the hollow eyes of death', *Richard
II* II, i, 270–71). Perdita–Flora–spring peers; and her mother,
we later learn, 'lived peerless' (V, iii, 14). (Antony and Cleopatra 'stand up peerless', *Antony and Cleopatra* I, i, 40 – it is a
word for rare and special, and Shakespeare uses it sparingly
of people.) After the cold and wintry sterility of Leontes' court,
new life is beginning to 'peer' ('to look out keenly or with
difficulty; peep out; come into view, appear' – OED: all
meanings apply here), and Shakespeare signals this in the first
line of the first song of the play (no singing at Leontes' court,
but there will be music in Paulina's chapel at the end).

Switching to his other skill, Autolycus, pretending he has
been beaten and robbed, picks the pocket of the too trusting
Clown who is going shopping for the sheep-shearing feast (he
runs through what he has to get – saffron, pies, mace, dates,
nutmegs, ginger, prunes, raisins; such listing and itemizing,
out of place in the placeless idealities of conventional pastoral,
help to give a thick sense of the local, the real). Unaware of
his loss, Clown offers to give Autolycus what 'little money' he
has. Autolycus is a rogue (not the dark and evil figure some
tremulous critics have found him), and his rogueries, along
with his singing and ballads and peddling, liven up this whole
act, just as they animate the whole sheep-shearing feast and
the little rural community. But Clown's instinctive little gesture

of kindness and compassion means that he 'glisters' through Autolycus's 'rust' – as Leontes admitted that Camillo did through the royal rust (III, ii, 167–8). It is surely not insignificant that Autolycus boasts he has spent time at court – where he no doubt learned to refine his skills of deception. But, as the Shepherd wearily accepted, stealing was as much a part of country life as wenching; and the roving energy and 'snapping-up' activities of the amorally opportunistic, though invariably merry, Autolycus (a touch of the *picaro* here) adds a realistic saltiness (how appropriate that he breaks into a list of spices!) to a scene which might have become *too* 'sweet'. I do not intend to track the comings-and-goings of Autolycus, but one of his ballads is worth noting. It is a ballad supposedly sung by a lamenting fish which appeared off the coast: 'It was thought she was a woman, and was turned into a cold fish for she would not exchange flesh with one that loved her. The ballad is very pitiful, and as true' (IV, iv, 280–83). It's like a distant, distorted echo from another world – where a king turned himself into a cold tyrant because he did not trust one that loved him and thought that she had exchanged flesh with someone else; where a king turned a woman into a cold corpse because he ceased to love her. Can these cold fish live?

The feast at the Shepherd's cottage opens with the first appearance of Perdita, whom *Flori*zel has dressed up as *Flor*a (revealing his merging intentions?). Flora was the Roman goddess of *flowers*, and there is no scene in Shakespeare as full of flowers as the one that follows. Prince Florizel is playing at classical pastoral:

> This your sheep-shearing
> Is as a meeting of the petty gods,
> And you the Queen on't.

> (IV, iv, 3–5)

Perdita is, though, uneasy that he has 'obscured' his 'high self' with 'a swain's wearing; and me, poor lowly maid,/Most goddesslike pranked up' (IV, iv, 7–10) – and she is right to be uneasy at being thus 'pranked up' (Shakespeare's only use of the word). No matter how sincere his love, Florizel is playing a dangerous pastoral 'prank' on her. There is certainly myth in the air. Florizel invokes the gods 'humbling their deities to love', and cites the 'transformations' of Jupiter to a bull, Neptune to a ram, Apollo to a swain – though even he realizes that these metamorphoses are not particularly happy auguries as far as a woman is concerned, and he hastens to distinguish his own honourable 'desire' from their hot, unchaste 'lusts'. But as well as myth, there are more insistent proximate realities, some of them unpastorally harsh and cruel, as the scene will bear out. The old Shepherd (now, supposedly her father) immediately comments on the inappropriateness of her dress (he says she looks like 'a feasted one, and not/The hostess', IV, iv, 63–4), and gives a picture of the more ungoddess-like behaviour and deportment required in this setting:

> Fie daughter! When my old wife lived, upon
> This day, she was both pantler, butler, cook;
> Both dame and servant; welcomed all, served all;
> Would sing her song, and dance her turn ...
>
> (IV, iv, 55–8)

and so on – affording a vivid cameo of an actual rural festival.

The whole prolonged episode serves to show the kind of world Perdita grew up in – not her royal birth but her rural nurturing. It is not a brief interlude in the 'green world', nor does it take place in a magic wood. It is an extended scene – at some nine hundred lines it must be the longest in Shakespeare (there is none of this in Greene, simply half a dozen lines referring to a 'meeting of all the Farmers Daughters in Sycilia' where Fawnia appears as 'mistres of the feast'), and through it all there is an accumulating sense of the realities of country life. After three oppessive, sterile acts in the court of Sicilia, we need a good long dose, or draft, of the freedoms and fertilities of rural Bohemia – if only to make us feel that this world has sufficient weight and reality to counterbalance Sicilia's winter-world

With the arrival of the guests to the feast (including the disguised Polixenes and Camillo), Perdita commences her obligations as hostess – by giving everyone flowers. She starts by handing rosemary and rue to the unknown visitors, and Polixenes comments that these 'flow'rs of winter' fit well 'our ages' (IV, iv, 78–9). Here we may just note that there is what

must be a deliberate indeterminacy about the time of year
this is taking place. Sheep-shearing would be in mid-June, and
there is certainly a feeling of late-spring burgeoning in the air.
Yet Perdita replies to Polixenes:

> Sir, the year growing ancient,
> Not yet on summer's death, nor on the birth
> Of trembling winter ...
>
> (IV, iv, 79–81)

which suggests the near approach of autumn. The reason for
this, I suggest, is that while Perdita is certainly a Proserpina-
like figure of returning spring, her mother will of necessity be
in the autumn of her life at the time of the reunion which this
scene is preparing for. I think Shakespeare wants to mix or
merge a sense both of rising sap and mature ripening – the
non-wintry phases of creative life.

Perdita continues her speech to Polixenes:

> the fairest flow'rs o' th' season,
> Are our carnations, and streaked gillyvors [pinks],
> Which some call Nature's bastards: of that kind
> Our rustic garden's barren; and I care not
> To get slips of them.
>
> (IV, iv, 81–5)

This precipitates what has been called the 'great debate', and
it certainly leads to a major exchange, when Polixenes asks
Perdita why she 'neglects' such flowers:

> *Perdita.*   For I have heard it said,
> There is an art, which in their piedness shares
> With great creating nature.
>
> *Polixenes.*   Say there be;
> Yet Nature is made better by no mean
> But Nature makes that mean; so over that art,
> Which you say adds to Nature, is an art,
> That Nature makes. You see, sweet maid, we marry
> A gentler scion to the wildest stock,
> And make conceive a bark of baser kind
> By bud of nobler race. This is an art

Which does mend Nature, change it rather; but
The art itself is Nature.

(IV, iv, 87-97)

The Elizabethans loved discussing the relationship between
Art and Nature, and throughout his work Shakespeare found
many occasions and formulations to deepen and further that
discussion. There is nothing particularly original in Polixenes'
argument, which from one point of view is unassailable –
Nature that made the carpenter, made the house, as Emerson
succinctly put it. Compare this, from Puttenham's *The Arte of
English Poesie* (1589): 'In some cases we say arte is an ayde and
coadiutor to nature, or peradventure a meane to supply her
wants ... In another respect arte is not only an aide and
coadiutor to nature in all her actions, but an alterer of them,
and in some sort a surmounter of her skill ...', a description
which fits nicely with what Shakespeare is doing as a playwright. But it was also felt that men, with their 'artificiall
devises', had in some ways corrupted and 'bastardized' 'our
great and puissant mother Nature' (see Montaigne's essay 'Of
the Cannibales' – Florio's translation appeared in 1603). The
grafting and cross-breeding of plants, in which there was much
contemporary interest, offered a fine focus to such discussions
– as it does here. It could be said that they are both 'right',
inasmuch as Perdita is deprecating (bad) artificiality, while
Polixenes is defending (good) art. The more general point is
that the whole matter of the relations between nature and art
is both vital and endless – is itself generative. 'Piedness' (from
the miscellaneous objects jumbled together by the magpie)
here means the multi-coloured results achieved by cross-
breeding flowers, and Perdita feels that there is something
unnatural about it (how nature can produce something felt to
be 'unnatural' occupies Shakespeare from start to finish).

The more immediate dramatic effect of the scene is of a
profound irony, partly retrospective, partly proleptic. We
heard the baby Perdita many times execrated as a 'bastard'
by Leontes, and she was cast out as one – yet here she is
taking a principled stand against bastardy. While Polixenes
here argues positively in favour of the practice whereby 'we
marry/A gentler scion to the wildest stock'; but when it comes

to grafting the (supposedly) base-born Perdita onto his own noble twig ('scion') Florizel (which *is*, after all, what Perdita is hoping for, despite opposition to graftings), his horticultural approval vanishes in a fury of rejection. For the moment, Perdita continues to distribute flowers – hot lavender, mints, savory, marjoram, marigolds, 'these are the flow'rs/Of middle summer' (IV, iv, 106–7). She specifically regrets that she lacks 'some flow'rs o' th' spring' which would be more fitting, both for Florizel and the shepherdesses – virgins all. But, in the poetry of her regret she effectively brings in spring:

> Daffodils,
> That come before the swallow dares, and take
> The winds of March with beauty; violets, dim,
> But sweeter than the lids of Juno's eyes,
> Or Cytherea's breath; pale primroses,
> That die unmarried ere they can behold
> Bright Phoebus in his strength ...
>
> (IV, iv, 118–24)

Nothing else could evoke an actual English spring more immediately than those quite astonishingly lovely opening lines. At the same time, the young maid's fancy lightly turns to myth; and Juno, Cytherea and Phoebus are somehow hovering over the flowers. It is in this speech that Perdita specifically invokes Proserpina, and the flowers she let fall 'from Dis's wagon' (IV, iv, 118), and of course the Ceres–Proserpina relationship is the most important mythic enlargement of the central drama of the mother and the daughter in *The Winter's Tale*. It is perhaps because Shakespeare wanted to strengthen this enriching analogy that he switched the geography, thereby having Perdita born in Sicily which was the birthplace of Proserpina and from whence she was abducted. This is the story from Ovid with the most influence on the play. I hardly need rehearse it here in full, but one detail is worth noting. When Ceres learns from Arethusa that her daughter is now a queen in hell –

> The mother heard in horror, thunderstruck
> It seemed and turned to stone.

The mother is 'turned to stone' in Shakespeare's play as

well, though in quite different circumstances and to quite different ends.

Florizel is, understandably, enchanted by the demeanour and words of Perdita, and he is moved to this ardent hymn of appreciation:

> What you do
> Still betters what is done. When you speak, sweet,
> I'd have you do it ever; when you sing,
> I'd have you buy and sell so; so give alms,
> Pray so; and for the ord'ring your affairs,
> To sing them too. When you do dance, I wish you
> A wave o' th' sea, that you might ever do
> Nothing but that – move still, still so,
> And own no other function. Each your doing,
> So singular in each particular,
> Crowns what you are doing in the present deeds,
> That all your acts are queens.
>
> (IV, iv, 135–46)

The poetry of this, and of Perdita's immediately preceding speeches, is at times blindingly beautiful – there is hardly a more regal compliment in the whole of Shakespeare than that last one; and – among other things – it contributes greatly to our sense of Perdita's very special beauty. This, it has to be said, is her most important quality: she has none of the wit and sparkle and intelligence of Beatrice, Viola and Rosalind (she is more like Pastorella in Spenser's *Fairie Queene*), and she is, indeed, effectively a mute for the whole of the last act. But in this play her preternatural beauty is everything; she is, as it were, the almost divine representative of great creating Nature herself.

But Florizel's speech also touches on a deeper longing that runs through the play – that the beauties of life should last; here, that youth's blooming grace and loveliness should be somehow perpetuated and preserved – not once and gone, but now and 'ever'. That nature, which is forever moving, indeed 'dancing', should also, somehow, be 'still'. Shakespeare, of course, fastens on just that phenomenon in nature which seems to enact that contradictory condition – a wave, which, as it moves towards the shore is always and never the same.

Shakespeare catches this with marvellous economy – 'move still, still so': movement and stillness, movement *in* stillness, stillness moving – these four words anticipate the climax of the play. But it is and can be only *seems*. The wave must break on the shore; Perdita must acquire her mother's wrinkles, and her spring will pass away into winter. But the yearning and striving for eternity – the desire that the mutable natural should yield the unchanging eternal – is a profound one, and Shakespeare taps more deeply into it in this play than ever before. Shakespeare knows as well as every other human being that things pass away, that even a memory cannot be made to last forever; that 'thy grave [must] give way to what's seen now', as Paulina says to the supposedly dead Hermione (V, i, 97–8). But just there we stop. Paulina has seen to it that Hermione has *not* passed away, and, until the final stunning surprise, it appears that she has been preserved in and through art. Shakespeare, being Shakespeare, has one further step to take. Of course, when Hermione steps out of art into life, she is still in theatre. But Shakespeare gives play to the great and unending question of to what extent art can appease or satisfy man's desire for what Yeats called 'monuments of unageing intellect', whether it can provide, or substitute for, or act as 'the artifice of eternity'. Yeats articulates and explores this desire in 'Sailing to Byzantium', and again in 'Byzantium' where the 'glory of changeless metal' and the 'marbles of the dancing floor' seem to offer an immutable value, as opposed to 'the fury and the mire of human veins' and the 'dolphin-torn' sea. Art, it might be, allows life to produce 'monuments of its own magnificence' ('Sailing to Byzantium'). All these matters come to a head in the concluding moments of the play.

The rural pleasures continue for some time, and the amorousness of the young lovers rises to the point where they wish to formally commit themselves to each other, and Florizel asks the unknown visitors to act as witnesses to 'mark our contract'. 'Mark your divorce' says his furious father, now dropping his disguise (IV, iv, 421). Polixenes has been so courteous, and so appreciative of Perdita's beauty and seemingly innate nobility, that when he now starts spewing hatred, anger and cruel threats around, it is as sudden and frightening as Leontes' earlier incomprehensible eruption. Perdita becomes a 'piece of excellent witchcraft', his own son a 'royal fool', while the old Shepherd he will have hanged. The viciousness with which he turns on Perdita is truly shocking:

> I'll have thy beauty scratched with briers and made
> More homely than thy state.
>
> (IV, iv, 429–30)

As children Leontes and Polixenes were 'as twinned lambs'; as adults they are as twinned – what? wolves, maddened bears? Polixenes has brought a Sicilian winter to the Bohemian country, and what was so promisingly in the bud seems blighted. Perdita was right to be apprehensive – some intimation of the potentially dark behaviour of father–kings must have been born in her blood. The rest of the act is take with the plotting and arrangements which will bring all those involved back to Sicilia. Perdita doesn't know it, but she is going home.

Back in Sicilia, in the first scene of the last act, the whole issue of 'issue' is becoming increasingly urgent. After sixteen years of, as one gathers, pretty stiff penance, Leontes still has no heir. His courtiers are pressing him to marry again, but Paulina – still acting as the uncompromising voice of conscience and the sleepless guardian of memory – reminds the King that the wife he killed was 'unparalleled', and repeats the oracle's prophecy that he will have no heir 'Till his lost child be found' (V, i, 40). Leave it to the gods:

> Care not for issue,
> The crown will find an heir.
>
> (V, i, 46–7)

As for his marrying again – never; unless another 'As like Hermione as is her picture' appears. Paulina makes a binding request of the King:

> give me the office
> To choose you a queen; she shall not be so young
> As was your former, but she shall be such
> As walked your first queen's ghost, it should take joy
> To see her in your arms.
>
> (V, i, 73–81)

Not that Leontes, or we, should have an inkling of the fact, but Paulina is preparing her ground. A final exchange emphasizes what will be a crucial word:

> *Leontes.*   My true Paulina,
> We shall not marry till thou bidd'st us.
> *Paulina.*   That
> Shall be when your first queen's again *in breath*;
> Never till then.
>
> (V, i, 81–4 – my italics)

Then Florizel makes his entrance with Perdita, presented as a princess from Libya. To Leontes, she looks a 'goddess' (V, i, 131), and he invokes blessings upon the pair:

> The blessèd gods
> Purge all infection from our air whilst you
> Do climate here!
>
> (V, i, 168–70)

In fact it is they who will be the disinfecting agents of the Sicilian climate, purging an air poisoned and made sterile by Leontes. But when a lord announces the arrival of a furious Polixenes, threatening 'divers deaths in death' (V, i, 202 – which means tortures) to poor Shepherd and Clown, and hell-bent on catching the young couple and preventing their marriage, it seems that winter has come again and infection returned to the air.

All the more surprising, then, that the next scene brings us a series of excited gentlemen telling of royal recognitions and reunions. Suddenly, the air is clear, all anger lost in grateful celebration.

Nothing but bonfires. The oracle is fulfilled; the King's daughter is found; such a deal of wonder is broken out within this hour that ballad-makers cannot be able to express it.

> (V, ii, 24–7)

The identity of Perdita is revealed, though the whole matter strains credulity.

This news, which is called true, is so like an old tale that the verity of it is in strong suspicion. Has the King found his heir?

> (V, ii, 29–32)

Again that problem – can it really be *proved*? The confident
Third Gentleman answers with an arresting image:

Most true, if ever truth were pregnant by circumstance; that which
you hear you'll swear you see, there is such unity in the proofs.

(V, ii, 33–5)

The usual gloss on the opening image is 'if ever truth was
made convincing by evidence'; but, as we have seen, pregnancy
and birth are at the centre of this play, and we can look a
little closer than that. 'Circumstance' is circumstances, and
circumstantial evidence. This news is true *if* these have ever
made truth pregnant, swelled it out (note that it is 'by', not
'with'). Truth will then presumably deliver, in time, a child of
truth; or, as here, a true child. But it has to be prefaced by
that conditional 'if'. The 'proofs' and 'many other evidences'
(V, ii, 41) certainly seem conclusive, and no one would wish
to doubt them. We, of course, have been privileged to see
enough to know that it *is* true. But for the gentlemen of Sicilia,
and for the King, the 'evidences' can only be 'circumstance',
circumstantial – a jewel, a mantle, some letters, (handkerchief
and rings to establish the fate of Antigonus), a facial resemblance; again, the 'proof' depends on materialities. Here, it
seems overwhelming, and the wonder is only temporarily
laced with doubt ('the verity of it is in strong suspicion').
But Posthumus thought the 'evidences' presented to him by
Iachimo were overwhelming as well. Shakespeare is not trying
to spread scepticism. There is, it seems to me, simply an
unspoken reminder that, no matter how great our hunger for
certainties, there is a point when trust must take over. 'Proofs'
can only go so far; love must go further.

Third Gentleman asks Second if he saw the meeting of the
two kings. He did not. 'Then have you lost a sight which was
to be seen, cannot be spoken of' (V, ii, 45–6). Nevertheless,
speak of it is what he does, at length and to enthralling effect.
As he promised, 'that which you hear you'll swear you see'.
First Gentleman has described the meeting of Leontes and
Camillo – 'There was speech in their dumbness, language in
their very gesture' (V, ii, 14–15). A speaking dumbness and the
language of gesture – this applies to the main participants in

the great scene of reunion. But why does not Shakespeare give us the scene direct? Why these, entirely amiable, chattering gentlemen? Why narration, rather than drama – or let us say, narration *as* drama? Why can't *we* see the meeting of the kings? It is quite instructive, even amusing, to see the explanations which have been offered. The usual line is that Shakespeare must have felt that he had done the father–daughter reunion in *Pericles*, so here he relegated it in order to highlight the reunion of the husband and the wife. But Shakespeare is surely a more resourceful and imaginative playwright than that. If he fills the stage with breathless talk for a whole scene, prior to a scene which will centre on stone, silence and sight, you may be sure he is after a particular effect. As far as I am concerned, only Leonard Barkan has appreciated what Shakespeare is doing.

The lack of dramatic three-dimensionality here sets the stage for the scene in which the three-dimensional medium of sculpture becomes that of drama by metamorphosis. The speech-without-drama of this scene is contrasted with the statue-with-silence of the following scene. The verbal without the visual is empty, while the visual without the verbal is frozen. Only Shakespeare's medium can effect the marriage.

Exactly.

In fact, the gentlemen refer to the statue of Hermione (it is the first we have heard of it) just before they leave. The reference is perfectly placed. It comes immediately after Third has described the moving moment when Perdita learned the details of her mother's death and wept, with a dolorous 'Alas'. 'I am sure my heart wept blood. Who was most marble there changed color, some swooned, all sorrowed' (V, ii, 95–7). He then proceeds to tell them that Perdita has gone to see 'her mother's statue, which is in the keeping of Paulina':

a piece many years in doing and now newly performed by that rare Italian master, Julio Romano, who, had he himself eternity and could put breath into his work, would beguile Nature of her custom, so perfectly he is her ape: he so near to Hermione hath done Hermione, that they say one would speak to her and stand in hope of answer.

(V, ii, 101–9)

With hindsight, one may say that this is preparing us for the final scene. But there is a lot more going on than that.

With the return of Perdita – let us say – the people of the Sicilian court who have been, effectively, turned to marble through the disastrous life-destroying nihilism of Leontes, are flushed with life-returning blood again. Her mother, most regrettably, was terminally frozen out of life by Leontes. But, it appears, she has been memorialized, monumentalized, as a statue – turned to marble in another sense. And by Julio Romano. Now it is not often that Shakespeare refers to an actual Renaissance artist by name in his plays, so this departure from practice invites our attention. Never mind that it is another unashamed anachronism (Romano's dates are 1492–1546), it must be signalling something directly relevant to the play at this stage. By common agreement, Shakespeare's most likely source for the name, and his reason for using it, lies in Vasari's *Lives* (published in 1550). There he would have found – in Latin – a transcription of the epitaph on Giulio Romano's tomb, which, translated, is:

Jupiter saw sculpted and painted bodies breathe and the earthly buildings made equal to those in heaven by the skill of Giulio Romano. Thus angered he then summoned a council of all the gods, and he removed that man from the earth, lest he be exposed, conquered, or equalled by an earth-born man.

Sculpted bodies that seem to breathe; works of art which rival (and thus threaten) divine powers of creation – Shakespeare is further preparing for his last act, which, among other things, effects perhaps his most profound plumbing of the provenance, the power, the privilege, and finally the limitations, of art, in miraculously compacted form.

To get some sense of how much lies behind this short final scene, it will help to have before us passages from two stories in Ovid's *Metamorphoses*. I have mentioned the general importance of the Pygmalion story for late Shakespeare; now, some of the details become particularly pertinent. They concern the actual period of transition when Pygmalion's master-work passes from ivory to flesh and blood, and the statue moves into life.

> It seemed to be alive,
> Its face to be a real girl's, a girl

Who wished to *move* ...
... is it flesh
Or ivory? Not ivory still, he's sure!
...
And he kissed her as she lay, and she seemed *warm*
... beneath his touch the flesh
Grew *soft*, its ivory hardness vanishing
...
His heart was torn wonder and misgiving,
Delight and terror that it was not true
...
She was alive! The *pulse* beat in her veins!
... she ... shyly raised
Her eyes to his and saw the world and him.   (my italics)

The other story is that of Deucalion, curiously enough referred to earlier (for only the second time in Shakespeare) by Polixenes in an entirely different context. Shakespeare leaves his traces in unexpected places. Deucalion and his wife Pyrrha are the sole survivors of the great Deluge visited by an irate Jupiter on an impious people. Facing a desolate, unpeopled world after the waters subside, Deucalion longs for some of his father's (Prometheus) magic to 'restore/Mankind again and in the moulded clay/Breathe life'. Consulting the oracle of Themis as to how to repair the loss of mankind, they are instructed – 'cast behind you your great mother's bones'. Initially baffled, they decide that this can only refer to the stones which lie around them on the ground, and they duly throw them over their shoulders.

Those stones (who would believe did ancient lore
Not testify the truth?) gave up their hardness;
Their rigidness grew slowly soft, and, softened,
Assumed a shape, and as they grew and felt
A gentler nature's touch, a semblance seemed
To appear, still indistinct, of human form,
Like the first rough-hewn marble of a statue,
Scarce modelled, or old old uncouth images.
The earthy part, damp with some trace of moisture
Was turned to flesh; what was inflexible
And solid changed to bone; what in the stones
Had been the veins retained the name of veins.

In a brief while, by Heaven's mysterious power,
The stones the man had thrown were formed as men,
Those from the woman's hand reshaped as women.
Hence we are hard, we children of the earth,
And in our lives of toil we prove our birth.

These two 'magic' moments of stone gradually giving way to/ becoming life – moments which should give us what Thomas Mann referred to as 'the archaic shudder of myth' – the hard becoming soft, the cold acquiring warmth, stillness beginning to move – these moments are vital for Shakespeare. And the gradualness is important: these are not sudden jumps – now stone; hey presto, now life. Rather, the one almost imperceptibly gives way to the other, so that it would be very difficult to mark a point at which the actual transformation took place, albeit that the time it takes is 'brief'.

When the last scene opens in the chapel in Paulina's house, a remark from Leontes makes it clear that they – which means all the main characters and some courtiers – have already spent some time looking at works of art – 'Your gallery/ Have we passed through, not without much content/In many singularities' (V, iii, 10–12). They have, as it were, had a preliminary immersion in the realm of aesthetic artefacts. And *now* Paulina '*draws a curtain and discovers Hermione standing like a statue*'; or, for the onlookers and the audience, we should, at this point, more accurately say – a statue standing like Hermione. We are to take it that they all stand still and silent – rapt, is perhaps the word. (Paulina – 'I like your silence; it the more shows off your wonder', V, iii, 21–2.) It is then that Leontes remarks that his Hermione was not so wrinkled, which Paulina turns into a further compliment to the artist who 'makes her/As she lived now' (V, iii, 31–2). The artifices of eternity must somehow incorporate the inexorabilities of time.

Leontes addresses the 'statue'; indirectly (you don't talk to stone), and then directly (you may if it seems to be the life it images):

> Oh, thus she stood,
> Even with such life of majesty – warm life,
> As now it coldly stands – when first I wooed her.
> I am ashamed: does not the stone rebuke me,

> For being more stone than it? O royal piece!
> There's magic in thy majesty, which has
> My evils conjured to remembrance, and
> From thy admiring daughter took the spirits,
> Standing like stone with thee.
>
> (V, iii, 34-42)

This is a peak moment, before the scene begins to move on. We are to imagine Perdita standing next to the 'statue' of her mother – in her almost divine beauty, she represents 'perfection of the life'; while the mother, through the almost divine art of the maker, represents 'perfection of the work' (the terms are again from Yeats). Art and life, for one impossible tremblingly arrested moment, seem momentarily identical, indistinguishable, at one. While Leontes realizes that the statue forces him to confront the question – who, in their relationship, was *really* the 'stone' one? Penance and time have brought softening (as well as wrinkles), and it is time for some frozen hearts to melt.

For a while, Leontes wants to prolong the arrested moment – 'Do not draw the curtain ... Let be, let be!' (V, iii, 59, 61) – 'gazing on this sphinx-like boundary between art and life' as Wilson Knight has it. He permits himself what, at this stage, must seem like Pygmalion-esque fantasies:

> See, my lord,
> Would you not deem it *breathed*? And that those *veins*
> Did verily bear blood?
> *Polixenes.*   Masterly done!
> The very life seems *warm* upon her *lip*.
> *Leontes.* The fixure of her *eye* has *motion* in 't,
> As we are mocked with art.
>
> (V, iii, 63-8 – my italics)

His now positive and appreciative gaze seems almost to be reassembling his wife's body part by part, conferring warmth on what he had once frozen into stone. Paulina purports to be anxious that Leontes will soon be 'so far transported that/ He'll think anon it lives' (V, iii, 68-9), and Leontes replies that he would like to live in that delusion (that the stone seems to be hovering on the brink of life) indefinitely – 'Make me to think so twenty years together' (V, iii, 71). Then he pushes his fantasy to the limit – 'methinks,/There is an air comes from her' (the 'it' of the statue has become 'her'): 'What fine chisel/ Could ever yet cut breath?' (V, iii, 77–8). Romano's genius was that he carved statues that seemed to breathe (lifelikeness was the supreme merit of art for the ancients). Leontes determines to take this literally and he moves to put flesh on stone – 'Let no man mock me,/For I will kiss her' (V, iii, 79–80). At which point Paulina, now curator, director and priestess all together, makes her final moye; and remember that this should be as much of a shock and surprise to us as it is to the people gathered in the chapel.

> Either forbear,
> Quit presently the chapel, or resolve you
> For more amazement. If you can behold it,
> I'll make the statue move indeed, descend,
> And take you by the hand – but then you'll think,
> Which I protest against, I am assisted
> By wicked powers.
>
> (V, iii, 85–91)

Black magic, white magic? We are in a 'chapel', which suggests Christian transforming grace; but we are in pre-Christian times, foregrounding pagan metamorphosing power. Leontes is content to accept any new miracles Paulina can effect with the Hermione–statue, 'for 'tis as easy/To make her speak, as move' (V, iii, 94–5). Here is the moment which marks and acknowledges the essential difference – art can do *almost* anything; but only (human) life can breathe, and speak, and move. Paulina (telling anyone who thinks 'it is unlawful business I am about' to leave – no one moves, the onlookers have become statuesque: V, iii, 95–7) makes her master-stroke and works her (white) magic.

> Music awake her: strike.
> 'Tis time, descend; be stone no more; approach;
> Strike all that look upon with marvel; come;
> I'll fill your grave up. *Stir*; nay come away;
> Bequeath to death your numbness, for from him
> Dear life redeems you. You perceive she *stirs*.
>
> (V, iii, 98–103 – my italics)

There it is, the key word: everything that had been stilled, frozen, arrested into a long sterile winter now 'stirs' as '*Hermione comes down*'. As she steps out of art back into life – and time – it is as if Hermione had simply been standing still for sixteen years in a state of suspended animation (Barkan's term). In this, she also stands for – embodies, figures – the kingdom of Sicilia of which she is Queen. But Perdita has returned. And it is to her, and only to her, that Hermione addresses her one speech (not one word for Leontes):

> You gods look down,
> And from your sacred vials pour your graces
> Upon my daughter's head
> ...
> thou shalt hear that I,
> Knowing by Paulina that the oracle
> Gave hope thou wast in being, have preserved
> Myself to see the issue.
>
> (V, iii, 121–8)

Ceres and Proserpina are reunited. Perdita is the 'issue' in every sense.

When Hermione steps down, Leontes gasps:

> Oh, she's warm!
> If this be magic, let it be an art
> Lawful as eating.
>
> (V, iii, 109–11)

It may seem strange to invoke 'eating' at this point, but then we recognize just how apposite it is. Eating is what every living body has to do, if it is to stay 'warm' with circulating blood. A magic as lawful as eating has nothing supernatural about it. There has been no divine – much less nefarious – intervention. Hermione's body has been a living body throughout, only arrested and concealed for sixteen long, barren years. The only 'magic' is Paulina's 'art', and her thaumaturgy is that of a dramatist. The last scene, with its stunning *coup de théâtre*, is stage-managed by Paulina (note the importance of music). Shakespeare is quite self-consciously putting his own art on stage – Paulina's chapel is Shakespeare's theatre in little. 'If you can behold it,/I'll make the statue move' (V, iii, 87–8) – Shakespeare is effectively speaking to his own audience through Paulina. When Leontes first sees the statue, he asks, in amazement – 'What was he that did make it?' (V, iii, 63). For that moment, Hermione is at once a statue, a woman and an actor. So how should we answer Leontes' question? Julio Romano? Shakespeare? Great creating nature? or ... But no – finally it is *the* unanswerable question.

When the First Gentleman describes the meeting of Leontes and Camillo he says:

> they looked as they had heard of a world ransomed, or one destroyed. A notable passion of wonder appeared in them ...
>
> (V, ii, 15–18)

or one destroyed: there are some phenomena – events, spectacles – which cause a response in which the wonderful is indistinguishable from the terrible. There is a description of Tolstoy's face while he listened to great music – an expression of *horror* came into it. Just so with this play. It does not merely please and entertain. It should leave us *aghast*, uncertain of just what sort of extraordinary thing it is we have just witnessed. In these last plays Shakespeare is touching on ultimate matters in quite amazing ways. Indeed, he might even have surprised himself.

THE TEMPEST (1611)

those infortunate (yet fortunate) Ilands
(*The True Declaration of the Estate of the Colonie in Virginia*, anon., 1610)

> I might call him
> A thing divine; for nothing natural
> I ever saw so noble.
>
> (I, ii, 418–20)

> That a monster should be such a natural!
>
> (III, ii, 34–5)

> These are not natural events; they strengthen
> From strange to stranger.
>
> (V, i, 227–8)

INTRODUCTION

Where are we? In the three previous plays we have adjusted ourselves, imaginatively, to the worlds of classical antiquity, Roman Britain, and pre-Christian Sicily. But here there are no offered orientations. Most unusually, the Folio has a written indication of locality – 'An un-inhabited Island' – though this may have been added by a scrivener, Ralph Crane, who worked for Shakespeare's company and perhaps made the transcript. Whoever wrote it, it is an indication pointing to nowhere, or no-known-where I should say. Coleridge had it right when he wrote 'in this play Shakespeare did not appeal to any sensuous impression of time and place but to the imagination'. It opens in the middle of what seems like an Atlantic storm and shipwreck, on what turns out to be a Mediterranean island, though by the end we must feel that we have passed out of geography altogether.

In a strange, late essay on the play, Henry James maintained that 'The story in *the Tempest* is a thing of naught, for any story will provide a remote island, a shipwreck and a coincidence.' Well! But this is not as breathtakingly dismissive as it sounds. James stresses, rather, the final triumph of Shakespeare's *style* – 'its rich simplicity and its free elegance ... its refinement of power ... It renders the poverties and obscurities of our world in the dazzling terms of a richer and better.' He, rightly, admires the wonderful economy of this (surprisingly short) play – 'the economy not of poverty, but of wealth *a little weary of congestion*' (my italics). That too feels right, for there is a sense in this play of sorting things out, summarizing essentials, eschewing the distractions of life's plenitudes. James says that the play reflects Shakespeare's 'charged inspiration and clarified experience', and 'clarified' is just the appropriate word. At the same time, no play is more blurring and blurred. I shall try to explain this, only apparent, contradiction.

To be sure, *The Tempest* has many of the features we associate with the Last Plays – an initial outbreak of disruptive evil and discord (in this play recounted, not shown); ensuing separations and voyages; miraculous salvation from shipwreck; reconciliations and reunions; and the coming together of almost divinely beautiful royal children who finally unite in a marriage presaging future harmony and renewal. What was *lost* – kingdoms, children – is found; though, as always, lost years cannot be retrieved. But, somehow, it's all very different. Recognitions and reconciliations are almost passionless and automatic; there is almost no repentance and what there is is off-hand, minimal; the forgiveness is brusque and unconvincing; there is no sense of regeneration, renewal, restoration – certainly not of redemption. Patience is mentioned, but only as not being practised. There is no sense of the seasonal replenishment afforded by 'great creating nature' – it is figured in a masque, but made to seem unbelievably insubstantial, a diaphanous sketch at two or three removes from reality. In fact, *everything* seems faint and somehow far away. The verse carries very few metaphors such as usually bring powerful extra life and presence to the words and set off cascades of meanings in the mind. The beat of the iambic lines is so unemphatic as to be almost inaudible. Indeed, I would venture another paradox and suggest that in a curious way it is almost as though we don't distinctly hear the words at all but rather a strange, almost hypnotic 'humming' such as Gonzalo hears while sleeping on the island. I say this in the full knowledge that the word 'roar' (and cognates) occurs more often here than in any other play. For there is a 'roaring' (a strange, semantically empty, hollow-throated word) which is a kind of silence – like the hissing, humming, 'oh-ing' noise you hear on the radio when the programmes are over. It's what you hear in sea-shells; and when you have been too long under water.

The story which for James was 'a thing of naught' was a thing of many romances, and many folk and fairy tales with a recurrent theme of a magician living in solitude and bringing up a daughter – on an island, or even under the sea (note). As with the play in some ways most closely related to it, *A Midsummer Night's Dream*, there is no specific source for *The Tempest*. Shakespeare has made his own mix wherein the genres blend into each other so that the play is, variously and at once, a romance, a pastoral, a tragicomedy, a morality, an allegorical history, a comedy influenced by *commedia dell'arte*, and a masque. Or, if you like, none of the above but something else again. But, beyond all reasonable doubt, a number of

INTRODUCTION

contemporary documents acted as some sort of immediate triggering influence. These were what have become known as the Bermuda Pamphlets, and here I must recount what, for some, might be a familiar story. From the time of 1582, when Richard Hakluyt the elder published *Divers Voyages touching the Discovery of America* – which starts 'I marvel not a little that since the first discovery of America (which is now full four-score-and-ten years), after so great conquest and plantings of the Spaniards and Portugals there, that we of England could never have the grace to set fast footing in such fertile and temperate places as are left as yet unpossessed by them' – the Elizabethans grew increasingly excited at the idea of settling North America. Hawkins investigated the coast of Florida, Drake found his way to California, and in 1585 Ralegh sent out his first colony to Virginia (so named to honour Elizabeth) under the command of Sir Richard Grenville. For various reasons this colony did not take and the failed and much-reduced colonists were taken home by Drake in the following year. But the hunt was irreversibly on, and in 1607 another colony was settled in Virginia at the now appropriately named Jamestown. Interest in reports sent or brought back from the New World (containing details of the voyages, the local flora and fauna, the indigenous natives, and the many difficulties and problems among the colonizers) was at a peak in the early years of the seventeenth century – just, of course, when Shakespeare was writing his play (which is his only play to contain the word 'plantation').

More immediately, an expedition to Virginia in 1609 led by Sir Thomas Gates had disappeared at sea. But he returned safely from Virginia in 1610, with a tale to tell of a terrible storm and shipwreck in the Bermudas; an almost miraculous escape to land; a period of surprisingly easy survival on a strange island; and finally the troubling state of the Virginian settlement when he managed to get there. The story occasioned various accounts by actual survivors and others, including a long letter by William Strachey giving '*A True Repertory of the Wracke and Redemption of Sir Thomas Gates ... the Ilands of the Bermudas: his comming to Virginia, and the estate of that Colonie ...*', which was not published until 1625 but which Shakespeare must have read (he had many friends on the Virginian Council, for whom the letter was written). It is on these pamphlets and this letter that Shakespeare draws for his play, though, as always, submitting the material to his own alchemy. I will quote a series of extracts which, I think, throw an interesting light on the play and, more importantly, on the alchemy.

And first, from that *True Repertory* – 'a most dreadfull Tempest'.

A dreadfull storme and hideous began to blow from out the North-east, which swelling, and roaring as it were by fits ... at length did beate all light from heaven ... so much the more fuller of horror, as in such cases horror and feare use to overrunne the troubled, and overmastered sences of all which (taken up with amazement) the cares lay so sensible to the terrible cries, and murmurs of the windes, and distraction of our Company ... our clamours dround in the windes, and the windes in thunder ... Windes and Seas were as mad, as fury and rage could make them ... there was not a moment in which the sodaine splitting, or instant over-setting of the Shippe was not expected ... For my part I thought her alreadie in the bottome of the Sea ...

which is perhaps where the play takes place; but more of that in time. You will recognize the details of Shakespeare's own tempest with which the play opens; and here is the origin of Ariel's fire:

an apparition of a little round light, like a faint Starre, trembling, and streaming along with a sparkling blaze, halfe the height upon the Maine Mast, and shooting sometimes from Shroud to Shroud ...

Then, the providential escape or salvation:

it wanted little ... to have shut up hatches, and commending our sinfull soules to God, committed the Shippe to the mercy of the Sea ... but see the goodnesse and sweet introduction of better hope, by our mercifull God given unto us. Sir George Summers, when no man dreamed of such happinesse, had discovered, and cried Land.

(As they seem to be foundering, Gonzalo cries out a longing 'for an acre of barren ground – long heath, brown furze, anything', I, i, 65–6.)

Indeede the morning now three quarters spent, had wonne a little cleerenesse from the dayes before, and it being better surveyed, the

very trees were scene to move with the winde upon the shoare side
— and by the mercy of God unto us, making out our Boates, we had
ere night brought all our men, women, and children, about the
number of one hundred and fifty, safe unto the Iland.

(In another pamphlet, *A Discovery of the Barmudas, otherwise called
the Ile of Divels*, Sylvester Jourdain expresses more wonder: 'But
our delivery was not more strange, in falling so opportunely
and happily upon the land, as our feeding and preservation
was beyond our hopes and all men's expectations most
admirable.')

The island turns out not to be as rumour, or seamen's
superstition, has it.

We found it to be the dangerous and dreaded Iland, or rather Ilands
of the Bermudas ... they be called commonly, The Devils Ilands,
and are feared and avoyded of all sea travellers alive, above any
other place in the world. Yet it pleased our mercifull God, to make
even this hideous and hated place, both the place of our safetie, and
meanes of our deliverance.

And hereby also, I hope to deliver the world from a foule and
generall errour: it being counted of most, that they can be no
habitation for Men, but rather given over to Devils and wicked
Spirits; whereas indeed wee find them now by experience, to bee as
habitable and commodious as most Countries of the same climate
and situation.

(Jourdain, who says the island is reputed to be an 'enchanted'
place, is even more enthusiastic: 'Wherefore my opinion is
that whereas it hath been and is still accounted the most
dangerous, infortunate, and most forlorn place of the world,
it is in truth the richest, healthfullest, and pleasing land ...
and merely natural, as ever man set foot upon.')

Strachey goes on to list all the trees, berries, fruits, birds, fish,
crustaceans and other animals the island affords – including a
'reasonable toothsom (some say) Tortoyse' (Prospero calls
Caliban a 'tortoise'). There are no rivers or springs; you have
to dig to find 'certaine gushings and soft burblings' of water
(Caliban can show you where). He notes the absence of 'any
venemous thing' – certainly, he never saw a snake; which is
somehow appropriate in this somewhat anamorphic version
of Paradise. And all the venom on Prospero's island is secreted

by men. These observations are apt for Shakespeare's own ambiguous and enchanted island. But we should remember that, in the play, the Bermudas are mentioned just once – fleetingly, peripherally: Ariel was once sent by Prospero 'to fetch dew/From the still-vexed Bermoothes' (I, ii, 228–9). The action is a long way elsewhere.

There are two more sections in the letter, both having relevance for the play. Once they were all safely landed and the danger was over, the men started to fall out and go wrong, as men will unless they are properly 'governed' by some good authority, however legitimated or derived. (The prospect of mobs of 'masterless men' was a nightmare for the Elizabethans and Jacobeans.) 'Loe, what are our affections and passions, if not rightly squared? ... some dangerous and secret discontents nourished amongst us, had like to have bin the parents of bloudy issues and mischiefes ... a conspiracy was discovered [led by] a mutinous and dissembling Imposter.'

In these dangers and divellish disquiets (whilest the almighty God wrought for us, and sent us miraculously delivered from the calamities of the Sea, all blessings upon the shoare, to content and binde us to gratefulnesse) thus inraged amongst our selves, to the destruction each of other, into what a mischiefe and misery had wee bin given up, had wee not had a Governour with his authority, to have suppressed the same? Yet was there a worse practise, faction, and conjuration a foote, deadly and bloudy, in which the life of our Governour, with many others were threatened, and could not but miscarry in his fall ... But as all giddy and lawlesse attempts, have always something of imperfection, and that as well by the property of the action, which holdeth of disobedience and rebellion ... as through the ignorance of the devisers themselves ...

Just so: this plot collapsed and came to nothing; as will a similar 'foul conspiracy' against Governor Prospero's life, hopelessly botched by Stephano and Trinculo, 'giddy and lawlesse' with drink.

They finally reach the Jamestown colony in Virgina, and find it to be 'full of misery and misgovernment'. In the absence of good government, 'the headlesse multitude' had fallen into 'wastful courses' and 'Idlenesse'. There was 'no husbandry'; they couldn't even be bothered 'to sowe Corne for their owne bellies'. Captain John Smith, writing about Virginia in 1608, describes how difficult it was to get the settlers to do any of the necessary plantation work. Neglecting agriculture and carpentry, all they wanted to do was look for non-existent gold. (A lot of these greedy, lazy wastrels were young gallants hoping for easy riches, not honest labourers.) Thus Strachey: 'Unto such calamity can sloath, riot and vanity, bring the most setled and plentifull estate.' Another contemporary anonymous pamphlet about Virginia makes the same point even more vigorously. 'So that, if it bee considered that without industry no land is sufficient to the Inhabitants: and that the trade to which they trusted, betrayed them to loose the opportunity of seed-time, and so to rust and weare out themselves.' Yet another anonymous pamphlet known as *The True Declaration of the Estate of the Colonie in Virginia* (1610) makes a definitive statement:

The ground of all those miseries, was the permissive providence of God, who, in the fore-mentioned violent storme, separated the head from the bodie, all the vital powers of regiment being exiled with *Sir Thomas Gates* in those infortunate (yet fortunate) Ilands. The broken remainder of those supplies made a greater shipwrack in the continent of *Virginia*, by the tempest of dissension: every man overvaluing his own worth, would be a Commander: every man underprizing an others value, denied to be commanded ... it is no wonder that so many in our colony perished: it is a wonder, that all were not devoured.

More than one kind of shipwreck; more than one kind of tempest. The importance of work, and agriculture and husbandry; and the whole question of good and necessary 'government', and 'the vitall powers of regiment' – these are central matters in Shakespeare's play. One more quotation from the *True Declaration*:

The next Fountaine of woes was secure negligence, and improvidence, when every man sharked for his present bootie, but was altogether carelesse of succeeding penurie. Now, I demand whether Sicilia, or Sardinia could hope for increase without manuring? A Colony is therefore denominated, because they should be Coloni, the Tillers of the Earth, and Stewards of fertilitie: our mutinous Loyterers would not sow with providence, and therefore they reaped the fruits of too deeere bought Repentance.

You will hardly find a better phrase for Stephano and Trinculo than 'mutinous Loyterers' sharking for booty (Caliban is something else). Shakespeare's play is not a study of imperialism and colonialism as currently understood. But it does engage with basic issues concerning what is involved in being proper *coloni* and in establishing 'plantations' in the New World. On this matter, a final quotation from a later essay by Francis Bacon entitled 'Of Plantations' (1625):

It is a shameful and unblessed thing to take the scum of people, and wicked condemned men, to be the people with whom you plant: and not only so, but it spoileth the plantation; for they will ever live like rogues, and not fall to work, but be lazy, and do mischief, and spend victuals, and be quickly weary, and then certify over to their country to the discredit of the plantation ... For government, let it be in the hands of one, assisted with some counsel ... And above all, let men make that profit of being in the wilderness, as they have God always, and his service, before their eyes.

With extraordinary economy, Shakespeare's play encompasses, or glances at, all these matters.

The Strachey letter was published in 1625 in *Purchas His Pilgrimes* with marginal notes by Samuel Purchas. I have not yet mentioned any of the remarks made by the commentators on Virginia concerning the indigenous inhabitants, the miscalled Indians. Suffice it to say that they were found to be credulous and adoring (treating the colonizers as gods); helpful (many of the colonies were completely dependent on the natives for food and instruction about the terrain, in their early years); and treacherous (there are some terrible massacres, often *but not always* provoked by the disgraceful behaviour of the colonists) – sometimes in that order. You will readily see that this exactly describes the range of responses that Caliban goes through with regard to Prospero. Strachey describes an episode of treachery on the part of the Indians, suddenly turned hostile. Purchas adds a marginal comment: 'Can a Leopard change his spots? Can a Savage remayning a Savage be civill? Were not wee our selves made and not borne civill in our Progenitors days? and were not Caesars Britaines as brutish as Virginians? The Romane swords were best teachers of civilitie to this & other Countries neere us.'

This last point, you may remember, was taken up in *Cymbeline*. More generally, it can be readily understood that the discovery of apparently totally uncivilized and 'primitive' (=first of its kind) natives in the New World lent enormous new impetus to that favourite Elizabethan topic of debate, and a concern central to all Shakespeare's drama – the relationship of savagery to civility, of nature to nurture; indeed, the *nature* of Nature itself. When Prospero describes Caliban as 'a born devil, on whose nature/Nurture can never stick' (IV, i, 188–9), he is raising all the questions. (We should not, incidentally, take Prospero's statements and definitions as veridical and definitive. It would be a mistake to assume that Shakespeare's view of Caliban is coextensive with Prospero's.) Leaving aside Caliban's role in the play for a moment – he is in a way the pivot; the figure against whom all the others are measured – we can see that he incorporates attributes associated with, at least, the European figure of the wild or 'salvage' man (of the woods) and the native of the New World. About this native, travellers' reports were continuously ambiguous – he was innocent, essentially uncorrupted, naturally happy; he was a cannibal, truly savage, naturally brutal. In Spenser's *Fairie Queene* Books IV and V, there is 'a wilde and salvage man', a cannibalistic monster, who lecherously abducts Amoret; but there is also a gentle 'wilde man' who, though without human speech, takes pity on Serena and saves her. Just so. Caliban has his lecherousness and murderousness; but he also has his sensitivities and delicacies (even though Prospero reserves that word exclusively for Ariel). His name is, effectively, an anagram of 'cannibal'; it might owe something to the Romany word for blackness – *caliban*; it could refer to the Caribbean. Whatever he is – born devil; monster (nature *un*natural); enslaved native; or just 'natural man' (man *in* a state of nature) – it is of particular interest that Prospero *needs* him.

> We cannot miss him. He does make our fire,
> Fetch in our wood, and serves in offices
> That profit us.
>
> (I, ii, 311–13)

(It is perhaps worth noting that the one task we see imposed on him, and after him on Ferdinand, namely 'fetching wood', was exactly the work which the insubordinate settlers initially refused to do for Sir Thomas Gates – though he wanted the wood to build a boat to escape from the island, where the mutinous loiterers preferred to remain in idleness.) You would have thought that a magician with Prospero's so potent powers (he can raise the dead!) would have been able to whisk a bit of firewood into his 'cell' at the flick of a wand. But no – Shakespeare wants to mark a curious and perhaps significant reliance and dependence. This is not a reprehensible implausibility, but a matter to think on.

Columbus himself was sure he had encountered cannibals in the Caribbean, and he contrasted them with the 'meke and humayne people' on other islands – 'they seeme to lyve in that goulden worlde of the whiche owlde wryters speake so much; wherein men lyved simplye and innocentlye without enforcement of lawes, without quarrelling Judges and libelles, content onely to satisfy nature ...' It was reports like this which helped to inspire Montaigne's essay 'Of the Cannibales' (John Florio's translation of the *Essais* was published in 1603 – a work which Shakespeare certainly knew and whose copy is almost certainly even now in the British Museum). I will quote some relevant passage; and you can see a tolerant and provocative relativism creeping in which surely appealed to the ironic Shakespeare.

I finde (as farre as I have been informed) there is nothing in that nation [the newly discovered America], that is either barbarous or savage, unlesse man call that barbarisme which is not common to them [point taken!] ... They are even savage, as we call those fruits wilde, which nature of her selfe, and of her ordinarie progresse hath produced: whereas indeed, they are those which our selves have altered by our artificiall devices, and diverted from their common order, we should rather terme savage [well, all right – an agreeable and refreshing inversion and oxymoron; the product, of course, of civilized casuistry] ... me seemeth that what in those nations we see by experience, doth not only exceed all the pictures wherewith licentious Poesie hath proudly imbellished the golden age and all her quaint inventions to faine a happy condition of man, but also the conception and desire of Philosophy [a nod there to the 'Golden Age' as described by 'licentious' Ovid] ... It is a nation, would I answer Plato, that hath no kinde of traffike, no knowledge of Letters, no intelligence of numbers, no name of magistrate, nor of politike superioritie; no use of service, of riches or of povertie; no contracts, no successions, no partitions, no occupation but idle; no respect of kindred, but common, no apparell but naturall, no manuring of lands, no use of wine, corne, or mettle ...

And as for cannibalism, continues Montaigne, compared to the indescribable tortures we 'civilized' people inflict on living bodies, the eating of a dead body is infinitely less 'barbarous' – and we can take that point, too. Shakespeare, of course, allows the good Gonzalo to articulate much of this passage from Montaigne (see II, i, 148–73), making it clear that his wistful evocation of the 'Golden Age' is full of impossible contradictions, easily pounced on by the sneering, worldly derision of Antonio and Sebastian. But where Gonzalo's confused and unrealizable fantasy is benign ('holy Gonzalo, honorable man'), the jeering malice of Antonio and Sebastian does them little credit, trenchant and telling though it is. As Coleridge very rightly observed: 'Shakespeare never puts habitual scorn into the mouths of other than bad men.'

But Ovid's Golden Age can hardly be squared with, or mapped on to, the 'New Land like unto That of the Golden Age', as one contemporary traveller described America. For one thing, there was no voyaging in it ('man knew no shores except their own'); for another, the sowing and farming neces-sary for plantation survival (even if some of those work-shy early settlers did try to regress to a Golden Age idleness) are innovations of the Silver Age ('then in long furrows first were set the seeds'); and for a third, not only voyaging ('men sailed the sea'), but also all the evil of 'deceit and treachery/And violence and wicked greed' and the 'hands of blood' which the travellers bring with them to the island, are the distinctive features of the Age of Iron. The 'brave new world' which Miranda so innocently wonders at is in fact the varyingly corrupt old world of Europe. Even Sycorax was from Algiers, and Caliban is not an indigenous native, not a Virginian or a Caribbean savage. From this point of view, the island *is* 'uninhabited' (the implication being, perhaps, that the only golden worlds are unpeopled ones), and whether Caliban is innately disposed to evil or was corrupted by his encounter and enforced servitude with Prospero, all the malign and infecting influences in the world of this play are importations, sourced elsewhere – wherever it *is* that evil is sourced; on this point Antonio is as unyieldingly silent as Iago.

So, while his opening shipwreck and aftermath has something more than echoes of the Atlantic adventure of Sir Thomas Gates and his crew, Shakespeare locates his island squarely in the Mediterranean, as we gather between Naples and Tunis. Italy, for Shakespeare and the Elizabethans, meant the glories of Renaissance civilization (here figured as Prospero's 'liberal arts without a parallel'), and the horrors of unscrupulous Machiavellian politics (Antonio's ruthless usurpation of Prospero's dukedom). Tunis, from where they are returning after what was clearly a completely political marriage of Alonso's daughter to the Tunisian king (the play's alertness to the importance to royal families of astute dynastic marriages may have some contemporary relevance), allows a backward reference to Carthage and some seemingly pointless banter about 'Widow Dido' and 'Widower Aeneas'. Carthage may be allowed to evoke a memory of the lost civilization of the ancient world ('Delenda est Carthago'), while Aeneas is, of course, the most famous founder of Empire of all. There are small echoes of the *Aeneid* in the play, and these have a quiet, marginal relevance. But the exiled Prospero is not an empire builder, no matter how relevant the settlement of Virginia is to his background in the play. It is the more general resonance gained by suspending this mysterious island between, or off, a sort of palimpsest of European civilization which is more cardinally suggestive.

Thus far, I have stood somewhat outside the play, identifying rather aridly possible thematic concerns; but, as we feel our way gently into the mysteries of the play, all this material, like Ferdinand's father (and much else), 'doth suffer a sea change/Into something rich and strange' (I, ii, 401–2). The opening scene of the storm and wreck shows confusion and disorder: the angry sea makes social hierarchy irrelevant ('What cares these roarers for the name of king?' – (I, i, 16–17), and it is no longer clear who is 'the master'.

The overworked Boatswain, annoyed at the useless courtiers in his way, sounds a note of insubordination, saying to Gonzalo 'if you can command these elements ... use your authority' (I, i, 22–4). Straight away questions of mastery and authority and command – and mutiny and insurrection – are raised which will recur in a different form on the island, where Prospero 'commands the elements' in his own special way, and where the roaring sea will merge into Prospero's anger. There is desperate talk of 'sinking', a literal downward movement which, again transmuted, will affect figures in scenes to come. Furious, unpleasant Antonio shouts at the Boatswain 'would thou mightst lie drowning/ The washing of ten tides!' (I, i, 57–8). Pirates were hanged on the beach and left there until they had been covered by three tides. The sea has much more work than that to do in this play, and the tidal washing continues, in various forms, throughout. For as well as being capable of stormy 'roarers', this is a cleansing and a 'clarifying' sea. And, in a curious way, it is as if the characters from the wreck *do* 'lie drowning' (not drown*ed*, note) during the play. This entirely realistic little scene ushers in what is to be the 'strangest' play Shakespeare ever wrote.

The second scene, it seems to me, marks an absolute alteration in mood and atmosphere, rather like the sudden change you experience if you are swimming in a noisy pool and suddenly duck your head down into submarine silence. Miranda refers to 'the wild waters in this roar' (I, ii, 2), but I don't think we can hear them. The world has gone quiet – the magisterial figure of Prospero is in complete command. It is indeed almost as if the play is taking place under the sea (as someone once remarked to Philip Brockbank); certainly there is something 'unearthly' about this island, and we soon learn that we have left the world of known and recognizable actualities behind. Miranda immediately reveals her 'piteous heart' by her instinctive sympathy with the shipwrecked men – 'I have suffered/With those that I saw suffer' (I, ii, 5–6). This pity must be innate since there is no one to teach it her, no 'piteous' precedent to learn from on this island. Miranda's compassion is absolutely vital; it bespeaks her inherent 'nobility', and is part of her 'better nature' which is essential to off-set and compensate for the bad nature which will soon be abroad on the island (and is perhaps incorporate in Caliban). From what we see of him, the austere and imperious Prospero is given more to anger than to pity, though pity is a lesson he will have to learn.

Prospero embarks on his long account of what befell him in Milan, the treacherous conspiracy against him, and how they were bundled into a boat and abandoned:

> To cry to th' sea that roared to us; to sigh
> To th' winds, whose pity, sighing back again,
> Did us but loving wrong.
>
> (I, ii, 149–51)

This sea always seems to be 'roaring', but within the tumult there is a wind sighing with pity – so the elements *can* set 'piteous' precedents. The apparent oxymoron of 'loving wrong' (which will be distortedly echoed by Caliban when he yearns for 'good mischief', by which he means the murder of Prospero: IV, i, 217) is important to the atmosphere and resolution of the play. When Miranda asks her father whether their coming to the island was 'foul play' or 'blessed' he replies:

> Both, both, my girl!
> By foul play, as thou say'st, were we heaved thence,
> But blessedly holp hither.
>
> (I, ii, 61–4)

When, near the end, Ferdinand is reunited with the father he thought drowned, he exclaims:

> Though the seas threaten, they are merciful.
> I have cursed them without cause.
>
> (V, i, 178–9)

This is a restatement of Viola's 'Tempests are kind, and salt waves fresh with love!' (*Twelfth Night* III, iv, 396), though in a somehow more sombre key. In this play, Nature *can* 'bless', as is clearly figured in the masque when Ceres says to Miranda and Ferdinand 'Ceres' blessing so is on you' (IV, i, 117), and more generally by the seemingly miraculous rescues and restorations on the island. But the word 'foul' occurs much more often; more often indeed than in any other play apart from *King Lear*. This is very much a Nature of 'both, both' with ultimately, as it were, no sure and lasting winner. As long (but only as long) as Prospero has his magic, the 'blessing' will seem to triumph. It is as if he works with the elements to bring about the mental renewal or spiritual cleansing of the errant courtiers. As he releases them from their charmed state, he comments:

> Their understanding
> Begins to swell, and the approaching tide
> Will shortly fill the reasonable shore,
> That now lies foul and muddy.
>
> (V, i, 79–82)

The cleansing sea has entered their very being. But not all the foulness can be washed away, as the mutely, contemptuously unrepentant Antonio sufficiently reminds us. And who can say what might yet happen to Prospero back in Milan – without his magic and, as it were, as vulnerable as the next man to the abiding foulness of the world.

As Prospero begins to recount their history, he announces 'The hour's now come'; most unusually, we are told exactly what time the play takes place (between 2.00 and 6.00 pm), and, for only the second time in Shakespeare, the duration of the action is the same as the length of the play (the other is *The Comedy of Errors*). Something is coming to a head; and the words spoken later by Antonio to Sebastian, with reference to his plan to murder Alonso, might more fittingly have been said by Prospero to Miranda:

> We all were sea-swallowed, though some cast again,
>   And, by that destiny, to perform an act
> Whereof what's past is prologue, what to come,
>   In yours and my discharge.
>
> (II, i, 255–8)

The past which is prologue to Prospero's final 'performance' reveals that he was foully treated by his usurping brother, but also that he was not without some responsibility for what happened. We have encountered the figure of the negligent or absconding ruler before (most notably in *Measure for Measure*), and, by his own account, Prospero was guilty of an irresponsible dereliction of duty while he pursued his 'liberal arts'.

> Those being all my study,
> The government I cast upon my brother
> And to my state grew stranger, being transported
> And rapt in secret studies.
>
> (I, ii, 74–7)

Not 'good government', whatever else it was. In a roundabout way, Prospero actually admits his responsibility:

> *I* thus neglecting worldly ends, all dedicated
> To closeness and the bettering of my mind –
> . . .   in my false brother
> *Awaked an evil nature*, and my trust,
> Like a good parent, did beget of him
> A falsehood in its contrary as great
> As my trust was, which had indeed no limit,
> A confidence sans bound.
>
> (I, ii, 89–97 – my italics)

So *he* did the 'awaking' of an evil latent in nature; just as his trust did the 'begetting' of falsehood. (I note in passing that for trust to be constructively operative it should not be limitless, any more than confidence should be simply boundless – to the extent that they are, they become indistinguishable from indifference.) A lot of things go by their 'contraries' in this play: there's a good father and a bad mother (Sycorax. Miranda's mother has one indirect reference which leaves her entirely without presence); a good brother and a bad brother; a noble child and a 'monstrous' child; a holy courtier and a foul one; a good servant and a bad servant; white magic and black magic. These contraries do not all remain stable and clear-cut – they wouldn't in Shakespeare; but there's a curious sense in which things somehow 'beget' their seeming opposites, a not-to-be-explained feeling that, say, Caliban is there because Ariel is there, that we have Sycorax because we have Prospero – or vice versa. As though people engender and awaken shadow selves. It is a very strange island.

INTRODUCTION

One of Prospero's many complaints about the conduct of his brother is the way in which he used the power Prospero had allowed him to win Prospero's own followers over to him; but the way Prospero describes this treacherous feat points to a larger mystery:

> new-created
> The creatures that were mine, I say – or changed 'em,
> Or else new-formed 'em
>
> (I, ii, 81–3)

New-created, new-formed, changed creatures – this is what we have been watching throughout Shakespeare's comedies, and here the mysteries of metamorphosis and change are an essential part of the island's atmosphere. Antonio changed creatures for the worse; Prospero seeks to new-create and new-form them for the better – in a Nature of 'both', people can always go either way. Prospero emerges as the better maker (as T. S. Eliot called Ezra Pound – *il miglior fabbro*), though his instructive failures with Caliban and Antonio mark a limit to his magic.

Nearing the end of his account, Prospero says:

> Now I arise.
> Sit still, and hear the last of our sea sorrow.
>
> (I, ii, 169–70)

Perhaps he stands up; but more importantly, he senses the approach of his 'zenith', and this starts the ascending movement, with a slight resurrectionary air, which counters the prevalent sinking tendency in the play. The 'sea sorrow' is over, and the 'roarers' will soon convert to music. Prospero is now in every sense the Governor. It is notable that he ascribes his sea-salvation to 'providence divine', and the propitious conditions for his coming triumph to 'bountiful Fortune'.

> By accident most strange, bountiful Fortune
> (Now my dear lady) hath mine enemies
> Brought to this shore; and by my prescience
> I find my zenith doth depend upon
> A most auspicious star, whose influence

cxlv

If now I court not, but omit, my fortunes
Will ever after droop.

(I, ii, 178–84)

Destiny, Providence, Fortune, accidents, stars, his own 'prescience' (not to mention his science) – it is impossible to fix just
who or what runs things, where the shaping and determining
powers come from. But everything is somehow at work, and
things are coming together.

Prospero starts his long narration by asking what images
Miranda 'hath kept with thy remembrance' (i, ii, 44). The
words 'remember', 'remembrance' occur more often in this
play than elsewhere, and there is a great deal of retrospective
peering into 'the dark backward and abysm of time' (I, ii, 50).
The most of life, one feels, was back there. Here, Prospero
has to educate Miranda's memory (as later he will Ariel's
and Caliban's) since for her it is as if it all happened in
another world.

'Tis far off,
And rather like a dream than an assurance
That my remembrance warrants.

(I, ii, 44–6)

This dream-like quality pervades the play; even as Prospero
recounts the real, waking world of Italian history to Miranda,
it seems to have a narcotic, even hypnotic effect on her (thus
his repeated jogging of her attention as she, presumably, keeps
dropping off – 'The strangeness of your story put/Heaviness
in me', I, ii, 306–7). Finishing his account he concludes:

Thou art inclined to sleep. 'Tis a good dullness,
And give it way. I know thou canst not choose. [*Miranda sleeps.*]

(I, ii, 185–6)

This particular dormition cannot have required a very strong
spell. This is not a facetious point. The island is full of sleep,
could itself be asleep and dreaming. A 'strange drowsiness',
'wondrous heavy' (II, i, 202–3) is everywhere. Many scenes
end in sleep or trance ('They fell together all ... they dropped
as by a thunderstroke', II, i, 207–8), and by the end you feel
the difference between waking and dreaming is terminally

blurred. Can you any longer be sure which is which? Thus
Sebastian to Antonio:

> What? Art thou waking?
> *Antonio.* Do you not hear me speak?
> *Sebastian.*   I do; and surely
> It is a sleepy language, and thou speak'st
> Out of thy sleep. What is it thou didst say?
> This is a strange repose, to be asleep
> With eyes wide open; standing, speaking, moving
> And yet so fast asleep.

(II, i, 213-19)

As it happens, the murderously plotting, and the slothfully bid-
dable, two courtiers are wickedly awake; yet Sebastian's words
aptly evoke the curious liminal state the characters seem to
find themselves in, speaking a 'sleepy language', falling into a
'strange repose'. When the Boatswain appears in the final scene,
he tells how they were 'dead of sleep'; then 'awaked' (with more
'roaring' sounds); then 'even in a dream ... brought moping
[dulled] hither' (V, i, 230-39). By this time, the characters
hardly know if they are asleep or awake, or suspended in some
waking dream. And nor do we. We (and they) might, by the
same token, wonder if they are alive or dead, or in some sort of
transitional limbo between the two states. Nobody dies in this
play. Unless, that is, they are all dead already, all 'sea-swallowed'
from the start. As Brockbank so pertinently commented, 'there
is no death after death'.

While Miranda is asleep, Prospero summons Ariel (nobody
apart from Prospero ever 'sees' Ariel, which makes him a very
different kind of presence from the grossly corporeal Caliban,
unpleasingly visible to all). Throughout this scene Prospero
constantly addresses Ariel as 'spirit', another word occurring
far more often in this play than elsewhere (twenty-nine times);
and clearly enough he (I don't know if spirits are gendered, but
'it' sounds rude) represents some kind of elemental opposite to
Caliban, who is invariably associated with (and even addressed
as) 'earth'. However, it soon becomes clear that Ariel is
quicksilvery volatile, at ease in all the elements. In the air, of
the air, obviously; but also doing Prospero's 'business in the
veins o' th' earth/When it is baked with frost' (I, ii, 255-6).

Of course he can fly, and swim, and 'ride on the curled clouds' (I, ii, 192); he can also 'dive into the fire', and on the King's ship 'I flamed amazement' (I, ii, 198). I am not sure that we need to know that he has the qualities allowed to Intelligences in medieval theology; or that in some angelogy he is one of the planetry spirits – superhuman but lower than the angels; or that he is 'a rational Platonic demon'. He has some of the fairy qualities of Puck, and while he is clearly under the control of Prospero, he seems to enjoy and exercise a certain degree of moral autonomy, acting responsibly as Prospero's agent.

But when Prospero tells him there is more work to do and he exhibits signs of reluctance – 'Is there more toil?' (I, ii, 242) – Prospero turns on him in fury, calling him 'malignant thing' and, tellingly, 'my slave' (I, ii, 257, 270). Since Prospero also calls Caliban his 'slave', we have to bear in mind that, whatever their extreme manifest differences, Ariel and Caliban have at least that status in common. Ariel wants 'my liberty' from Prospero; while Caliban, severally intoxicated by Stephano, deliriously, though utterly mistakenly, celebrates his new-found 'Freedom, high day, freedom!' (I, ii, 245; II, ii, 195). It wouldn't do to make too much of the fact that a number of Elizabethans had already made fortunes by introducing slavery into the West Indies, though it may well be relevant; and, given the horror that slavery in the New World was to become, we might wish to allow Shakespeare a disturbing prescience. But more relevant for the play is the fact that Shakespeare is reactivating, and of course richly transforming, a situation and theme from the old world of classical Plautine comedy. Bernard Knox has written an important article on this subject, and I can do no better than summarize his contribution.

Classical comedy derives a good deal of its humour from exploiting the absolute difference, crucial in the society of the time, between the free man and the slave (for Aristotle they were different natures). However callous we may find it, the crude activities and base proclivities of the slave were phenomena to be laughed at. But there were, for the purposes of the comedies, two kinds of slave: the stupid, sullen, cursing, drunken, lecherous, thievish, cowardly – let us say 'foul' –

slave, who makes clumsy attempts to rebel, and is humiliated and punished; but there was also the clever, adroit, intelligent – let us say 'delicate' – slave, who would actually help his master and solve his problems, thereby gaining his freedom. The master in these comedies was invariably an irascible and rough-tongued *senex*, or old man, who turns out in the end to be good-hearted and generous. You can see what Shakespeare has done with these crude stereotypes in the infinitely richer and more complex figures of Caliban, Ariel and Prospero. And in some of the comedies there could be an ironic twist whereby free men show themselves as thinking and acting like slaves, while a slave might prove superior to his master in intelligence, taste, and emotion. We have an echo of this in a crucial moment at the beginning of the last act (Prospero's last act – as Prospero – in every sense). Prospero's former foes are now completely in his power – 'At this hour/Lies at my mercy all mine enemies' (IV, i, 262–3). The long-awaited, long-prepared-for moment has come and the hour has struck. Prospero asks Ariel (now again addressed as 'my spirit') how the King and his followers are faring: 'all prisoners, sir ... They cannot budge till your release.' The three guilty men are still 'distracted', while the others are mourning bemusedly over them (V, i, 9–13). Then Ariel continues:

> Your charm so strongly works 'em,
> That if you now beheld them, your affections
> Would become tender.
> *Prospero.*   Dost thou think so, spirit?
> *Ariel.* Mine would, sir, were I human.
> *Prospero.*   And mine shall.
> Hast thou, which art but air, a touch, a feeling
> Of their afflictions, and shall not myself,
> One of their kind, that relish all as sharply,
> Passion as they, be kindlier moved than thou art?
> Though with their high wrongs I am struck to th' quick,
> Yet with my nobler reason 'gainst my fury
> Do I take part. The rarer action is
> In virtue than in vengeance.
>
>   (V, i, 17–28)

This is a key moment in Shakespeare, first to last – vengeance is abjured or transcended; pity and forgiveness prevail. Some critics have spent fruitless time speculating whether angry old Prospero was intending to give his 'enemies' a good stiff dose of their own malignant medicine, before Ariel's irresistibly cadenced intercession. Maybe he was, and maybe he wasn't. Be content that Shakespeare has made sure we can never know. What he *does* show us is the supposedly non-human servant tentatively presuming to give his master a lesson in humanity. It is another 'rare' moment on this enchanted island.

Venting his fury on the hapless Ariel, Prospero reminds him that he was previously enslaved by the 'damned witch Sycorax' who had been banished to the island from 'Argier' (I, ii, 263). Because Ariel was 'a spirit too *delicate*/To act her *earthy* and abhorred commands' (I, ii, 272–3, my italics), he refused to obey her orders; as punishment

> she did confine thee,
> By help of her more potent ministers
> And in her most unmitigable rage,
> Into a cloven pine
>
> (I, ii, 274–7)

and left him there until she died. It was only Prospero's 'art' which released him. And if Ariel goes on showing a disinclination to follow Prospero's instructions – 'I will rend an oak/And peg thee in his knotty entrails till/Thou hast howled away twelve winters' (I, ii, 294–6). Ariel is reduced to the abject pleas for mercy of a cowed slave threatened with a whipping. Prospero, the majestic Italian mage and royal magician, master of high Renaissance Arts, whose daughter is a 'wonder', must seem a kind of absolute opposite to Sycorax, the disgraced North African 'hag', 'damned witch' and wicked sorceress, whose offspring is a 'monster'. Of course we are prompted to say – white magic opposed to black magic. But they are both banished figures; they both depend on slaves and 'ministers'; and Prospero in *his* 'most unmitigable rage' threatens a rebellious Ariel with a punishment almost identical to the one visited on him by Sycorax (for, as between being confined in a cloven pine and pegged in an oak's entrails, it must be very much a case of six of one, half a dozen of the

other). Prospero's 'Art' (always with a capital A in the First
Folio) is constantly stressed – it is *another* word used more
frequently in this play than elsewhere; and it is registered as
being akin to an occult mystic science, while Sycorax dabbled
diabolically in the merest witchery. Yet in his final invocation
of all his 'elves' and 'demi-puppets', prior to abjuring his
special powers, Prospero is made to echo, in detail, the
invocation of Medea in Ovid's *Metamorphoses* (V, i, 33–50).
Now it is true that on this occasion Medea wants some magic
to restore the youth of Jason's aged father, Aeson. But this is
perhaps the only occasion on which she uses her strange skills
for re-creative purposes. Even though she does finish up in
pagan heaven, her life is littered with dismembered or otherwise
butchered corpses, including those of her own children. Understandably, Medea came to be the prototypical name for the
witch of terrifying, dark destructive power. And if, as it were,
Prospero draws on some of her spells and recipes, we must at
least wonder whether his 'rough magic' contains some elements
from the Medea brew. Of course Prospero and Sycorax are very
different; but worrying similarities begin to appear, and what
looked like a separation and a clarification – white here, black
there – turns out to be a proximity and a blurring.

After Ariel, of course Caliban, as night follows day. He,
too, shows a reluctance to respond to Prospero's orders (on
the not unreasonable grounds that (a) 'There's enough wood
within', and (b) 'I must eat my dinner', I, ii, 314, 330). Clearly
it is a day for slaves to be recalcitrant, and Prospero is in what
might be called a 'foul' temper. First, he promises Caliban a
pretty painful night of cramps and stinging pinches (the
punishments Prospero metes out sound sort of fairy-folksy,
but, if read carefully, they would seem to be, not exactly
tortures, but at least 'cruel and unusual'; for instance, being
wound round with adders which 'hiss me into madness', II, ii,
14). Then, as with Miranda and Ariel, he reminds Caliban of
the past. 'I have used thee (filth as thou art)' – always the kind
word – 'with humane care' (I, ii, 345–6), trying to educate
him, as he was educating his own child. Miranda, indeed,
reminds Caliban, in some uncharacteristically harsh words
(she sounds like her father – 'abhorred slave' and so on), that

she taught him language. This continued 'till thou didst seek to violate/The honor of my child' (I, ii, 347–8) – 'O ho, O ho! Would't had been done!' cries Caliban, revealing the unrepentant lechery of the savage (I, ii, 349) – at which point the 'humane care' very promptly stopped, and Caliban was 'confined into this rock' – another of Prospero's prisoners.

Caliban has another view of what happened:

> This island's mine by Sycorax my mother,
> Which thou tak'st from me.

> (I, ii, 331–2)

Disregarding the fact that all talk of 'property rights' on this 'uninhabited island' seems faintly absurd, Caliban's claim to, as it were, legitimate ownership is dubious. It will not do to see him as representing the expropriated native of shameful colonial history. The banished Sycorax (with child) has no more 'right' to the island than the exiled Prospero (with child). They are both alien interlopers (call them witches, call them settlers) on a land hitherto outside of history. Admittedly she was there first; but he seems to have made a better fist of things. What *is* certain is that Caliban – however he was while running wild and free – is *considerably* worse off as the solitary 'subject' under (usurping?) 'king' Prospero. Caliban's famous retort on being reminded of what we call the 'gift' of language is unanswerably compact – 'You taught me language, and my profit on't/Is, I know how to curse' (I, ii, 363–4). So he does; and so he curses, inventively and volubly, throughout. But his cursing is, must be, some kind of derivative of the abominable language of execration, disgust and vilification regularly bestowed on him by his ferocious-sounding master. Prospero may be many things, and I will come to that; but, here, let us notice one little detail. Shakespeare had a particular feeling for dogs' names, and when Ariel and Prospero finally set the '*divers Spirits in the shape of dogs and hounds*' on doomed, drunken and thieving Stephano, Trinculo and Caliban, the dogs summoned by Ariel are 'Mountain' and 'Silver' – which seems appropriate enough since Ariel is equally at home in shining light and 'heavy' earth; while the dogs called up by Prospero are 'Fury' and 'Tyrant' (IV, i, 255–7). Point taken – ask Ariel and Caliban.

INTRODUCTION

Caliban also reveals that, initially, Prospero was kind or, at least, conciliatory in his treatment of him – 'Thou strok'st me and made much of me' (I, ii, 333); though perhaps this is rather as one might pet a dog of uncertain temper. In response 'I loved thee/And showed thee all the qualities o' th' isle,/ The fresh springs, brine pits, barren place and fertile' (I, ii, 336-8). Just as the native Indians were indispensable to the first settlers. And notice that the island is barren *and* fertile. Both. You can read it either way, according to your temperament and predisposition – holy Gonzalo and good Adrian see the fertility ('see how lush and lusty the grass looks', etc.); rank-minded and sour-souled Antonio and Sebastian stress the fen-like barrenness ('the ground indeed is tawny', etc. – see II, i, 37-60). The island as a whole says different things to different people, who duly experience it in different ways.

It is notable that Caliban reveals himself as capable of 'love'; for the rest, the talk of love is, rightly enough, exclusively between Ferdinand and Miranda – except for a curiously touching moment shortly before the end when Ariel quite unexpectedly asks Prospero, 'Do you love me, master? No?' ('Dearly, my delicate Ariel' – Prospero's response is perhaps his tenderest utterance in the play, IV, i, 48-9.) It seems that there is a surprising capacity for 'love' in these non-human, or sub-human, slaves that you will look for in vain in worldly-wise, worldly-withered courtiers like Antonio and Sebastian. Caliban has had this 'love' whipped out of him ('lying slave,/ Whom stripes may move, not kindness!', I, ii, 344-5); but we see him pathetically eager to transfer it to Stephano. It will not do to interpret this as some sort of instinctive, animal-like, tail-wagging servility. The need and desire to love is the very mark of the human. And as well as the (acquired – thank you Prospero and Miranda) ability to curse, Caliban also reveals an (innate) sensitivity, which manifests itself in one of the most beautiful speeches in the play – not, surely, something that Shakespeare would have given him if he wanted us to share the unqualifiedly negative Prospero view of Caliban.

> Be not afeard; the isle is full of noises,
> Sounds and sweet airs that give delight and hurt not.
> Sometimes a thousand twanging instruments

Will hum about mine ears; and sometimes voices
That, if I then had waked after long sleep,
Will make me sleep again; and then, in dreaming,
The clouds methought would open and show riches
Ready to drop upon me, that, when I waked,
I cried to dream again.

(III, ii, 140–48)

It is a moment of 'rare' sensibility.

I have no desire to sentimentalize Caliban; there is clearly much of the savage about him, and there was that sexual attempt on Miranda (not that *that* makes him sub-human, alas!). But it simply will not do to see Prospero as embodying or representing Art, civility, law and order, the most advanced western civilized thought and skill, having to bring to heel raw, recalcitrant wild nature in the misshapen shape of the 'beast', Caliban. *Something* of that, certainly; but, as I have intimated, in this play all such schematic, diagrammatic clarifications are, finally, out. Caliban is called 'monster' often (it is yet another word which occurs more frequently than elsewhere), but only by Stephano and Trinculo (they also compare him to 'a dead Indian', II, ii, 34 – which *may* be a Virginian hint) – never by Prospero, who stays with 'beast'. And Stephano and Trinculo are pickled silly most of the time; certainly not qualified to pronounce on the more or less monstrous in man or nature. They reveal an inferiority to Caliban when they allow themselves to be distracted from their plot by the useless finery set out to snare them. 'Let it alone, thou fool! It is but trash' (IV, i, 224) says unacquisitive Caliban. He is primitive; they are degenerate. The real 'monsters' on the island are, of course Sebastian and, particularly, Antonio. They are both effectively speechless and notably unrepentant during the final reconciliation scene. Antonio really *is* an utterly recalcitrant piece of degraded nature; impervious to, and contemptuous of, any grace or kindness. He may have the bearing of a courtier, but in him we see nature *de*natured, the last humanizing flicker extinguished. There are worse things in heaven and earth than Caliban. True, he does instigate the plot to kill Prospero, thus initiating the parodic version of Antonio's planned regicide which, in

turn, is a repetition, this time thwarted, of the distant usurpation of Prospero. (Unlike Scott Fitzgerald's Gatsby, Prospero
can repeat the past – and change it.) Certainly, you should
not assassinate Governors, and we must never forget the
importance of 'the vital power of regiment'; but one has heard
of justified, or at least justifiable, slave revolts. Just how much
'nurture' will, or can, 'stick' on Caliban's 'nature' remains an
open question. Clearly there are some natures on which it
won't – one of the mysteries we live amongst. At the end,
Caliban seems resolved to have another go – 'I'll be wise
hereafter,/And seek for grace' (V, i, 295–6). At the same time,
Prospero acknowledges some sort of responsibility for Caliban
which remains terminally ambiguous – 'this thing of darkness
I/Acknowledge mine' (V, i, 275–6). Why his?

If I have not wanted to promote Caliban as a version of the
mythical 'noble savage', I have, by the same token, no desire
to *de*mote Prospero into an *ig*noble slave-driver. 'Nobility' –
and it is very important – in this play appertains exclusively
to the Italian courts, and Prospero must be registered as
noble, even though disquietingly prone to anger. As Miranda
watches, as she thinks, the ship go down, she instinctively
guesses that it 'had no doubt some noble creature in her' (I,
ii, 7); and so it does – Ferdinand:

> I might call him
> A thing divine; for nothing natural
> I ever saw so noble.

(I, ii, 418–20)

This is Miranda's response to her first sight of him (she in
turn will be thought a 'goddess' by Ferdinand's father; this is
par for romance, and together they make a 'noble' pair). Just
as nature can produce monsters, so it can engender nobles.
Though, to define true nobility (when it doesn't just mean
rank or title) may be said to be an ongoing matter, always to
be explored in Shakespeare's plays. Certainly, some of the
'goodly creatures' that Miranda wonders at when the courtiers
are assembled at the end, are neither so good, nor indeed so
'beauteous', as she generously assumes (V, i, 182–3).

But Ferdinand is presented as genuinely noble (this is

demonstrated in his courteous and chivalric courting of Miranda, enduring the test of penal servitude for her sake). Like Caliban, he also hears some of the 'sounds and sweet airs' of the isle, which again prompt some beautiful lines:

> Where should this music be? I' th' air or th' earth?
> It sounds no more; and sure it waits upon
> Some god o' th' island. Sitting on a bank,
> Weeping again the King my father's wrack,
> This music crept by me upon the waters,
> Allaying both their fury and my passion
> With its sweet air.

(I, ii, 388–94)

The last word nicely elides air–oxygen with air–melody; the sounds are Ariel's, but it is as if Ferdinand is breathing in the music of the elements – earth, air, waters. And the grammar allows the music to be weeping with Ferdinand. The threatening roaring of the sea has modulated to a consoling, placating singing. A second song effectively distils the atmosphere and process of the whole play.

> Full fathom five thy father lies;
>   Of his bones are coral made;
> Those are pearls that were his eyes;
>   Nothing of him that doth fade
> But doth suffer a sea change
> Into something rich and strange.

(I, ii, 397–402)

This is the magical metamorphosis which seems to spread through the play.

Ariel also makes sounds specially for Alonso, Antonio and Sebastian – this time, a moral indictment:

> You are three men of sin, whom destiny –
> That hath to instrument this lower world
> And what is in't – the never-surfeited sea
> Hath caused to belch up you and on this island,
> Where man doth not inhabit–

(III, iii, 53–7)

It is as if these indigestible sinners have caused the very sea

to vomit them out. Ariel reminds them of their 'great guilt'
and their treatment of Prospero –

> for which foul deed
> The pow'rs, delaying, not forgetting, have
> Incensed the seas and shores, yea, all the creatures,
> Against your peace.
>
> (III, iii, 72–5)

'The powers' – unspecified; it is as if they were under the
supervision of the seas and shores, which are 'instrumenting'
this 'lower world'. To Alonso, it is as if the sea had spoken:

> O, it is monstrous, monstrous!
> Methought the billows spoke and told me of it;
> The winds did sing it to me; and the thunder,
> That deep and dreadful organ pipe, pronounced
> The name of Prosper; it did bass my trespass.
> Therefore my son i' th' ooze is bedded; and
> I'll seek him deeper than e'er plummet sounded
> And with him there lie mudded.
>
> (III, iii, 95–102)

The elements of nature, mediated by Prospero, refracted
through Ariel, yield a moral music.

When Ferdinand has passed his test and is honourably
betrothed to Miranda, Prospero, through Ariel, puts on a
masque for them, which he calls 'some vanity of my art' (IV,
i, 41); and much of his art is, indeed, theatrical. Ceres and
Juno appear to bestow 'Honor, riches, marriage blessing' (IV,
i, 106) on the pair, and Ceres invokes the seasonal bounty of
great creating Nature:

> Earth's increase, foison plenty,
> Barns and garners never empty
> Vines with clust'ring branches growing,
> Plants with goodly burden bowing,
> Spring come to you at the farthest
> In the very end of harvest.
>
> (IV, i, 110–15)

It is important that Venus is kept away, since virginity is
essential for a royal marriage; and this is a marriage Prospero

very much wants (so that his child's children will inherit Milan *and* Naples). Hence his stress on the necessity for 'all sanctimonious ceremonies' and his almost hysterical hands-off warnings to Ferdinand. The masque does celebrate a more familiar pastoral nature; but it is as if in a dream within a dream. And it ends suddenly with '*a strange, hollow, and confused noise*' as the dancing Nymphs and Reapers '*heavily vanish*' (more 'hollowness' and 'heaviness' on the isle). He has foiled one plot, but he has another to deal with. 'I had forgot that foul conspiracy/Of the beast Caliban and his confederates/Against my life. The minute of their plot/Is almost come' (IV, i, 139–42). He must go carefully by the clock, and can't really afford much dalliance with pastoral illusionism. But the thought of Caliban's malevolence brings back his old fury, and Ferdinand and Miranda are dismayed to see him 'with anger so distempered' (IV, i, 145). He seeks to reassure them with what is, I suppose, the most famous speech in Shakespeare:

> be cheerful, sir.
> Our revels now are ended. These our actors,
> As I foretold you, were all spirits and
> Are melted into air, into thin air;
> And, like the baseless fabric of this vision,
> The cloud-capped towers, the gorgeous palaces,
> The solemn temples, the great globe itself,
> Yea, all which it inherit, shall dissolve,
> And, like this insubstantial pageant faded,
> Leave not a rack behind. We are such stuff
> As dreams are made on, and our little life
> Is rounded with a sleep. Sir, I am vexed.
> Bear with my weakness; my old brain is troubled.
> Be not disturbed with my infirmity ...

(IV, i, 147–60)

This was how masques 'dissolved', and Shakespeare had seen a number. Here it leads easily on to a vision of cosmic dissolution. Prospero is a magician; but he is also a vexed old man, with his thoughts turning towards the grave. (People have understandably wondered whether this is also Shakespeare, not so old – forty-seven – and, as one hopes, not so vexed, with his thoughts turning towards retirement.)

From now on his 'project doth gather to a head' (V, i, 1).
The King and courtiers are drawn into a circle where they
'*stand charmed*', 'spell-stopped' (V, i, 61). They have indeed
been 'justled from your senses' (V, i, 158), but now Prospero
commences the breaking of the spell and the clearing of
the mind.

> The charm dissolves apace;
> And as the morning steals upon the night,
> Melting the darkness, so their rising senses
> Begin to chase the ignorant fumes that mantle
> The clearer reason ...
>
> (V, i, 64–8)

The senses are rising, the understanding is swelling – the
refreshing tide of renewed sanity is coming in. The reconciliations, reunions and restorations are perfunctorily managed,
and a quick forgiveness is dispensed. (Even to 'unnatural'
Antonio, though with some asperity and quite a touch of the
old temper – 'For you, most wicked sir, whom to call brother/
Would even infect my mouth, I do forgive/Thy rankest fault
– all of them', V, i, 130–32. He gets no reply.) It is as if
Shakespeare through Prospero is saying – these are the familiar
conventions of the genre; let's just quickly run through them.
Time is running out – and the absconding playwright shows
his hand through the retiring Governor. Good Gonzalo, always
positive, is the most appreciative:

> O, rejoice
> Beyond a common joy, and set it down
> With gold on lasting pillars. In one voyage
> Did Claribel her husband find at Tunis,
> And Ferdinand her brother found a wife
> Where he himself was lost; Prospero his dukedom
> In a poor isle; and all of us ourselves
> When no man was his own.
>
> (V, i, 206–13)

Truly to 'find' yourself is the best benefit afforded by this
island.

But they can still 'taste/Some subtleties o' th' isle, that will
not let you/Believe things certain' (V, i, 123–5), and as seeming

miracle follows seeming miracle – a curtain drawn revealing Ferdinand and Miranda playing chess (more theatrics); the news that the wrecked ship is, in fact, as good as new – it is the sheer 'strangeness' of the whole experience which overwhelms them.

> These are not natural events; they strengthen
> From strange to stranger.
>
> (V, i, 227–8)

> This is as strange a maze as e'er men trod,
> And there is more in this business than nature
> Was ever conduct of.
>
> (V, i, 242–4)

'Strange to stranger' – to strangest (appropriately enough, 'strange' is yet another word which occurs more often in this play than elsewhere – the last one I will mention); what cannot happen here? These are, indeed, not 'natural' events – they are theatrical events. Which brings us to Prospero and Shakespeare.

The inclination to identify Prospero and his creator goes back a long way. In 1838 Thomas Campbell wrote of *The Tempest* that it 'has a sort of sacredness as the last work of the mighty workman. Shakespeare, as if conscious that it would be his last, and as if to typify himself, has made its hero a natural, a dignified, a benevolent magician.' This view of Prospero prevailed at least up to and including Frank Kermode's landmark, and still indispensable, Arden edition of 1954 (few editions have weathered the years so well). But more recent commentaries have knocked quite a few spots off that dignity and benevolence, and a second look has been taken at Prospero's magic. This seems to me to be correct; though when he is made out to be a megalomaniacal fascist imperialist, one begins to yearn for the old sanities. Prospero is a complex character in his own right, and we must leave him firmly embedded in the play rather than trying to transport him to Stratford. Having said that, there are some clear parallels between Prospero and Shakespeare, just as there is an unmistakable sense of concludingness in the famous lines of relinquishment, and in the generally penumbral air of the last scene, which is at once a new dawn and an old dusk (both).

> I'll break my staff,
> Bury it certain fathoms in the earth,
> And deeper than did ever plummet sound
> I'll drown my book.
>
> (V, i, 54–7)

Marlowe's Doctor Faustus promises to 'burn my books' in his very last words, and there is surely, here, a distant echo: but Shakespeare's is, rather, a drowned and drowning play; though it is worth noting that Faustus also prayed that his soul should be:

> changed into little water-drops,
> And fall into the ocean, ne'er to be found!
>
> (*Doctor Faustus* V, ii, 118–19)

Prospero's 'project' and Shakespeare's play last exactly the same length of time because, finally, they are one and the same thing. At the end, Prospero must put on his Milanese clothes, leave his island, and return to his unmagical ducal daily duties in Italy; just so, playwright and audience must leave the theatre and return to their less bewitching, 'real' lives. Even Shakespeare's magic can only work in the theatre and for so long. That is why Prospero (and there is a nice legend that Shakespeare played the role) comes forward to speak the Epilogue; post-play, minus magic, in the hands of God – and the audience.

> Now my charms are all o'erthrown,
> And what strength I have's mine own,
> Which is most faint.
> ...   Now I want
> Spirits to enforce, art to enchant;
> And my ending is despair
> Unless I be relieved by prayer.
>
> (1–3, 13–16)

Prospero can put on spectacular, spell-binding shows, he can 'justle' the senses this way and that; but, if you remember, his 'art' cannot get the daily chores done (like bringing in the wood), and it cannot convert the unconvertible (Antonio). And, we have to say, that goes for Shakespeare and his art, too. (He, too, can wake 'sleepers' from their graves by *his* 'so potent art', V, i, 50 – Theseus, Caesar, Cleopatra, Henry V – you name it.) It is irrelevant, and certainly undiscoverable, whether Shakespeare was here consciously saying goodbye to the theatre. But he was, by this time, far too self-conscious an artist for it not to be the case that in depicting and delimiting Prospero's magic he was both displaying and examining his own art. There has never been an art like it, before or since.

When I started to write these introductions, I made a point of acknowledging the enduring influence of the man who taught me how to read Shakespeare at Cambridge (and, in effect, for the rest of my life), the late Philip Brockbank. As a very small concluding piety I want to let him answer my opening question, and have the last word on the last play.

Where is the island of *The Tempest*? The final answer to this question must be, 'in the theatre' ... Every Shakespearian play is 'islanded' from the flux of life to which the epilogue returns us at the end of *The Tempest*, and having left the island–theatre we know that the fuller significance of our lost lives was there brought home to us.

Tony Tanner
King's College, Cambridge, April 1996

SELECT BIBLIOGRAPHY

BIOGRAPHY

The standard biography is now Samuel Schoenbaum, *William Shakespeare: A Documentary Life*, Oxford University Press, Oxford, 1975. A shortened version of this excellent volume was published in 1977. For those interested in Shakespearian mythology, Schoenbaum has also produced *Shakespeare's Lives*, Clarendon Press, Oxford, 1970, a witty dissection of the myriad theories, concerning the playwright's identity and the authorship of the plays. Rather in the same vein is Anthony Burgess, *Shakespeare*, Penguin, London, 1972, a lively introduction to the presumed facts of the poet's life, enhanced by novelistic licence.

BIBLIOGRAPHY

Among the vast quantity of Shakespeare criticism it is probably only useful to list texts which are both outstanding and easily available. This I do below. For further information the serious student may consult the bibliographies of works listed. There are also three major journals which record the flow of critical work: the *Shakespeare Quarterly*; and the *Shakespeare Survey* and *Shakespeare Studies* which are published annually.

CRITICISM

The two indispensable Shakespearian critics are Johnson and Coleridge. Their dispersed comments are collected in *Samuel Johnson on Shakespeare*, ed., H. R. Woodhuysen, Penguin, London, 1989, and S. T. Coleridge, *Shakespearian Criticism*, two vols., Everyman's Library, London, 1960.

ROMANCE, THE LAST PLAYS: GENERAL

BARKAN, LEONARD, *The Gods Made Flesh*, 1986.
BATE, JONATHAN, *Shakespeare and Ovid*, 1993.
BERGERON, DAVID M., *Shakespeare's Romances and the Royal Family*, 1985.
BLAND, D. S., 'The Heroine and the Sea: an Aspect of Shakespeare's Last Plays', Essays in Criticism 3, 1953.
BROWN, JOHN R. (ed.), *Later Shakespeare*, 1966.
CAVE, TERENCE, *Recognitions*, 1988.
CUTTS, JOHN P., *Rich and Strange: A Study of Shakespeare's Last Plays*, 1968.
DANBY, JOHN F., *Poets on Fortune's Hill*, 1952.

ROMANCES

DUNN, C. M., 'The Function of Music in Shakespeare's Romances', Shakespeare Quarterly 20, 1969.

EDWARDS, PHILIP, 'Shakespeare's Romances: 1900–1957', Shakespeare Survey 11, 1958.

FELPERIN, HOWARD, Shakespearean Romance, 1972.

FOAKES, R. A., The Dark Comedies to the Last Plays, 1971.

FRYE, NORTHROP, A Natural Perspective, 1955.

GESNER, CAROL, Shakespeare and the Greek Romance, 1970.

HOENIGER, F. D., 'Shakespeare's Romances since 1958', Shakespeare Survey 29, 1976.

HUNTER, G. K., Shakespeare: The Late Comedies, 1962.

HUNTER, R. G., Shakespeare and the Comedy of Forgiveness, 1965.

KERMODE, FRANK, Shakespeare and the Final Plays, 1963.

KNIGHT, G. WILSON, The Crown of Life, 1947.

LONG, J. H., Shakespeare's Use of Music: The Final Comedies, 1961.

JAMES, HENRY, Literary Criticism Vol. 2, 1984.

MOWAT, BARBARA A., The Dramaturgy of Shakespeare's Romances, 1976.

MUIR, KENNETH, 'Theophanies in the Last Plays', in Shakespeare's Late Plays, ed. Tobias and Zolbrod, 1974.

PETERSON, D. L., Time, Tide and Tempest: A Study of Shakespeare's Romances, 1973.

PETTET, E. C., Shakespeare and the Romance Tradition, 1949.

SALINGAR, L. G., 'Time and Art in Shakespeare's Romances', Renaissance Drama 9, 1966.

SANDERS, NORMAN, 'An Overview of Critical Approaches to the Romances', in Shakespeare's Romances Reconsidered, ed. Kay and Jacobs, 1978.

SMITH, HALLETT, Shakespeare's Romances: A Study of Some Ways of the Imagination, 1972.

SPENCER, THEODORE, 'Appearance and Reality in Shakespeare's Last Plays', Modern Philology 39, 1942.

TILLYARD, E. M. W., Shakespeare's Last Plays, 1938.

TRAVERSI, DEREK A., Shakespeare: The Last Phase, 1954.

UPHAUS, R. W., Beyond Tragedy: Structure and Experiment in Shakespeare's Romances, 1981.

WELLS, STANLEY, 'Shakespeare and Romance' in Later Shakespeare, ed. Brown and Harris, 1966.

YATES, FRANCIS A., Shakespeare's Last Plays: A New Approach, 1975.

YOUNG, DAVID, The Heart's Forest: A Study of Shakespeare's Pastoral Plays, 1972.

SELECT BIBLIOGRAPHY

PERICLES

ARTHOS, JOHN, 'Pericles: A Study in the Dramatic Use of Romantic Narrative', Shakespeare Quarterly 4, 1953.

BARBER, C. L., '"Thou that Beget'st Him That Did Thee Beget": Transformation in Pericles and The Winter's Tale', Shakespeare Quarterly 22, 1969.

BARKER, G. A., 'Themes and Variations in Shakespeare's Pericles', English Studies 44, 1963.

BROCKBANK, J. P., 'Pericles and the Dream of Immortality', in On Shakespeare, 1989.

CRAIG, HARDIN, 'Pericles and the Painfull Adventures', Studies in Philology 45, 1948.

CUTTS, JOHN P., 'Pericles, "Downright Violence"', Shakespeare Survey 4, 1968.

EWBANK, INGA-STINA, '"My name is Marina"; The Language of Recognition' in Shakespeare's Styles, ed. P. Edwards, 1980.

GREENFIELD, THELMA N., 'A Re-Examination of the "Patient" Pericles', Shakespeare Survey 3, 1967.

MANLY, J. M., 'The Miracle Play in Mediaeval England', in Essays by Divers Hands, 1927.

MUIR, KENNETH, 'The Problem of Pericles', English Studies 30, 1949.

NEELY, CAROL THOMAS, Broken Nuptials in Shakespeare's Plays, 1985.

PARROTT, THOMAS M., 'Pericles: The Play and the Novel', Shakespeare Assocation Bulletin 23, 1948.

PRESTON, CLAIRE, 'The Emblematic Structure of Pericles', Word and Image 8, 1992.

SCHANZER, ERNEST, Introduction to the Signet edition, 1965.

TOMPKINS, J. M. S., 'Why Pericles?', Review of English Studies 3, 1952.

CYMBELINE

BROCKBANK, J. P., 'History and Histrionics in Cymbeline', in On Shakespeare, 1989.

HARRIS, BERNARD, '"What's Past is Prologue": Cymbeline and Henry VIII', in Later Shakespeare, 1966.

HOENIGER, F. D., 'Irony and Romance in Cymbeline', Studies in English Literature 2, 1962.

HUNT, MAURICE, 'Shakespeare's Empirical Romance: Cymbeline and Modern Knowledge', Texas Studies in Language and Literature 22, 1980.

JONES, EMRYS, 'Stuart Cymbeline', Essays in Criticism 11, 1961.

KIRSCH, ARTHUR C., 'Cymbeline and Coterie Dramaturgy', Journal of English Literary History 34, 1967.

LAWRENCE, W. W., Shakespeare's Problem Comedies, 1931.

ROMANCES

MARSH, D. R. C., *The Recurring Miracle: A Study of Cymbeline and the Last Plays*, 1962.

MOFFETT, ROBIN, '*Cymbeline* and the Nativity', Shakespeare Quarterly 13, 1962.

MOWAT, BARBARA A., '*Cymbeline*: Crude Dramaturgy and Aesthetic Distance', Renaissance Papers, 1966.

PETERSON, DOUGLAS, '*Cymbeline*: Legendary History and Arcadian Romance', in *Time, Tide and Tempest*, 1973.

RIBNER, IRVING, 'Shakespeare and Legendary History: *Lear* and *Cymbeline*', Shakespeare Quarterly 7, 1956.

SHAHEEN, NASEEB, 'The Use of Scripture in *Cymbeline*', Shakespeare Survey 4, 1968.

STEPHENSON, A. A., 'The Significance of *Cymbeline*', Scrutiny 10, 1941–2.

SWANDER, HOMER D., '*Cymbeline* and the "Blameless Hero"', Journal of England Literary History 31, 1964.

TAYLOR, MICHAEL, 'The Pastoral Reckoning in *Cymbeline*', Shakespeare Survey 36, 1983.

THORNE, WILLIAM B., '*Cymbeline*: "Lopp'd Branches" and the Concept of Regeneration', Shakespeare Quarterly 20, 1969.

WICKHAM, GLYNNE, 'Riddle and Emblem: A Study in the Dramatic Structure of *Cymbeline*', in *English Renaissance Studies*, ed. John Carey, 1980.

THE WINTER'S TALE

BARBER, C. L., '*The Winter's Tale* and Jacobean Society', in *Shakespeare in a Changing World*, ed. Kettle, 1964.

BARTON, ANNE, 'Leontes and the Spider: Language and Speaker in Shakespeare's Last Plays', in *Shakespeare's Styles*, ed. P. Edwards, 1980.

BETHELL, SAMUEL L., *The Winter's Tale: A Study*, 1947.

BIGGINS, DENNIS, '"Exit pursued by a Beare": A Problem in *The Winter's Tale*', Shakespeare Quarterly 13, 1962.

BONJOUR, ADRIEN, 'Polixenes and the Winter of His Discontent', English Studies 50, 1969.

BRYANT, JERRY H., '*The Winter's Tale*, and the Pastoral Tradition', Shakespeare Quarterly 14, 1963.

BRYANT, JOSEPH A., 'Shakespeare's Allegory: *The Winter's Tale*', Sewanee Review 63, 1955.

ELLIS, JOHN, 'Rooted Affection: The Genesis of Jealousy in *The Winter's Tale*', College English 25, 1964.

EWBANK, INGA-STINA, 'The Triumph of Time in *The Winter's Tale*', Review of English Studies 5, 1964.

FREY, CHARLES, *Shakespeare's Vast Romance: A Study of 'The Winter's Tale'*, 1980.

GOURLAY, PATRICIA S., ' "O my most sacred lady": Female Metaphor in *The Winter's Tale*', English Literary Renaissance 5, 1975.

HARTWIG, JOAN, 'The Tragicomic Perspective of *The Winter's Tale*', Journal of English Literary History 37, 1970.

LAWLOR, JOHN, '*Pandosto* and the Nature of Dramatic Romance', Philological Quarterly 41, 1962.

LIVINGSTON, MARY L., 'The Natural Art of *The Winter's Tale*', Modern Language Quarterly 30, 1969.

MARTZ, LOUIS, 'Shakespeare's Humanist Enterprise: *The Winter's Tale*', in *English Renaissance Studies*, ed. John Carey, 1984.

MATCHETT, WILLIAM H., 'Some Dramatic Techniques in *The Winter's Tale*', Shakespeare Survey 22, 1969.

MOWAT, BARBARA A., 'A Tale of Sprights and Goblins', Shakespeare Quarterly 20, 1969.

MUIR, KENNETH (ed.), *The Winter's Tale: A Casebook*, 1968.

NEELY, CAROL THOMAS, '*The Winter's Tale*: The Triumph of Speech', Studies in English Literature 15, 1975.

NUTTALL, A. D., *Shakespeare: The Winter's Tale*, 1966.

PYLE, FITZROY, *The Winter's Tale: A Commentary on the Structure*, 1969.

SCHWARTZ, MURRAY M., '*The Winter's Tale*: Loss and Transformation', in *Psychoanalysis and Literary Process*, ed. F. Crews, 1970.

SMITH, JONATHAN, 'The Language of Leontes', Shakespeare Quarterly 19, 1968.

TINKLER, F. C., '*The Winter's Tale*', Scrutiny 5, 1936–7.

WILLIAMS, JOHN A., *The Natural Work of Art: The Experience of Romance in Shakespeare's The Winter's Tale*, 1967.

THE TEMPEST

ABRAMS, RICHARD, '*The Tempest* and the Concept of the Machiavellian Playwright', English Literary Renaissance 8, 1978.

AUDEN, W. H., 'The Sea and the Mirror: A Commentary on Shakespeare's *The Tempest*', *The Collected Poetry*, 1945.

BERGER, HARRY, 'Miraculous Harp: A Reading of Shakespeare's *The Tempest*', Shakespeare Studies 5, 1969.

BROCKBANK, J. P., '*The Tempest*: Conventions of Art and Empire' and 'Island of *The Tempest*', both in *On Shakespeare*, 1989.

BROWER, REUBEN, 'The Mirror of Analogy', in *The Fields of Light*, 1951.

BROWN, JOHN R., *Shakespeare: The Tempest*, 1969.

BROWN, PAUL, ' "This thing of darkness I acknowledge mine": *The Tempest* and the Discourse of Colonialism', in *Political Shakespeare*, ed. Dollimore and Sinfield, 1985.

ROMANCES

CANTOR, PAUL, 'Prospero's Republic: The Politics of Shakespeare's *The Tempest*', in *Shakespeare as Political Thinker*, ed. Alvis and West, 1981.

CARTELLI, THOMAS, 'Prospero in Africa', in *Shakespeare Reproduced*, ed. Howard and O'Connor, 1987.

COURSEN, HERBERT, 'Prospero and the Drama of the Soul', Shakespeare Survey 4, 1968.

CRAIG, HARDIN, 'Magic in *The Tempest*', Philological Quarterly 47, 1968.

DAVIDSON, FRANK, '*The Tempest*: An Interpretation', Journal of English and Germanic Philology, 62, 1963.

DEVEREUX, E. J., 'Sacramental Imagery in *The Tempest*', Humanities Association Bulletin 19.1, 1968.

DRIVER, TOM F., 'The Shakespearean Clock: Time and the Vision of Reality in *Romeo and Juliet* and *The Tempest*', Shakespeare Quarterly 15, 1964.

EBNER, DEAN, '*The Tempest*: Rebellion and the Ideal State', Shakespeare Quarterly 16, 1965.

FELPERIN, HOWARD, 'Shakespeare's Miracle Play', Shakespeare Quarterly 18, 1967.

GESNER, CAROL, '*The Tempest* as Pastoral Romance', Shakespeare Quarterly 10, 1959.

GILBERT, ALLAN, '*The Tempest*: Parallelism in Characters and Situations', Journal of English and Germanic Philology 14, 1915.

GOHN, ERNEST, '*The Tempest*: Theme and Structure', English Studies 45, 1964.

GRAZIA, MARGRETA DE, '*The Tempest*: Gratuitous Movement or Action without Kibes and Pinches', Shakespeare Studies 14, 1981.

GREENBLATT, STEPHEN, 'Learning to Curse', in *First Images of America*, ed. F. Chiapelli, 1976.

HANKINS, JOHN E., 'Caliban the Bestial Man', Publications of the Modern Language Association 62, 1947.

HART, JEFFREY P., 'Prospero and Faustus', Boston University Studies in English 2, 1956.

HILLMAN, RICHARD, '*The Tempest* as Romance and Anti-Romance', University of Toronto Quarterly 55, 1985–6.

HOENIGER, F. D., 'Prospero's Storm and Miracle', Shakespeare Quarterly 7, 1956.

HUNT, JOHN D., *A Critical Commentary on Shakespeare's The Tempest*, 1968.

JAMES, DAVID, *The Dream of Prospero*, 1967.

JEWKES, WILFRED T., 'Excellent Dumb Discourse: The Limits of the Language in *The Tempest*', in *Essays on Shakespeare*, 1963.

JOHNSON, WENDELL S., 'The Genesis of Ariel', Shakespeare Quarterly 2, 1951.

SELECT BIBLIOGRAPHY

KAHN, COPPELIA, 'The Providential Tempest and the Shakespearean Family', in *Representing Shakespeare*, ed. Schwartz and Kahn, 1980.

KERMODE, FRANK, *The Tempest*, Arden edition, 1954.

KERNAN, ALVIN B., *The Playwright as Magician*, 1979.

KNOX, BERNARD, '*The Tempest* and the Ancient Comic Tradition', English Institute Essays, 1954.

LEININGER, LORIE, 'The Miranda Trap: Sexism and Racism in Shakespeare's *The Tempest*', in *The Woman's Part*, ed. C. Lenz, 1980.

LEVIN, HARRY, 'Two Magician Comedies, *The Tempest* and *The Alchemist*', Shakespeare Survey 22, 1969.

MARX, LEO, 'Shakespeare's American Fable', Massachusetts Review 2, 1960–61.

NOSWORTHY, JAMES M., 'The Narrative Sources of *The Tempest*', Review of English Studies 24, 1948.

NUTTALL, A. D., *Two Concepts of Allegory: A Study of Shakespeare's The Tempest*, 1967.

ORGEL, STEPHEN, *The Tempest*, World's Classics edition, 1994.

PHILLIPS, JAMES E., '*The Tempest* and the Renaissance Idea of Man', in *Shakespeare 400*, ed. J. McManaway, 1964.

ROBINSON, JAMES E., 'Time and *The Tempest*', Journal of English and Germanic Philology 63, 1964.

RYKEN, LELAND, 'The Temptation Theme in *The Tempest* and the Question of Dramatic Suspense', Tennessee Studies in Literature 14, 1969.

SEIDEN, MELVIN, 'Utopianism in *The Tempest*', Modern Language Quarterly 31, 1970.

SEMON, KENNETH J., 'Shakespeare's *The Tempest*: Beyond a Common Joy', English Literary History 40, 1973.

SISSON, CHARLES J., 'The Magic of Prospero', Shakespeare Survey 11, 1958.

SMITH, HALLETT (ed.), *Twentieth Century Interpretations of The Tempest*, 1969.

SRIGLEY, MICHAEL, *Images of Regeneration: A Study of Shakespeare's The Tempest and Its Cultural Background*, 1985.

STILL, COLIN, *Shakespeare's Mystery Play: A Study of the Tempest*, 1921.

STOLL, ELMER, '*The Tempest*', Publications of the Modern Language Assocation 47, 1932.

SUNDELSON, DAVID, 'So Rare a Wonder'd Father: Prospero's *Tempest*', in *Representing Shakespeare*, ed. Schwartz and Kahn, 1980.

WAGNER, EMMA, *Shakespeare's The Tempest: An Allegorical Interpretation*, 1933.

WEST, ROBERT H., 'Ceremonial Magic in *The Tempest*', in Shakespearean Essays, 1964.

ROMANCES

WRIGHT, LOUIS (ed.), *The Elizabethans' America*, 1965.

WILSON, HAROLD S., 'Action and Symbol in *Measure for Measure* and *The Tempest*', Shakespeare Quarterly 4, 1953.

WILSON, J. DOVER, *The Meaning of The Tempest*, 1936.

ZIMBARDO, ROSE A., 'Form and Disorder in *The Tempest*', Shakespeare Quarterly 14, 1963.

CHRONOLOGY

DATE	AUTHOR'S LIFE	LITERARY CONTEXT
1564	Born in Stratford, Warwickshire, the eldest surviving son of John Shakespeare, glover and occasional dealer in wool, and Mary Arden, daughter of a prosperous farmer.	Birth of Christopher Marlowe.
1565	John Shakespeare elected Alderman of Stratford.	Clinthio: *Hecatommithi*. Edwards: *Damon and Pythias*.
1566	Birth of Shakespeare's brother Gilbert.	Gascoigne: *Supposes*.
1567		Udall: *Roister Doister*. Golding: *The Stories of Venus and Adonis and of Hermaphroditus and Salamcis*.
1568	His father is elected bailiff.	Gascoigne: *Jocasta*. Wilmot: *Tancred and Gismunda*. Second Edition of Vasari's *Lives of the Artists*.
1569	Probably starts attending the petty school attached to the King's New School in Stratford. Birth of his sister Joan.	
1570	His father involved in money-lending.	
1571	John Shakespeare is elected Chief Alderman and deputy to the new bailiff.	
1572		Whitgift's *Answer* to the 'Admonition' receives Cartwright's *Reply*, beginning the first literary debate between Anglicans and Puritans.
1573		Tasso: *Aminta*.
1574	Probably enters the Upper School (where studies include rhetoric, logic, the Latin poets, and a little Greek). Birth of his brother Richard.	
1575		*Gammer Gurton's Needle* is printed.

Death of Michelangelo. Birth of Galileo.

Rebellion against Spain in the Netherlands. Birth of the actor Edward Alleyn.
Birth of the actor Richard Burbage.

Mary Stuart flees to England from Scotland.

Northern Rebellion.

Excommunication of Elizabeth. *Baïf's* Academy founded in Paris to promote poetry, music and dance.
Ridolfi Plot. Puritan 'Admonition' to Parliament.

Dutch rebels conquer Holland and Zeeland. Massacre of St Bartholomew's Day in Paris.

Accession of Henry III and new outbreak of civil war in France. First Catholic missionaries arrive in England from Douai. Earl of Leicester's Men obtain licence to perform within the City of London.

Kenilworth Revels.

DATE	AUTHOR'S LIFE	LITERARY CONTEXT
1576		Castiglione's *The Book of the Courtier* banned by the Spanish Inquisition. George Gascoigne: *The Steel Glass.*
1577		John Northbrooke's attack in *Treatise wherein Dicing, Dancing, Vain Plays etc are reproved.*
1578	Shakespeare family fortunes are in decline, and John is having to sell off property to pay off his increasing debts.	Sidney writes *The Lady of May* and begins the 'Old' *Arcadia.* George Whetstone: *Promos and Cassandra.* John Lyly: *Euphues, the Anatomy of Wit.* Pierre de Ronsard, leader of the Pléiade, publishes his *Sonnets pour Hélène.* He is said to have exercised a considerable influence on the English sonnet-writers of the sixteenth century.
1579		Spenser: *The Shepherd's Calendar.* North: translation of Plutarch. Gossen: *The School of Abuse, and Pleasant Invective against Poets, Pipers, Players etc.* First visit to England of the duc d'Alençon as a suitor to Elizabeth, provoking much opposition to a French match. The Corral de la Cruz built in Madrid.
1580	Birth of Shakespeare's brother Edmund.	Sidney: *Apologie for Poetrie.* Lodge: *Defense of Plays.*
1581		John Newton's translation of Seneca's *Ten Tragedies.* Barnaby Rich: *Apolonius and Silla.* Stricter enforcement of treason laws and increased penalties on recusants. Campion captured and executed. Northern provinces of the Netherlands renounce their allegiance to Phillip II, and invite the duc d'Alençon to be their sovereign.

HISTORICAL EVENTS

Restricted by the City of London's order that no plays be performed within the City boundaries, James Burbage of The Earl of Leicester's Men builds The Theatre only just outside the boundaries in Shoreditch. The Blackfriars Theatre is built. End of civil war in France. Observatory of Uraniborg built for the Danish astronomer, Tycho Brahe. Death of Titian.

Drake's circumnavigation of the world. The Curtain Theatre built. Birth of Rubens.

Spanish conquest of Portugal. Jesuit mission arrives in England from Rome led by Edmund Campion and Parsons.

DATE	AUTHOR'S LIFE	LITERARY CONTEXT
1583	Birth of their daughter Susanna.	
1583-4	The players' companies of the Earls of Essex, Oxford and Leicester perform in Stratford.	Giordarno Bruno visits England.
1584		Bruno publishes *La cena de le Ceneri* and *Spaccio della bestia trionfante*. Reginald Scott: *The Discovery of Witchcraft*.
1585	Birth of Shakespeare's twins Hamnet and Judith. The following years until 1592 are the 'Lost Years' for which no documentary records of his life survive, only legends such as the one of deer-stealing and flight from prosecution, and conjectures such as ones that he became a schoolmaster, travelled in Europe, or went to London to be an actor as early as the mid 1580s.	Death of Pierre de Ronsard. Bruno: *De gli eroici furori*, dedicated to Sidney.
1586		Timothy Bright: *A Treatise of Melancholy*.
1586-7	Five players' companies visit Stratford, including the Queen's, Essex's, Leicester's and Stafford's.	
1587		Holinshed: *Chronicles of England, Scotland and Ireland*. Marlowe: First part of *Tamburlaine the Great* acted. New edition of *The Mirror for Magistrates*.
1588		Marlowe: Second part of *Tamburlaine*. Thomas Kyd: *The Spanish Tragedy*. Lope de Vega, serving with the Armada, writes some of *The Beauty of Angelica*.

CHRONOLOGY

First meeting of the Durham House Set led by Ralegh, Northumberland and Harriot, to promote mathematics, astronomy and navigation. Archbishop Whitgift leads more extreme anti-Puritan policy. Throckmorton plot, involving the Spanish ambassador.

Death of d'Alençon. Assassination of William of Orange. The Teatro Olimpico, Vicenza, built by Palladio.

England sends military aid to the Dutch rebels under the command of Leicester. Ralegh organizes the colonization of Virginia.

Babington plot. Death of Sir Philip Sidney. Rise of the Earl of Essex. Colonization of Munster.

Execution of Mary Stuart. Drake's raid on Cadiz.

Defeat of the Armada. Death of the Earl of Leicester. The first of the Puritan Marprelate Tracts published.

DATE	AUTHOR'S LIFE	LITERARY CONTEXT
1589	The earliest likely date at which Shakespeare began composition of his first play (1 *Henry VI*) when he would have been working as an actor at The Theatre, with Burbage's company.	Marlowe: *The Jew of Malta*. Thomas Nashe: *The Anatomy of Absurdity*. Richard Hakluyt: *Principal Navigations, Voyages and Discoveries of the English nation*.
1590	2 *Henry VI*, 3 *Henry VI*.	Spenser: first 3 books of *The Faerie Queen*. Publication of Sidney's 'New' *Arcadia*. Nashe: *An Almond for a Parrot*, one of the Marprelate Tracts. Greene: *Menaphon*. Guarina: *The Faithful Shepherd*.
1590–92	Performances of *Henry VI*, parts 2 and 3, *Titus* and *The Shrew* by the Earl of Pembroke's Men.	
1591	*Richard III* and *The Comedy of Errors* written.	Spenser's *Complaints* which includes his translation of fifteen of Joachim du Bellay's sonnets – du Bellay was a member of the Pléiade and responsible for its manifesto. Sir John Harington's translation of *Orlando Furioso*. Publication of Sidney's *Astrophel and Stella*.
1592	First recorded reference to Shakespeare as an actor and playwright in Greene's attack in *The Groatsworth of Wit* describing him as 'an upstart crow'.	Samuel Daniel: *Delia*. Marlowe's *Edward II* and *Doctor Faustus* performed. *Arden of Feversham* printed. Nashe: *Strange News*.
1592–4	*Titus Andronicus* written.	
1593	Publication of *Venus and Adonis*, dedicated to the Earl of Southampton. The *Sonnets* probably begun.	Marlowe: *Massacre of Paris*. *The Phoenix Nest*, miscellany of poems including ones by Ralegh, Lodge and Breton. Barnabe Barnes: *Parthenophil and Parthenope*. George Peele: *The Honour of the Garter*. Lodge: *Phillis*. Nashe: *Christ's Tears over Jerusalem*.

CHRONOLOGY

HISTORICAL EVENTS

Failure of the Portugal expedition. Henry III of France assassinated. English military aid sent to Henry of Navarre. Marlowe's tutor, Francis Ket, burned at the stake for atheism.

English government discovers and suppresses the Puritan printing press.

Earl of Essex given command of the English army in France. The last fight of the *Revenge* under Spanish attack.

Capture of Madre de Dios. Split in the main players' company. Shakespeare and Burbage's group remain at The Theatre, Alleyn's move to the Rose on Bankside. Plague in London: the theatres closed.

Marlowe arrested on blasphemy charges and murdered two weeks later. Kyd arrested for libel. Henry of Navarre converts to Catholicism in order to unite France.

DATE	AUTHOR'S LIFE	LITERARY CONTEXT
1593–4	*The Taming of the Shrew; The Two Gentlemen of Verona.*	
1593–6		John Donne writing his early poems, the Satires and Elegies.
1594	*The Rape of Lucrece* dedicated to his patron Southampton. *The Comedy of Errors* and *Titus Andronicus* performed at the Rose. Shakespeare established as one of the shareholders in his company, The Chamberlain's Men, which performs before the Queen during the Christmas festivities.	Daniel: *Cleopatra.* Spenser: *Amoretti* and *Epithalamion.* Drayton: *Idea's Mirror.* Nashe: *The Terrors of the Night, The Unfortunate Traveller.* Greene: *Friar Bacon and Friar Bungay.*
1594–5	*Love's Labor's Lost* and *Romeo and Juliet* written.	
1595	*Richard II.*	Daniel: *The First Four Books of the Civil Wars between the two houses of Lancaster and York.* Sidney: *Defence of Poesy* published. Ralegh: *The Discovery of the Empire of Guiana.*
1595–6	*A Midsummer Night's Dream.*	
1596	Death of his son, Hamnet. *The Merchant of Venice.* Shakespeare living in Bishopsgate ward. His father, John, is granted a coat of arms. *King John* written.	Lodge: *Wits Miserie.* First complete edition of Spenser's *Faerie Queen.*
1597	*Henry IV* Part 1. First performance of *The Merry Wives of Windsor.* Shakespeare's company now under the patronage of the new Lord Chamberlain, Hunsdon. In Stratford, Shakespeare buys New Place, the second largest house in the town, with its own orchards and vines.	John Donne writes 'The Storme' and 'The Calme'. Francis Bacon: first edition of *Essays.* Jonson and Nashe imprisoned for writing *The Isle of Dogs.*
1597–8	*Henry IV* Part 2.	
1598	*Much Ado About Nothing.* Shakespeare one of the 'principal comedians' with Richard Burbage, Heminge and Cordell in Jonson's *Every Man in*	Publication of Sidney's *Works* and of Marlowe's *Hero and Leander* (together with Chapman's continuation). *Seven Books of the Iliads* (first of

Henry of Navarre accepted as King in Paris. Rebellion in Ireland. The London theatres re-open. The Swan Theatre is built. Ralegh accused of blasphemy.

France declares war on Spain. Failure of the Indies voyage and death of Hawkins. Ralegh's expedition to Guiana.

England joins France in the war against Spain. Death of Drake. Raid on Cadiz led by Essex. In long-standing power struggle with Essex, Robert Cecil is appointed Secretary of State.

Islands Voyage led by Essex and Ralegh. The government suppresses the *Isle of Dogs* at the Swan and closes the theatres. Despite the continued hostility of the City of London, they soon re-open. James Burbage builds the second Blackfriars Theatre. Death of James Burbage.

Peace between France and Spain. Death of Philip II. Tyrone defeats the English at Armagh. Essex appointed Lord Deputy of Ireland.

DATE	AUTHOR'S LIFE	LITERARY CONTEXT
1598 *cont.*	*his Humour.* For the second year, Shakespeare is listed as having failed to pay tax levied on all householders.	Chapman's Homeric translations). Meres: *Palladia Tamia.* New edition of Lodge's *Rosalynde.* Lope de Vega: *La Arcadia.* James VI of Scotland: *The True Law of Free Monarchies.*
1599	*As You Like It, Henry V, Julius Caesar.* Shakespeare one of the shareholders in the Globe Theatre. He moves lodgings to Bankside. Publication of *The Passionate Pilgrim*, a miscellany of 20 poems, at least 5 by Shakespeare.	Jonson: *Every Man out of his Humour.* Dekker: *The Shoemaker's Holiday.* Sir John Hayward: *The First Part of the Life and Reign of King Henry IV.* Greene's translation of *Orlando Furioso.*
1600		'England's Helicon'.
1601	*Twelfth Night. Hamlet* (performed with Burbage as the Prince and Shakespeare as the Ghost). *The Phoenix and the Turtle.* The Lord Chamberlain's Men paid by one of Essex's followers to perform *Richard II* on the day before the rebellion. Death of John Shakespeare.	
1601–2	*Troilus and Cressida.*	
1602	Shakespeare buys more property in Stratford.	
1603–4	*All's Well That Ends Well.*	
1603	Shakespeare's company now under the patronage of King James. Shakespeare is one of the principal tragedians in Jonson's *Sejanus.*	Montaigne's *Essays* translated into English. Thomas Heywood: *A Woman Killed with Kindness.*
1604	Shakespeare known to be lodging in Silver Street with a Huguenot family called Mountjoy. *Othello*; first performance of *Measure for Measure.*	Chapman: *Bussy d'Ambois.* Marston: *The Malcontent.*
1604–5	Ten of his plays performed at court by the King's Men.	
1605	First performance of *King Lear* at the Globe, with Burbage as the King, and Robert Armin as the Fool.	

CHRONOLOGY

The Burbage brothers, Richard and Cuthbert, pull down The Theatre and, with its timbers, build the Globe on Bankside. Essex's campaign fails in Ireland, and after returning without permission to court he is arrested. The government suppresses satirical writings, and burns pamphlets by Nashe and Harvey.

Essex released but still in disgrace. The Fortune Theatre built by Alleyn and Henslowe. Bruno executed for heresy by the Inquisition in Rome.
Essex's Rebellion. Essex and Southampton arrested, and the former executed. Spanish invasion of Ireland. Monopolies debates in Parliament.

Spanish troops defeated in Ireland.

Death of Elizabeth, and accession of James I. Ralegh imprisoned in the Tower. Plague in London. Sir Thomas Bodley re-founds the library of Oxford University.

Peace with Spain. Hampton Court Conference.

DATE	AUTHOR'S LIFE	LITERARY CONTEXT
1605	First performance of *King Lear* at the Globe, with Burbage as the King, and Robert Armin as the Fool. Shakespeare makes further investments in Stratford, buying a half interest in a lease of tithes.	Cervantes: *Don Quixote* (part one). Bacon: *The Proficience and Advancement of Learning.* Jonson and Inigo Jones: *The Masque of Blackness.* Jonson and co-authors imprisoned for libellous references to the court in *Eastward Ho.*
1605–6		Jonson: *Volpone.*
1606	First performance of *Macbeth.*	John Ford's masque *Honour Triumphant.*
1607	*Antony and Cleopatra.* Susanna marries John Hall, a physician. Death of Shakespeare's brother Edmund, an actor.	Tourneur's *The Revenger's Tragedy* printed. Barnes: *The Devil's Charter.*
1607–8	*Timon of Athens, Coriolanus, Pericles.*	
1608	Shakespeare one of the sharcholders in the Blackfriars Theatre. Death of his mother.	Lope de Vega: *Peribanez.* Beaumont and Fletcher: *Philaster.* Jonson and Jones: *The Masque of Beauty.* Donne writes *La Corona.* Twelve books of Homer's *Iliad* (Chapman's translation).
1609	Publication, probably unauthorized, of the quarto edition of the *Sonnets* and *A Lover's Complaint.*	Jonson and Jones: *The Masque of Queens.* Donne's 'The Expiration' printed; 'Liturgie' and 'On the Annunciation' written. Bacon: *De Sapientia Veterum.* Lope de Vega: *New Art of Writing Plays for the Theatre.*
1609–10	*Cymbeline.*	
1610		Donne: *Pseudo-Martyr* printed and *The First Anniversarie* written. Jonson: *The Alchemist.* Beaumont and Fletcher: *The Maid's Tragedy.*
1610–11	*The Winter's Tale.*	
1611	*The Tempest* performed in the Banqueting House, Whitehall. Simon Forman records seeing performances of *Macbeth, The Winter's Tale* and *Cymbeline.*	Beaumont and Fletcher: *A King and No King, The Knight of the Burning Pestle.* Tourneur: *The Atheist's Tragedy.* Jonson and Jones: *Masque of Oberon.* Authorized Version of the Bible.

CHRONOLOGY

HISTORICAL EVENTS

Gunpowder Plot.

Monteverdi: *Orfeo*.
Bacon appointed Solicitor General.

Galileo's experiments with the telescope confirm the Copernican theory.
Kepler draws up 'Laws of Planetary Motion'. Twelve-year Truce between
Spain and Netherlands.

Galileo: *The Starry Messenger*. Assassination of Henry IV of France.
Parliament submits the Petition of Grievances.

DATE	AUTHOR'S LIFE	LITERARY CONTEXT
1611 *cont.*		Sir John Davies: *The Scourge of Folly.*
1612	Shakespeare appears as a witness in a Court of Requests case involving a dispute over a dowry owed by his former landlord, Mountjoy, to his son-in-law, Belott. Death of his brother Gilbert.	Webster: *The White Devil* printed. Tourneur: *The Nobleman.* Lope de Vega: *Fuente Ovejuna.*
1613	At a performance of his last play, *Henry VIII*, the Globe Theatre catches fire and is destroyed. As part of the court celebrations for the marriage of Princess Elizabeth, The King's Men perform 14 plays, including *Much Ado, Othello, The Winter's Tale* and *The Tempest*. Death of his brother Richard.	Sir Thomas Overbury: *The Wife.* Donne: 'Good Friday' and 'Epithalamion' on Princess Elizabeth's marriage. Cervantes: *Novelas ejemplares* – a collection of short stories.
1614	In Stratford, Shakespeare protects his property interests during a controversy over a threat to enclose the common fields.	Jonson: *Bartholomew Fair.* Webster: *The Duchess of Malfi.* Ralegh: *The History of the World.*
1615	The Warwick Assizes issue an order to prevent enclosures, which ends the dispute in Stratford.	Cervantes publishes 8 plays and *Don Quixote* (part two).
1616	Marriage of his daughter Judith to Thomas Quincy, a vintner, who a month later is tried for fornication with another woman whom he had made pregnant. Death of Shakespeare (23 April).	Jonson: *The Devil is an Ass.* Jonson publishes his *Works.*
1623	The players Heminge and Condell publish the plays of the First Folio.	

CHRONOLOGY

HISTORICAL EVENTS

The Inquisition of Rome begins investigating Galileo. Donne writes the *The Second Anniversarie* and a 'A Valediction: forbidding mourning'.
Death of Henry, Prince of Wales.

Marriage of Princess Elizabeth to Frederick, Elector Palatine. Bacon appointed Attorney-General.

The second Globe and the Hope Theatre built.

Inquiry into the murder of Sir Thomas Overbury in the Tower implicates the wife of the King's favourite, Somerset.

Ralegh released from the Tower to lead an expedition to Guiana; on his return he is executed.

WILLIAM SHAKESPEARE

PERICLES, PRINCE OF TYRE

Edited by Ernest Schanzer

GOWER, as Chorus
ANTIOCHUS, King of Antioch
PERICLES, Prince of Tyre
HELICANUS ⎱
ESCANES ⎰ two lords of Tyre
SIMONIDES, King of Pentapolis
CLEON, Governor of Tharsus
LYSIMACHUS, Governor of Mytilene
CERIMON, a lord of Ephesus
THALIARD, a lord of Antioch
PHILEMON, servant to Cerimon
LEONINE, servant to Dionyza
MARSHAL
A PANDER
BOULT, his servant
THE DAUGHTER OF ANTIOCHUS
DIONYZA, wife to Cleon
THAISA, daughter to Simonides
MARINA, daughter to Pericles and Thaisa
LYCHORIDA, nurse to Marina
A BAWD
DIANA

LORDS, LADIES, KNIGHTS, GENTLEMEN, SAILORS, PIRATES, FISHERMEN, AND MESSENGERS

Scene: Dispersedly in various Mediterranean countries]

PERICLES
PRINCE OF TYRE

[ACT I

*Before the king's palace at Antioch, with heads
displayed upon its walls.*]

Enter Gower.

GOWER To sing a song that old was sung,
   From ashes ancient Gower is come,
   Assuming man's infirmities,
   To glad your ear, and please your eyes.
   It hath been sung at festivals,   5
   On ember-eves and holidays,
   And lords and ladies in their lives
   Have read it for restoratives.
   The purchase is to make men glorious;
   Et bonum quo antiquius eo melius.   10
   If you, born in those latter times,
   When wit's more ripe, accept my rhymes,
   And that to hear an old man sing
   May to your wishes pleasure bring,
   I life would wish, and that I might   15

Text references are printed in **bold** type; the annotation follows in roman type.
I.s.d. **Gower** John Gower, fourteenth-century poet 1 **old** of old 3 **Assuming
man's infirmities** putting on man's infirm body 6 **ember-eves** evenings before
the fasts known as "ember days" 9 **purchase** gain 10 **Et ... melius** and the
more ancient a good thing is the better it is (Latin)

3

Waste it for you, like taper-light.
This Antioch, then; Antiochus the great
Built up this city for his chiefest seat,
The fairest in all Syria –
20 I tell you what mine authors say.
This king unto him took a peer,
Who died, and left a female heir,
So buxom, blithe, and full of face,
As heaven had lent her all his grace;
25 With whom the father liking took,
And her to incest did provoke.
Bad child, worse father, to entice his own
To evil should be done by none.
But custom what they did begin
30 Was with long use accounted no sin.
The beauty of this sinful dame
Made many princes thither frame,
To seek her as a bedfellow,
In marriage pleasures playfellow;
35 Which to prevent he made a law,
To keep her still, and men in awe:
That whoso asked her for his wife,
His riddle told not, lost his life.
So for her many a wight did die,
40 As yon grim looks do testify.   [*Points to the heads.*]
What now ensues, to the judgment of your eye
I give my cause, who best can justify.   *Exit.*

---

17 **This Antioch** this is Antioch   21 **peer** companion, consort   23 **buxom** gay,
lively   23 **full of face** beautiful (?) with a round face (?)   28 **should** which
should   29 **custom** through custom   32 **frame** direct their course   36 **To …**
awe to keep her always to himself, and to keep others from demanding her in
marriage   38 **told** expounded   41–42 **What … justify** in what now ensues I
submit my case to the judgment of your eye, as you are best able to acquit me (of
the charge of having told an incredible tale)

[Scene I. *Before the palace of Antioch.*]

Enter Antiochus, Prince Pericles, and followers.

ANTIOCHUS Young Prince of Tyre, you have at large
received
The danger of the task you undertake.

PERICLES I have, Antiochus, and, with a soul
Embold'ned with the glory of her praise,
Think death no hazard in this enterprise.   5

ANTIOCHUS Music!   [*Music sounds.*]
Bring in our daughter, clothèd like a bride,
For the embracements even of Jove himself;
At whose conception, till Lucina reigned,
Nature this dowry gave to glad her presence.   10
The senate house of planets all did sit,
To knit in her their best perfections.

Enter Antiochus' daughter.

PERICLES See where she comes, appareled like the
spring,
Graces her subjects, and her thoughts the king
Of every virtue gives renown to men!   15
Her face the book of praises, where is read
Nothing but curious pleasures, as from thence
Sorrow were ever razed, and testy wrath
Could never be her mild companion.
You gods that made me man, and sway in love;   20

I.i.1 **at large received** learned fully   9 **till Lucina reigned** i.e., before her birth
(Lucina is the goddess of childbirth)   10 **this dowry** i.e., her beauty   10 **to glad
her presence** to make her presence delightful (?)   15 **gives** which gives
17 **curious** exquisite   18 **razed** erased   19 **her mild companion** the companion of her mildness   20 **and sway in love** and who govern in love

That have enflamed desire in my breast
To taste the fruit of yon celestial tree
Or die in th' adventure, be my helps,
As I am son and servant to your will,
25 To compass such a boundless happiness!

ANTIOCHUS Prince Pericles—

PERICLES That would be son to great Antiochus.

ANTIOCHUS Before thee stands this fair Hesperides,
With golden fruit, but dangerous to be touched;
30 For deathlike dragons here affright thee hard.
Her face like heaven enticeth thee to view
Her countless glory, which desert must gain;
And which without desert, because thine eye
Presumes to reach, all the whole heap must die.
35 Yon sometimes famous princes, like thyself,
Drawn by report, advent'rous by desire,
Tell thee, with speechless tongues and semblance
    pale,
That without covering, save yon field of stars,
Here they stand martyrs slain in Cupid's wars;
40 And with dead cheeks advise thee to desist
For going on death's net, whom none resist.

PERICLES Antiochus, I thank thee, who hath taught
My frail mortality to know itself,
And by those fearful objects to prepare
45 This body, like to them, to what I must;
For death remembered should be like a mirror,
Who tells us life's but breath, to trust it error.
I'll make my will, then; and, as sick men do,
Who know the world, see heaven, but, feeling woe,
50 Gripe not at earthly joys as erst they did,
So I bequeath a happy peace to you
And all good men, as every prince should do;

24 As as surely as   28 Hesperides the daughters of Hesperus, the evening star
(but here, by confusion, the garden containing the golden apples, which, with the
aid of a dragon, they were appointed to watch)   34 the whole heap the whole
body   35 sometimes once   41 For for fear of   50 gripe grasp

6

My riches to the earth from whence they came;
[*To the Princess*] But my unspotted fire of love to
   you.
Thus, ready for the way of life or death,   55
I wait the sharpest blow, Antiochus.

ANTIOCHUS Scorning advice, read the conclusion
      then: [*He throws down the riddle.*]
Which read and not expounded, 'tis decreed,
As these before thee thou thyself shalt bleed.

DAUGHTER Of all 'sayed yet, mayst thou prove
      prosperous!   60
Of all 'sayed yet, I wish thee happiness.

PERICLES Like a bold champion I assume the lists,
Nor ask advice of any other thought
But faithfulness and courage.

               [*He reads*] *the riddle.*

I am no viper, yet I feed   65
On mother's flesh, which did me breed.
I sought a husband, in which labor
I found that kindness in a father.
He's father, son, and husband mild;
I mother, wife, and yet his child.   70
How they may be, and yet in two,
As you will live, resolve it you.
[*Aside*] Sharp physic is the last. But O, you
      powers,
That gives heaven countless eyes to view men's
      acts:
Why cloud they not their sights perpetually,   75
If this be true which makes me pale to read it?

---

57 **conclusion** riddle   60 **'sayed yet** who have yet assayed   62 **assume the lists**
undertake the contest   65 **I am no viper** (vipers were believed to be born by
eating their way out of the mother's body)   68 **kindness** (1) kinship (2) affection
71 **How ... two** how these things may be, and yet all be found in two persons
73 **Sharp physic is the last** the last condition of the riddle is an unpleasant
medicine   74 **gives** give (the third person plural in *s* is not unusual)

7

Fair glass of light, I loved you, and could still,
Were not this glorious casket stored with ill.
But I must tell you, now my thoughts revolt;
80   For he's no man on whom perfections wait
That, knowing sin within, will touch the gate.
You are a fair viol, and your sense the strings;
Who, fingered to make man his lawful music,
Would draw heaven down, and all the gods to
      hearken;
85   But being played upon before your time,
Hell only danceth at so harsh a chime.
Good sooth, I care not for you.

                              [*He turns towards the Princess.*]

ANTIOCHUS Prince Pericles, touch not, upon thy life,
For that's an article within our law
90   As dangerous as the rest. Your time's expired.
Either expound now, or receive your sentence.

PERICLES Great King,
Few love to hear the sins they love to act;
'Twould braid yourself too near for me to tell it.
95   Who has a book of all that monarchs do,
He's more secure to keep it shut than shown;
For vice repeated is like the wand'ring wind
Blows dust in others' eyes to spread itself;
And yet the end of all is bought thus dear:
100   The breath is gone, and the sore eyes see clear
To stop the air would hurt them. The blind mole
      casts
Copped hills towards heaven, to tell the earth is
      thronged
By man's oppression; and the poor worm doth die
      for't.
Kings are earth's gods; in vice their law's their will;
105   And if Jove stray, who dares say Jove doth ill?

77 **glass of light** i.e., one who reflects light, as does a mirror, but does not contain it 82 **sense** senses (?) 87 **Good sooth** truly 90 **dangerous** rigorous 94 **braid** upbraid 94 **too near** touching you too closely 97 **repeated** talked about 98 **Blows** which blows 98 **to spread** in spreading 102 **Copped** peaked 102 **thronged** crushed 103 **worm** creature

It is enough you know; and it is fit,
What being more known grows worse, to smother it.
  All love the womb that their first being bred;
Then give my tongue like leave to love my head.

ANTIOCHUS [*Aside*] Heaven, that I had thy head! He
  has found the meaning.   110
But I will gloze with him. [*Aloud*] Young Prince
  of Tyre,
Though by the tenor of our strict edict,
Your exposition misinterpreting,
We might proceed to cancel of your days,
Yet hope, succeeding from so fair a tree   115
As your fair self, doth tune us otherwise.
Forty days longer we do respite you;
If by which time our secret be undone,
This mercy shows we'll joy in such a son.
And until then your entertain shall be   120
As doth befit our honor and your worth.
                              [*Exeunt all but Pericles.*]

PERICLES How courtesy would seem to cover sin,
  When what is done is like an hypocrite,
The which is good in nothing but in sight!
If it be true that I interpret false,   125
Then were it certain you were not so bad
As with foul incest to abuse your soul;
Where now you're both a father and a son
By your uncomely claspings with your child,
Which pleasures fits a husband, not a father;   130
And she an eater of her mother's flesh
By the defiling of her parents' bed;
And both like serpents are, who though they feed
On sweetest flowers, yet they poison breed.
Antioch, farewell, for wisdom sees, those men   135

---

111 **gloze** talk speciously 114 **cancel of** the canceling of 115 **succeeding**
resulting 118 **secret be undone** riddle be solved 120 **entertain** entertainment,
reception 122 **seem** make a specious appearance 124 **sight** outward
appearance 129 **uncomely** improper

Blush not in actions blacker than the night,
Will 'schew no course to keep them from the light.
One sin, I know, another doth provoke;
Murder's as near to lust as flame to smoke.
140 Poison and treason are the hands of sin,
Ay, and the targets, to put off the shame.
Then, lest my life be cropped to keep you clear,
By flight I'll shun the danger which I fear.   *Exit.*

Enter Antiochus.

ANTIOCHUS He hath found the meaning,
145 For which we mean to have his head. He must
Not live to trumpet forth my infamy,
Nor tell the world Antiochus doth sin
In such a loathèd manner.
And therefore instantly this prince must die;
150 For by his fall my honor must keep high.
Who attends us there?

Enter Thaliard.

THALIARD   Doth your Highness call?

ANTIOCHUS Thaliard,
You are of our chamber, Thaliard, and our mind
    partakes
Her private actions to your secrecy;
155 And for your faithfulness we will advance you.
Thaliard, behold, here's poison, and here's gold!
We hate the Prince of Tyre, and thou must kill him.
It fits thee not to ask the reason why.
Because we bid it. Say, is it done?

THALIARD My lord, 'tis done.

160 ANTIOCHUS   Enough.

Enter a Messenger.

Let your breath cool yourself telling your haste.

136 **Blush** who blush 137 **'schew** eschew, avoid 141 **targets** shields 141 **put off** avert 153 **of our chamber** our chamberlain 153 **partakes** imparts

MESSENGER My lord, Prince Pericles is fled.   [*Exit.*]

ANTIOCHUS As thou wilt live, fly after; and like an
    arrow shot from a well-experienced archer hits the
    mark his eye doth level at, so thou never return   165
    unless thou say Prince Pericles is dead.

THALIARD My lord, if I can get him within my pistol's
    length, I'll make him sure enough. So farewell to
    your Highness.

ANTIOCHUS Thaliard, adieu! [*Exit Thaliard.*] Till
    Pericles be dead   170
    My heart can lend no succor to my head.   [*Exit.*]

[Scene II. *Tyre. A room in the palace.*]

Enter Pericles.

PERICLES [*To Servants without*] Let none disturb us.
    Why should this change of thoughts,
    The sad companion, dull-eyed melancholy,
    Be my so used a guest as not an hour
    In the day's glorious walk or peaceful night,   5
    The tomb where grief should sleep, can breed me
        quiet?
    Here pleasures court mine eyes, and mine eyes shun
        them,
    And danger, which I feared, is at Antioch,
    Whose arm seems far too short to hit me here;
    Yet neither pleasure's art can joy my spirits,   10
    Nor yet the other's distance comfort me.
    Then it is thus: the passions of the mind,

165 level aim   168 sure unable to do harm   I.ii.4 used customary   10 joy give
joy to

That have their first conception by misdread,
Have after-nourishment and life by care;
15   And what was first but fear what might be done,
Grows elder now and cares it be not done.
And so with me: the great Antiochus,
'Gainst whom I am too little to contend,
Since he's so great can make his will his act,
20   Will think me speaking, though I swear to silence;
Nor boots it me to say I honor him,
If he suspect I may dishonor him.
And what may make him blush in being known
He'll stop the course by which it might be known.
25   With hostile forces he'll o'erspread the land,
And with th' ostent of war will look so huge,
Amazement shall drive courage from the state,
Our men be vanquished ere they do resist,
And subjects punished that ne'er thought offense;
30   Which care of them, not pity of myself,
Who am no more but as the tops of trees
Which fence the roots they grow by and defend them,
Makes both my body pine and soul to languish,
And punish that before that he would punish.

Enter [Helicanus and] all the Lords to
Pericles.

35   FIRST LORD Joy and all comfort in your sacred breast!

SECOND LORD And keep your mind, till you return
    to us,
Peaceful and comfortable!

---

13 **misdread** dread of evil   16 **cares** is anxious that   19 **can** that he can
21 **boots it me** does it avail me   23 **in being known** if it were known
26 **th' ostent** the display   27 **Amazement** consternation   32 **fence** protect
36–37 **And keep ... comfortable** (these lines must be either corrupt or
misplaced, as Pericles' decision to leave Tyre is not taken till the end of the scene)
37 **comfortable** cheerful (a passage in which Helicanus reproves Pericles for
wasting "his body there with pining sorrow, upon whose safety depended the lives
and prosperity of a whole kingdom" [Wilkins] and is sternly rebuked by him for
his presumption, must have preceded the next speech, but is missing from the text)

HELICANUS Peace, peace, and give experience tongue.
  They do abuse the King that flatter him,
  For flattery is the bellows blows up sin;   40
  The thing the which is flattered but a spark
  To which that blast gives heat and stronger glowing;
  Whereas reproof, obedient and in order,
  Fits kings, as they are men, for they may err.
  When Signor Sooth here does proclaim a peace   45
  He flatters you, makes war upon your life.
  Prince, pardon me, or strike me, if you please;
  I cannot be much lower than my knees.
                        [*He kneels.*]

PERICLES All leave us else! But let your cares
    o'erlook
  What shipping and what lading's in our haven,   50
  And then return to us.   [*Exeunt Lords.*]
                  Helicanus,
  Thou hast moved us. What seest thou in our looks?

HELICANUS An angry brow, dread lord.

PERICLES If there be such a dart in princes' frowns,
  How durst thy tongue move anger to our face?   55

HELICANUS How dares the plants look up to heaven,
    from whence
  They have their nourishment?

PERICLES   Thou knowest I have power
  To take thy life from thee.

HELICANUS   I have ground the ax myself;
  Do but you strike the blow.

PERICLES   Rise, prithee, rise.
                  [*He raises him.*]
  Sit down. Thou art no flatterer.   60
  I thank thee for't; and heaven forbid

---

38 **give experience tongue** allow experience to speak 39 **abuse** ill-use
40 **blows up** which fans into flame 45 **Signor Sooth** Sir Flattery 49 **All leave
us else** everybody else leave us 49 **o'erlook** look into 50 **lading** cargo

That kings should let their ears hear their faults
   hid!
Fit counselor and servant for a prince,
Who by thy wisdom makes a prince thy servant,
What wouldst thou have me do?

65 HELICANUS   To bear with patience
Such griefs as you do lay upon yourself.

PERICLES Thou speak'st like a physician, Helicanus,
That ministers a potion unto me
That thou wouldst tremble to receive thyself.

70   Attend me then: I went to Antioch,
Where, as thou know'st, against the face of death
I sought the purchase of a glorious beauty,
From whence an issue I might propagate
Are arms to princes and brings joys to subjects.

75   Her face was to mine eye beyond all wonder;
The rest—hark in thine ear—as black as incest;
Which by my knowledge found, the sinful father
Seemed not to strike, but smooth; but thou
   know'st this:
'Tis time to fear when tyrants seems to kiss.

80   Which fear so grew in me, I hither fled,
Under the covering of a careful night,
Who seemed my good protector; and, being here,
Bethought me what was past, what might succeed.
I knew him tyrannous; and tyrants' fears

85   Decrease not, but grow faster than the years;
And should he doubt, as no doubt he doth,
That I should open to the list'ning air
How many worthy princes' bloods were shed
To keep his bed of blackness unlaid ope,

90   To lop that doubt, he'll fill this land with arms,
And make pretense of wrong that I have done him;

62 **hear their faults hid** i.e., hear the flattery which hides their faults
70 **Attend** listen to   72 **purchase** acquisition   74 **Are arms** which are arms
78 **Seemed** pretended   78 **smooth** flatter   81 **careful** taking good care
86 **And should ... he doth** (the first "doubt," meaning "fear", is pronounced as a
disyllable)   87 **open** reveal   89 **unlaid ope** undisclosed   90 **doubt** dread, fear

When all for mine, if I may call, offense
Must feel war's blow, who spares not innocence;
Which love to all, of which thyself art one,
Who now reprovedst me for't—

HELICANUS   Alas, sir!   95

PERICLES Drew sleep out of mine eyes, blood from my
        cheeks,
    Musings into my mind, with thousand doubts
    How I might stop this tempest ere it came;
    And finding little comfort to relieve them,
    I thought it princely charity to grieve them.   100

HELICANUS Well, my lord, since you have given me
        leave to speak,
    Freely will I speak. Antiochus you fear,
    And justly, too, I think, you fear the tyrant
    Who either by public war or private treason
    Will take away your life.   105
    Therefore, my lord, go travel for a while,
    Till that his rage and anger be forgot,
    Or till the Destinies do cut his thread of life.
    Your rule direct to any; if to me,
    Day serves not light more faithful than I'll be.   110

PERICLES I do not doubt thy faith.
    But should he wrong my liberties in my absence?

HELICANUS We'll mingle our bloods together in the
        earth,
    From whence we had our being and our birth.

PERICLES Tyre, I now look from thee then, and to
        Tharsus   115
    Intend my travel, where I'll hear from thee,
    And by whose letters I'll dispose myself.

93 who which   95 now just now   100 grieve them grieve for them   109 direct
assign   110 Day ... faithful day is not served by light more faithfully
112 liberties prerogatives   116 Intend direct   117 dispose myself direct my
actions

15

The care I had and have of subjects' good
On thee I lay, whose wisdom's strength can bear it.
120   I'll take thy word for faith, not ask thine oath:
Who shuns not to break one will crack both.
But in our orbs we'll live so round and safe,
That time of both this truth shall ne'er convince:
Thou showed'st a subject's shine, I a true prince.

Exit [with Helicanus].

[Scene III. *The palace at Tyre.*]

Enter Thaliard solus.

THALIARD So this is Tyre, and this the court. Here
must I kill King Pericles; and if I do it not, I am
sure to be hanged at home. 'Tis dangerous. Well,
I perceive he was a wise fellow and had good dis-
5   cretion that, being bid to ask what he would of the
King, desired he might know none of his secrets.
Now do I see he had some reason for't: for if a
king bid a man be a villain, he's bound by the indenture of his oath to be one. Husht, here comes
10   the lords of Tyre.

Enter Helicanus, Escanes, with other Lords.

HELICANUS You shall not need, my fellow peers of
Tyre,

---

121 **one** (pronounced as a disyllable)   122 **we'll live so round** (1) we'll live
so honestly (2) we'll move in such a perfect circle   122 **safe** trustworthily
123 **of both ... convince** shall never confute this truth regarding both of us
124 **Thou ... prince** you showed a subject's luster, I showed myself a true
prince   I.iii.s.d. **solus** alone (Latin)   8–9 **indenture** contract binding servant to
master

Further to question me of your king's departure.
His sealed commission left in trust with me
Does speak sufficiently he's gone to travel.

THALIARD [*Aside*] How? The King gone?   15

HELICANUS If further yet you will be satisfied
Why, as it were, unlicensed of your loves
He would depart, I'll give some light unto you.
Being at Antioch—

THALIARD   [*Aside*] What from Antioch?

HELICANUS Royal Antiochus—on what cause I know
not—   20
Took some displeasure at him; at least he judged
so;
And doubting lest he had erred or sinned,
To show his sorrow, he'd correct himself;
So puts himself unto the shipman's toil,
With whom each minute threatens life or death.   25

THALIARD [*Aside*] Well, I perceive I shall not be
hanged now
Although I would.
But since he's gone, the King's ears it must please
He scaped the land, to perish at the seas.
I'll present myself. [*Aloud*] Peace to the lords of
Tyre!   30

HELICANUS Lord Thaliard from Antiochus is welcome.

THALIARD From him I come
With message unto princely Pericles.
But since my landing I have understood
Your lord has betook himself to unknown travels.   35
Now message must return from whence it came.

---

17 **unlicensed of your loves** without your loving assent 22 **doubting lest**
fearing that ("doubting" is here trisyllabic) 23 **he'd correct** he wanted to punish

HELICANUS We have no reason to desire it,
　　　Commended to our master, not to us.
　　　Yet, ere you shall depart, this we desire:
40　　As friends to Antioch we may feast in Tyre.

　　　　　　　　　　　　Exit [with the rest].

　　　　　　　[Scene IV. *Tharsus.*]

　　　　*Enter Cleon, the Governor of Tharsus, with
　　　　his wife [Dionyza] and others.*

CLEON My Dionyza, shall we rest us here,
　　　And by relating tales of others' griefs,
　　　See if 'twill teach us to forget our own?

DIONYZA That were to blow at fire in hope to quench
　　　　it,
5　　For who digs hills because they do aspire
　　　Throws down one mountain to cast up a higher.
　　　O my distressed lord, even such our griefs are;
　　　Here they are but felt and seen with mischief's
　　　　eyes,
　　　But like to groves, being topped, they higher rise.

10　CLEON O Dionyza,
　　　Who wanteth food and will not say he wants it,
　　　Or can conceal his hunger till he famish?
　　　Our tongues and sorrows cease not to sound deep

38 **Commended** since it is commended I.iv.5 **digs** digs down 8 **mischief's**
misfortune's 13–14 **Our tongues ... to weep** let our sorrowful tongues
(hendiadys) not cease to ..., let our eyes not cease to weep

Our woes into the air, our eyes to weep,
Till tongues fetch breath that may proclaim them
    louder,   15
That, if heaven slumber while their creatures want,
They may awake their helps to comfort them.
I'll then discourse our woes, felt several years,
And wanting breath to speak help me with tears.

DIONYZA I'll do my best, sir.   20

CLEON This Tharsus, o'er which I have the govern-
    ment,
A city on whom plenty held full hand,
For riches strewed herself even in her streets;
Whose towers bore heads so high they kissed the
    clouds,
And strangers ne'er beheld but wond'red at;   25
Whose men and dames so jetted and adorned,
Like one another's glass to trim them by;
Their tables were stored full, to glad the sight,
And not so much to feed on as delight;
All poverty was scorned, and pride so great,   30
The name of help grew odious to repeat.

DIONYZA O, 'tis too true!

CLEON But see what heaven can do by this our change:
These mouths who but of late earth, sea, and air
Were all too little to content and please,   35
Although they gave their creatures in abundance,
As houses are defiled for want of use,
They are now starved for want of exercise;
Those palates who, not yet two summers younger,
Must have inventions to delight the taste,   40
Would now be glad of bread, and beg for it;

---

19 **help me** do you help me   22 **on** over   23 **riches strewed herself** ("riches"
is a feminine singular)   26 **jetted and adorned** strutted and dressed themselves
up   27 **glass to trim them by** pattern according to which to array themselves
31 **repeat** mention   40 **inventions** ingenious novelties

Those mothers who, to nuzzle up their babes,
Thought nought too curious, are ready now
To eat those little darlings whom they loved.
45   So sharp are hunger's teeth that man and wife
Draw lots who first shall die to lengthen life.
Here stands a lord, and there a lady weeping;
Here many sink, yet those which see them fall
Have scarce strength left to give them burial.
50   Is not this true?

DIONYZA Our cheeks and hollow eyes do witness it.

CLEON O, let those cities that of plenty's cup
And her prosperities so largely taste,
With their superfluous riots, hear these tears!
55   The misery of Tharsus may be theirs.

Enter a Lord.

LORD Where's the Lord Governor?

CLEON Here.
Speak out thy sorrows which thou bring'st in haste,
For comfort is too far for us to expect.

60   LORD We have descried, upon our neighboring shore,
A portly sail of ships make hitherward.

CLEON I thought as much.
One sorrow never comes but brings an heir
That may succeed as his inheritor;
65   And so in ours: some neighboring nation,
Taking advantage of our misery,
Hath stuffed the hollow vessels with their power,
To beat us down, the which are down already,
And make a conquest of unhappy me,
70   Whereas no glory's got to overcome.

LORD That's the least fear; for, by the semblance
Of their white flags displayed, they bring us peace,
And come to us as favorers, not as foes.

42 **nuzzle up** bring up   43 **curious** exquisite   54 **superfluous riots** inordinate
revels   61 **portly sail** stately fleet   67 **power** armed force   70 **Whereas** where

CLEON Thou speak'st like him's untutored to repeat:
Who makes the fairest show means most deceit.   75
But bring they what they will, what need we fear?
On ground's the lowest, and we are halfway there.
Go tell their general we attend him here,
To know for what he comes, and whence he comes,
And what he craves.   80

LORD I go, my lord.   [*Exit.*]

CLEON Welcome is peace, if he on peace consist;
If wars, we are unable to resist.

Enter Pericles, with Attendants.

PERICLES Lord Governor, for so we hear you are,
Let not our ships and number of our men   85
Be like a beacon fired t' amaze your eyes.
We have heard your miseries as far as Tyre,
And seen the desolation of your streets;
Nor come we to add sorrow to your tears,
But to relieve them of their heavy load;   90
And these our ships you happily may think
Are like the Trojan horse was stuffed within
With bloody veins expecting overthrow,
Are stored with corn to make your needy bread,
And give them life whom hunger starved half dead.   95

ALL The gods of Greece protect you!
And we'll pray for you.   [*They kneel.*]

PERICLES   Arise, I pray you, rise;
We do not look for reverence but for love,
And harborage for ourself, our ships, and men.

CLEON The which when any shall not gratify,   100
Or pay you with unthankfulness in thought,

74 **him's untutored to repeat** him who has never been taught to recite 77 **On
ground's the lowest** i.e., he that lies upon the ground can fall no lower
78 **attend** await 80 **craves** desires 82 **on peace consist** stands on peace
91 **you happily may think** you may perhaps think 92 **was** which was
93 **With ... overthrow** i.e., with bloodthirsty warriors waiting for the overthrow
(of Troy) 94 **your needy bread** bread for your needy citizens 100 **gratify**
show gratitude for

Be it our wives, our children, or ourselves,
The curse of heaven and men succeed their evils!
Till when—the which I hope shall ne'er be seen—
105 Your Grace is welcome to our town and us.

PERICLES Which welcome we'll accept; feast here awhile,
Until our stars that frown lend us a smile.

Exeunt.

[ACT II]

Enter Gower.

GOWER Here have you seen a mighty king
　　His child iwis to incest bring;
　　A better prince and benign lord
　　That will prove awful both in deed and word.
　　Be quiet, then, as men should be,   5
　　Till he hath passed necessity.
　　I'll show you those in trouble's reign
　　Losing a mite, a mountain gain.
　　The good in conversation,
　　To whom I give my benison,   10
　　Is still at Tharsus, where each man
　　Thinks all is writ he spoken can;
　　And, to remember what he does,
　　Built his statue to make him glorious.
　　But tidings to the contrary   15
　　Are brought your eyes; what need speak I?

II.2 **iwis** assuredly　4 **awful** commanding profound respect　6 **passed necessity** experienced extreme hardship　7 **those in trouble's reign** those who under
the dominion of trouble　9 **conversation** conduct, way of life　12 **all ... can** all
his words are holy writ　13 **remember** commemorate

Dumb Show

*Enter at one door Pericles, talking with Cleon;
all the train with them. Enter at another door
a Gentleman with a letter to Pericles; Pericles
shows the letter to Cleon. Pericles gives the
Messenger a reward and knights him. Exit
Pericles at one door, and Cleon at another.*

Good Helicane, that stayed at home,
Not to eat honey like a drone
From others' labors, for he strives
20   To killen bad, keep good alive,
And to fulfill his prince' desire,
Sends word of all that haps in Tyre:
How Thaliard came full bent with sin
And hid intent to murder him;
25   And that in Tharsus was not best
Longer for him to make his rest.
He, doing so, put forth to seas,
Where when men been there's seldom ease;
For now the wind begins to blow;
30   Thunder above and deeps below
Makes such unquiet that the ship
Should house him safe is wracked and split;
And he, good prince, having all lost,
By waves from coast to coast is tossed.
35   All perishen of man, of pelf,
Ne aught escapend but himself;
Till fortune, tired with doing bad,
Threw him ashore, to give him glad.
And here he comes. What shall be next,
40   Pardon old Gower—this 'longs the text.   [*Exit.*]

23 **bent with** intent upon   24 **And hid intent** and with hidden intent
27 **doing so** i.e., acting as advised   32 **Should** which should   35 **pelf**
possessions   36 **escapend** escaping   38 **glad** gladness   40 **'longs** belongs to

[Scene I. *Pentapolis, at the seashore.*]

Enter Pericles, wet.

PERICLES Yet cease your ire, you angry stars of heaven!
　Wind, rain, and thunder, remember, earthly man
　Is but a substance that must yield to you;
　And I, as fits my nature, do obey you.
　Alas, the seas hath cast me on the rocks,　　　　　5
　Washed me from shore to shore, and left me breath
　Nothing to think on but ensuing death.
　Let it suffice the greatness of your powers
　To have bereft a prince of all his fortunes;
　And having thrown him from your wat'ry grave,　10
　Here to have death in peace is all he'll crave.

Enter three Fishermen.

FIRST FISHERMAN What ho, Pilch!

SECOND FISHERMAN Ha, come and bring away the
　nets!

FIRST FISHERMAN What, Patchbreech, I say!　　　15

THIRD FISHERMAN What say you, master?

FIRST FISHERMAN Look how thou stirr'st now! Come
　away, or I'll fetch thee with a wanion.

THIRD FISHERMAN Faith, master, I am thinking of the
　poor men that were cast away before us even now.　20

FIRST FISHERMAN Alas, poor souls, it grieved my heart
　to hear what pitiful cries they made to us to help

II.i.12 **Pilch** (a coarse outer garment made of leather or skin, here used, like
Patchbreech, jestingly as a name)　13 **bring away** bring here without delay
17 **how thou stirr'st now!** what a stock you are!　17–18 **Come away** come here
right away　18 **with a wanion** with a vengeance

25

them, when, well-a-day, we could scarce help ourselves.

25 THIRD FISHERMAN Nay, master, said not I as much
when I saw the porpoise how he bounced and
tumbled? They say they're half fish, half flesh. A
plague on them! They ne'er come but I look to be
washed. Master, I marvel how the fishes live in the
30 sea.

FIRST FISHERMAN Why, as men do a-land: the great
ones eat up the little ones. I can compare our rich
misers to nothing so fitly as to a whale; 'a plays
and tumbles, driving the poor fry before him, and
35 at last devours them all at a mouthful: Such whales
have I heard on a' th' land, who never leave gap-
ing till they swallowed the whole parish, church,
steeple, bells, and all.

PERICLES [*Aside*] A pretty moral.

40 THIRD FISHERMAN But, master, if I had been the sex-
ton, I would have been that day in the belfry.

SECOND FISHERMAN Why, man?

THIRD FISHERMAN Because he should have swallowed
me too; and when I had been in his belly, I would
45 have kept such a jangling of the bells that he should
never have left till he cast bells, steeple, church,
and parish up again. But if the good King Simonides were of my mind—

PERICLES [*Aside*] Simonides!

50 THIRD FISHERMAN We would purge the land of these
drones that rob the bee of her honey.

PERICLES [*Aside*] How from the finny subject of the sea
These fishers tell the infirmities of men;
And from their wat'ry empire recollect

---

23 **well-a-day** alas   33 **'a** he   36 **heard on a' th' land** heard of on land
39 **moral** tale conveying a moral lesson   52 **subject** subjects, citizens
54 **recollect** gather up

All that may men approve or men detect!   55
[*Aloud*] Peace be at your labor, honest fishermen!

SECOND FISHERMAN Honest good fellow, what's that?
  If it be a day fits you, scratch it out of the calendar,
  and nobody look after it.

PERICLES May see the sea hath cast upon your coast—   60

SECOND FISHERMAN What a drunken knave was the
  sea to cast thee in our way!

PERICLES A man whom both the waters and the wind
  In that vast tennis court hath made the ball
  For them to play upon entreats you pity him.   65
  He asks of you that never used to beg.

FIRST FISHERMAN No, friend, cannot you beg? Here's
  them in our country of Greece gets more with begging than we can do with working.

SECOND FISHERMAN Canst thou catch any fishes, then?   70

PERICLES I never practiced it.

SECOND FISHERMAN Nay, then, thou wilt starve, sure;
  for here's nothing to be got nowadays unless thou
  canst fish for't.

PERICLES What I have been I have forgot to know;   75
  But what I am want teaches me to think on:
  A man thronged up with cold. My veins are chill,
  And have no more of life than may suffice
  To give my tongue that heat to ask your help;
  Which if you shall refuse, when I am dead,   80
  For that I am a man, pray you see me burièd.

FIRST FISHERMAN Die, quoth-a? Now gods forbid't!

---

55 **approve** commend   55 **detect** expose (in wrongdoing)   57–59 **Honest ...
after it** (a lost line in which Pericles wishes the fishermen a good day appears to
have preceded this passage. The fisherman rudely replies that if the day fitted
Pericles' wretched appearance it ought to be removed from the calendar)   60 **May
you** may   62 **cast** (1) cast up, vomit (2) throw   77 **thronged up** overwhelmed
81 **For that** because   82 **quoth-a** did he say

And I have a gown here! Come, put it on; keep
thee warm. Now, afore me, a handsome fellow!
85   Come, thou shalt go home, and we'll have flesh for
holidays, fish for fasting days, and moreo'er pud-
dings and flapjacks, and thou shalt be welcome.

PERICLES I thank you, sir.

SECOND FISHERMAN Hark you, my friend: you said
90   you could not beg.

PERICLES I did but crave.

SECOND FISHERMAN But crave? Then I'll turn craver
too, and so I shall 'scape whipping.

PERICLES Why, are your beggars whipped, then?

95 SECOND FISHERMAN O, not all, my friend, not all! For
if all your beggars were whipped, I would wish no
better office than to be beadle. But, master, I'll go
draw up the net.   [Exit with Third Fisherman.]

PERICLES [Aside] How well this honest mirth becomes
100   their labor!

FIRST FISHERMAN Hark you, sir, do you know where
ye are?

PERICLES Not well.

FIRST FISHERMAN Why, I'll tell you: this is called
105   Pentapolis, and our king the good Simonides.

PERICLES The good Simonides do you call him?

FIRST FISHERMAN Ay, sir; and he deserves so to be
called, for his peaceable reign and good government.

PERICLES He is a happy king, since he gains from his
110   subjects the name of good by his government. How
far is his court distant from this shore?

---

84 afore me upon my word 87 flapjacks pancakes 92–93 Then I'll ...
whipping i.e., through not calling himself a beggar (whipping, administered by
the beadle, was the regular punishment of beggars in Shakespeare's day)
99 becomes suits with

FIRST FISHERMAN Marry, sir, half a day's journey.
And I'll tell you, he hath a fair daughter, and tomorrow is her birthday; and there are princes and
knights come from all parts of the world to joust   115
and tourney for her love.

PERICLES Were my fortunes equal to my desires, I
could wish to make one there.

FIRST FISHERMAN O, sir, things must be as they may;
and what a man cannot get he may lawfully deal   120
for his wife's soul.

Enter the two Fishermen, drawing up a net.

SECOND FISHERMAN Help, master, help! Here's a fish
hangs in the net like a poor man's right in the
law: 'twill hardly come out. Ha, bots on't, 'tis
come at last; and 'tis turned to a rusty armor.   125

PERICLES An armor, friends! I pray you, let me see it.
Thanks, Fortune, yet, that after all thy crosses
Thou givest me somewhat to repair myself;
And though it was mine own, part of my heritage
Which my dead father did bequeath to me,   130
With this strict charge, even as he left his life:
"Keep it, my Pericles; it hath been a shield
'Twixt me and death"—and pointed to this
    brace—
"For that it saved me, keep it; in like necessity—
The which the gods protect thee from!—may't
    defend thee."   135
It kept where I kept, I so dearly loved it;
Till the rough seas, that spares not any man,
Took it in rage, though calmed have given't again.
I thank thee for't. My shipwrack now's no ill,
Since I have here my father gave in his will.   140

112 **Marry** why (a mild oath, from "By the Virgin Mary") 120–21 **he may ...
wife's soul** (no sense can be made of the text as it stands, nor has it been plausibly
emended) 123 **right** just claim 124 **bots on't** a plague upon it 128 **repair**
renew, restore 133 **brace** armor covering the arms 140 **my father gave** that
which my father gave

FIRST FISHERMAN What mean you, sir?

PERICLES To beg of you, kind friends, this coat of
        worth,
    For it was sometime target to a king;
    I know it by this mark. He loved me dearly,
145 And for his sake I wish the having of it;
    And that you'd guide me to your sovereign's court,
    Where with it I may appear a gentleman.
    And if that ever my low fortune's better,
    I'll pay your bounties; till then rest your debtor.

150 FIRST FISHERMAN Why, wilt thou tourney for the lady?

PERICLES I'll show the virtue I have borne in arms.

FIRST FISHERMAN Why, d' ye take it, and the gods give
    thee good on't!

SECOND FISHERMAN Ay, but hark you, my friend:
155 'twas we that made up this garment through the
    rough seams of the waters. There are certain con-
    dolements, certain vails. I hope, sir, if you thrive,
    you'll remember from whence you had them.

PERICLES Believe't, I will!
160 By your furtherance I am clothed in steel;
    And spite of all the rapture of the sea,
    This jewel holds his building on my arm.
    Unto thy value I will mount myself
    Upon a courser, whose delightful steps
165 Shall make the gazer joy to see him tread.
    Only, my friend, I yet am unprovided
    Of a pair of bases.

SECOND FISHERMAN We'll sure provide. Thou shalt

---

143 **target** literally, light shield, hence protection   151 **virtue** valor   156–57 **con-
dolements** (probably a malapropism through confusion with "dole" meaning
"distribution of gifts")   157 **vails** perquisites, tips   158 **them** i.e., the armor
161 **rapture** act of plunder, seizure   162 **building** fixed place   163 **Unto thy
value** to as high a value (as the jewel will fetch)   167 **bases** pleated skirt, worn by
knights on horseback

have my best gown to make thee a pair; and I'll
bring thee to the court myself.   170

PERICLES Then honor be but equal to my will,
This day I'll rise, or else add ill to ill.   [*Exeunt.*]

[Scene II. *Pentapolis. The court of Simonides.*
A public way leading to the lists. A pavilion
near it.]

Enter Simonides, with [Lords,] Attendants, and
Thaisa.

SIMONIDES Are the knights ready to begin the
triumph?

FIRST LORD They are, my liege,
And stay your coming to present themselves.

SIMONIDES Return them we are ready; and our
daughter,
In honor of whose birth these triumphs are,   5
Sits here like Beauty's child, whom Nature gat
For men to see and seeing wonder at.
                              [*Exit a Lord.*]

THAISA It pleaseth you, my royal father, to express
My commendations great, whose merit's less.

SIMONIDES It's fit it should be so; for princes are   10
A model which heaven makes like to itself:

II.ii.1 **triumph** festivity, here tournament   4 **Return** tell by way of answer
6 **gat** begat   11 **model** likeness in little

As jewels lose their glory if neglected,
So princes their renowns if not respected.
'Tis now your honor, daughter, to entertain
15 The labor of each knight in his device.

THAISA Which, to preserve mine honor, I'll perform.

[*Simonides and Thaisa take seats in the pavilion.*]
The first Knight passes by. [*As each Knight
passes, his page, who goes before him, presents
his shield to the Princess.*]

SIMONIDES Who is the first that doth prefer himself?

THAISA A knight of Sparta, my renownèd father;
And the device he bears upon his shield
20 Is a black Ethiop reaching at the sun.
The word, *Lux tua vita mihi.*

SIMONIDES He loves you well that holds his life of
you.

The second Knight [*passes*].

Who is the second that presents himself?

THAISA A prince of Macedon, my royal father;
25 And the device he bears upon his shield
Is an armed knight that's conquered by a lady;
The motto thus, in Spanish, *Più per dolcezza che
per forza.*

[*The*] *third Knight* [*passes*].

SIMONIDES And what's the third?

THAISA   The third of Antioch;
And his device a wreath of chivalry.
30 The word, *Me pompae provexit apex.*

---

14 **honor** honorable duty   14 **entertain** receive   15 **device** emblematic figure,
accompanied by a motto, inscribed on the shield   17 **prefer** present   21 **word**
motto   21 **Lux tua vita mihi** thy light is life to me (Latin)   27 **Più ... forza**
more by gentleness than by force (Italian)   29 **wreath of chivalry** the twisted
band by which, in heraldry, the crest is joined to the knight's helmet   30 **Me
pompae provexit apex** the crown of the triumph has led me on (Latin)

[The] fourth Knight [passes].

SIMONIDES What is the fourth?

THAISA A burning torch that's turnèd upside down.
The word, *Qui me alit me extinguit.*

SIMONIDES Which shows that beauty hath his power
and will,
Which can as well inflame as it can kill.   35

[The] fifth Knight [passes].

THAISA The fifth, an hand environèd with clouds,
Holding out gold that's by the touchstone tried.
The motto thus, *Sic spectanda fides.*

*[The] sixth Knight, [Pericles, passes, without
page].*

SIMONIDES And what's the sixth and last, the which
the knight himself
With such a graceful courtesy delivered?   40

THAISA He seems to be a stranger; but his present is
A withered branch, that's only green at top;
The motto, *In hac spe vivo.*

SIMONIDES A pretty moral.
From the dejected state wherein he is,   45
He hopes by you his fortunes yet may flourish.

FIRST LORD He had need mean better than his
outward show
Can any way speak in his just commend;
For by his rusty outside he appears
To have practiced more the whipstock than the
lance.   50

---

33 **Qui ... extinguit** who feeds me puts me out (Latin)   34 **his** its   38 **Sic spectanda fides** thus is faithfulness to be tried (Latin)   40 **delivered** presented   41 **present** object presented   43 **In hac spe vivo** in this hope I live (Latin)   48 **commend** commendation   50 **To have practiced more the whipstock** to have wielded more the handle of a whip, i.e., worked as a carter

SECOND LORD He well may be a stranger, for he comes
　　To an honored triumph strangely furnishèd.

THIRD LORD And on set purpose let his armor rust
　　Until this day to scour it in the dust.

55 SIMONIDES Opinion's but a fool that makes us scan
　　The outward habit for the inward man.
　　But stay, the knights are coming!
　　We will withdraw into the gallery.   [*Exeunt.*]
　　　　　　　　　　　　Great shouts [*within*], *and all cry*
　　　　　　　　　　　　　　"The mean Knight!"

[*Scene III. Pentapolis. A hall of state.*]

Enter the King, [*Thaisa, Marshal, Lords, Ladies,*]
and Knights from tilting, [*and Attendants*].

SIMONIDES Knights,
　　To say you're welcome were superfluous.
　　To place upon the volume of your deeds,
　　As in a title page, your worth in arms,
5　　Were more than you expect, or more than's fit,
　　Since every worth in show commends itself.
　　Prepare for mirth, for mirth becomes a feast.
　　You are princes and my guests.

THAISA But you my knight and guest;
10　　To whom this wreath of victory I give,
　　And crown you king of this day's happiness.

55 **Opinion** public opinion   55 **scan** scrutinize, examine   58s.d. **mean** shabby
II.iii.4 **As ... arms** (title pages of early printed books often proclaimed the
excellence of their contents)

PERICLES 'Tis more by fortune, lady, than my merit.

SIMONIDES Call it by what you will, the day is yours;
　　And here, I hope, is none that envies it.
　　In framing an artist, art hath thus decreed: 15
　　To make some good, but others to exceed;
　　And you are her labored scholar. Come, queen
　　　　o' th' feast—
　　For, daughter, so you are—here take your place.
　　Marshal, the rest as they deserve their grace.

KNIGHTS We are honored much by good Simonides.   20

SIMONIDES Your presence glads our days. Honor we
　　love;
　　For who hates honor hates the gods above.

MARSHAL Sir, yonder is your place.

PERICLES   Some other is more fit.

FIRST KNIGHT Contend not, sir; for we are gentlemen
　　Have neither in our hearts nor outward eyes   25
　　Envied the great, nor shall the low despise.

PERICLES You are right courteous knights.

SIMONIDES   Sit, sir, sit.
　　[Aside] By Jove I wonder, that is king of thoughts,
　　These cates resist me, he but thought upon.

THAISA [Aside] By Juno, that is queen of marriage,   30
　　All viands that I eat
　　Do seem unsavory, wishing him my meat.
　　[To Simonides] Sure he's a gallant gentleman.

SIMONIDES He's but a country gentleman;
　　Has done no more than other knights have done;   35
　　Has broken a staff or so; so let it pass.

THAISA [Aside] To me he seems like diamond to glass.

---

15 **framing** molding   17 **her labored scholar** the scholar over whom art took
special pains   19 **grace** favor   25 **Have** that have   29 **cates** delicacies
29 **resist ... upon** repel me (?) when I but think of him

PERICLES [*Aside*] Yon king's to me like to my father's
    picture,
    Which tells me in that glory once he was;
40   Had princes sit like stars about his throne,
    And he the sun for them to reverence;
    None that beheld him but, like lesser lights,
    Did vail their crowns to his supremacy;
    Where now his son's a glowworm in the night,
45   The which hath fire in darkness, none in light.
    Whereby I see that Time's the king of men;
    He's both their parent and he is their grave,
    And gives them what he will, not what they crave.

SIMONIDES What, are you merry, knights?

50 KNIGHTS Who can be other in this royal presence?

SIMONIDES Here, with a cup that's stored unto the
    brim—
    As you do love, fill to your mistress' lips—
    We drink this health to you.

KNIGHTS   We thank your Grace.

SIMONIDES Yet pause awhile.
55   Yon knight doth sit too melancholy,
    As if the entertainment in our court
    Had not a show might countervail his worth.
    Note it not you, Thaisa?

THAISA What is't to me, my father?

60 SIMONIDES O, attend, my daughter:
    Princes, in this, should live like gods above,
    Who freely give to everyone that come
    To honor them.
    And princes not doing so are like to gnats,
65   Which make a sound, but killed are wond'red at.
    Therefore, to make his entrance more sweet,

---

43 **vail** lower 52 **to** in honor of 57 **countervail** be equal to 65 **but killed are
wond'red at** i.e., when they are found to be such small animals, after making so
great a noise 66 **entrance** (trisyllabic)

Here, say we drink this standing-bowl of wine to
  him.

THAISA Alas, my father, it befits not me
  Unto a stranger knight to be so bold:
  He may my proffer take for an offense,   70
  Since men take women's gifts for impudence.

SIMONIDES How?
  Do as I bid you, or you'll move me else!

THAISA [*Aside*] Now, by the gods, he could not please
  me better.

SIMONIDES And furthermore tell him we desire to
  know of him   75
  Of whence he is, his name and parentage.

THAISA The King my father, sir, has drunk to you.

PERICLES I thank him.

THAISA Wishing it so much blood unto your life.

PERICLES I thank both him and you, and pledge him
  freely.   80

THAISA And further he desires to know of you
  Of whence you are, your name and parentage.

PERICLES A gentleman of Tyre; my name Pericles;
  My education been in arts and arms;
  Who, looking for adventures in the world,   85
  Was by the rough seas reft of ships and men,
  And after shipwrack driven upon this shore.

THAISA He thanks your Grace; names himself Pericles,
  A gentleman of Tyre,
  Who only by misfortune of the seas,   90
  Bereft of ships and men, cast on this shore.

SIMONIDES Now, by the gods, I pity his misfortune,
  And will awake him from his melancholy.
  Come, gentlemen, we sit too long on trifles,
  And waste the time which looks for other revels.   95

67 **standing-bowl** bowl resting on a foot   84 **been** has been

Even in your armors, as you are addressed,
Will well become a soldier's dance.
I will not have excuse with saying this:
Loud music is too harsh for ladies' heads,
100 Since they love men in arms as well as beds.

They dance.

So, this was well asked, 'twas so well performed.
Come, sir, here's a lady that wants breathing too;
And I have heard you knights of Tyre
Are excellent in making ladies trip,
105 And that their measures are as excellent.

PERICLES In those that practice them they are, my lord.

SIMONIDES O, that's as much as you would be denied
Of your fair courtesy.

They dance.

Unclasp, unclasp!
Thanks, gentlemen, to all; all have done well,
[*To Pericles*] But you the best. Pages and lights, to
110   conduct
These knights unto their several lodgings! Yours,
     sir,
We have given order be next our own.

PERICLES I am at your Grace's pleasure.

SIMONIDES Princes, it is too late to talk of love,
115 And that's the mark I know you level at.

96 **addressed** accoutered   97 **Will well** (two such words as "your steps" must
have originally preceded this)   99 **Loud music** i.e., the loud noise made by the
clashing of their armor (?)   100 **arms** (a pun is presumably intended)
100s.d. **They dance** (most editors assume that the first dance is performed by the
Knights alone, the second by the Knights and Ladies. The text, especially line 102,
suggests rather that both dances are mixed. In the first dance Thaisa and, perhaps,
Pericles do not participate; in the second they dance together)   102 **breathing**
exercise   104 **trip** dance a light dance (with a *double entendre*)   105 **measures**
dances   107–8 **denied/Of your fair courtesy** refused permission to show your
courtesy (by dancing with Thaisa) (?)   115 **level** aim

Therefore each one betake him to his rest;
Tomorrow all for speeding do their best.

> [*Exeunt.*]

[Scene IV. *Tyre*].

Enter Helicanus and Escanes.

HELICANUS No, Escanes, know this of me:
Antiochus from incest lived not free;
For which, the most high gods not minding longer
To withhold the vengeance that they had in store,
Due to this heinous capital offense,   5
Even in the height and pride of all his glory,
When he was seated in a chariot
Of an inestimable value, and
His daughter with him, a fire from heaven came,
And shriveled up their bodies, even to loathing.   10
For they so stunk
That all those eyes adored them ere their fall
Scorn now their hand should give them burial.

ESCANES 'Twas very strange.

HELICANUS And yet but justice; for though this king
    were great,   15
His greatness was no guard to bar heaven's shaft,
But sin had his reward.

ESCANES   'Tis very true.

---

117 **speeding** success   II.iv.3 **minding** being inclined   12 **adored** that adored
17 **his** its

Enter two or three Lords.

FIRST LORD See, not a man in private conference
Or council has respect with him but he.

SECOND LORD It shall no longer grieve without
20   reproof.

THIRD LORD And cursed be he that will not second it.

FIRST LORD Follow me then. Lord Helicane, a word.

HELICANUS With me? And welcome. Happy day, my
lords!

FIRST LORD Know that our griefs are risen to the top,
25   And now at length they overflow their banks.

HELICANUS Your griefs, for what? Wrong not your
prince you love.

FIRST LORD Wrong not yourself, then, noble Helicane;
But if the Prince do live, let us salute him,
Or know what ground's made happy by his breath.
30   If in the world he live, we'll seek him out;
If in his grave he rest, we'll find him there;
And be resolved he lives to govern us,
Or, dead, gives cause to mourn his funeral,
And leaves us to our free election.

SECOND LORD Whose death's indeed the strongest in
35   our censure.
And knowing this: kingdoms without a head,
Like goodly buildings left without a roof
Soon fall to ruin, your noble self,
That best know how to rule and how to reign,
40   We thus submit unto—our sovereign.

ALL Live, noble Helicane!

HELICANUS For honor's cause, forbear your suffrages.
If that you love Prince Pericles, forbear.

---

20 grieve be a grievance   24 griefs grievances   32 resolved satisfied   35 the
strongest in our censure the more likely supposition in our judgment

Take I your wish, I leap into the seas
Where's hourly trouble for a minute's ease.   45
A twelvemonth longer let me entreat you
To forbear the absence of your king;
If in which time expired he not return,
I shall with agèd patience bear your yoke.
But if I cannot win you to this love,   50
Go search like nobles, like noble subjects,
And in your search spend your adventurous worth;
Whom if you find, and win unto return,
You shall like diamonds sit about his crown.

FIRST LORD To wisdom he's a fool that will not yield;   55
And since Lord Helicane enjoineth us,
We with our travels will endeavor it.

HELICANUS Then you love us, we you, and we'll clasp
      hands:
When peers thus knit, a kingdom ever stands.
                                              [*Exeunt.*]

[Scene V. *Pentapolis. A room in the palace.*]

Enter the King reading of a letter at one door;
the Knights meet him.

FIRST KNIGHT Good morrow to the good Simonides.

SIMONIDES Knights, from my daughter this I let you
      know:

44 **Take I** if I should accept   47 **forbear** tolerate, endure   50 **love** act of
kindness

That for this twelvemonth she'll not undertake
A married life.
5   Her reason to herself is only known,
Which from her by no means can I get.

SECOND KNIGHT May we not get access to her, my lord?

SIMONIDES Faith, by no means. She hath so strictly
      tied her
To her chamber that 'tis impossible.
One twelve moons more she'll wear Diana's
10   livery.
This by the eye of Cynthia hath she vowed,
And on her virgin honor will not break it.

THIRD KNIGHT Loath to bid farewell, we take our
      leaves.   [*Exeunt Knights.*]

SIMONIDES So, they are well dispatched.
15   Now to my daughter's letter:
She tells me here she'll wed the stranger knight,
Or never more to view nor day nor light.
'Tis well, mistress; your choice agrees with mine.
I like that well! Nay, how absolute she's in't,
20   Not minding whether I dislike or no!
Well, I do commend her choice,
And will no longer have it be delayed.
Soft, here he comes! I must dissemble it.

Enter Pericles.

PERICLES All fortune to the good Simonides!

SIMONIDES To you as much. Sir, I am beholding to
25   you
For your sweet music this last night. I do
Protest my ears were never better fed
With such delightful pleasing harmony.

II.v.6 **means** (here pronounced as a disyllable) 10 **One twelve moons** one year
10 **wear Diana's livery** i.e., remain a virgin 11 **Cynthia** the moon 13 **Loath**
(here pronounced as a disyllable) 19 **absolute** positive, decided 23 **Soft** hold
(an interjection) 25 **beholding** indebted

PERICLES It is your Grace's pleasure to commend;
   Not my desert.

SIMONIDES   Sir, you are music's master.   30

PERICLES The worst of all her scholars, my good lord.

SIMONIDES Let me ask you one thing: What do you
      think of
   My daughter, sir?

PERICLES   A most virtuous princess.

SIMONIDES And she is fair too, is she not?

PERICLES As a fair day in summer, wondrous fair.   35

SIMONIDES Sir, my daughter thinks very well of you;
   Ay, so well that you must be her master,
   And she will be your scholar: therefore look to it.

PERICLES I am unworthy for her schoolmaster.

SIMONIDES She thinks not so; peruse this writing else.   40

PERICLES [Aside] What's here?
   A letter that she loves the knight of Tyre!
   'Tis the King's subtlety to have my life.
   [Kneels] O, seek not to entrap me, gracious lord,
   A stranger and distressèd gentleman,   45
   That never aimed so high to love your daughter,
   But bent all offices to honor her.

SIMONIDES Thou hast bewitched my daughter, and
      thou art
   A villain!

PERICLES By the gods, I have not.
   Never did thought of mine levy offense;   50
   Nor never did my actions yet commence
   A deed might gain her love or your displeasure.

SIMONIDES Traitor, thou liest!

PERICLES   Traitor?

40 else if you do not believe it   46 to as to   47 bent all offices turned all my
services   50 levy (apparently misused for "level," i.e., aim)   52 might that
might

SIMONIDES   Ay, traitor!

PERICLES Even in his throat—unless it be the King—
55   That calls me traitor I return the lie.

SIMONIDES [*Aside*] Now, by the gods, I do applaud
        his courage.

PERICLES My actions are as noble as my thoughts,
        That never relished of a base descent.
        I came unto your court for honor's cause,
60   And not to be a rebel to her state;
        And he that otherwise accounts of me,
        This sword shall prove he's honor's enemy.

SIMONIDES No?
        Here comes my daughter, she can witness it.

                    Enter Thaisa.

65 PERICLES Then, as you are as virtuous as fair,
        Resolve your angry father if my tongue
        Did e'er solicit, or my hand subscribe
        To any syllable that made love to you.

THAISA Why, sir, say if you had,
70   Who takes offense at that would make me glad?

SIMONIDES Yea, mistress, are you so peremptory?
        (*Aside*) I am glad on't with all my heart.—
        I'll tame you; I'll bring you in subjection!
        Will you, not having my consent,
75   Bestow your love and your affections
        Upon a stranger?—(*aside*) who, for aught I know,
        May be, nor can I think the contrary,
        As great in blood as I myself—
        Therefore hear you, mistress: either frame
80   Your will to mine—and you, sir, hear you:
        Either be ruled by me, or I'll make you—
        Man and wife.
        Nay, come, your hands and lips must seal it too!

---

58 **relished of** had a trace of   60 **her state** honor's domain   66 **Resolve** inform
70 **would** which would   71 **peremptory** determined

And being joined, I'll thus your hopes destroy;
And for further grief—God give you joy!   85
What, are you both pleased?

THAISA   Yes, if you love me, sir.

PERICLES Even as my life my blood that fosters it.

SIMONIDES What, are you both agreed?

BOTH Yes, if 't please your Majesty.

SIMONIDES It pleaseth me so well that I will see you
    wed;   90
And then, with what haste you can, get you to bed.
                                        Exeunt.

87 **my blood** i.e., loves my blood

45

[ACT III]

Enter Gower.

GOWER Now sleep y-slackèd hath the rout;
　　　No din but snores the house about,
　　　Made louder by the o'erfed breast
　　　Of this most pompous marriage feast.
5　　The cat, with eyne of burning coal,
　　　Now couches 'fore the mouse's hole;
　　　And crickets sing at the oven's mouth
　　　All the blither for their drouth.
　　　Hymen hath brought the bride to bed,
10　　Where by the loss of maidenhead
　　　A babe is molded. Be attent,
　　　And time that is so briefly spent
　　　With your fine fancies quaintly eche.
　　　What's dumb in show I'll plain with speech.

III.1 **y-slackèd** reduced to inactivity 1 **rout** company of revelers 4 **pompous** magnificent 5 **eyne** eyes (archaic plural) 8 **drouth** dryness 9 **Hymen** the god of marriage 11 **attent** attentive 12 **briefly** quickly 13 **fancies** imaginings 13 **quaintly** skillfully 13 **eche** augment (old spelling of "eke") 14 **plain** explain

[Dumb Show]

*Enter Pericles and Simonides at one door, with Attendants;
a Messenger meets them, kneels, and gives Pericles a letter;
Pericles shows it Simonides; the Lords kneel to him. Then
enter Thaisa with child, with Lychorida, a nurse; the King
shows her the letter; she rejoices; she and Pericles take leave
of her father, and depart [with Lychorida and their Attendants. Then exeunt Simonides and the rest].*

By many a dern and painful perch   15
Of Pericles the careful search
By the four opposing coigns
Which the world together joins
Is made with all due diligence
That horse and sail and high expense   20
Can stead the quest. At last from Tyre,
Fame answering the most strange inquire,
To th' court of King Simonides
Are letters brought, the tenor these:
Antiochus and his daughter dead,   25
The men of Tyrus on the head
Of Helicanus would set on
The crown of Tyre, but he will none.
The mutiny he there hastes t' appease;
Says to 'em, if King Pericles   30
Come not home in twice six moons,
He, obedient to their dooms,
Will take the crown. The sum of this,
Brought hither to Pentapolis,
Y-ravishèd the regions round,   35
And everyone with claps can sound,
"Our heir-apparent is a king!
Who dreamt, who thought of such a thing?"
Brief, he must hence depart to Tyre.

---

15 **dern** wild, drear 15 **painful** toilsome 15 **perch** measure of land
17 **opposing coigns** opposite corners 21 **stead** be of use to 22 **Fame** ...
inquire Rumor having responded to inquiries in the most distant regions (?)
32 **dooms** judgments 33 **sum** gist 35 **Y-ravishèd** enraptured 36 **can** began (a
Middle English variant of "gan") 36 **sound** proclaim, declare 39 **Brief** in short

40   His queen with child makes her desire—
        Which who shall cross?—along to go.
        Omit we all their dole and woe.
        Lychorida, her nurse, she takes,
        And so to sea. Their vessel shakes
45   On Neptune's billow; half the flood
        Hath their keel cut; but Fortune's mood
        Varies again: the grislèd north
        Disgorges such a tempest forth
        That, as a duck for life that dives,
50   So up and down the poor ship drives.
        The lady shrieks and, well-a-near,
        Does fall in travail with her fear;
        And what ensues in this fell storm
        Shall for itself itself perform.
55   I nill relate, action may
        Conveniently the rest convey;
        Which might not what by me is told.
        In your imagination hold
        This stage the ship, upon whose deck
60   The sea-tossed Pericles appears to speak.   [*Exit.*]

[Scene I.]

Enter Pericles, a-shipboard.

PERICLES The god of this great vast rebuke these
            surges,
        Which wash both heaven and hell; and thou that hast

___

42 **dole** grief 45–46 **half … cut** i.e., half the voyage has been completed
47 **grislèd** horrible, grisly 51 **well-a-near** alas 55 **nill** will not (Middle
English) 55 **action** (here pronounced as a trisyllable) III.i.1 **vast** boundless
expanse

Upon the winds command, bind them in brass,
Having called them from the deep! O, still
Thy deaf'ning dreadful thunders; gently quench   5
Thy nimble sulphurous flashes! O, how, Lychorida,
How does my queen? Thou stormest venomously;
Wilt thou spit all thyself? The seaman's whistle
Is as a whisper in the ears of death,
Unheard. Lychorida!—Lucina, O   10
Divinest patroness and midwife gentle
To those that cry by night, convey thy deity
Aboard our dancing boat; make swift the pangs
Of my queen's travails! Now, Lychorida!

Enter Lychorida [with an infant].

LYCHORIDA Here is a thing too young for such a place,   15
  Who, if it had conceit, would die, as I
  Am like to do. Take in your arms this piece
  Of your dead queen.

PERICLES   How? How, Lychorida?

LYCHORIDA Patience, good sir; do not assist the storm.
  Here's all that is left living of your queen—   20
  A little daughter. For the sake of it
  Be manly, and take comfort.

PERICLES   O you gods!
  Why do you make us love your goodly gifts,
  And snatch them straight away? We here below
  Recall not what we give, and therein may   25
  Vie honor with you.

LYCHORIDA   Patience, good sir,
  Even for this charge.

PERICLES   Now, mild may be thy life!
  For a more blusterous birth had never babe;

6 **nimble** swift   10 **Lucina** the goddess of childbirth   16 **conceit** capacity to
understand   26 **Vie honor with you** compete with you in respect of honor
27 **Even for this charge** for the sake of the babe left in your care

Quiet and gentle thy conditions! For
30   Thou art the rudeliest welcome to this world
That ever was prince's child. Happy what follows!
Thou hast as chiding a nativity
As fire, air, water, earth and heaven can make,
To herald thee from the womb. Even at the first
35   Thy loss is more than can thy portage quit,
With all thou canst find here. Now the good gods
Throw their best eyes upon't!

Enter two Sailors.

FIRST SAILOR   What courage, sir? God save you!

PERICLES   Courage enough. I do not fear the flaw:
40   It hath done to me the worst. Yet, for the love
Of this poor infant, this fresh, new seafarer,
I would it would be quiet.

FIRST SAILOR   Slack the bolins there! Thou wilt not,
wilt thou? Blow, and split thyself!

45   SECOND SAILOR   But sea-room, and the brine and cloudy
billow kiss the moon, I care not.

FIRST SAILOR   Sir, your queen must overboard; the sea
works high, the wind is loud, and will not lie
till the ship be cleared of the dead.

50   PERICLES   That's your superstition.

FIRST SAILOR   Pardon us, sir; with us at sea it hath been
still observed; and we are strong in custom. Therefore briefly yield her; for she must overboard
straight.

55   PERICLES   As you think meet. Most wretched queen!

LYCHORIDA   Here she lies, sir.

---

35 **than can thy portage quit** than your cargo (i.e., all that you are going to
possess in the course of the voyage of life) can compensate for (?)   39 **flaw** gust of
wind   41 **fresh** raw, inexperienced   43 **bolins** ropes from weather-side of square
sail to bow   45 **and** if   48 **works** rages   48 **lie** subside   52 **still** always   52 **strong
in custom** steadfast in observing customs   53 **briefly** quickly

PERICLES A terrible childbed hast thou had, my dear;
  No light, no fire. Th' unfriendly elements
  Forgot thee utterly; nor have I time
  To give thee hallowed to thy grave, but straight   60
  Must cast thee, scarcely coffined, in the ooze;
  Where, for a monument upon thy bones,
  And e'er-remaining lamps, the belching whale
  And humming water must o'erwhelm thy corpse,
  Lying with simple shells. O Lychorida,   65
  Bid Nestor bring me spices, ink and paper,
  My casket and my jewels; and bid Nicander
  Bring me the satin coffin. Lay the babe
  Upon the pillow. Hie thee, whiles I say
  A priestly farewell to her. Suddenly, woman!   70
                             [*Exit Lychorida.*]

SECOND SAILOR Sir, we have a chest beneath the
  hatches,
  Caulked and bitumèd ready.

PERICLES I thank thee. Mariner, say, what coast is this?

SECOND SAILOR We are near Tharsus.

PERICLES   Thither, gentle mariner,
  Alter thy course for Tyre. When canst thou reach it?   75

SECOND SAILOR By break of day, if the wind cease.

PERICLES O make for Tharsus!
  There will I visit Cleon, for the babe
  Cannot hold out to Tyrus. There I'll leave it
  At careful nursing. Go thy ways, good mariner.   80
  I'll bring the body presently.   *Exit* [*with Sailors*].

---

62 **for** instead of   68 **coffin** case, box   70 **Suddenly** at once   72 **bitumèd** made
watertight with bitumen   80 **careful** full of good care   80 **Go thy ways** come
along   81 **presently** immediately

[Scene II. *Ephesus. A room in Cerimon's house.*]

Enter Lord Cerimon with a Servant.

CERIMON Philemon, ho!

Enter Philemon.

PHILEMON Doth my lord call?

CERIMON Get fire and meat for those poor men:
'T 'as been a turbulent and stormy night.

[*Exit Philemon.*]

5   SERVANT I have been in many; but such a night as this
Till now I ne'er endured.

CERIMON Your master will be dead ere you return.
There's nothing can be minist'red to nature
That can recover him. Give this to the 'pothecary,
And tell me how it works.   [*Exit Servant.*]

Enter two Gentlemen.

10   FIRST GENTLEMAN   Good morrow.

SECOND GENTLEMAN Good morrow to your lordship.

CERIMON   Gentlemen,
Why do you stir so early?

FIRST GENTLEMAN Sir,
Our lodgings, standing bleak upon the sea,
15   Shook as the earth did quake;
The very principals did seem to rend
And all to topple. Pure surprise and fear
Made me to quit the house.

III.ii.9–10 **Give ... works** (this prescription must be intended for someone other than the servant's master)   16 **principals** chief rafters of a house

52

SECOND GENTLEMAN That is the cause we trouble you
    so early;
  'Tis not our husbandry.

CERIMON   O, you say well.   20

FIRST GENTLEMAN But I much marvel that your
    lordship, having
  Rich tire about you, should at these early hours
  Shake off the golden slumber of repose.
  'Tis most strange,
  Nature should be so conversant with pain,   25
  Being thereto not compelled.

CERIMON   I held it ever
  Virtue and cunning were endowments greater
  Than nobleness and riches: careless heirs
  May the two latter darken and expend,
  But immortality attends the former,   30
  Making a man a god. 'Tis known, I ever
  Have studied physic, through which secret art,
  By turning o'er authorities, I have,
  Together with my practice, made familiar
  To me and to my aid the blest infusions   35
  That dwells in vegetives, in metals, stones;
  And I can speak of the disturbances
  That nature works, and of her cures; which gives
    me
  A more content in course of true delight
  Than to be thirsty after tottering honor,   40
  Or tie my treasure up in silken bags,
  To please the Fool and Death.

SECOND GENTLEMAN Your honor has through Ephesus
    poured forth
  Your charity, and hundreds call themselves
  Your creatures, who by you have been restored;   45

20 **husbandry** zeal for work   22 **tire** belongings   25 **pain** trouble, labor
27 **cunning** skill   28 **nobleness** nobility (i.e., social rank)   30 **attends** awaits
35 **my aid** my assistant (?)   36 **vegetives** vegetables, herbs   39 **more** greater
42 **the Fool and Death** (probably an allusion to the Dance of Death, in which
these two figures often appeared as companions)

And not your knowledge, your personal pain, but
    even
Your purse, still open, hath built Lord Cerimon
Such strong renown as time shall never raze.

Enter two or three [Servants] with a chest.

FIRST SERVANT So; lift there!

CERIMON   What's that?

FIRST SERVANT   Sir, even now
50   Did the sea toss up upon our shore this chest.
    'Tis of some wrack.

CERIMON   Set't down, let's look upon't.

SECOND GENTLEMAN 'Tis like a coffin, sir.

CERIMON   Whate'er it be,
    'Tis wondrous heavy. Wrench it open straight.
    If the sea's stomach be o'ercharged with gold,
55   'Tis a good constraint of fortune
    It belches upon us.

SECOND GENTLEMAN 'Tis so, my lord.

CERIMON How close 'tis caulked and bitumed!
    Did the sea cast it up?

FIRST SERVANT I never saw so huge a billow, sir,
    As tossed it upon shore.

60 CERIMON   Wrench it open: soft! It smells
    Most sweetly in my sense.

SECOND GENTLEMAN   A delicate odor.

CERIMON As ever hit my nostril. So; up with it!
    O you most potent gods! What's here, a corse!

SECOND GENTLEMAN Most strange!

CERIMON   Shrouded in cloth of state;

46 **not** not only 46 **pain** trouble 47 **still** always 53 **straight** immediately
56 **It belches upon us** that it belches this chest upon us 64 **cloth of state**
magnificent fabric

Balmed, and entreasured with full bags of spices!   65
A passport too! Apollo, perfect me
In the characters!   [*Reads from a scroll.*]

> Here I give to understand,
> If e'er this coffin drives a-land,
> I, King Pericles, have lost   70
> This queen, worth all our mundane cost.
> Who finds her, give her burying;
> She was the daughter of a king.
> Besides this treasure for a fee,
> The gods requite his charity!   75

If thou livest, Pericles, thou hast a heart
That even cracks for woe! This chanced tonight.

SECOND GENTLEMAN Most likely, sir.

CERIMON   Nay, certainly tonight;
For look how fresh she looks! They were too rough
That threw her in the sea. Make a fire within.   80
Fetch hither all my boxes in my closet.
                              [*Exit Servant.*]
Death may usurp on nature many hours,
And yet the fire of life kindle again
The o'erpressed spirits. [I have read
Of some Egyptians, who after four hours' death   85
Have raised impoverished bodies, like to this,
Unto their former health.]

> *Enter one [Servant] with napkins and fire.*

                              Well said, well said;
The fire and cloths.
The still and woeful music that we have,
Cause it to sound, beseech you. [*Music.*]   90
The viol once more! How thou stirr'st, thou block!

65 **Balmed** anointed with fragrant oil 66 **perfect me** instruct me fully
67 **characters** writing (the stress falls here on the second syllable) 71 **mundane
cost** worldly riches 77 **tonight** last night 82 **nature** man's physical
constitution 86 **impoverished** deprived of their native strength 87 **Well said**
well done 88 **cloths** napkins 91 **How thou stirr'st** how quick you are! (used
ironically)

The music there! [*Music.*] I pray you, give her air.
Gentlemen,
This queen will live: nature awakes; a warmth
95 Breathes out of her. She hath not been entranced
Above five hours. See how she 'gins to blow
Into life's flower again!

FIRST GENTLEMAN   The heavens
Through you increase our wonder, and sets up
Your fame forever.

CERIMON   She is alive! Behold,
100 Her eyelids, cases to those heavenly jewels
Which Pericles hath lost, begin to part
Their fringes of bright gold; the diamonds
Of a most praisèd water doth appear
To make the world twice rich. Live,
105 And make us weep to hear your fate, fair creature,
Rare as you seem to be.   *She moves.*

THAISA   O dear Diana,
Where am I? Where's my lord? What world is this?

SECOND GENTLEMAN Is not this strange?

FIRST GENTLEMAN   Most rare!

CERIMON   Hush, my gentle neighbors!
Lend me your hands; to the next chamber bear her.
110 Get linen. Now this matter must be looked to,
For her relapse is mortal. Come, come;
And Aesculapius guide us!
                              They carry her away. Exeunt Omnes.

94 **nature** the vital powers   95 **entranced** in a swoon   96 **blow** bloom
103 **water** luster   111 **is mortal** would be fatal   112 **Aesculapius** Greek god of
medicine   112s.d. **Omnes** all (Latin)

[Scene III. *Tharsus*.]

Enter Pericles at Tharsus with Cleon and Dionyza,
[and Lychorida with Marina in her arms].

PERICLES Most honored Cleon, I must needs be gone:
My twelve months are expired, and Tyrus stands
In a litigious peace. You and your lady,
Take from my heart all thankfulness! The gods
Make up the rest upon you!

CLEON   Your shafts of fortune,   5
Though they hurt you mortally, yet glance
Full woundingly on us.

DIONYZA   O your sweet queen!
That the strict fates had pleased you had brought
    her hither
To have blest mine eyes with her!

PERICLES   We cannot but
Obey the powers above us. Could I rage   10
And roar as doth the sea she lies in, yet
The end must be as 'tis. My gentle babe,
Marina, whom, for she was born at sea,
I have named so, here I charge
Your charity withal, leaving her   15
The infant of your care; beseeching you
To give her princely training, that she may
Be mannered as she is born.

CLEON   Fear not, my lord, but think
Your Grace, that fed my country with your corn,
For which the people's prayers still fall upon you,   20
Must in your child be thought on. If neglection

III.iii.3 **litigious** productive of contention 7 **full** very 13 **for** because
15 **withal** with   21 **neglection** neglect

57

Should therein make me vile, the common body,
By you relieved, would force me to my duty.
But if to that my nature need a spur,
25   The gods revenge it upon me and mine,
To the end of generation!

PERICLES   I believe you.
Your honor and your goodness teach me to't,
Without your vows. Till she be married, madam,
By bright Diana, whom we honor all,
30   Unscissored shall this hair of mine remain,
Though I show ill in't. So I take my leave.
Good madam, make me blessèd in your care
In bringing up my child.

DIONYZA   I have one myself,
Who shall not be more dear to my respect
Than yours, my lord.

35   PERICLES   Madam, my thanks and prayers.

CLEON We'll bring your Grace e'en to the edge o' th'
    shore,
Then give you up to the masked Neptune and
The gentlest winds of heaven.

PERICLES   I will embrace
Your offer. Come, dearest madam. O, no tears,
40   Lychorida, no tears!
Look to your little mistress, on whose grace
You may depend hereafter. Come, my lord.

                                        [Exeunt.]

---

22 **common body** common people   26 **To the end of generation** i.e., until the
human race ceases to procreate (?)   34 **respect** care   37 **masked** deceptively
calm (?)   41 **grace** favor

[Scene IV. *Ephesus*.]

Enter Cerimon and Thaisa.

CERIMON Madam, this letter, and some certain jewels,
Lay with you in your coffer; which are
At your command. Know you the character?

THAISA It is my lord's. That I was shipped at sea
I well remember, even on my eaning time;   5
But whether there delivered, by the holy gods,
I cannot rightly say. But since King Pericles,
My wedded lord, I ne'er shall see again,
A vestal livery will I take me to,
And never more have joy.   10

CERIMON Madam, if this you purpose as ye speak,
Diana's temple is not distant far,
Where you may abide till your date expire.
Moreover, if you please, a niece of mine
Shall there attend you.   15

THAISA My recompense is thanks, that's all;
Yet my good will is great, though the gift small.
                                        Exit [with Cerimon].

III.iv.3 **character** handwriting   5 **eaning time** time of childbirth   9 **vestal** ...
to i.e., I will live the life of a vestal virgin   13 **date** term of life

[ACT IV]

Enter Gower.

GOWER Imagine Pericles arrived at Tyre,
 Welcomed and settled to his own desire.
 His woeful queen we leave at Ephesus,
 Unto Diana there's a votaress.
5 Now to Marina bend your mind,
 Whom our fast-growing scene must find
 At Tharsus, and by Cleon trained
 In music's letters; who hath gained
 Of education all the grace,
10 Which makes her both the heart and place
 Of general wonder. But, alack,
 That monster, Envy, oft the wrack
 Of earnèd praise, Marina's life
 Seeks to take off by treason's knife.
15 And in this kind: Our Cleon hath
 One daughter, and a full grown wench,
 Even ripe for marriage rite. This maid
 Hight Philoten; and it is said
 For certain in our story, she
20 Would ever with Marina be.

IV.4 **there's** there as   8 **music's letters** the study of music   10 **place** dwelling
12 **wrack** ruin   14 **treason's** treachery's   15 **in this kind** in the following way
18 **hight** is named

Be't when she weaved the sleided silk
With fingers long, small, white as milk;
Or when she would with sharp needle wound
The cambric, which she made more sound
By hurting it; or when to th' lute   25
She sung, and made the night-bird mute,
That still records with moan; or when
She would with rich and constant pen
Vail to her mistress Dian; still
This Philoten contends in skill   30
With absolute Marina: so
With dove of Paphos might the crow
Vie feathers white. Marina gets
All praises, which are paid as debts,
And not as given. This so darks   35
In Philoten all graceful marks
That Cleon's wife, with envy rare,
A present murderer does prepare
For good Marina, that her daughter
Might stand peerless by this slaughter.   40
The sooner her vile thoughts to stead,
Lychorida, our nurse, is dead;
And cursèd Dionyza hath
The pregnant instrument of wrath
Prest for this blow. The unborn event   45
I do commend to your content;
Only I carry wingèd time
Post on the lame feet of my rhyme;
Which never could I so convey
Unless your thoughts went on my way.   50
Dionyza does appear,
With Leonine, a murderer.   *Exit*.

21 **sleided** (a variant of "sleaved," i.e., divided into filaments)   22 **small** slender
23 **needle** (here pronounced as a monosyllable)   26 **night-bird** nightingale
27 **still records with moan** ever sings dolefully   29 **Vail** do homage
31 **absolute** free from imperfection   32 **dove of Paphos** Venus' dove
33 **Vie** compete in respect of   35 **darks** darkens, puts in the shade   38 **present**
speedy   38 **prepare** provide   41 **stead** aid   44 **pregnant** disposed, inclined
45 **Prest** ready   45 **event** outcome   46 **commend to your content** commend to
you, hoping that it will please you   48 **Post** in post haste

[Scene I. *Tharsus, near the seashore.*]

Enter Dionyza with Leonine.

DIONYZA Thy oath remember; thou hast sworn to do't.
'Tis but a blow, which never shall be known.
Thou canst not do a thing in the world so soon
To yield thee so much profit. Let not conscience,
5   Which is but cold, or flaming love thy bosom
Enslave too nicely; nor let pity, which
Even women have cast off, melt thee, but be
A soldier to thy purpose.

LEONINE I will do't. But yet she is a goodly creature!

10   DIONYZA The fitter then the gods should have her.
Here she comes weeping her old nurse's death!
Thou art resolved?

LEONINE   I am resolved.

Enter Marina with a basket of flowers.

MARINA No, I will rob Tellus of her weed
To strew thy green with flowers; the yellows, blues,
15   The purple violets, and marigolds,
Shall as a carpet hang upon thy grave,
While summer days doth last. Ay me, poor maid,
Born in a tempest, when my mother died,
This world to me is as a lasting storm,
20   Whirring me from my friends.

DIONYZA How now, Marina, why do you keep alone?
How chance my daughter is not with you?

IV.i.6 **nicely** scrupulously 8 **A soldier to** wholly devoted to 11 **weeping**
lamenting 13 **Tellus** the earth 13 **weed** garment (of flowers) 14 **green** i.e.,
the green turf of Lychorida's grave 16 **carpet** piece of tapestry 20 **Whirring**
whirling, hurrying along 20 **friends** relations

Do not consume your blood with sorrowing.
Have you a nurse of me! Lord, how your favor
Is changed with this unprofitable woe!   25
Come, give me your flowers.
On the sea margent walk with Leonine.
The air is quick there and it pierces, and
Sharpens the stomach. Come, Leonine, take
Her by the arm, walk with her.

MARINA   No, I pray you.   30
I'll not bereave you of your servant.

DIONYZA   Come, come!
I love the King your father and yourself
With more than foreign heart. We every day
Expect him here. When he shall come, and find
Our paragon to all reports thus blasted,   35
He will repent the breadth of his great voyage;
Blame both my lord and me, that we have taken
No care to your best courses. Go, I pray you,
Walk, and be cheerful once again; reserve
That excellent complexion, which did steal   40
The eyes of young and old. Care not for me;
I can go home alone.

MARINA   Well, I will go;
But yet I have no desire to it.

DIONYZA   Come, come,
I know 'tis good for you.
Walk half an hour, Leonine, at the least.   45
Remember what I have said.

LEONINE   I warrant you, madam.

DIONYZA I'll leave you, my sweet lady, for a while.
Pray, walk softly, do not heat your blood. What!
I must have care of you.

23 Do ... sorrowing (alluding to the ancient notion that each sigh takes a drop of
blood from the heart) 24 favor face, looks 28 quick sharp 33 foreign not of
one's family 35 to all reports according to all reports 36 breadth extent
38 to your best courses to what was best for you 39 reserve preserve, guard
46 warrant promise 48 softly slowly

MARINA   My thanks, sweet madam.
                                            [*Exit Dionyza*.]
        Is this wind westerly that blows?

50 LEONINE   Southwest.

    MARINA When I was born the wind was north.

    LEONINE   Was't so?

    MARINA My father, as nurse says, did never fear,
        But cried "Good seamen!" to the sailors, galling
        His kingly hands haling ropes;
55   And, clasping to the mast, endured a sea
        That almost burst the deck.

    LEONINE   When was this?

    MARINA When I was born.
        Never was waves nor wind more violent;
        And from the ladder-tackle washes off
60   A canvas-climber. "Ha!" says one, "wolt out?"
        And with a dropping industry they skip
        From stem to stern; the boatswain whistles, and
        The master calls and trebles their confusion.

    LEONINE Come, say your prayers!

65 MARINA What mean you?

    LEONINE If you require a little space for prayer,
        I grant it. Pray; but be not tedious, for
        The gods are quick of ear, and I am sworn
        To do my work with haste.

    MARINA   Why will you kill me?

70 LEONINE To satisfy my lady.

    MARINA Why would she have me killed?
        Now, as I can remember, by my troth,
        I never did her hurt in all my life.

---

53 **galling** making sore by chafing 55 **clasping** clinging 60 **canvas-climber**
sailor climbing aloft to trim sails 60 **wolt** wilt 61 **dropping** dripping wet
72 **as** as far as

I never spake bad word nor did ill turn
To any living creature. Believe me, la,   75
I never killed a mouse, nor hurt a fly;
I trod upon a worm against my will,
But I wept for't. How have I offended,
Wherein my death might yield her any profit,
Or my life imply her any danger?   80

LEONINE My commission
Is not to reason of the deed, but do't.

MARINA You will not do't for all the world, I hope.
You are well-favored, and your looks foreshow
You have a gentle heart. I saw you lately,   85
When you caught hurt in parting two that fought.
Good sooth, it showed well in you. Do so now.
Your lady seeks my life: come you between,
And save poor me, the weaker!

LEONINE   I am sworn,
And will dispatch.   [Seizes her.]

                    Enter Pirates.

FIRST PIRATE   Hold, villain!
                              [Leonine runs away.]

SECOND PIRATE   A prize! A prize!   90

THIRD PIRATE Half-part, mates, half-part! Come, let's
have her aboard suddenly.
                          [They carry off Marina.]

                    Enter Leonine.

LEONINE These roguing thieves serve the great pirate
    Valdes,
And they have seized Marina. Let her go;
There's no hope she'll return. I'll swear she's
    dead,   95
And thrown into the sea. But I'll see further:

75 la (exclamation to emphasize a statement) 84 well-favored good-looking
87 good sooth truly 91 Half-part go shares 92 suddenly at once
93 roguing vagrant 95 hope i.e., fear

65

Perhaps they will but please themselves upon her,
Not carry her aboard. If she remain,
Whom they have ravished must by me be slain.

Exit.

[Scene II. *Mytilene. In front of a brothel.*]

*Enter the three Bawds [i.e. a Pander, his servant
Boult, and a Bawd].*

PANDER Boult!

BOULT Sir?

PANDER Search the market narrowly! Mytilene is full
of gallants. We lost too much money this mart by
5   being too wenchless.

BAWD We were never so much out of creatures. We
have but poor three, and they can do no more than
they can do; and they with continual action are
even as good as rotten.

10   PANDER Therefore let's have fresh ones, whate'er we
pay for them. If there be not a conscience to be
used in every trade, we shall never prosper.

BAWD Thou say'st true: 'tis not our bringing up of
poor bastards—as, I think, I have brought up some
15   eleven—

BOULT Ay, to eleven; and brought them down again.
But shall I search the market?

IV.ii.4 **mart** market-time   16 **to eleven** up to the age of eleven   16 **brought
them down again** i.e., by prostituting them

BAWD What else, man? The stuff we have, a strong
wind will blow it to pieces, they are so pitifully
sodden.   20

PANDER Thou sayest true; they're too unwholesome,
o' conscience. The poor Transylvanian is dead that
lay with the little baggage.

BOULT Ay, she quickly pooped him; she made him
roast meat for worms. But I'll go search the market.   25
                                                    Exit.

PANDER Three or four thousand chequins were as
pretty a proportion to live quietly, and so give
over.

BAWD Why to give over, I pray you? Is it a shame
to get when we are old?   30

PANDER O, our credit comes not in like the commodity, nor the commodity wages not with the
danger. Therefore, if in our youths we could pick
up some pretty estate, 'twere not amiss to keep our
door hatched. Besides, the sore terms we stand   35
upon with the gods will be strong with us for giving o'er.

BAWD Come, other sorts offend as well as we.

PANDER As well as we? Ay, and better too; we offend
worse. Neither is our profession any trade; it's no   40
calling. But here comes Boult.

Enter Boult, with the Pirates and Marina.

BOULT Come your ways, my masters! You say she's
a virgin?

18 **stuff** goods for sale   20 **sodden** grown rotten by soaking (referring to the
treatment of venereal disease by means of the sweating tub)   22 **o' conscience** on
my conscience   24 **pooped** foundered (?)   26 **chequins** sequins, Italian gold coins
27 **proportion** portion, share   27–28 **give over** give up, retire   30 **get** acquire
money   31 **credit** reputation   32 **commodity** profit   32 **wages not** is not
commensurate   35 **hatched** with the hatch (the lower half of a divided door) shut
38 **sorts** classes of people   40 **trade** recognized business   42 **Come your ways**
come along

FIRST PIRATE O, sir, we doubt it not.

45   BOULT Master, I have gone through for this piece
you see. If you like her, so; if not, I have lost my
earnest.

BAWD Boult, has she any qualities?

BOULT She has a good face, speaks well, and has ex-
50   cellent good clothes. There's no farther necessity of
qualities can make her be refused.

BAWD What's her price, Boult?

BOULT It cannot be bated one doit of a thousand
pieces.

55   PANDER Well, follow me, my masters; you shall have
your money presently. Wife, take her in. Instruct
her what she has to do, that she may not be raw
in her entertainment.

[Exeunt Pander and Pirates.]

BAWD Boult, take you the marks of her, the color of
60   her hair, complexion, height, her age, with warrant
of her virginity; and cry "He that will give most
shall have her first!" Such a maidenhead were no
cheap thing, if men were as they have been. Get
this done as I command you.

65   BOULT Performance shall follow.   Exit.

MARINA Alack that Leonine was so slack, so slow!
He should have struck, not spoke; or that these
        pirates,
Not enough barbarous, had not o'erboard
Thrown me to seek my mother!

70   BAWD Why lament you, pretty one?

45 gone through completed the process of bargaining (?) 45 piece girl
47 earnest money given as a deposit   48 qualities accomplishments   51 can
that can   53 bated reduced   53 doit smallest coin, worth half a farthing
56 presently immediately   57 raw inexperienced   58 entertainment manner of
reception

MARINA That I am pretty.

BAWD Come, the gods have done their part in you.

MARINA I accuse them not.

BAWD You are light into my hands, where you are
like to live.   75

MARINA The more my fault
To 'scape his hands where I was like to die.

BAWD Ay, and you shall live in pleasure.

MARINA No.

BAWD Yes, indeed shall you, and taste gentlemen of   80
all fashions. You shall fare well: you shall have the
difference of all complexions. What do you stop
your ears?

MARINA Are you a woman?

BAWD What would you have me be, and I be not a   85
woman?

MARINA An honest woman, or not a woman.

BAWD Marry, whip thee, gosling! I think I shall
have something to do with you. Come, you're a
young foolish sapling, and must be bowed as I   90
would have you.

MARINA The gods defend me!

BAWD If it please the gods to defend you by men,
then men must comfort you, men must feed you,
men stir you up. Boult's returned.   95

[*Enter Boult.*]

Now, sir, hast thou cried her through the market?

74 **are light** have fallen   82 **difference** variety   82 **complexions** colors of skin,
i.e., men of every race   82 **What** why   85 **and** if   87 **honest** chaste   88 **Marry**
(interjection expressing indignation)   88 **whip thee, gosling** hang thee, green-
horn   89 **have … you** have trouble with you   95 **stir you up** excite you
96 **cried** (1) advertised by loud cries (2) extolled

BOULT I have cried her almost to the number of her hairs; I have drawn her picture with my voice.

BAWD And I prithee tell me, how dost thou find the
100 inclination of the people, especially of the younger sort?

BOULT Faith, they listened to me as they would have hearkened to their father's testament. There was a Spaniard's mouth wat'red and he went to bed to
105 her very description.

BAWD We shall have him here tomorrow with his best ruff on.

BOULT Tonight, tonight. But, mistress, do you know the French knight that cowers i' the hams?

110 BAWD Who, Monsieur Veroles?

BOULT Ay, he: he offered to cut a caper at the proclamation; but he made a groan at it, and swore he would see her tomorrow.

BAWD Well, well; as for him, he brought his disease
115 hither. Here he does but repair it. I know he will come in our shadow, to scatter his crowns of the sun.

BOULT Well, if we had of every nation a traveler, we should lodge them with this sign.

120 BAWD [To Marina] Pray you, come hither awhile. You have fortunes coming upon you. Mark me: you must seem to do that fearfully which you commit willingly; despise profit where you have most gain. To weep that you live as ye do makes
125 pity in your lovers: seldom but that pity begets you a good opinion, and that opinion a mere profit.

97–98 almost ... hairs any number of times   104 and as if   110 Veroles (from French *vérole* = pox)   111 offered attempted   115 repair renew   116 shadow shelter   116–17 crowns of the sun French gold coins   119 this sign i.e., Marina's charms   126 mere downright

MARINA I understand you not.

BOULT O, take her home, mistress, take her home! These blushes of hers must be quenched with some 130 present practice.

BAWD Thou sayest true, i' faith, so they must. For your bride goes to that with shame which is her way to go with warrant.

BOULT Faith, some do, and some do not. But, mistress, 135 if I have bargained for the joint—

BAWD Thou mayest cut a morsel off the spit.

BOULT I may so?

BAWD Who should deny it? Come, young one, I like the manner of your garments well. 140

BOULT Ay, by my faith, they shall not be changed yet.

BAWD Boult, spend thou that in the town. Report what a sojourner we have: you'll lose nothing by custom. When nature framed this piece, she 145 meant thee a good turn. Therefore say what a paragon she is, and thou hast the harvest out of thine own report.

BOULT I warrant you, mistress, thunder shall not so awake the beds of eels as my giving out her 150 beauty stirs up the lewdly inclined. I'll bring home some tonight.

BAWD Come your ways! Follow me.

MARINA If fires be hot, knives sharp, or waters deep, Untied I still my virgin knot will keep. 155 Diana aid my purpose!

---

129 **take her home** tell her your mind (?) 131 **present** immediate 133–34 **which ... warrant** to which she is entitled to go 144–45 **by custom** i.e., by our getting customers 145 **framed** shaped 149–50 **thunder ... eels** (thunder was supposed to rouse eels from the mud)

BAWD What have we to do with Diana? Pray you,
will you go with us?   *Exit [with the rest].*

[Scene III. *Tharsus.*]

Enter Cleon and Dionyza.

DIONYZA Why are you foolish? Can it be undone?

CLEON O Dionyza, such a piece of slaughter
The sun and moon ne'er looked upon!

DIONYZA I think you'll turn a child again.

5 CLEON Were I chief lord of all this spacious world,
I'd give it to undo the deed. A lady
Much less in blood than virtue, yet a princess
To equal any single crown o' th' earth
I' th' justice of compare! O villain Leonine!
10 Whom thou hast pois'ned too.
If thou hadst drunk to him, 't had been a
kindness
Becoming well thy fact. What canst thou say
When noble Pericles shall demand his child?

DIONYZA That she is dead. Nurses are not the fates
. . . .

IV.iii.7 **Much ... virtue** even more so in point of virtue than of descent   9 **I' th'
justice of compare** in a just comparison   11 **If ... him** i.e., if thou hadst
poisoned thyself in pledging him   11 **a kindness** (1) a kind action (2) an
appropriate action   12 **Becoming** befitting   12 **fact** deed   14 **fates** (a line
seems to have dropped out here, to the effect that the nurse's power over human
life is merely "To foster it ...")

To foster it, not ever to preserve.   15
She died at night. I'll say so. Who can cross it?
Unless you play the pious innocent,
And for an honest attribute cry out
"She died by foul play."

CLEON   O, go to. Well, well.
Of all the faults beneath the heavens the gods   20
Do like this worst.

DIONYZA   Be one of those that thinks
The petty wrens of Tharsus will fly hence
And open this to Pericles. I do shame
To think of what a noble strain you are,
And of how coward a spirit.

CLEON   To such proceeding   25
Whoever but his approbation added,
Though not his prime consent, he did not flow
From honorable sources.

DIONYZA   Be it so, then.
Yet none does know but you how she came dead,
Nor none can know, Leonine being gone.   30
She did distain my child, and stood between
Her and her fortunes: none would look on her,
But cast their gazes on Marina's face;
Whilst ours was blurted at, and held a malkin,
Not worth the time of day. It pierced me thorough;   35
And though you call my course unnatural,
You not your child well loving, yet I find
It greets me as an enterprise of kindness
Performed to your sole daughter.

CLEON   Heavens forgive it!

DIONYZA And as for Pericles, what should he say?   40

16 cross contradict   18 an honest attribute the reputation of honesty   19 go to
(an expression of disapproval)   22–23 The petty ... Pericles (an allusion to the
popular belief in the revelation of hidden murders by a telltale bird)
27 prime initial   27 flow issue   31 distain cast a slur on   34 blurted at
treated with scorn   34 malkin slut   35 the time of day a greeting   38 greets
me presents itself to me   38 kindness love

We wept after her hearse, and yet we mourn.
Her monument
Is almost finished, and her epitaphs
In glitt'ring golden characters express
45   A general praise to her, and care in us
At whose expense 'tis done.

CLEON   Thou art like the harpy,
Which, to betray, dost, with thine angel's face,
Seize with thine eagle's talents.

DIONYZA Ye're like one that superstitiously
50   Do swear to th' gods that winter kills the flies.
But yet I know you'll do as I advise.   [*Exeunt.*]

[Scene IV. *Before Marina's monument at Tharsus.*

Enter Gower.]

GOWER Thus time we waste, and long leagues make
      short;
Sail seas in cockles, have and wish but for't;
Making, to take our imagination,
From bourn to bourn, region to region.
5   By you being pardoned, we commit no crime

---

42 **monument** (probably a few words, such as "which stands i' the market-place," have here dropped out)   44 **characters** letters   47–48 **dost ... talents** i.e., dost, while smiling at thy victim with thine angel's face, seize it with thine eagle's talents (a common variant of talons)   49–50 **Ye're ... flies** i.e., you are so much afraid of divine vengeance that you even swear to the gods that it is not you but winter which is guilty of the death of flies   IV.iv.1 **waste** annihilate   2 **cockles** cockleshells   2 **have ... for't** have by merely wishing for it   3 **Making** making our way   3 **take** captivate, delight   4 **bourn** frontier

To use one language in each several clime
Where our scene seems to live. I do beseech you
To learn of me, who stand i' th' gaps to teach you
The stages of our story. Pericles
Is now again thwarting the wayward seas,   10
Attended on by many a lord and knight,
To see his daughter, all his life's delight.
Old Helicanus goes along. Behind
Is left to govern it, you bear in mind,
Old Escanes, whom Helicanus late   15
Advanced in Tyre to great and high estate.
Well-sailing ships and bounteous winds have
    brought
This king to Tharsus—think his pilot thought;
So with his steerage shall your thoughts go on—
To fetch his daughter home, who first is gone.   20
Like motes and shadows see them move awhile.
Your ears unto your eyes I'll reconcile.

[*Dumb Show*]

*Enter Pericles at one door, with all his train; Cleon and
Dionyza at the other. Cleon shows Pericles the tomb;
whereat Pericles makes lamentation, puts on sackcloth,
and in a mighty passion departs. [Then Cleon, Dionyza,
and the rest go also.]*

See how belief may suffer by foul show!
This borrowed passion stands for true-owed woe.
And Pericles, in sorrow all devoured,   25
With sighs shot through and biggest tears
    o'ershowered,
Leaves Tharsus and again embarks. He swears
Never to wash his face, nor cut his hairs.
He puts on sackcloth, and to sea. He bears

---

7 **scene** dramatic performance   10 **thwarting** crossing   15 **late** recently
18 **think his pilot thought** think that his pilot is thought   19 **with his steerage**
with the course held by Pericles   20 **first** before him   23 **suffer by foul show**
be abused by hypocrisy   24 **borrowed passion** counterfeit grief   24 **true-owed**
sincerely owned

30 A tempest, which his mortal vessel tears,
    And yet he rides it out. Now please you wit
    The epitaph is for Marina writ
    By wicked Dionyza.

            [*Reads the inscription on Marina's monument.*]

    "The fairest, sweetest, and best lies here,
35 Who withered in her spring of year.
    She was of Tyrus the King's daughter,
    On whom foul death hath made this slaughter.
    Marina was she called; and at her birth
    Thetis, being proud, swallowed some part o' th'
        earth.
40 Therefore the earth, fearing to be o'erflowed,
    Hath Thetis' birth-child on the heavens
        bestowed;
    Wherefore she does—and swears she'll never
        stint—
    Make raging battery upon shores of flint."

    No visor does become black villainy
45 So well as soft and tender flattery.
    Let Pericles believe his daughter's dead,
    And bear his courses to be orderèd
    By Lady Fortune; while our scene must play
    His daughter's woe and heavy well-a-day
50 In her unholy service. Patience, then,
    And think you now are all in Mytilen.   *Exit.*

---

30 **vessel** i.e., his body   31 **he rides it out** i.e., he survives it   31 **wit** know
32 **is** that is   36 **of Tyrus the King's daughter** daughter of the King of Tyrus
39 **Thetis** a sea nymph (here, as commonly in Elizabethan literature, confused
with Tethys, wife of Oceanus, hence the sea personified)   41 **birth-child** person
born in a particular place   42 **she** i.e., the sea   44 **visor** mask, disguise   47 **bear**
... **orderèd** suffer his actions to be regulated   48 **scene** performance   49 **well-a-
day** grief

[Scene V. *Mytilene. A street before the brothel.*]

Enter, [from the brothel,] two Gentlemen.

FIRST GENTLEMAN Did you ever hear the like?

SECOND GENTLEMAN No, nor never shall do in such a
place as this, she being once gone.

FIRST GENTLEMAN But to have divinity preached there!
Did you ever dream of such a thing?   5

SECOND GENTLEMAN No, no. Come, I am for no more
bawdy houses. Shall's go hear the vestals sing?

FIRST GENTLEMAN I'll do anything now that is virtuous; but I am out of the road of rutting forever.
Exit [with the other].

[Scene VI. *Mytilene. A room in the brothel.*

Enter Pander, Bawd, and Boult.]

PANDER Well, I had rather than twice the worth of
her she had ne'er come here.

BAWD Fie, fie upon her! She's able to freeze the god

IV.v.7 **vestals** virgin priestesses   9 **rutting** fornication

Priapus, and undo a whole generation. We must
5   either get her ravished or be rid of her. When she
should do for clients her fitment and do me the
kindness of our profession, she has me her quirks,
her reasons, her master-reasons, her prayers, her
knees; that she would make a puritan of the devil,
10   if he should cheapen a kiss of her.

BOULT Faith, I must ravish her, or she'll disfurnish
us of all our cavalleria and make our swearers
priests.

PANDER Now, the pox upon her green-sickness for
15   me!

BAWD Faith, there's no way to be rid on't but by the
way to the pox. Here comes the Lord Lysimachus
disguised.

BOULT We should have both lord and lown, if the
20   peevish baggage would but give way to customers.

Enter Lysimachus.

LYSIMACHUS How now! How a dozen of virginities?

BAWD Now, the gods to-bless your Honor!

BOULT I am glad to see your Honor in good health.

LYSIMACHUS You may so; 'tis the better for you that
25   your resorters stand upon sound legs. How now,
wholesome iniquity, have you that a man may
deal withal and defy the surgeon?

BAWD We have here one, sir, if she would—but there
never came her like in Mytilene.

IV.vi.4 **Priapus** the classical god of fertility   6 **fitment** duty   6–7 **do me ...
has me** (the "ethical dative," frequently used in narrative by Shakespeare)
10 **cheapen** bargain for   11 **disfurnish** deprive   12 **cavalleria** body of gentlemen (Italian)   14 **green-sickness** squeamishness   14–15 **for me** say I   17 **pox**
syphilis   19 **lown** loon, lowborn fellow   21 **How** at what price   22 **to-bless**
bless entirely ("to" is an intensive prefix)   26 **wholesome** health-giving (used
ironically)   26 **that** that which   27 **deal withal** have sexual relations with

LYSIMACHUS If she'd do the deeds of darkness, thou   30
wouldst say.

BAWD Your Honor knows what 'tis to say well
enough.

LYSIMACHUS Well, call forth, call forth.

BOULT For flesh and blood, sir, white and red, you   35
shall see a rose; and she were a rose indeed, if
she had but—

LYSIMACHUS What, prithee?

BOULT O, sir, I can be modest.

LYSIMACHUS That dignifies the renown of a bawd no   40
less than it gives a good report to a punk to be
chaste.   [*Exit Boult.*]

BAWD Here comes that which grows to the stalk—
never plucked yet, I can assure you.

[*Enter Boult with Marina.*]

Is she not a fair creature?   45

LYSIMACHUS Faith, she would serve after a long voyage at sea. Well, there's for you. Leave us.

BAWD I beseech your Honor, give me leave: a word,
and I'll have done presently.

LYSIMACHUS I beseech you, do.   50

BAWD [*To Marina*] First, I would have you note, this
is an honorable man.

MARINA I desire to find him so, that I may worthily
note him.

BAWD Next, he's the governor of this country, and   55
a man whom I am bound to.

32 what 'tis to say how to express my meaning   41–42 it gives ... chaste to be
chaste gives a good reputation to a prostitute (the whole speech is ironic)
43 grows to is an integral part of   49 presently at once   54 note respect

MARINA If he govern the country, you are bound to him indeed; but how honorable he is in that I know not.

60 BAWD Pray you, without any more virginal fencing, will you use him kindly? He will line your apron with gold.

MARINA What he will do graciously, I will thankfully receive.

65 LYSIMACHUS Ha' you done?

BAWD My lord, she's not paced yet; you must take some pains to work her to your manage. Come, we will leave his Honor and her together. Go thy ways.   [Exeunt Bawd, Pander, and Boult.]

70 LYSIMACHUS Now, pretty one, how long have you been at this trade?

MARINA What trade, sir?

LYSIMACHUS Why, I cannot name't but I shall offend.

MARINA I cannot be offended with my trade. Please 75 you to name it.

LYSIMACHUS How long have you been of this profession?

MARINA E'er since I can remember.

LYSIMACHUS Did you go to't so young? Were you a 80 gamester at five or at seven?

MARINA Earlier too, sir, if now I be one.

LYSIMACHUS Why, the house you dwell in proclaims you to be a creature of sale.

MARINA Do you know this house to be a place of 85 such resort, and will come into't? I hear say you're

57 **bound** subject (another example of Marina's "quirks" of which the bawd complained)   66 **paced** taught her paces   67 **manage** action and paces to which a horse is trained   68–69 **Go thy ways** come along   79 **go to't** copulate
80 **gamester** one addicted to amorous sport

of honorable parts and are the governor of this
place.

LYSIMACHUS Why, hath your principal made known
unto you who I am?

MARINA Who is my principal?   90

LYSIMACHUS Why, your herb-woman; she that sets
seeds and roots of shame and iniquity. O, you have
heard something of my power, and so stand aloof
for more serious wooing. But I protest to thee,
pretty one, my authority shall not see thee, or else   95
look friendly upon thee. Come, bring me to some
private place. Come, come.

MARINA If you were born to honor, show it now;
If put upon you, make the judgment good
That thought you worthy of it.   100

LYSIMACHUS How's this? How's this? Some more;
    be sage.

MARINA   For me,
That am a maid, though most ungentle fortune
Have placed me in this sty, where, since I came,
Diseases have been sold dearer than physic—
That the gods   105
Would set me free from this unhallowed place,
Though they did change me to the meanest bird
That flies i' th' purer air!

LYSIMACHUS   I did not think
Thou couldst have spoke so well; ne'er dreamt thou
    couldst.
Had I brought hither a corrupted mind,   110
Thy speech had altered it. Hold, here's gold for
    thee:
Persever in that clear way thou goest,
And the gods strengthen thee!

MARINA   The good gods preserve you!

88 **principal** employer 99 **If put upon you** if honor was bestowed upon you
112 **clear** free from blame

LYSIMACHUS For me, be you thoughten
115   That I came with no ill intent; for to me
        The very doors and windows savor vilely.
        Fare thee well. Thou art a piece of virtue, and
        I doubt not but thy training hath been noble.
        Hold, here's more gold for thee.
120   A curse upon him, die he like a thief,
        That robs thee of thy goodness! If thou dost
        Hear from me, it shall be for thy good.

                        [*Enter Boult.*]

BOULT I beseech your Honor, one piece for me.

LYSIMACHUS Avaunt, thou damned doorkeeper!
125   Your house, but for this virgin that doth prop it,
        Would sink, and overwhelm you. Away!   [*Exit.*]

BOULT How's this? We must take another course with
you. If your peevish chastity, which is not worth
a breakfast in the cheapest country under the
130   cope, shall undo a whole household, let me be
gelded like a spaniel. Come your ways.

MARINA Whither would you have me?

BOULT I must have your maidenhead taken off, or
the common hangman shall execute it. Come your
135   ways. We'll have no more gentlemen driven away.
Come your ways, I say.

                        Enter Bawd.

BAWD How now! What's the matter?

BOULT Worse and worse, mistress: she has here spoken
holy words to the Lord Lysimachus.

140 BAWD O abominable!

---

114 **For me, be you thoughten** (this line, like much else in this scene, is
undoubtedly corrupt, but the true reading seems irrecoverable) 116 **savor**
smell 124 **Avaunt** be off 124 **doorkeeper** pander 128 **peevish** refractory
130 **cope** sky 133–34 **or the ... execute it** (with a play on the "head" of
"maidenhead")

BOULT She makes our profession as it were to stink
    afore the face of the gods.

BAWD Marry, hang her up forever!

BOULT The nobleman would have dealt with her like
    a nobleman, and she sent him away as cold as a   145
    snowball; saying his prayers too.

BAWD Boult, take her away! Use her at thy pleasure.
    Crack the glass of her virginity, and make the rest
    malleable.

BOULT And if she were a thornier piece of ground   150
    than she is, she shall be ploughed.

MARINA Hark, hark, you gods!

BAWD She conjures! Away with her! Would she
    had never come within my doors! Marry, hang
    you! She's born to undo us. Will you not go the   155
    way of womenkind? Marry come up, my dish of
    chastity with rosemary and bays!   [Exit.]

BOULT Come, mistress; come your ways with me.

MARINA Whither wilt thou have me?

BOULT To take from you the jewel you hold so dear.   160

MARINA Prithee, tell me one thing first.

BOULT Come now, your one thing.

MARINA What canst thou wish thine enemy to be?

BOULT Why, I could wish him to be my master, or,
    rather, my mistress.   165

MARINA Neither of these are so bad as thou art,
    Since they do better thee in their command.
    Thou hold'st a place for which the pained'st fiend

150 **And if** even if   153 **conjures** invokes supernatural aid (with the suggestion of
black magic)   156 **Marry come up** (an expression of contempt akin to our
"hoity-toity")   156–57 **dish ... bays** (a gibe at Marina's ostentatious virtue;
dishes at Christmas were thus garnished)   167 **do better ... command** are
superior to you through their position of authority   168 **pained'st** most tormented

Of hell would not in reputation change.
170 Thou art the damnèd doorkeeper to every
Coistrel that comes inquiring for his Tib;
To the choleric fisting of every rogue
Thy ear is liable; thy food is such
As hath been belched on by infected lungs.

175 BOULT What would you have me do? Go to the wars,
would you? Where a man may serve seven years
for the loss of a leg, and have not money enough
in the end to buy him a wooden one?

MARINA Do any thing but this thou doest. Empty
180 Old receptacles, or common shores, of filth;
Serve by indenture to the common hangman.
Any of these ways are yet better than this.
For what thou professest a baboon, could he
speak,
Would own a name too dear. That the gods
185 Would safely deliver me from this place!
Here, here's gold for thee.
If that thy master would gain by me,
Proclaim that I can sing, weave, sew, and dance,
With other virtues which I'll keep from boast;
190 And I will undertake all these to teach.
I doubt not but this populous city will
Yield many scholars.

BOULT But can you teach all this you speak of?

MARINA Prove that I cannot, take me home again,
195 And prostitute me to the basest groom
That doth frequent your house.

BOULT Well, I will see what I can do for thee. If I
can place thee, I will.

171 **Coistrel** base fellow   171 **Tib** strumpet   172 **fisting** punching   179 **doest**
(pronounced as a disyllable)   180 **receptacles** (the stress here falls on the first
syllable)   180 **common shores** i.e., the no-man's-land by the sea, where filth was
allowed to be deposited for the tide to wash away   181 **by indenture** i.e., as
apprentice   183 **thou professest** you have as an occupation   184 **Would ...
dear** would claim to possess too high a reputation   189 **virtues** accomplishments
195 **groom** menial

MARINA But amongst honest women?

BOULT Faith, my acquaintance lies little amongst them.   200
    But since my master and mistress hath bought you,
    there's no going but by their consent. Therefore
    I will make them acquainted with your purpose,
    and I doubt not but I shall find them tractable
    enough. Come, I'll do for thee what I can; come   205
    your ways.   *Exeunt*.

203 **purpose** proposition

[ACT V]

Enter Gower.

GOWER Marina thus the brothel 'scapes, and chances
    Into an honest house, our story says.
    She sings like one immortal, and she dances
    As goddesslike to her admired lays;
    Deep clerks she dumbs, and with her neele
5   composes
    Nature's own shape of bud, bird, branch, or berry,
    That even her art sisters the natural roses;
    Her inkle, silk, twin with the rubied cherry;
    That pupils lacks she none of noble race,
10   Who pour their bounty on her; and her gain
    She gives the cursèd bawd. Here we her place;
    And to her father turn our thoughts again,
    Where we left him on the sea. We there him lost;
    Whence, driven before the winds, he is arrived
15   Here where his daughter dwells; and on this coast
    Suppose him now at anchor. The city's hived

V.5 **Deep clerks** men of profound learning   5 **neele** needle   7 **sisters** is exactly
like   8 **inkle** linen thread   16 **The city's hived** i.e., the citizens are gathered like
bees in a hive

God Neptune's annual feast to keep; from whence
Lysimachus our Tyrian ship espies,
His banners sable, trimmed with rich expense;
And to him in his barge with fervor hies.   20
In your supposing once more put your sight:
Of heavy Pericles think this his bark;
Where what is done in action, more, if might,
Shall be discovered. Please you, sit and hark.

Exit.

[Scene I. *On board Pericles' ship, off Mytilene.*
A pavilion on deck, with a curtain before it;
Pericles within, unkempt and clad in sackcloth,
reclining on a couch.]

Enter Helicanus, to him two Sailors, [one be-
longing to the Tyrian vessel, the other of
Mytilene.]

TYRIAN SAILOR Where is Lord Helicanus?
He can resolve you. O, here he is.
Sir, there is a barge put off from Mytilene,
And in it is Lysimachus, the Governor,
Who craves to come aboard. What is your will?   5

HELICANUS That he have his. Call up some gentlemen.

TYRIAN SAILOR Ho, gentlemen! my lord calls.

19-20 **His ... him** its ... it   21 **In your supposing** under the guidance of your
imagination   22 **heavy** sorrowful   23 **more, if might** and more if it were
possible   24 **discovered** disclosed   V.i.2 **resolve** free from uncertainty

Enter two or three Gentlemen.

FIRST GENTLEMAN Doth your lordship call?

HELICANUS Gentlemen, there is some of worth would
    come aboard.

10   I pray, greet him fairly.   *[Exeunt the Gentlemen.]*

*Enter Lysimachus [and Lords, with the
Gentlemen].*

MYTILENIAN SAILOR *[To Lysimachus]* Sir,
    This is the man that can, in aught you would,
    Resolve you.

LYSIMACHUS Hail, reverend sir! The gods preserve
    you!

15 HELICANUS And you, sir, to outlive the age I am,
    And die as I would do.

LYSIMACHUS   You wish me well.
    Being on shore, honoring of Neptune's triumphs,
    Seeing this goodly vessel ride before us,
    I made to it, to know of whence you are.

HELICANUS First, what is your place?

20 LYSIMACHUS   I am the Governor of
    This place you lie before.

HELICANUS Sir,
    Our vessel is of Tyre, in it the King;
    A man who for this three months hath not spoken
25   To anyone, nor taken sustenance
    But to prorogue his grief.

LYSIMACHUS Upon what ground is his distempera-
    ture?

HELICANUS 'Twould be too tedious to repeat;
    But the main grief springs from the loss
30   Of a belovèd daughter and a wife.

9 **some** someone 10 **fairly** courteously 17 **triumphs** festivities 20 **place**
official position 26 **prorogue** prolong 27 **distemperature** mental disturbance

LYSIMACHUS May we not see him?

HELICANUS You may;
   But bootless is your sight; he will not speak
   To any.

LYSIMACHUS   Yet let me obtain my wish.

HELICANUS [*Draws back the curtain*] Behold him. This
      was a goodly person   35
   Till the disaster that, one mortal night,
   Drove him to this.

LYSIMACHUS Sir King, all hail! The gods preserve
      you!
   Hail, royal sir!

HELICANUS It is in vain; he will not speak to you.   40

LORD Sir,
   We have a maid in Mytilene, I durst wager,
   Would win some words of him.

LYSIMACHUS   'Tis well bethought.
   She questionless, with her sweet harmony,
   And other chosen attractions, would allure,   45
   And make a batt'ry through his deafened ports,
   Which now are midway stopped.
   She is all happy as the fairest of all,
   And with her fellow maid is now upon
   The leafy shelter that abuts against   50
   The island's side.
                  [*He whispers to a Lord, who leaves*.]

HELICANUS Sure, all effectless; yet nothing we'll omit
   That bears recovery's name. But since your kindness
   We have stretched thus far, let us beseech you
   That for our gold we may provision have,   55
   Wherein we are not destitute for want,
   But weary for the staleness.

33 **bootless** unavailing   36 **mortal** fatal   45 **chosen** choice   46 **ports** inlets
52 **all** entirely

LYSIMACHUS   O sir, a courtesy
    Which if we should deny, the most just God
    For every graff would send a caterpillar,
60   And so inflict our province. Yet once more
    Let me entreat to know at large the cause
    Of your king's sorrow.

HELICANUS Sit, sir, I will recount it to you.
    But see, I am prevented.

    [*Enter Lord with Marina and another girl.*]

65   LYSIMACHUS O, here's the lady that I sent for.
    Welcome, fair one! Is't not a goodly presence?

HELICANUS She's a gallant lady.

LYSIMACHUS She's such a one that, were I well
        assured
    Came of a gentle kind and noble stock,
    I'd wish no better choice, and think me rarely
70   wed.
    [*To Marina*] Fair one, all goodness that consists
        in bounty
    Expect even here, where is a kingly patient.
    If that thy prosperous and artificial feat
    Can draw him but to answer thee in aught,
75   Thy sacred physic shall receive such pay
    As thy desires can wish.

MARINA   Sir, I will use
    My utmost skill in his recovery,
    Provided
    That none but I and my companion maid
    Be suffered to come near him.

80   LYSIMACHUS   Come, let us leave her;
    And the gods make her prosperous!

59 **graff** graft, grafted plant 60 **inflict** afflict 61 **at large** in full 64 **prevented** forestalled 66 **presence** person 67 **gallant** excellent 69 **Came** she came 69 **kind** family 70 **rarely** splendidly 71 **goodness that consists in** good things that inhere in 73 **prosperous** successful 73 **artificial** skillful

[They withdraw. Marina sings.]

LYSIMACHUS Marked he your music?

MARINA   No, nor looked on us.

LYSIMACHUS See, she will speak to him.

MARINA Hail, sir! My lord, lend ear.

PERICLES Hum, ha!   [*He pushes her back.*] 85

MARINA I am a maid,
  My lord, that ne'er before invited eyes,
  But have been gazed on like a comet. She speaks,
  My lord, that, may be, hath endured a grief
  Might equal yours, if both were justly weighed. 90
  Though wayward fortune did malign my state,
  My derivation was from ancestors
  Who stood equivalent with mighty kings:
  But time hath rooted out my parentage,
  And to the world and awkward casualties 95
  Bound me in servitude. [*Aside*] I will desist.
  But there is something glows upon my cheek,
  And whispers in mine ear "Go not till he speak."

PERICLES My fortunes—parentage—good parentage—
  To equal mine—was it not thus? What say you? 100

MARINA I said, my lord, if you did know my
    parentage,
  You would not do me violence.

PERICLES   I do think so.
  Pray you, turn your eyes upon me.
  You're like something that—what countrywoman?
  Here of these shores?

MARINA   No, nor of any shores. 105
  Yet I was mortally brought forth, and am
  No other than I appear.

---

87 **invited eyes** i.e., invited anyone to look at her   91 **malign** treat malignantly
95 **awkward casualties** adverse chances   104 **what countrywoman?** of what
country?   106 **mortally** humanly

PERICLES I am great with woe, and shall deliver
    weeping.
My dearest wife was like this maid, and such
My daughter might have been: my queen's square
110   brows;
Her stature to an inch; as wandlike straight;
As silver-voiced; her eyes as jewel-like
And cased as richly; in pace another Juno;
Who starves the ears she feeds, and makes them
    hungry
The more she gives them speech. Where do you
115   live?

MARINA Where I am but a stranger: from the deck
You may discern the place.

PERICLES   Where were you bred?
And how achieved you these endowments, which
You make more rich to owe?

120 MARINA If I
Should tell my history, it would seem like lies
Disdained in the reporting.

PERICLES   Prithee, speak.
Falseness cannot come from thee; for thou lookest
Modest as Justice, and thou seemest a palace
For the crowned Truth to dwell in. I will believe
125   thee,
And make my senses credit thy relation
To points that seem impossible; for thou lookest
Like one I loved indeed. What were thy friends?
Didst thou not say when I did push thee back—
Which was when I perceived thee—that thou
130   cam'st
From good descending?

MARINA   So indeed I did.

---

108 **great** pregnant   108 **deliver** give birth to   113 **cased** encased   113 **pace** gait
119 **to owe** by owning them   122 **in the reporting** in the very act of utterance
128 **friends** relations   131 **descending** lineage

PERICLES Report thy parentage. I think thou said'st
  Thou hadst been tossed from wrong to injury,
  And that thou thought'st thy griefs might equal
      mine,
  If both were opened.

MARINA   Some such thing I said,   135
  And said no more but what my thoughts
  Did warrant me was likely.

PERICLES   Tell thy story.
  If thine, considered, prove the thousandth part
  Of my endurance, thou art a man, and I
  Have suffered like a girl; yet thou dost look   140
  Like Patience gazing on kings' graves, and smiling
  Extremity out of act. What were thy friends?
  How lost thou them? Thy name, my most kind
      virgin?
  Recount, I do beseech thee: come, sit by me.

MARINA My name is Marina.

PERICLES   O, I am mocked,   145
  And thou by some incensèd god sent hither
  To make the world to laugh at me.

MARINA   Patience, good sir,
  Or here I'll cease.

PERICLES   Nay, I'll be patient.
  Thou little know'st how thou dost startle me
  To call thyself Marina.

MARINA   The name   150
  Was given me by one that had some power:
  My father, and a king.

PERICLES   How, a king's daughter?
  And called Marina?

MARINA   You said you would believe me;

135 **opened** disclosed   139 **my endurance** what I have endured   142 **Extremity out of act** extreme calamity out of striking (?) extreme despair out of committing suicide (?)   142 **friends** relations

But, not to be a troubler of your peace,
I will end here.

155 PERICLES   But are you flesh and blood?
Have you a working pulse, and are no fairy?
Motion as well? Speak on. Where were you born?
And wherefore called Marina?

MARINA   Called Marina
For I was born at sea.

PERICLES   At sea! What mother?

160 MARINA My mother was the daughter of a king;
Who died the minute I was born,
As my good nurse Lychorida hath oft
Delivered weeping.

PERICLES   O, stop there a little!
This is the rarest dream that e'er dulled sleep
165 Did mock sad fools withal. This cannot be:
My daughter's buried. Well, where were you bred?
I'll hear you more, to th' bottom of your story,
And never interrupt you.

MARINA You scorn. Believe me, 'twere best I did give
     o'er.

170 PERICLES I will believe you by the syllable
Of what you shall deliver. Yet, give me leave:
How came you in these parts? Where were you
     bred?

MARINA The King my father did in Tharsus leave me;
Till cruel Cleon, with his wicked wife,
175 Did seek to murder me;
And having wooed a villain to attempt it,
Who having drawn to do't,
A crew of pirates came and rescued me;
Brought me to Mytilene. But, good sir,

157 **Motion** i.e., the movement of the blood and spirits through the body
163 **Delivered** reported   165 **withal** with   179 **Mytilene** (the final syllable is here sounded)

Whither will you have me? Why do you weep? It
    may be   180
You think me an impostor: no, good faith!
I am the daughter to King Pericles,
If good King Pericles be.

PERICLES   Ho, Helicanus!

HELICANUS Calls my lord?

PERICLES Thou art a grave and noble counselor,   185
    Most wise in general. Tell me, if thou canst,
    What this maid is, or what is like to be,
    That thus hath made me weep?

HELICANUS   I know not;
    But here's the regent, sir, of Mytilene
    Speaks nobly of her.

LYSIMACHUS   She never would tell   190
    Her parentage; being demanded that,
    She would sit still and weep.

PERICLES O Helicanus, strike me, honored sir!
    Give me a gash, put me to present pain;
    Lest this great sea of joys rushing upon me   195
    O'erbear the shores of my mortality,
    And drown me with their sweetness. O, come
      hither,
    Thou that beget'st him that did thee beget;
    Thou that wast born at sea, buried at Tharsus,
    And found at sea again! O Helicanus,   200
    Down on thy knees; thank the holy gods as loud
    As thunder threatens us: this is Marina!
    What was thy mother's name? Tell me but that,
    For truth can never be confirmed enough,
    Though doubts did ever sleep.

MARINA   First, sir, I pray,   205
    What is your title?

---

183 **be** i.e., be alive   187 **like** likely   190 **Speaks** that speaks   192 **still** always
196 **O'erbear** overwhelm   198 **beget'st** i.e., gives new life to

PERICLES I am Pericles of Tyre: but tell me now
　　　My drowned queen's name, as in the rest you said
　　　Thou hast been godlike perfect, and thou art
210　　The heir of kingdoms and another life
　　　To Pericles, thy father.

MARINA [*Kneels*] Is it no more to be your daughter than
　　　To say my mother's name was Thaisa?
　　　Thaisa was my mother, who did end
215　　The minute I began.

PERICLES Now blessing on thee! Rise; thou art my child.
　　　Give me fresh garments. [*To Marina*] Mine own! Helicanus,
　　　She is not dead at Tharsus, as she should have been
　　　By savage Cleon. She shall tell thee all;
220　　When thou shalt kneel, and justify in knowledge
　　　She is thy very princess. Who is this?

HELICANUS Sir, 'tis the Governor of Mytilene,
　　　Who, hearing of your melancholy state,
　　　Did come to see you.

PERICLES　　　　　　　　I embrace you.
225　　Give me my robes. I am wild in my beholding.
　　　O heavens bless my girl! [*Music*.] But hark, what music?
　　　Tell Helicanus, my Marina, tell him
　　　O'er, point by point, for yet he seems to doubt,
　　　How sure you are my daughter. But what music?

230 HELICANUS My lord, I hear none.

PERICLES None?
　　　The music of the spheres! List, my Marina.

---

209 **and thou art** (these words are missing in the text) 218 **should have been** was said to be 219 **By** at the hands of 220 **justify in knowledge** affirm in recognition of her claim 225 **beholding** appearance, looks (?)

LYSIMACHUS It is not good to cross him; give him
    way.

PERICLES Rarest sounds! Do ye not hear?

LYSIMACHUS   Music, my lord?

PERICLES I hear most heavenly music.   235
    It nips me unto list'ning, and thick slumber
    Hangs upon mine eyes. Let me rest.   [*He sleeps.*]

LYSIMACHUS A pillow for his head. So leave him all.
    Well, my companion friends,
    If this but answer to my just belief,   240
    I'll well remember you.   [*Exeunt all but Pericles.*]

      Diana [*appears to Pericles in a vision*].

DIANA My temple stands in Ephesus. Hie thee thither,
    And do upon mine altar sacrifice.
    There, when my maiden priests are met together,
    Before the people all,   245
    Reveal how thou at sea didst lose thy wife.
    To mourn thy crosses, with thy daughter's, call,
    And give them repetition to the life.
    Perform my bidding, or thou livest in woe;
    Do't, and happy, by my silver bow!   250
    Awake, and tell thy dream.   [*She vanishes.*]

PERICLES Celestial Dian, goddess argentine,
    I will obey thee. Helicanus!

    [*Enter Helicanus, Lysimachus, and Marina.*]

HELICANUS   Sir?

PERICLES My purpose was for Tharsus, there to strike
    The inhospitable Cleon; but I am   255
    For other service first: toward Ephesus

---

236 **nips me unto** compels me to   240–41 **If this ... you** i.e., if Marina is really
a princess (and therefore a fit match for me) I shall well reward you (?) (lines 239–
41 read like the reporter's addition and ought, probably, to be omitted)
247 **crosses** misfortunes   248 **repetition to the life** lifelike recital   250 **happy**
i.e., thou livest happy   252 **argentine** silvery

Turn our blown sails; eftsoons I'll tell thee why.
[*To Lysimachus*] Shall we refresh us, sir, upon your
    shore,
And give you gold for such provision as
260   Our intents will need?

LYSIMACHUS Sir,
With all my heart; and when you come ashore
I have another suit.

PERICLES   You shall prevail,
Were it to woo my daughter; for it seems
265   You have been noble towards her.

LYSIMACHUS Sir, lend me your arm.

PERICLES   Come, my Marina.
                                        Exeunt.

[Scene II. *The temple of Diana at Ephesus;
Thaisa and several maidens standing near the
altar, all appareled as priestesses; Cerimon and
other inhabitants of Ephesus attending.*

Enter Gower.]

GOWER Now our sands are almost run;
More a little, and then dumb.
This, my last boon, give me—
For such kindness must relieve me—
5   That you aptly will suppose

257 **blown** inflated by the wind   257 **eftsoons** afterwards, shortly   260 **intents**
purposes   V.ii.5 **aptly** readily

What pageantry, what feats, what shows,
What minstrelsy and pretty din,
The regent made in Mytilin
To greet the King. So he thrived
That he is promised to be wived   10
To fair Marina; but in no wise
Till he had done his sacrifice,
As Dian bade: whereto being bound,
The interim, pray you, all confound.
In feathered briefness sails are filled,   15
And wishes fall out as they're willed.
At Ephesus the temple see
Our king and all his company.
That he can hither come so soon
Is by your fancies' thankful doom.   20

                                                          [*Exit.*]

[Scene III. *The temple of Diana. Enter Pericles,
    with Lysimachus, Helicanus, and Marina.*]

PERICLES Hail, Dian! To perform thy just command,
    I here confess myself the King of Tyre;
    Who, frighted from my country, did wed
    At Pentapolis the fair Thaisa.

---

7 **pretty** pleasing   12 **he** i.e., Pericles, whereas in lines 9–10 Lysimachus is
referred to   13 **bound** on his way   14 **all confound** entirely consume   15 **In
feathered briefness** with winged speed   17 **Ephesus the temple** the temple of
Ephesus   20 **your fancies' thankful doom** the thanks-deserving verdict of your
imaginations

5   At sea in childbed died she, but brought forth
       A maid–child called Marina; who, O goddess,
       Wears yet thy silver livery. She at Tharsus
       Was nursed with Cleon; whom at fourteen years
       He sought to murder; but her better stars
10   Brought her to Mytilene; 'gainst whose shore
       Riding, her fortunes brought the maid aboard us,
       Where, by her own most clear remembrance, she
       Made known herself my daughter.

THAISA   Voice and favor!
       You are, you are—O royal Pericles!   [Swoons.]

PERICLES What means the nun? She dies! Help,
15   gentlemen!

CERIMON Noble sir,
       If you have told Diana's altar true,
       This is your wife.

PERICLES   Reverend appearer, no.
       I threw her overboard with these very arms.

CERIMON Upon this coast, I warrant you.

20 PERICLES   'Tis most certain.

CERIMON Look to the lady. O, she's but overjoyed.
       Early one blustering morn this lady
       Was thrown upon this shore. I oped the coffin,
       Found there rich jewels; recovered her, and placed
          her
       Here in Diana's temple.

25 PERICLES   May we see them?

CERIMON Great sir, they shall be brought you to my
          house,
       Whither I invite you. Look, Thaisa is
       Recoverèd.

V.iii.7 **Wears yet thy silver livery** i.e., is still a virgin   8 **with Cleon** in Cleon's
family   11 **Riding** as we rode at anchor   13 **favor** looks, face   17 **true** the truth
18 **appearer** one who appears   24 **recovered her** restored her to consciousness

THAISA   O, let me look!
If he be none of mine, my sanctity
Will to my sense bend no licentious ear,   30
But curb it, spite of seeing. O, my lord,
Are you not Pericles? Like him you spake,
Like him you are. Did you not name a tempest,
A birth and death?

PERICLES   The voice of dead Thaisa!

THAISA That Thaisa am I, supposèd dead and
          drowned.   35

PERICLES Immortal Dian!

THAISA   Now I know you better.
When we with tears parted Pentapolis,
The King my father gave you such a ring.
                                        [*Points to his ring.*]

PERICLES This, this! No more. You gods, your
          present kindness
Makes my past miseries sports. You shall do well   40
That on the touching of her lips I may
Melt and no more be seen. O come, be buried
A second time within these arms.

MARINA   My heart
Leaps to be gone into my mother's bosom.
                                        [*Kneels to Thaisa.*]

PERICLES Look who kneels here: flesh of thy flesh,
          Thaisa;   45
Thy burden at the sea, and called Marina,
For she was yielded there.

29-30 **If he ... licentious ear** if he is not my husband, my holiness will not listen
licentiously to my desire   37 **parted** departed from   39 **No more** i.e., no more
confirmation is needed that you are Thaisa (alternatively one could punctuate "No
more, you gods!" and interpret: give me no greater happiness, you gods!)
40-41 **You shall do well/That** you would do well if   47 **yielded** brought forth

THAISA   Blest, and mine own!

HELICANUS Hail, madam, and my queen!

THAISA   I know you not.

PERICLES You have heard me say, when I did fly from
      Tyre
50   I left behind an ancient substitute.
      Can you remember what I called the man?
      I have named him oft.

THAISA   'Twas Helicanus then.

PERICLES Still confirmation.
      Embrace him, dear Thaisa; this is he.
55   Now do I long to hear how you were found;
      How possibly preserved; and who to thank,
      Besides the gods, for this great miracle.

THAISA Lord Cerimon, my lord: this man,
      Through whom the gods have shown their power;
          that can
      From first to last resolve you.

60   PERICLES   Reverend sir,
      The gods can have no mortal officer
      More like a god than you. Will you deliver
      How this dead queen re-lives?

CERIMON   I will, my lord.
      Beseech you first, go with me to my house,
65   Where shall be shown you all was found with her;
      How she came placed here in the temple;
      No needful thing omitted.

PERICLES   Pure Dian,
      I bless thee for thy vision, and will offer
      Nightly oblations to thee. Thaisa,
70   This Prince, the fair betrothèd of your daughter,
      Shall marry her at Pentapolis. And now,
      This ornament

60 **resolve you** free you from doubt   62 **deliver** relate

Makes me look dismal will I clip to form;
And what this fourteen years no razor touched,
To grace thy marriage-day I'll beautify.   75

THAISA Lord Cerimon hath letters of good credit,
　　sir,
My father's dead.

PERICLES Heavens make a star of him! Yet there, my
　　queen,
We'll celebrate their nuptials, and ourselves
Will in that kingdom spend our following days.   80
Our son and daughter shall in Tyrus reign.
Lord Cerimon, we do our longing stay
To hear the rest untold. Sir, lead's the way.

　　　　　　　　　　　　　　　　[_Exeunt._]

[_Enter_] _Gower._

[GOWER] In Antiochus and his daughter you have
　　heard
Of monstrous lust the due and just reward.   85
In Pericles, his queen and daughter, seen,
Although assailed with fortune fierce and keen,
Virtue preserved from fell destruction's blast,
Led on by heaven, and crowned with joy at last.
In Helicanus may you well descry   90
A figure of truth, of faith, of loyalty.
In reverent Cerimon there well appears
The worth that learnèd charity aye wears.
For wicked Cleon and his wife, when fame
Had spread his cursèd deed, the honored name   95
Of Pericles to rage the city turn,
That him and his they in his palace burn;
The gods for murder seemèd so content

---

73 **Makes** which makes　73 **form** proper shape　76 **credit** trustworthiness
82 **stay** delay　83 **untold** i.e., that is yet untold　88 **blast** blowing up (?) stroke
of lightning (?) blight (?)　94 **fame** report　94–96 **when fame ... city turn** i.e.,
holding Pericles' name in such honor, the citizens are enraged by the report of the
murder of his child　97 **his** i.e., his family

To punish them, although not done but meant.
100   So, on your patience evermore attending,
New joy wait on you! Here our play has ending.

[Exit.]

FINIS

---

99 **although not done but meant** although the murder was not carried out but merely intended

Textual Note

The booke of Pericles Prynce of Tyre (i.e., presumably, the promptbook) was entered, together with *Antony and Cleopatra*, in the Stationers' Register on May 20, 1608. Both plays were entered to Edward Blount, and, as neither of them was published by him, it has been supposed that these were "blocking entries," designed to prevent piracy. If so, this proved unsuccessful in the case of *Pericles*, for what is certainly a pirated version of the play was brought out in 1609 by another publisher, Henry Gosson. It proved so popular that a second quarto edition of the play was published by him in the same year, a third appeared in 1611, a fourth in 1619, a fifth in 1630, and a sixth in 1635 (Q2–Q6). As all of these are merely reprints of each other, they have no independent textual authority. *Pericles* was not included in the first collected edition of Shakespeare's plays, the First Folio of 1623, and was not added to any collected edition until the second impression of the Third Folio, in 1664, where it was reprinted from Q6. Varying explanations of the reason for the play's exclusion from the First Folio have been put forward: copyright difficulties; the absence of a good text available to the editors; the fact that the play is only partly Shakespeare's. The last would seem the most probable reason, and is only weakened by the inclusion in the Folio of *Henry VIII*.

The only authoritative text of *Pericles* is therefore that of the first Quarto of 1609 (Q). It is unfortunately a very poor text, as the list below of some hundred and eight corrupt readings makes immediately apparent. At least some twenty of these would seem to be auditory errors, due to a mishearing by the reporter of the words spoken on the stage (apparent instances of this are found at I.i.114; I.ii.86; II.ii.30; IV Chorus 26; IV.iv.24; V.i. 228). Most scholars are agreed that the text derives from a report of the play as performed by Shakespeare's company. It is the degree of badness of the report about which they are divided. Some would group it with the "bad" Quartos, such as those of *Romeo and Juliet* and *Hamlet*; others insist that, in spite of numerous corruptions, many of them due to the compositors, the text is basically a good one. My own view is that the Quarto of *Pericles* stands somewhere between the good and the bad Quartos: too faithful to its original to be classed as a "bad" Quarto; too full of errors (both graphic and auditory), of omissions, and additions, to be accounted a good one.

Next to the errors due to mishearing, the reporter seems responsible for a variety of other deficiencies in the text:

1) In the Shakespearian part, after—for the most part impeccably—setting out the verse of III.i, he apparently found the task too demanding, and wrote out the remaining blank verse as prose; and that is how most of it was set by the compositors. 2) He occasionally seems to have added words, or even whole lines, that can scarcely have been in the Shakespearian original (e.g. V.i.240–1). 3) There are two scenes in the play in which an evident gap in the report is to be found: in I.ii, where some dialogue between Pericles and Helicanus is evidently missing (before line 38. See gloss on lines 38–48); and in IV.vi, where some dialogue between Marina and Lysimachus appears to have been lost (after line 109). In the first case the reporter seems to have made little attempt to fill the gap; in the second case he apparently tried to fill it by reconstructing the missing lines from memory—a memory which must have been exceedingly dim.

But apart from this instance, there is no indication in the text that—as in all the "bad" Quartos proper—the report was a memorial reconstruction. On the contrary— at least in the Shakespearian part—the report must have been made at the theater, probably during repeated visits to performances of the play. Long scenes such as III.i and V.i, in which the text has every appearance of adhering faithfully to the Shakespearian original, cannot have been reported from memory.[1] In the non-Shakespearian

1 I do not share Philip Edwards' pessimistic view that "we have in these later acts

part it is much more difficult to be sure of this, and there are some grounds for supposing that its fidelity to the original text is not as great (notably in II.i).

The majority of the corrupt readings in Q seem, in fact, to have been introduced not by the reporter but by the compositors (Philip Edwards has shown them to have been three in number), who were uniformly slovenly and careless at their task (except in II.v, which seems to be free from compositorial errors). They misread words, misassigned speeches, occasionally omitted speech prefixes, sometimes set prose as verse, and made only sporadic—and then quite inept—attempts to reestablish Shakespeare's blank verse division. The occasional omission of words within a line (as at I.iv.13), or of a whole line (as, apparently, after line 14 in IV.iii and probably after line 122 in I.ii), would also seem to be attributable to them rather than to the reporter.

The text of this edition diverges on a number of points from preceding ones: 1) Where the Quarto text is manifestly corrupt and we are left with nonsense, I have not hesitated to emend, even when we cannot be sure that the chosen emendation is necessarily the right one and when previous modern editors have retained the original reading. Instances of this are found at I.iv.13; III.ii.84–87; IV.i.11; and V.i.209. On the other hand, Q readings have, on a very few occasions, been retained where previous editors have emended, e.g. at III.i.67, where editors have unnecessarily emended Q's "coffin" to "coffer," since the two words were used interchangeably in Shakespeare's day.

2) Like other editors, I have for the most part followed Malone's relineation of Shakespeare's blank verse in the passages where it was set as prose. But occasionally, where better and more Shakespearian verse seemed to result, I have introduced line divisions not found in previous editions, e.g., at III.iii.9–15; IV.i.27–30; V.i.20–21.

only the *disjecta membra* of once powerful verse," that "we lose sight, presumably forever, of the genuine version of the last three acts, from the opening of III.ii." (*Shakespeare Survey 5*, 1952, 38.)

3) Sometimes I have departed from the punctuation adopted by previous editors, and thereby imposed a different meaning on the text. An example of this is found at I.i.7–12:

> Bring in our daughter, clothèd like a bride,
> For the embracements even of Jove himself;
> At whose conception, till Lucina reigned,
> Nature this dowry gave to glad her presence.
> The senate house of planets all did sit,
> To knit in her their best perfections.

The last four lines are a major crux in the play, and have been much emended and discussed. Most editors put a colon in 1.10, either after "gave" or after "presence" (Q puts a semicolon after "gave" and a comma after "presence"), thus making the planetary influence itself Nature's dowry. But this does not make astrological sense, as a) beauty was considered the gift of Nature, not of the planets; b) planetary influence would be thought of as exerted at birth, not between conception and birth; c) such planetary influence would not be believed to be in the gift of Nature. By punctuating as above, I have separated Nature's gift from that of the planets, interpreting: "between conception and birth Nature gave her her beauty as dowry ['this dowry': the beauty you are about to behold]; then, at her birth, the planets bestowed upon her, other, non-physical, perfections over which they have control." The change in punctuation thus restores sense to the passage, and to Nature and the stars what is the due of each.

4) Not infrequently the explanations given in the glosses differ from those of previous editors. For example at I Chorus 42 the word "justify," instead of having its modern meaning, is, I believe, one of a series of legal metaphors, and has the archaic meaning of "acquit, absolve" (*Oxford English Dictionary* 4); while at V.i.220 I believe it has another archaic meaning, that of "affirm" (*Oxford English Dictionary* 5b).

5) I have parted company from previous editors over

several stage directions, which they have taken over from Malone's edition, and which seem quite unjustified. There are two chief instances of this. At the opening of III.ii Q's direction reads, *Enter Lord Cerymon with a seruant*. Malone, followed by most subsequent editors, added to this *and some Persons who have been shipwrecked*, because of Cerimon's line, "Get fire and meat for these poor men" (line 3). But to march several characters onto the stage, only to march them off again a few lines later (line 10) without their having uttered a word, would be a most un-Shakespearian piece of dramaturgy. I have, therefore, adhered to Q's direction, and emended "these" in line 3 to "those," so that Pericles is speaking of some poor men —there is not the slightest indication that they are shipwrecked—who are never brought on stage, but are merely mentioned in order to display Cerimon in his role of benefactor. The other instance occurs at the opening of V.i. We are on board Pericles' ship, having just been told by Gower:

> In your supposing once more put your sight:
> Of heavy Pericles think this his bark. (V. Chorus 21–22)

Malone, with evidently little faith in the audience's capacity for supposing, has added to the required direction (*"On board Pericles' Ship"*, etc.), "A Barge lying beside the Tyrian Vessel." At line 10 he introduced the direction, *The Gentlemen and the Two Sailors descend, and go on board the Barge. Enter, from thence, Lysimachus and Lords*; at line 51, *Exit Lord, in the Barge of Lysimachus*; and at line 64, *Enter, from the Barge, Lord, Marina, and a young Lady*. And all these directions have been taken over by subsequent editors. It is not clear how Malone envisaged the staging of this, but he evidently imagined the barge—by means of some piece of stage machinery—departing, and returning a few minutes later with Marina, all in full view of the audience. There is neither need nor warrant for all this, and in the present edition Malone's barge has been silently dropped.

TEXTUAL NOTE

In the Quartos of *Pericles* the text is not divided into
acts and scenes. The act division was introduced by the
Third Folio, and the scene division by Malone. In the
present text spelling and punctuation have been modern-
ized, and speech prefixes expanded and regularized. All
additions to Q's stage directions are indicated by square
brackets. Purely typographical errors have been silently
corrected. All other departures from the Quarto text are
listed below, with the adopted reading, in bold, given
first, followed by Q's reading, in roman.

I Chorus 39 **a** of

I.i.8 **For the embracements** For embracements 18 **razed** racte 57 **Antiochus** [Q omits] 112 **our** your 114 **cancel** counsell 121s.d. **Exeunt ... Pericles** Manet Pericles solus 128 **you're** you 129 **uncomely** vntimley
170 **Antiochus** [Q omits]

I.ii.s.d. **Enter Pericles** Enter Pericles with his Lords 4 **Be my** By me
21 **honor him** honour 26 **th' ostent** the stint 31 **am once** 42 **blast** sparke
45 **a peace** peace 66 **you** you yourselfe 82 **Bethought me** Bethought
84 **fears** feare 86 **doubt** doo't 100 **grieve them** griue for them 122 **we'll** will

I.iii.1 **Thaliard** [Q omits] 28 **ears it** seas 29 **seas** Sea 31 **Helicanus** [Q
omits] 35 **betook** betake

I.iv.13 **sorrows cease not** sorrowes 17 **helps** helpers 36 **they** thy 39 **two
summers** too sauers 58 **thou** thee 67 **Hath** That 74 **him's** himnes
76–7 **will, what need we fear?/On ground's the lowest,** will, and what they
can,/What need wee leaue our grounds the lowest?

II Chorus 11 **Tharsus** Tharstill 19 **for he strives** for though he striue
22 **Sends word** Sau'd one 24 **hid intent to murder** hid in Tent to murdred
[changed in some copies of Q to "had intent to murder"]

II.i.6 **me breath** my breath 12 **What ho, Pilch!** What, to pelch? 18 **fetch
thee** fetch'th 35 **devours** deuowre 43 **Third Fisherman. I.** 58 **scratch it**
Search 82 **quoth-a** ke-tha 86 **holidays** all day 86 **moreo'er** more; or
94 **your** you 103 **is called Pentapolis** I cald Pantapoles 127 **thy crosses**
crosses 135 **thee from!—may't** thee, Fame may 161 **rapture** rupture
164 **delightful** delight 171 **equal a** Goale

II.ii.4 **daughter** daughter heere 27 **Più per dolcezza che per forza** Pue Per
doleera kee per forsa 28 **what's** with 29 **chivalry** Chiually 30 **pompae**
Pompey 56 **for** by

II.iii.3 **To** I 13 **yours** your 26 **Envied** Enuies 29 **but** not 38 **Yon** You
39 **tells me** tels 44 **son's** sonne like 51 **stored** stur'd 52 **you do** do you
114 **Simonides** [Q omits]

II.iv.10 **their** those   33 **gives** giue's   34 **leaves** leaue   35 **death's indeed** death in deed,   36 **this: kingdoms** this Kingdome is   42 **For** Try   57 **endeavor it** endeauour

III Chorus 2 **the house about** about the house   6 **'fore** from   7 **crickets** Cricket   8 **All** Are   17 **coigns** Crignes   29 **t'appease** t'oppresse   35 **Y-ravishèd** Iranyshed   46 **fortune's mood** fortune mou'd   60 **sea-tossed** seas tost

III.i.7 **Thou stormest** then storme   11 **midwife** my wife   26 **Vie** Vse   52 **custom** easterne   53–54 **for ... straight** [In Q this is printed after "meet" in the next line]   61 **in the ooze** in oare   63 **And** The   66 **paper** Taper

III.ii.3 **those** these   26 **held** hold   37 **And I can** and can   38 **gives** doth giue   41 **treasure** pleasure   48 **never raze** neuer   57 **bitumed** bottomed   77 **even** euer   84–7 **I have read/Of some Egyptians, who after four hours' death/Have raised impoverished bodies, like to this,/Unto their former health** I heard of an Egiptian that had 9. howers lien dead,/Who was by good applyaunce recouered   89 **still** rough   95 **Breathes** breath

III.iii.5 **shafts** shakes   6 **hurt** hant   7 **woundingly** wondringly   29–30 **honor all,/Unscissored** honour,/All vnsisterd   31 **ill** will

III.iv.5 **eaning** learning

IV Chorus 10 **her** hie   10 **heart** art   14 **Seeks** Seeke   17 **ripe** right   17 **rite** sight   21 **she** they   26 **night-bird** night bed   32 **With dove of Paphos might the crow** The Doue of Paphos might with the crow   47 **carry** carried

IV.i.5–6 **or flaming love thy bosom/ Enslave** in flaming, thy loue bosome, enflame   11 **weeping her old nurse's** weeping for her onely Mistresse   19 **is as a** is a   24–5 **favor/Is** fauours   27 **On the sea margent** ere the sea marre it   62 **stem** sterne   92s.d. **They ... Marina** Exit   95 **she'll** shee will

IV.ii.4 **much** much much   21 **they're too** ther's two   53 **It** I   69 **me to** me, for to   77 **was like to** was to   109 **i' the** ethe   116 **crowns of** crownes in   132 **Bawd.** Mari.

IV.iii.1 **are** ere   6 **A** O   12 **fact** face   17 **pious** impious   27 **prime** prince   28 **sources** courses   31 **distain** disdaine   33 **Marina's** Marianas

IV.iv.7 **scene** sceanes   8 **i' th' gaps** with gappes   10 **the** thy   112 **life's** liues   16 **Tyre** time   18 **his** this   19 **go on** grone   24 **true-owed** true olde   29 **puts** put   48 **scene** Steare

IV.vi.s.d. **Enter ... Boult** Enter Bawdes   3   40 **dignifies** dignities   41 **punk** number   73 **name't** name   93 **aloof** aloft   135 **ways** way   141 **She** He   158 **ways** way   190 **I will** will   199 **women** woman

V Chorus 8 **silk, twin** Silke Twine,   13 **lost** left   14 **Whence** Where   16 **city's hived** Citie striu'de

V.i.11 **Mytilenian Sailor.** Hell. [changed in some copies of Q to I. Say.]   15 **you, sir, to** you to   34–6 **Lys. Yet ... wish./Hel. Behold ... Till yet ... wish./Lys. Behold ... person./Hell. Till** 36 **night** wight   46 **ports** parts   49 **And with her fellow maid is now** and her fellow maides, now   66 **presence** present   70 **I'd** I do   70 **rarely wed** rarely to wed   71 **Fair one, all** Faire on all   71 **bounty**

TEXTUAL NOTE

beautie 73 **feat** fate 81s.d. **They ... sings** The Song 82 **Marked** Marke
104 **countrywoman** Countrey women 105 **shores? ... shores** shewes? ...
shewes 109 **such** sucha one 126 **make my senses** make senses 129 **say**
stay 143 **thou** them? **Thy** thou thy 157 **Motion as well?** Motion
well, 165–66 **be: My daughter's buried.** be my daughter, buried;
183 **Pericles** Hell. 209–10 **perfect, and thou art/The** perfit, the 210 **life like**
216 **thou art** th' art 228 **doubt** doat 235 **Pericles. I hear most heavenly
music** Lys. I heare./Per. Most heauenly Musicke 248–49 **life./ Perform** like, or
performe 263 **suit** sleight

V.iii.6 **who** whom 8 **whom** who 15 **nun** mum 22 **one** in 49 **Pericles.**
Hell. 68 **I bless** blesse 69 **Nightly** night 83 [Q has *FINIS* after this line, as well
as after line 101] 88 **preserved** preferd 99 **punish them** punish

WILLIAM SHAKESPEARE

CYMBELINE

Edited by Richard Hosley

CYMBELINE, King of Britain

IMOGEN, daughter to Cymbeline by a former wife, later disguised under the name of Fidele

POSTHUMUS LEONATUS, a gentleman, husband to Imogen

GUIDERIUS ⎰ sons to Cymbeline, disguised under the names
ARVIRAGUS ⎱ of Polydore and Cadwal, supposed sons to Morgan

BELARIUS, a banished lord, disguised under the name of Morgan

THE QUEEN, wife to Cymbeline

CLOTEN, son to the Queen by a former husband

CORNELIUS, a physician employed by the Queen

PISANIO, servant to Posthumus

LORDS attending on Cymbeline

LADIES attending on the Queen

HELEN, a lady attending on Imogen

TWO LORDS, friends to Cloten

TWO GENTLEMEN of Cymbeline's court

TWO BRITON CAPTAINS   MUSICIANS employed by Cloten
MESSENGERS   TWO JAILERS

CAIUS LUCIUS, Roman ambassador, later general of the Roman forces

TWO ROMAN SENATORS

ROMAN TRIBUNES   ROMAN CAPTAINS

A SOOTHSAYER, named Philharmonus

PHILARIO, an Italian friend to Posthumus

IACHIMO, an Italian friend to Philario

A FRENCHMAN, friend to Philario

JUPITER

GHOST OF SICILIUS LEONATUS, father to Posthumus

GHOST OF THE MOTHER TO POSTHUMUS

GHOSTS OF THE TWO YOUNG BROTHERS TO POSTHUMUS, called Leonati

BRITON SOLDIERS, ROMAN SOLDIERS, ATTENDANTS, a DUTCHMAN and a SPANIARD (friends to Philario)

Scene: Britain, Rome, Wales]

CYMBELINE

ACT I

Scene I. [*Britain.*]

Enter two Gentlemen.

FIRST GENTLEMAN You do not meet a man but frowns.
  Our bloods
  No more obey the heavens than our courtiers
  Still seem as does the King's.

SECOND GENTLEMAN   But what's the matter?

FIRST GENTLEMAN His daughter, and the heir of's
    kingdom, whom
  He purposed to his wife's sole son—a widow   5
  That late he married—hath referred herself
  Unto a poor but worthy gentleman. She's wedded,
  Her husband banished, she imprisoned. All
  Is outward sorrow, though I think the King
  Be touched at very heart.

Text references are printed in **boldface** type; the annotation follows in roman
type.
I.i.1 **bloods** moods 3 **seem as does the King's** wear expressions like the
King's 6 **referred** given

10 SECOND GENTLEMAN   None but the King?

FIRST GENTLEMAN He that hath lost her too. So is the
    Queen,
    That most desired the match. But not a courtier,
    Although they wear their faces to the bent
    Of the King's looks, hath a heart that is not
    Glad at the thing they scowl at.

15 SECOND GENTLEMAN   And why so?

FIRST GENTLEMAN He that hath missed the Princess is a
    thing
    Too bad for bad report, and he that hath her—
    I mean, that married her, alack good man,
    And therefore banished—is a creature such
20 As, to seek through the regions of the earth
    For one his like, there would be something failing
    In him that should compare. I do not think
    So fair an outward and such stuff within
    Endows a man but he.

SECOND GENTLEMAN   You speak him far.

25 FIRST GENTLEMAN I do extend him, sir, within himself,
    Crush him together rather than unfold
    His measure duly.

SECOND GENTLEMAN What's his name and birth?

FIRST GENTLEMAN I cannot delve him to the root. His
    father
    Was called Sicilius, who did join his honor
30 Against the Romans with Cassibelan,
    But had his titles by Tenantius, whom
    He served with glory and admired success,
    So gained the sur-addition Leonatus;
    And had, besides this gentleman in question,
35 Two other sons, who in the wars o' th' time

13 **bent** inclination   24 **speak him far** praise him much   25 **do extend** . . .
himself i.e., do not exaggerate his real merit   29 **honor** reputation (as a
soldier)   32 **admired** wondered at   33 **sur-addition** additional title

Died with their swords in hand; for which their
    father,
Then old and fond of issue, took such sorrow
That he quit being, and his gentle lady,
Big of this gentleman our theme, deceased
As he was born. The King he takes the babe   40
To his protection, calls him Posthumus Leonatus,
Breeds him and makes him of his bedchamber,
Puts to him all the learnings that his time
Could make him the receiver of, which he took
As we do air, fast as 'twas minist'red,   45
And in's spring became a harvest, lived in court—
Which rare it is to do—most praised, most loved,
A sample to the youngest, to th' more mature
A glass that feated them, and to the graver
A child that guided dotards. To his mistress,   50
For whom he now is banished—her own price
Proclaims how she esteemed him and his virtue.
By her election may be truly read
What kind of man he is.

SECOND GENTLEMAN   I honor him
Even out of your report. But pray you tell me,   55
Is she sole child to th' King?

FIRST GENTLEMAN   His only child.
He had two sons—if this be worth your hearing,
Mark it—the eldest of them at three years old,
I' th' swathing clothes the other, from their nursery
Were stol'n, and to this hour no guess in knowledge 60
Which way they went.

SECOND GENTLEMAN   How long is this ago?

FIRST GENTLEMAN Some twenty years.

SECOND GENTLEMAN That a king's children should be
    so conveyed,

37 **fond of issue** doting on children 42 **of his bedchamber** i.e., a
chamberlain 43 **Puts to him** sets him to work at 43 **time** age 49 **glass that
feated them** mirror that reflected their features 51 **price** what she is willing to
undergo for his sake 53 **election** choice 55 **out of** beyond 63 **conveyed** stolen

So slackly guarded, and the search so slow
That could not trace them!

65 FIRST GENTLEMAN   Howsoe'er 'tis strange,
Or that the negligence may well be laughed at,
Yet is it true, sir.

SECOND GENTLEMAN I do well believe you.

FIRST GENTLEMAN We must forbear. Here comes the
    gentleman,
The Queen, and Princess.   *Exeunt.*

Enter the Queen, Posthumus, and Imogen.

70 QUEEN No, be assured you shall not find me, daughter,
After the slander of most stepmothers,
Evil-eyed unto you. You're my prisoner, but
Your jailer shall deliver you the keys
That lock up your restraint. For you, Posthumus,
75 So soon as I can win th' offended King,
I will be known your advocate. Marry, yet
The fire of rage is in him, and 'twere good
You leaned unto his sentence with what patience
Your wisdom may inform you.

POSTHUMUS   Please your Highness,
I will from hence today.

80 QUEEN   You know the peril.
I'll fetch a turn about the garden, pitying
The pangs of barred affections, though the King
Hath charged you should not speak together.   *Exit.*

IMOGEN   O
Dissembling courtesy! How fine this tyrant
85 Can tickle where she wounds! My dearest husband,
I something fear my father's wrath, but nothing—

68 **forbear** withdraw 68 **Here comes** (this entrance-announcement shows that,
though the stage is technically "clear" at line 69 [at which point F marks a new
scene], the oncoming players enter before the offgoing ones have completed their
exit) 71 **slander** ill repute 76 **Marry** indeed (by the Virgin Mary) 78 **leaned
unto** deferred to 85 **tickle** (pretend to) please

Always reserved my holy duty—what
His rage can do on me. You must be gone,
And I shall here abide the hourly shot
Of angry eyes, not comforted to live   90
But that there is this jewel in the world
That I may see again.

POSTHUMUS   My queen, my mistress.
O lady, weep no more, lest I give cause
To be suspected of more tenderness
Than doth become a man. I will remain   95
The loyal'st husband that did e'er plight troth;
My residence, in Rome at one Philario's,
Who to my father was a friend, to me
Known but by letter. Thither write, my queen,
And with mine eyes I'll drink the words you send,   100
Though ink be made of gall.

Enter Queen.

QUEEN   Be brief, I pray you.
If the King come, I shall incur I know not
How much of his displeasure. [Aside] Yet I'll move
   him
To walk this way. I never do him wrong
But he does buy my injuries, to be friends;   105
Pays dear for my offenses.   [Exit.]

POSTHUMUS   Should we be taking leave
As long a term as yet we have to live,
The loathness to depart would grow. Adieu.

IMOGEN Nay, stay a little.
Were you but riding forth to air yourself,   110
Such parting were too petty. Look here, love;
This diamond was my mother's. [Giving a ring]
   Take it, heart,
But keep it till you woo another wife,
When Imogen is dead.

87 reserved excepting   87 duty i.e., of child to parent   105 buy i.e., gladly
accept   113 But only

POSTHUMUS   How, how? Another?
115   You gentle gods, give me but this I have,
       And cere up my embracements from a next
       With bonds of death! Remain, remain thou here
       While sense can keep it on. And, sweetest, fairest,
       As I my poor self did exchange for you
120   To your so infinite loss, so in our trifles
       I still win of you. For my sake wear this.

                                [*Giving a bracelet*]

       It is a manacle of love; I'll place it
       Upon this fairest prisoner.

IMOGEN   O the gods!
       When shall we see again?

                        Enter Cymbeline and Lords.

POSTHUMUS   Alack, the King!

CYMBELINE Thou basest thing, avoid hence, from my
125   sight!
       If after this command thou fraught the court
       With thy unworthiness, thou diest. Away!
       Thou'rt poison to my blood.

POSTHUMUS   The gods protect you,
       And bless the good remainders of the court.
       I am gone.   *Exit.*

130   IMOGEN   There cannot be a pinch in death
       More sharp than this is.

CYMBELINE   O disloyal thing
       That shouldst repair my youth, thou heap'st
       A year's age on me.

IMOGEN   I beseech you, sir,
       Harm not yourself with your vexation.
135   I am senseless of your wrath; a touch more rare
       Subdues all pangs, all fears.

CYMBELINE   Past grace? obedience?

116 **cere up** shroud 125 **avoid** go 126 **fraught** freight, burden
129 **remainders of** those who remain at 132 **repair** renew 135 **am senseless of** do not feel 135 **touch more rare** finer anxiety

120

IMOGEN Past hope, and in despair; that way, past
grace.

CYMBELINE That mightst have had the sole son of my
queen.

IMOGEN O blessed that I might not! I chose an eagle
And did avoid a puttock.   140

CYMBELINE Thou took'st a beggar, wouldst have made
my throne
A seat for baseness.

IMOGEN   No, I rather added
A luster to it.

CYMBELINE   O thou vile one!

IMOGEN   Sir,
It is your fault that I have loved Posthumus.
You bred him as my playfellow, and he is   145
A man worth any woman; overbuys me
Almost the sum he pays.

CYMBELINE   What, art thou mad?

IMOGEN Almost, sir. Heaven restore me! Would I were
A neatherd's daughter, and my Leonatus
Our neighbor shepherd's son.

Enter Queen.

CYMBELINE   Thou foolish thing!   150
[*To Queen*] They were again together. You have
done
Not after our command. Away with her
And pen her up.

QUEEN   Beseech your patience. Peace,
Dear lady daughter, peace! Sweet sovereign,

140 puttock kite (bird of prey)   146-47 overbuys me . . . pays he exceeds me
in worth by almost the price which he is now called upon to pay, i.e., banishment
(J. M. Nosworthy)   149 neatherd's cowherd's   153 Beseech I beseech

Leave us to ourselves, and make yourself some
155   comfort
Out of your best advice.

CYMBELINE   Nay, let her languish
A drop of blood a day and, being aged,
Die of this folly.

Exeunt [Cymbeline and Lords].

Enter Pisanio.

QUEEN   Fie, you must give way.—
Here is your servant. How now, sir? What news?

PISANIO My lord your son drew on my master.

160 QUEEN   Ha!
No harm, I trust, is done?

PISANIO   There might have been
But that my master rather played than fought
And had no help of anger. They were parted
By gentlemen at hand.

QUEEN   I am very glad on't.

IMOGEN Your son's my father's friend; he takes his
165   part
To draw upon an exile. O brave sir!
I would they were in Afric both together,
Myself by with a needle that I might prick
The goer-back. Why came you from your master?

170 PISANIO On his command. He would not suffer me
To bring him to the haven, left these notes
Of what commands I should be subject to
When't pleased you to employ me.

QUEEN   This hath been
Your faithful servant. I dare lay mine honor
He will remain so.

175 PISANIO   I humbly thank your Highness.

156 **advice** consideration   165 **takes his part** plays his usual role   168 **needle**
(pronounced "neel")   174 **lay** stake

QUEEN Pray walk awhile.   [*Exit Queen.*]

IMOGEN About some half-hour hence, pray you speak
  with me.
  You shall at least go see my lord aboard.
  For this time leave me.   *Exeunt* [*severally*].

Scene II. [*Britain.*]

Enter Cloten and two Lords.

FIRST LORD Sir, I would advise you to shift a shirt; the
  violence of action hath made you reek as a sacrifice. Where air comes out, air comes in; there's none
  abroad so wholesome as that you vent.

CLOTEN If my shirt were bloody, then to shift it. Have   5
  I hurt him?

SECOND LORD [*Aside*] No, faith, not so much as his
  patience.

FIRST LORD Hurt him? His body's a passable carcass
  if he be not hurt. It is a throughfare for steel if it be   10
  not hurt.

SECOND LORD [*Aside*] His steel was in debt. It went o'
  th' backside the town.

CLOTEN The villain would not stand me.

SECOND LORD [*Aside*] No, but he fled forward still, to-   15
  ward your face.

FIRST LORD Stand you? You have land enough of your

179s.d. **severally** by different tiring-house doors (Imogen follows the Queen
offstage while Pisanio exits by the other door) I.ii.s.d. **Cloten** (rhymes with
"rotten"; cf. "Cloten's clotpoll," IV.ii.184) 2 **reek** give off vapors 4 **vent** give
off 9 **passable** affording passage (quibble on "tolerable") 12–13 **It went . . .
the town** like a debtor avoiding a creditor by taking a back street (i.e., his rapier
missed) 14 **stand** confront

own, but he added to your having, gave you some
ground.

20 SECOND LORD [*Aside*] As many inches as you have
oceans. Puppies!

CLOTEN I would they had not come between us.

SECOND LORD [*Aside*] So would I, till you had measured how long a fool you were upon the ground.

25 CLOTEN And that she should love this fellow and refuse
me!

SECOND LORD [*Aside*] If it be a sin to make a true election, she is damned.

FIRST LORD Sir, as I told you always, her beauty and
30 her brain go not together. She's a good sign, but I
have seen small reflection of her wit.

SECOND LORD [*Aside*] She shines not upon fools, lest
the reflection should hurt her.

CLOTEN Come, I'll to my chamber. Would there had
35 been some hurt done!

SECOND LORD [*Aside*] I wish not so—unless it had
been the fall of an ass, which is no great hurt.

CLOTEN You'll go with us?

FIRST LORD I'll attend your lordship.

40 CLOTEN Nay, come, let's go together.

SECOND LORD Well, my lord.   *Exeunt*.

27–28 **election** choice   30 **She's** she has   30 **sign** appearance

Scene III. [*Britain.*]

Enter Imogen and Pisanio.

IMOGEN I would thou grew'st unto the shores o' th'
    haven
  And questioned'st every sail. If he should write,
  And I not have it, 'twere a paper lost
  As offered mercy is. What was the last
  That he spake to thee?

PISANIO   It was his queen, his queen.   5

IMOGEN Then waved his handkerchief?

PISANIO   And kissed it, madam.

IMOGEN Senseless linen, happier therein than I!
  And that was all?

PISANIO   No, madam. For so long
  As he could make me with this eye or ear
  Distinguish him from others, he did keep   10
  The deck, with glove or hat or handkerchief
  Still waving, as the fits and stirs of's mind
  Could best express how slow his soul sailed on,
  How swift his ship.

IMOGEN   Thou shouldst have made him
  As little as a crow or less, ere left   15
  To after-eye him.

PISANIO   Madam, so I did.

IMOGEN I would have broke mine eyestrings, cracked
  them but

I.iii.3–4 'twere . . . mercy is i.e., a letter gone astray would be as great a loss as mercy that fails to reach its object   7 Senseless without feeling   12 as as if   15–16 ere . . . after-eye before you stopped looking after

To look upon him till the diminution
Of space had pointed him sharp as my needle;
20   Nay, followed him till he had melted from
The smallness of a gnat to air, and then
Have turned mine eye and wept. But, good Pisanio,
When shall we hear from him?

PISANIO   Be assured, madam,
With his next vantage.

25   IMOGEN I did not take my leave of him, but had
Most pretty things to say. Ere I could tell him
How I would think on him at certain hours
Such thoughts and such; or I could make him swear
The shes of Italy should not betray
30   Mine interest and his honor; or have charged him
At the sixth hour of morn, at noon, at midnight,
T'encounter me with orisons, for then
I am in heaven for him; or ere I could
Give him that parting kiss which I had set
35   Betwixt two charming words—comes in my father,
And like the tyrannous breathing of the north
Shakes all our buds from growing.

Enter a Lady.

LADY   The Queen, madam,
Desires your Highness' company.

IMOGEN Those things I bid you do, get them dispatched.
I will attend the Queen.

40   PISANIO   Madam, I shall.   *Exeunt.*

---

19 **space** i.e., distance   24 **vantage** opportunity   32 **T'encounter . . . orisons**
join me in prayers   35 **charming** protecting from evil   37s.d. (the Lady's
message has the theatrical function of motivating Imogen's exit)

Scene IV. [*Rome.*]

Enter Philario, Iachimo, a Frenchman, a Dutchman,
and a Spaniard.

IACHIMO Believe it, sir, I have seen him in Britain. He
was then of a crescent note, expected to prove so
worthy as since he hath been allowed the name of.
But I could then have looked on him without the
help of admiration, though the catalogue of his en-   5
dowments had been tabled by his side and I to
peruse him by items.

PHILARIO You speak of him when he was less furnished
than now he is with that which makes him both
without and within.   10

FRENCHMAN I have seen him in France. We had very
many there could behold the sun with as firm eyes
as he.

IACHIMO This matter of marrying his king's daughter,
wherein he must be weighed rather by her value   15
than his own, words him, I doubt not, a great deal
from the matter.

FRENCHMAN And then his banishment.

IACHIMO Ay, and the approbation of those that weep
this lamentable divorce under her colors are won-   20
derfully to extend him, be it but to fortify her
judgment, which else an easy battery might lay flat

I.iv.s.d. **Iachimo** (probably pronounced "Yákimo"; cf. "yellow Iachimo," II.v.14;
but possibly pronounced "Jáckimo" since the name is a variant of the Italian
Giacomo) 2 **crescent note** growing reputation 5 **admiration** wonder 6
tabled tabulated 9 **makes** is the making of 12 **behold the sun** (as the eagle—
noblest of birds—was thought to do) 16–17 **words him . . . matter** makes him
out better than he truly is 20 **colors** banner 21 **extend him** enlarge his
reputation

for taking a beggar without less quality. But how
comes it he is to sojourn with you? How creeps
25 acquaintance?

PHILARIO His father and I were soldiers together, to
whom I have been often bound for no less than my
life.

Enter Posthumus.

Here comes the Briton. Let him be so entertained
30 amongst you as suits, with gentlemen of your knowing, to a stranger of his quality. I beseech you all
be better known to this gentleman, whom I commend to you as a noble friend of mine. How worthy
he is I will leave to appear hereafter, rather than
35 story him in his own hearing.

FRENCHMAN Sir, we have known together in Orleans.

POSTHUMUS Since when I have been debtor to you for
courtesies which I will be ever to pay and yet pay
still.

40 FRENCHMAN Sir, you o'errate my poor kindness. I was
glad ı did atone my countryman and you. It had
been pity you should have been put together with
so mortal a purpose as then each bore, upon importance of so slight and trivial a nature.

45 POSTHUMUS By your pardon, sir, I was then a young
traveler; rather shunned to go even with what I
heard than in my every action to be guided by
others' experiences. But upon my mended judgment,
if I offend not to say it is mended, my quarrel was
50 not altogether slight.

FRENCHMAN Faith, yes, to be put to the arbitrament of
swords, and by such two that would be all likeli-

23 **without less** i.e., with less (double negative)   23 **quality** inherent worth
29 **entertained** welcomed   31 **stranger** foreigner   31 **quality** rank   36 **known
together** been acquainted   41 **atone** reconcile   42 **put together** i.e., in a
duel   43–44 **importance** a matter   46 **shunned . . . even** refused to agree

hood have confounded one the other or have fall'n
both.

IACHIMO Can we with manners ask what was the dif-   55
ference?

FRENCHMAN Safely, I think. 'Twas a contention in
public, which may without contradiction suffer the
report. It was much like an argument that fell out last
night, where each of us fell in praise of our coun-   60
try mistresses; this gentleman at that time vouch-
ing—and upon warrant of bloody affirmation—his
to be more fair, virtuous, wise, chaste, constant,
qualified, and less attemptable than any the rarest
of our ladies in France.   65

IACHIMO That lady is not now living, or this gentleman's opinion, by this, worn out.

POSTHUMUS She holds her virtue still, and I my mind.

IACHIMO You must not so far prefer her 'fore ours of
Italy.   70

POSTHUMUS Being so far provoked as I was in France,
I would abate her nothing, though I profess myself
her adorer, not her friend.

IACHIMO As fair and as good—a kind of hand-in-
hand comparison—had been something too fair   75
and too good for any lady in Britain. If she went
before others I have seen, as that diamond of yours
outlusters many I have beheld, I could not but believe she excelled many; but I have not seen the
most precious diamond that is, nor you the lady.   80

POSTHUMUS I praised her as I rated her. So do I my
stone.

---

53 confounded destroyed   58 contradiction objection   60–61 country i.e., of
our own countries (with bawdy quibble)   62 warrant . . . affirmation pledge to
support by shedding blood (R. B. Heilman)   64 qualified endowed with good
qualities   67 by this by this time   72 abate depreciate   73 friend paramour
74–75 hand-in-hand claiming equality   76–77 went before excelled

IACHIMO What do you esteem it at?

POSTHUMUS More than the world enjoys.

85 IACHIMO Either your unparagoned mistress is dead, or
she's outprized by a trifle.

POSTHUMUS You are mistaken. The one may be sold or
given, or if there were wealth enough for the purchase or merit for the gift. The other is not a thing
90 for sale, and only the gift of the gods.

IACHIMO Which the gods have given you?

POSTHUMUS Which by their graces I will keep.

IACHIMO You may wear her in title yours, but you
know strange fowl light upon neighboring ponds.
95 Your ring may be stol'n too. So your brace of unprizable estimations, the one is but frail and the
other casual. A cunning thief, or a that-way-
accomplished courtier, would hazard the winning
both of first and last.

100 POSTHUMUS Your Italy contains none so accomplished
a courtier to convince the honor of my mistress,
if, in the holding or loss of that, you term her frail.
I do nothing doubt you have store of thieves; notwithstanding, I fear not my ring.

105 PHILARIO Let us leave here, gentlemen.

POSTHUMUS Sir, with all my heart. This worthy signior,
I thank him, makes no stranger of me; we are
familiar at first.

IACHIMO With five times so much conversation I
110 should get ground of your fair mistress, make her
go back even to the yielding, had I admittance, and
opportunity to friend.

84 **enjoys** possesses 86 **outprized** exceeded in value 88 **or** either
95–96 **unprizable estimations** inestimable values 97 **casual** liable to accident 101 **convince the honor** conquer the chastity 105 **leave** leave off
108 **at first** from the first 110 **get ground of** gain an advantage over (a dueling
metaphor followed by bawdy quibbles on "go back" and "yielding") · 112 **to** as a

POSTHUMUS No, no.

IACHIMO I dare thereupon pawn the moiety of my
estate to your ring, which in my opinion o'ervalues   115
it something. But I make my wager rather against
your confidence than her reputation; and, to bar
your offense herein too, I durst attempt it against
any lady in the world.

POSTHUMUS You are a great deal abused in too bold   120
a persuasion, and I doubt not you sustain what
y'are worthy of by your attempt.

IACHIMO What's that?

POSTHUMUS A repulse—though your attempt, as you
call it, deserve more: a punishment too.   125

PHILARIO Gentlemen, enough of this. It came in too
suddenly; let it die as it was born, and I pray you
be better acquainted.

IACHIMO Would I had put my estate and my neighbor's on th' approbation of what I have spoke!   130

POSTHUMUS What lady would you choose to assail?

IACHIMO Yours, whom in constancy you think stands
so safe. I will lay you ten thousand ducats to your
ring that, commend me to the court where your lady
is, with no more advantage than the opportunity of 135
a second conference, and I will bring from thence
that honor of hers which you imagine so reserved.

POSTHUMUS I will wage against your gold, gold to it.
My ring I hold dear as my finger; 'tis part of it.

IACHIMO You are a friend, and therein the wiser. If 140
you buy ladies' flesh at a million a dram, you cannot preserve it from tainting. But I see you have
some religion in you, that you fear.

114 moiety half   120 abused deceived   121 persuasion opinion   130 approbation proof   138 wage wager   143 that since

POSTHUMUS This is but a custom in your tongue. You
145   bear a graver purpose, I hope.

IACHIMO I am the master of my speeches, and would
       undergo what's spoken, I swear.

POSTHUMUS Will you? I shall but lend my diamond till
       your return. Let there be covenants drawn be-
150   tween's. My mistress exceeds in goodness the huge-
       ness of your unworthy thinking. I dare you to this
       match: here's my ring.

PHILARIO I will have it no lay.

IACHIMO By the gods, it is one. If I bring you no suffi-
155   cient testimony that I have enjoyed the dearest
       bodily part of your mistress, my ten thousand ducats
       are yours; so is your diamond too. If I come off and
       leave her in such honor as you have trust in, she
       your jewel, this your jewel, and my gold are yours
160   —provided I have your commendation for my
       more free entertainment.

POSTHUMUS I embrace these conditions. Let us have
       articles betwixt us. Only, thus far you shall answer:
       if you make your voyage upon her and give me di-
165   rectly to understand you have prevailed, I am no
       further your enemy; she is not worth our debate. If
       she remain unseduced, you not making it appear
       otherwise, for your ill opinion and th' assault you
       have made to her chastity you shall answer me with
170   your sword.

IACHIMO Your hand; a covenant. We will have these
       things set down by lawful counsel, and straight
       away for Britain, lest the bargain should catch cold
       and starve. I will fetch my gold and have our two
175   wagers recorded.

POSTHUMUS Agreed.   [*Exeunt Posthumus and Iachimo.*]

144 **This** i.e., what you say   147 **undergo** undertake   149 **covenants** a legal
agreement   153 **lay** wager   160 **commendation** introduction to her
161 **entertainment** welcome   164–65 **directly** plainly   172–73 **straight away**
immediately I shall leave   174 **starve** die

132

FRENCHMAN Will this hold, think you?

PHILARIO Signior Iachimo will not from it. Pray let us
follow 'em.   *Exeunt.*

Scene V. [*Britain.*]

Enter Queen, Ladies, and Cornelius.

QUEEN Whiles yet the dew's on ground, gather those
    flowers.
  Make haste. Who has the note of them?

LADY   I, madam.

QUEEN Dispatch.   *Exeunt Ladies.*
  Now, Master Doctor, have you brought those drugs?

CORNELIUS Pleaseth your Highness, ay. Here they are,
    madam.   [*Presenting a box*]   5
  But I beseech your Grace, without offense—
  My conscience bids me ask—wherefore you have
  Commanded of me these most poisonous
    compounds,
  Which are the movers of a languishing death,
  But, though slow, deadly.

QUEEN   I wonder, Doctor,   10
  Thou ask'st me such a question. Have I not been
  Thy pupil long? Hast thou not learned me how
  To make perfumes? distil? preserve? yea, so
  That our great king himself doth woo me oft
  For my confections? Having thus far proceeded—   15
  Unless thou think'st me devilish—is't not meet
  That I did amplify my judgment in
  Other conclusions? I will try the forces

I.v.2 note list 3 **Dispatch** make haste 8 **compounds** drugs 12 **learned**
taught 15 **confections** drugs 17 **judgment** knowledge 18 **conclusions**
experiments

Of these thy compounds on such creatures as
20 We count not worth the hanging—but none human—
To try the vigor of them and apply
Allayments to their act, and by them gather
Their several virtues and effects.

CORNELIUS   Your Highness
Shall from this practice but make hard your heart.
25 Besides, the seeing these effects will be
Both noisome and infectious.

QUEEN   O, content thee.

Enter Pisanio.

[*Aside*] Here comes a flattering rascal. Upon him
Will I first work. He's for his master,
And enemy to my son.—How now, Pisanio?—
30 Doctor, your service for this time is ended;
Take your own way.

CORNELIUS [*Aside*]   I do suspect you, madam,
But you shall do no harm.

QUEEN [*To Pisanio*]   Hark thee, a word.

CORNELIUS [*Aside*] I do not like her. She doth think she
    has
Strange ling'ring poisons. I do know her spirit
35 And will not trust one of her malice with
A drug of such damned nature. Those she has
Will stupefy and dull the sense awhile,
Which first perchance she'll prove on cats and
    dogs,
Then afterward up higher; but there is
40 No danger in what show of death it makes,
More than the locking up the spirits a time,
To be more fresh, reviving. She is fooled
With a most false effect, and I the truer
So to be false with her.

22 **Allayments to their act** antidotes to their action 22 **them** i.e., the
experiments 23 **Their** i.e., of the compounds 38 **prove** test

QUEEN   No further service, Doctor,
  Until I send for thee.

CORNELIUS   I humbly take my leave.   *Exit.*   45

QUEEN Weeps she still, say'st thou? Dost thou think in
    time
  She will not quench and let instructions enter
  Where folly now possesses? Do thou work.
  When thou shalt bring me word she loves my son,
  I'll tell thee on the instant thou art then   50
  As great as is thy master; greater, for
  His fortunes all lie speechless and his name
  Is at last gasp. Return he cannot nor
  Continue where he is. To shift his being
  Is to exchange one misery with another,   55
  And every day that comes comes to decay
  A day's work in him. What shalt thou expect
  To be depender on a thing that leans,
  Who cannot be new built, nor has no friends
  So much as but to prop him?
              [*Dropping the box; Pisanio picks it up*.]
                          Thou tak'st up   60
  Thou know'st not what, but take it for thy labor.
  It is a thing I made which hath the King
  Five times redeemed from death. I do not know
  What is more cordial. Nay, I prithee take it.
  It is an earnest of a farther good   65
  That I mean to thee. Tell thy mistress how
  The case stands with her; do't as from thyself.
  Think what a chance thou changest on, but think
  Thou hast thy mistress still—to boot, my son,
  Who shall take notice of thee. I'll move the King   70
  To any shape of thy preferment such
  As thou'lt desire; and then myself, I chiefly,
  That set thee on to this desert, am bound
  To load thy merit richly. Call my women.

47 **quench** cool down   54 **being** location   56 **decay** destroy   64 **cordial**
restorative   65 **earnest** pledge   68 **chance thou changest on** i.e., opportunity
you have to change service (?)   71 **preferment** advancement   73 **desert** action
meriting reward

Think on my words.   *Exit Pisanio.*
75   A sly and constant knave,
Not to be shaked; the agent for his master,
And the remembrancer of her to hold
The handfast to her lord. I have given him that
Which, if he take, shall quite unpeople her
80   Of liegers for her sweet, and which she after,
Except she bend her humor, shall be assured
To taste of too.

                    Enter Pisanio and Ladies.

                         So, so. Well done, well done.
The violets, cowslips, and the primroses
Bear to my closet. Fare thee well, Pisanio.
Think on my words.   *Exeunt Queen and Ladies.*

85   PISANIO   And shall do.
But when to my good lord I prove untrue,
I'll choke myself. There's all I'll do for you.   *Exit.*

                    Scene VI. [*Britain.*]

                    Enter Imogen alone.

IMOGEN   A father cruel and a stepdame false,
A foolish suitor to a wedded lady
That hath her husband banished. O, that husband,
My supreme crown of grief, and those repeated
5   Vexations of it! Had I been thief-stol'n,
As my two brothers, happy; but most miserable
Is the desire that's glorious. Blessed be those,

---

77 **remembrancer** person employed to remind someone (legal term)   78 **hand-fast** marriage contract   80 **liegers** ambassadors   80 **sweet** lover   81 **bend her humor** change her mind   84 **closet** private room   I.vi.4 **repeated** (already) enumerated   7 **desire that's glorious** i.e., unfulfilled longing that aspires to great things (Nosworthy)

How mean soe'er, that have their honest wills,
Which seasons comfort. Who may this be? Fie!

Enter Pisanio and Iachimo.

PISANIO Madam, a noble gentleman of Rome,   10
Comes from my lord with letters.

IACHIMO   Change you, madam:
The worthy Leonatus is in safety
And greets your Highness dearly.

                                        [*Presenting a letter*]

IMOGEN   Thanks, good sir.
You're kindly welcome.

IACHIMO [*Aside*] All of her that is out of door most
    rich!   15
If she be furnished with a mind so rare,
She is alone th' Arabian bird, and I
Have lost the wager. Boldness be my friend!
Arm me, audacity, from head to foot,
Or like the Parthian I shall flying fight—   20
Rather, directly fly.

IMOGEN *(Reads)* "He is one of the noblest note, to
whose kindnesses I am most infinitely tied. Reflect
upon him accordingly, as you value your trust—
                                        Leonatus."   25
So far I read aloud.
But even the very middle of my heart
Is warmed by th' rest and takes it thankfully.
You are as welcome, worthy sir, as I
Have words to bid you, and shall find it so   30
In all that I can do.

IACHIMO   Thanks, fairest lady.
What, are men mad? Hath nature given them eyes

8 **mean** low-ranking   8 **honest wills** plain desires   9 **seasons** give relish to
11 **Comes** who comes   11 **you** i.e., your expression   14 **out of door** external,
visible   17 **Arabian bird** phoenix (of which species only one example existed at a
time)   20 **Parthian** mounted archer who shot arrows behind him while in flight
(Iachimo will resort to indirect methods)   22 **note** reputation   23 **Reflect** bestow
attention

To see this vaulted arch and the rich crop
Of sea and land, which can distinguish 'twixt
35   The fiery orbs above and the twinned stones
Upon the numbered beach, and can we not
Partition make with spectacles so precious
'Twixt fair and foul?

IMOGEN   What makes your admiration?

IACHIMO It cannot be i' th' eye, for apes and monkeys,
40   'Twixt two such shes, would chatter this way and
Contemn with mows the other; nor i' th' judgment,
For idiots, in this case of favor, would
Be wisely definite; nor i' th' appetite—
Sluttery, to such neat excellence opposed,
45   Should make desire vomit emptiness,
Not so allured to feed.

IMOGEN What is the matter, trow?

IACHIMO   The cloyèd will—
That satiate yet unsatisfied desire, that tub
Both filled and running—ravening first the lamb,
Longs after for the garbage.

50   IMOGEN   What, dear sir,
Thus raps you? Are you well?

IACHIMO   Thanks, madam, well.
[To Pisanio] Beseech you, sir, desire
My man's abode where I did leave him.
He's strange and peevish.

PISANIO   I was going, sir,
55   To give him welcome.   *Exit*.

---

33 **crop** harvest 35 **twinned** exactly alike 36 **numbered** abounding (in
stones) 37 **Partition** distinction 37 **spectacles so precious** i.e., eyesight
38 **admiration** wonder 40 **this way** towards Imogen 41 **mows** grimaces
42 **ease of favor** question of beauty 43 **definite** decisive 43 **appetite** physical
desire 45 **make . . . emptiness** i.e., destroy desire 47 **What . . . trow** what
are you talking about, I wonder 47 **will** sexual desire 51 **raps** transports
52–53 **desire . . . abode** request that my servant remain 54 **strange and
peevish** a foreigner and skittish

IMOGEN Continues well my lord? His health, beseech
    you?

IACHIMO Well, madam.

IMOGEN Is he disposed to mirth? I hope he is.

IACHIMO Exceeding pleasant; none a stranger there
    So merry and so gamesome. He is called   60
    The Briton reveler.

IMOGEN   When he was here
    He did incline to sadness, and ofttimes
    Not knowing why.

IACHIMO   I never saw him sad.
    There is a Frenchman his companion, one
    An eminent monsieur that, it seems, much loves   65
    A Gallian girl at home. He furnaces
    The thick sighs from him, whiles the jolly Briton—
    Your lord, I mean—laughs from's free lungs, cries
        "O,
    Can my sides hold to think that man who knows
    By history, report, or his own proof   70
    What woman is, yea, what she cannot choose
    But must be, will's free hours languish for
    Assurèd bondage?"

IMOGEN   Will my lord say so?

IACHIMO Ay, madam, with his eyes in flood with
    laughter.
    It is a recreation to be by   75
    And hear him mock the Frenchman. But heavens
    know
    Some men are much to blame.

IMOGEN   Not he, I hope.

IACHIMO Not he—but yet heaven's bounty towards him
    might

59 **none a stranger** there is no foreigner 62 **sadness** seriousness 66 **Gallian**
French 66 **furnaces** exhales like a furnace 67 **thick** frequent 70 **proof**
experience 72 **languish** pass in languishing

Be used more thankfully. In himself 'tis much;
80 In you, which I account his, beyond all talents.
Whilst I am bound to wonder, I am bound
To pity too.

IMOGEN   What do you pity, sir?

IACHIMO Two creatures heartily.

IMOGEN   Am I one, sir?
You look on me. What wrack discern you in me
Deserves your pity?

85 IACHIMO   Lamentable! What,
To hide me from the radiant sun and solace
I' th' dungeon by a snuff!

IMOGEN   I pray you, sir,
Deliver with more openness your answers
To my demands. Why do you pity me?

90 IACHIMO That others do,
I was about to say, enjoy your—but
It is an office of the gods to venge it,
Not mine to speak on't.

IMOGEN   You do seem to know
Something of me or what concerns me. Pray you,
95 Since doubting things go ill often hurts more
Than to be sure they do—for certainties
Either are past remedies, or, timely knowing,
The remedy then born—discover to me
What both you spur and stop.

IACHIMO   Had I this cheek
100 To bathe my lips upon; this hand, whose touch,
Whose every touch, would force the feeler's soul
To th' oath of loyalty; this object, which
Takes prisoner the wild motion of mine eye,
Fixing it only here; should I, damned then,

79 'tis i.e., heaven's bounty is 80 beyond all talents beyond all natural
endowments, i.e., inestimable 84 wrack disaster 86 solace find pleasure
87 snuff candle-end 92 office duty 95 doubting fearing 97 timely knowing if one knows in time 98 discover reveal 99 What why

Slaver with lips as common as the stairs   105
That mount the Capitol; join gripes with hands
Made hard with hourly falsehood (falsehood, as
With labor); then bye-peeping in an eye
Base and illustrous as the smoky light
That's fed with stinking tallow—it were fit   110
That all the plagues of hell should at one time
Encounter such revolt.

IMOGEN   My lord, I fear,
Has forgot Britain.

IACHIMO   And himself. Not I
Inclined to this intelligence pronounce
The beggary of his change, but 'tis your graces   115
That from my mutest conscience to my tongue
Charms this report out.

IMOGEN   Let me hear no more.

IACHIMO O dearest soul, your cause doth strike my
          heart
With pity that doth make me sick. A lady
So fair, and fastened to an empery   120
Would make the great'st king double, to be
          partnered
With tomboys hired with that self exhibition
Which your own coffers yield; with diseased
          ventures
That play with all infirmities for gold
Which rottenness can lend nature; such boiled stuff   125
As well might poison poison! Be revenged,
Or she that bore you was no queen, and you
Recoil from your great stock.

IMOGEN   Revenged?

106 **gripes** grips 108 **bye-peeping** peeping sidelong 109 **illustrous**
lackluster 112 **Encounter** confront 112 **revolt** inconstancy 113–14 **Not I ...**
pronounce I, though disinclined to bring this news, report 115 **beggary**
meanness 116 **conscience** knowledge 120 **empery** empire 121 **Would** which
would 122 **tomboys** whores 122 **self exhibition** self-same allowance 123
ventures whores 125 **boiled stuff** i.e., women who have been "sweated" for
venereal disease 128 **Recoil** decline

How should I be revenged? If this be true—
130 As I have such a heart that both mine ears
Must not in haste abuse—if it be true,
How should I be revenged?

IACHIMO   Should he make me
Live like Diana's priest betwixt cold sheets,
Whiles he is vaulting variable ramps,
135 In your despite, upon your purse? Revenge it.
I dedicate myself to your sweet pleasure,
More noble than that runagate to your bed,
And will continue fast to your affection,
Still close as sure.

IMOGEN   What ho, Pisanio!

140 IACHIMO Let me my service tender on your lips.

IMOGEN Away, I do condemn mine ears that have
So long attended thee. If thou wert honorable,
Thou wouldst have told this tale for virtue, not
For such an end thou seek'st, as base as strange.
145 Thou wrong'st a gentleman who is as far
From thy report as thou from honor, and
Solicits here a lady that disdains
Thee and the devil alike. What ho, Pisanio!
The King my father shall be made acquainted
150 Of thy assault. If he shall think it fit
A saucy stranger in his court to mart
As in a Romish stew and to expound
His beastly mind to us, he hath a court
He little cares for and a daughter who
155 He not respects at all. What ho, Pisanio!

IACHIMO O happy Leonatus! I may say
The credit that thy lady hath of thee
Deserves thy trust, and thy most perfect goodness

134 **variable ramps** fickle whores 137 **runagate** traitor 139 **close** secret
142 **attended thee** listened to you (in anger Imogen shifts from formal "you" to
familiar "thee," thus treating Iachimo as an inferior; at line 168 she reverts to
"you") 151 **to mart** should do business 152 **Romish stew** Roman
bawdyhouse 157 **credit** trust 157 **of** in

142

Her assured credit. Blessèd live you long,
A lady to the worthiest sir that ever   160
Country called his, and you his mistress, only
For the most worthiest fit. Give me your pardon.
I have spoke this to know if your affiance
Were deeply rooted, and shall make your lord
That which he is, new o'er; and he is one   165
The truest mannered, such a holy witch
That he enchants societies into him.
Half all men's hearts are his.

IMOGEN   You make amends.

IACHIMO He sits 'mongst men like a descended god.
He hath a kind of honor sets him off   170
More than a mortal seeming. Be not angry,
Most mighty Princess, that I have adventured
To try your taking of a false report, which hath
Honored with confirmation your great judgment
In the election of a sir so rare,   175
Which you know cannot err. The love I bear him
Made me to fan you thus, but the gods made you,
Unlike all others, chaffless. Pray your pardon.

IMOGEN All's well, sir. Take my pow'r i' th' court for
    yours.

IACHIMO My humble thanks. I had almost forgot   180
T' entreat your grace but in a small request,
And yet of moment too, for it concerns
Your lord, myself, and other noble friends
Are partners in the business.

IMOGEN   Pray what is't?

IACHIMO Some dozen Romans of us and your lord—   185
The best feather of our wing—have mingled sums
To buy a present for the Emperor;
Which I, the factor for the rest, have done

161 **his** its own   163 **affiance** faith   165 **one** above all   166 **truest mannered**
most honestly behaved   166 **witch** charmer   167 **into** to   171 **mortal seeming**
human appearance   173 **try your taking** test your reception   176 **Which**
who   177 **fan** winnow   184 **Are** i.e., who are   188 **factor** agent

143

In France. 'Tis plate of rare device, and jewels
190   Of rich and exquisite form, their values great,
And I am something curious, being strange,
To have them in safe stowage. May it please you
To take them in protection?

IMOGEN   Willingly;
And pawn mine honor for their safety. Since
195   My lord hath interest in them, I will keep them
In my bedchamber.

IACHIMO   They are in a trunk
Attended by my men. I will make bold
To send them to you, only for this night.
I must aboard tomorrow.

IMOGEN   O, no, no.

200 IACHIMO Yes, I beseech, or I shall short my word
By length'ning my return. From Gallia
I crossed the seas on purpose and on promise
To see your grace.

IMOGEN   I thank you for your pains.
But not away tomorrow!

IACHIMO   O, I must, madam.
205   Therefore I shall beseech you, if you please
To greet your lord with writing, do't tonight.
I have outstood my time, which is material
To th' tender of our present.

IMOGEN   I will write.
Send your trunk to me; it shall safe be kept
210   And truly yielded you. You're very welcome.
                              Exeunt [severally].

191 **curious** anxious 191 **strange** a foreigner 200 **short** fall short of
201 **Gallia** France 208 **tender** giving 210s.d. **severally** by different tiring-
house doors

ACT II

Scene I. [*Britain.*]

Enter Cloten and the two Lords.

CLOTEN Was there ever man had such luck? When I
kissed the jack, upon an upcast to be hit away! I
had a hundred pound on't. And then a whoreson
jackanapes must take me up for swearing, as if I
borrowed mine oaths of him and might not spend   5
them at my pleasure.

FIRST LORD What got he by that? You have broke his
pate with your bowl.

SECOND LORD [*Aside*] If his wit had been like him
that broke it, it would have run all out.   10

CLOTEN When a gentleman is disposed to swear, it is
not for any standers-by to curtail his oaths. Ha?

SECOND LORD No, my lord—[*Aside*] nor crop the ears
of them.

CLOTEN Whoreson dog, I gave him satisfaction! Would 15
he had been one of my rank.

SECOND LORD [*Aside*] To have smelled like a fool.

II.i.2 **kissed the jack** came close to the target ball (in the game of bowls)
2 **upcast** chance   4 **take me up** rebuke me   16 **of my rank** i.e., so I might have
challenged him to a duel (the Second Lord quibbles)

CLOTEN I am not vexed more at anything in th' earth.
A pox on't! I had rather not be so noble as I am.
20   They dare not fight with me because of the Queen
my mother. Every jack-slave hath his bellyful of
fighting, and I must go up and down like a cock that
nobody can match.

SECOND LORD [*Aside*] You are cock and capon too,
25   and you crow, cock, with your comb on.

CLOTEN Sayest thou?

SECOND LORD It is not fit your lordship should undertake every companion that you give offense to.

CLOTEN No, I know that, but it is fit I should commit
30   offense to my inferiors.

SECOND LORD Ay, it is fit for your lordship only.

CLOTEN Why, so I say.

FIRST LORD Did you hear of a stranger that's come
to court tonight?

35   CLOTEN A stranger, and I not know on't?

SECOND LORD [*Aside*] He's a strange fellow himself,
and knows it not.

FIRST LORD There's an Italian come, and, 'tis thought,
one of Leonatus' friends.

40   CLOTEN Leonatus? A banished rascal, and he's another,
whatsoever he be. Who told you of this stranger?

FIRST LORD One of your lordship's pages.

CLOTEN Is it fit I went to look upon him? Is there no
derogation in't?

45   SECOND LORD You cannot derogate, my lord.

21 **jack-slave** lout   25 **and** if   27–28 **undertake** take on   28 **companion** low
fellow   29–30 **commit offense** offer battle   33 **stranger** foreigner   44 **derogation** loss of dignity   45 **cannot derogate** do anything derogatory to your rank
(with quibble on "have no dignity to lose")

CLOTEN Not easily, I think.

SECOND LORD [*Aside*] You are a fool, granted; therefore your issues, being foolish, do not derogate.

CLOTEN Come, I'll go see this Italian. What I have lost
today at bowls I'll win tonight of him. Come, go.   50

SECOND LORD I'll attend your lordship.
                        Exeunt [*Cloten and First Lord*].
That such a crafty devil as is his mother
Should yield the world this ass! A woman that
Bears all down with her brain, and this her son
Cannot take two from twenty, for his heart,   55
And leave eighteen. Alas, poor princess,
Thou divine Imogen, that thou endur'st,
Betwixt a father by thy stepdame governed,
A mother hourly coining plots, a wooer
More hateful than the foul expulsion is   60
Of thy dear husband, than that horrid act
Of the divorce he'ld make. The heavens hold firm
The walls of thy dear honor, keep unshaked
That temple, thy fair mind, that thou mayst stand,
T' enjoy thy banished lord and this great land! *Exit*. 65

Scene II. [*Britain*.]

Enter Imogen in her bed, and a Lady.

IMOGEN Who's there? My woman Helen?

LADY   Please you, madam.

IMOGEN What hour is it?

48 **issues** deeds 54 **Bears all down** overcomes everything 55 **for his heart** to
save his life II.ii.s.d. **Enter . . . bed** (in Elizabethan open-stage production the
bed is "thrust out" upon the stage by attendants and the trunk is carried on; in
modern proscenium-arch production the bed and trunk are usually "discovered"
by raising the front curtain)

LADY   Almost midnight, madam.

IMOGEN I have read three hours then. Mine eyes are
    weak.
    Fold down the leaf where I have left. To bed.
5   Take not away the taper, leave it burning;
    And if thou canst awake by four o' th' clock,
    I prithee call me. Sleep hath seized me wholly.
                                [*Exit Lady*.]
    To your protection I commend me, gods.
    From fairies and the tempters of the night
10   Guard me, beseech ye!
              Sleeps. Iachimo [comes] from the trunk.

IACHIMO The crickets sing, and man's o'erlabored
    sense
    Repairs itself by rest. Our Tarquin thus
    Did softly press the rushes ere he wakened
    The chastity he wounded. Cytherea,
15   How bravely thou becom'st thy bed, fresh lily,
    And whiter than the sheets! That I might touch!
    But kiss, one kiss! Rubies unparagoned,
    How dearly they do't! 'Tis her breathing that
    Perfumes the chamber thus. The flame o' th' taper
20   Bows toward her and would underpeep her lids
    To see th' enclosèd lights, now canopied
    Under these windows, white and azure-laced
    With blue of heaven's own tinct. But my design:
    To note the chamber. I will write all down:
25   Such and such pictures; there the window; such
    Th' adornment of her bed; the arras, figures,
    Why, such and such; and the contents o' th' story.
    Ah, but some natural notes about her body
    Above ten thousand meaner movables
30   Would testify, t' enrich mine inventory.
    O sleep, thou ape of death, lie dull upon her.

---

9 **fairies** i.e., malignant fairies 12 **Tarquin** (who raped Lucrece) 13 **rushes**
Elizabethan floor-covering 14 **Cytherea** Venus 15 **bravely** magnificently
15 **lily** emblem of chastity 22 **windows** shutters, i.e., eyelids 27 **th' story** i.e.,
the story depicted on the arras (cf. II.iv.69) 28 **notes** marks 29 **meaner**
movables lesser furnishings 31 **ape** mimic 31 **dull** heavy

And be her sense but as a monument,
Thus in a chapel lying. Come off, come off—
                  [*Removing her bracelet*]
As slippery as the Gordian knot was hard.
'Tis mine, and this will witness outwardly,   35
As strongly as the conscience does within,
To th' madding of her lord. On her left breast
A mole cinque-spotted, like the crimson drops
I' th' bottom of a cowslip. Here's a voucher
Stronger than ever law could make. This secret   40
Will force him think I have picked the lock and
   ta'en
The treasure of her honor. No more. To what end?
Why should I write this down that's riveted,
Screwed to my memory? She hath been reading late
The tale of Tereus. Here the leaf's turned down   45
Where Philomel gave up. I have enough.
To th' trunk again, and shut the spring of it.
Swift, swift, you dragons of the night, that dawning
May bare the raven's eye. I lodge in fear.
Though this a heavenly angel, hell is here.   50
                        Clock strikes.
One, two, three. Time, time!   [*Goes into the trunk.*]
                              Exeunt.

---

32 **monument** recumbent effigy on a tomb   36 **conscience** knowledge
38 **cinque-spotted** having five spots   39 **voucher** guarantee   45 **Tereus** (who
raped Philomela; apparently the book is Ovid's *Metamorphoses*)   49 **bare the**
raven's eye (the raven supposedly being an early bird)   51s.d. **Exeunt** (the bed
and trunk are carried offstage or concealed by dropping the front curtain)

Scene III. [*Britain.*]

Enter Cloten and Lords.

FIRST LORD Your lordship is the most patient man in loss, the most coldest that ever turned up ace.

CLOTEN It would make any man cold to lose.

FIRST LORD But not every man patient after the noble
5   temper of your lordship. You are most hot and furious when you win.

CLOTEN Winning will put any man into courage. If I could get this foolish Imogen, I should have gold enough. It's almost morning, is't not?

10 FIRST LORD Day, my lord.

CLOTEN I would this music would come. I am advised to give her music a-mornings; they say it will penetrate.

Enter Musicians.

Come on, tune. If you can penetrate her with your
15   fingering, so; we'll try with tongue too. If none will do, let her remain, but I'll never give o'er. First, a very excellent good-conceited thing; after, a wonderful sweet air with admirable rich words to it— and then let her consider.

Song.

20   Hark, hark, the lark at heaven's gate sings,
          And Phoebus gins arise,

II.iii.2 **coldest** calmest   2 **ace** one, the lowest throw at dice (pun on "ass")
3 **cold** gloomy   12–13 **penetrate** affect emotionally (with bawdy quibble)
16 **give o'er** give up   17 **good-conceited** well-devised   21 **Phoebus gins**
Apollo (the sun) begins to

His steeds to water at those springs
  On chaliced flowers that lies;
And winking Mary-buds begin
  To ope their golden eyes.   25
With every thing that pretty is,
  My lady sweet, arise,
    Arise, arise!

CLOTEN So, get you gone. If this penetrate, I will consider your music the better; if it do not, it is a   30
vice in her ears which horsehairs and calves'
guts, nor the voice of unpaved eunuch to boot,
can never amend.

                      [*Exeunt Musicians.*]

      Enter Cymbeline and Queen.

SECOND LORD Here comes the King.

CLOTEN I am glad I was up so late, for that's the reason   35
I was up so early. He cannot choose but take this
service I have done fatherly. Good morrow to your
Majesty and to my gracious mother.

CYMBELINE Attend you here the door of our stern
daughter? Will she not forth?   40

CLOTEN I have assailed her with musics, but she vouch-
safes no notice.

CYMBELINE The exile of her minion is too new;
She hath not yet forgot him. Some more time
Must wear the print of his remembrance out,   45
And then she's yours.

QUEEN   You are most bound to th' King,
Who lets go by no vantages that may
Prefer you to his daughter. Frame yourself
To orderly solicits, and be friended

24 **winking Mary-buds** closed marigold buds   29–30 **consider** reward
31 **vice** flaw   31 **horsehairs** bowstrings   31–32 **calves' guts** fiddle-strings
32 **unpaved** unstoned (i.e., castrated)   43 **minion** darling   47 **vantages**
opportunities   48 **Prefer** recommend   48 **Frame** prepare   49 **solicits**
solicitations

50   With aptness of the season. Make denials
        Increase your services. So seem as if
        You were inspired to do those duties which
        You tender to her; that you in all obey her,
        Save when command to your dismission tends,
        And therein you are senseless.

55 CLOTEN   Senseless? Not so.

                    [*Enter a Messenger.*]

    MESSENGER So like you, sir, ambassadors from Rome.
        The one is Caius Lucius.

    CYMBELINE   A worthy fellow,
        Albeit he comes on angry purpose now.
        But that's no fault of his. We must receive him
60   According to the honor of his sender,
        And towards himself, his goodness forespent on us,
        We must extend our notice. Our dear son,
        When you have given good morning to your
            mistress,
        Attend the Queen and us. We shall have need
        T" employ you towards this Roman. Come, our
65   queen.   *Exeunt [all but Cloten].*

    CLOTEN If she be up, I'll speak with her; if not,
        Let her lie still and dream. By your leave, ho!
                                        [*Knocks.*]
        I know her women are about her. What
        If I do line one of their hands? 'Tis gold
        Which buys admittance—oft it doth—yea, and
70   makes
        Diana's rangers false themselves, yield up
        Their deer to th' stand o' th' stealer; and 'tis gold
        Which makes the true man killed and saves the
            thief,
        Nay, sometime hangs both thief and true man. What

54 **dismission** rejection 55 **senseless** insensible 56 **So like you** if you
please 61 **forespent** having earlier been spent 69 **line** i.e., with money
71 **rangers** gamekeepers 71 **false** betray 72 **stand o' th' stealer** standing-
place of the hunter (quibble on "erection of the phallus")

Can it not do and undo? I will make   75
One of her women lawyer to me, for
I yet not understand the case myself.
By your leave.   *Knocks.*

Enter a Lady.

LADY Who's there that knocks?

CLOTEN   A gentleman.

LADY   No more?

CLOTEN Yes, and a gentlewoman's son.

LADY   That's more   80
Than some whose tailors are as dear as yours
Can justly boast of. What's your lordship's pleasure?

CLOTEN Your lady's person. Is she ready?

LADY   Ay,
To keep her chamber.

CLOTEN   There is gold for you.
Sell me your good report.   85

LADY How? My good name? Or to report of you
What I shall think is good? The Princess!

Enter Imogen. [Exit Lady.]

CLOTEN Good morrow, fairest sister. Your sweet hand.

IMOGEN Good morrow, sir. You lay out too much
    pains
For purchasing but trouble. The thanks I give   90
Is telling you that I am poor of thanks
And scarce can spare them.

CLOTEN   Still I swear I love you.

IMOGEN If you but said so, 'twere as deep with me.
If you swear still, your recompense is still
That I regard it not.

76 **lawyer** to quibble on "lower to," i.e., lie down for 77 **understand** quibble
on "stand under," i.e., penetrate 83 **ready** dressed 93 **deep** effective 94 **still**
continually

95 CLOTEN   This is no answer.

IMOGEN But that you shall not say I yield, being
      silent,
    I would not speak. I pray you spare me. Faith,
    I shall unfold equal discourtesy
    To your best kindness. One of your great knowing
100   Should learn, being taught, forbearance.

CLOTEN To leave you in your madness, 'twere my sin.
    I will not.

IMOGEN Fools are not mad folks.

CLOTEN   Do you call me fool?

IMOGEN As I am mad, I do.
105   If you'll be patient, I'll no more be mad;
    That cures us both. I am much sorry, sir,
    You put me to forget a lady's manners
    By being so verbal; and learn now for all
    That I, which know my heart, do here pronounce
110   By th' very truth of it, I care not for you,
    And am so near the lack of charity
    To accuse myself I hate you—which I had rather
    You felt than make't my boast.

CLOTEN   You sin against
    Obedience, which you owe your father. For
115   The contract you pretend with that base wretch,
    One bred of alms and fostered with cold dishes,
    With scraps o' th' court—it is no contract, none.
    And though it be allowed in meaner parties—
    Yet who than he more mean?—to knit their souls,
120   On whom there is no more dependency
    But brats and beggary, in self-figured knot;
    Yet you are curbed from that enlargement by

96 But so 98 unfold display 98 equal discourtesy i.e., discourtesy equal
99 knowing knowledge 108 verbal talkative 112 To accuse . . . hate that I
accuse myself of hating 114–15 For . . . pretend as for the marriage contract you
claim 118 meaner lower-ranking 120 dependency retinue 121 self-figured
shaped by one's self 122 enlargement freedom

The consequence o' th' crown, and must not foil
The precious note of it with a base slave,
A hilding for a livery, a squire's cloth,   125
A pantler—not so eminent.

IMOGEN   Profane fellow!
Wert thou the son of Jupiter, and no more
But what thou art besides, thou wert too base
To be his groom. Thou wert dignified enough,
Even to the point of envy, if 'twere made   130
Comparative to your virtues to be styled
The under-hangman of his kingdom, and hated
For being preferred so well.

CLOTEN   The south fog rot him!

IMOGEN He never can meet more mischance than
come
To be but named of thee. His meanest garment   135
That ever hath but clipped his body is dearer
In my respect than all the hairs above thee,
Were they all made such men. How now, Pisanio?

Enter Pisanio.

CLOTEN "His garment"? Now the devil—

IMOGEN To Dorothy my woman hie thee presently.   140

CLOTEN "His garment"?

IMOGEN   I am sprited with a fool,
Frighted, and angered worse. Go bid my woman
Search for a jewel that too casually
Hath left mine arm. It was thy master's. Shrew me
If I would lose it for a revenue   145
Of any king's in Europe. I do think
I saw't this morning; confident I am

123 **consequence** importance 123 **foil** defile 124 **note** eminence, importance
125 **hilding for** good-for-nothing fit only for 126 **pantler** pantry-servant
129 **dignified** given honor 130–32 **if 'twere . . . kingdom** if, according to the
virtue of each of you, you were made under-hangman and he king (Heilman)
133 **preferred** advanced 133 **The south fog** the damp, supposedly unhealthy,
south wind 136 **clipped** embraced 137 **respect** regard 140 **presently**
immediately 141 **sprited** haunted 144 **Shrew** curse

Last night 'twas on mine arm; I kissed it.
I hope it be not gone to tell my lord
That I kiss aught but he.

150 PISANIO   'Twill not be lost.

IMOGEN I hope so. Go and search.   [*Exit Pisanio.*]

CLOTEN   You have abused me.
"His meanest garment"?

IMOGEN   Ay, I said so, sir.
If you will make't an action, call witness to't.

CLOTEN I will inform your father.

IMOGEN   Your mother too.
155   She's my good lady and will conceive, I hope,
But the worst of me. So I leave you, sir,
To th' worst of discontent.   *Exit.*

CLOTEN   I'll be revenged.
"His meanest garment"? Well.   *Exit.*

Scene IV. [*Rome.*]

Enter Posthumus and Philario.

POSTHUMUS Fear it not, sir. I would I were so sure
To win the King as I am bold her honor
Will remain hers.

PHILARIO   What means do you make to him?

POSTHUMUS Not any, but abide the change of time,
5   Quake in the present winter's state, and wish
That warmer days would come. In these feared
      hopes

151 **so** i.e., not 153 **action** lawsuit 155 **conceive** come to believe
158s.d. **Exit** (by the other door) II.iv.2 **bold** confident 3 **means** overtures
6 **feared** fear-laden

I barely gratify your love; they failing,
I must die much your debtor.

PHILARIO Your very goodness and your company
    O'erpays all I can do. By this, your king   10
    Hath heard of great Augustus; Caius Lucius
    Will do's commission throughly. And I think
    He'll grant the tribute, send th' arrearages,
    Or look upon our Romans, whose remembrance
    Is yet fresh in their grief.

POSTHUMUS   I do believe,   15
    Statist though I am none, nor like to be,
    That this will prove a war; and you shall hear
    The legions now in Gallia sooner landed
    In our not-fearing Britain than have tidings
    Of any penny tribute paid. Our countrymen   20
    Are men more ordered than when Julius Caesar
    Smiled at their lack of skill but found their courage
    Worthy his frowning at. Their discipline,
    Now mingled with their courages, will make known
    To their approvers they are people such   25
    That mend upon the world.

Enter Iachimo.

PHILARIO   See, Iachimo!

POSTHUMUS The swiftest harts have posted you by
    land,
    And winds of all the corners kissed your sails
    To make your vessel nimble.

PHILARIO   Welcome, sir.

POSTHUMUS I hope the briefness of your answer made   30
    The speediness of your return.

IACHIMO   Your lady
    Is one of the fairest that I have looked upon.

7 **gratify** repay 10 **this** this time 16 **Statist** politician 25 **approvers** testers
26 **That mend upon** whose reputation grows with 27 **have posted** must have
sped 28 **corners** i.e., of the earth 30 **your answer** the answer you received

POSTHUMUS And therewithal the best, or let her beauty
   Look through a casement to allure false hearts
   And be false with them.

35 IACHIMO   Here are letters for you.

POSTHUMUS Their tenor good, I trust.

IACHIMO   'Tis very like.

POSTHUMUS Was Caius Lucius in the Briton court
   When you were there?

IACHIMO   He was expected then,
   But not approached.

POSTHUMUS   All is well yet.
40 Sparkles this stone as it was wont, or is't not
   Too dull for your good wearing?

IACHIMO   If I have lost it,
   I should have lost the worth of it in gold.
   I'll make a journey twice as far t' enjoy
   A second night of such sweet shortness which
45 Was mine in Britain—for the ring is won.

POSTHUMUS The stone's too hard to come by.

IACHIMO   Not a whit,
   Your lady being so easy.

POSTHUMUS   Make not, sir,
   Your loss your sport. I hope you know that we
   Must not continue friends.

IACHIMO   Good sir, we must,
50 If you keep covenant. Had I not brought
   The knowledge of your mistress home, I grant
   We were to question farther, but I now
   Profess myself the winner of her honor,
   Together with your ring, and not the wronger
55 Of her or you, having proceeded but
   By both your wills.

35 **are letters** is a letter   51 **knowledge** carnal knowledge   52 **question** dispute
(as in a duel)

POSTHUMUS   If you can make't apparent
That you have tasted her in bed, my hand
And ring is yours. If not, the foul opinion
You had of her pure honor gains or loses
Your sword or mine, or masterless leave both   60
To who shall find them.

IACHIMO   Sir, my circumstances,
Being so near the truth as I will make them,
Must first induce you to believe; whose strength
I will confirm with oath, which I doubt not
You'll give me leave to spare when you shall find   65
You need it not.

POSTHUMUS   Proceed.

IACHIMO   First, her bedchamber—
Where I confess I slept not, but profess
Had that was well worth watching—it was hanged
With tapestry of silk and silver; the story
Proud Cleopatra, when she met her Roman   70
And Cydnus swelled above the banks, or for
The press of boats or pride: a piece of work
So bravely done, so rich, that it did strive
In workmanship and value; which I wondered
Could be so rarely and exactly wrought,   75
Since the true life on't was—

POSTHUMUS   This is true,
And this you might have heard of here, by me
Or by some other.

IACHIMO   More particulars
Must justify my knowledge.

POSTHUMUS   So they must,
Or do your honor injury.

IACHIMO   The chimney   80

60 **leave** let it leave   61 **circumstances** details   65 **spare** omit   68 **watching**
remaining awake for   70 **Roman** Antony   71 **or** either   73 **bravely** finely
73–74 **it did strive ... value** it was doubtful whether the workmanship or the
intrinsic value was greater   79 **justify** prove   80 **chimney** fireplace

Is south the chamber, and the chimney-piece
Chaste Dian bathing. Never saw I figures
So likely to report themselves. The cutter
Was as another Nature, dumb; outwent her,
Motion and breath left out.

85 POSTHUMUS   This is a thing
Which you might from relation likewise reap,
Being, as it is, much spoke of.

IACHIMO   The roof o' th' chamber
With golden cherubins is fretted. Her andirons—
I had forgot them—were two winking Cupids
90 Of silver, each on one foot standing, nicely
Depending on their brands.

POSTHUMUS   This is her honor!
Let it be granted you have seen all this—and praise
Be given to your remembrance—the description
Of what is in her chamber nothing saves
The wager you have laid.

95 IACHIMO   Then, if you can
                              [*Showing the bracelet*]
Be pale, I beg but leave to air this jewel. See!
And now 'tis up again. It must be married
To that your diamond; I'll keep them.

POSTHUMUS   Jove!
Once more let me behold it. Is it that
Which I left with her?

100 IACHIMO   Sir, I thank her, that.
She stripped it from her arm; I see her yet.
Her pretty action did outsell her gift,
And yet enriched it too. She gave it me and said
She prized it once.

---

81 **chimney-piece** sculpture placed over the fireplace   83 **likely to report** apt to
identify   83 **cutter** sculptor   84 **as … dumb** like Nature in creative power
although unable to make the sculpture speak   84 **outwent** surpassed   86 **relation** report   88 **fretted** carved   89 **winking** with closed eyes, i.e., blind
91 **Depending on their brands** leaning on their torches   96 **Be pale** remain
unflushed, i.e., calm   97 **up** put up, pocketed   102 **outsell** exceed in value

POSTHUMUS   May be she plucked it off
  To send it me.

IACHIMO   She writes so to you, doth she?   105

POSTHUMUS O, no, no, no, 'tis true. Here, take this too.
                              [*Giving the ring*]
  It is a basilisk unto mine eye,
  Kills me to look on't. Let there be no honor
  Where there is beauty; truth, where semblance;
        love,
  Where there's another man. The vows of women   110
  Of no more bondage be to where they are made
  Than they are to their virtues, which is nothing.
  O, above measure false!

PHILARIO   Have patience, sir,
  And take your ring again; 'tis not yet won.
  It may be probable she lost it, or   115
  Who knows if one her women, being corrupted,
  Hath stol'n it from her?

POSTHUMUS   Very true,
  And so I hope he came by't. Back my ring;
  Render to me some corporal sign about her
  More evident than this, for this was stol'n.   120

IACHIMO By Jupiter, I had it from her arm.

POSTHUMUS Hark you, he swears; by Jupiter he swears.
  'Tis true—nay, keep the ring—'tis true. I am sure
  She would not lose it. Her attendants are
  All sworn and honorable. They induced to steal it?   125
  And by a stranger? No, he hath enjoyed her.
  The cognizance of her incontinency
  Is this. She hath bought the name of whore thus
        dearly.

---

107 **basilisk** monster supposedly capable of killing by look   110–12 **The vows ... nothing** let the vows of women be no more binding to the recipients of them than women are bound to their own virtues—which is not at all (Nosworthy)   115 **probable** provable   116 **one** one of   120 **evident** conclusive   125 **sworn** i.e., to loyalty   127 **cognizance** badge   128 **this** the bracelet

There, take thy hire, and all the fiends of hell
Divide themselves between you!

130 PHILARIO   Sir, be patient.
This is not strong enough to be believed
Of one persuaded well of.

POSTHUMUS   Never talk on't.
She hath been colted by him.

IACHIMO   If you seek
For further satisfying, under her breast—
135 Worthy the pressing—lies a mole, right proud
Of that most delicate lodging. By my life,
I kissed it, and it gave me present hunger
To feed again, though full. You do remember
This stain upon her?

POSTHUMUS   Ay, and it doth confirm
140 Another stain, as big as hell can hold,
Were there no more but it.

IACHIMO   Will you hear more?

POSTHUMUS Spare your arithmetic; never count the
    turns.
Once, and a million!

IACHIMO   I'll be sworn.

POSTHUMUS   No swearing.
If you will swear you have not done't, you lie,
145 And I will kill thee if thou dost deny
Thou'st made me cuckold.

IACHIMO   I'll deny nothing.

POSTHUMUS O that I had her here, to tear her limb-
    meal!
I will go there and do't i' th' court, before
Her father. I'll do something.   *Exit.*

PHILARIO   Quite besides

129 **hire** reward   132 **persuaded** that we are persuaded to think   133 **colted**
possessed sexually   137 **present** immediate   139 **stain** mark   140 **stain**
corruption   147 **limb-meal** limb from limb

The government of patience! You have won.   150
Let's follow him and pervert the present wrath
He hath against himself.

IACHIMO   With all my heart.   *Exeunt.*

[Scene V. *Rome.*]

Enter Posthumus.

POSTHUMUS Is there no way for men to be, but
      women
   Must be half-workers? We are all bastards,
   And that most venerable man which I
   Did call my father was I know not where
   When I was stamped. Some coiner with his tools   5
   Made me a counterfeit; yet my mother seemed
   The Dian of that time. So doth my wife
   The nonpareil of this. O, vengeance, vengeance!
   Me of my lawful pleasure she restrained
   And prayed me oft forbearance—did it with   10
   A pudency so rosy, the sweet view on't
   Might well have warmed old Saturn—that I
      thought her
   As chaste as unsunned snow. O, all the devils!
   This yellow Iachimo in an hour, was't not?
   Or less? At first? Perchance he spoke not, but,   15
   Like a full-acorned boar, a German one,
   Cried "O!" and mounted; found no opposition
   But what he looked for should oppose and she
   Should from encounter guard. Could I find out
   The woman's part in me! For there's no motion   20

150 **government** control   151 **pervert** divert   II.v.1 **be** exist   2 **half-workers**
i.e., in begetting   5 **stamped** minted   5 **coiner** counterfeiter   7 **Dian** Diana
(goddess of chastity)   8 **nonpareil** one without equal   11 **pudency** modesty
11 **on't** of it   12 **Saturn** (considered to be cold and gloomy)   14 **yellow** i.e., of
complexion   15 **At first** immediately   16 **full-acorned** fed full with acorns
20 **motion** impulse

That tends to vice in man but I affirm
It is the woman's part. Be it lying, note it,
The woman's; flattering, hers; deceiving, hers;
Lust and rank thoughts, hers, hers; revenges, hers;
25 Ambitions, covetings, change of prides, disdain,
Nice longing, slanders, mutability,
All faults that have a name, nay, that hell knows,
Why, hers, in part or all, but rather all.
For even to vice
30 They are not constant, but are changing still
One vice but of a minute old for one
Not half so old as that. I'll write against them,
Detest them, curse them. Yet 'tis greater skill
In a true hate to pray they have their will;
35 The very devils cannot plague them better.   *Exit*.

24 **rank** lascivious   25 **change of prides** varying extravagances   26 **Nice**
wanton   26 **mutability** inconstancy   33 **skill** reason

ACT III

Scene I. [*Britain.*]

Enter in state Cymbeline, Queen, Cloten, and Lords at one door and, at another, Caius Lucius and Attendants.

CYMBELINE Now say, what would Augustus Caesar
    with us?

LUCIUS When Julius Caesar, whose remembrance yet
    Lives in men's eyes and will to ears and tongues
    Be theme and hearing ever, was in this Britain
    And conquered it, Cassibelan thine uncle,   5
    Famous in Caesar's praises no whit less
    Than in his feats deserving it, for him
    And his succession granted Rome a tribute,
    Yearly three thousand pounds, which by thee lately
    Is left untendered.

QUEEN   And, to kill the marvel,   10
    Shall be so ever.

CLOTEN   There be many Caesars
    Ere such another Julius. Britain's a world
    By itself, and we will nothing pay
    For wearing our own noses.

III.i.10 **kill the marvel** end the astonishment (caused by non-payment)

QUEEN   That opportunity
15   Which then they had to take from's, to resume
      We have again. Remember, sir, my liege,
      The kings your ancestors, together with
      The natural bravery of your isle, which stands
      As Neptune's park, ribbèd and palèd in
20   With rocks unscalable and roaring waters,
      With sands that will not bear your enemies' boats
      But suck them up to th' topmast. A kind of
          conquest
      Caesar made here, but made not here his brag
      Of "Came and saw and overcame." With shame,
25   The first that ever touched him, he was carried
      From off our coast, twice beaten; and his shipping,
      Poor ignorant baubles on our terrible seas,
      Like eggshells moved upon their surges, cracked
      As easily 'gainst our rocks. For joy whereof
30   The famed Cassibelan, who was once at point—
      O giglot Fortune!—to master Caesar's sword,
      Made Lud's Town with rejoicing fires bright
      And Britons strut with courage.

CLOTEN Come, there's no more tribute to be paid. Our
35   kingdom is stronger than it was at that time, and, as
      I said, there is no moe such Caesars. Other of them
      may have crooked noses, but to owe such straight
      arms, none.

CYMBELINE Son, let your mother end.

40   CLOTEN We have yet many among us can gripe as
      hard as Cassibelan. I do not say I am one, but I
      have a hand. Why tribute? Why should we pay
      tribute? If Caesar can hide the sun from us with a
      blanket or put the moon in his pocket, we will pay
45   him tribute for light; else, sir, no more tribute, pray
      you now.

---

19 **ribbèd** enclosed   19 **palèd** fenced   27 **ignorant** inexperienced   30 **at point** at the point   31 **giglot** wanton   31 **to master** of mastering   32 **Lud's Town** London   37 **crooked** i.e., Roman   37 **owe** own   40 **gripe** grasp

CYMBELINE You must know,
    Till the injurious Romans did extort
    This tribute from us, we were free. Caesar's
        ambition,
    Which swelled so much that it did almost stretch   50
    The sides o' th' world, against all color here
    Did put the yoke upon's; which to shake off
    Becomes a warlike people, whom we reckon
    Ourselves to be. We do say then to Caesar,
    Our ancestor was that Mulmutius which   55
    Ordained our laws, whose use the sword of Caesar
    Hath too much mangled, whose repair and
        franchise
    Shall, by the power we hold, be our good deed,
    Though Rome be therefore angry. Mulmutius made
        our laws,
    Who was the first of Britain which did put   60
    His brows within a golden crown and called
    Himself a king.

LUCIUS   I am sorry, Cymbeline,
    That I am to pronounce Augustus Caesar—
    Caesar, that hath moe kings his servants than
    Thyself domestic officers—thine enemy.   65
    Receive it from me then: war and confusion
    In Caesar's name pronounce I 'gainst thee. Look
    For fury not to be resisted. Thus defied,
    I thank thee for myself.

CYMBELINE   Thou art welcome, Caius.
    Thy Caesar knighted me; my youth I spent   70
    Much under him; of him I gathered honor,
    Which he to seek of me again, perforce,
    Behooves me keep at utterance. I am perfect
    That the Pannonians and Dalmatians for
    Their liberties are now in arms, a precedent   75

48 **injurious** insulting   51 **against all color** without any right   57 **franchise**
free exercise   64 **his** as his   66 **confusion** destruction   72 **he to seek** his seeking
73 **keep at utterance** defend to the last ditch   73 **perfect** well aware
74 **Pannonians and Dalmatians** inhabitants of present-day Hungary and what
was formerly Yugoslavia

Which not to read would show the Britons cold.
So Caesar shall not find them.

LUCIUS   Let proof speak.

CLOTEN His Majesty bids you welcome. Make pastime
with us a day or two, or longer. If you seek us after-
80   wards in other terms, you shall find us in our salt-
water girdle; if you beat us out of it, it is yours. If
you fall in the adventure, our crows shall fare the
better for you, and there's an end.

LUCIUS So, sir.

CYMBELINE I know your master's pleasure, and he
85   mine.
All the remain is, welcome.   *Exeunt.*

Scene II. [*Britain.*]

Enter Pisanio reading of a letter.

PISANIO How? of adultery? Wherefore write you not
What monsters her accuse? Leonatus,
O master, what a strange infection
Is fall'n into thy ear! What false Italian,
5   As poisonous-tongued as handed, hath prevailed
On thy too ready hearing? Disloyal? No.
She's punished for her truth and undergoes,
More goddess-like than wife-like, such assaults
As would take in some virtue. O my master,
10   Thy mind to her is now as low as were
Thy fortunes. How? That I should murder her,
Upon the love and truth and vows which I
Have made to thy command? I her? Her blood?
If it be so to do good service, never

76 **cold** deficient in spirit   77 **proof** experience   86 **the remain** that remains
III.ii.3 **strange** foreign   7 **truth** fidelity   7 **undergoes** endures   9 **take in**
conquer   10 **to** compared with

Let me be counted serviceable. How look I   15
That I should seem to lack humanity
So much as this fact comes to? [*Reading*] "Do't!
  The letter
That I have sent her, by her own command
Shall give thee opportunity." O damned paper,
Black as the ink that's on thee! Senseless bauble,   20
Art thou a fedary for this act, and look'st
So virgin-like without? Lo, here she comes.

Enter Imogen.

I am ignorant in what I am commanded.

IMOGEN How now, Pisanio?

PISANIO Madam, here is a letter from my lord.   25

IMOGEN Who, thy lord? That is my lord Leonatus?
O, learn'd indeed were that astronomer
That knew the stars as I his characters;
He'ld lay the future open. You good gods,
Let what is here contained relish of love,   30
Of my lord's health, of his content—yet not
That we two are asunder; let that grieve him.
Some griefs are med'cinable; that is one of them,
For it doth physic love—of his content
All but in that. Good wax, thy leave. Blest be   35
You bees that make these locks of counsel. Lovers
And men in dangerous bonds pray not alike;
Though forfeiters you cast in prison, yet
You clasp young Cupid's tables. Good news, gods!
                                            [*Reading*]
    "Justice and your father's wrath, should he take   40
me in his dominion, could not be so cruel to me as
you, O the dearest of creatures, would even renew
me with your eyes. Take notice that I am in Cambria

17 fact crime   20 Senseless inanimate   21 fedary for accomplice in   23 am
ignorant in will pretend ignorance of   27 astronomer astrologer   28 characters handwriting   31 not not content   33 med'cinable curative   34 physic
love keep love healthy   36 locks of counsel waxen seals   37 in dangerous
bonds under contracts imposing penalties   38 forfeiters contract-violators
39 tables notebooks   41 as but that   43 Cambria Wales

at Milford Haven. What your own love will
45   out of this advise you, follow. So he wishes you all
happiness, that remains loyal to his vow, and your
increasing in love.

                                Leonatus Posthumus."
O, for a horse with wings! Hear'st thou, Pisanio?
50   He is at Milford Haven. Read, and tell me
How far 'tis thither. If one of mean affairs
May plod it in a week, why may not I
Glide thither in a day? Then, true Pisanio,
Who long'st like me to see thy lord, who long'st—
55   O, let me bate—but not like me, yet long'st,
But in a fainter kind—O, not like me!
For mine's beyond beyond: say, and speak thick—
Love's counselor should fill the bores of hearing,
To th' smothering of the sense—how far it is
60   To this same blessèd Milford. And by th' way
Tell me how Wales was made so happy as
T' inherit such a haven. But first of all,
How we may steal from hence, and for the gap
That we shall make in time from our hence-going
65   And our return, to excuse. But first, how get hence?
Why should excuse be born or ere begot?
We'll talk of that hereafter. Prithee speak,
How many score of miles may we well rid
'Twixt hour and hour?

PISANIO   One score 'twixt sun and sun,
70   Madam, 's enough for you, and too much too.

IMOGEN Why, one that rode to's execution, man,
Could never go so slow. I have heard of riding
    wagers
Where horses have been nimbler than the sands
That run i' th' clock's behalf. But this is fool'ry.
75   Go bid my woman feign a sickness, say

---

51 **mean affairs** ordinary business   55 **bate** abate, modify (the statement)
57 **thick** profusely   58 **bores of hearing** ears   60 **by th' way** on the way
66 **or ere begot** i.e., before conception (of the deed which makes excuse
necessary)   68 **rid** cover   74 **i' th' clock's behalf** in place of a clock

She'll home to her father; and provide me presently
A riding suit, no costlier than would fit
A franklin's housewife.

PISANIO   Madam, you're best consider.

IMOGEN I see before me, man. Nor here, nor here,
Nor what ensues, but have a fog in them   80
That I cannot look through. Away, I prithee;
Do as I bid thee. There's no more to say.
Accessible is none but Milford way.

                                   Exeunt [severally].

Scene III. [*Wales.*]

Enter Belarius, Guiderius, and Arviragus.

BELARIUS A goodly day not to keep house with such
Whose roof's as low as ours! Stoop, boys. This gate
Instructs you how t' adore the heavens and bows
    you
To a morning's holy office. The gates of monarchs
Are arched so high that giants may jet through   5
And keep their impious turbans on without
Good morrow to the sun. Hail, thou fair heaven!
We house i' th' rock, yet use thee not so hardly
As prouder livers do.

GUIDERIUS   Hail, heaven!

ARVIRAGUS   Hail, heaven!

BELARIUS Now for our mountain sport. Up to yond hill;   10
    Your legs are young. I'll tread these flats. Consider,

76 **presently** immediately   78 **franklin** small landowner   78 **housewife** (pronounced "huzzif")   79 **before me** i.e., what is immediately ahead   79 **Nor
here, nor here** neither to this side nor that   80 **what ensues** the eventual outcome
III.iii.2 **This gate** one of the tiring-house doors (representing the "cave")
3 **bows you** makes you bow   5 **jet** strut   8 **hardly** badly

When you above perceive me like a crow,
That it is place which lessens and sets off,
And you may then revolve what tales I have told
    you
15 Of courts, of princes, of the tricks in war.
This service is not service, so being done,
But being so allowed. To apprehend thus
Draws us a profit from all things we see,
And often, to our comfort, shall we find
20 The sharded beetle in a safer hold
Than is the full-winged eagle. O, this life
Is nobler than attending for a check,
Richer than doing nothing for a bribe,
Prouder than rustling in unpaid-for silk:
25 Such gain the cap of him that makes him fine
Yet keeps his book uncrossed. No life to ours.

GUIDERIUS Out of your proof you speak. We poor
    unfledged
Have never winged from view o' th' nest, nor know
    not
What air's from home. Haply this life is best
30 If quiet life be best, sweeter to you
That have a sharper known, well corresponding
With your stiff age; but unto us it is
A cell of ignorance, traveling abed,
A prison, or a debtor that not dares
To stride a limit.

35 ARVIRAGUS   What should we speak of
When we are old as you? When we shall hear
The rain and wind beat dark December, how
In this our pinching cave shall we discourse
The freezing hours away? We have seen nothing.

13 **place** position 13 **sets off** displays to advantage 16 **This** any particular
17 **allowed** approved 20 **sharded** provided with wing-cases 20 **hold**
stronghold 22 **attending for a check** doing service at court only to receive a
rebuke 25 **gain the cap** win approval 25 **makes him fine** dresses
elegantly 26 **keeps ... uncrossed** does not cancel the debts in his account
book 27 **proof** experience 33 **abed** i.e., in imagination 35 **stride a limit** step
over a boundary 38 **pinching** distressingly cold

We are beastly: subtle as the fox for prey,   40
Like warlike as the wolf for what we eat.
Our valor is to chase what flies. Our cage
We make a choir, as doth the prisoned bird,
And sing our bondage freely.

BELARIUS   How you speak!
Did you but know the city's usuries   45
And felt them knowingly; the art o' th' court,
As hard to leave as keep, whose top to climb
Is certain falling, or so slipp'ry that
The fear's as bad as falling; the toil o' th' war,
A pain that only seems to seek out danger   50
I' th' name of fame and honor, which dies i' th'
    search
And hath as oft a sland'rous epitaph
As record of fair act; nay, many times
Doth ill deserve by doing well; what's worse,
Must curtsy at the censure. O boys, this story   55
The world may read in me. My body's marked
With Roman swords, and my report was once
First with the best of note. Cymbeline loved me,
And when a soldier was the theme, my name
Was not far off. Then was I as a tree   60
Whose boughs did bend with fruit. But in one night
A storm or robbery, call it what you will,
Shook down my mellow hangings, nay, my leaves,
And left me bare to weather.

GUIDERIUS   Uncertain favor!

BELARIUS My fault being nothing, as I have told you
    oft,   65
But that two villains, whose false oaths prevailed
Before my perfect honor, swore to Cymbeline
I was confederate with the Romans. So
Followed my banishment, and this twenty years
This rock and these demesnes have been my world,   70
Where I have lived at honest freedom, paid

40 **beastly** beast-like   41 **Like** as   47 **keep** remain at   50 **pain** labor
54 **deserve** earn   57 **report** reputation   58 **note** reputation   63 **hangings** fruit

More pious debts to heaven than in all
The fore-end of my time. But up to th' mountains!
This is not hunters' language. He that strikes
75 The venison first shall be the lord o' th' feast;
To him the other two shall minister,
And we will fear no poison, which attends
In place of greater state. I'll meet you in the valleys.
            Exeunt [Guiderius and Arviragus].
How hard it is to hide the sparks of nature!
80 These boys know little they are sons to th' King,
Nor Cymbeline dreams that they are alive.
They think they are mine, and though trained up
            thus meanly
I' th' cave wherein they bow, their thoughts do hit
The roofs of palaces, and Nature prompts them
85 In simple and low things to prince it much
Beyond the trick of others. This Polydore,
The heir of Cymbeline and Britain, who
The King his father called Guiderius—Jove!
When on my three-foot stool I sit and tell
90 The warlike feats I have done, his spirits fly out
Into my story; say "Thus mine enemy fell,
And thus I set my foot on's neck," even then
The princely blood flows in his cheek, he sweats,
Strains his young nerves, and puts himself in
            posture
95 That acts my words. The younger brother Cadwal,
Once Arviragus, in as like a figure
Strikes life into my speech and shows much more
                                    [Horn.]
His own conceiving. Hark, the game is roused!
O Cymbeline, heaven and my conscience knows
100 Thou didst unjustly banish me; whereon,
At three and two years old, I stole these babes,
Thinking to bar thee of succession as
Thou refts me of my lands. Euriphile,

73 **fore-end** early part   77 **attends** is present   86 **trick** capacity   94 **nerves**
sinews   96 **in ... figure** playing his part equally well   98 **conceiving**
interpretation   103 **refts** robbed

Thou wast their nurse; they took thee for their
   mother,
And every day do honor to her grave.   105
Myself, Belarius, that am Morgan called,
They take for natural father. The game is up.

                                   Exit.

Scene IV. [*Wales*.]

Enter Pisanio and Imogen.

IMOGEN Thou told'st me, when we came from horse,
   the place
Was near at hand. Ne'er longed my mother so
To see me first as I have now. Pisanio, man,
Where is Posthumus? What is in thy mind
That makes thee stare thus? Wherefore breaks that
   sigh   5
From th' inward of thee? One but painted thus
Would be interpreted a thing perplexed
Beyond self-explication. Put thyself
Into a havior of less fear, ere wildness
Vanquish my staider senses. What's the matter?   10
Why tender'st thou that paper to me with
A look untender? If't be summer news,
Smile to't before; if winterly, thou need'st
But keep that count'nance still. My husband's hand?
That drug-damned Italy hath outcraftied him,   15
And he's at some hard point. Speak, man! Thy
   tongue
May take off some extremity, which to read
Would be even mortal to me.

107 **up** roused III.iv.3 **have** i.e., have longing (to see Posthumus) 7 **perplexed**
troubled 9 **havior** appearance 9 **wildness** panic 10 **matter** business
15 **outcraftied** outwitted 16 **at some hard point** in some difficult situation
17 **take ... extremity** lessen the shock

PISANIO   Please you read,
And you shall find me, wretched man, a thing
20   The most disdained of fortune.

IMOGEN *(Reads)* "Thy mistress, Pisanio, hath played
the strumpet in my bed, the testimonies whereof lies
bleeding in me. I speak not out of weak surmises,
but from proof as strong as my grief and as certain
25   as I expect my revenge. That part thou, Pisanio,
must act for me, if thy faith be not tainted with the
breach of hers. Let thine own hands take away her
life. I shall give thee opportunity at Milford Haven
—she hath my letter for the purpose—where, if
30   thou fear to strike and to make me certain it is
done, thou art the pander to her dishonor and
equally to me disloyal."

PISANIO What shall I need to draw my sword? The
          paper
Hath cut her throat already. No, 'tis slander,
Whose edge is sharper than the sword, whose
35   tongue
Outvenoms all the worms of Nile, whose breath
Rides on the posting winds and doth belie
All corners of the world. Kings, queens, and states,
Maids, matrons, nay, the secrets of the grave
40   This viperous slander enters. What cheer, madam?

IMOGEN False to his bed? What is it to be false?
To lie in watch there and to think on him?
To weep 'twixt clock and clock? If sleep charge
          nature,
To break it with a fearful dream of him
45   And cry myself awake? That's false to's bed, is it?

PISANIO Alas, good lady!

IMOGEN I false? Thy conscience witness! Iachimo,

36 **worms** serpents   37 **posting** speeding   37 **belie** fill with lies   38 **states**
lords   42 **in watch** awake   43 **'twixt clock and clock** from hour to hour
43 **charge** burden   44 **fearful** frightening   47 **Thy** i.e., Posthumus'

Thou didst accuse him of incontinency.
Thou then looked'st like a villain; now, methinks,
Thy favor's good enough. Some jay of Italy,   50
Whose mother was her painting, hath betrayed
    him.
Poor I am stale, a garment out of fashion,
And, for I am richer than to hang by th' walls,
I must be ripped. To pieces with me! O,
Men's vows are women's traitors! All good seeming,   55
By thy revolt, O husband, shall be thought
Put on for villainy, not born where't grows,
But worn a bait for ladies.

PISANIO   Good madam, hear me.

IMOGEN True honest men, being heard like false
    Aeneas,
Were in his time thought false, and Sinon's weeping   60
Did scandal many a holy tear, took pity
From most true wretchedness. So thou, Posthumus,
Wilt lay the leaven on all proper men;
Goodly and gallant shall be false and perjured
From thy great fail. Come, fellow, be thou honest;   65
Do thou thy master's bidding. When thou seest him,
A little witness my obedience. Look,
I draw the sword myself. Take it, and hit
The innocent mansion of my love, my heart.
Fear not, 'tis empty of all things but grief.   70
Thy master is not there, who was indeed
The riches of it. Do his bidding, strike!
Thou mayst be valiant in a better cause,
But now thou seem'st a coward.

---

50 favor appearance   50 jay whore   51 Whose ... painting i.e., dependent
upon make-up   53 for ... walls i.e., since I am too valuable to be set aside
55 seeming appearance   56 revolt turning away   57 not ... grows i.e., trans-
planted (hence assumed)   59 heard heard to speak   59 Aeneas (who jilted
Dido)   60 Sinon (who persuaded Troy to admit the Trojan Horse)   61 scandal
make disreputable   63 lay ... men cause all honorable men to be thought
corrupt   64 Goodly handsome   65 fail failure

PISANIO   Hence, vile instrument!
   Thou shalt not damn my hand.

75   IMOGEN   Why, I must die,
   And if I do not by thy hand, thou art
   No servant of thy master's. Against self-slaughter
   There is a prohibition so divine
   That cravens my weak hand. Come, here's my
      heart—
80   Something's afore't; soft, soft, we'll no defense—
   Obedient as the scabbard. What is here?
   The scriptures of the loyal Leonatus
   All turned to heresy? Away, away,
   Corrupters of my faith! You shall no more
85   Be stomachers to my heart. Thus may poor fools
   Believe false teachers. Though those that are
      betrayed
   Do feel the treason sharply, yet the traitor
   Stands in worse case of woe.
   And thou, Posthumus, that didst set up
90   My disobedience 'gainst the King my father
   And make me put into contempt the suits
   Of princely fellows, shalt hereafter find
   It is no act of common passage, but
   A strain of rareness; and I grieve myself
95   To think, when thou shalt be disedged by her
   That now thou tirest on, how thy memory
   Will then be panged by me. Prithee dispatch,
   The lamb entreats the butcher. Where's thy knife?
   Thou art too slow to do thy master's bidding
   When I desire it too.

100 PISANIO   O gracious lady,
   Since I received command to do this business
   I have not slept one wink.

79 **cravens** makes cowardly 80 **Something** Posthumus' letter 80 **soft** wait
81 **Obedient** i.e., as ready to receive the sword 82 **scriptures** writings
85 **stomachers** ornamental cloth worn under lacing of the bodice (she has been
holding the letter against her breast) 93–94 **It ... rareness** i.e., my choice of you
was not an everyday matter but resulted from rare qualities 95 **be disedged** have
lost the edge (of appetite) 96 **tirest** feedest ravenously (hawking term)
97 **panged** tormented

IMOGEN   Do't, and to bed then.

PISANIO I'll wake mine eyeballs out first.

IMOGEN   Wherefore then
Didst undertake it? Why hast thou abused
So many miles with a pretense? This place?   105
Mine action and thine own? Our horses' labor?
The time inviting thee? The perturbed court
For my being absent? whereunto I never
Purpose return. Why hast thou gone so far,
To be unbent when thou hast ta'en thy stand,   110
Th' elected deer before thee?

PISANIO   But to win time
To lose so bad employment, in the which
I have considered of a course. Good lady,
Hear me with patience.

IMOGEN   Talk thy tongue weary, speak.
I have heard I am a strumpet, and mine ear,   115
Therein false struck, can take no greater wound,
Nor tent to bottom that. But speak.

PISANIO   Then, madam,
I thought you would not back again.

IMOGEN   Most like,
Bringing me here to kill me.

PISANIO   Not so, neither.
But if I were as wise as honest, then   120
My purpose would prove well. It cannot be
But that my master is abused. Some villain,
Ay, and singular in his art, hath done you both
This cursèd injury.

IMOGEN Some Roman courtesan.

PISANIO   No, on my life: 125

103 wake ... out remain awake till my eyes drop out   110 unbent with bow
unbent, unprepared   110 stand hunting station   111 elected chosen   117 tent
... that probe reaching to bottom of the wound   118 back go back   122 abused
deceived   123 singular unique   125 courtesan courtier

179

I'll give but notice you are dead, and send him
Some bloody sign of it, for 'tis commanded
I should do so. You shall be missed at court,
And that will well confirm it.

IMOGEN   Why, good fellow,
130 What shall I do the while? Where bide? How live?
Or in my life what comfort when I am
Dead to my husband?

PISANIO   If you'll back to th' court—

IMOGEN No court, no father, nor no more ado
With that harsh, noble, simple nothing,
135 That Cloten, whose love suit hath been to me
As fearful as a siege.

PISANIO   If not at court,
Then not in Britain must you bide.

IMOGEN   Where then?
Hath Britain all the sun that shines? Day, night,
Are they not but in Britain? I' th' world's volume
140 Our Britain seems as of it, but not in't;
In a great pool a swan's nest. Prithee think
There's livers out of Britain.

PISANIO   I am most glad
You think of other place. Th' ambassador,
Lucius the Roman, comes to Milford Haven
145 Tomorrow. Now if you could wear a mind
Dark as your fortune is, and but disguise
That which, t' appear itself, must not yet be
But by self-danger, you should tread a course
Pretty and full of view; yea, haply, near
150 The residence of Posthumus, so nigh, at least,
That though his actions were not visible, yet
Report should render him hourly to your ear
As truly as he moves.

127 it your death   139 not but only   140 of it ... in't i.e., part of the world yet
separated from it   146 Dark inscrutable   147 That her sex   147 itself i.e., as
itself   149 full of view with good prospects   149 haply perhaps   152 render
describe

IMOGEN   O, for such means,
Though peril to my modesty, not death on't,
I would adventure.

PISANIO   Well then, here's the point: 155
You must forget to be a woman; change
Command into obedience, fear and niceness—
The handmaids of all women, or more truly
Woman it pretty self—into a waggish courage;
Ready in gibes, quick-answered, saucy, and   160
As quarrelous as the weasel. Nay, you must
Forget that rarest treasure of your cheek,
Exposing it—but O, the harder heart!
Alack, no remedy—to the greedy touch
Of common-kissing Titan, and forget   165
Your laborsome and dainty trims, wherein
You made great Juno angry.

IMOGEN   Nay, be brief.
I see into thy end and am almost
A man already.

PISANIO   First, make yourself but like one.
Forethinking this, I have already fit—   170
'Tis in my cloak-bag—doublet, hat, hose, all
That answer to them. Would you, in their serving,
And with what imitation you can borrow
From youth of such a season, 'fore noble Lucius
Present yourself, desire his service, tell him   175
Wherein you're happy, which will make him
    know,
If that his head have ear in music; doubtless
With joy he will embrace you, for he's honorable,

154 **modesty** chastity   157 **Command** habit of commanding (as a person of rank)   157 **niceness** fastidiousness   159 **it** its   160 **quick-answered** quick-answering   161 **quarrelous** quarrelsome   163 **harder** too hard   165 **common-kissing Titan** the sun which kisses everything alike   166 **laborsome** elaborate   166 **trims** apparel   167 **angry** i.e., with jealousy   168 **end** purpose   170 **Forethinking** planning in advance for   170 **fit** prepared   172 **answer** correspond   172 **in their serving** with their aid   174 **season** age   175 **his service** employment as his servant   176 **happy** accomplished   176 **make him know** satisfy him   178 **embrace** welcome

And, doubling that, most holy. Your means
          abroad—
180 You have me, rich, and I will never fail
Beginning nor supplyment.

IMOGEN   Thou art all the comfort
The gods will diet me with. Prithee away.
There's more to be considered, but we'll even
All that good time will give us. This attempt
185 I am soldier to, and will abide it with
A prince's courage. Away, I prithee.

PISANIO   Well, madam, we must take a short farewell,
Lest, being missed, I be suspected of
Your carriage from the court. My noble mistress,
190 Here is a box; I had it from the Queen.
What's in't is precious. If you are sick at sea
Or stomach-qualmed at land, a dram of this
Will drive away distemper. To some shade,
And fit you to your manhood. May the gods
Direct you to the best.

IMOGEN   Amen. I thank thee.
                              Exeunt [severally].

Scene V. [*Britain.*]

*Enter Cymbeline, Queen, Cloten, Lucius, [a
Messenger, Attendants,] and Lords.*

CYMBELINE   Thus far, and so farewell.

LUCIUS   Thanks, royal sir.
My emperor hath wrote: I must from hence,
And am right sorry that I must report ye
My master's enemy.

179 means i.e., of subsistence   183 even keep pace with   185 soldier to brave
enough for   185 abide face   189 Your carriage removing you   193 distemper
illness

CYMBELINE   Our subjects, sir,
Will not endure his yoke, and for ourself   5
To show less sovereignty than they, must needs
Appear unkinglike.

LUCIUS   So, sir. I desire of you
A conduct overland to Milford Haven.
Madam, all joy befall your Grace, and you.

CYMBELINE   My lords, you are appointed for that
     office;   10
The due of honor in no point omit.
So farewell, noble Lucius.

LUCIUS   Your hand, my lord.

CLOTEN   Receive it friendly, but from this time forth
I wear it as your enemy.

LUCIUS   Sir, the event
Is yet to name the winner. Fare you well.   15

CYMBELINE   Leave not the worthy Lucius, good my
     lords,
Till he have crossed the Severn. Happiness!

                   Exeunt Lucius et ceteri.

QUEEN   He goes hence frowning, but it honors us
That we have given him cause.

CLOTEN   'Tis all the better;
Your valiant Britons have their wishes in it.   20

CYMBELINE   Lucius hath wrote already to the Emperor
How it goes here. It fits us therefore ripely
Our chariots and our horsemen be in readiness.
The pow'rs that he already hath in Gallia
Will soon be drawn to head, from whence he
     moves   25
His war for Britain.

III.v.8 **conduct** escort   9 **you** Cymbeline   10 **office** duty   14 **event** outcome
17s.d. **et ceteri** and others (Attendants and Lords)   22 **fits . . . ripely** behooves
us therefore strongly   25 **drawn to head** gathered into an army

QUEEN   'Tis not sleepy business,
But must be looked to speedily and strongly.

CYMBELINE Our expectation that it would be thus
Hath made us forward. But, my gentle queen,
30   Where is our daughter? She hath not appeared
Before the Roman, nor to us hath tendered
The duty of the day. She looks us like
A thing more made of malice than of duty.
We have noted it.—Call her before us, for
We have been too slight in sufferance.

[*Exit Messenger.*]

35   QUEEN   Royal sir,
Since the exile of Posthumus, most retired
Hath her life been; the cure whereof, my lord,
'Tis time must do. Beseech your Majesty,
Forbear sharp speeches to her. She's a lady
40   So tender of rebukes that words are strokes,
And strokes death to her.

Enter Messenger.

CYMBELINE   Where is she, sir? How
Can her contempt be answered?

MESSENGER   Please you, sir,
Her chambers are all locked, and there's no answer
That will be given to th' loud of noise we make.

45   QUEEN My lord, when last I went to visit her,
She prayed me to excuse her keeping close;
Whereto constrained by her infirmity,
She should that duty leave unpaid to you
Which daily she was bound to proffer. This
50   She wished me to make known, but our great court
Made me to blame in memory.

CYMBELINE   Her doors locked?

32 **looks** seems to   35 **slight in sufferance** remiss in permissiveness   40 **tender of** sensitive to   42 **answered** accounted for   46 **close** to herself   50 **our great court** i.e., state affairs   51 **to blame in memory** fail to remember

Not seen of late? Grant, heavens, that which I fear
Prove false!   *Exit*.

QUEEN   Son, I say, follow the King.

CLOTEN That man of hers, Pisanio, her old servant,
I have not seen these two days.

QUEEN   Go, look after. *Exit [Cloten]*.   55
Pisanio, thou that stand'st so for Posthumus—
He hath a drug of mine. I pray his absence
Proceed by swallowing that, for he believes
It is a thing most precious. But for her,
Where is she gone? Haply despair hath seized her,   60
Or, winged with fervor of her love, she's flown
To her desired Posthumus. Gone she is
To death or to dishonor, and my end
Can make good use of either. She being down,
I have the placing of the British crown.   65

                    Enter Cloten.

How now, my son?

CLOTEN   'Tis certain she is fled.
Go in and cheer the King. He rages; none
Dare come about him.

QUEEN [*Aside*]   All the better. May
This night forestall him of the coming day!
                                    Exit Queen.

CLOTEN I love and hate her, for she's fair and royal,   70
And that she hath all courtly parts more exquisite
Than lady, ladies, woman. From every one
The best she hath, and she, of all compounded,
Outsells them all. I love her therefore, but
Disdaining me and throwing favors on   75
The low Posthumus slanders so her judgment
That what's else rare is choked; and in that point

56 **stand'st so for** so much supportest 58 **Proceed by** result from
69 **forestall** deprive 70 **for** because 71 **that** because 71 **parts** qualities
74 **Outsells** outvalues 76 **slanders** denigrates

I will conclude to hate her, nay, indeed,
To be revenged upon her. For, when fools
Shall—

Enter Pisanio.

80   Who is here? What, are you packing, sirrah?
Come hither. Ah, you precious pander! Villain,
Where is thy lady? In a word, or else
Thou art straightway with the fiends.

PISANIO   O good my lord!

CLOTEN Where is thy lady? Or, by Jupiter,
85   I will not ask again. Close villain,
I'll have this secret from thy heart or rip
Thy heart to find it. Is she with Posthumus?
From whose so many weights of baseness cannot
A dram of worth be drawn.

PISANIO   Alas, my lord,
90   How can she be with him? When was she missed?
He is in Rome.

CLOTEN   Where is she, sir? Come nearer.
No farther halting. Satisfy me home
What is become of her.

PISANIO O my all-worthy lord!

CLOTEN   All-worthy villain!
95   Discover where thy mistress is at once,
At the next word. No more of "worthy lord"!
Speak, or thy silence on the instant is
Thy condemnation and thy death.

PISANIO   Then, sir,
This paper is the history of my knowledge
Touching her flight.   *[Presenting a letter]*

100 CLOTEN   Let's see't. I will pursue her
Even to Augustus' throne.

80 **packing** plotting   80 **sirrah** (term of address to an inferior)   85 **Close** secretive
91 **nearer** to the point   92 **home** thoroughly   95 **Discover** reveal   99 **This paper** (cf. line 131 and V.v.279)

PISANIO [*Aside*]   Or this, or perish.
She's far enough, and what he learns by this
May prove his travel, not her danger.

CLOTEN   Hum!

PISANIO [*Aside*] I'll write to my lord she's dead. O
    Imogen,
Safe mayst thou wander, safe return again!   105

CLOTEN Sirrah, is this letter true?

PISANIO Sir, as I think.

CLOTEN It is Posthumus' hand, I know't. Sirrah, if thou
    wouldst not be a villain, but do me true service, un-
    dergo those employments wherein I should have   110
    cause to use thee with a serious industry—that is,
    what villainy soe'er I bid thee do, to perform it di-
    rectly and truly—I would think thee an honest man.
    Thou shouldst neither want my means for thy relief
    nor my voice for thy preferment.   115

PISANIO Well, my good lord.

CLOTEN Wilt thou serve me? For since patiently and
    constantly thou hast stuck to the bare fortune of that
    beggar Posthumus, thou canst not, in the course of
    gratitude, but be a diligent follower of mine. Wilt   120
    thou serve me?

PISANIO Sir, I will.

CLOTEN Give me thy hand. Here's my purse. Hast any
    of thy late master's garments in thy possession?

PISANIO I have, my lord, at my lodging the same suit   125
    he wore when he took leave of my lady and mis-
    tress.

CLOTEN The first service thou dost me, fetch that suit
    hither. Let it be thy first service. Go.

PISANIO I shall, my lord.   *Exit.*   130

101 **Or** either   109–10 **undergo** undertake   115 **preferment** advancement

CLOTEN Meet thee at Milford Haven! I forgot to ask
him one thing; I'll remember't anon. Even there,
thou villain Posthumus, will I kill thee. I would
these garments were come. She said upon a time—
135 the bitterness of it I now belch from my heart—that
she held the very garment of Posthumus in more
respect than my noble and natural person, together
with the adornment of my qualities. With that suit
upon my back will I ravish her; first kill him, and in
140 her eyes. There shall she see my valor, which will then
be a torment to her contempt. He on the ground,
my speech of insultment ended on his dead body,
and when my lust hath dined—which, as I say, to
vex her I will execute in the clothes that she so
145 praised—to the court I'll knock her back, foot
her home again. She hath despised me rejoicingly,
and I'll be merry in my revenge.

Enter Pisanio [with the clothes].

Be those the garments?

PISANIO Ay, my noble lord.

150 CLOTEN How long is't since she went to Milford
Haven?

PISANIO She can scarce be there yet.

CLOTEN Bring this apparel to my chamber; that is the
second thing that I have commanded thee. The third
155 is that thou wilt be a voluntary mute to my design.
Be but duteous, and true preferment shall tender
itself to thee. My revenge is now at Milford. Would
I had wings to follow it! Come, and be true.   *Exit.*

PISANIO Thou bid'st me to my loss, for true to thee
160 Were to prove false, which I will never be,
To him that is most true. To Milford go,

142 **insultment** scornful triumph   145 **knock her back** beat her home
145 **foot** kick   159 **loss** i.e., of honor   161 **him** Posthumus

And find not her whom thou pursuest. Flow, flow,
You heavenly blessings, on her. This fool's speed
Be crossed with slowness; labor be his meed.   *Exit.*

Scene VI. [*Wales.*]

Enter Imogen alone [*in boy's clothes*].

IMOGEN I see a man's life is a tedious one.
 I have tired myself, and for two nights together
 Have made the ground my bed. I should be sick
 But that my resolution helps me. Milford,
 When from the mountain-top Pisanio showed thee,   5
 Thou wast within a ken. O Jove, I think
 Foundations fly the wretched—such, I mean,
 Where they should be relieved. Two beggars told me
 I could not miss my way. Will poor folks lie,
 That have afflictions on them, knowing 'tis   10
 A punishment or trial? Yes. No wonder,
 When rich ones scarce tell true. To lapse in fulness
 Is sorer than to lie for need, and falsehood
 Is worse in kings than beggars. My dear lord,
 Thou art one o' th' false ones. Now I think on thee   15
 My hunger's gone, but even before, I was
 At point to sink for food. But what is this?
 Here is a path to't. 'Tis some savage hold.
 I were best not call; I dare not call. Yet famine,
 Ere clean it o'erthrow nature, makes it valiant.   20
 Plenty and peace breeds cowards; hardness ever
 Of hardiness is mother. Ho! Who's here?
 If anything that's civil, speak; if savage,
 Take or lend. Ho! No answer? Then I'll enter.

164 **crossed** thwarted   164 **meed** reward   III.vi.6 **a ken** view   7 **Foundations** security (quibble on "hospitals")   12 **lapse in fulness** i.e., lie when prosperous   13 **sorer** worse   16 **even** just   17 **At point** about   17 **for** for lack of   18 **hold** stronghold   20 **clean** completely   21 **hardness** hardship   23 **civil** civilized   24 **Take or lend** take (what I have) or give (what you will)

25   Best draw my sword, and if mine enemy
      But fear the sword like me, he'll scarcely look on't.
      Such a foe, good heavens!   *Exit*.

             Enter Belarius, Guiderius, and Arviragus.

BELARIUS You, Polydore, have proved best woodman
      and
      Are master of the feast. Cadwal and I
30   Will play the cook and servant; 'tis our match.
      The sweat of industry would dry and die
      But for the end it works to. Come, our stomachs
      Will make what's homely savory. Weariness
      Can snore upon the flint when resty sloth
35   Finds the down pillow hard. Now peace be here,
      Poor house, that keep'st thyself.

GUIDERIUS   I am throughly weary.

ARVIRAGUS I am weak with toil, yet strong in appetite.

GUIDERIUS There is cold meat i' th' cave. We'll browse
      on that
      Whilst what we have killed be cooked.

BELARIUS [*Looking through door*]   Stay, come not in.
40   But that it eats our victuals, I should think
      Here were a fairy.

GUIDERIUS   What's the matter, sir?

BELARIUS By Jupiter, an angel; or, if not,
      An earthly paragon. Behold divineness
      No elder than a boy.

                    Enter Imogen.

45   IMOGEN Good masters, harm me not.
      Before I entered here, I called and thought
      To have begged or bought what I have took. Good
      troth,

27 **Such a foe** i.e., may I have (if any) such a foe   27s.d. **Exit** (at this point, since
the stage is cleared, F marks a new scene)   28 **woodman** hunter   30 **match**
agreement   33 **homely** plain   34 **resty** lazy   41 **matter** subject (of your remark)
47 **Good troth** in truth

I have stol'n naught, nor would not, though I had
  found
Gold strewed i' th' floor. Here's money for my meat.
I would have left it on the board so soon   50
As I had made my meal, and parted
With pray'rs for the provider.

GUIDERIUS   Money, youth?

ARVIRAGUS All gold and silver rather turn to dirt,
As 'tis no better reckoned but of those
Who worship dirty gods.

IMOGEN   I see you're angry.   55
Know, if you kill me for my fault, I should
Have died had I not made it.

BELARIUS   Whither bound?

IMOGEN To Milford Haven.

BELARIUS What's your name?

IMOGEN Fidele, sir. I have a kinsman who   60
Is bound for Italy; he embarked at Milford;
To whom being going, almost spent with hunger,
I am fall'n in this offense.

BELARIUS   Prithee, fair youth,
Think us no churls, nor measure our good minds
By this rude place we live in. Well encountered!   65
'Tis almost night; you shall have better cheer
Ere you depart, and thanks to stay and eat it.
Boys, bid him welcome.

GUIDERIUS   Were you a woman, youth,
I should woo hard but be your groom in honesty.
I'ld bid for you as I do buy.

ARVIRAGUS   I'll make't my comfort   70
He is a man. I'll love him as my brother,
And such a welcome as I'ld give to him

66 **cheer** entertainment 67 **thanks** i.e., our thanks 69 **but be** ere I should fail
to be (E. Dowden) 70 **I'ld bid ... buy** i.e., I'd seek your hand in earnest

After long absence, such is yours. Most welcome.
Be sprightly, for you fall 'mongst friends.

IMOGEN   'Mongst friends?
75 —If brothers. [*Aside*] Would it had been so that they
Had been my father's sons! Then had my prize
Been less, and so more equal ballasting
To thee, Posthumus.

BELARIUS   He wrings at some distress.

GUIDERIUS Would I could free't!

ARVIRAGUS   Or I, whate'er it be,
What pain it cost, what danger. Gods!

80 BELARIUS   Hark, boys. [*Whispers.*]

IMOGEN Great men
That had a court no bigger than this cave,
That did attend themselves and had the virtue
Which their own conscience sealed them, laying by
85 That nothing-gift of differing multitudes,
Could not outpeer these twain. Pardon me, gods,
I'ld change my sex to be companion with them,
Since Leonatus false.

BELARIUS   It shall be so.
Boys, we'll go dress our hunt. Fair youth, come in.
90 Discourse is heavy, fasting. When we have supped,
We'll mannerly demand thee of thy story,
So far as thou wilt speak it.

GUIDERIUS   Pray draw near.

74 **sprightly** in good spirits   75 **If brothers** i.e., yes, if we were indeed brothers
76 **prize** price, value (quibble on "captured ship")   77 **less** (since then she would
not be heir apparent)   77 **ballasting** weight   78 **wrings** writhes   83 **attend**
themselves i.e., get along without attendants   84 **sealed them** authenticated for
them (as in affixing a waxen seal to a legal document)   84 **laying by** setting aside
85 **nothing-gift** worthless gift (flattery)   85 **differing** fickle   86 **outpeer** surpass
89 **hunt** quarry

ARVIRAGUS The night to th' owl and morn to th' lark
    less welcome.

IMOGEN Thanks, sir.

ARVIRAGUS I pray draw near.   *Exeunt.*   95

Scene VII. [*Rome.*]

Enter two Roman Senators and Tribunes.

FIRST SENATOR This is the tenor of the Emperor's writ:
    That since the common men are now in action
    'Gainst the Pannonians and Dalmatians,
    And that the legions now in Gallia are
    Full weak to undertake our wars against   5
    The fall'n-off Britons, that we do incite
    The gentry to this business. He creates
    Lucius proconsul, and to you the tribunes,
    For this immediate levy, he commends
    His absolute commission. Long live Caesar!   10

TRIBUNE Is Lucius general of the forces?

SECOND SENATOR   Ay.

TRIBUNE Remaining now in Gallia?

FIRST SENATOR   With those legions
    Which I have spoke of, whereunto your levy
    Must be supplyant. The words of your commission
    Will tie you to the numbers and the time   15
    Of their dispatch.

TRIBUNE   We will discharge our duty.
                               Exeunt.

III.vii.1 **writ** dispatch   6 **fall'n-off** revolted   9 **commends** entrusts   10 **absolute commission** full authority   14 **supplyant** supplementary   15 **tie you to** confirm for you

ACT IV

Scene I. [*Wales.*]

Enter Cloten alone.

CLOTEN I am near to th' place where they should meet,
if Pisanio have mapped it truly. How fit his garments serve me! Why should his mistress, who was
made by him that made the tailor, not be fit too?
5   The rather, saving reverence of the word, for 'tis
said a woman's fitness comes by fits. Therein I
must play the workman. I dare speak it to myself,
for it is not vainglory for a man and his glass to
confer in his own chamber—I mean, the lines of my
10   body are as well drawn as his; no less young, more
strong, not beneath him in fortunes, beyond him in
the advantage of the time, above him in birth, alike
conversant in general services, and more remarkable in single oppositions. Yet this imperceiverant
15   thing loves him in my despite. What mortality is!
Posthumus, thy head, which now is growing upon
thy shoulders, shall within this hour be off, thy
mistress enforced, thy garments cut to pieces be-

IV.i.2 **fit** suitably 4 **fit** suitable 5 **saving reverence of** begging pardon for
5 **for** since 6 **fitness** sexual inclination 8 **glass** looking-glass 12 **advantage
of the time** social opportunities 13 **general** i.e., military 14 **single oppositions** duels 14 **imperceiverant** imperceptive 15 **mortality** life 18 **enforced**
raped

fore her face; and all this done, spurn her home to
her father, who may haply be a little angry for my   20
so rough usage; but my mother, having power of
his testiness, shall turn all into my commendations.
My horse is tied up safe. Out, sword, and to a sore
purpose! Fortune put them into my hand. This is the
very description of their meeting place, and the fel-   25
low dares not deceive me.   *Exit*.

Scene II. [*Wales.*]

*Enter Belarius, Guiderius, Arviragus, and Imogen
from the cave.*

BELARIUS You are not well. Remain here in the cave;
  We'll come to you after hunting.

ARVIRAGUS   Brother, stay here.
  Are we not brothers?

IMOGEN   So man and man should be,
  But clay and clay differs in dignity,
  Whose dust is both alike. I am very sick.   5

GUIDERIUS Go you to hunting, I'll abide with him.

IMOGEN So sick I am not, yet I am not well,
  But not so citizen a wanton as
  To seem to die ere sick. So please you, leave me;
  Stick to your journal course; the breach of custom   10
  Is breach of all. I am ill, but your being by me
  Cannot amend me; society is no comfort
  To one not sociable. I am not very sick,
  Since I can reason of it. Pray you trust me here—

21 **power of** control over   23 **sore** causing suffering (quibble on "wound," i.e.,
vagina)   IV.ii.4 **clay and clay** one person and another   4 **dignity** rank   5 **dust**
remains after death   8 **citizen** city-bred, bourgeois   8 **wanton** spoilt child
10 **journal** daily   12 **amend** cure

15   I'll rob none but myself—and let me die,
        Stealing so poorly.

GUIDERIUS   I love thee—I have spoke it—
        How much the quantity, the weight as much
        As I do love my father.

BELARIUS   What? How, how?

ARVIRAGUS If it be sin to say so, sir, I yoke me
20   In my good brother's fault. I know not why
        I love this youth, and I have heard you say
        Love's reason's without reason. The bier at door,
        And a demand who is't shall die, I'ld say
        "My father, not this youth."

BELARIUS [*Aside*]   O noble strain!
25   O worthiness of nature, breed of greatness!
        Cowards father cowards and base things sire base;
        Nature hath meal and bran, contempt and grace.
        I'm not their father; yet who this should be
        Doth miracle itself, loved before me.—
        'Tis the ninth hour o' th' morn.

30 ARVIRAGUS   Brother, farewell.

IMOGEN I wish ye sport.

ARVIRAGUS   You health.—So please you, sir.

IMOGEN [*Aside*] These are kind creatures. Gods, what
        lies I have heard!
        Our courtiers say all's savage but at court.
        Experience, O, thou disprov'st report!
35   Th' imperious seas breeds monsters; for the dish
        Poor tributary rivers as sweet fish.
        I am sick still, heartsick. Pisanio,
        I'll now taste of thy drug.

GUIDERIUS   I could not stir him.

16 **poorly** i.e., from myself only   17 **How much** as much   24 **strain** heredity
28–29 **who this ... before me** that this person, whoever he is, should be loved
more than I is miraculous   31 **So please you** at your service   35 **imperious**
imperial   36 **as** just as   38 **stir him** move him (to tell his story)

He said he was gentle, but unfortunate;
Dishonestly afflicted, but yet honest.   40

ARVIRAGUS Thus did he answer me, yet said hereafter
I might know more.

BELARIUS   To th' field, to th' field.—
We'll leave you for this time; go in and rest.

ARVIRAGUS We'll not be long away.

BELARIUS   Pray be not sick,
For you must be our housewife.

IMOGEN   Well or ill,   45
I am bound to you.   *Exit.*

BELARIUS   And shalt be ever.
This youth, howe'er distressed, appears he hath
    had
Good ancestors.

ARVIRAGUS   How angel-like he sings!

GUIDERIUS But his neat cookery! He cut our roots in
    characters,
And sauced our broths as Juno had been sick   50
And he her dieter.

ARVIRAGUS   Nobly he yokes
A smiling with a sigh, as if the sigh
Was that it was for not being such a smile;
The smile mocking the sigh that it would fly
From so divine a temple to commix   55
With winds that sailors rail at.

GUIDERIUS   I do note
That grief and patience, rooted in them both,
Mingle their spurs together.

ARVIRAGUS   Grow patience,

---

39 **gentle** well-born 46 **bound** indebted (Belarius quibbles on "tied by affection") 47 **appears** appears as though 49 **neat** elegant 49 **characters** designs 53 **that** what 58 **spurs** chief roots

And let the stinking elder, grief, untwine
60   His perishing root with the increasing vine.

BELARIUS It is great morning. Come away.—Who's
        there?

Enter Cloten.

CLOTEN I cannot find those runagates. That villain
        Hath mocked me. I am faint.

BELARIUS   "Those runagates"?
        Means he not us? I partly know him. 'Tis
65   Cloten, the son o' th' Queen. I fear some ambush.
        I saw him not these many years, and yet
        I know 'tis he. We are held as outlaws. Hence!

GUIDERIUS He is but one. You and my brother search
        What companies are near. Pray you, away.
        Let me alone with him.
                    [*Exeunt Belarius and Arviragus.*]

70   CLOTEN   Soft, what are you
        That fly me thus? Some villain mountaineers?
        I have heard of such. What slave art thou?

GUIDERIUS   A thing
        More slavish did I ne'er than answering
        A "slave" without a knock.

CLOTEN   Thou art a robber,
75   A lawbreaker, a villain. Yield thee, thief.

GUIDERIUS To who? To thee? What art thou? Have
        not I
        An arm as big as thine? A heart as big?
        Thy words, I grant, are bigger, for I wear not
        My dagger in my mouth. Say what thou art,
        Why I should yield to thee.

---

59 **elder** elder tree   60 **perishing** destructive   60 **with** from   61 **great morn-ing** broad daylight   62 **runagates** runaways   69 **companies** companions
70 **Let ... him** leave him to me   70 **Soft** wait   71 **villain** low-born

CLOTEN   Thou villain base,   80
  Know'st me not by my clothes?

GUIDERIUS   No, nor thy tailor, rascal,
  Who is thy grandfather. He made those clothes,
  Which, as it seems, make thee.

CLOTEN   Thou precious varlet,
  My tailor made them not.

GUIDERIUS   Hence then, and thank
  The man that gave them thee. Thou art some fool;   85
  I am loath to beat thee.

CLOTEN   Thou injurious thief,
  Hear but my name and tremble.

GUIDERIUS   What's thy name?

CLOTEN Cloten, thou villain.

GUIDERIUS Cloten, thou double villain, be thy name,
  I cannot tremble at it. Were it Toad, or Adder,
    Spider,   90
  'Twould move me sooner.

CLOTEN   To thy further fear,
  Nay, to thy mere confusion, thou shalt know
  I am son to th' Queen.

GUIDERIUS   I am sorry for't; not seeming
  So worthy as thy birth.

CLOTEN   Art not afeard?

GUIDERIUS Those that I reverence, those I fear—the
    wise;   95
  At fools I laugh, not fear them.

CLOTEN   Die the death!
  When I have slain thee with my proper hand,
  I'll follow those that even now fled hence

81 **me** i.e., my rank   83 **precious varlet** egregious knave   86 **injurious** insulting
92 **mere** utter   93 **not seeming** since you do not seem   97 **proper** own

And on the gates of Lud's Town set your heads.
100   Yield, rustic mountaineer.   *Fight and exeunt.*

Enter Belarius and Arviragus.

BELARIUS No company's abroad?

ARVIRAGUS None in the world. You did mistake him
      sure.

BELARIUS I cannot tell. Long is it since I saw him,
      But time hath nothing blurred those lines of favor
105   Which then he wore. The snatches in his voice,
      And burst of speaking, were as his. I am absolute
      'Twas very Cloten.

ARVIRAGUS   In this place we left them.
      I wish my brother make good time with him,
      You say he is so fell.

BELARIUS   Being scarce made up,
110   I mean to man, he had not apprehension
      Of roaring terrors; for defect of judgment
      Is oft the cause of fear.

Enter Guiderius [with Cloten's head].

                          But see, thy brother.

GUIDERIUS This Cloten was a fool, an empty purse;
      There was no money in't. Not Hercules
115   Could have knocked out his brains, for he had none.
      Yet I not doing this, the fool had borne
      My head as I do his.

BELARIUS   What hast thou done?

GUIDERIUS I am perfect what: cut off one Cloten's
      head,
      Son to the Queen, after his own report;

101 **abroad** about   104 **lines of favor** contours of his face   105 **snatches**
hesitations   106 **absolute** certain   107 **very Cloten** Cloten himself   108 **make
good time** have good fortune   109 **fell** fierce   109 **made up** grown
111–12 **for defect … fear** (sense unclear and frequently emended; Belarius seems
to be saying that Cloten lacked the intelligence to be frightened)   118 **perfect**
well aware

Who called me traitor, mountaineer, and swore   120
With his own single hand he'ld take us in,
Displace our heads where—thank the gods—they
    grow,
And set them on Lud's Town.

BELARIUS   We are all undone.

GUIDERIUS Why, worthy father, what have we to lose
But that he swore to take, our lives? The law   125
Protects not us. Then why should we be tender
To let an arrogant piece of flesh threat us,
Play judge and executioner all himself,
For we do fear the law? What company
Discover you abroad?

BELARIUS   No single soul   130
Can we set eye on, but in all safe reason
He must have some attendants. Though his humor
Was nothing but mutation—ay, and that
From one bad thing to worse—not frenzy, not
Absolute madness could so far have raved   135
To bring him here alone. Although perhaps
It may be heard at court that such as we
Cave here, hunt here, are outlaws, and in time
May make some stronger head; the which he
    hearing—
As it is like him—might break out, and swear   140
He'ld fetch us in; yet is't not probable
To come alone, either he so undertaking,
Or they so suffering. Then on good ground we
    fear,
If we do fear this body hath a tail
More pèrilous than the head.

ARVIRAGUS   Let ordinance   145
Come as the gods foresay it. Howsoe'er,
My brother hath done well.

121 **take us in** overcome us   125 **that** what   126–27 **tender/To** so considerate
as to   129 **For** because   132 **humor** chief characteristic   139 **make** make up
139 **head** force   142 **To come** for him to come   143 **suffering** allowing
144 **tail** i.e., followers   145 **ordinance** whatever is ordained   146 **foresay**
foretell, determine

BELARIUS　　　　　　　　　　I had no mind
To hunt this day. The boy Fidele's sickness
Did make my way long forth.

GUIDERIUS　　　　　　　　　With his own sword,
150 Which he did wave against my throat, I have ta'en
His head from him. I'll throw't into the creek
Behind our rock, and let it to the sea
And tell the fishes he's the Queen's son, Cloten.
That's all I reck.　　　　　　　　　　　　*Exit*.

BELARIUS　　　　　　　I fear 'twill be revenged.
155 Would, Polydore, thou hadst not done't, though valor
Becomes thee well enough.

ARVIRAGUS　　　　　　　　　Would I had done't,
So the revenge alone pursued me. Polydore,
I love thee brotherly, but envy much
Thou hast robbed me of this deed. I would revenges
That possible strength might meet would seek us
160　　through
And put us to our answer.

BELARIUS　　　　　　　　　　Well, 'tis done.
We'll hunt no more today, nor seek for danger
Where there's no profit. I prithee, to our rock;
You and Fidele play the cooks. I'll stay
165 Till hasty Polydore return, and bring him
To dinner presently.

ARVIRAGUS　　　　　　　Poor sick Fidele,
I'll willingly to him. To gain his color
I'ld let a parish of such Clotens blood
And praise myself for charity.　　　　　　*Exit*.

BELARIUS　　　　　　　　　O thou goddess,
170 Thou divine Nature, thou thyself thou blazon'st
In these two princely boys! They are as gentle
As zephyrs blowing below the violet,

149 **way long forth** i.e., way forth seem long　154 **reck** care　157 **So** so that
157 **pursued** would have pursued　160 **possible** our available　160 **seek us
through** search thoroughly for us　167 **gain** restore　168 **let ... blood** kill a
parish-full of Clotens　170 **blazon'st** proclaimest

Not wagging his sweet head; and yet as rough,
Their royal blood enchafed, as the rud'st wind
That by the top doth take the mountain pine   175
And make him stoop to th' vale. 'Tis wonder
That an invisible instinct should frame them
To royalty unlearned, honor untaught,
Civility not seen from other, valor
That wildly grows in them but yields a crop   180
As if it had been sowed. Yet still it's strange
What Cloten's being here to us portends,
Or what his death will bring us.

Enter Guiderius.

GUIDERIUS   Where's my brother?
I have sent Cloten's clotpoll down the stream
In embassy to his mother; his body's hostage   185
For his return.   *Solemn music.*

BELARIUS   My ingenious instrument!
Hark, Polydore, it sounds. But what occasion
Hath Cadwal now to give it motion? Hark!

GUIDERIUS Is he at home?

BELARIUS   He went hence even now.

GUIDERIUS What does he mean? Since death of my
     dear'st mother   190
It did not speak before. All solemn things
Should answer solemn accidents. The matter?
Triumphs for nothing and lamenting toys
Is jollity for apes and grief for boys.
Is Cadwal mad?

*Enter Arviragus with Imogen, dead, bearing her in his
arms.*

BELARIUS   Look, here he comes,   195

174 **enchafed** heated 177 **frame** dispose 178 **royalty** regal conduct
179 **Civility** civilized behavior 180 **wildly grows** grows wild 184 **clotpoll**
blockhead 186 **ingenious** skillfully constructed 192 **answer** correspond to
192 **accidents** events 193 **Triumphs** public festivities 193 **lamenting toys**
lamenting over trifles

And brings the dire occasion in his arms
Of what we blame him for.

ARVIRAGUS   The bird is dead
That we have made so much on. I had rather
Have skipped from sixteen years of age to sixty,
200   To have turned my leaping time into a crutch,
Than have seen this.

GUIDERIUS   O sweetest, fairest lily!
My brother wears thee not the one half so well
As when thou grew'st thyself.

BELARIUS   O Melancholy,
Who ever yet could sound thy bottom, find
205   The ooze, to show what coast thy sluggish crayer
Might eas'liest harbor in? Thou blessèd thing,
Jove knows what man thou mightst have made;
   but I,
Thou diedst, a most rare boy, of melancholy.
How found you him?

ARVIRAGUS   Stark, as you see,
210   Thus smiling, as some fly had tickled slumber,
Not as Death's dart being laughed at; his right
   cheek
Reposing on a cushion.

GUIDERIUS   Where?

ARVIRAGUS   O' th' floor;
His arms thus leagued. I thought he slept, and put
My clouted brogues from off my feet, whose
   rudeness
Answered my steps too loud.

215 GUIDERIUS   Why, he but sleeps.
If he be gone, he'll make his grave a bed;
With female fairies will his tomb be haunted,
And worms will not come to thee.

198 **on** of 205 **crayer** small trading vessel 207 **I** i.e., what I know is
209 **Stark** stiff (as in death) 210 **as** as if 211 **as . . . at** as if laughing at Death's
arrow 213 **leagued** folded 214 **clouted brogues** heavy, nail-studded shoes
214 **rudeness** roughness

ARVIRAGUS   With fairest flowers,
   Whilst summer lasts and I live here, Fidele,
   I'll sweeten thy sad grave. Thou shalt not lack   220
   The flower that's like thy face, pale primrose; nor
   The azured harebell, like thy veins; no, nor
   The leaf of eglantine, whom not to slander,
   Outsweet'ned not thy breath. The ruddock would
   With charitable bill—O bill sore shaming   225
   Those rich-left heirs that let their fathers lie
   Without a monument!—bring thee all this;
   Yea, and furred moss besides, when flow'rs are
     none,
   To winter-ground thy corse—

GUIDERIUS   Prithee have done,
   And do not play in wench-like words with that   230
   Which is so serious. Let us bury him,
   And not protract with admiration what
   Is now due debt. To th' grave.

ARVIRAGUS   Say, where shall's lay him?

GUIDERIUS By good Euriphile, our mother.

ARVIRAGUS   Be't so.
   And let us, Polydore, though now our voices   235
   Have got the mannish crack, sing him to th' ground,
   As once to our mother; use like note and words,
   Save that Euriphile must be Fidele.

GUIDERIUS Cadwal,
   I cannot sing. I'll weep, and word it with thee,   240
   For notes of sorrow out of tune are worse
   Than priests and fanes that lie.

ARVIRAGUS   We'll speak it then.

BELARIUS Great griefs, I see, med'cine the less, for
     Cloten
   Is quite forgot. He was a queen's son, boys,

222 **azured harebell** sky-blue wild hyacinth 223 **eglantine** sweet-briar
224 **ruddock** robin 229 **winter-ground** protect in winter (?) 233 **shall's** shall
us (we) 240 **word** speak 242 **fanes** temples 243 **med'cine** cure

245 And though he came our enemy, remember
     He was paid for that. Though mean and mighty,
       rotting
     Together, have one dust, yet reverence,
     That angel of the world, doth make distinction
     Of place 'tween high and low. Our foe was princely,
250 And though you took his life as being our foe,
     Yet bury him as a prince.

GUIDERIUS   Pray you fetch him hither.
     Thersites' body is as good as Ajax'
     When neither are alive.

ARVIRAGUS   If you'll go fetch him,
     We'll say our song the whilst. Brother, begin.
                              [*Exit Belarius.*]

GUIDERIUS Nay, Cadwal, we must lay his head to th'
255   east;
     My father hath a reason for't.

ARVIRAGUS   'Tis true.

GUIDERIUS Come on then and remove him.

ARVIRAGUS   So. Begin.

                    Song.

GUIDERIUS Fear no more the heat o' th' sun
               Nor the furious winter's rages;
260   Thou thy worldly task hast done,
               Home art gone and ta'en thy wages.
          Golden lads and girls all must,
          As chimney-sweepers, come to dust.

ARVIRAGUS Fear no more the frown o' th' great;
265   Thou art past the tyrant's stroke.
          Care no more to clothe and eat;
               To thee the reed is as the oak.

246 **paid** punished   250 **as being** because he was   251 **as** as being, because he
was   252 **Thersites** (the vituperative Greek warrior of the Trojan War)
252 **Ajax** (one of the Greek heroes at Troy)   255 **to th' east** (the reverse of
Christian practice)   263 **As** like

                    The scepter, learning, physic, must
                    All follow this and come to dust.

GUIDERIUS Fear no more the lightning flash,   270

ARVIRAGUS   Nor th' all-dreaded thunder-stone;

GUIDERIUS Fear not slander, censure rash;

ARVIRAGUS   Thou hast finished joy and moan.

BOTH   All lovers young, all lovers must
                    Consign to thee and come to dust.   275

GUIDERIUS No exorciser harm thee,

ARVIRAGUS Nor no witchcraft charm thee.

GUIDERIUS Ghost unlaid forbear thee;

ARVIRAGUS Nothing ill come near thee.

BOTH   Quiet consummation have,   280
                    And renownèd be thy grave.

Enter Belarius with the body of Cloten.

GUIDERIUS We have done our obsequies. Come, lay
    him down.

BELARIUS Here's a few flowers, but 'bout midnight,
    more.
    The herbs that have on them cold dew o' th' night
    Are strewings fitt'st for graves. Upon their faces.   285
    You were as flow'rs, now withered; even so
    These herblets shall which we upon you strew.
    Come on, away; apart upon our knees.
    The ground that gave them first has them again.
    Their pleasures here are past, so is their pain.   290
              Exeunt [Belarius, Guiderius, and Arviragus].

IMOGEN (*Awakes*) Yes, sir, to Milford Haven. Which
    is the way?

268 **scepter, learning, physic** i.e., kings, scholars, physicians   275 **Consign to**
co-sign with (i.e., meet the same fate)   276 **exorciser** spirit-raiser   278 **forbear
thee** let thee alone   280 **consummation** fulfillment, end   285 **faces** fronts
287 **shall** shall be

I thank you. By yond bush? Pray, how far thither?
'Ods pittikins, can it be six mile yet?
I have gone all night. Faith, I'll lie down and sleep.
                                        [*Seeing Cloten*]
295 But, soft, no bedfellow! O gods and goddesses!
These flow'rs are like the pleasures of the world;
This bloody man, the care on't. I hope I dream,
For so I thought I was a cave-keeper
And cook to honest creatures. But 'tis not so;
300 'Twas but a bolt of nothing, shot at nothing,
Which the brain makes of fumes. Our very eyes
Are sometimes like our judgments, blind. Good
     faith,
I tremble still with fear, but if there be
Yet left in heaven as small a drop of pity
305 As a wren's eye, feared gods, a part of it!
The dream's here still. Even when I wake it is
Without me, as within me; not imagined, felt.
A headless man? The garments of Posthumus?
I know the shape of's leg; this is his hand,
310 His foot Mercurial, his Martial thigh,
The brawns of Hercules; but his Jovial face—
Murder in heaven? How? 'Tis gone. Pisanio,
All curses madded Hecuba gave the Greeks,
And mine to boot, be darted on thee! Thou,
315 Conspired with that irregulous devil Cloten,
Hath here cut off my lord. To write and read
Be henceforth treacherous! Damned Pisanio
Hath with his forgèd letters—damned Pisanio—
From this most bravest vessel of the world
320 Struck the maintop. O Posthumus, alas,
Where is thy head? Where's that? Ay me, where's
     that?

---

293 **'Ods pittikins** God's little pity, God have mercy   294 **gone** walked   298 **so**
i.e., while dreaming   300 **bolt** arrow   301 **fumes** bodily vapors thought to rise to
the brain and cause dreams   305 **a part** i.e., grant me a part   310 **Mercurial**
quick (like Mercury's)   310 **Martial** powerful (like Mars's)   311 **brawns** muscles
311 **Jovial** majestic (like Jove's)   313 **madded** maddened   313 **Hecuba** (wife of
Priam, king of Troy)   315 **Conspired** having conspired   315 **irregulous** lawless

Pisanio might have killed thee at the heart
And left this head on. How should this be? Pisanio?
'Tis he and Cloten. Malice and lucre in them
Have laid this woe here. O, 'tis pregnant, pregnant!   325
The drug he gave me, which he said was precious
And cordial to me, have I not found it
Murd'rous to th' senses? That confirms it home.
This is Pisanio's deed, and Cloten. O,
Give color to my pale cheek with thy blood,   330
That we the horrider may seem to those
Which chance to find us. O my lord, my lord!

                              [*Falling on the body.*]

Enter Lucius and Captains; a Soothsayer to them.

CAPTAIN The legions garrisoned in Gallia
After your will have crossed the sea, attending
You here at Milford Haven with your ships.   335
They are in readiness.

LUCIUS   But what from Rome?

CAPTAIN The Senate hath stirred up the confiners
And gentlemen of Italy, most willing spirits
That promise noble service, and they come
Under the conduct of bold Iachimo,   340
Siena's brother.

LUCIUS   When expect you them?

CAPTAIN With the next benefit o' th' wind.

LUCIUS   This forwardness
Makes our hopes fair. Command our present num-
    bers
Be mustered; bid the captains look to't.—Now, sir,

---

324 **lucre** greed   325 **pregnant** evident   327 **cordial** restorative   328 **home** thoroughly   329 **Cloten** i.e., Cloten's   332 **Which** who   332s.d. **to them** (presumably the Soothsayer enters, a moment later, at another door)   334 **After** according to   334 **attending** waiting for   337 **confiners** inhabitants   341 **Siena's** i.e., the Duke of Siena's   342 **forwardness** promptness

What have you dreamed of late of this war's
345　　purpose?

SOOTHSAYER Last night the very gods showed me a
　　　vision—
I fast and prayed for their intelligence—thus:
I saw Jove's bird, the Roman eagle, winged
From the spongy south to this part of the west,
350　　There vanished in the sunbeams; which portends,
Unless my sins abuse my divination,
Success to th' Roman host.

LUCIUS　　　　　　　　Dream often so,
And never false. Soft, ho, what trunk is here?
Without his top? The ruin speaks that sometime
355　　It was a worthy building. How, a page?
Or dead or sleeping on him? But dead rather,
For nature doth abhor to make his bed
With the defunct or sleep upon the dead.
Let's see the boy's face.

CAPTAIN　　　　　　　He's alive, my lord.

LUCIUS He'll, then, instruct us of this body. Young
360　　one,
Inform us of thy fortunes, for it seems
They crave to be demanded. Who is this
Thou mak'st thy bloody pillow? Or who was he
That, otherwise than noble nature did,
365　　Hath altered that good picture? What's thy interest
In this sad wrack? How came't? Who is't? What
　　　art thou?

IMOGEN I am nothing, or if not,
Nothing to be were better. This was my master,
A very valiant Briton and a good,
370　　That here by mountaineers lies slain. Alas,
There is no more such masters. I may wander

347 **fast** fasted　347 **intelligence** communication　349 **spongy** damp
351 **abuse** render inaccurate　353 **false** falsely　354 **sometime** once　356 **Or**
either　357 **nature doth abhor** man naturally abhors (Heilman)　364 **did** i.e.,
painted (J. C. Maxwell)　366 **wrack** ruin of a man

From east to occident, cry out for service,
Try many, all good, serve truly, never
Find such another master.

LUCIUS   'Lack, good youth,
Thou mov'st no less with thy complaining than   375
Thy master in bleeding. Say his name, good friend.

IMOGEN Richard du Champ. [*Aside*] If I do lie and do
No harm by it, though the gods hear, I hope
They'll pardon it.—Say you, sir?

LUCIUS   Thy name?

IMOGEN   Fidele, sir.

LUCIUS Thou dost approve thyself the very same;   380
Thy name well fits thy faith, thy faith thy name.
Wilt take thy chance with me? I will not say
Thou shalt be so well mastered, but be sure
No less beloved. The Roman emperor's letters
Sent by a consul to me should not sooner   385
Than thine own worth prefer thee. Go with me.

IMOGEN I'll follow, sir. But first, and't please the gods,
I'll hide my master from the flies, as deep
As these poor pickaxes can dig; and when
With wild wood-leaves and weeds I ha' strewed his
    grave   390
And on it said a century of prayers,
Such as I can, twice o'er, I'll weep and sigh,
And leaving so his service, follow you,
So please you entertain me.

LUCIUS   Ay, good youth,
And rather father thee than master thee.   395
My friends,
The boy hath taught us manly duties. Let us
Find out the prettiest daisied plot we can
And make him with our pikes and partisans

380 **approve** prove   386 **prefer** recommend   389 **pickaxes** i.e., fingers
391 **century of** hundred   392 **can** know   394 **So** if it   394 **entertain** employ
399 **partisans** halberds

400   A grave. Come, arm him. Boy, he's preferred
      By thee to us, and he shall be interred
      As soldiers can. Be cheerful; wipe thine eyes.
      Some falls are means the happier to arise.   *Exeunt.*

                    Scene III. [*Britain.*]

              Enter Cymbeline, Lords, and Pisanio.

      CYMBELINE Again, and bring me word how 'tis with her.
                                          [*Exit a Lord.*]
      A fever with the absence of her son,
      A madness, of which her life's in danger. Heavens,
      How deeply you at once do touch me! Imogen,
5   The great part of my comfort, gone; my queen
      Upon a desperate bed, and in a time
      When fearful wars point at me; her son gone,
      So needful for this present. It strikes me past
      The hope of comfort.—But for thee, fellow,
10   Who needs must know of her departure and
      Dost seem so ignorant, we'll enforce it from thee
      By a sharp torture.

      PISANIO   Sir, my life is yours,
      I humbly set it at your will; but for my mistress,
      I nothing know where she remains, why gone,
      Nor when she purposes return. Beseech your
15   Highness,
      Hold me your loyal servant.

      LORD   Good my liege,
      The day that she was missing he was here.
      I dare be bound he's true and shall perform
      All parts of his subjection loyally. For Cloten,

400 **arm** carry 400 **preferred** recommended IV.iii.2 **with** resulting from
4 **touch** wound 6 **Upon ... bed** i.e., desperately ill 14 **nothing** not at all
19 **subjection** duty as a subject

There wants no diligence in seeking him,   20
And will no doubt be found.

CYMBELINE   The time is troublesome.
  [*To Pisanio*] We'll slip you for a season, but our
    jealousy
  Does yet depend.

LORD   So please your Majesty,
  The Roman legions, all from Gallia drawn,
  Are landed on your coast, with a supply   25
  Of Roman gentlemen by the Senate sent.

CYMBELINE Now for the counsel of my son and
    queen!
  I am amazed with matter.

LORD   Good my liege,
  Your preparation can affront no less
  Than what you hear of. Come more, for more
    you're ready.
  The want is but to put those pow'rs in motion   30
  That long to move.

CYMBELINE   I thank you. Let's withdraw,
  And meet the time as it seeks us. We fear not
  What can from Italy annoy us, but
  We grieve at chances here. Away.   35
                      Exeunt [all but Pisanio].

PISANIO I heard no letter from my master since
  I wrote him Imogen was slain. 'Tis strange.
  Nor hear I from my mistress, who did promise
  To yield me often tidings. Neither know I
  What is betid to Cloten, but remain   40
  Perplexed in all. The heavens still must work.
  Wherein I am false I am honest; not true, to be true.

---

21 **will he will**   21 **troublesome** full of troubles   22 **slip you** let you go free
22 **jealousy** suspicion   23 **depend** remain   27 **Now for** would I had
28 **amazed with matter** confounded by business   29 **preparation** armed forces
29 **affront no less** i.e., face larger forces   30 **Come more** if more come
31 **The want is but** the only thing needed is   34 **annoy** harm   36 **no letter** i.e.,
not at all   40 **is betid** has happened

These present wars shall find I love my country,
Even to the note o' th' King, or I'll fall in them.
45   All other doubts, by time let them be cleared;
Fortune brings in some boats that are not steered.

                                          Exit.

Scene IV. [*Wales.*]

Enter Belarius, Guiderius, and Arviragus.

GUIDERIUS The noise is round about us.

BELARIUS   Let us from it.

ARVIRAGUS What pleasure, sir, find we in life, to lock it
    From action and adventure?

GUIDERIUS   Nay, what hope
    Have we in hiding us? This way the Romans
5   Must or for Britons slay us or receive us
    For barbarous and unnatural revolts
    During their use, and slay us after.

BELARIUS   Sons,
    We'll higher to the mountains, there secure us.
    To the King's party there's no going. Newness
    Of Cloten's death—we being not known, not
10   mustered
    Among the bands—may drive us to a render
    Where we have lived, and so extort from's that
    Which we have done, whose answer would be
       death
    Drawn on with torture.

GUIDERIUS   This is, sir, a doubt

---

44 **note** knowledge IV.iv.2 **lock** preclude 4 **This way** i.e., if we do so
5 **Must or** must either 6 **revolts** rebels 7 **During their use** while they have
use for us 11 **render** account 13 **answer** requital 14 **Drawn on** brought
about

In such a time nothing becoming you 15
Nor satisfying us.

ARVIRAGUS It is not likely
That when they hear the Roman horses neigh,
Behold their quartered fires, have both their eyes
And ears so cloyed importantly as now,
That they will waste their time upon our note, 20
To know from whence we are.

BELARIUS O, I am known
Of many in the army. Many years,
Though Cloten then but young, you see, not wore
him
From my remembrance. And besides, the King
Hath not deserved my service nor your loves, 25
Who find in my exile the want of breeding,
The certainty of this hard life; aye hopeless
To have the courtesy your cradle promised,
But to be still hot summer's tanlings and
The shrinking slaves of winter.

GUIDERIUS Than be so 30
Better to cease to be. Pray, sir, to th' army.
I and my brother are not known; yourself
So out of thought, and thereto so o'ergrown,
Cannot be questioned.

ARVIRAGUS By this sun that shines,
I'll thither. What thing is't that I never 35
Did see man die, scarce ever looked on blood
But that of coward hares, hot goats, and venison!
Never bestrid a horse, save one that had
A rider like myself, who ne'er wore rowel
Nor iron on his heel! I am ashamed 40
To look upon the holy sun, to have

18 **quartered fires** camp fires   19 **cloyed importantly** burdened with important matters   20 **upon our note** on noticing us   23 **then** i.e., was then   26 **Who**
... breeding you who through sharing my exile experience a lack of education
27 **certainty** inescapability   29 **tanlings** tanned persons   33 **o'ergrown** re-
placed in their thoughts   37 **hot** lecherous   39 **rowel** the wheel on a spur

The benefit of his blest beams, remaining
So long a poor unknown.

GUIDERIUS   By heavens, I'll go.
If you will bless me, sir, and give me leave,
45 I'll take the better care, but if you will not,
The hazard therefore due fall on me by
The hands of Romans!

ARVIRAGUS   So say I. Amen.

BELARIUS No reason I, since of your lives you set
So slight a valuation, should reserve
My cracked one to more care. Have with you,
50   boys!
If in your country wars you chance to die,
That is my bed too, lads, and there I'll lie.
Lead, lead. [*Aside*] The time seems long; their
    blood thinks scorn
Till it fly out and show them princes born.   *Exeunt.*

---

46 **hazard therefore due** risk attendant upon being unblessed   50 **cracked** i.e.,
since old   51 **country** country's

ACT V

Scene I. [*Britain.*]

Enter Posthumus alone [with a bloody handkerchief].

POSTHUMUS Yea, bloody cloth, I'll keep thee, for I
    wished
  Thou shouldst be colored thus. You married ones,
  If each of you should take this course, how many
  Must murder wives much better than themselves
  For wrying but a little! O Pisanio,   5
  Every good servant does not all commands;
  No bond but to do just ones. Gods, if you
  Should have ta'en vengeance on my faults, I never
  Had lived to put on this; so had you saved
  The noble Imogen to repent, and struck   10
  Me, wretch more worth your vengeance. But alack,
  You snatch some hence for little faults; that's love,
  To have them fall no more; you some permit
  To second ills with ills, each elder worse,
  And make them dread it, to the doers' thrift.   15
  But Imogen is your own. Do your best wills,
  And make me blest to obey. I am brought hither

V.i.2 **You married ones** (he addresses the audience)   5 **wrying** deviating, going
wrong   7 **No bond but** i.e., he is bound only   9 **put on this** instigate this crime
13 **fall** i.e., from virtue   14 **second** follow up   14 **elder** i.e., later   15 **them** the
doers   15 **dread it** repent the evil course   15 **thrift** profit

217

Among th' Italian gentry, and to fight
Against my lady's kingdom. 'Tis enough
20   That, Britain, I have killed thy mistress; peace,
I'll give no wound to thee. Therefore, good heavens,
Hear patiently my purpose. I'll disrobe me
Of these Italian weeds and suit myself
As does a Briton peasant. So I'll fight
25   Against the part I come with; so I'll die
For thee, O Imogen, even for whom my life
Is every breath a death; and thus, unknown,
Pitied nor hated, to the face of peril
Myself I'll dedicate. Let me make men know
30   More valor in me than my habits show.
Gods, put the strength o' th' Leonati in me.
To shame the guise o' th' world, I will begin
The fashion, less without and more within.   *Exit.*

Scene II. [*Britain.*]

*Enter Lucius, Iachimo, and the Roman Army at one
door, and the Briton Army at another, Leonatus
Posthumus following like a poor soldier. They
march over and go out. Then enter again in skirmish Iachimo and Posthumus. He vanquisheth and
disarmeth Iachimo and then leaves him.*

IACHIMO   The heaviness and guilt within my bosom
Takes off my manhood. I have belied a lady,
The princess of this country, and the air on't
Revengingly enfeebles me; or could this carl,
5   A very drudge of nature's, have subdued me
In my profession? Knighthoods and honors, borne
As I wear mine, are titles but of scorn.

25 **part** side   30 **habits** clothes   32 **guise** custom   V.ii.s.d. **They march ... go
out** (each group marches about the stage and exits by the other door)   2 **Takes
off** destroys   2 **belied** slandered   3 **on't** of it   4 **or** otherwise   4 **carl** churl

If that thy gentry, Britain, go before
This lout as he exceeds our lords, the odds
Is that we scarce are men and you are gods.   *Exit.*   10

*The battle continues. The Britons fly; Cymbeline is
taken. Then enter to his rescue Belarius, Guiderius,
and Arviragus.*

BELARIUS Stand, stand! We have th' advantage of the
 ground.
The lane is guarded. Nothing routs us but
The villainy of our fears.

GUIDERIUS, ARVIRAGUS   Stand, stand, and fight!

*Enter Posthumus and seconds the Britons. They rescue
Cymbeline and exeunt. Then enter Lucius, Iachimo,
and Imogen.*

LUCIUS Away, boy, from the troops, and save thyself,
For friends kill friends, and the disorder's such   15
As War were hoodwinked.

IACHIMO   'Tis their fresh supplies.

LUCIUS It is a day turned strangely; or betimes
Let's reinforce or fly.   *Exeunt.*

Scene III. [*Britain.*]

Enter Posthumus and a Briton Lord.

LORD Cam'st thou from where they made the stand?

POSTHUMUS   I did;
Though you, it seems, come from the fliers.

LORD   I did.

8 **go before** excell   16 **hoodwinked** blindfolded   17 **or betimes** either quickly

POSTHUMUS No blame be to you, sir, for all was lost,
But that the heavens fought. The King himself
5   Of his wings destitute, the army broken,
And but the backs of Britons seen, all flying
Through a strait lane; the enemy full-hearted,
Lolling the tongue with slaught'ring, having work
More plentiful than tools to do't, struck down
10   Some mortally, some slightly touched, some falling
Merely through fear, that the strait pass was
          dammed
With dead men hurt behind, and cowards living
To die with lengthened shame.

LORD   Where was this lane?

POSTHUMUS Close by the battle, ditched, and walled
          with turf;
15   Which gave advantage to an ancient soldier,
An honest one I warrant, who deserved
So long a breeding as his white beard came to,
In doing this for's country. Athwart the lane
He with two striplings—lads more like to run
20   The country base than to commit such slaughter;
With faces fit for masks, or rather fairer
Than those for preservation cased or shame—
Made good the passage, cried to those that fled,
"Our Britain's harts die flying, not our men.
25   To darkness fleet souls that fly backwards. Stand,
Or we are Romans and will give you that
Like beasts which you shun beastly, and may save
But to look back in frown. Stand, stand!" These
          three,

V.iii.7 **strait** narrow 7 **full-hearted** full of courage 10 **touched** wounded
12 **behind** i.e., while running away 17 **So long ... came to** i.e., to live
(renowned) as long after this day as he had lived before in growing his beard
19–20 **run/The country base** play the game of prisoner's base 21 **masks** for
protection from sunburn (so used by ladies) 22 **for preservation ... shame**
covered for protection or modesty 25 **fleet** are wafted 26 **are Romans** i.e., will
behave like Romans 27 **beastly** i.e., like cowards 27–28 **save/But to look
back in frown** i.e., prevent only by looking back defiantly

Three thousand confident, in act as many—
For three performers are the file when all   30
The rest do nothing—with this word "Stand, stand,"
Accommodated by the place, more charming
With their own nobleness, which could have turned
A distaff to a lance, gilded pale looks,
Part shame, part spirit renewed; that some, turned
    coward   35
But by example—O, a sin in war,
Damned in the first beginners!—gan to look
The way that they did and to grin like lions
Upon the pikes o' th' hunters. Then began
A stop i' th' chaser, a retire; anon   40
A rout, confusion thick. Forthwith they fly
Chickens, the way which they stooped eagles;
    slaves,
The strides they victors made; and now our cowards,
Like fragments in hard voyages, became
The life o' th' need. Having found the back door
    open   45
Of the unguarded hearts, heavens, how they wound!
Some slain before, some dying, some their friends
O'erborne i' th' former wave, ten chased by one
Are now each one the slaughterman of twenty.
Those that would die or ere resist are grown   50
The mortal bugs o' th' field.

LORD   This was strange chance:
A narrow lane, an old man, and two boys.

POSTHUMUS Nay, do not wonder at it. You are made
Rather to wonder at the things you hear

---

30 **file** whole force   32 **more charming** i.e., winning over others   34 **gilded**
brought color to   35 **Part** some   36 **by example** by imitating others   38 **they**
the three men   38 **grin** bare the teeth   40 **stop . . . chaser** sudden check (as of a
horse) on the part of the pursuer   40 **anon** soon   42 **stooped** swooped (hawking
term)   44 **fragments** scraps (of food)   45 **life o' th' need** a source of life in time
of need   47 **slain before** i.e., who had feigned death   47 **some** some of   50 **or
ere** before   51 **mortal bugs** deadly terrors   51 **field** battle

55   Than to work any. Will you rhyme upon't
        And vent it for a mock'ry? Here is one:
        "Two boys, an old man twice a boy, a lane,
        Preserved the Britons, was the Romans' bane."

    LORD Nay, be not angry, sir.

    POSTHUMUS   'Lack, to what end?
60   Who dares not stand his foe, I'll be his friend;
        For if he'll do as he is made to do,
        I know he'll quickly fly my friendship too.
        You have put me into rhyme.

    LORD   Farewell. You're angry. *Exit.*

    POSTHUMUS Still going? This is a lord! O noble misery,
65   To be i' th' field, and ask "What news?" of me!
        Today how many would have given their honors
        To have saved their carcasses, took heel to do't,
        And yet died too! I, in mine own woe charmed,
        Could not find Death where I did hear him groan
        Nor feel him where he struck. Being an ugly
70   monster,
        'Tis strange he hides him in fresh cups, soft beds,
        Sweet words, or hath moe ministers than we
        That draw his knives i' th' war. Well, I will find
        him,
        For being now a favorer to the Briton,
75   No more a Briton. I have resumed again
        The part I came in. Fight I will no more,
        But yield me to the veriest hind that shall
        Once touch my shoulder. Great the slaughter is
        Here made by th' Roman; great the answer be

---

55 **work** any perform any such deeds 56 **vent it** make it known 60 **stand** withstand 61 **made** naturally inclined 63 **put** forced 64 **going** running away 64 **noble misery** wretchedness of false nobility 68 **charmed** preserved as by a charm 74 **being ... favorer to** since he now favors 75 **No more a Briton** i.e., I will seek Death among the Romans 77 **hind** peasant 78 **touch my shoulder** as in a formal arrest 79 **answer** retaliation

Britons must take. For me, my ransom's death.   80
On either side I come to spend my breath,
Which neither here I'll keep nor bear again,
But end it by some means for Imogen.

Enter two [Briton] Captains and Soldiers.

FIRST CAPTAIN Great Jupiter be praised, Lucius is
taken.
'Tis thought the old man and his sons were angels.   85

SECOND CAPTAIN There was a fourth man, in a silly
habit,
That gave th' affront with them.

FIRST CAPTAIN   So 'tis reported,
But none of 'em can be found. Stand, who's there?

POSTHUMUS A Roman,
Who had not now been drooping here if seconds   90
Had answered him.

SECOND CAPTAIN   Lay hands on him. A dog,
A leg of Rome shall not return to tell
What crows have pecked them here. He brags his
service
As if he were of note. Bring him to th' King.

*Enter Cymbeline, Belarius, Guiderius, Arviragus,
Pisanio, and Roman Captives [guarded]. The Captains present Posthumus to Cymbeline, who delivers
        him over to a Jailer.   [Exeunt.]*

81 **spend my breath** give up my life   86 **a silly habit** lowly clothing
87 **affront** attack   90 **seconds** supporters   91 **answered him** acted as he
did   94 **note** reputation

Scene IV. [*Britain.*]

Enter Posthumus and [two] Jailers.

FIRST JAILER You shall not now be stol'n; you have
    locks upon you.
So graze as you find pasture.

SECOND JAILER   Ay, or a stomach.
                              [*Exeunt Jailers.*]

POSTHUMUS Most welcome, bondage, for thou art a
    way,
I think, to liberty. Yet am I better
5   Than one that's sick o' th' gout, since he had rather
Groan so in perpetuity than be cured
By th' sure physician, Death, who is the key
T' unbar these locks. My conscience, thou art
    fettered
More than my shanks and wrists. You good gods,
    give me
10   The penitent instrument to pick that bolt,
Then free for ever. Is't enough I am sorry?
So children temporal fathers do appease;
Gods are more full of mercy. Must I repent,
I cannot do it better than in gyves,
15   Desired more than constrained. To satisfy,
If of my freedom 'tis the main part, take
No stricter render of me than my all.

V.iv.s.d. **Enter** (the action may be continuous from V.iii, Posthumus and the
Jailers remaining on stage after the exit of Cymbeline at the end of that scene; in
any case at the beginning of V.iv the locale of the action changes from open
country to a prison) **2 stomach** appetite (for grazing) **10 penitent . . . bolt** tool
of repentance which will unfetter my conscience **11 free** i.e., in death **14 gyves**
fetters **15 constrained** forced upon me **15 satisfy** make atonement **16 If . . .
main part** i.e., if atonement is essential to my freedom of conscience **17 stricter
render** sterner repayment **17 all** i.e., life

I know you are more clement than vile men,
Who of their broken debtors take a third,
A sixth, a tenth, letting them thrive again   20
On their abatement. That's not my desire.
For Imogen's dear life take mine; and though
'Tis not so dear, yet 'tis a life; you coined it.
'Tween man and man they weigh not every stamp;
Though light, take pieces for the figure's sake;   25
You rather mine, being yours. And so, great
    pow'rs,
If you will take this audit, take this life
And cancel these cold bonds. O Imogen,
I'll speak to thee in silence.   [*Sleeps.*]

Solemn music. Enter, as in an apparition, Sicilius
Leonatus, father to Posthumus, an old man attired
like a warrior; leading in his hand an ancient
Matron, his wife and mother to Posthumus with
Music before them. Then, after other Music, fol-
lows the two young Leonati, brothers to Posthumus,
with wounds as they died in the wars. They circle
Posthumus round as he lies sleeping.

SICILIUS No more, thou Thunder-master, show thy
    spite on mortal flies.   30
With Mars fall out, with Juno chide, that thy
    adulteries
      Rates and revenges.
Hath my poor boy done aught but well, whose face
    I never saw?
I died whilst in the womb he stayed attending
    Nature's law;
Whose father then, as men report thou orphans'
    father art,   35

21 **abatement** reduced amount   23 **dear** valuable   24 **stamp** coin   25 **figure**
the ruler's image stamped on the "piece" (coin)   26 **You ... being yours** i.e., you
should take my life the sooner since (though light coin) it is at least stamped in
your image   27 **take this audit** accept this account   28 **cancel ... bonds** i.e.,
remove (through letting me die) these iron shackles (quibble on "void these
worthless contracts")   29s.d. **Music** musicians   30 **Thunder-master** Jupiter
32 **Rates** scolds   34 **Attending** awaiting

Thou shouldst have been, and shielded him from this earth-vexing smart.

MOTHER Lucina lent not me her aid, but took me in my throes,
That from me was Posthumus ripped, came crying 'mongst his foes,
    A thing of pity.

SICILIUS Great Nature like his ancestry moulded the
40   stuff so fair
That he deserved the praise o' th' world, as great Sicilius' heir.

FIRST BROTHER When once he was mature for man, in Britain where was he
That could stand up his parallel, or fruitful object be
In eye of Imogen, that best could deem his dignity?

MOTHER With marriage wherefore was he mocked, to
45   be exiled and thrown
From Leonati seat and cast from her his dearest one, Sweet Imogen?

SICILIUS Why did you suffer Iachimo, slight thing of Italy,
To taint his nobler heart and brain with needless jealousy,
And to become the geck and scorn o' th' other's
50   villainy?

SECOND BROTHER For this from stiller seats we come, our parents and us twain,
That striking in our country's cause fell bravely and were slain,

---

36 **earth-vexing smart** suffering which plagues the life of man   37 **Lucina** Juno Lucina (goddess of childbirth)   40 **stuff** substance   42 **mature for man** fully matured   43 **fruitful** ripe, mature   44 **deem his dignity** judge his worth 48 **you** Jupiter   48 **slight** worthless   50 **geck** dupe   51 **stiller seats** quieter abodes (in the Elysian Fields)

Our fealty and Tenantius' right with honor to
maintain.

FIRST BROTHER Like hardiment Posthumus hath to
Cymbeline performed.
Then, Jupiter, thou King of gods, why hast thou
thus adjourned   55
The graces for his merits due, being all to dolors
turned?

SICILIUS Thy crystal window ope; look out. No longer
exercise
Upon a valiant race thy harsh and potent injuries.

MOTHER Since, Jupiter, our son is good, take off his
miseries.

SICILIUS Peep through thy marble mansion. Help, or
we poor ghosts will cry   60
To th' shining synod of the rest against thy deity.

BROTHERS Help, Jupiter, or we appeal and from thy
justice fly.

*Jupiter descends in thunder and lightning, sitting
upon an eagle. He throws a thunderbolt. The Ghosts
fall on their knees.*

JUPITER No more, you petty spirits of region low,
Offend our hearing. Hush! How dare you ghosts
Accuse the Thunderer, whose bolt, you know,   65
Sky-planted, batters all rebelling coasts?
Poor shadows of Elysium, hence, and rest
Upon your never-withering banks of flow'rs.
Be not with mortal accidents opprest.
No care of yours it is; you know 'tis ours.   70
Whom best I love I cross; to make my gift,
The more delayed, delighted. Be content.
Your low-laid son our godhead will uplift;

53 **Tenantius** Sicilius   54 **hardiment** bold exploits   55 **adjourned** deferred
61 **the rest** the other gods   62s.d. **descends** (Jupiter is lowered by suspension-
gear from stage cover to stage)   63 **region low** Hades   66 **Sky-planted** based in
the sky   69 **accidents** occurrences   71 **cross** thwart

His comforts thrive, his trials well are spent.
75   Our Jovial star reigned at his birth, and in
        Our temple was he married. Rise, and fade.
He shall be lord of Lady Imogen,
        And happier much by his affliction made.
This tablet lay upon his breast, wherein
80   Our pleasure his full fortune doth confine.
And so, away; no farther with your din
        Express impatience, lest you stir up mine.
        Mount, eagle, to my palace crystalline.   *Ascends*.

SICILIUS He came in thunder; his celestial breath
85   Was sulphurous to smell; the holy eagle
        Stooped, as to foot us. His ascension is
        More sweet than our blest fields; his royal bird
        Prunes the immortal wing and cloys his beak,
        As when his god is pleased.

ALL   Thanks, Jupiter.

90 SICILIUS The marble pavement closes; he is entered
        His radiant roof. Away, and, to be blest,
        Let us with care perform his great behest.

                              [*The Ghosts*] *vanish*.

POSTHUMUS [*Waking*] Sleep, thou hast been a grandsire
        and begot
A father to me, and thou hast created
95   A mother and two brothers; but, O scorn,
Gone! They went hence so soon as they were born.
And so I am awake. Poor wretches that depend
On greatness' favor, dream as I have done,
Wake, and find nothing. But, alas, I swerve.
100   Many dream not to find, neither deserve,
And yet are steeped in favors. So am I,
That have this golden chance and know not why.

74 **spent** ended   75 **Jovial star** the planet Jupiter   80 **confine** i.e., state precisely
86 **Stooped ... us** swooped (hawking term) as if to seize us in his talons
87 **More sweet** (in contrast to his angry, sulphurous descent)   87 **our blest
fields** the Elysian Fields   88 **Prunes** preens   88 **cloys** claws   90 **closes** (apparently in allusion to the trap door in the underside of the stage cover through which
Jupiter has ascended)   92s.d. **vanish** i.e., exit rapidly   95 **scorn** mockery
99 **swerve** err

What fairies haunt this ground? A book? O rare
  one,
Be not, as is our fangled world, a garment
Nobler than that it covers. Let thy effects   105
So follow to be most unlike our courtiers,
As good as promise.   *Reads.*
  "Whenas a lion's whelp shall, to himself unknown, without seeking find, and be embraced by a
piece of tender air; and when from a stately cedar   110
shall be lopped branches which, being dead many
years, shall after revive, be jointed to the old stock,
and freshly grow; then shall Posthumus end his
miseries, Britain be fortunate and flourish in peace
and plenty."   115
'Tis still a dream, or else such stuff as madmen
Tongue, and brain not; either, both, or nothing;
Or senseless speaking, or a speaking such
As sense cannot untie. Be what it is,
The action of my life is like it, which   120
I'll keep, if but for sympathy.

Enter Jailer.

JAILER Come, sir, are you ready for death?

POSTHUMUS Over-roasted rather; ready long ago.

JAILER Hanging is the word, sir. If you be ready for
that, you are well cooked.   125

POSTHUMUS So, if I prove a good repast to the spectators, the dish pays the shot.

JAILER A heavy reckoning for you, sir. But the comfort
is, you shall be called to no more payments, fear no
more tavern bills, which are as often the sadness of   130
parting as the procuring of mirth. You come in faint

104 **fangled** addicted to finery   106 **to** as to   108 **Whenas** when   117 **Tongue**
speak   117 **brain** understand   118 **Or senseless** either irrational   119 **sense**
the power of reason   120 **like it** i.e., without meaning or incapable of understanding
121 **sympathy** the resemblance   124 **Hanging** (the Jailer, picking up the
metaphor in "Over-roasted," quibbles on "hanging of meat")   127 **the dish ...
shot** i.e., the excellence of the food justifies its cost

for want of meat, depart reeling with too much
drink; sorry that you have paid too much, and sorry
that you are paid too much; purse and brain both
135   empty; the brain the heavier for being too light, the
purse too light, being drawn of heaviness. O, of
this contradiction you shall now be quit. O, the
charity of a penny cord! It sums up thousands in a
trice. You have no true debitor and creditor but it;
140   of what's past, is, and to come, the discharge. Your
neck, sir, is pen, book, and counters; so the acquittance follows.

POSTHUMUS I am merrier to die than thou art to live.

JAILER Indeed, sir, he that sleeps feels not the tooth-
145   ache; but a man that were to sleep your sleep, and
a hangman to help him to bed, I think he would
change places with his officer; for, look you, sir,
you know not which way you shall go.

POSTHUMUS Yes indeed do I, fellow.

150   JAILER Your death has eyes in's head then. I have not
seen him so pictured. You must either be directed
by some that take upon them to know, or to take
upon yourself that which I am sure you do not
know, or jump the after-inquiry on your own peril.
155   And how you shall speed in your journey's end, I
think you'll never return to tell on.

POSTHUMUS I tell thee, fellow, there are none want
eyes to direct them the way I am going but such as
wink and will not use them.

160   JAILER What an infinite mock is this, that a man should
have the best use of eyes to see the way of blind-
ness! I am sure hanging's the way of winking.

134 **are paid too much** have been subdued by too much liquor 136 **drawn**
emptied 139 **debitor and creditor** account book 140 **discharge** payment
141 **counters** (used for reckoning) 141–42 **acquittance** receipt 145 **a man**
that were i.e., if a man were destined 147 **officer** executioner 150 **Your death**
... head i.e., you seem to be informed about what will happen to you after
death 151 **pictured** (in the traditional skull or death's head) 154 **jump** gamble
on 155 **speed in** fare at 156 **on** of 159 **wink** close

Enter a Messenger.

MESSENGER Knock off his manacles; bring your prisoner to the King.

POSTHUMUS Thou bring'st good news; I am called to be   165
made free.

JAILER I'll be hanged then.

POSTHUMUS Thou shalt be then freer than a jailer. No
bolts for the dead.
                          [*Exeunt Posthumus and Messenger.*]

JAILER Unless a man would marry a gallows and beget   170
young gibbets, I never saw one so prone. Yet, on
my conscience, there are verier knaves desire to live,
for all he be a Roman; and there be some of them
too that die against their wills. So should I, if I were
one. I would we were all of one mind, and one mind   175
good. O, there were desolation of jailers and gallowses! I speak against my present profit, but my
wish hath a preferment in't.   *Exit.*

Scene V. [*Britain.*]

Enter Cymbeline, Belarius, Guiderius, Arviragus,
Pisanio, and Lords.

CYMBELINE Stand by my side, you whom the gods have
made
Preservers of my throne. Woe is my heart
That the poor soldier that so richly fought,
Whose rags shamed gilded arms, whose naked
breast
Stepped before targes of proof, cannot be found.   5

166 **made free** i.e., by death   171 **prone** eager   173 **for all** even though
173 **them** Romans   178 **preferment** promotion (for myself)   V.v.5 **targes of
proof** shields of proven strength

231

He shall be happy that can find him, if
Our grace can make him so.

BELARIUS   I never saw
Such noble fury in so poor a thing,
Such precious deeds in one that promised naught
But beggary and poor looks.

10 CYMBELINE   No tidings of him?

PISANIO He hath been searched among the dead and
     living,
But no trace of him.

CYMBELINE   To my grief, I am
The heir of his reward, which I will add
To you, the liver, heart, and brain of Britain,
15 By whom I grant she lives. 'Tis now the time
To ask of whence you are. Report it.

BELARIUS   Sir,
In Cambria are we born, and gentlemen.
Further to boast were neither true nor modest,
Unless I add we are honest.

CYMBELINE   Bow your knees.
20 Arise my knights o' th' battle; I create you
Companions to our person and will fit you
With dignities becoming your estates.

Enter Cornelius and Ladies.

There's business in these faces. Why so sadly
Greet you our victory? You look like Romans
And not o' th' court of Britain.

25 CORNELIUS   Hail, great King!
To sour your happiness I must report
The Queen is dead.

CYMBELINE   Who worse than a physician
Would this report become? But I consider

---

14 **liver, heart, and brain** (the vital parts—Belarius, Guiderius, and Arviragus)
20 **knights o' th' battle** knights created on the battlefield 21 **fit** equip
22 **estates** ranks

By med'cine life may be prolonged, yet death
Will seize the doctor too. How ended she?   30

CORNELIUS With horror, madly dying, like her life,
Which, being cruel to the world, concluded
Most cruel to herself. What she confessed
I will report, so please you. These her women
Can trip me if I err, who with wet cheeks   35
Were present when she finished.

CYMBELINE   Prithee say.

CORNELIUS First, she confessed she never loved you,
only,
Affected greatness got by you, not you;
Married your royalty, was wife to your place,
Abhorred your person.

CYMBELINE   She alone knew this,   40
And but she spoke it dying, I would not
Believe her lips in opening it. Proceed.

CORNELIUS Your daughter, whom she bore in hand to
love
With such integrity, she did confess
Was as a scorpion to her sight, whose life,   45
But that her flight prevented it, she had
Ta'en off by poison.

CYMBELINE   O most delicate fiend!
Who is't can read a woman? Is there more?

CORNELIUS More, sir, and worse. She did confess she
had
For you a mortal mineral, which, being took,   50
Should by the minute feed on life and, ling'ring,
By inches waste you. In which time she purposed,
By watching, weeping, tendance, kissing, to
O'ercome you with her show and, in time,

35 **trip me** expose inaccuracy   38 **Affected** loved   40 **your person** you as a
person   41 **but** except that   42 **opening** disclosing   43 **bore in hand** pretended
47 **Ta'en off** destroyed   47 **delicate** subtle   50 **mortal mineral** deadly poison
51 **by the minute** minute by minute   53 **tendance** attention   54 **show** simula-
tion (of devotion)

55 When she had fitted you with her craft, to work
    Her son into th' adoption of the crown;
    But failing of her end by his strange absence,
    Grew shameless desperate, opened, in despite
    Of heaven and men, her purposes, repented
60 The evils she hatched were not effected, so
    Despairing died.

CYMBELINE   Heard you all this, her women?

LADIES We did, so please your Highness.

CYMBELINE   Mine eyes
    Were not in fault, for she was beautiful;
    Mine ears, that heard her flattery; nor my heart,
    That thought her like her seeming. It had been
65   vicious
    To have mistrusted her. Yet, O my daughter,
    That it was folly in me thou mayst say,
    And prove it in thy feeling. Heaven mend all!

*Enter Lucius, Iachimo, [the Soothsayer,] and other
Roman Prisoners, [guarded; the Messenger and
Posthumus] Leonatus behind; and Imogen.*

    Thou com'st not, Caius, now for tribute. That
70 The Britons have razed out, though with the loss
    Of many a bold one; whose kinsmen have made suit
    That their good souls may be appeased with
        slaughter
    Of you their captives, which ourself have granted.
    So think of your estate.

75 LUCIUS Consider, sir, the chance of war. The day
    Was yours by accident; had it gone with us,
    We should not, when the blood was cool, have
        threatened

55 **fitted you** shaped you to her purpose   65 **seeming** appearance   65 **had been
vicious** would have been morally wrong   67 **it** trusting her   68 **prove ...
feeling** experience the effect of my folly in your suffering   68s.d. **behind**
(Posthumus remains apart from the main group of players till line 209)   70 **razed
out** erased   72 **their** i.e., of those slain in battle   74 **your estate the** condition of
your souls

Our prisoners with the sword. But since the gods
Will have it thus, that nothing but our lives
May be called ransom, let it come. Sufficeth   80
A Roman with a Roman's heart can suffer.
Augustus lives to think on't—and so much
For my peculiar care. This one thing only
I will entreat: my boy, a Briton born,
Let him be ransomed. Never master had   85
A page so kind, so duteous, diligent,
So tender over his occasions, true,
So feat, so nurse-like. Let his virtue join
With my request, which I'll make bold your
    Highness
Cannot deny. He hath done no Briton harm,   90
Though he have served a Roman. Save him, sir,
And spare no blood beside.

CYMBELINE   I have surely seen him;
His favor is familiar to me. Boy,
Thou hast looked thyself into my grace
And art mine own. I know not why, wherefore,   95
To say "Live, boy." Ne'er thank thy master. Live,
And ask of Cymbeline what boon thou wilt,
Fitting my bounty and thy state; I'll give it,
Yea, though thou do demand a prisoner,
The noblest ta'en.

IMOGEN   I humbly thank your Highness.   100

LUCIUS I do not bid thee beg my life, good lad,
And yet I know thou wilt.

IMOGEN   No, no, alack,
There's other work in hand. I see a thing
Bitter to me as death; your life, good master,
Must shuffle for itself.

LUCIUS   The boy disdains me;   105

83 **peculiar** individual   87 **tender over his occasions** sensitive to his wants
88 **feat** dexterous   93 **favor** face   94 **looked thyself into** gained by thy looks
96 **To say** I am saying   103 **thing** the ring on Iachimo's finger   105 **shuffle** shift

235

He leaves me, scorns me. Briefly die their joys
That place them on the truth of girls and boys.
Why stands he so perplexed?

CYMBELINE   What wouldst thou, boy?
I love thee more and more. Think more and more
What's best to ask. Know'st him thou look'st on?
110   Speak.
Wilt have him live? Is he thy kin? Thy friend?

IMOGEN He is a Roman, no more kin to me
Than I to your Highness; who, being born your
     vassal,
Am something nearer.

CYMBELINE   Wherefore ey'st him so?

115 IMOGEN I'll tell you, sir, in private, if you please
To give me hearing.

CYMBELINE   Ay, with all my heart,
And lend my best attention. What's thy name?

IMOGEN Fidele, sir.

CYMBELINE   Thou'rt my good youth, my page;
I'll be thy master. Walk with me; speak freely.

BELARIUS Is not this boy revived from death?

120 ARVIRAGUS   One sand another
Not more resembles that sweet rosy lad
Who died, and was Fidele. What think you?

GUIDERIUS The same dead thing alive.

BELARIUS Peace, peace, see further. He eyes us not;
     forbear.
125 Creatures may be alike. Were't he, I am sure
He would have spoke to us.

GUIDERIUS   But we saw him dead.

BELARIUS Be silent, let's see further.

PISANIO [*Aside*]   It is my mistress.

106 **Briefly** quickly   107 **truth** loyalty

236

Since she is living, let the time run on
To good or bad.

CYMBELINE   Come, stand thou by our side;
Make thy demand aloud.—Sir, step you forth,   130
Give answer to this boy, and do it freely;
Or, by our greatness and the grace of it,
Which is our honor, bitter torture shall
Winnow the truth from falsehood.—On, speak to
  him.

IMOGEN My boon is that this gentleman may render   135
Of whom he had this ring.

POSTHUMUS [Aside]   What's that to him?

CYMBELINE That diamond upon your finger, say
How came it yours.

IACHIMO Thou'lt torture me to leave unspoken that
Which to be spoke would torture thee.

CYMBELINE   How? Me?   140

IACHIMO I am glad to be constrained to utter that
Which torments me to conceal. By villainy
I got this ring. 'Twas Leonatus' jewel,
Whom thou didst banish, and—which more may
  grieve thee,
As it doth me—a nobler sir ne'er lived   145
'Twixt sky and ground. Wilt thou hear more, my
  lord?

CYMBELINE All that belongs to this.

IACHIMO   That paragon, thy daughter,
For whom my heart drops blood and my false
  spirits
Quail to remember—Give me leave, I faint.

CYMBELINE My daughter? What of her? Renew thy
  strength.   150

135 render state   139 to leave for leaving   148 and and whom

I had rather thou shouldst live while nature will
Than die ere I hear more. Strive, man, and speak.

IACHIMO Upon a time—unhappy was the clock
That struck the hour!—it was in Rome—accursed
155 The mansion where!—'twas at a feast—O, would
Our viands had been poisoned, or at least
Those which I heaved to head!—the good
      Posthumus—
What should I say? He was too good to be
Where ill men were, and was the best of all
160 Amongst the rar'st of good ones—sitting sadly,
Hearing us praise our loves of Italy
For beauty that made barren the swelled boast
Of him that best could speak; for feature, laming
The shrine of Venus or straight-pight Minerva,
165 Postures beyond brief nature; for condition,
A shop of all the qualities that man
Loves woman for; besides that hook of wiving,
Fairness which strikes the eye—

CYMBELINE   I stand on fire.
Come to the matter.

IACHIMO   All too soon I shall,
170 Unless thou wouldst grieve quickly. This Posthumus
Most like a noble lord in love and one
That had a royal lover, took his hint,
And not dispraising whom we praised—therein
He was as calm as virtue—he began
His mistress' picture; which by his tongue being
175   made,
And then a mind put in't, either our brags

---

151 **while nature will** i.e., the rest of your natural life   157 **heaved to head**
lifted to mouth   163 **feature** shapeliness   163 **laming/The shrine** making
deformed (by comparison) the image   164 **straight-pight** tall, erect   165 **Postures** forms   165 **beyond brief nature** i.e., more richly endowed than mortal
beings   165 **condition** character   166 **shop** repository   167 **hook** fishhook
169 **matter** point   172 **hint** opportunity   176 **And then ... in't** i.e., added to
which was a good mind

Were cracked of kitchen trulls, or his description
Proved us unspeaking sots.

CYMBELINE   Nay, nay, to th' purpose.

IACHIMO Your daughter's chastity—there it begins.
He spake of her as Dian had hot dreams   180
And she alone were cold; whereat I, wretch,
Made scruple of his praise and wagered with him
Pieces of gold 'gainst this which then he wore
Upon his honored finger, to attain
In suit the place of 's bed and win this ring   185
By hers and mine adultery. He, true knight,
No lesser of her honor confident
Than I did truly find her, stakes this ring;
And would so, had it been a carbuncle
Of Phoebus' wheel, and might so safely had it   190
Been all the worth of 's car. Away to Britain
Post I in this design. Well may you, sir,
Remember me at court, where I was taught
Of your chaste daughter the wide difference
'Twixt amorous and villainous. Being thus
    quenched   195
Of hope, not longing, mine Italian brain
Gan in your duller Britain operate
Most vilely; for my vantage, excellent.
And, to be brief, my practice so prevailed
That I returned with simular proof enough   200
To make the noble Leonatus mad
By wounding his belief in her renown
With tokens thus and thus; averring notes
Of chamber hanging, pictures, this her bracelet—
O cunning, how I got it!—nay, some marks   205
Of secret on her person, that he could not

177 **cracked** boasted   178 **unspeaking sots** inarticulate fools   180 **as** as if
181 **cold** chaste   182 **Made scruple of** expressed doubt about, disputed
185 **suit** amorous solicitation (Maxwell)   189 **carbuncle** red precious stone
190 **Of Phoebus' wheel** (decorating the sun-god's chariot)   194 **Of** by
195 **amorous** i.e., faithful   195-96 **Being thus ... longing** the fire of hope
(though not of desire) being thus put out   198 **vantage** profit   199 **practice**
plot   200 **simular** simulated, specious   202 **renown** good name   203 **averring**
avouching

But think her bond of chastity quite cracked,
I having ta'en the forfeit. Whereupon—
Methinks I see him now—

POSTHUMUS [*Advancing*]   Ay, so thou dost,
210 Italian fiend! Ay me, most credulous fool,
Egregious murderer, thief, anything
That's due to all the villains past, in being,
To come! O, give me cord or knife or poison,
Some upright justicer! Thou, King, send out
215 For torturers ingenious. It is I
That all th' abhorrèd things o' th' earth amend
By being worse than they. I am Posthumus,
That killed thy daughter—villain-like, I lie—
That caused a lesser villain than myself,
220 A sacrilegious thief, to do't. The temple
Of Virtue was she; yea, and she herself.
Spit, and throw stones, cast mire upon me, set
The dogs o' th' street to bay me; every villain
Be called Posthumus Leonatus, and
225 Be villainy less than 'twas! O Imogen!
My queen, my life, my wife! O Imogen,
Imogen, Imogen!

IMOGEN   Peace, my lord. Hear, hear—

POSTHUMUS Shall's have a play of this? Thou scornful
    page,
There lie thy part.   [*Striking her; she falls.*]

PISANIO   O gentlemen, help!
230 Mine and your mistress! O my lord Posthumus,
You ne'er killed Imogen till now. Help, help!
Mine honored lady!

CYMBELINE   Does the world go round?

POSTHUMUS How comes these staggers on me?

208 **forfeit** that which was forfeited for breach of contract   211–12 **anything/
That's due** i.e., any word that's appropriate   214 **justicer** judge   216 **amend**
make better (by contrast)   221 **she herself** Virtue herself   225 **less** i.e., by
comparison with my villainy   228 **Shall's** shall us (we)   229 **There lie thy part**
play your role lying there   233 **staggers** dizziness

PISANIO   Wake, my mistress!

CYMBELINE If this be so, the gods do mean to strike me
   To death with mortal joy.

PISANIO   How fares my mistress?   235

IMOGEN O, get thee from my sight;
   Thou gav'st me poison. Dangerous fellow, hence;
   Breathe not where princes are.

CYMBELINE   The tune of Imogen!

PISANIO Lady,
   The gods throw stones of sulphur on me if   240
   That box I gave you was not thought by me
   A precious thing; I had it from the Queen.

CYMBELINE New matter still.

IMOGEN   It poisoned me.

CORNELIUS   O gods!
   I left out one thing which the Queen confessed,
   Which must approve thee honest. "If Pisanio   245
   Have," said she, "given his mistress that confection
   Which I gave him for cordial, she is served
   As I would serve a rat."

CYMBELINE   What's this, Cornelius?

CORNELIUS The Queen, sir, very oft importuned me
   To temper poisons for her, still pretending   250
   The satisfaction of her knowledge only
   In killing creatures vile, as cats and dogs
   Of no esteem. I, dreading that her purpose
   Was of more danger, did compound for her
   A certain stuff which, being ta'en, would cease   255
   The present pow'r of life, but in short time
   All offices of nature should again
   Do their due functions. Have you ta'en of it?

235 **mortal** deadly, fatal   238 **tune** voice   240 **stones of sulphur** thunderbolts
242 **precious** i.e., beneficial   245 **approve** prove   246 **confection** drug
250 **temper** mix   250 **still pretending** always alleging as her purpose
253 **esteem** value   255 **cease** suspend   257 **offices of nature** bodily parts

IMOGEN Most like I did, for I was dead.

BELARIUS   My boys,
There was our error.

260 GUIDERIUS   This is sure Fidele.

IMOGEN Why did you throw your wedded lady from
    you?
Think that you are upon a rock, and now
Throw me again.   [*Embracing him*]

POSTHUMUS   Hang there like fruit, my soul,
Till the tree die!

CYMBELINE   How now, my flesh, my child?
265 What, mak'st thou me a dullard in this act?
Wilt thou not speak to me?

IMOGEN [*Kneeling*]   Your blessing, sir.

BELARIUS Though you did love this youth, I blame ye
    not;
You had a motive for't.

CYMBELINE   My tears that fall
Prove holy water on thee. Imogen,
270 Thy mother's dead.

IMOGEN   I am sorry for't, my lord.

CYMBELINE O, she was naught, and long of her it
    was
That we meet here so strangely; but her son
Is gone, we know not how nor where.

PISANIO   My lord,
Now fear is from me, I'll speak troth. Lord Cloten,
275 Upon my lady's missing, came to me
With his sword drawn, foamed at the mouth, and
    swore,

259 **like** probably   259 **dead** as if dead   262 **upon a rock** (sense unclear; "rock"
is sometimes emended to "lock," a hold in wrestling)   265 **mak'st ... dullard**
treat me like a fool (by ignoring me)   265 **act** action, scene   268 **motive** cause
270 **mother** step-mother   271 **naught** wicked   271 **long of** because of
274 **troth** truth

242

If I discovered not which way she was gone,
It was my instant death. By accident
I had a feignèd letter of my master's
Then in my pocket, which directed him   280
To seek her on the mountains near to Milford;
Where, in a frenzy, in my master's garments,
Which he enforced from me, away he posts
With unchaste purpose and with oath to violate
My lady's honor. What became of him   285
I further know not.

GUIDERIUS   Let me end the story:
I slew him there.

CYMBELINE   Marry, the gods forfend!
I would not thy good deeds should from my lips
Pluck a hard sentence. Prithee, valiant youth,
Deny't again.

GUIDERIUS   I have spoke it, and I did it.   290

CYMBELINE He was a prince.

GUIDERIUS A most incivil one. The wrongs he did me
Were nothing princelike, for he did provoke me
With language that would make me spurn the sea
If it could so roar to me. I cut off's head,   295
And am right glad he is not standing here
To tell this tale of mine.

CYMBELINE   I am sorry for thee.
By thine own tongue thou art condemned and must
Endure our law. Thou'rt dead.

IMOGEN   That headless man
I thought had been my lord.

CYMBELINE   Bind the offender   300
And take him from our presence.

BELARIUS   Stay, sir King.

277 **discovered** revealed   287 **Marry** indeed (by the Virgin Mary)   287 **forfend**
forbid   288 **thy good deeds** i.e., in view of thy good deeds (in battle) that
thou   290 **Deny't again** speak again and deny what you have said (Nosworthy)
292 **incivil** unmannerly

This man is better than the man he slew,
As well descended as thyself, and hath
More of thee merited than a band of Clotens
Had ever scar for.—Let his arms alone;
They were not born for bondage.

CYMBELINE   Why, old soldier:
Wilt thou undo the worth thou art unpaid for
By tasting of our wrath? How of descent
As good as we?

ARVIRAGUS   In that he spake too far.

CYMBELINE And thou shalt die for't.

BELARIUS   We will die all three
But I will prove that two on's are as good
As I have given out him. My sons, I must
For mine own part unfold a dangerous speech,
Though haply well for you.

ARVIRAGUS   Your danger's ours.

GUIDERIUS And our good his.

BELARIUS   Have at it then. By leave,
Thou hadst, great King, a subject who
Was called Belarius.

CYMBELINE   What of him? He is
A banished traitor.

BELARIUS   He it is that hath
Assumed this age; indeed a banished man,
I know not how a traitor.

CYMBELINE   Take him hence.
The whole world shall not save him.

BELARIUS   Not too hot.

305 **Had ever scar for** ever earned by wounds   307 **the worth ... for** thy not
yet rewarded esteem (?)   310 **thou** Belarius   311 **But I will prove** if I do not
prove (Maxwell)   311 **on's** of us   315 **By leave** by your permission
319 **Assumed** attained to   321 **hot** fast

First pay me for the nursing of thy sons,
And let it be confiscate all, so soon
As I have received it.

CYMBELINE   Nursing of my sons?

BELARIUS I am too blunt and saucy; here's my knee.   325
Ere I arise I will prefer my sons;
Then spare not the old father. Mighty sir,
These two young gentlemen that call me father
And think they are my sons are none of mine;
They are the issue of your loins, my liege,   330
And blood of your begetting.

CYMBELINE   How? My issue?

BELARIUS So sure as you your father's. I, old Morgan,
Am that Belarius whom you sometime banished.
Your pleasure was my mere offense, my punishment
Itself, and all my treason; that I suffered   335
Was all the harm I did. These gentle princes—
For such and so they are—these twenty years
Have I trained up; those arts they have as I
Could put into them. My breeding was, sir, as
Your Highness knows. Their nurse, Euriphile,   340
Whom for the theft I wedded, stole these children
Upon my banishment. I moved her to't,
Having received the punishment before
For that which I did then. Beaten for loyalty
Excited me to treason. Their dear loss,   345
The more of you 'twas felt, the more it shaped
Unto my end of stealing them. But, gracious sir,
Here are your sons again, and I must lose
Two of the sweet'st companions in the world.
The benediction of these covering heavens   350

---

323 **it** the payment   326 **prefer** promote (in rank)   333 **sometime** once
334 **mere** entire   338 **arts** accomplishments   342 **moved** incited   344 **Beaten**
my having been beaten   346 **of** by   346–47 **shaped/ Unto** served

Fall on their heads like dew, for they are worthy
To inlay heaven with stars.

CYMBELINE   Thou weep'st and speak'st.
The service that you three have done is more
Unlike than this thou tell'st. I lost my children;
355   If these be they, I know not how to wish
A pair of worthier sons.

BELARIUS   Be pleased awhile.
This gentleman whom I call Polydore,
Most worthy prince, as yours, is true Guiderius;
This gentleman, my Cadwal, Arviragus,
360   Your younger princely son. He, sir, was lapped
In a most curious mantle, wrought by th' hand
Of his queen mother, which for more probation
I can with ease produce.

CYMBELINE   Guiderius had
Upon his neck a mole, a sanguine star;
It was a mark of wonder.

365 BELARIUS   This is he,
Who hath upon him still that natural stamp.
It was wise Nature's end in the donation
To be his evidence now.

CYMBELINE   O, what am I?
A mother to the birth of three? Ne'er mother
370   Rejoiced deliverance more. Blest pray you be,
That, after this strange starting from your orbs,
You may reign in them now! O Imogen,
Thou hast lost by this a kingdom.

IMOGEN   No, my lord,
I have got two worlds by't. O my gentle brothers,
375   Have we thus met? O, never say hereafter
But I am truest speaker. You called me brother

---

353 **service** i.e., in battle   354 **Unlike** improbable   360 **lapped** wrapped
361 **curious** elaborately wrought   362 **probation** proof   364 **sanguine** blood-red
367 **end** purpose   371 **orbs** spheres, orbits (of planets)

When I was but your sister, I you brothers
When ye were so indeed.

CYMBELINE Did you e'er meet?

ARVIRAGUS Ay, my good lord.

GUIDERIUS And at first meeting loved,
Continued so until we thought he died. 380

CORNELIUS By the Queen's dram she swallowed.

CYMBELINE O rare instinct!
When shall I hear all through? This fierce abridg-
ment
Hath to it circumstantial branches, which
Distinction should be rich in. Where, how lived
you?
And when came you to serve our Roman captive? 385
How parted with your brothers? How first met
them?
Why fled you from the court? And whither? These,
And your three motives to the battle, with
I know not how much more, should be demanded,
And all the other bye-dependences 390
From chance to chance; but nor the time nor
place
Will serve our long inter'gatories. See,
Posthumus anchors upon Imogen,
And she like harmless lightning throws her eye
On him, her brothers, me, her master, hitting 395
Each object with a joy; the counterchange
Is severally in all. Let's quit this ground
And smoke the temple with our sacrifices.
Thou art my brother; so we'll hold thee ever.

---

382 **fierce** drastic 383 **circumstantial** detailed 383–84 **which ... rich in**
which deserves to be elaborately discriminated (Maxwell) 388 **your three
motives** the motives of you three 390 **bye-dependences** connected circumstances 391 **chance** event 391 **but nor** but neither 396 **counterchange**
exchange 397 **severally in all** in each and in all 398 **smoke** fill with smoke
399 **Thou** Belarius

400 IMOGEN You are my father too, and did relieve me
       To see this gracious season.

    CYMBELINE   All o'erjoyed
       Save these in bonds; let them be joyful too,
       For they shall taste our comfort.

    IMOGEN   My good master,
       I will yet do you service.

    LUCIUS   Happy be you!

405 CYMBELINE The forlorn soldier, that so nobly fought,
       He would have well becomed this placed and graced
       The thankings of a king.

    POSTHUMUS   I am, sir,
       The soldier that did company these three
       In poor beseeming; 'twas a fitment for
410   The purpose I then followed. That I was he,
       Speak, Iachimo. I had you down and might
       Have made you finish.

    IACHIMO [*Kneeling*]   I am down again,
       But now my heavy conscience sinks my knee,
       As then your force did. Take that life, beseech you,
415   Which I so often owe; but your ring first,
       And here the bracelet of the truest princess
       That ever swore her faith.

    POSTHUMUS   Kneel not to me.
       The pow'r that I have on you is to spare you;
       The malice towards you to forgive you. Live,
       And deal with others better.

420 CYMBELINE   Nobly doomed!
       We'll learn our freeness of a son-in-law:
       Pardon's the word to all.

---

400 **You** Belarius   400 **relieve** aid   401 **gracious season** joyful occasion
403 **taste our comfort** share in our joy   405 **forlorn** lost, missing
409 **beseeming** appearance, clothing   409 **fitment** suitable device   412 **finish**
die   413 **sinks** lowers   415 **often** many times over   420 **doomed** judged
421 **freeness** generosity

ARVIRAGUS   You holp us, sir,
As you did mean indeed to be our brother.
Joyed are we that you are.

POSTHUMUS Your servant, princes. Good my lord of
  Rome,   425
Call forth your soothsayer. As I slept, methought
Great Jupiter, upon his eagle backed,
Appeared to me, with other spritely shows
Of mine own kindred. When I waked, I found
This label on my bosom, whose containing   430
Is so from sense in hardness that I can
Make no collection of it. Let him show
His skill in the construction.

LUCIUS   Philharmonus!

SOOTHSAYER Here, my good lord.

LUCIUS   Read, and declare the meaning.

SOOTHSAYER (*Reads*) "Whenas a lion's whelp shall, to   435
himself unknown, without seeking find, and be embraced by a piece of tender air; and when from a
stately cedar shall be lopped branches which, being
dead many years, shall after revive, be jointed to the
old stock, and freshly grow; then shall Posthumus   440
end his miseries, Britain be fortunate and flourish
in peace and plenty."
Thou, Leonatus, art the lion's whelp;
The fit and apt construction of thy name,
Being *Leo-natus*, doth import so much.—   445
The piece of tender air, thy virtuous daughter,
Which we call *mollis aer*, and *mollis aer*
We term it *mulier*.—Which *mulier* I divine
Is thy most constant wife, who even now

423 As as if   427 upon his eagle backed upon the back of his eagle
428 spritely ghostly   430 label piece of paper   430 containing contents
431 from remote from   432 collection of conclusion about   433 construction
interpretation   445 Leo-natus lion-born   447 mollis aer tender air
448 mulier woman (thought to derive from *mollis*, soft)   449 who thou who
(Posthumus)

450 Answering the letter of the oracle,
   Unknown to you, unsought, were clipped about
   With this most tender air.

CYMBELINE   This hath some seeming.

SOOTHSAYER The lofty cedar, royal Cymbeline,
   Personates thee, and thy lopped branches point
455 Thy two sons forth; who, by Belarius stol'n,
   For many years thought dead, are now revived,
   To the majestic cedar joined, whose issue
   Promises Britain peace and plenty.

CYMBELINE   Well,
   My peace we will begin. And, Caius Lucius,
460 Although the victor, we submit to Caesar
   And to the Roman empire, promising
   To pay our wonted tribute, from the which
   We were dissuaded by our wicked queen,
   Whom heavens in justice, both on her and hers,
465 Have laid most heavy hand.

SOOTHSAYER The fingers of the pow'rs above do tune
   The harmony of this peace. The vision
   Which I made known to Lucius ere the stroke
   Of this yet scarce-cold battle, at this instant
470 Is full accomplished; for the Roman eagle,
   From south to west on wing soaring aloft,
   Lessened herself and in the beams o' th' sun
   So vanished; which foreshadowed our princely eagle,
   Th' imperial Caesar, should again unite
475 His favor with the radiant Cymbeline,
   Which shines here in the west.

CYMBELINE   Laud we the gods,
   And let our crooked smokes climb to their nostrils
   From our blest altars. Publish we this peace
   To all our subjects. Set we forward; let
480 A Roman and a British ensign wave

451 **clipped** embraced 452 **seeming** plausibility 454 **Personates** represents
464 **Whom** on whom 464 **hers** i.e., Cloten 477 **crooked** curling 479 **Set we
forward** let us march

Friendly together. So through Lud's Town march,
And in the temple of great Jupiter
Our peace we'll ratify, seal it with feasts.
Set on there! Never was a war did cease,
Ere bloody hands were washed, with such a peace.   485
                                        Exeunt.

FINIS

484 Set on there begin marching

Textual Note

There is only one "substantive" edition of *Cymbeline*, the Shakespeare Folio of 1623. Because of incomplete notation of properties and music in the stage directions of F, it seems clear that the printer's copy for F was not a promptbook or the faithful transcript of one; and several directions are phrased in the "fictive" language characteristic of an author writing his own stage directions. Probably therefore the copy for F consisted of an authorial manuscript or the faithful transcript of one: either (1) "foul papers" (the author's last working draft of the play before preparation of a promptbook) in unusually clean condition (like the copy for *Antony and Cleopatra*); (2) authorial "fair copy" (the author's faithful transcript of his own foul papers); or (3) a faithful scribal transcript of foul papers or authorial fair copy. The type for F was set by a single compositor, Jaggard's Compositor B. (See Charlton Hinman, *The Printing and Proof-Reading of the First Folio of Shakespeare*, 1963.) F provides, in general, a good text, correctly lined and with relatively few corruptions. In the present edition "accidental" errors in F have been emended silently; "substantive" errors requiring emendation are listed at the end of this note.

F is divided into acts and scenes. Division into acts presumably derives from original production of the play with four intervals for nondramatic music. (Cf. Wilfred T. Jewkes, *Act Division in Elizabethan and Jacobean Plays*, 1958.) Division into scenes presumably derives from annotation of the printer's copy by a Folio editor wishing to give the text a semblance of neoclassical style. The present edition follows the act divisions of F and, for convenience of reference, the scene divisions of the Globe edition, although at three points these vary (both correctly and incorrectly) from those of F. Globe I.i combines F I.i and ii, incorrectly since the stage (despite notice by players going off of those coming on) is technically clear at I.i.69

(the "overlap" of players is paralleled at I.ii.118 of *Measure for Measure*). Globe II.iv and v divide F II.iv, correctly since the stage is clear at II.iv.152. And Globe III.vi combines F III.vi and vii, incorrectly since the stage is clear at III.vi.27. Both Globe and F fail to mark a new scene at IV.ii.100, incorrectly since the stage is clear at that point.

F contains no place headings, for the reason that the play was originally produced without changeable scenery. (Cf. Richard Southern, *Changeable Scenery: Its Origin and Development in the British Theatre*, 1952.) Place headings have been added to the present edition in accordance with a general requirement of the Signet Classic Shakespeare Series, but such headings designate only the three general locales of the action, Britain, Rome, and Wales. A more specific designation is impossible in at least three instances (I.ii, II.i, II.v); and in any case specific designations are misleading since they suggest a change of scenery for each scene with a particular locale different from that of the preceding scene.

In the following list of substantive emendations the reading of the present edition is given in bold type, that of F in roman type.

I.i.4 **First Gentleman** 1 [so throughout balance of scene]   10 **Second Gentleman** 2 [so throughout balance of scene]   158 **Exeunt** Exit

I.ii.1 **First Lord** 1 [so throughout balance of scene and in II.i and II.iii]   7 **Second Lord** 2 [so throughout balance of scene and in II.i and II.iii]

I.iii.9 **this** his

I.iv.49 **not** [not in F]   76 **Britain** Britanie   78–79 **but believe** beleeue   88–89 **purchase** purchases   133 **thousand** thousands

I.v.3s.d. **Exeunt** Exit   75s.d. [occurs after l.74 in F]   85s.d. **Exeunt** Exit

I.vi.7 **desire** desires   28 **takes** take   104 **Fixing** Fiering   109 **illustrous** illustrious   168 **men's** men   169 **descended** defended

II.i.27 **your** you   34 **tonight** night   51s.d. **Exeunt** Exit   61 **husband, than** Husband. Then   62 **make. The** make the   65s.d. **Exit** Exeunt

II.ii.49 **bare** beare   51s.d. **Exeunt** Exit

II.iii.7 **Cloten** [not in F]   29 **Cloten** [not in F]   31 **vice** voyce   45 **out** on't
49 **solicits** solicity   139 **garment** Garments   156 **you** your

II.iv.6 **hopes** hope   18 **legions** Legion   24 **mingled** wing-led   47 **not** note
100–01 **that. She** that She   135 **the** her

II.v.16 **German** Iarmen   27 **have a** [not in F]

III.i.19 **ribbèd ... palèd** ribb'd ... pal'd   20 **rocks** Oakes   54 **be. We do say**
be, we do. Say

III.ii.68 **score** store   79 **here, nor** heere, not

III.iii.2 **Stoop** Sleepe   23 **bribe** Babe   28 **know** knowes   83 **wherein they**
whereon the

III.iv.80 **afore't** a-foot   91 **make** makes   103 **out** [not in F]   125 **courtesan.**
Curtezan?   149 **haply** happily

III.v.17s.d. **Exeunt** Exit   32 **looks** looke   40 **strokes** stroke   41s.d. **Messenger**
a Messenger   55s.d. [occurs after "days" in F]   142 **insultment** insulment

III.vi.70 **I'ld** I

III.vii.9 **commends** commands

IV.i.19 **her** thy   20 **haply** happily

IV.ii.49 [speech heading Arui. precedes "He" in F]   58 **patience** patient
122 **thank** thanks   132 **humor** Honor   186 **ingenious** ingenuous   205 **crayer**
care   206 **Might** Might'st   290 **is** are   332s.d.–333 **Enter Lucius and Cap-**
tains; a Soothsayer to them. Captain. The legions Enter Lucius, Captaines,
and a Soothsayer. Cap. To them, the Legions   336 **are in** are heere in

IV.iv.2 **find we** we finde   8 **us** v.   17 **the** their   27 **hard** heard

V.i.1 **wished** am wisht

V.iii.24 **harts** hearts   42 **stooped** stopt   43 **they** the   84 **First Captain** 1 [so
throughout balance of scene]   86 **Second Captain** 2 [so throughout balance of
scene]

V.iv.s.d. **Jailers** Gaoler   1 **First Jailer** Gao   51 **come** came   57 **look** looke,
looke   130 **are as often** are often   141 **sir** Sis   156 **on** one   178s.d. **Exit**
Exeunt

V.v.62 **Ladies** La   64 **heard** heare   126 **saw** see   134 **On One**   205 **it** [not in
F]   297 **sorry** sorrow   334 **mere** neere   378 **ye** we   386 **brothers**
Brother   392 **inter'gatories** Interrogatories   405 **so** no   435 **Soothsayer** [not
in F]   445 **Leo-natus** Leonatus   449 **thy** this   469 **this** yet yet this

WILLIAM SHAKESPEARE

THE WINTER'S TALE

Edited by Frank Kermode

The Names of the Actors

LEONTES, King of Sicilia
MAMILLIUS, Young Prince of Sicilia
CAMILLO ⎫
ANTIGONUS ⎪
        ⎬ four Lords of Sicilia
CLEOMENES ⎪
DION ⎭
HERMIONE, Queen to Leontes
PERDITA, daughter to Leontes and Hermione
PAULINA, wife to Antigonus
EMILIA, a Lady [attending on Hermione]
POLIXENES, King of Bohemia
FLORIZEL, Prince of Bohemia
OLD SHEPHERD, reputed father of Perdita
CLOWN, his son
AUTOLYCUS, a rogue
ARCHIDAMUS, a Lord of Bohemia
[A MARINER]
[A JAILER]
[MOPSA ⎫
       ⎬ shepherdesses]
DORCAS ⎭
OTHER LORDS AND GENTLEMEN, [LADIES, OFFICERS OF THE
COURT,] AND SERVANTS
SHEPHERDS AND SHEPHERDESSES
[TIME, as Chorus]

[*Scene:* Sicilia and Bohemia]

THE WINTER'S TALE

ACT I

Scene I. [*Sicilia, the Court of Leontes.*]

Enter Camillo and Archidamus.

ARCHIDAMUS If you shall chance, Camillo, to visit
Bohemia, on the like occasion whereon my services
are now on foot, you shall see, as I have said, great
difference betwixt our Bohemia and your Sicilia.

CAMILLO I think this coming summer the King of   5
Sicilia means to pay Bohemia the visitation which
he justly owes him.

ARCHIDAMUS Wherein our entertainment shall shame
us we will be justified in our loves; for indeed—

CAMILLO Beseech you—   10

ARCHIDAMUS Verily I speak it in the freedom of my
knowledge: we cannot with such magnificence—
in so rare—I know not what to say.... We will
give you sleepy drinks, that your senses, unintelligent of our insufficience, may, though they can-   15
not praise us, as little accuse us.

Text references are printed in **bold** type; the annotation follows in roman type.
I.i.8–9 **Wherein ... loves** our entertainment may fall short of yours, but we shall
make up for it by the strength of our affection   14–15 **unintelligent** unaware

CAMILLO You pay a great deal too dear for what's given freely.

ARCHIDAMUS Believe me, I speak as my understanding
20   instructs me, and as mine honesty puts it to utterance.

CAMILLO Sicilia cannot show himself overkind to Bohemia. They were trained together in their childhoods; and there rooted betwixt them then such
25   an affection, which cannot choose but branch now. Since their more mature dignities and royal necessities made separation of their society, their encounters, though not personal, have been royally attorneyed with interchange of gifts, letters, lov-
30   ing embassies, that they have seemed to be together, though absent: shook hands, as over a vast; and embraced as it were from the ends of opposed winds. The heavens continue their loves!

ARCHIDAMUS I think there is not in the world either
35   malice or matter to alter it. You have an unspeakable comfort of your young Prince Mamillius; it is a gentleman of the greatest promise that ever came into my note.

CAMILLO I very well agree with you in the hopes of
40   him. It is a gallant child; one that, indeed, physics the subject, makes old hearts fresh; they that went on crutches ere he was born desire yet their life to see him a man.

ARCHIDAMUS Would they else be content to die?

45   CAMILLO Yes, if there were no other excuse why they should desire to live.

ARCHIDAMUS If the King had no son, they would desire to live on crutches till he had one.

Exeunt.

25 **branch** i.e., flourish   27 **society** companionship   29 **attorneyed** supplied by substitutes   31 **vast** desolate space   40–41 **physics the subject** is good medicine for the people

Scene II. [*The Court of Leontes.*]

Enter Leontes, Hermione, Mamillius, Polixenes,
Camillo, [and Attendants].

POLIXENES Nine changes of the wat'ry star hath been
   The shepherd's note since we have left our throne
   Without a burden: time as long again
   Would be filled up, my brother, with our thanks,
   And yet we should for perpetuity   5
   Go hence in debt. And therefore, like a cipher,
   Yet standing in rich place, I multiply
   With one "We thank you," many thousands moe
   That go before it.

LEONTES   Stay your thanks awhile,
   And pay them when you part.   10

POLIXENES   Sir, that's tomorrow.
   I am questioned by my fears of what may chance
   Or breed upon our absence, that may blow
   No sneaping winds at home, to make us say,
   "This is put forth too truly." Besides, I have stayed
   To tire your royalty.

LEONTES   We are tougher, brother,   15
   Than you can put us to 't.

I.ii.1 **wat'ry star** i.e., the moon 8 **moe** more 3–9 **time as long ... before it** it
would take us the same length of time to thank you, and even then we should leave
here forever your debtors. So I offer you one more thank-you, which, though it is
in itself nothing, works like a zero on the end of a number and multiplies all the
thanks I've given you before (instead of merely adding to them) 11–14 **I am**
questioned ... too truly i.e., I'm worried about what may happen at home,
perhaps as a result of my absence—worried in case blighting influences may not be
at work which we shall regret, saying "We went away only too well" 16 **put us**
to 't drive us to extremities

POLIXENES   No longer stay.

LEONTES One sev'night longer.

POLIXENES   Very sooth, tomorrow.

LEONTES We'll part the time between 's then; and in
    that
    I'll no gainsaying.

POLIXENES   Press me not, beseech you, so.
    There is no tongue that moves, none, none i' th'
20   world
    So soon as yours could win me; so it should now,
    Were there necessity in your request, although
    'Twere needful I denied it. My affairs
    Do even drag me homeward; which to hinder
25   Were, in your love, a whip to me; my stay,
    To you a charge and trouble: to save both,
    Farewell, our brother.

LEONTES   Tongue-tied, our Queen? Speak you.

HERMIONE I had thought, sir, to have held my peace
    until
    You had drawn oaths from him not to stay. You,
    sir,
30   Charge him too coldly. Tell him you are sure
    All in Bohemia's well; this satisfaction,
    The bygone day proclaimed. Say this to him,
    He's beat from his best ward.

LEONTES   Well said, Hermione.

HERMIONE To tell he longs to see his son were strong;
35   But let him say so then, and let him go;
    But let him swear so, and he shall not stay,
    We'll thwack him hence with distaffs.
    Yet of your royal presence, I'll adventure
    The borrow of a week. When at Bohemia
40   You take my lord, I'll give him my commission

19 **I'll no gainsaying** I'll not accept a refusal 25 **Were … to me** i.e., though
doing it out of love, you would be tormenting me by making me stay in these
circumstances 33 **ward** defensive posture in fencing

To let him there a month behind the gest
Prefixed for 's parting, yet, good deed, Leontes,
I love thee not a jar o' th' clock behind
What lady she her lord. You'll stay?

POLIXENES   No, madam.

HERMIONE Nay, but you will?

POLIXENES   I may not, verily.   45

HERMIONE Verily?
You put me off with limber vows; but I,
Though you would seek t' unsphere the stars with
    oaths,
Should yet say, "Sir, no going." Verily,
You shall not go; a lady's "Verily" is   50
As potent as a lord's. Will you go yet?
Force me to keep you as prisoner,
Not like a guest; so you shall pay your fees
When you depart, and save your thanks. How say
    you?
My prisoner or my guest? By your dread "Verily,"   55
One of them you shall be.

POLIXENES   Your guest, then, madam:
To be your prisoner should import offending;
Which is for me less easy to commit,
Than you to punish.

HERMIONE   Not your jailer, then,
But your kind hostess. Come, I'll question you   60
Of my lord's tricks, and yours, when you were boys:
You were pretty lordings then?

POLIXENES   We were, fair Queen,
Two lads that thought there was no more behind
But such a day tomorrow as today,
And to be boy eternal.

HERMIONE   Was not my lord   65
The verier wag o' th' two?

41 **gest** stage of royal progress; time allocated to one place on the route 42 **good deed** indeed, in very deed 43 **jar** tick 44 **lady she** gentlewoman 47 **limber** limp 53 **fees** (which were always due from prisoner to jailer) 57 **import offending** mean that I had committed some crime 63 **behind** to come

POLIXENES We were as twinned lambs, that did frisk
    i' th' sun,
    And bleat the one at th' other; what we changed
    Was innocence for innocence; we knew not
70   The doctrine of ill-doing, nor dreamed
    That any did; had we pursued that life,
    And our weak spirits ne'er been higher reared
    With stronger blood, we should have answered
      heaven
    Boldly, "not guilty"; the imposition cleared,
    Hereditary ours.

75 HERMIONE   By this we gather
    You have tripped since.

POLIXENES   O my most sacred lady,
    Temptations have since then been born to 's, for
    In those unfledged days was my wife a girl;
    Your precious self had then not crossed the eyes
    Of my young playfellow.

80 HERMIONE   Grace to boot!
    Of this make no conclusion, lest you say
    Your queen and I are devils. Yet go on,
    Th' offenses we have made you do we'll answer,
    If you first sinned with us, and that with us
    You did continue fault, and that you slipped not
    With any but with us.

85 LEONTES   Is he won yet?

HERMIONE He'll stay, my lord.

LEONTES   At my request he would not.
    Hermione, my dearest, thou never spok'st
    To better purpose.

HERMIONE   Never?

---

68 **changed** exchanged   72–75 **our weak spirits ... Hereditary ours** i.e., had
the weakness of our animal spirits not been fortified by the passionate blood of
maturity, our wills would never have been corrupted, and we should have been
able to claim exemption from the taint of original sin   80 **Grace to boot!** Heaven
help me!   81 **make no conclusion** don't pursue that line of argument

LEONTES   Never but once.

HERMIONE What! Have I twice said well? When was 't
    before?   90
I prithee tell me; cram 's with praise, and make 's
As fat as tame things: one good deed, dying
    tongueless,
Slaughters a thousand waiting upon that.
Our praises are our wages—you may ride 's
With one soft kiss a thousand furlongs, ere   95
With spur we heat an acre. But to th' goal:
My last good deed was to entreat his stay.
What was my first? It has an elder sister,
Or I mistake you; O, would her name were Grace!
But once before I spoke to th' purpose? When?   100
Nay, let me have 't; I long.

LEONTES   Why, that was when
Three crabbèd months had soured themselves to
    death,
Ere I could make thee open thy white hand
And clap thyself my love; then didst thou utter
"I am yours forever."

HERMIONE   'Tis Grace indeed.   105
Why, lo you now, I have spoke to th' purpose twice:
The one forever earned a royal husband;
Th' other, for some while a friend.

LEONTES   [Aside] Too hot, too hot!
To mingle friendship far is mingling bloods.
I have tremor cordis on me; my heart dances,   110
But not for joy, not joy. This entertainment
May a free face put on, derive a liberty
From heartiness, from bounty, fertile bosom,
And well become the agent—'t may, I grant;
But to be paddling palms and pinching fingers,   115
As now they are, and making practiced smiles
As in a looking glass; and then to sigh, as 'twere

96 heat an acre race over a furlong   104 clap offer the handclasp that seals a
bargain   110 tremor cordis palpitation of the heart   113 fertile bosom generous affection

The mort o' th' deer—oh, that is entertainment
My bosom likes not, nor my brows. Mamillius,
Art thou my boy?

MAMILLIUS   Ay, my good lord.

120 LEONTES   I' fecks!
Why, that's my bawcock. What, hast smutched thy
    nose?
They say it is a copy out of mine. Come, Captain,
We must be neat—not neat, but cleanly, Captain:
And yet the steer, the heifer, and the calf,
125 Are all called neat. Still virginaling
Upon his palm? How now, you wanton calf,
Art thou my calf?

MAMILLIUS   Yes, if you will, my lord.

LEONTES Thou want'st a rough pash, and the shoots
    that I have
To be full like me: yet they say we are
130 Almost as like as eggs; women say so,
That will say anything. But were they false
As o'er-dyed blacks, as wind, as waters; false
As dice are to be wished, by one that fixes
No bourn 'twixt his and mine—yet were it true
135 To say this boy were like me. Come, Sir Page,
Look on me with your welkin eye. Sweet villain,
Most dear'st, my collop! Can thy dam, may 't be?
Affection! Thy intention stabs the center.
Thou dost make possible things not so held,
140 Communicat'st with dreams—how can this be?—
With what's unreal thou coactive art,

117–18 as 'twere/The mort o' th' deer like the horn call signifying the death of
the deer 119 brows (alluding to the myth of the horns that grow on the
foreheads of cuckolds) 120 fecks (a mild oath, derived from "i' faith")
121 bawcock fine fellow (Fr. *beau coq*) 123 neat (Leontes rejects the word
because it also means "horned cattle") 125 virginaling i.e., as if playing the
virginals (a small keyboard instrument) 128 pash head 132 o'er-dyed blacks
black garments worn out by too much dyeing 134 bourn boundary 136 welkin
blue (like the sky) 137 collop a cut off his own flesh 137 dam mother
(Leontes' thoughts still run on cattle) 138 Affection passion 138 intention
purpose 138 center i.e., of the world (?) of my heart (?)

And fellow'st nothing. Then 'tis very credent
Thou mayst co-join with something, and thou dost,
And that beyond commission, and I find it,
And that to the infection of my brains,   145
And hardening of my brows.

POLIXENES   What means Sicilia?

HERMIONE He something seems unsettled.

POLIXENES   How, my lord?

LEONTES What cheer? How is 't with you, best brother?

HERMIONE   You look
As if you held a brow of much distraction;
Are you moved, my lord?

LEONTES   No, in good earnest.   150
How sometimes Nature will betray its folly,
Its tenderness, and make itself a pastime
To harder bosoms! Looking on the lines
Of my boy's face, methoughts I did recoil
Twenty-three years, and saw myself unbreeched,   155
In my green velvet coat; my dagger muzzled,
Lest it should bite its master, and so prove,
As ornaments oft do, too dangerous.
How like, methought, I then was to this kernel,
This squash, this gentleman. Mine honest friend,   160
Will you take eggs for money?

MAMILLIUS No, my lord, I'll fight.

LEONTES You will? Why, happy man be 's dole! My
    brother,

142 **credent** credible   138–46 **Affection ... brows** (may be corrupt. Paraphrase:
"Passion! Your desire for fulfillment can pierce to the heart of things. You deal
with matters normally thought of as illusory—with dreams and fantasies, impossible as that sounds. You collaborate with the unreal; so it isn't improbable that
you should do so with what really exists; this is what has happened, as my mental
disturbance and cuckold's horns indicate." The passion is jealousy; Leontes
recognizes that it is sometimes baseless, but argues that it is not so in his
case)   160 **squash** unripe peapod (young person)   161 **take eggs for money**
allow yourself to be imposed upon   163 **happy man be 's dole** may it be his lot
to be a happy man

Are you so fond of your young prince as we
Do seem to be of ours?

165 POLIXENES   If at home, sir,
He's all my exercise, my mirth, my matter;
Now my sworn friend, and then mine enemy;
My parasite, my soldier, statesman, all.
He makes a July's day short as December,
170 And with his varying childness, cures in me
Thoughts that would thick my blood.

LEONTES   So stands this squire
Officed with me. We two will walk, my lord,
And leave you to your graver steps. Hermione,
How thou lov'st us, show in our brother's welcome;
175 Let what is dear in Sicily, be cheap;
Next to thyself and my young rover, he's
Apparent to my heart.

HERMIONE   If you would seek us,
We are yours i' th' garden; shall 's attend you there?

LEONTES To your own bents dispose you; you'll be
       found,
180 Be you beneath the sky. [*Aside*] I am angling now,
Though you perceive me not how I give line.
Go to, go to!
How she holds up the neb, the bill to him!
And arms her with the boldness of a wife
To her allowing husband!
       [*Exeunt Polixenes, Hermione, and Attendants.*]
185   Gone already!
Inch-thick, knee-deep, o'er head and ears a forked
       one!
Go play, boy, play: thy mother plays, and I
Play too—but so disgraced a part, whose issue
Will hiss me to my grave; contempt and clamor

171 **thick my blood** make me melancholy 171–72 **So stands … me** My son
has a similar post in my household 177 **Apparent** heir apparent 180 **angling**
giving them scope, "playing" them 183 **neb** beak 185 **allowing** approving
186 **forked** (alluding to the branching cuckold's horns) 188 **issue** exit (following
the idea of the actor not capable of his part)

Will be my knell. Go play, boy, play. There have
   been,   190
Or I am much deceived, cuckolds ere now,
And many a man there is, even at this present,
Now, while I speak this, holds his wife by th' arm,
That little thinks she has been sluiced in 's absence,
And his pond fished by his next neighbor, by   195
Sir Smile, his neighbor, nay, there's comfort in 't,
Whiles other men have gates, and those gates
   opened,
As mine, against their will. Should all despair,
That have revolted wives, the tenth of mankind
Would hang themselves. Physic for 't there's none;   200
It is a bawdy planet, that will strike
Where 'tis predominant; and 'tis powerful, think it,
From east, west, north, and south. Be it concluded,
No barricado for a belly. Know 't
It will let in and out the enemy,   205
With bag and baggage. Many thousand on 's
Have the disease, and feel 't not. How now, boy!

MAMILLIUS I am like you, they say.

LEONTES   Why, that's some comfort.
What! Camillo there?

CAMILLO Ay, my good lord.   210

LEONTES Go play, Mamillius; thou 'rt an honest man.
                         [*Exit Mamillius.*]
Camillo, this great sir will yet stay longer.

CAMILLO You had much ado to make his anchor hold;
When you cast out, it still came home.

LEONTES   Didst note it?

CAMILLO He would not stay at your petitions, made   215
His business more material.

LEONTES   Didst perceive it?

199 **revolted** unfaithful   202 **predominant** in the ascendant (a technical term in astrology)

269

[*Aside*] They're here with me already: whispering,
    rounding:
"Sicilia is a so-forth": 'tis far gone,
When I shall gust it last. How came 't, Camillo,
That he did stay?

220 CAMILLO   At the good Queen's entreaty.

LEONTES "At the Queen's" be 't: "Good" should be
    pertinent,
But so it is, it is not. Was this taken
By any understanding pate but thine?
For thy conceit is soaking, will draw in
225 More than the common blocks. Not noted, is 't,
But of the finer natures? By some severals
Of headpiece extraordinary? Lower messes
Perchance are to this business purblind? Say.

CAMILLO Business, my lord? I think most understand
Bohemia stays here longer.

LEONTES   Ha?

230 CAMILLO   Stays here longer.

LEONTES Ay, but why?

CAMILLO To satisfy your Highness, and the entreaties
Of our most gracious mistress.

LEONTES   Satisfy
Th' entreaties of your mistress? Satisfy?
235 Let that suffice. I have trusted thee, Camillo,
With all the nearest things to my heart, as well
My chamber-counsels, wherein, priestlike, thou
Hast cleansed my bosom—ay, from thee departed
Thy penitent reformed; but we have been
240 Deceived in thy integrity, deceived
In that which seems so.

217 **They're here** They (onlookers) have already caught on to my situation
217 **rounding** speaking in secret   218 **so-forth** i.e., they slyly avoid the word
"cuckold"   219 **gust** taste, hear of   222 **taken** observed   224 **conceit is soaking** intelligence is absorbent   225 **blocks** blockheads   226 **severals** individuals
227 **Lower messes** inferior people ("mess" in the sense of a group who dine
together and would be of the same—low—rank)   237 **chamber-counsels** con-
fessions of secret sins

270

CAMILLO   Be it forbid, my lord!

LEONTES To bide upon 't. Thou art not honest; or
 If thou inclin'st that way, thou art a coward,
 Which hoxes honesty behind, restraining
 From course required; or else thou must be counted 245
 A servant, grafted in my serious trust,
 And therein negligent; or else a fool,
 That seest a game played home, the rich stake
  drawn,
 And tak'st it all for jest.

CAMILLO   My gracious lord,
 I may be negligent, foolish, and fearful, 250
 In every one of these no man is free
 But that his negligence, his folly, fear,
 Among the infinite doings of the world,
 Sometime puts forth. In your affairs, my lord,
 If ever I were willful negligent, 255
 It was my folly; if industriously
 I played the fool, it was my negligence,
 Not weighing well the end: if ever fearful
 To do a thing, where I the issue doubted,
 Whereof the execution did cry out 260
 Against the nonperformance, 'twas a fear
 Which oft infects the wisest. These, my lord,
 Are such allowed infirmities, that honesty
 Is never free of. But beseech your Grace,
 Be plainer with me, let me know my trespass 265
 By its own visage; if I then deny it,
 'Tis none of mine.

LEONTES   Ha' not you seen, Camillo—
 But that's past doubt, you have, or your eyeglass
 Is thicker than a cuckold's horn—or heard—
 For to a vision so apparent, rumor 270
 Cannot be mute—or thought—for cogitation
 Resides not in that man that does not think—

242 **bide** insist 244 **hoxes** hamstrings 248 **played home ... stake drawn**
played earnestly, great stakes being won 254 **puts forth** shows itself 266 **by its
own visage** under its true name 268 **eyeglass** the lens of the eye

My wife is slippery? If thou wilt confess,
Or else be impudently negative,
275 To have nor eyes, nor ears, nor thought, then say
My wife's a hobbyhorse, deserves a name
As rank as any flax-wench, that puts to
Before her troth-plight; say 't, and justify 't.

CAMILLO I would not be a stander-by to hear
280 My sovereign mistress clouded so, without
My present vengeance taken; 'shrew my heart,
You never spoke what did become you less
Than this; which to reiterate, were sin
As deep as that, though true.

LEONTES   Is whispering nothing?
285 Is leaning cheek to cheek? Is meeting noses?
Kissing with inside lip? Stopping the career
Of laughter with a sigh (a note infallible
Of breaking honesty)? Horsing foot on foot?
Skulking in corners? Wishing clocks more swift?
290 Hours, minutes? Noon, midnight? And all eyes
Blind with the pin and web, but theirs; theirs only,
That would unseen be wicked? Is this nothing?
Why, then the world and all that's in 't is nothing,
The covering sky is nothing, Bohemia nothing,
295 My wife is nothing, nor nothing have these nothings,
If this be nothing.

CAMILLO   Good my lord, be cured
Of this diseased opinion, and betimes,
For 'tis most dangerous.

LEONTES   Say it be, 'tis true.

CAMILLO No, no, my lord.

LEONTES   It is; you lie, you lie.

267–73 **Ha' not you … slippery?** Have you not seen—you must have, or your
sight is grossly thick—or heard—as you must, since Hermione's conduct is so
open that there must be gossip about it—or thought—and unless you have you
can't think at all—that my wife is unfaithful?   276 **hobbyhorse** loose woman
277 **flax-wench** low-bred girl   281 **present** immediate   284 **As deep as that,
though true** i.e., as wicked as her adultery if it were a fact, which it is not
286 **career** gallop   288 **honesty** chastity   291 **pin and web** cataract

I say thou liest, Camillo, and I hate thee,   300
Pronounce thee a gross lout, a mindless slave,
Or else a hovering temporizer, that
Canst with thine eyes at once see good and evil,
Inclining to them both. Were my wife's liver
Infected as her life, she would not live   305
The running of one glass.

CAMILLO   Who does infect her?

LEONTES Why, he that wears her like her medal,
    hanging
About his neck, Bohemia, who, if I
Had servants true about me, that bare eyes
To see alike mine honor as their profits,   310
Their own particular thrifts, they would do that
Which should undo more doing. Ay, and thou,
His cupbearer, whom I from meaner form
Have benched and reared to worship, who mayst
    see
Plainly as heaven sees earth, and earth see heaven,   315
How I am gallèd, mightst bespice a cup,
To give mine enemy a lasting wink;
Which draught to me were cordial.

CAMILLO   Sir, my lord,
I could do this, and that with no rash potion,
But with a lingering dram that should not work   320
Maliciously, like poison; but I cannot
Believe this crack to be in my dread mistress,
So sovereignly being honorable.
I have loved thee——

LEONTES Make that thy question, and go rot!   325

302 **hovering** vacillating   304 **liver** (since this was the seat of the passions, it
presumably was infected; transposition of "liver" and "life" has been proposed)
306 **glass** hourglass   307 **medal** (here a portrait miniature worn about the neck)
311 **particular** thrifts special gains   314 **benched** i.e., raised to place of dignity
317 **give ... lasting wink**, i.e., close his eyes forever   318 **cordial** medicine
320 **lingering dram** slow-working dose   324 **I have loved thee** (difficult to
explain: Camillo may be about to protest his long loyalty, or threaten withdrawal of
his love, but he would hardly address the King as "thou." Some editors give the
words to Leontes, which hardly helps)   325 **Make ... rot** i.e., if you doubt the
Queen's infidelity, go to hell

Dost think I am so muddy, so unsettled,
To appoint myself in this vexation? Sully
The purity and whiteness of my sheets—
Which to preserve is sleep; which being spotted,
330 Is goads, thorns, nettles, tails of wasps—
Give scandal to the blood o' th' prince, my son,
Who I do think is mine, and love as mine,
Without ripe moving to 't? Would I do this?
Could man so blench?

CAMILLO   I must believe you, sir;
335 I do, and will fetch off Bohemia for 't:
Provided that when he's removed, your Highness
Will take again your queen as yours at first,
Even for your son's sake, and thereby for sealing
The injury of tongues, in courts and kingdoms
Known and allied to yours.

340 LEONTES   Thou dost advise me,
Even so as I mine own course have set down.
I'll give no blemish to her honor, none.

CAMILLO My lord,
Go then; and with a countenance as clear
345 As friendship wears at feasts, keep with Bohemia,
And with your queen: I am his cupbearer;
If from me he have wholesome beverage,
Account me not your servant.

LEONTES   This is all:
Do 't, and thou hast the one half of my heart;
Do 't not, thou split'st thine own.

350 CAMILLO   I'll do 't, my lord.

LEONTES I will seem friendly, as thou hast advised me.
                                                    Exit.

CAMILLO O miserable lady! But for me,
What case stand I in? I must be the poisoner
Of good Polixenes, and my ground to do 't
355 Is the obedience to a master—one
Who, in rebellion with himself, will have
All that are his so too. To do this deed,

327 **appoint** establish   333 **ripe** adequate, matured   334 **blench** swerve

Promotion follows; if I could find example
Of thousands that had struck anointed kings,
And flourished after, I'd not do 't; but since   360
Nor brass, nor stone, nor parchment bears not one,
Let villainy itself forswear 't. I must
Forsake the court; to do 't, or no, is certain
To me a break-neck. Happy star reign now!
Here comes Bohemia.

Enter Polixenes.

POLIXENES   This is strange: methinks   365
My favor here begins to warp. Not speak?
Good day, Camillo.

CAMILLO   Hail, most royal sir.

POLIXENES What is the news i' th' court?

CAMILLO   None rare, my lord.

POLIXENES The King hath on him such a countenance,
As he had lost some province, and a region   370
Loved as he loves himself; even now I met him
With customary compliment, when he,
Wafting his eyes to th' contrary, and falling
A lip of much contempt, speed from me, and
So leaves me to consider what is breeding   375
That changes thus his manners.

CAMILLO I dare not know, my lord.

POLIXENES How, dare not? Do not? Do you know, and
    dare not
Be intelligent to me? 'Tis thereabouts;
For to yourself, what you do know, you must,   380
And cannot say you dare not. Good Camillo,
Your changed complexions are to me a mirror,
Which shows me mine changed too: for I must be
A party in this alteration, finding

358–62 **if I could example ... forswear 't** if the records showed that king-killers
prospered, I would not do it; but since they prove the contrary, villainy itself
should forswear regicide   373 **Wafting his eyes to th' contrary** looking (contemptuously) away   378–81 **How, dare not? ... you dare not** What do you
mean, dare not? That you do not? Can it be that you know, and dare not tell me?
That must be the explanation, since you can't say you don't dare tell yourself what
you know

                    Myself thus altered with 't.

385 CAMILLO   There is a sickness
                    Which puts some of us in distemper; but
                    I cannot name the disease; and it is caught
                    Of you, that yet are well.

     POLIXENES   How caught of me?
                    Make me not sighted like the basilisk.
390   I have looked on thousands, who have sped the better
                    By my regard, but killed none so. Camillo,
                    As you are certainly a gentleman, thereto
                    Clerklike experienced, which no less adorns
                    Our gentry than our parents' noble names
395   In whose success we are gentle: I beseech you,
                    If you know aught which does behoove my knowledge
                    Thereof to be informed, imprison 't not
                    In ignorant concealment.

     CAMILLO   I may not answer.

     POLIXENES A sickness caught of me, and yet I well?
400   I must be answered. Dost thou hear, Camillo,
                    I conjure thee, by all the parts of man,
                    Which honor does acknowledge, whereof the least
                    Is not this suit of mine, that thou declare
                    What incidency thou dost guess of harm
405   Is creeping toward me; how far off, how near,
                    Which way to be prevented, if to be;
                    If not, how best to bear it.

     CAMILLO   Sir, I will tell you,
                    Since I am charged in honor, and by him
                    That I think honorable. Therefore mark my counsel,
410   Which must be ev'n as swiftly followed as
                    I mean to utter it; or both yourself and me,
                    Cry lost, and so good night.

     POLIXENES   On, good Camillo.

     CAMILLO I am appointed him to murder you.

_____

389 **basilisk** a mythical serpent which killed by looking   390 **sped** prospered
393 **Clerklike experienced** with the experience of an educated man
395 **success** succession   395 **gentle** well born   401 **conjure** adjure   401 **parts**
duties, functions   404 **incidency** threat   413 **him** i.e., by Leontes

POLIXENES By whom, Camillo?

CAMILLO   By the King.

POLIXENES   For what?

CAMILLO He thinks, nay with all confidence he swears,   415
    As he had seen 't, or been an instrument
    To vice you to 't, that you have touched his queen
    Forbiddenly.

POLIXENES   Oh then my best blood turn
    To an infected jelly, and my name
    Be yoked with his, that did betray the Best!   420
    Turn then my freshest reputation to
    A savor that may strike the dullest nostril
    Where I arrive, and my approach be shunned,
    Nay, hated too, worse than the great'st infection
    That e'er was heard, or read!

CAMILLO   Swear his thought over   425
    By each particular star in heaven, and
    By all their influences; you may as well
    Forbid the sea for to obey the moon,
    As or by oath remove or counsel shake
    The fabric of his folly, whose foundation   430
    Is piled upon his faith, and will continue
    The standing of his body.

POLIXENES   How should this grow?

CAMILLO I know not: but I am sure 'tis safer to
    Avoid what's grown than question how 'tis born.
    If therefore you dare trust my honesty,   435
    That lies enclosèd in this trunk, which you
    Shall bear along impawned, away tonight.
    Your followers I will whisper to the business,

417 To vice to force   420 his, that did betray the Best i.e., Judas   422 savor
alluding to the idea that infection (e.g., of the plague) could be smelled (hence the
use of flowers in posies as a prophylactic)   425 Swear his thought over deny his
suspicion with oaths   429–32 As or by oath ... of his body i.e., you may as well
attempt the obviously impossible as try to remove by your oaths or pull down by
your advice the structure of his crazy delusion which has its foundations on settled
belief, and will last as long as his life (stand up as long as he can)   432 How
should this grow? How can this have grown up   437 impawned as a pledge of
good faith (Camillo points to his body, which is the "trunk")

277

And will by twos and threes, at several posterns,
440   Clear them o' th' city. For myself, I'll put
My fortunes to your service, which are here
By this discovery lost. Be not uncertain,
For by the honor of my parents, I
Have uttered truth; which if you seek to prove,
445   I dare not stand by; nor shall you be safer,
Than one condemned by the King's own mouth,
        thereon
His execution sworn.

POLIXENES   I do believe thee:
I saw his heart in 's face. Give me thy hand,
Be pilot to me, and thy places shall
450   Still neighbor mine. My ships are ready, and
My people did expect my hence departure
Two days ago. This jealousy
Is for a precious creature; as she's rare,
Must it be great; and, as his person's mighty,
455   Must it be violent: and, as he does conceive,
He is dishonored by a man, which ever
Professed to him, why his revenges must
In that be made more bitter. Fear o'ershades me;
Good expedition be my friend, and comfort
460   The gracious Queen, part of his theme, but nothing
Of his ill-ta'en suspicion. Come, Camillo,
I will respect thee as a father, if
Thou bear'st my life off hence; let us avoid.

CAMILLO It is in mine authority to command
465   The keys of all the posterns: please your Highness
To take the urgent hour. Come, sir, away.   *Exeunt.*

439 **posterns** gates   444 **prove** test   446–47 **mouth ... sworn** i.e., the King
having condemned him has sworn that the sentence will be death (Corrupt? See
list of emendations)   449 **places** offices, functions, dignities   457 **Professed**
made professions (of friendship)   459 **expedition** speed   460–61 **part of his
theme ... suspicion** (obscure: Shakespeare's sense has perhaps not quite got
through. "May my speedy departure also help the Queen, who is involved in
Leontes' fantasy though she has no rightful place in his suspicions." But this fails
to explain why Polixenes thought his departure would help Hermione. Perhaps
"expedition" is not the subject of "comfort"—then he is merely wishing the
Queen comfort in the troubles he is leaving her to, and the vagueness of the
expression matches the emptiness of the wish)   463 **avoid** depart

ACT II

Scene I. [*Sicilia, the Court of Leontes.*]

Enter Hermione, Mamillius, Ladies.

HERMIONE Take the boy to you; he so troubles me,
'Tis past enduring.

FIRST LADY   Come, my gracious lord,
Shall I be your playfellow?

MAMILLIUS   No, I'll none of you.

FIRST LADY Why, my sweet lord?

MAMILLIUS You'll kiss me hard, and speak to me, as if   5
I were a baby still. I love you better.

SECOND LADY And why so, my lord?

MAMILLIUS   Not for because
Your brows are blacker; yet black brows, they say,
Become some women best, so that there be not
Too much hair there, but in a semicircle,   10
Or a half-moon, made with a pen.

SECOND LADY   Who taught' this?

MAMILLIUS I learned it out of women's faces. Pray now,
What color are your eyebrows?

FIRST LADY   Blue, my lord.

II.i.11 **taught'** taught you

279

MAMILLIUS Nay, that's a mock. I have seen a lady's nose
That has been blue, but not her eyebrows.

15 FIRST LADY   Hark ye,
The Queen, your mother, rounds apace; we shall
Present our services to a fine new prince
One of these days, and then you'd wanton with us,
If we would have you.

SECOND LADY   She is spread of late
20 Into a goodly bulk; good time encounter her!

HERMIONE What wisdom stirs amongst you? Come, sir, now
I am for you again; pray you sit by us,
And tell 's a tale.

MAMILLIUS   Merry or sad shall 't be?

HERMIONE As merry as you will.

25 MAMILLIUS A sad tale's best for winter; I have one
Of sprites and goblins.

HERMIONE   Let's have that, good sir.
Come on, sit down; come on, and do your best,
To fright me with your sprites; you're powerful at it.

MAMILLIUS There was a man.

HERMIONE   Nay, come sit down; then on.

30 MAMILLIUS Dwelt by a churchyard—I will tell it softly,
Yond crickets shall not hear it.

HERMIONE Come on, then, and give 't me in mine ear.

[*Enter Leontes, Antigonus, and Lords.*]

LEONTES Was he met there? His train? Camillo with
him?

LORD Behind the tuft of pines I met them, never
35 Saw I men scour so on their way. I eyed them
Even to their ships.

LEONTES   How blest am I

18 **wanton** play   31 **yond crickets** i.e., the chattering ladies   35 **scour** hurry

In my just censure, in my true opinion!
Alack, for lesser knowledge! How accursed,
In being so blest! There may be in the cup
A spider steeped, and one may drink, depart,   40
And yet partake no venom, for his knowledge
Is not infected; but if one present
Th' abhorred ingredient to his eye, make known
How he hath drunk, he cracks his gorge, his sides,
With violent hefts. I have drunk, and seen the
    spider.   45
Camillo was his help in this, his pander.
There is a plot against my life, my crown;
All's true that is mistrusted; that false villain,
Whom I employed, was pre-employed by him;
He has discovered my design, and I   50
Remain a pinched thing; yea, a very trick
For them to play at will. How came the posterns
So easily open?

LORD   By his great authority;
Which often hath no less prevailed than so
On your command.

LEONTES   I know 't too well.   55
[*To Hermione*] Give me the boy. I am glad you did
    not nurse him;
Though he does bear some signs of me, yet you
Have too much blood in him.

HERMIONE   What is this? Sport?

LEONTES Bear the boy hence, he shall not come about
    her;

                    [*Exit Mamillius and a Lady.*]
Away with him, and let her sport herself
With that she's big with; for 'tis Polixenes   60
Has made thee swell thus.

HERMIONE   But I'd say he had not;

37 **censure** judgment 40 **spider** (spiders were thought of as venomous; there
seems to have been a superstition that this was so only if one saw the spider)
45 **hefts** retchings 50 **discovered** revealed 51 **pinched thing** puppet, toy

And I'll be sworn you would believe my saying,
Howe'er you lean to th' nayward.

LEONTES   You, my lords,
65 Look on her, mark her well; be but about
To say, "She is a goodly lady," and
The justice of your hearts will thereto add,
" 'Tis pity she's not honest, honorable";
Praise her but for this her without-door form,
70 Which on my faith deserves high speech, and straight
The shrug, the hum or ha, these petty brands
That calumny doth use—oh, I am out!
That mercy does, for calumny will sear
Virtue itself—these shrugs, these hum's and ha's,
75 When you have said she's goodly, come between,
Ere you can say she's honest. But be 't known,
From him that has most cause to grieve it should be,
She's an adult'ress.

HERMIONE   Should a villain say so,
The most replenished villain in the world,
80 He were as much more villain; you, my lord,
Do but mistake.

LEONTES   You have mistook, my lady,
Polixenes for Leontes. O thou thing,
Which I'll not call a creature of thy place,
Lest barbarism, making me the precedent,
85 Should a like language use to all degrees,
And mannerly distinguishment leave out
Betwixt the prince and beggar. I have said
She's an adult'ress, I have said with whom.
More, she's a traitor, and Camillo is
90 A federary with her, and one that knows
What she should shame to know herself
But with her most vile principal—that she's
A bed-swerver, even as bad as those

64 nayward negative 69 without-door form external appearance 72 I am
out I have lost my place, got my speech wrong 75 come between pause,
interrupt, break off 79 replenished complete, perfect 83 place rank
85 degrees social ranks 90 federary confederate, accomplice 92 principal
partner (i.e., Polixenes) 93 bed-swerver adulteress

That vulgars give bold'st titles; ay, and privy
To this their late escape.

HERMIONE   No, by my life,   95
Privy to none of this; how will this grieve you,
When you shall come to clearer knowledge, that
You thus have published me! Gentle my lord,
You scarce can right me throughly then to say
You did mistake.

LEONTES   No; if I mistake   100
In those foundations which I build upon,
The center is not big enough to bear
A schoolboy's top. Away with her to prison.
He who shall speak for her is afar off guilty,
But that he speaks.

HERMIONE   There's some ill planet reigns;   105
I must be patient, till the heavens look
With an aspect more favorable. Good my lords,
I am not prone to weeping, as our sex
Commonly are; the want of which vain dew
Perchance shall dry your pities. But I have   110
That honorable grief lodged here which burns
Worse than tears drown. Beseech you all, my lords,
With thoughts so qualified as your charities
Shall best instruct you, measure me; and so
The King's will be performed!

LEONTES   Shall I be heard?   115

HERMIONE Who is 't that goes with me? Beseech your
      Highness
My women may be with me, for you see
My plight requires it. Do not weep, good fools;
There is no cause; when you shall know your
      mistress
Has deserved prison, then abound in tears,   120
As I come out; this action I now go on

98 **published** publicly proclaimed or denounced   102 **center** (of the earth, and so
of the universe), i.e., "If I am mistaken, no foundation can be trusted"
105 **But that he speaks** i.e., in merely speaking he is found guilty as a remote
accomplice   113 **qualified** tempered, moderated

Is for my better grace. Adieu, my lord.
I never wished to see you sorry; now
I trust I shall. My women come, you have leave.

125 LEONTES Go, do our bidding: hence.

[*Exeunt Queen and Ladies.*]

LORD Beseech your Highness, call the Queen again.

ANTIGONUS Be certain what you do, sir, lest your justice
Prove violence, in the which three great ones suffer,
Yourself, your queen, your son.

LORD   For her, my lord,
130 I dare my life lay down, and will do 't, sir,
Please you t' accept it, that the Queen is spotless
I' th' eyes of heaven, and to you—I mean,
In this, which you accuse her.

ANTIGONUS   If it prove
She's otherwise, I'll keep my stables where
135 I lodge my wife; I'll go in couples with her;
Than when I feel and see her, no farther trust her;
For every inch of woman in the world,
Ay, every dram of woman's flesh is false,
If she be.

LEONTES Hold your peaces.

LORD   Good my lord.

140 ANTIGONUS It is for you we speak, not for ourselves.
You are abused, and by some putter-on
That will be damned for 't. Would I knew the villain,
I would land-damn him! Be she honor-flawed,
I have three daughters: the eldest is eleven;
145 The second and the third, nine and some five:
If this prove true, they'll pay for 't. By mine honor,

121–22 **this action ... grace** by contrast with one who goes to prison to be
disgraced, I embark on this course to add to my honesty and credit   134–35 **I'll
keep my stables ... wife** (obscure but certainly coarse. He will keep his stallions
locked up when his wife is near?)   135 **go in couples** be coupled by a leash to
her, for safety's sake (of course, he means that if the Queen is unchaste, other
women must be even more so)   141 **putter-on** plotter, one who instigates
143 **land-damn** severely beat (?)

I'll geld 'em all; fourteen they shall not see
To bring false generations. They are co-heirs,
And I had rather glib myself than they
Should not produce fair issue.

LEONTES   Cease, no more!   150
You smell this business with a sense as cold
As is a dead man's nose; but I do see 't, and feel 't,
As you feel doing thus; and see withal
The instruments that feel.

ANTIGONUS   If it be so,
We need no grave to bury honesty;   155
There's not a grain of it the face to sweeten
Of the whole dungy earth.

LEONTES   What? Lack I credit?

LORD I had rather you did lack than I, my lord,
Upon this ground; and more it would content me
To have her honor true than your suspicion,   160
Be blamed for 't how you might.

LEONTES   Why, what need we
Commune with you of this, but rather follow
Our forceful instigation? Our prerogative
Calls not your counsels, but our natural goodness
Imparts this; which, if you, or stupefied,   165
Or seeming so, in skill, cannot, or will not,
Relish a truth like us, inform yourselves,
We need no more of your advice. The matter,
The loss, the gain, the ord'ring on 't,
Is all properly ours.

ANTIGONUS   And I wish, my liege,   170
You had only in your silent judgment tried it,
Without more overture.

148 **false generations** illegitimate children   149 **glib** castrate   152–54 **but I do see … that feel** (Leontes here strikes either Antigonus or himself. "But I see it and feel it with immediate, vital force, as you do when you strike yourself thus [or, when I strike you thus]—you feel it and see the hands that inflicted the pain")   157 **Lack I credit?** am I not believed   163–65 **Our prerogative … imparts this** i.e., I'm not obliged to seek your advice; it's out of the goodness of my heart that I tell you this (Leontes, on his dignity, uses the royal "we")   166 **skill** reason

LEONTES   How could that be?
    Either thou art most ignorant by age,
    Or thou wert born a fool. Camillo's flight,
175   Added to their familiarity—
    Which was as gross as ever touched conjecture,
    That lacked sight only, naught for approbation
    But only seeing, all other circumstances
    Made up to th' deed—doth push on this proceeding.
180   Yet, for a greater confirmation—
    For in an act of this importance, 'twere
    Most piteous to be wild—I have dispatched in post
    To sacred Delphos, to Apollo's temple,
    Cleomenes and Dion, whom you know
185   Of stuffed sufficiency. Now, from the oracle
    They will bring all, whose spiritual counsel had,
    Shall stop, or spur me. Have I done well?

LORD Well done, my lord.

LEONTES Though I am satisfied, and need no more
190   Than what I know, yet shall the oracle
    Give rest to th' minds of others—such as he,
    Whose ignorant credulity will not
    Come up to th' truth. So have we thought it good
    From our free person she should be confined,
195   Lest that the treachery of the two fled hence
    Be left her to perform. Come, follow us,
    We are to speak in public: for this business
    Will raise us all.

ANTIGONUS   [*Aside*] To laughter, as I take it,
    If the good truth were known.   *Exeunt*.

---

176 **as ever touched conjecture** as ever conjecture reached to   177 **approbation** proof   182 **wild** rash   183 **Delphos** Delos (Shakespeare mistakenly
thought the oracle of Apollo was there rather than at Delphi. In this error he
follows his source, *Pandosto*)   185 **stuffed sufficiency** more than adequate
dependability   186 **all** the whole truth   191 **such as he** i.e., Antigonus
195–96 **Lest that ... perform** (referring to the "plot against his life and crown"
of which he accuses all three)   198 **raise** rouse

Scene II. [*Sicilia, a prison.*]

Enter Paulina, a Gentleman, [*and Attendants*].

PAULINA The keeper of the prison, call to him;
Let him have knowledge who I am.
                              [*Exit Gentleman.*]
                              Good lady,
No court in Europe is too good for thee—
What dost thou then in prison?

        [*Enter Gentleman with the*] *Jailer*.

                              Now, good sir,
You know me, do you not?

JAILER   For a worthy lady,   5
And one whom much I honor.

PAULINA   Pray you, then,
Conduct me to the Queen.

JAILER   I may not, madam,
To the contrary I have express commandment.

PAULINA Here's ado, to lock up honesty and honor
from
Th' access of gentle visitors! Is 't lawful, pray you,   10
To see her women? Any of them? Emilia?

JAILER So please you, madam,
To put apart these your attendants, I
Shall bring Emilia forth.

PAULINA   I pray now call her.
Withdraw yourselves.
                    [*Exit Gentleman and Attendants.*]

JAILER   And, madam,   15
I must be present at your conference.

287

PAULINA Well, be 't so, prithee.   [*Exit Jailer.*]
Here's such ado to make no stain a stain,
As passes coloring.

[*Enter Jailer, with*] *Emilia.*

                              Dear gentlewoman,
20 How fares our gracious lady?

EMILIA As well as one so great and so forlorn
May hold together. On her frights and griefs
(Which never tender lady hath borne greater)
She is, something before her time, delivered.

PAULINA A boy?

25 EMILIA   A daughter, and a goodly babe,
Lusty, and like to live; the Queen receives
Much comfort in 't; says, "My poor prisoner,
I am innocent as you."

PAULINA   I dare be sworn.
These dangerous, unsafe lunes i' th' King, beshrew
     them!
30 He must be told on 't, and he shall; the office
Becomes a woman best. I'll take 't upon me.
If I prove honey-mouthed, let my tongue blister,
And never to my red-looked anger be
The trumpet any more. Pray you, Emilia,
35 Commend my best obedience to the Queen;
If she dares trust me with her little babe,
I'll show 't the King, and undertake to be
Her advocate to th' loud'st. We do not know
How he may soften at the sight o' th' child;
40 The silence often of pure innocence
Persuades, when speaking fails.

EMILIA   Most worthy madam,
Your honor and your goodness is so evident,

II.ii.19 **coloring** the art of dyeing (thus giving a specious appearance)   23 **Which**
than which   29 **lunes** fits of lunacy   32 **tongue blister** (because lies were
supposed to blister the tongue)   33–34 **red-looked ... trumpet** (the figure is of
an angry face as a herald dressed in red and preceded by a trumpet[er])

That your free undertaking cannot miss
A thriving issue: there is no lady living
So meet for this great errand. Please your ladyship   45
To visit the next room, I'll presently
Acquaint the Queen of your most noble offer,
Who but today hammered of this design,
But durst not tempt a minister of honor
Lest she should be denied.

PAULINA   Tell her, Emilia,   50
I'll use that tongue I have; if wit flow from 't
As boldness from my bosom, let 't not be doubted
I shall do good.

EMILIA   Now be you blest for it!
I'll to the Queen. Please you come something nearer.

JAILER Madam, if 't please the Queen to send the babe,   55
I know not what I shall incur to pass it,
Having no warrant.

PAULINA   You need not fear it, sir:
This child was prisoner to the womb and is
By law and process of great Nature thence
Freed, and enfranchised; not a party to   60
The anger of the King, nor guilty of,
If any be, the trespass of the Queen.

JAILER I do believe it.

PAULINA Do not you fear—upon mine honor, I
Will stand betwixt you and danger.   *Exeunt*.   65

45 **meet** fitting   46 **presently** immediately   48 **hammered of** deliberated upon
49 **tempt** make trial of   51 **wit** wisdom   56 **to pass it** (as a result of allowing it
to pass)

Scene III. [*Sicilia, the Court of Leontes.*]

Enter Leontes, Servants, Antigonus, and Lords.

LEONTES Nor night nor day no rest: it is but weakness
To bear the matter thus, mere weakness. If
The cause were not in being—part o' th' cause,
She, th' adult'ress (for the harlot king
5   Is quite beyond mine arm, out of the blank
And level of my brain, plot-proof); but she,
I can hook to me—say that she were gone,
Given to the fire, a moiety of my rest
Might come to me again. Who's there?

SERVANT   My lord!

LEONTES How does the boy?

10 FIRST ATTENDANT He took good rest tonight; 'tis hoped
His sickness is discharged.

LEONTES   To see his nobleness!
Conceiving the dishonor of his mother,
He straight declined, drooped, took it deeply,
Fastened, and fixed the shame on 't in himself;
15 Threw off his spirit, his appetite, his sleep,
And downright languished. Leave me solely; go,
See how he fares.   [*Exit Servant.*]
                  Fie, fie, no thought of him!
The very thought of my revenges that way
Recoil upon me—in himself too mighty,
20 And in his parties, his alliance; let him be,

II.iii.3 **th' cause** (Leontes interrupts himself, remembering that Polixenes is inaccessible, so that only part of the cause of his agony is within his power to destroy)   4 **harlot** lewd   5–6 **out of the blank/ And level** beyond my range ("blank" is the center of the target; "level" means "aim." The reference is to archery)   8 **moiety** half   17 **no thought of him** i.e., of Polixenes

Until a time may serve. For present vengeance
Take it on her. Camillo and Polixenes
Laugh at me, make their pastime at my sorrow;
They should not laugh if I could reach them, nor
Shall she within my power.

Enter Paulina [with the Baby].

LORD   You must not enter.   25

PAULINA Nay, rather, good my lords, be second to me.
Fear you his tyrannous passion more, alas,
Than the Queen's life? A gracious innocent soul,
More free than he is jealous.

ANTIGONUS   That's enough.

SERVANT Madam, he hath not slept tonight, commanded   30
None should come at him.

PAULINA   Not so hot, good sir;
I come to bring him sleep. 'Tis such as you
That creep like shadows by him, and do sigh
At each his needless heavings—such as you
Nourish the cause of his awaking. I   35
Do come with words as medicinal as true,
Honest as either, to purge him of that humor
That presses him from sleep.

LEONTES   What noise there, ho?

PAULINA No noise, my lord, but needful conference
About some gossips for your Highness.

LEONTES   How?   40
Away with that audacious lady! Antigonus,
I charged thee that she should not come about me;
I knew she would.

ANTIGONUS   I told her so, my lord,
On your displeasure's peril, and on mine,
She should not visit you.

LEONTES   What? Canst not rule her?   45

26 **be second to** support 29 **free** innocent 37 **humor** illness 40 **gossips**
godparents

PAULINA From all dishonesty he can: in this,
　　　　Unless he take the course that you have done—
　　　　Commit me for committing honor, trust it,
　　　　He shall not rule me.

ANTIGONUS　　　　　　La you now, you hear,
50　　When she will take the rein, I let her run;
　　　　But she'll not stumble.

PAULINA　　　　　　　Good my liege, I come—
　　　　And I beseech you hear me, who profess
　　　　Myself your loyal servant, your physician,
　　　　Your most obedient counselor; yet that dares
55　　Less appear so in comforting your evils,
　　　　Than such as most seem yours—I say, I come
　　　　From your good queen.

LEONTES　　　　　　Good queen!

PAULINA Good queen, my lord, good queen, I say good
　　　　queen,
　　　　And would by combat make her good, so were I
　　　　A man, the worst about you.

60　LEONTES　　　　　　　Force her hence.

PAULINA Let him that makes but trifles of his eyes
　　　　First hand me. On mine own accord I'll off,
　　　　But first I'll do my errand. The good queen
　　　　(For she is good) hath brought you forth a daughter;
　　　　Here 'tis; commends it to your blessing.
　　　　　　　　　　　　[*She lays down the Baby.*]

65　LEONTES　　　　　　　　Out!
　　　　A mankind witch! Hence with her, out o' door!
　　　　A most intelligencing bawd!

---

48 Commit ... committing (the word is used in a punning sense, first meaning
"send to prison," and secondly, "performing")　**50–51 rein ... run ... stumble**
(Antigonus, as usual, speaks of his wife as if she were a horse)　**55 comforting**
abetting, countenancing　**56 as most seem yours** as are nearest to you　**59 by
combat** in a trial by combat (which would, in the code of chivalry, vindicate a
lady's honor)　**60 the worst** the lowest in degree　**66 mankind** male, ferocious,
violent　**67 intelligencing** i.e., acting as a pander

PAULINA   Not so;
  I am as ignorant in that as you
  In so entitling me; and no less honest
  Than you are mad; which is enough, I'll warrant,   70
  As this world goes, to pass for honest.

LEONTES   Traitors!
  Will you not push her out? [*To Antigonus*] Give
    her the bastard,
  Thou dotard, thou art woman-tired, unroosted
  By thy Dame Partlet here. Take up the bastard,
  Take 't up, I say; give 't to thy crone.

PAULINA   Forever   75
  Unvenerable be thy hands, if thou
  Tak'st up the Princess, by that forcèd baseness
  Which he has put upon 't!

LEONTES   He dreads his wife.

PAULINA So I would you did; then 'twere past all doubt
  You'd call your children yours.

LEONTES   A nest of traitors.   80

ANTIGONUS I am none, by this good light.

PAULINA   Nor I: nor any
  But one that's here, and that's himself; for he,
  The sacred honor of himself, his queen's,
  His hopeful son's, his babe's, betrays to slander,
  Whose sting is sharper than the sword's; and will not   85
  (For as the case now stands, it is a curse
  He cannot be compelled to 't) once remove
  The root of his opinion, which is rotten
  As ever oak or stone was sound.

LEONTES   A callat
  Of boundless tongue, who late hath beat her
    husband,   90

---

73 **woman-tired** henpecked   74 **Dame Partlet** (traditionally the name of the
hen; compare Reynard the fox, etc.)   77 **forcèd baseness** falsely base name
(bastard)   89 **callat** scold

And now baits me! This brat is none of mine;
It is the issue of Polixenes.
Hence with it, and together with the dam,
Commit them to the fire.

PAULINA   It is yours:
95 And might we lay th' old proverb to your charge,
So like you, 'tis the worse. Behold, my lords,
Although the print be little, the whole matter
And copy of the father: eye, nose, lip,
The trick of 's frown, his forehead, nay, the valley,
The pretty dimples of his chin and cheek; his
100   smiles;
The very mold and frame of hand, nail, finger.
And thou, good goddess Nature, which hast made it
So like to him that got it, if thou hast
The ordering of the mind too, 'mongst all colors
105 No yellow in 't, lest she suspect, as he does,
Her children not her husband's.

LEONTES   A gross hag!
And lozel, thou art worthy to be hanged,
That wilt not stay her tongue.

ANTIGONUS   Hang all the husbands
That cannot do that feat, you'll leave yourself
Hardly one subject.

110 LEONTES   Once more, take her hence.

PAULINA A most unworthy and unnatural lord
Can do no more.

LEONTES   I'll ha' thee burned.

PAULINA   I care not;
It is an heretic that makes the fire,
Not she which burns in 't. I'll not call you tyrant;
115 But this most cruel usage of your queen
(Not able to produce more accusation

90–91 beat ... baits (pronounced alike)   95 th' old proverb i.e., "They are so
like that they are the worse for it"   97–98 print ... matter ... copy (the figure is
derived from printing)   103 got begot   105 yellow (the color of jealousy)
107 lozel worthless fellow

Than your own weak-hinged fancy) something
  savors
Of tyranny, and will ignoble make you,
Yea, scandalous to the world.

LEONTES   On your allegiance,
  Out of the chamber with her! Were I a tyrant,   120
  Where were her life? She durst not call me so,
  If she did know me one. Away with her.

PAULINA I pray you do not push me, I'll be gone.
  Look to your babe, my lord, 'tis yours: Jove send her
  A better guiding spirit. What needs these hands?   125
  You, that are thus so tender o'er his follies,
  Will never do him good, not one of you.
  So, so; farewell, we are gone.   *Exit*.

LEONTES Thou, traitor, hast set on thy wife to this.
  My child? Away with 't! Even thou, that hast   130
  A heart so tender o'er it, take it hence,
  And see it instantly consumed with fire.
  Even thou, and none but thou. Take it up straight;
  Within this hour bring me word 'tis done,
  And by good testimony, or I'll seize thy life,   135
  With what thou else call'st thine; if thou refuse,
  And wilt encounter with my wrath, say so;
  The bastard brains with these my proper hands
  Shall I dash out. Go, take it to the fire,
  For thou sett'st on thy wife.

ANTIGONUS   I did not, sir;   140
  These lords, my noble fellows, if they please,
  Can clear me in 't.

LORDS   We can: my royal liege,
  He is not guilty of her coming hither.

LEONTES You're liars all.

117 **weak-hinged** ill-supported (a door hangs on its hinges) 119 **On your
allegiance** (the ultimate command; to disobey it is treason) 120 **tyrant** (Paulina
avoided calling him tyrant, but in coming close to so doing reminded him that this
interpretation might all too easily be put upon his actions) 135 **seize** confiscate
138 **proper** own

145 LORD Beseech your Highness, give us better credit.
We have always truly served you, and beseech
So to esteem of us; and on our knees we beg,
As recompense of our dear services
Past, and to come, that you do change this purpose,
150   Which being so horrible, so bloody, must
Lead on to some foul issue. We all kneel.

LEONTES I am a feather for each wind that blows.
Shall I live on to see this bastard kneel
And call me father? Better burn it now
155   Than curse it then. But be it; let it live.
It shall not neither. You, sir, come you hither:
You that have been so tenderly officious
With Lady Margery, your midwife there,
To save this bastard's life—for 'tis a bastard,
So sure as this beard's gray—what will you
160   adventure,
To save this brat's life?

ANTIGONUS   Anything, my lord,
That my ability may undergo,
And nobleness impose—at least thus much:
I'll pawn the little blood which I have left,
165   To save the innocent—anything possible.

LEONTES It shall be possible. Swear by this sword
Thou wilt perform my bidding.

ANTIGONUS   I will, my lord.

LEONTES Mark, and perform it: seest thou? For the
      fail
Of any point in 't, shall not only be
170   Death to thyself, but to thy lewd-tongued wife,
Whom for this time we pardon. We enjoin thee,
As thou art liegeman to us, that thou carry
This female bastard hence, and that thou bear it
To some remote and desert place, quite out

158 **Lady Margery** (another facetious name of the hen) 160 **this beard's gray**
(Leontes here, presumably, refers to—perhaps touches—the beard of Antigonus)
164 **pawn** pledge 166 **by this sword** by the cross on the handle, or that formed
by the hilt and the blade 168 **fail** failure

Of our dominions; and that there thou leave it,   175
Without more mercy, to its own protection
And favor of the climate. As by strange fortune
It came to us, I do in justice charge thee,
On thy soul's peril, and thy body's torture,
That thou commend it strangely to some place,   180
Where chance may nurse or end it. Take it up.

ANTIGONUS I swear to do this, though a present death
Had been more merciful. Come on, poor babe,
Some powerful spirit instruct the kites and ravens
To be thy nurses! Wolves and bears, they say,   185
Casting their savageness aside, have done
Like offices of pity. Sir, be prosperous
In more than this deed does require! And blessing
Against this cruelty fight on thy side,
Poor thing, condemned to loss. *Exit [with the Baby].*

LEONTES   No, I'll not rear   190
Another's issue.

Enter a Servant.

SERVANT   Please your Highness, posts
From those you sent to th' oracle are come
An hour since: Cleomenes and Dion,
Being well arrived from Delphos, are both landed,
Hasting to th' court.

LORD   So please you, sir, their speed   195
Hath been beyond accompt.

LEONTES   Twenty-three days
They have been absent; 'tis good speed; foretells
The great Apollo suddenly will have
The truth of this appear. Prepare you, lords,
Summon a session, that we may arraign   200
Our most disloyal lady; for as she hath
Been publicly accused, so shall she have
A just and open trial. While she lives,
My heart will be a burden to me. Leave me,
And think upon my bidding.   *Exeunt.*   205

180 **strangely** as a stranger   188 **require** deserve   196 **beyond accompt**
unprecedented   200 **session** judicial trial or investigation

ACT III

Scene I. [*Sicilia. On a high road.*]

Enter Cleomenes and Dion.

CLEOMENES   The climate's delicate, the air most sweet,
Fertile the isle, the temple much surpassing
The common praise it bears.

DION   I shall report,
For most it caught me, the celestial habits
5   (Methinks I so should term them) and the reverence
Of the grave wearers. O, the sacrifice,
How ceremonious, solemn, and unearthly
It was i' th' off'ring!

CLEOMENES   But of all, the burst
And the ear-deaf'ning voice o' th' oracle,
10   Kin to Jove's thunder, so surprised my sense,
That I was nothing.

DION   If th' event o' th' journey
Prove as successful to the Queen (O be 't so!)
As it hath been to us rare, pleasant, speedy,
The time is worth the use on 't.

CLEOMENES   Great Apollo
15   Turn all to th' best; these proclamations,

III.i.2 **the isle** i.e., Delos (as in II.i.183; again by mistake for Delphi)
4 **celestial habits** heavenly clothing   11 **event** outcome

So forcing faults upon Hermione,
I little like.

DION   The violent carriage of it
Will clear or end the business when the oracle,
Thus by Apollo's great divine sealed up,
Shall the contents discover, something rare   20
Even then will rush to knowledge. Go; fresh horses,
And gracious be the issue!   *Exeunt.*

Scene II. [*Sicilia, a court of justice.*]

Enter Leontes, Lords, Officers.

LEONTES This session, to our great grief we pronounce,
Even pushes 'gainst our heart. The party tried,
The daughter of a king, our wife, and one
Of us too much beloved. Let us be cleared
Of being tyrannous, since we so openly   5
Proceed in justice, which shall have due course,
Even to the guilt or the purgation.
Produce the prisoner.

OFFICER It is his Highness' pleasure that the Queen
Appear in person here in court.

[*Enter*] Hermione, as to her trial, [*Paulina and*]
Ladies.

          Silence.   10

LEONTES Read the indictment.

OFFICER "Hermione, Queen to the worthy Leontes, King
of Sicilia, thou art here accused and arraigned of high

17 **carriage** management   19 **great divine** chief priest   III.ii.7 **purgation**
acquittal   10 s.d. **as to her trial** (this direction occurs in the Folio at the head of
the scene)   10 **Silence** (italic in Folio, as if a stage direction. But presumably the
Officer calls out the word)

treason, in committing adultery with Polixenes, King
15 of Bohemia, and conspiring with Camillo to take away
the life of our sovereign lord the King, thy royal husband; the pretense whereof being by circumstances
partly laid open, thou, Hermione, contrary to the faith
and allegiance of a true subject, didst counsel and aid
20 them, for their better safety, to fly away by night."

HERMIONE Since what I am to say must be but that
    Which contradicts my accusation, and
    The testimony on my part no other
    But what comes from myself, it shall scarce boot me
25   To say, "Not guilty"; mine integrity
    Being counted falsehood, shall, as I express it,
    Be so received. But thus: if powers divine
    Behold our human actions—as they do—
    I doubt not then, but Innocence shall make
30   False Accusation blush, and Tyranny
    Tremble at Patience. You, my lord, best know—
    Who least will seem to do so—my past life
    Hath been as continent, as chaste, as true,
    As I am now unhappy; which is more
35   Than history can pattern, though devised
    And played to take spectators. For behold me,
    A fellow of the royal bed, which owe
    A moiety of the throne, a great king's daughter,
    The mother to a hopeful prince, here standing
40   To prate and talk for life and honor, 'fore
    Who please to come and hear. For life, I prize it
    As I weigh grief, which I would spare; for honor,
    'Tis a derivative from me to mine,
    And only that I stand for. I appeal
45   To your own conscience, sir, before Polixenes
    Came to your court, how I was in your grace,
    How merited to be so; since he came,
    With what encounter so uncurrent, I

17 **pretense** design   24 **boot** assist   35 **can pattern** can offer parallels   36 **take**
move   37 **owe** own   43 **'Tis ... mine** i.e., it is my son's inheritance   48–49
With what ... appear thus by what outrageous conduct I have acted so unlike
myself as to bring upon myself the ordeal of this appearance in court

Have strained t' appear thus; if one jot beyond
The bound of honor, or in act or will   50
That way inclining, hardened be the hearts
Of all that hear me, and my near'st of kin
Cry fie upon my grave!

LEONTES   I ne'er heard yet
That any of these bolder vices wanted
Less impudence to gainsay what they did,   55
Than to perform it first.

HERMIONE   That's true enough,
Though 'tis a saying, sir, not due to me.

LEONTES You will not own it.

HERMIONE   More than mistress of
Which comes to me in name of fault, I must not
At all acknowledge. For Polixenes,   60
With whom I am accused, I do confess
I loved him, as in honor he required;
With such a kind of love, as might become
A lady like me; with a love, even such,
So, and no other, as yourself commanded;   65
Which not to have done, I think had been in me
Both disobedience and ingratitude
To you, and toward your friend, whose love had
     spoke,
Even since it could speak, from an infant, freely,
That it was yours. Now, for conspiracy,   70
I know not how it tastes, though it be dished
For me to try how; all I know of it,
Is that Camillo was an honest man;
And why he left your court, the gods themselves,
Wotting no more than I, are ignorant.   75

50–51 **or in act ... inclining** either in performance or intention approaching the
bounds of honor   55–56 **Less impudence ... first** (the point is that if one is
bold enough to commit the crime one will be bold enough to deny it; but the
expression is not very clear)   58–60 **More than mistress ... acknowledge** I
must refuse to acknowledge as my own, faults which I do not in fact possess
62 **required** was entitled to   71 **dished** served (as of food)   75 **Wotting** if they
know

LEONTES You knew of his departure, as you know
What you have underta'en to do in 's absence.

HERMIONE   Sir,
You speak a language that I understand not.
My life stands in the level of your dreams,
Which I'll lay down.

80 LEONTES   Your actions are my dreams.
You had a bastard by Polixenes,
And I but dreamed it. As you were past all shame—
Those of your fact are so—so past all truth;
Which to deny concerns more than avails; for as
85 Thy brat hath been cast out, like to itself,
No father owning it (which is indeed
More criminal in thee than it) so thou
Shalt feel our justice; in whose easiest passage
Look for no less than death.

HERMIONE   Sir, spare your threats:
90 The bug which you would fright me with, I seek.
To me can life be no commodity.
The crown and comfort of my life, your favor,
I do give lost, for I do feel it gone,
But know not how it went. My second joy,
95 And first fruits of my body, from his presence
I am barred, like one infectious. My third comfort,
Starred most unluckily, is from my breast,
The innocent milk in its most innocent mouth,
Haled out to murder. Myself on every post
100 Proclaimed a strumpet; with immodest hatred
The childbed privilege denied, which 'longs
To women of all fashion. Lastly, hurried
Here to this place, i' th' open air, before

---

79 **level** range (archery) 83 **Those of your fact** those guilty of your crime
84 **concerns more than avails** is more trouble to you than it's worth 85 **like to
itself** i.e., appropriately, since it has no father 90 **bug** bogey, bugbear
91 **commodity** advantage, asset 93 **give** reckon as 97 **starred** fated 99 **post**
(on which public notices and advertisements were placed. In Greene's novel the
King issues a proclamation concerning his wife's guilt, which is "blazed through
the country") 101 **longs** belongs 102 **fashion** rank

I have got strength of limit. Now, my liege,
Tell me, what blessings I have here alive,   105
That I should fear to die? Therefore proceed.
But yet hear this—mistake me not: for life,
I prize it not a straw, but for mine honor,
Which I would free—if I shall be condemned
Upon surmises, all proofs sleeping else   110
But what your jealousies awake, I tell you
'Tis rigor, and not law. Your honors all,
I do refer me to the oracle:
Apollo be my judge!

LORD   This your request
Is altogether just; therefore bring forth,   115
And in Apollo's name, his oracle. [*Exeunt Officers.*]

HERMIONE The Emperor of Russia was my father.
Oh that he were alive, and here beholding
His daughter's trial! That he did but see
The flatness of my misery; yet with eyes   120
Of pity, not revenge!

        [*Enter Officers, with*] Cleomenes [*and*] Dion.

OFFICER You here shall swear upon this sword of
    justice,
That you, Cleomenes and Dion, have
Been both at Delphos, and from thence have brought
This sealed-up oracle, by the hand delivered   125
Of great Apollo's priest; and that since then
You have not dared to break the holy seal,
Nor read the secrets in 't.

CLEOMENES, DION   All this we swear.

LEONTES Break up the seals and read.

OFFICER "Hermione is chaste, Polixenes blameless,   130
Camillo a true subject, Leontes a jealous tyrant, his
innocent babe truly begotten, and the King shall live
without an heir, if that which is lost be not found."

---

104 **strength of limit** strength to go out   112 **rigor, and not law** tyranny, not
justice   117 **Emperor of Russia** (in *Pandosto* it is the wife of Polixenes who is
daughter of this emperor)   120 **flatness** completeness

303

LORDS Now blessèd be the great Apollo!

HERMIONE   Praised!

LEONTES Hast thou read truth?

135 OFFICER   Ay, my lord, even so
As it is here set down.

LEONTES There is no truth at all i' th' oracle.
The sessions shall proceed; this is mere falsehood.

[*Enter a Servant.*]

SERVANT My lord, the King, the King!

LEONTES   What is the business?

140 SERVANT O sir, I shall be hated to report it.
The Prince, your son, with mere conceit and fear
Of the Queen's speed, is gone.

LEONTES   How? Gone?

SERVANT   Is dead.

LEONTES Apollo's angry, and the heavens themselves
Do strike at my injustice. [*Hermione faints.*] How
now there!

PAULINA This news is mortal to the Queen—look
145   down
And see what death is doing.

LEONTES   Take her hence;
Her heart is but o'ercharged, she will recover.
I have too much believed mine own suspicion.
Beseech you tenderly apply to her
Some remedies for life.

[*Exeunt Paulina and Ladies, with Hermione.*]

150   Apollo, pardon
My great profaneness 'gainst thine oracle.
I'll reconcile me to Polixenes,
New woo my queen, recall the good Camillo—

141 **conceit** concept, thought   142 **speed** fortune, success   145 **mortal** deadly

Whom I proclaim a man of truth, of mercy.
For, being transported by my jealousies   155
To bloody thoughts and to revenge, I chose
Camillo for the minister to poison
My friend Polixenes; which had been done,
But that the good mind of Camillo tardied
My swift command, though I with death and with   160
Reward did threaten and encourage him,
Not doing it and being done. He, most humane,
And filled with honor, to my kingly guest
Unclasped my practice, quit his fortunes here—
Which you knew great—and to the hazard   165
Of all incertainties himself commended,
No richer than his honor. How he glisters
Through my rust! And how his piety
Does my deeds make the blacker!

[*Enter Paulina.*]

PAULINA   Woe the while!
O cut my lace, lest my heart, cracking it,   170
Break too!

LORD What fit is this, good lady?

PAULINA What studied torments, tyrant, hast for me?
What wheels, racks, fires? What flaying, boiling
In leads or oils? What old or newer torture   175
Must I receive, whose every word deserves
To taste of thy most worst. Thy tyranny,
Together working with thy jealousies,
Fancies too weak for boys, too green and idle
For girls of nine—O, think what they have done,   180
And then run mad indeed, stark mad; for all

160–62 **though I ... being done** though I threatened him with death for not doing it, and promised him rewards for doing it   164 **Unclasped my practice** revealed my plot   165 **Which ... hazard** (the line apparently lacks a foot, which the Second Folio—with the approval of some editors—supplies by inserting the word "certain" before "hazard")   168 **Through my rust** (again, to mend the meter, F2 reads "through my dark rust." Some editors read "Thorough," which is interchangeable with "Through")   170 **cut my lace** (to give her more breath)

Thy bygone fooleries were but spices of it.
That thou betrayedst Polixenes, 'twas nothing;
That did but show thee, of a fool, inconstant,
185 And damnable ingrateful. Nor was 't much
Thou wouldst have poisoned good Camillo's honor,
To have him kill a king—poor trespasses,
More monstrous standing by; whereof I reckon
The casting forth to crows thy baby daughter
190 To be or none, or little; though a devil
Would have shed water out of fire, ere done 't;
Nor is 't directly laid to thee the death
Of the young Prince, whose honorable thoughts,
Thoughts high for one so tender, cleft the heart
195 That could conceive a gross and foolish sire
Blemished his gracious dam. This is not, no,
Laid to thy answer; but the last—O lords,
When I have said, cry "woe": the Queen, the Queen,
The sweet'st, dear'st creature's dead; and vengeance
    for 't
Not dropped down yet.

200 LORDS   The higher pow'rs forbid!

PAULINA I say she's dead; I'll swear 't. If word nor oath
Prevail not, go and see; if you can bring
Tincture or luster in her lip, her eye,
Heat outwardly or breath within, I'll serve you
205 As I would do the gods. But, O thou tyrant,
Do not repent these things, for they are heavier
Than all thy woes can stir; therefore betake thee
To nothing but despair. A thousand knees,
Ten thousand years together, naked, fasting,
210 Upon a barren mountain, and still winter
In storm perpetual, could not move the gods
To look that way thou wert.

LEONTES   Go on, go on;

182 **spice** samples 184 **of a fool** for a fool 188 **standing by** i.e., and so
available for comparison 191 **shed water out of fire** wept out of burning eyes
198 **said** said it 207 **all thy woes can stir** all thy penitence can remove
210 **still winter** forever winter

Thou canst not speak too much, I have deserved
All tongues to talk their bitt'rest.

LORD   Say no more;
  Howe'er the business goes, you have made fault   215
  I' th' boldness of your speech.

PAULINA   I am sorry for 't;
  All faults I make, when I shall come to know them,
  I do repent. Alas, I have showed too much
  The rashness of a woman; he is touched
  To th' noble heart. What's gone and what's past
    help   220
  Should be past grief; do not receive affliction
  At my petition; I beseech you, rather
  Let me be punished that have minded you
  Of what you should forget. Now, good my liege,
  Sir, royal sir, forgive a foolish woman.   225
  The love I bore your queen—lo, fool again!
  I'll speak of her no more, nor of your children;
  I'll not remember you of my own lord,
  Who is lost too. Take your patience to you,
  And I'll say nothing.

LEONTES   Thou didst speak but well,   230
  When most the truth which I receive much better
  Than to be pitied of thee. Prithee bring me
  To the dead bodies of my queen and son.
  One grave shall be for both; upon them shall
  The causes of their death appear, unto   235
  Our shame perpetual. Once a day I'll visit
  The chapel where they lie, and tears shed there
  Shall be my recreation. So long as nature
  Will bear up with this exercise, so long
  I daily vow to use it. Come, and lead me   240
  To these sorrows.   *Exeunt.*

221–22 **do not receive ... petition** I would not have you suffer because I prayed
that you should   228 **remember** remind   230–31 **Thou didst ... the truth**
You spoke well only when most telling the truth   238 **recreation** diversion (to do
so will be his only pastime)

Scene III. [*Bohemia, the seacoast.*]

Enter Antigonus [and] a Mariner, [with a] Babe.

ANTIGONUS Thou art perfect then our ship hath
            touched upon
      The deserts of Bohemia?

MARINER   Ay, my lord, and fear
      We have landed in ill time; the skies look grimly,
      And threaten present blusters. In my conscience,
5   The heavens with that we have in hand are angry
      And frown upon 's.

ANTIGONUS Their sacred wills be done! Go get aboard,
      Look to thy bark, I'll not be long before
      I call upon thee.

MARINER   Make your best haste, and go not
10   Too far i' th' land; 'tis like to be loud weather;
      Besides, this place is famous for the creatures
      Of prey that keep upon 't.

ANTIGONUS   Go thou away,
      I'll follow instantly.

MARINER   I am glad at heart
      To be so rid o' th' business.   *Exit.*

ANTIGONUS   Come, poor babe;
15   I have heard, but not believed, the spirits o' th' dead
      May walk again; if such thing be, thy mother
      Appeared to me last night; for ne'er was dream

III.iii.s.d. **Bohemia** (substituted for the Sicily of *Pandosto*. Bohemia, as is
notorious, had no seacoast) 1 **perfect** certain 4 **conscience** knowledge, awareness (but with something of the modern meaning also) 12 **keep** live 16 **if such
thing be** (Antigonus takes the skeptical Protestant view as a rule, but is convinced
of the reality of the vision. Possibly Shakespeare, when he wrote this scene, had
not yet had the idea of reanimating Hermione)

So like awaking. To me comes a creature,
Sometimes her head on one side, some another;
I never saw a vessel of like sorrow   20
So filled, and so becoming. In pure white robes,
Like very sanctity, she did approach
My cabin where I lay; thrice bowed before me,
And, gasping to begin some speech, her eyes
Became two spouts; the fury spent, anon   25
Did this break from her: "Good Antigonus,
Since fate, against thy better disposition,
Hath made thy person for the thrower-out
Of my poor babe, according to thine oath,
Places remote enough are in Bohemia,   30
There weep, and leave it crying; and for the babe
Is counted lost forever, Perdita
I prithee call 't. For this ungentle business
Put on thee by my lord, thou ne'er shalt see
Thy wife Paulina more." And so, with shrieks,   35
She melted into air. Affrighted much,
I did in time collect myself, and thought
This was so, and no slumber. Dreams are toys;
Yet for this once, yea superstitiously,
I will be squared by this. I do believe   40
Hermione hath suffered death, and that
Apollo would (this being indeed the issue
Of King Polixenes) it should here be laid
Either for life, or death, upon the earth
Of its right father. Blossom, speed thee well!   45

                    [*He lays down the Baby.*]

There lie, and there thy character: there these,

                    [*Lays down a bundle.*]

Which may, if Fortune please, both breed thee,
    pretty,

21 **so filled and so becoming** so filled with sorrow, and so beautiful in sorrow
22 **very sanctity** sanctity itself   23 **cabin** berth   32 **Perdita** (meaning "the lost
girl")   38 **This was so** this was real   38 **toys** trifles   39 **superstitiously** (again
the Protestant view of ghosts)   40 **squared** regulated, ordered   46 **character**
description (by which Perdita is later to be recognized)   47 **breed thee** raise you,
pay for your upbringing

And still rest thine. The storm begins; poor wretch,
That for thy mother's fault art thus exposed
50   To loss, and what may follow! Weep I cannot,
But my heart bleeds; and most accursed am I
To be by oath enjoined to this. Farewell,
The day frowns more and more; thou 'rt like to have
A lullaby too rough; I never saw
55   The heavens so dim by day. A savage clamor!
Well may I get aboard! This is the chase;
I am gone forever.   *Exit, pursued by a bear.*

[Enter] Shepherd.

SHEPHERD I would there were no age between ten and
three-and-twenty, or that youth would sleep out the
60   rest; for there is nothing in the between but getting
wenches with child, wronging the ancientry, stealing,
fighting. Hark you now! Would any but these
boiled brains of nineteen and two-and-twenty hunt
this weather? They have scared away two of my
65   best sheep, which I fear the wolf will sooner find
than the master; if anywhere I have them, 'tis by
the seaside, browsing of ivy. Good luck, an 't be
thy will, what have we here? Mercy on 's, a barne!
A very pretty barne; a boy or a child, I wonder?
70   A pretty one, a very pretty one; sure, some scape;
though I am not bookish, yet I can read waiting-
gentlewoman in the scape. This has been some stair-
work, some trunk-work, some behind-door-work;
they were warmer that got this than the poor thing
75   is here. I'll take it up for pity; yet I'll tarry till my
son come; he hallowed but even now. Whoa-ho-
hoa!

---

48 **And still rest thine** there will be something over   50 **Weep I cannot** (though
the ghost had told him to)   55 **savage clamor** the noise of the hunters
56 **chase** the bear   63 **boiled** seething, hot   67 **browsing of ivy** ("whereon they
do greatly feed," according to *Pandosto*)   68 **barne** child (compare mod. Scots
"bairn")   69 **a boy or a child** a boy or a girl ("child" for "girl" is a dialect form
and presumably was so in 1610)   70 **scape** sexual misadventure   73 **trunk-work**
secret or clandestine action

Enter Clown.

CLOWN Hilloa, loa!

SHEPHERD What? Art so near? If thou 'lt see a thing to
talk on, when thou art dead and rotten, come hither.   80
What ail'st thou, man?

CLOWN I have seen two such sights, by sea and by land!
But I am not to say it is a sea, for it is now the sky;
betwixt the firmament and it, you cannot thrust a
bodkin's point.   85

SHEPHERD Why, boy, how is it?

CLOWN I would you did but see how it chafes, how
it rages, how it takes up the shore, but that's not
to the point. O, the most piteous cry of the poor
souls! Sometimes to see 'em, and not to see 'em;   90
now the ship boring the moon with her mainmast,
and anon swallowed with yeast and froth, as you'd
thrust a cork into a hogshead. And then for the
land-service, to see how the bear tore out his
shoulder bone, how he cried to me for help, and   95
said his name was Antigonus, a nobleman! But to
make an end of the ship, to see how the sea flap-
dragoned it; but first, how the poor souls roared,
and the sea mocked them; and how the poor
gentleman roared, and the bear mocked him, both   100
roaring louder than the sea or weather.

SHEPHERD Name of mercy, when was this, boy?

CLOWN Now, now; I have not winked since I saw these
sights; the men are not yet cold under water, nor
the bear half dined on the gentleman; he's at it now.   105

SHEPHERD Would I had been by, to have helped the
old man!

CLOWN I would you had been by the ship's side, to have

---

88 **takes up** rebukes   94 **land-service** i.e., the soldier who serves on land
(Antigonus) as opposed to the seamen aboard the ship (perhaps with a pun on
"service" meaning "dish"—Antigonus being food for the bear)   97–98 **flap-
dragoned** swallowed down (as drinkers swallowed flapdragons [raisins, etc.] out of
burning brandy)

helped her; there your charity would have lacked
110　footing.

SHEPHERD Heavy matters, heavy matters! But look
thee here, boy. Now bless thyself; thou met'st with
things dying, I with things new born. Here's a sight
for thee; look thee, a bearing-cloth for a squire's
115　child; look thee here, take up, take up, boy; open
it; so, let's see; it was told me I should be rich by
the fairies. This is some changeling; open 't; what's
within, boy?

CLOWN You're a made old man; if the sins of your
120　youth are forgiven you, you're well to live. Gold,
all gold!

SHEPHERD This is fairy gold, boy, and 'twill prove so;
up with 't, keep it close; home, home, the next
way! We are lucky, boy, and to be so still requires
125　nothing but secrecy. Let my sheep go; come, good
boy, the next way home.

CLOWN Go you the next way with your findings, I'll go
see if the bear be gone from the gentleman, and
how much he hath eaten. They are never curst but
130　when they are hungry. If there be any of him left,
I'll bury it.

SHEPHERD That's a good deed. If thou mayest discern
by that which is left of him what he is, fetch me to
th' sight of him.

135　CLOWN Marry will I; and you shall help to put him
i' th' ground.

SHEPHERD 'Tis a lucky day, boy, and we'll do good
deeds on 't.

Exeunt.

109–10 charity ... footing (alluding to the establishment of charitable
foundations) 114 bearing-cloth christening robe 117 changeling (usually the
inferior child left by the fairies; here the child they stole, found with their gold,
which must be kept secret) 119 made (Folio reads "mad," but this emendation
of Theobald is supported by the parallel passage in *Pandosto*) 123 close secret
123 next nearest 124 still always 129 curst vicious 135 Marry indeed (from
"By Mary")

ACT IV

Scene I.

Enter Time, the Chorus.

TIME I that please some, try all, both joy and terror
  Of good and bad; that makes and unfolds error,
  Now take upon me, in the name of Time,
  To use my wings. Impute it not a crime
  To me, or my swift passage, that I slide   5
  O'er sixteen years, and leave the growth untried
  Of that wide gap, since it is in my pow'r
  To o'erthrow law, and in one self-born hour
  To plant, and o'erwhelm custom. Let me pass;
  The same I am, ere ancient'st order was   10
  Or what is now received. I witness to
  The times that brought them in; so shall I do
  To th' freshest things now reigning, and make stale
  The glistering of this present, as my tale
  Now seems to it. Your patience this allowing,   15
  I turn my glass, and give my scene such growing

IV.i.1 **try** test **6 growth untried** (Time asks to be excused from detailed accounts of the interim period and its developments, for instance Perdita's childhood) **8–9 law ... custom** (note the distinction: Time "plants" Custom but not Law. Custom lacks the authority of Law, and relates to erroneous Opinion; hence the contemporary use of the word in attacks on such ceremonies of the Roman Church as seemed to Protestants without Scriptural authority) **9 Let me pass ...** (not clear in detail, but the sense is: Let me pass over that gap; I alone remain unchanged from the beginning—and have passed over that far greater gap) **14–15 as my tale ... to it** as my tale seems stale compared with the play it interrupts

As you had slept between. Leontes leaving—
Th' effects of his fond jealousies so grieving,
That he shuts up himself—imagine me,
20 Gentle spectators, that I now may be
In fair Bohemia; and remember well,
I mentioned a son o' th' King's, which Florizel
I now name to you; and with speed so pace
To speak of Perdita, now grown in grace
25 Equal with wond'ring. What of her ensues
I list not prophesy; but let Time's news
Be known when 'tis brought forth. A shepherd's
        daughter,
And what to her adheres, which follows after,
Is th' argument of Time. Of this allow,
30 If ever you have spent time worse, ere now;
If never, yet that Time himself doth say,
He wishes earnestly you never may.   *Exit*.

Scene II. [*Bohemia, the Court of Polixenes.*]

Enter Polixenes and Camillo.

POLIXENES I pray thee, good Camillo, be no more
importunate. 'Tis a sickness denying thee anything,
a death to grant this.

CAMILLO It is fifteen years since I saw my country;
5   though I have, for the most part, been aired
abroad, I desire to lay my bones there. Besides,
the penitent King, my master, hath sent for me, to
whose feeling sorrows I might be some allay, or I

---

18 fond foolish   22 mentioned (unless the whole play is thought of as Time's
report, this is not so; various emendations have been suggested, of which the best
is "A mentioned son ...")   25 Equal with wond'ring to a degree demanding
admiration   26 I list not I do not care to   28 adheres belongs   28 after (at this
period an acceptable rhyme for "daughter")   29 argument story

314

o'erween to think so, which is another spur to my
departure.   10

POLIXENES As thou lov'st me, Camillo, wipe not out the
rest of thy services by leaving me now. The need I
have of thee, thine own goodness hath made. Better
not to have had thee, than thus to want thee; thou,
having made me businesses, which none, without   15
thee, can sufficiently manage, must either stay to
execute them thyself, or take away with thee the
very services thou hast done; which if I have not
enough considered—as too much I cannot—to be
more thankful to thee shall be my study, and my   20
profit therein the heaping friendships. Of that fatal
country Sicilia, prithee speak no more, whose very
naming punishes me with the remembrance of that
penitent (as thou call'st him) and reconciled king,
my brother, whose loss of his most precious queen   25
and children are even now to be afresh lamented.
Say to me, when saw'st thou the Prince Florizel, my
son? Kings are no less unhappy, their issue not
being gracious, than they are in losing them when
they have approved their virtues.   30

CAMILLO Sir, it is three days since I saw the Prince.
What his happier affairs may be are to me unknown;
but I have missingly noted, he is of late much
retired from court, and is less frequent to his
princely exercises than formerly he hath appeared.   35

POLIXENES I have considered so much, Camillo, and
with some care, so far that I have eyes under my
service, which look upon his removedness; from
whom I have this intelligence, that he is seldom
from the house of a most homely shepherd—a man,   40
they say, that from very nothing, and beyond the

IV.ii.9 o'erween am boastful enough to 14 want be without 21 friendships
friendly offices 28–30 Kings ... virtues it is as hard for kings to bear the
disobedience and ill conduct of their children as to lose them when convinced of
their virtues 33 missingly (because he noted not the Prince but his absence)
35 exercises military and sporting activities 37–38 so far that ... removedness to the extent that I'm having him watched in the place where he is hiding
himself 39 intelligence report

imagination of his neighbors, is grown into an unspeakable estate.

CAMILLO I have heard, sir, of such a man, who hath
45   a daughter of most rare note; the report of her is
extended more than can be thought to begin from
such a cottage.

POLIXENES That's likewise part of my intelligence; but,
I fear, the angle that plucks our son thither. Thou
50   shalt accompany us to the place, where we will, not
appearing what we are, have some question with
the shepherd; from whose simplicity I think it not
uneasy to get the cause of my son's resort thither.
Prithee be my present partner in this business, and
55   lay aside the thoughts of Sicilia.

CAMILLO I willingly obey your command.

POLIXENES My best Camillo! We must disguise ourselves.

                              Exit [Polixenes with Camillo].

Scene III. [*A road near the Shepherd's cottage.*]

                    Enter Autolycus, singing.

When daffodils begin to peer,
With heigh the doxy over the dale,
Why, then comes in the sweet o' the year,
For the red blood reigns in the winter's pale.

5   The white sheet bleaching on the hedge,
With heigh the sweet birds, O how they sing!

49 **angle** fishhook   51 **question** talk   IV.iii.2 **doxy** beggar's mistress   4 **pale**
(1) enclosure (2) paleness

Doth set my pugging tooth an edge,
For a quart of ale is a dish for a king.

The lark, that tirra-lirra chants,
With heigh, with heigh, the thrush and the jay!   10
Are summer songs for me and my aunts
While we lie tumbling in the hay.

I have served Prince Florizel, and in my time wore
three-pile, but now I am out of service.

But shall I go mourn for that, my dear?   15
    The pale moon shines by night;
And when I wander here and there
    I then do most go right.
If tinkers may have leave to live,
    And bear the sow-skin budget,   20
Then my account I well may give,
    And in the stocks avouch it.

My traffic is sheets; when the kite builds, look to
lesser linen. My father named me Autolycus, who
being, as I am, littered under Mercury, was like-   25
wise a snapper-up of unconsidered trifles. With die
and drab, I purchased this caparison, and my
revenue is the silly cheat. Gallows and knock
are too powerful on the highway. Beating and hanging are terrors to me; for the life to come, I sleep   30
out the thought of it. A prize, a prize.

---

7 **pugging** thieving (to "pug" means to "pull off"; perhaps Autolycus is thinking
of his sheet-stealing; he is all set to begin snatching them off the hedges)
11 **aunts** whores   14 **three-pile** the best velvet   20 **sow-skin budget** pigskin
toolbag   22 **avouch** corroborate   23–24 **when the kite ... linen** (this is a
warning. The kite will use bits of household linen for its nest; Autolycus will
snatch your sheets)   24 **Autolycus** (son of Chione by Mercury, grandfather of
Ulysses; Homer says he excelled in thieving, and Ovid that "in theft and filching"
he "had no peers")   25 **under Mercury** under the influence of the planet
Mercury (Mercury was the patron of thieves)   26–27 **die and drab** (dice and
whores are responsible for my having no clothes but these)   28 **silly cheat** simple
(petty) theft   28 **knock** beating (the risks of highway robbery, death, or combat
on the road seem too great)

317

Enter Clown.

CLOWN Let me see, every 'leven wether tods, every
tod yields pound and odd shilling; fifteen hundred
shorn, what comes the wool to?

35   AUTOLYCUS [*Aside*] If the springe hold, the cock's mine.

CLOWN I cannot do 't without counters. Let me see,
what am I to buy for our sheep-shearing feast?
Three pound of sugar, five pound of currants, rice—
40   what will this sister of mine do with rice? But my
father hath made her mistress of the feast, and she
lays it on. She hath made me four-and-twenty nose-
gays for the shearers (three-man song-men all, and
very good ones), but they are most of them means
45   and basses; but one Puritan amongst them, and he
sings psalms to hornpipes. I must have saffron to
color the warden pies; mace; dates, none, that's
out of my note; nutmegs, seven; a race or two of
ginger, but that I may beg; four pound of prunes,
50   and as many of raisins o' th' sun.

AUTOLYCUS Oh, that ever I was born!

CLOWN I' th' name of me!

AUTOLYCUS Oh help me, help me; pluck but off these
rags; and then, death, death!

55   CLOWN Alack, poor soul, thou hast need of more rags
to lay on thee, rather than have these off.

AUTOLYCUS Oh sir, the loathsomeness of them offends
me more than the stripes I have received, which are
mighty ones and millions.

60   CLOWN Alas, poor man, a million of beating may come
to a great matter.

32 **every 'leven wether tods** every eleven sheep yield a tod (28 lbs.) of wool
35 **springe** snare   35 **cock's** woodcock's   43 **three-man song-men** singers of
lively catches for three voices   44 **means** tenors   46 **psalms to hornpipes** i.e.,
he is an unusually cheerful Puritan   47 **warden pies** pies made of warden pears
47 **mace** spice made of nutmeg   50 **o' th' sun** sun-dried

AUTOLYCUS I am robbed, sir, and beaten; my money
and apparel ta'en from me, and these detestable
things put upon me.

CLOWN What, by a horseman or a footman?   65

AUTOLYCUS A footman, sweet sir, a footman.

CLOWN Indeed, he should be a footman, by the garments he has left with thee; if this be a horseman's
coat, it hath seen very hot service. Lend me thy
hand, I'll help thee. Come, lend me thy hand.   70
                                        [Helps him up.]

AUTOLYCUS Oh good sir, tenderly, oh!

CLOWN Alas, poor soul!

AUTOLYCUS Oh good sir, softly, good sir; I fear, sir,
my shoulder blade is out.

CLOWN How now? Canst stand?   75

AUTOLYCUS Softly, dear sir; good sir, softly; you ha'
done me a charitable office.
                                        [Picks his pocket.]

CLOWN Dost lack any money? I have a little money
for thee.

AUTOLYCUS No, good sweet sir; no, I beseech you, sir;   80
I have a kinsman not past three-quarters of a mile
hence, unto whom I was going. I shall there have
money, or anything I want; offer me no money, I
pray you; that kills my heart.

CLOWN What manner of fellow was he that robbed   85
you?

AUTOLYCUS A fellow, sir, that I have known to go about
with troll-my-dames; I knew him once a servant
of the Prince. I cannot tell, good sir, for which of
his virtues it was, but he was certainly whipped out   90
of the court.

CLOWN His vices, you would say; there's no virtue

---

65 **footman** foot soldier   88 **troll-my-dames** a game played by women, rather
like bagatelle   92 **vices** (the Clown fails to see Autolycus' little joke)

whipped out of the court; they cherish it to make it
stay there; and yet it will no more but abide.

95   AUTOLYCUS Vices, I would say, sir. I know this man
well; he hath been since an ape-bearer; then a
process-server, a bailiff: then he compassed a motion of the Prodigal Son, and married a tinker's
wife within a mile where my land and living lies;
100   and, having flown over many knavish professions,
he settled only in rogue. Some call him Autolycus.

CLOWN Out upon him! Prig, for my life, prig! He
haunts wakes, fairs, and bear-baitings.

105   AUTOLYCUS Very true, sir; he, sir, he; that's the rogue
that put me into this apparel.

CLOWN Not a more cowardly rogue in all Bohemia; if
you had but looked big, and spit at him, he'd have
run.

110   AUTOLYCUS I must confess to you, sir, I am no fighter;
I am false of heart that way, and that he knew, I
warrant him.

CLOWN How do you now?

AUTOLYCUS Sweet sir, much better than I was. I can
115   stand and walk. I will even take my leave of you,
and pace softly towards my kinsman's.

CLOWN Shall I bring thee on the way?

AUTOLYCUS No, good-faced sir, no, sweet sir.

CLOWN Then fare thee well; I must go buy spices for
120   our sheep-shearing.   Exit.

AUTOLYCUS Prosper you, sweet sir! Your purse is not
hot enough to purchase your spice. I'll be with you
at your sheep-shearing too; if I make not this cheat

---

94 **abide** make a brief stay   96 **ape-bearer** one who carries a monkey about for
exhibition   97 **process-server** server of writs, bailiff   97–98 **compassed a
motion** got possession of a puppet show   98 **Prodigal Son** (a favorite theme for
representation)   99 **land and living** (Autolycus refers grandly to his estates)
103 **Prig** thief

bring out another, and the shearers prove sheep, let
me be unrolled, and my name put in the book of 125
virtue!

Song.

Jog on, jog on, the footpath way,
And merrily hent the stile-a;
A merry heart goes all the day,
Your sad tires in a mile-a.   130

Exit.

Scene IV. [*Bohemia, the Shepherd's cottage*.]

Enter Florizel [*and*] *Perdita*.

FLORIZEL These your unusual weeds to each part of
    you
Do give a life; no shepherdess, but Flora,
Peering in April's front. This your sheep-shearing
Is as a meeting of the petty gods,
And you the Queen on 't.

PERDITA   Sir, my gracious lord,   5
To chide at your extremes it not becomes me—
Oh pardon, that I name them! Your high self,
The gracious mark o' th' land, you have obscured
With a swain's wearing; and me, poor lowly maid,
Most goddesslike pranked up. But that our feasts   10
In every mess have folly, and the feeders
Digest it with a custom, I should blush

125 **unrolled** struck off the honorable list of vagabonds   128 **hent** take hold of (to
leap over)   IV.iv.1 **unusual weeds** unaccustomed garments (Perdita is dressed to
be mistress of the feast)   2 **Flora** (Perdita's costume may have resembled that of
the Roman goddess)   3 **Peering in April's front** i.e., Flora in April, when the
flowers peep out rather than boldly appear   6 **extremes** exaggerations   8 **mark**
the object of everyone's attention   10–12 **our feasts ... custom** our feasts, at
every social level, admit licensed folly, which the guests tolerate, calling it a custom

To see you so attired; swoon, I think,
To show myself a glass.

FLORIZEL   I bless the time
15   When my good falcon made her flight across
Thy father's ground.

PERDITA   Now Jove afford you cause!
To me the difference forges dread; your greatness
Hath not been used to fear. Even now I tremble
To think your father by some accident
20   Should pass this way, as you did: oh, the fates!
How would he look to see his work, so noble,
Vilely bound up? What would he say? Or how
Should I, in these my borrowed flaunts, behold
The sternness of his presence?

FLORIZEL   Apprehend
25   Nothing but jollity. The gods themselves,
Humbling their deities to love, have taken
The shapes of beasts upon them. Jupiter
Became a bull, and bellowed; the green Neptune
A ram, and bleated; and the fire-robed god,
30   Golden Apollo, a poor humble swain,
As I seem now. Their transformations
Were never for a piece of beauty rarer,
Nor in a way so chaste, since my desires
Run not before mine honor, nor my lusts
Burn hotter than my faith.

35   PERDITA   Oh, but sir,
Your resolution cannot hold when 'tis
Opposed, as it must be, by th' power of the King.
One of these two must be necessities,
Which then will speak, that you must change this
          purpose,
Or I my life.

17 **difference** i.e., in our ranks   22 **Vilely bound up** (the analogy is with a good
book shabbily bound)   23 **flaunts** finery   27–30 **Jupiter … swain** (Jupiter took
the shape of a bull to carry off Europa; Neptune became a ram to woo Theophane;
Apollo served as a shepherd to help Admetus win Alcestis)   32 **piece** work of
art   33 **in a way** (he refers to the chastity of his intentions, not to Perdita herself)
38–40 **One of these two … I my life** i.e., the time will come when Florizel will
have to give up his plans, or Perdita will lose her life

FLORIZEL   Thou dearest Perdita,   40
  With these forced thoughts, I prithee, darken not
  The mirth o' th' feast: or I'll be thine, my fair,
  Or not my father's. For I cannot be
  Mine own, nor anything to any, if
  I be not thine. To this I am most constant,   45
  Though destiny say no. Be merry, gentle;
  Strangle such thoughts as these, with anything
  That you behold the while. Your guests are coming;
  Lift up your countenance, as it were the day
  Of celebration of that nuptial, which   50
  We two have sworn shall come.

PERDITA   O Lady Fortune,
  Stand you auspicious!

FLORIZEL   See, your guests approach.
  Address yourself to entertain them sprightly,
  And let's be red with mirth.
        [*Enter*] *Shepherd, Clown, Polixenes, Camillo*
        [*disguised*], *Mopsa, Dorcas, Servants.*

SHEPHERD Fie, daughter! When my old wife lived, upon   55
  This day, she was both pantler, butler, cook;
  Both dame and servant; welcomed all, served all;
  Would sing her song, and dance her turn; now here
  At upper end o' th' table, now i' th' middle;
  On his shoulder, and his; her face o' fire   60
  With labor and the thing she took to quench it,
  She would to each one sip. You are retired,
  As if you were a feasted one, and not
  The hostess of the meeting. Pray you bid
  These unknown friends to 's welcome, for it is   65
  A way to make us better friends, more known.
  Come, quench your blushes, and present yourself
  That which you are, mistress o' th' feast. Come on,
  And bid us welcome to your sheep-shearing,
  As your good flock shall prosper.

PERDITA   [*To Polixenes*] Sir,
  welcome.   70

41 **forced** strained, unduly fearful   42–43 **or ... Or** either ... or   56 **pantler**
keeper of the pantry   60 **on his shoulder** at his shoulder   62 **retired** withdrawn

It is my father's will I should take on me
The hostess-ship o' th' day. [*To Camillo*] You're
    welcome, sir.
Give me those flow'rs there, Dorcas. Reverend sirs,
For you there's rosemary and rue; these keep
75   Seeming and savor all the winter long.
Grace and remembrance be to you both,
And welcome to our shearing!

POLIXENES   Shepherdess—
A fair one are you—well you fit our ages
With flow'rs of winter.

PERDITA   Sir, the year growing ancient,
80   Not yet on summer's death, nor on the birth
Of trembling winter, the fairest flow'rs o' th' season
Are our carnations, and streaked gillyvors,
Which some call Nature's bastards; of that kind
Our rustic garden's barren; and I care not
To get slips of them.

85   POLIXENES   Wherefore, gentle maiden,
Do you neglect them?

PERDITA   For I have heard it said,
There is an art, which in their piedness shares
With great creating Nature.

POLIXENES   Say there be;
Yet Nature is made better by no mean
90   But Nature makes that mean; so over that art,
Which you say adds to Nature, is an art,
That Nature makes. You see, sweet maid, we marry
A gentler scion to the wildest stock,
And make conceive a bark of baser kind
95   By bud of nobler race. This is an art

---

75 **Seeming and savor** color and scent   76 **Grace and remembrance** (rue is
for grace and repentance; rosemary for remembrance, because the fragrance lasted
indefinitely)   82 **gillyvors** pinks (sometimes in modern regional usage, "wall-
flowers"; but here Perdita means carnations, pinks, sweet william—the blooms
have streaks of color, and for this reason were associated with loose women)

Which does mend Nature, change it rather; but
The art itself is Nature.

PERDITA   So it is.

POLIXENES Then make your garden rich in gillyvors,
And do not call them bastards.

PERDITA   I'll not put
The dibble in earth, to set one slip of them;   100
No more than were I painted, I would wish
This youth should say 'twere well, and only therefore
Desire to breed by me. Here's flow'rs for you:
Hot lavender, mints, savory, marjoram,
The marigold that goes to bed wi' th' sun,   105
And with him rises, weeping; these are flow'rs
Of middle summer, and I think they are given
To men of middle age. You're very welcome.

CAMILLO I should leave grazing, were I of your flock,
And only live by gazing.

PERDITA   Out, alas!   110
You'd be so lean that blasts of January
Would blow you through and through. [*To Florizel*]
   Now, my fair'st friend,
I would I had some flow'rs o' th' spring, that might
Become your time of day—[*to Shepherdesses*] and
   yours, and yours,
That wear upon your virgin branches yet   115
Your maidenheads growing. O Proserpina,
For the flow'rs now, that, frighted, thou let'st fall
From Dis's wagon! Daffodils,
That come before the swallow dares, and take
The winds of March with beauty; violets, dim,   120
But sweeter than the lids of Juno's eyes,

---

100 **dibble** tool for making holes to plant seeds or cuttings   104 **Hot lavender** (the epithet has not been satisfactorily explained)   116–18 **Proserpina ... Dis's wagon** (the God of the Underworld bore off Proserpina as she gathered flowers with her mother, Ceres, in the Vale of Enna. Ovid's account [*Metamorphoses* V.398–99] mentions that she dropped the flowers she had picked)   119 **take** charm, captivate

Or Cytherea's breath; pale primroses,
That die unmarried ere they can behold
Bright Phoebus in his strength (a malady
125   Most incident to maids); bold oxlips, and
The crown imperial; lilies of all kinds,
The flower-de-luce being one. O, these I lack
To make you garlands of, and my sweet friend,
To strew him o'er and o'er!

FLORIZEL   What, like a corse?

130   PERDITA No, like a bank for Love to lie and play on;
Not like a corse; or if, not to be buried,
But quick and in mine arms. Come, take your
     flow'rs;
Methinks I play as I have seen them do
In Whitsun pastorals; sure this robe of mine
Does change my disposition.

135   FLORIZEL   What you do
Still betters what is done. When you speak, sweet,
I'd have you do it ever; when you sing,
I'd have you buy and sell so; so give alms,
Pray so; and for the ord'ring your affairs,
140   To sing them too. When you do dance, I wish you
A wave o' th' sea, that you might ever do
Nothing but that—move still, still so,
And own no other function. Each your doing,
So singular in each particular,
145   Crowns what you are doing in the present deeds,
That all your acts are queens.

PERDITA   O Doricles,
Your praises are too large; but that your youth
And the true blood which peeps fairly through 't,

122 **Cytherea's** Venus'   123 **die unmarried** (because it grows in shade, and in
spring, Milton has "the rathe primrose that forsaken dies")   129 **corse** corpse
132 **quick** alive   134 **Whitsun pastorals** (Whitsun was the season for games
related to old spring festivals, and Perdita refers probably to the King and Queen
in these games—identified with Robin Hood and Marian)   143–46 **Each your
doing ... queens** "Your manner in each act crowns the act" (Dr. Johnson)
146 **Doricles** (Florizel's pseudonym)   148 **peeps** shows

Do plainly give you out an unstained shepherd,
With wisdom I might fear, my Doricles,   150
You wooed me the false way.

FLORIZEL   I think you have
As little skill to fear, as I have purpose
To put you to 't. But come, our dance, I pray;
Your hand, my Perdita; so turtles pair
That never mean to part.

PERDITA   I'll swear for 'em.   155

POLIXENES This is the prettiest low-born lass that ever
Ran on the greensward; nothing she does or seems
But smacks of something greater than herself,
Too noble for this place.

CAMILLO   He tells her something
That makes her blood look out; good sooth she is   160
The queen of curds and cream.

CLOWN   Come on, strike up.

DORCAS Mopsa must be your mistress; marry, garlic
To mend her kissing with!

MOPSA   Now, in good time!

CLOWN Not a word, a word, we stand upon our manners.
Come, strike up.   165

Here a dance of Shepherds and Shepherdesses.

POLIXENES Pray, good shepherd, what fair swain is this,
Which dances with your daughter?

SHEPHERD They call him Doricles, and boasts himself
To have a worthy feeding; but I have it

151 **the false way** i.e., by flattery   152 **skill** reason   154 **turtles** doves
160 **blood look out** blush   160 **good sooth** in truth   161 **queen of curds and
cream** (J. D. Wilson argues that Camillo is calling Perdita a "white-pot queen"—
the name given in some May games to the queen, by association with a dish called
"white-pot," made of custard, cream, spices, apples, etc.)   162–63 **garlic . . .
kissing with** use garlic to overcome her bad breath   163 **in good time**
(expression of indignation)   169 **feeding** landed property

170 Upon his own report, and I believe it:
He looks like sooth. He says he loves my daughter;
I think so too; for never gazed the moon
Upon the water, as he'll stand and read,
As 'twere, my daughter's eyes; and, to be plain,
175 I think there is not half a kiss to choose
Who loves another best.

POLIXENES   She dances featly.

SHEPHERD So she does anything, though I report it
That should be silent. If young Doricles
Do light upon her, she shall bring him that
180 Which he not dreams of.

Enter Servant.

SERVANT O master, if you did but hear the peddler at
the door, you would never dance again after a
tabor and pipe; no, the bagpipe could not move
you. He sings several tunes faster than you'll tell
185 money; he utters them as he had eaten ballads,
and all men's ears grew to his tunes.

CLOWN He could never come better; he shall come in;
I love a ballad but even too well, if it be doleful
matter merrily set down; or a very pleasant thing
190 indeed, and sung lamentably.

SERVANT He hath songs for man or woman of all
sizes; no milliner can so fit his customers with gloves.
He has the prettiest love songs for maids, so without
bawdry, which is strange; with such delicate bur-
195 dens of dildos and fadings: "Jump her, and thump
her"; and where some stretch-mouthed rascal
would, as it were, mean mischief, and break a foul
gap into the matter, he makes the maid to answer,

176 **another** the other   176 **featly** nimbly   183 **tabor** little drum   184 **tell**
count   185 **ballads** broadsheet words and music, to familiar tunes and on topical
subjects   194–95 **burdens** refrains   195 **dildos and fadings** (dildos, often
mentioned in ballad refrains, are phalli; fadings are indecent refrains)
195–96 **Jump her and thump her** (familiar ballad refrains)   197–98 **foul gap**
i.e., a break in the song for obscene patter

"Whoop, do me no harm, good man"; puts him
off, slights him, with "Whoop, do me no harm, good   200
man."

POLIXENES This is a brave fellow.

CLOWN Believe me, thou talkest of an admirable
conceited fellow. Has he any unbraided wares?

SERVANT He hath ribbons of all the colors i' th' rain-   205
bow; points, more than all the lawyers in Bohemia
can learnedly handle, though they come to him
by th' gross; inkles, caddisses, cambrics, lawns.
Why, he sings 'em over, as they were gods or
goddesses; you would think a smock were a she-   210
angel, he so chants to the sleevehand, and the
work about the square on 't.

CLOWN Prithee bring him in, and let him approach
singing.

PERDITA Forewarn him that he use no scurrilous words   215
in 's tunes.

                                          [Exit Servant.]

CLOWN You have of these peddlers that have more
in them than you'd think, sister.

PERDITA Ay, good brother, or go about to think.

                Enter Autolycus, singing.

        Lawn as white as driven snow,   220
        Cypress black as e'er was crow,
        Gloves as sweet as damask roses,
        Masks for faces, and for noses;

199 Whoop ... good man (an extant ballad, coarse in character, has this refrain.
The joke in this speech lies in the servant's praising Autolycus for the decency of
his songs, and simultaneously betraying the fact of their indecency)   204 conceited witty   204 unbraided new ("braided wares" are shop-soiled)
206 points tagged laces, by which clothes were held up (with a pun on the sense of
"arguments")   208 gross twelve dozen points (also with reference to clerkly
"engrossing," the lawyer's fair copying)   208 inkles linen tapes   208 caddisses
worsted tapes for garters   211 sleevehand cuff   212 square embroidered yoke
217 You have of these peddlers there are peddlers   219 go about to intend
to   221 Cypress crape   222 Gloves ... roses (it was the fashion to perfume
gloves)   223 Masks ... noses (to protect ladies' faces or noses from the sun)

Bugle-bracelet, necklace-amber,
225   Perfume for a lady's chamber;
Golden quoifs and stomachers
For my lads to give their dears;
Pins and poking-sticks of steel;
What maids lack from head to heel!
230   Come buy of me, come, come buy, come buy,
Buy lads, or else your lasses cry; come buy!

CLOWN If I were not in love with Mopsa, thou shouldst
take no money of me; but being enthralled as I
am, it will also be the bondage of certain ribbons
235   and gloves.

MOPSA I was promised them against the feast, but
they come not too late now.

DORCAS He hath promised you more than that, or there
be liars.

240 MOPSA He hath paid you all he promised you; may
be he has paid you more, which will shame you to
give him again.

CLOWN Is there no manners left among maids? Will
they wear their plackets where they should bear
245   their faces? Is there not milking-time, when you are
going to bed, or kiln-hole, to whistle of these
secrets, but you must be tittle-tattling before all our
guests? 'Tis well they are whis'pring. Clammer
your tongues, and not a word more.

---

224 **Bugle-bracelet** bracelet of beads   226 **quoifs** head scarves   228 **poking-sticks** metal rods used in ironing starched ruffs   234 **bondage** i.e., he is a prisoner of Mopsa, and will take the fairings into captivity with him   236 **against** before   241–42 **paid you more ... give him again** (this girlish insult means: "Perhaps he has made you pregnant")   244 **plackets** petticoats, or slits in petticoats (often used indecently. Here the Clown merely means that they should not as it were wash their dirty linen in public)   246 **kiln-hole** the place containing the fire for malt making (convenient for confidential talk)   248 **Clammer** silence (technical term in bellringing)

MOPSA I have done. Come, you promised me a 250
tawdry-lace, and a pair of sweet gloves.

CLOWN Have I not told thee how I was cozened by the
way, and lost all my money?

AUTOLYCUS And indeed, sir, there are cozeners abroad;
therefore it behooves men to be wary. 255

CLOWN Fear not thou, man; thou shalt lose nothing
here.

AUTOLYCUS I hope so, sir, for I have about me many
parcels of charge.

CLOWN What hast here? Ballads? 260

MOPSA Pray now, buy some. I love a ballad in print,
a-life, for then we are sure they are true.

AUTOLYCUS Here's one to a very doleful tune, how a
usurer's wife was brought to bed of twenty money-
bags at a burden, and how she longed to eat adders' 265
heads and toads carbonadoed.

MOPSA Is it true, think you?

AUTOLYCUS Very true, and but a month old.

DORCAS Bless me from marrying a usurer!

AUTOLYCUS Here's the midwife's name to 't: one Mis- 270
tress Taleporter, and five or six honest wives that
were present. Why should I carry lies abroad?

MOPSA Pray you now, buy it.

CLOWN Come on, lay it by, and let's first see moe
ballads; we'll buy the other things anon. 275

AUTOLYCUS Here's another ballad, of a fish that appeared upon the coast on Wednesday the fourscore of April, forty thousand fathom above water,
and sung this ballad against the hard hearts of

251 **tawdry-lace** silk worn around the neck (called after St. Audrey [Ethelreda], who was punished for youthful ostentation—especially fine necklaces—by a tumor in the throat)   259 **parcels of charge** goods of value   262 **a-life** dearly   266 **carbonadoed** cut up and broiled   274 **moe** more   276 **of a fish** (records of very similar ballads survive)

331

280   maids; it was thought she was a woman, and was
       turned into a cold fish for she would not exchange
       flesh with one that loved her. The ballad is very
       pitiful, and as true.

DORCAS Is it true too, think you?

285 AUTOLYCUS Five justices' hands at it, and witnesses
       more than my pack will hold.

CLOWN Lay it by too; another.

AUTOLYCUS This is a merry ballad, but a very pretty
       one.

290 MOPSA Let's have some merry ones.

AUTOLYCUS Why, this is a passing merry one, and goes
       to the tune of "Two Maids Wooing a Man." There's
       scarce a maid westward but she sings it; 'tis in
       request, I can tell you.

295 MOPSA We can both sing it. If thou 'lt bear a part, thou
       shalt hear; 'tis in three parts.

DORCAS We had the tune on 't, a month ago.

AUTOLYCUS I can bear my part, you must know 'tis
       my occupation. Have at it with you.

Song.

300 AUTOLYCUS   Get you hence, for I must go
                    Where it fits not you to know.

    DORCAS   Whither?

    MOPSA   O whither?

    DORCAS   Whither?

305 MOPSA   It becomes thy oath full well,
                    Thou to me thy secrets tell.

    DORCAS   Me too; let me go thither.

    MOPSA   Or thou go'st to th' grange or mill,

    DORCAS   If to either thou dost ill.

310 AUTOLYCUS   Neither.

    DORCAS   What, neither?

332

AUTOLYCUS	Neither.
DORCAS	Thou hast sworn my love to be.
MOPSA	Thou hast sworn it more to me.
	Then whither goest? Say, whither? 315

CLOWN We'll have this song out anon by ourselves;
my father and the gentlemen are in sad talk, and
we'll not trouble them. Come bring away thy pack
after me; wenches, I'll buy for you both. Peddler,
let's have the first choice; follow me, girls.   320
                    [*Exeunt Clown, Dorcas, and Mopsa.*]

AUTOLYCUS And you shall pay well for 'em.

Song.

Will you buy any tape, or lace for your cape,
     My dainty duck, my dear-a?
Any silk, any thread, any toys for your head,
     Of the new'st, and fin'st fin'st wear-a?   325
Come to the peddler, money's a meddler,
     That doth utter all men's ware-a.

                                   Exit.

Enter Servant.

SERVANT Master, there is three carters, three shepherds,
three   neatherds,   three   swineherds   that   have
made themselves all men of hair; they call them-   330
selves saltiers, and they have a dance, which the
wenches say is a gallimaufry of gambols, because
they are not in 't; but they themselves are o' th'
mind, if it be not too rough for some that know
little but bowling, it will please plentifully.   335

SHEPHERD Away! We'll none on 't; here has been too
much homely foolery already. I know, sir, we weary
you.

POLIXENES You weary those that refresh us; pray let's
see these four threes of herdsmen.

317 **sad** serious   327 **utter** put forth   329 **neatherds** cowherds   330 **men of hair** hairy men, satyrs (or the wild men of medieval art and entertainment) 331 **saltiers**, satyrs (or perhaps leapers, vaulters, from Fr. *saultier*, "vaulter") 332 **gallimaufry** hodgepodge   335 **bowling** (here, a gentle activity, contrasted with the acrobatic dance)

340 SERVANT One three of them, by their own report, sir,
     hath danced before the King; and not the worst
     of the three but jumps twelve foot and a half by
     th' squier.

SHEPHERD Leave your prating; since these good men
345 are pleased, let them come in; but quickly now.

SERVANT Why, they stay at door, sir.   [*Exit.*]

Here a dance of twelve Satyrs.

POLIXENES [*To Shepherd*] O father, you'll know more
     of that hereafter.
     [*To Camillo*] Is it not too far gone? 'Tis time to part
     them.
     He's simple and tells much. How now, fair
     shepherd!
350 Your heart is full of something that does take
     Your mind from feasting. Sooth, when I was young,
     And handed love as you do, I was wont
     To load my she with knacks; I would have ransacked
     The peddler's silken treasury, and have poured it
355 To her acceptance: you have let him go,
     And nothing marted with him. If your lass
     Interpretation should abuse, and call this
     Your lack of love or bounty, you were straited
     For a reply, at least if you make a care
     Of happy holding her.

360 FLORIZEL   Old sir, I know
     She prizes not such trifles as these are;
     The gifts she looks from me are packed and locked
     Up in my heart, which I have given already,
     But not delivered. O, hear me breathe my life
365 Before this ancient sir, who, it should seem,
     Hath sometime loved: I take thy hand, this hand
     As soft as dove's down, and as white as it,

341 **before the King** (the performers of this dance had certainly done so, perhaps
in this very dance) 343 **squier** rule 352 **handed** dealt with 356 **marted with**
bought of 357 **Interpretation should abuse** choose to misunderstand
358 **straited** in difficulties 363–64 **given ... delivered** the deal is settled, but
the goods not yet handed over

Or Ethiopian's tooth, or the fanned snow that's
  bolted
By th' northern blasts twice o'er—

POLIXENES   What follows this?
How prettily th' young swain seems to wash   370
The hand was fair before! I have put you out;
But to your protestation: let me hear
What you profess.

FLORIZEL   Do, and be witness to 't.

POLIXENES And this my neighbor too?

FLORIZEL   And he, and more
Than he, and men; the earth, the heavens, and all: 375
That were I crowned the most imperial monarch,
Thereof most worthy; were I the fairest youth
That ever made eye swerve; had force and
  knowledge
More than was ever man's, I would not prize them
Without her love; for her, employ them all,   380
Commend them, and condemn them to her service,
Or to their own perdition.

POLIXENES   Fairly offered.

CAMILLO This shows a sound affection.

SHEPHERD   But, my daughter,
Say you the like to him?

PERDITA   I cannot speak
So well, nothing so well; no, nor mean better.   385
By th' pattern of mine own thoughts I cut out
The purity of his.

SHEPHERD   Take hands, a bargain;
And friends unknown, you shall bear witness to 't:
I give my daughter to him, and will make
Her portion equal his.

FLORIZEL   O, that must be   390

368 **bolted** sifted 371 **was fair** that was fair 381–82 **Commend ... perdition**
commend them to her service, or condemn them to their own perdition

I' th' virtue of your daughter. One being dead,
I shall have more than you can dream of yet,
Enough then for your wonder. But come on,
Contract us 'fore these witnesses.

SHEPHERD   Come, your hand;
And, daughter, yours.

395 POLIXENES   Soft, swain, awhile, beseech you,
Have you a father?

FLORIZEL   I have; but what of him?

POLIXENES Knows he of this?

FLORIZEL   He neither does, nor shall.

POLIXENES Methinks a father
Is at the nuptial of his son a guest
400 That best becomes the table. Pray you once more,
Is not your father grown incapable
Of reasonable affairs? Is he not stupid
With age and alt'ring rheums? Can he speak, hear?
Know man from man? Dispute his own estate?
405 Lies he not bed-rid? And again does nothing
But what he did being childish?

FLORIZEL   No, good sir;
He has his health, and ampler strength indeed
Than most have of his age.

POLIXENES   By my white beard,
You offer him, if this be so, a wrong
410 Something unfilial. Reason my son
Should choose himself a wife, but as good reason
The father, all whose joy is nothing else
But fair posterity, should hold some counsel
In such a business.

FLORIZEL   I yield all this;
415 But for some other reasons, my grave sir,
Which 'tis not fit you know, I not acquaint

392-93 **I shall have more ... your wonder** I shall have more than you can at
this time dream of, and enough to amaze you when you know of it   403 **alt'ring
rheums** i.e., rheumatic afflictions which disturb his judgment   410 **Reason my
son** there is reason that my son

My father of this business.

POLIXENES   Let him know 't.

FLORIZEL He shall not.

POLIXENES   Prithee, let him.

FLORIZEL   No, he must not.

SHEPHERD Let him, my son; he shall not need to grieve
At knowing of thy choice.

FLORIZEL   Come, come, he must not.   420
Mark our contract.

POLIXENES [*Discovering himself*] Mark your divorce,
    young sir,
Whom son I dare not call; thou art too base
To be acknowledged. Thou, a scepter's heir,
That thus affect'st a sheep-hook! Thou, old traitor,
I am sorry that by hanging thee, I can   425
But shorten thy life one week. And thou, fresh piece
Of excellent witchcraft, who of force must know
The royal fool thou cop'st with——

SHEPHERD   O my heart!

POLIXENES I'll have thy beauty scratched with briers
    and made
More homely than thy state. For thee, fond boy,   430
If I may ever know thou dost but sigh
That thou no more shalt see this knack—as never
I mean thou shalt—we'll bar thee from succession;
Not hold thee of our blood, no not our kin,
Farre than Deucalion off. Mark thou my words.   435
Follow us to the court. Thou, churl, for this time,
Though full of our displeasure, yet we free thee
From the dead blow of it. And you, enchantment,

---

421 **contract** (J. D. Wilson in the New Cambridge edition points out that "we
have here a description, all but the final solemn words, of one of those betrothal
ceremonies which were held as legally binding as marriage in church")
424 **affect'st** desirest, lovest   435 **Farre than Deucalion off** further back than
Deucalion (legendary ancient king of Thessaly)

Worthy enough a herdsman—yea him, too,
440   That makes himself, but for our honor therein,
Unworthy thee—if ever henceforth thou
These rural latches to his entrance open,
Or hoop his body more with thy embraces,
I will devise a death as cruel for thee
As thou art tender to 't.   *Exit*.

445   PERDITA   Even here undone!
I was not much afeard; for once or twice
I was about to speak and tell him plainly,
The selfsame sun that shines upon his court
Hides not his visage from our cottage, but
Looks on alike. [*To Florizel*] Will 't please you, sir,
450   be gone?
I told you what would come of this. Beseech you,
Of your own state take care: this dream of mine
Being now awake, I'll queen it no inch farther,
But milk my ewes, and weep.

CAMILLO   Why, how now, father!
Speak ere thou diest.

455   SHEPHERD   I cannot speak nor think,
Nor dare to know that which I know. [*To Florizel*]
       O sir,
You have undone a man of fourscore three,
That thought to fill his grave in quiet, yea,
To die upon the bed my father died,
460   To lie close by his honest bones; but now
Some hangman must put on my shroud, and lay me
Where no priest shovels in dust. Oh cursèd wretch,
That knew'st this was the Prince, and wouldst
       adventure
To mingle faith with him! Undone, undone!
465   If I might die within this hour, I have lived
To die when I desire.   *Exit*.

FLORIZEL   Why look you so upon me?

439–41 **yea him … Unworthy thee** indeed, you're worthy of Florizel—whose
conduct has made him, save for the fact of his being my son, unworthy of you
462 **Where no priest shovels in dust** (before the Reformation, and even in the
First Prayer Book of Edward VI, the priest was directed to do this. Felons were
buried by the gallows)

I am but sorry, not afeard; delayed,
But nothing altered. What I was, I am;
More straining on, for plucking back; not following
My leash unwillingly.

CAMILLO   Gracious my lord,   470
You know your father's temper; at this time
He will allow no speech—which I do guess
You do not purpose to him—and as hardly
Will he endure your sight as yet, I fear;
Then, till the fury of his Highness settle,   475
Come not before him.

FLORIZEL   I not purpose it.
I think, Camillo?

CAMILLO   Even he, my lord.

PERDITA How often have I told you 'twould be thus?
How often said my dignity would last
But till 'twere known?

FLORIZEL   It cannot fail, but by   480
The violation of my faith, and then
Let Nature crush the sides o' th' earth together,
And mar the seeds within. Lift up thy looks;
From my succession wipe me, father, I
Am heir to my affection.

CAMILLO   Be advised.   485

FLORIZEL I am, and by my fancy; if my reason
Will thereto be obedient, I have reason;
If not, my senses better pleased with madness,
Do bid it welcome.

CAMILLO   This is desperate, sir.

469–70 **More straining on ... unwillingly** (the image is of a hound. Florizel
continues on his chosen course, all the more strongly for having been dragged
back; he is not going to do as his father says against his will) 482–83 **Let Nature
... the seeds within** (for this image of the end of creation compare *Macbeth*
IV.i.59 and *Lear* III.ii.8) 486–88 **fancy ... reason ... madness** if the fancy,
which makes images, is not obedient to the reason—a higher mental power—the
result is madness or dream (Florizel wants his reason to obey his fancy; otherwise,
he says, he'd rather be mad. For the psychology involved, see *Midsummer Night's
Dream* V.i.2 ff.)

490 FLORIZEL So call it, but it does fulfill my vow;
          I needs must think it honesty. Camillo,
          Not for Bohemia, nor the pomp that may
          Be thereat gleaned; for all the sun sees or
          The close earth wombs or the profound seas hide
495   In unknown fathoms, will I break my oath
          To this my fair beloved. Therefore, I pray you,
          As you have ever been my father's honored friend,
          When he shall miss me, as in faith I mean not
          To see him any more, cast your good counsels
500   Upon his passion; let myself and Fortune
          Tug for the time to come. This you may know,
          And so deliver: I am put to sea
          With her whom here I cannot hold on shore;
          And most opportune to her need, I have
505   A vessel rides fast by, but not prepared
          For this design. What course I mean to hold
          Shall nothing benefit your knowledge, nor
          Concern me the reporting.

     CAMILLO   O my lord,
          I would your spirit were easier for advice,
          Or stronger for your need.

510 FLORIZEL   Hark, Perdita——
          [To Camillo] I'll hear you by and by.

     CAMILLO   He's irremovable,
          Resolved for flight. Now were I happy if
          His going I could frame to serve my turn,
          Save him from danger, do him love and honor,
515   Purchase the sight again of dear Sicilia,
          And that unhappy king, my master, whom
          I so much thirst to see.

     FLORIZEL   Now, good Camillo,
          I am so fraught with curious business that
          I leave out ceremony.

     CAMILLO   Sir, I think

501 **Tug** contend, strive 504 **opportune** (accent on second syllable)
518 **curious** needing great care 519 **ceremony** (Florizel is apologizing for
having broken away from Camillo to hold his urgent private talk with Perdita)

340

You have heard of my poor services i' th' love   520
That I have borne your father?

FLORIZEL   Very nobly
Have you deserved; it is my father's music
To speak your deeds, not little of his care
To have them recompensed, as thought on.

CAMILLO   Well, my lord,
If you may please to think I love the King,   525
And through him what's nearest to him, which is
Your gracious self, embrace but my direction,
If your more ponderous and settled project
May suffer alteration. On mine honor,
I'll point you where you shall have such receiving   530
As shall become your Highness, where you may
Enjoy your mistress; from the whom, I see
There's no disjunction to be made, but by—
As heavens forfend—your ruin; marry her;
And with my best endeavors, in your absence,   535
Your discontenting father strive to qualify
And bring him up to liking.

FLORIZEL   How, Camillo,
May this, almost a miracle, be done?
That I may call thee something more than man,
And after that trust to thee.

CAMILLO   Have you thought on   540
A place whereto you'll go?

FLORIZEL   Not any yet;
But as th' unthought-on accident is guilty
To what we wildly do, so we profess
Ourselves to be the slaves of chance, and flies
Of every wind that blows.

CAMILLO   Then list to me.   545
This follows, if you will not change your purpose,

527 **direction** advice   536 **discontenting** displeased   536 **qualify** appease,
moderate (used, for example, of tempering wine with water)   542–45 **But as ...
wind that blows** since we are compelled to this wild behavior by a chance we
never foresaw, we think of ourselves as the slaves of chance, and will go where it
sends us, like flies in a wind   545 **list** listen

But undergo this flight: make for Sicilia,
And there present yourself and your fair princess
(For so I see she must be) 'fore Leontes.
550   She shall be habited as it becomes
The partner of your bed. Methinks I see
Leontes opening his free arms and weeping
His welcomes forth; asks thee, the son, forgiveness,
As 'twere i' th' father's person; kisses the hands
555   Of your fresh princess; o'er and o'er divides him
'Twixt his unkindness and his kindness: th' one
He chides to hell, and bids the other grow
Faster than thought or time.

FLORIZEL   Worthy Camillo,
What color for my visitation shall I
Hold up before him?

560   CAMILLO   Sent by the King your father
To greet him, and to give him comforts. Sir,
The manner of your bearing towards him, with
What you, as from your father, shall deliver,
Things known betwixt us three, I'll write you down,
565   The which shall point you forth at every sitting
What you must say, that he shall not perceive,
But that you have your father's bosom there,
And speak his very heart.

FLORIZEL   I am bound to you;
There is some sap in this.

CAMILLO   A course more promising
570   Than a wild dedication of yourselves
To unpathed waters, undreamed shores, most certain
To miseries enough: no hope to help you,
But as you shake off one, to take another;
Nothing so certain as your anchors, who
575   Do their best office if they can but stay you,
Where you'll be loath to be. Besides, you know,
Prosperity's the very bond of love,

558 **Faster** firmer   559 **color** pretext   566–67 **perceive,/ But that** know otherwise than that   569 **sap** life fluid   575 **stay** hold

Whose fresh complexion and whose heart together
Affliction alters.

PERDITA   One of these is true:
I think affliction may subdue the cheek,   580
But not take in the mind.

CAMILLO   Yea? Say you so?
There shall not at your father's house these seven
      years
Be born another such.

FLORIZEL   My good Camillo,
She is as forward of her breeding as
She is i' th' rear our birth.

CAMILLO   I cannot say 'tis pity   585
She lacks instructions, for she seems a mistress
To most that teach.

PERDITA   Your pardon, sir; for this,
I'll blush you thanks.

FLORIZEL   My prettiest Perdita!
But O, the thorns we stand upon! Camillo—
Preserver of my father, now of me,   590
The medicine of our house—how shall we do?
We are not furnished like Bohemia's son,
Nor shall appear in Sicilia.

CAMILLO   My lord,
Fear none of this. I think you know my fortunes
Do all lie there; it shall be so my care   595
To have you royally appointed, as if
The scene you play were mine. For instance, sir,
That you may know you shall not want—one word.
                                        [*They talk aside.*]
                    Enter Autolycus.

AUTOLYCUS Ha, ha, what a fool Honesty is! And

582 **these seven years** (used to signify a long, indefinite period)   584–85 **She is
as forward ... our birth** she is as far in advance of the way of life she was reared
to as she is inferior to us in birth   591 **medicine** physician   593 **appear** appear
so (the second word may have dropped out)   596 **royally appointed** equipped
like a prince   599 **Ha, ha, what a fool** ... (these lines echo passages in Greene's
Second Part of Conny-catching [1592]. The character of Autolycus, and the account
of the tricks of his trade, is indebted to this book)

600   Trust, his sworn brother, a very simple gentleman. I
      have sold all my trumpery: not a counterfeit stone,
      not a ribbon, glass, pomander, brooch, table-book,
      ballad, knife, tape, glove, shoe-tie, bracelet, horn-
      ring, to keep my pack from fasting. They throng
605   who should buy first, as if my trinkets had been
      hallowed, and brought a benediction to the buyer;
      by which means I saw whose purse was best in
      picture, and what I saw to my good use I remem-
      bered. My clown, who wants but something to be
610   a reasonable man, grew so in love with the wenches'
      song, that he would not stir his pettitoes till he had
      both tune and words, which so drew the rest of the
      herd to me that all their other senses stuck in ears:
      you might have pinched a placket, it was senseless;
615   'twas nothing to geld a codpiece of a purse; I would
      have filed keys off that hung in chains. No hearing,
      no feeling, but my sir's song, and admiring the
      nothing of it. So that in this time of lethargy I
      picked and cut most of their festival purses; and had
620   not the old man come in with a hubbub against his
      daughter and the King's son, and scared my
      choughs from the chaff, I had not left a purse
      alive in the whole army.

              [*Camillo, Florizel, and Perdita come forward.*]

CAMILLO Nay, but my letters, by this means being there
625   So soon as you arrive, shall clear that doubt.

FLORIZEL And those that you'll procure from King
      Leontes?

CAMILLO Shall satisfy your father.

PERDITA   Happy be you!
      All that you speak shows fair.

CAMILLO [*Seeing Autolycus*] Who have we here?
      We'll make an instrument of this, omit

602 **table-book** notebook   606 **hallowed** sacred   607-8 **in picture** to look
at (?)   611 **pettitoes** toes (especially of a pig)   617 **my sir's** the Clown's
618 **nothing** nothingness, nonsense (with perhaps, as Wilson suggests, a pun on
"noting")   622 **choughs** fools

Nothing may give us aid.   630

AUTOLYCUS If they have overheard me now—why,
    hanging.

CAMILLO How now, good fellow, why shak'st thou so?
    Fear not, man; here's no harm intended to thee.

AUTOLYCUS I am a poor fellow, sir.

CAMILLO Why, be so still; here's nobody will steal that   635
    from thee. Yet for the outside of thy poverty we
    must make an exchange; therefore discase thee
    instantly—thou must think there's a necessity in 't
    —and change garments with this gentleman; though
    the pennyworth on his side be the worst, yet hold   640
    thee, there's some boot. [*Giving money.*]

AUTOLYCUS I am a poor fellow, sir. [*Aside*] I know ye
    well enough.

CAMILLO Nay, prithee dispatch; the gentleman is half
    flayed already.   645

AUTOLYCUS Are you in earnest, sir? [*Aside*] I smell
    the trick on 't.

FLORIZEL Dispatch, I prithee.

AUTOLYCUS Indeed, I have had earnest, but I cannot
    with conscience take it.   650

CAMILLO Unbuckle, unbuckle.

    [*Florizel and Autolycus exchange garments.*]

Fortunate mistress—let my prophecy
Come home to ye—you must retire yourself
Into some covert; take your sweetheart's hat
And pluck it o'er your brows, muffle your face,   655
Dismantle you, and, as you can, disliken
The truth of your own seeming, that you may

---

637 **discase** undress   641 **boot** extra reward   645 **flayed** skinned (undressed)
649 **earnest** money paid as installment, "deposit"   652 **prophecy** (the prophecy
is the form of address, "Fortunate mistress!")   656-57 **disliken ... seeming** (a
complicated way of saying "alter your usual appearance," which may indicate
Shakespeare's obsessive interest in problems related to "truth" and "seeming")

    (For I do fear eyes over) to shipboard
    Get undescried.

PERDITA   I see the play so lies
    That I must bear a part.

660 CAMILLO   No remedy.
    Have you done there?

FLORIZEL   Should I now meet my father,
    He would not call me son.

CAMILLO   Nay, you shall have no hat.
                  [*Giving hat to Perdita.*]
    Come, lady, come; farewell, my friend.

AUTOLYCUS   Adieu, sir.

FLORIZEL O Perdita, what have we twain forgot?
665   Pray you, a word.

CAMILLO [*Aside*] What I do next shall be to tell the
      King
    Of this escape, and whither they are bound;
    Wherein my hope is, I shall so prevail
    To force him after; in whose company
670   I shall re-view Sicilia, for whose sight
    I have a woman's longing.

FLORIZEL   Fortune speed us!
    Thus we set on, Camillo, to th' seaside.

CAMILLO The swifter speed, the better.
              Exit [*Camillo, with Florizel and Perdita*].

AUTOLYCUS I understand the business, I hear it. To have
675   an open ear, a quick eye, and a nimble hand, is
    necessary for a cutpurse; a good nose is requisite
    also, to smell out work for th' other senses. I see
    this is the time that the unjust man doth thrive. What
    an exchange had this been without boot! What a
680   boot is here, with this exchange! Sure, the gods do
    this year connive at us, and we may do anything

658 **eyes over** watching, spying eyes   681 **connive at** close their eyes to

extempore. The Prince himself is about a piece of
iniquity—stealing away from his father, with his
clog at his heels; if I thought it were a piece of
honesty to acquaint the King withal, I would not   685
do 't. I hold it the more knavery to conceal it; and
therein am I constant to my profession.

Enter Clown and Shepherd.

Aside, aside! Here is more matter for a hot brain.
Every lane's end, every shop, church, session,
hanging, yields a careful man work.   690

CLOWN See, see, what a man you are now! There is
no other way but to tell the King she's a changeling,
and none of your flesh and blood.

SHEPHERD Nay, but hear me.

CLOWN Nay, but hear me.   695

SHEPHERD Go to, then.

CLOWN She being none of your flesh and blood, your
flesh and blood has not offended the King, and so
your flesh and blood is not to be punished by him.
Show those things you found about her, those   700
secret things, all but what she has with her. This
being done, let the law go whistle; I warrant you.

SHEPHERD I will tell the King all, every word, yea, and
his son's pranks too; who, I may say, is no honest
man, neither to his father nor to me, to go about to   705
make me the King's brother-in-law.

CLOWN Indeed brother-in-law was the farthest off you
could have been to him; and then your blood had
been the dearer by I know not how much an ounce.

AUTOLYCUS [*Aside*] Very wisely, puppies!   710

SHEPHERD Well, let us to the King; there is that in this
fardel will make him scratch his beard.

AUTOLYCUS [*Aside*] I know not what impediment this
complaint may be to the flight of my master.

684 **clog** hindrance (Perdita)   712 **fardel** bundle

347

715 CLOWN Pray heartily he be at palace.

AUTOLYCUS [*Aside*] Though I am not naturally honest,
I am so sometimes by chance. Let me pocket up my
peddler's excrement. [*Takes off false beard.*] How
now, rustics, whither are you bound?

720 SHEPHERD To th' palace, an it like your worship.

AUTOLYCUS Your affairs there, what, with whom, the
condition of that fardel, the place of your dwelling,
your names, your ages, of what having, breeding,
and anything that is fitting to be known, discover.

725 CLOWN We are but plain fellows, sir.

AUTOLYCUS A lie: you are rough, and hairy. Let me
have no lying; it becomes none but tradesmen, and
they often give us soldiers the lie, but we pay them
for it with stamped coin, not stabbing steel; there-
730 fore they do not give us the lie.

CLOWN Your worship had like to have given us one,
if you had not taken yourself with the manner.

SHEPHERD Are you a courtier, an 't like you, sir?

AUTOLYCUS Whether it like me or no, I am a courtier.
735 Seest thou not the air of the court in these enfold-
ings? Hath not my gait in it the measure of the
court? Receives not thy nose court-odor from me?
Reflect I not on thy baseness court-contempt?
Think'st thou, for that I insinuate, or toaze from
740 thee thy business, I am therefore no courtier? I am
courtier cap-a-pé; and one that will either push

715 at palace (the Clown speaks of the King being "at palace" as he might of an
ordinary man being "at home" [Cambridge editors])   718 excrement i.e., his
false beard (hair, beard, and nails were called "excrement," from L. *excrescere*, to
grow out)   721 what, with whom (parodying a form of legal questioning to
terrify the rustics)   723 having property   727–30 it becomes none ... give us
the lie (tradesmen give the lie by giving short measure, but the simple soldier
nevertheless pays them for the lie with money, not with his sword—so the
tradesmen are not, after all, *giving* the lie; they are selling it [J. D. Wilson's
explanation])   732 with the manner in the act (at first Autolycus was about to lie
by saying "give" instead of "sell" when speaking of the tradesmen; but he caught
himself in the act and changed his statement)   733 courtier (Autolycus is wearing
Florizel's festive clothes)   736 measure stately tread   739 toaze tease,
worry, comb out   741 cap-a-pé head-to-foot (of armor; here, thorough, complete)

on or pluck back thy business there; whereupon I
command thee to open thy affair.

SHEPHERD My business, sir, is to the King.

AUTOLYCUS What advocate hast thou to him?   745

SHEPHERD I know not, an 't like you.

CLOWN Advocate's the court-word for a pheasant; say
you have none.

SHEPHERD None, sir; I have no pheasant, cock nor hen.

AUTOLYCUS How blessed are we that are not simple men!   750
Yet Nature might have made me as these are,
Therefore I will not disdain.

CLOWN This cannot be but a great courtier.

SHEPHERD His garments are rich, but he wears them
not handsomely.   755

CLOWN He seems to be the more noble in being fan-
tastical. A great man, I'll warrant; I know by the
picking on 's teeth.

AUTOLYCUS The fardel there? What's i' th' fardel?
Wherefore that box?   760

SHEPHERD Sir, there lies such secrets in this fardel and
box, which none must know but the King, and which
he shall know within this hour, if I may come to th'
speech of him.

AUTOLYCUS Age, thou hast lost thy labor.   765

SHEPHERD Why, sir?

AUTOLYCUS The King is not at the palace; he is gone
aboard a new ship, to purge melancholy and air
himself; for if thou be'st capable of things serious,
thou must know the King is full of grief.   770

SHEPHERD So 'tis said, sir—about his son, that should
have married a shepherd's daughter.

AUTOLYCUS If that shepherd be not in handfast, let
him fly; the curses he shall have, the tortures he
shall feel, will break the back of man, the heart of   775
monster.

CLOWN Think you so, sir?

747 Advocate's ... pheasant (the Clown, misunderstanding the word, thinks
Autolycus is referring to the practice of bribing the judge with a bird)
758 picking on 's teeth (regarded as an elegant practice)   773 handfast custody

AUTOLYCUS Not he alone shall suffer what wit can
make heavy, and vengeance bitter; but those that
780   are germane to him, though removed fifty times,
shall all come under the hangman; which, though
it be great pity, yet it is necessary. An old sheep-
whistling rogue, a ram-tender, to offer to have his
daughter come into grace! Some say he shall be
785   stoned; but that death is too soft for him, say I.
Draw our throne into a sheepcote! All deaths are
too few, the sharpest too easy.

CLOWN Has the old man e'er a son, sir, do you hear,
an 't like you, sir?

790   AUTOLYCUS He has a son—who shall be flayed alive,
then 'nointed over with honey, set on the head of a
wasp's nest; then stand till he be three-quarters and a
dram dead; then recovered again with aqua-vitae or
some other hot infusion; then, raw as he is, and in
795   the hottest day prognostication proclaims, shall he
be set against a brick wall, the sun looking with a
southward eye upon him, where he is to behold
him with flies blown to death. But what talk we of
these traitorly rascals, whose miseries are to be
800   smiled at, their offenses being so capital? Tell me,
for you seem to be honest plain men, what you have
to the King; being something gently considered,
I'll bring you where he is aboard, tender your
persons to his presence, whisper him in your be-
805   halfs; and if it be in man besides the King to effect
your suits, here is man shall do it.

CLOWN He seems to be of great authority. Close with
him, give him gold; and though authority be a
stubborn bear, yet he is oft led by the nose with
810   gold. Show the inside of your purse to the outside of
his hand, and no more ado. Remember—stoned,
and flayed alive.

SHEPHERD An 't please you, sir, to undertake the busi-

780 germane related   795 prognostication weather forecast in the almanac for
the year   802 being something gently considered if you bribe me like a
gentleman (handsomely)   803 tender present   807-8 Close with him accept his
offer

ness for us, here is that gold I have; I'll make it as
much more, and leave this young man in pawn till   815
I bring it you.

AUTOLYCUS After I have done what I promised?

SHEPHERD Ay, sir.

AUTOLYCUS Well, give me the moiety. Are you a
party in this business?   820

CLOWN In some sort, sir; but though my case be a
pitiful one, I hope shall not be flayed out of it.

AUTOLYCUS Oh, that's the case of the shepherd's son:
hang him, he'll be made an example.

CLOWN Comfort, good comfort! We must to the King,   825
and show our strange sights; he must know 'tis none
of your daughter, nor my sister; we are gone else.
Sir, I will give you as much as this old man does
when the business is performed, and remain, as he
says, your pawn till it be brought you.   830

AUTOLYCUS I will trust you. Walk before toward the
seaside, go on the right hand; I will but look upon
the hedge, and follow you.

CLOWN We are blessed, in this man, as I may say, even
blessed.   835

SHEPHERD Let's before, as he bids us. He was provided
to do us good.

[Exeunt Shepherd and Clown.]

AUTOLYCUS If I had a mind to be honest, I see Fortune
would not suffer me: she drops booties in my mouth.
I am courted now with a double occasion—gold,   840
and a means to do the Prince, my master, good;
which who knows how that may turn back to my
advancement? I will bring these two moles, these
blind ones, aboard him. If he think it fit to shore
them again, and that the complaint they have to the   845
King concerns him nothing, let him call me rogue
for being so far officious; for I am proof against that
title, and what shame else belongs to 't. To him will
I present them, there may be matter in it.   *Exit.*

819 moiety half   821–22 case ... flayed (punning on case/skin)   832–33 **look
upon the hedge** i.e., relieve himself   842 **turn back** redound

ACT V

Scene I. [*Sicilia, the Court of Leontes.*]

Enter Leontes, Cleomenes, Dion, Paulina, Servants.

CLEOMENES Sir, you have done enough, and have
    performed
A saintlike sorrow. No fault could you make
Which you have not redeemed; indeed paid down
More penitence than done trespass. At the last,
5 Do as the heavens have done: forget your evil;
With them forgive yourself.

LEONTES   Whilst I remember
Her and her virtues, I cannot forget
My blemishes in them, and so still think of
The wrong I did myself; which was so much,
10 That heirless it hath made my kingdom, and
Destroyed the sweet'st companion that e'er man
Bred his hopes out of.

PAULINA   True, too true, my lord.
If one by one you wedded all the world,
Or from the all that are took something good
15 To make a perfect woman, she you killed
Would be unparalleled.

LEONTES   I think so. Killed?
She I killed! I did so; but thou strik'st me
Sorely, to say I did—it is as bitter
Upon thy tongue as in my thought. Now, good now,
Say so but seldom.

20 CLEOMENES   Not at all, good lady:

You might have spoken a thousand things that would
Have done the time more benefit, and graced
Your kindness better.

PAULINA   You are one of those
Would have him wed again.

DION   If you would not so,
You pity not the state, nor the remembrance   25
Of his most sovereign name; consider little
What dangers, by his Highness' fail of issue,
May drop upon his kingdom, and devour
Incertain lookers-on. What were more holy
Than to rejoice the former queen is well?   30
What holier than, for royalty's repair,
For present comfort, and for future good,
To bless the bed of majesty again
With a sweet fellow to 't?

PAULINA   There is none worthy,
Respecting her that's gone; besides, the gods   35
Will have fulfilled their secret purposes;
For has not the divine Apollo said—
Is 't not the tenor of his oracle—
That King Leontes shall not have an heir
Till his lost child be found? Which that it shall,   40
Is all as monstrous to our human reason
As my Antigonus to break his grave,
And come again to me; who, on my life,
Did perish with the infant. 'Tis your counsel
My lord should to the heavens be contrary,   45
Oppose against their wills. [*To Leontes*] Care not
    for issue,
The crown will find an heir. Great Alexander
Left his to th' worthiest: so his successor
Was like to be the best.

LEONTES   Good Paulina,
Who hast the memory of Hermione,   50

V.i.22 **graced** suited   25 **remembrance** (he means the perpetuation of the
King's name in a son)   27 **fail** failure   29 **Incertain lookers-on** bystanders
whose uncertainty makes them incapable of action

    I know, in honor: O, that ever I
    Had squared me to thy counsel! Then, even now,
    I might have looked upon my queen's full eyes,
    Have taken treasure from her lips——

PAULINA   And left them
    More rich for what they yielded.

55   LEONTES   Thou speak'st truth;
    No more such wives, therefore no wife. One worse,
    And better used, would make her sainted spirit
    Again possess her corpse, and on this stage,
    Where we offenders now appear, soul-vexed,
    And begin, "Why to me?"

60   PAULINA   Had she such power,
    She had just cause.

LEONTES   She had, and would incense me
    To murder her I married.

PAULINA   I should so.
    Were I the ghost that walked, I'd bid you mark
    Her eye, and tell me for what dull part in 't
65   You chose her; then I'd shriek, that even your ears
    Should rift to hear me, and the words that followed
    Should be, "Remember mine."

LEONTES   Stars, stars,
    And all eyes else, dead coals! Fear thou no wife;
    I'll have no wife, Paulina.

PAULINA   Will you swear
70   Never to marry, but by my free leave?

LEONTES Never, Paulina, so be blessed my spirit.

PAULINA Then, good my lords, bear witness to his oath.

CLEOMENES You tempt him overmuch.

PAULINA   Unless another,

52 **squared me to** regulated myself by   59 **Where we offenders now appear**
(many attempts to emend this passage have given no better sense than the Folio.
The verb "appear" is needed both for the offenders and for the ghost of Hermione;
the obscurity arises from its doing duty for both. Compare the famous difficulty in
Hamlet IV.iv.53: "Rightly to be great/Is not to stir without great argument ...,"
where "not" stands for "not not") 60 **Why to me** Why do you offer such
treatment to me

As like Hermione as is her picture,
Affront his eye.

CLEOMENES   Good madam——

PAULINA   I have done;   75
Yet if my lord will marry, if you will, sir—
No remedy but you will—give me the office
To choose you a queen; she shall not be so young
As was your former, but she shall be such
As, walked your first queen's ghost, it should take
      joy   80
To see her in your arms.

LEONTES   My true Paulina,
We shall not marry till thou bidd'st us.

PAULINA   That
Shall be when your first queen's again in breath;
Never till then.

                Enter a Servant.

SERVANT One that gives out himself Prince Florizel,   85
Son of Polixenes, with his princess—she
The fairest I have yet beheld—desires access
To your high presence.

LEONTES   What with him? He comes not
Like to his father's greatness; his approach,
So out of circumstance, and sudden, tells us   90
'Tis not a visitation framed, but forced
By need and accident. What train?

SERVANT   But few,
And those but mean.

LEONTES   His princess, say you, with him?

SERVANT Ay, the most peerless piece of earth, I think,
That e'er the sun shone bright on.

PAULINA   O Hermione,   95
As every present time doth boast itself
Above a better, gone, so must thy grave

75 **affront** confront   90 **out of circumstance** lacking ceremony   91 **framed**
planned   92 **train** attendants

355

Give way to what's seen now. Sir, you yourself
Have said, and writ so; but your writing now
100 Is colder than that theme: "She had not been,
Nor was not to be equaled"; thus your verse
Flowed with her beauty once; 'tis shrewdly ebbed,
To say you have seen a better.

SERVANT   Pardon, madam:
The one I have almost forgot—your pardon—
105 The other, when she has obtained your eye,
Will have your tongue too. This is a creature,
Would she begin a sect, might quench the zeal
Of all professors else; make proselytes
Of who she but bid follow.

PAULINA   How! Not women?

110 SERVANT Women will love her that she is a woman
More worth than any man; men, that she is
The rarest of all women.

LEONTES   Go, Cleomenes,
Yourself, assisted with your honored friends,
Bring them to our embracement.
                          Exit [*Cleomenes with others*].
                          Still, 'tis strange,
He should thus steal upon us.

115 PAULINA   Had our prince,
Jewel of children, seen this hour, he had paired
Well with this lord; there was not full a month
Between their births.

LEONTES Prithee no more; cease; thou know'st
120 He dies to me again, when talked of. Sure
When I shall see this gentleman, thy speeches
Will bring me to consider that which may
Unfurnish me of reason. They are come.

Enter Florizel, Perdita, Cleomenes, and others.

Your mother was most true to wedlock, Prince,

100 **theme** Hermione herself   101 **verse** (he had presumably written verses of
compliment to Hermione)   108 **professors** those who profess zeal for religion
(especially Puritans)

For she did print your royal father off,   125
Conceiving you. Were I but twenty-one,
Your father's image is so hit in you,
His very air, that I should call you brother,
As I did him, and speak of something wildly
By us performed before. Most dearly welcome!   130
And your fair princess—goddess! Oh, alas!
I lost a couple that 'twixt heaven and earth
Might thus have stood begetting wonder as
You, gracious couple, do. And then I lost—
All mine own folly—the society,   135
Amity too, of your brave father, whom,
Though bearing misery, I desire my life
Once more to look on him.

FLORIZEL   By his command
Have I here touched Sicilia, and from him
Give you all greetings that a king, at friend,   140
Can send his brother; and but infirmity,
Which waits upon worn times, hath something
    seized
His wished ability, he had himself
The lands and waters 'twixt your throne and his
Measured to look upon you; whom he loves   145
(He bade me say so) more than all the scepters
And those that bear them living.

LEONTES   Oh, my brother—
Good gentleman!—the wrongs I have done thee stir
Afresh within me; and these thy offices,
So rarely kind, are as interpreters   150
Of my behindhand slackness. Welcome hither,
As is the spring to th' earth! And hath he too
Exposed this paragon to th' fearful usage,
At least ungentle, of the dreadful Neptune,

136–38 whom ... on him I wish to go on living, however miserably, in order to
look on him again (the final "him" is dispensable, but the construction is not
unique in Shakespeare) 140 at friend being in friendship with 142 worn
times advanced years 142 seized arrested 149 offices kindnesses, compli-
ments 150–51 interpreters ... slackness put into words feelings I've been too
slow in expressing

155 To greet a man not worth her pains, much less
Th' adventure of her person?

FLORIZEL   Good my lord,
She came from Libya.

LEONTES   Where the warlike Smalus,
That noble honored lord, is feared and loved?

FLORIZEL Most royal sir, from thence; from him, whose
daughter
160 His tears proclaimed his, parting with her; thence,
A prosperous south wind friendly, we have crossed,
To execute the charge my father gave me,
For visiting your Highness. My best train
I have from your Sicilian shores dismissed;
165 Who for Bohemia bend, to signify
Not only my success in Libya, sir,
But my arrival and my wife's in safety
Here where we are.

LEONTES   The blessèd gods
Purge all infection from our air whilst you
170 Do climate here! You have a holy father,
A graceful gentleman, against whose person,
So sacred as it is, I have done sin;
For which, the heavens, taking angry note,
Have left me issueless; and your father's blessed,
175 As he from heaven merits it, with you,
Worthy his goodness. What might I have been,
Might I a son and daughter now have looked on,
Such goodly things as you!

Enter a Lord.

LORD   Most noble sir,
That which I shall report will bear no credit,
180 Were not the proof so nigh. Please you, great sir,
Bohemia greets you from himself, by me;
Desires you to attach his son, who has—
His dignity and duty both cast off—

156 **adventure** risk   170 **climate** reside   171 **graceful** virtuous   182 **attach** arrest

Fled from his father, from his hopes, and with
A shepherd's daughter.

LEONTES   Where's Bohemia? Speak.   185

LORD Here in your city; I now came from him.
I speak amazedly, and it becomes
My marvel and my message. To your court
Whiles he was hast'ning—in the chase, it seems,
Of this fair couple—meets he on the way   190
The father of this seeming lady, and
Her brother, having both their country quitted,
With this young prince.

FLORIZEL   Camillo has betrayed me;
Whose honor and whose honesty till now
Endured all weathers.

LORD   Lay 't so to his charge;   195
He's with the King your father.

LEONTES   Who? Camillo?

LORD Camillo, sir; I spake with him; who now
Has these poor men in question. Never saw I
Wretches so quake; they kneel, they kiss the earth;
Forswear themselves as often as they speak.   200
Bohemia stops his ears, and threatens them
With divers deaths in death.

PERDITA   Oh my poor father!
The heaven sets spies upon us, will not have
Our contract celebrated.

LEONTES   You are married?

FLORIZEL We are not, sir, nor are we like to be;   205
The stars, I see, will kiss the valleys first;
The odds for high and low 's alike.

LEONTES   My lord,

187–88 becomes/My marvel suits my bewilderment   198 in question in talk,
in conference   200 Forswear deny on oath   202 divers deaths in death various
tortures   207 The odds ... alike (dicing terms. "Fortune is a cheater who
beguiles princes and shepherds alike with his false dice" [J. D. Wilson])

Is this the daughter of a king?

FLORIZEL   She is,
When once she is my wife.

210 LEONTES That once, I see by your good father's speed,
Will come on very slowly. I am sorry,
Most sorry, you have broken from his liking,
Where you were tied in duty; and as sorry
Your choice is not so rich in worth as beauty,
That you might well enjoy her.

215 FLORIZEL   Dear, look up.
Though Fortune, visible an enemy,
Should chase us, with my father, power no jot
Hath she to change our loves. Beseech you, sir,
Remember since you owed no more to Time
220 Than I do now; with thought of such affections,
Step forth mine advocate; at your request
My father will grant precious things as trifles.

LEONTES Would he do so, I'd beg your precious
          mistress,
Which he counts but a trifle.

PAULINA   Sir, my liege,
225 Your eye hath too much youth in 't; not a month
'Fore your queen died, she was more worth such
          gazes
Than what you look on now.

LEONTES   I thought of her,
Even in these looks I made. But your petition
Is yet unanswered. I will to your father.
230 Your honor not o'erthrown by your desires,
I am friend to them and you: upon which errand
I now go toward him. Therefore follow me,
And mark what way I make. Come, good my lord.
                                        Exeunt.

214 worth rank   217 chase persecute   230 Your honor ... desires (a certain
insistence on this point of prenuptial chastity is observable both in this play and in
The Tempest)   233 what way I make how far I succeed

Scene II. [*Sicilia, before the palace of Leontes.*]

Enter Autolycus and a Gentleman.

AUTOLYCUS Beseech you, sir, were you present at this
relation?

FIRST GENTLEMAN I was by at the opening of the fardel,
heard the old shepherd deliver the manner how he
found it; whereupon, after a little amazedness, we   5
were all commanded out of the chamber; only this,
methought I heard the shepherd say, he found the
child.

AUTOLYCUS I would most gladly know the issue of it.

FIRST GENTLEMAN I make a broken delivery of the   10
business, but the changes I perceived in the King
and Camillo were very notes of admiration. They
seemed almost, with staring on one another, to
tear the cases of their eyes. There was speech in
their dumbness, language in their very gesture; they   15
looked as they had heard of a world ransomed, or
one destroyed. A notable passion of wonder appeared in them; but the wisest beholder that knew
no more but seeing could not say if th' importance were joy, or sorrow—but in the extremity   20
of the one it must needs be.

Enter another Gentleman.

Here comes a gentleman that happily knows more:
the news, Rogero?

SECOND GENTLEMAN Nothing but bonfires. The oracle is
fulfilled; the King's daughter is found; such a deal   25

V.ii.12 **notes of admiration** exclamation points   14 **cases of their eyes** eyelids
19 **but seeing** but what he saw   19–20 **importance** significance   22 **happily**
haply, perhaps

of wonder is broken out within this hour that ballad-
makers cannot be able to express it.

Enter another Gentleman.

Here comes the Lady Paulina's steward; he can
deliver you more. How goes it now, sir? This news,
30 which is called true, is so like an old tale that the
verity of it is in strong suspicion. Has the King
found his heir?

THIRD GENTLEMAN Most true, if ever truth were pregnant by circumstance; that which you hear you'll
35 swear you see, there is such unity in the proofs. The
mantle of Queen Hermione; her jewel about the
neck of it; the letters of Antigonus found with it,
which they know to be his character; the majesty
of the creature, in resemblance of the mother; the
40 affection of nobleness, which nature shows above
her breeding and many other evidences—proclaim
her, with all certainty, to be the King's daughter.
Did you see the meeting of the two kings?

SECOND GENTLEMAN No.

45 THIRD GENTLEMAN Then have you lost a sight which
was to be seen, cannot be spoken of. There might
you have beheld one joy crown another, so and in
such manner that it seemed Sorrow wept to take
leave of them; for their joy waded in tears. There
50 was casting up of eyes, holding up of hands, with
countenance of such distraction that they were to
be known by garment, not by favor. Our king,
being ready to leap out of himself for joy of his
found daughter, as if that joy were now become a
55 loss, cries, "Oh, thy mother, thy mother"; then asks
Bohemia forgiveness, then embraces his son-in-law;
then again worries he his daughter with clipping
her. Now he thanks the old shepherd, which stands

33–34 **truth ... circumstance** made evident by, filled out by circumstances
38 **character** handwriting   40 **affection** natural disposition   51 **countenance**
(probably meant as a plural; a common orthographical feature in Shakespearean
texts)   52 **favor** features   57 **clipping** embracing

362

by, like a weather-bitten conduit of many kings'
reigns. I never heard of such another encounter,   60
which lames report to follow it, and undoes description to do it.

SECOND GENTLEMAN What, pray you, became of Antigonus, that carried hence the child?

THIRD GENTLEMAN Like an old tale still, which will   65
have matter to rehearse, though credit be asleep,
and not an ear open: he was torn to pieces with
a bear. This avouches the shepherd's son, who has
not only his innocence (which seems much) to
justify him, but a handkerchief and rings of his   70
that Paulina knows.

FIRST GENTLEMAN What became of his bark and his
followers?

THIRD GENTLEMAN Wracked the same instant of their
master's death, and in the view of the shepherd: 75
so that all the instruments which aided to expose the
child were even then lost when it was found. But
oh, the noble combat, that 'twixt joy and sorrow was
fought in Paulina! She had one eye declined for the
loss of her husband, another elevated that the oracle 80
was fulfilled. She lifted the Princess from the earth,
and so locks her in embracing as if she would pin
her to her heart, that she might no more be in danger
of losing.

FIRST GENTLEMAN The dignity of this act was worth   85
the audience of kings and princes, for by such was
it acted.

THIRD GENTLEMAN One of the prettiest touches of all,
and that which angled for mine eyes—caught the
water though not the fish—was, when at the rela-   90
tion of the Queen's death, with the manner how she
came to 't bravely confessed and lamented by the
King, how attentiveness wounded his daughter; till,

59 **weather-bitten conduit** weather-worn fountain (the old man's tears make him
resemble a fountain in human shape) 62 **do it** describe it 66 **credit** belief
67 **with** by 69 **innocence** simplicity 84 **losing** being lost

from one sign of dolor to another, she did, with an
95   "Alas"—I would fain say—bleed tears; for I am
sure my heart wept blood. Who was most marble
there changed color; some swooned, all sorrowed.
If all the world could have seen 't, the woe had been
universal.

100   FIRST GENTLEMAN Are they returned to the court?

THIRD GENTLEMAN No, the Princess, hearing of her
mother's statue, which is in the keeping of Paulina—
a piece many years in doing and now newly performed by that rare Italian master, Julio Ro-
105   mano, who, had he himself eternity and could put
breath into his work, would beguile Nature of her
custom, so perfectly he is her ape: he so near to
Hermione hath done Hermione, that they say one
would speak to her and stand in hope of answer.
110   Thither with all greediness of affection are they
gone, and there they intend to sup.

SECOND GENTLEMAN I thought she had some great matter there in hand, for she hath privately, twice or
thrice a day, ever since the death of Hermione,
115   visited that removed house. Shall we thither, and
with our company piece the rejoicing?

FIRST GENTLEMAN Who would be thence that has the
benefit of access? Every wink of an eye some new
grace will be born. Our absence makes us un-
120   thrifty to our knowledge. Let's along.

Exit [*with the other Gentlemen*].

AUTOLYCUS Now, had I not the dash of my former life
in me, would preferment drop on my head. I

103–4 **performed** completed 104–05 **Julio Romano** (Italian painter [1492–
1546]. This allusion has caused much debate, because of the anachronism, and
because Julio is remembered not as a sculptor but as a painter, though he probably
practiced sculpture as well) 105–07 **had he himself ... ape** had he this other
attribute of God and could put breath into his statues, he would cheat Nature of
her trade, so closely can he imitate her (the sentiment is a little confused)
116 **piece** i.e., add to 119–20 **unthrifty to our knowledge** careless in the
accumulation of knowledge

brought the old man and his son aboard the Prince;
told him I heard them talk of a fardel and I know
not what; but he at that time overfond of the shep-   125
herd's daughter (so he then took her to be), who
began to be much seasick, and himself little better,
extremity of weather continuing, this mystery remained undiscovered. But 'tis all one to me; for had
I been the finder-out of this secret, it would not have   130
relished among my other discredits.

Enter Shepherd and Clown.

Here come those I have done good to against my
will, and already appearing in the blossoms of their
fortune.

SHEPHERD Come, boy, I am past moe children; but thy   135
sons and daughters will be all gentlemen born.

CLOWN You are well met, sir. You denied to fight with
me this other day, because I was no gentleman
born. See you these clothes? Say you see them not
and think me still no gentleman born; you were   140
best say these robes are not gentlemen born. Give
me the lie, do; and try whether I am not now a
gentleman born.

AUTOLYCUS I know you are now, sir, a gentleman born.

CLOWN Ay, and have been so any time these four   145
hours.

SHEPHERD And so have I, boy.

CLOWN So you have; but I was a gentleman born before my father; for the King's son took me by the
hand and called me brother; and then the two   150
kings called my father brother; and then the Prince,
(my brother) and the Princess (my sister) called
my father father; and so we wept; and there was
the first gentlemanlike tears that ever we shed.

SHEPHERD We may live, son, to shed many more.   155

131 **relished** proved tasteful, acceptable

CLOWN Ay; or else 'twere hard luck, being in so preposterous estate as we are.

AUTOLYCUS I humbly beseech you, sir, to pardon me all the faults I have committed to your worship, and
160 to give me your good report to the Prince, my master.

SHEPHERD Prithee, son, do: for we must be gentle, now we are gentlemen.

CLOWN Thou wilt amend thy life?

165 AUTOLYCUS Ay, an it like your good worship.

CLOWN Give me thy hand. I will swear to the Prince thou art as honest a true fellow as any is in Bohemia.

SHEPHERD You may say it, but not swear it.

170 CLOWN Not swear it, now I am a gentleman? Let boors and franklins say it, I'll swear it.

SHEPHERD How if it be false, son?

CLOWN If it be ne'er so false, a true gentleman may swear it in the behalf of his friend; and I'll swear
175 to the Prince thou art a tall fellow of thy hands, and that thou wilt not be drunk; but I know thou art no tall fellow of thy hands, and that thou wilt be drunk; but I'll swear it, and I would thou wouldst be a tall fellow of thy hands.

180 AUTOLYCUS I will prove so, sir, to my power.

CLOWN Ay, by any means prove a tall fellow. If I do not wonder how thou dar'st venture to be drunk, not being a tall fellow, trust me not. Hark, the kings and the princes, our kindred, are going to see the
185 Queen's picture. Come, follow us; we'll be thy good masters.   *Exeunt*.

156–57 **preposterous** (malapropism for "prosperous")   165 **an it like** if it please
167 **true** honest (as opposed to thieving)   171 **boors and franklins** peasants and
yeomen   175 **a tall fellow of thy hands** a man of courage   180 **to my power** as
far as I am able

Scene III. [*Sicilia, a chapel in Paulina's house.*]

Enter Leontes, Polixenes, Florizel, Perdita, Camillo,
Paulina, Lords, etc.

LEONTES O grave and good Paulina, the great comfort
That I have had of thee!

PAULINA   What, sovereign sir,
I did not well, I meant well. All my services
You have paid home. But that you have
  vouchsafed,
With your crowned brother and these your
  contracted   5
Heirs of your kingdoms, my poor house to visit,
It is a surplus of your grace, which never
My life may last to answer.

LEONTES   O Paulina,
We honor you with trouble; but we came
To see the statue of our queen. Your gallery   10
Have we passed through, not without much content
In many singularities; but we saw not
That which my daughter came to look upon,
The statue of her mother.

PAULINA   As she lived peerless,
So her dead likeness I do well believe   15
Excels whatever yet you looked upon,
Or hand of man hath done; therefore I keep it
Lonely, apart. But here it is; prepare
To see the life as lively mocked, as ever
Still sleep mocked death: behold, and say 'tis well.   20

V.iii.4 **paid home** paid in full   5 **your contracted** (this "your" should possibly
be omitted; the compositor could have caught it from "your crowned" or from the
next line)   12 **singularities** varieties

367

[*Paulina draws a curtain and discovers*] *Hermione*
[*standing*] *like a statue*.

I like your silence; it the more shows off
Your wonder; but yet speak, first you, my liege.
Comes it not something near?

LEONTES   Her natural posture!
Chide me, dear stone, that I may say indeed
25   Thou art Hermione; or rather, thou art she
In thy not chiding; for she was as tender
As infancy and grace. But yet, Paulina,
Hermione was not so much wrinkled, nothing
So agèd as this seems.

POLIXENES   Oh, not by much.

30   PAULINA So much the more our carver's excellence,
Which lets go by some sixteen years, and makes her
As she lived now.

LEONTES   As now she might have done,
So much to my good comfort, as it is
Now piercing to my soul. Oh, thus she stood,
35   Even with such life of majesty—warm life,
As now it coldly stands—when first I wooed her.
I am ashamed: does not the stone rebuke me,
For being more stone than it? O royal piece!
There's magic in thy majesty, which has
40   My evils conjured to remembrance, and
From thy admiring daughter took the spirits,
Standing like stone with thee.

PERDITA   And give me leave,
And do not say 'tis superstition that
I kneel, and then implore her blessing. Lady,
45   Dear queen, that ended when I but began,
Give me that hand of yours to kiss.

PAULINA   O, patience!
The statue is but newly fixed, the color's
Not dry.

32 **As she lived** as if she lived   39-40 **magic ... conjured ... remembrance**
(the sight of the statue has called up his sins into his mind as a magician summons
demons)

CAMILLO My lord, your sorrow was too sore laid on,
Which sixteen winters cannot blow away,   50
So many summers dry. Scarce any joy
Did ever so long live; no sorrow
But killed itself much sooner.

POLIXENES   Dear my brother,
Let him that was the cause of this have power
To take off so much grief from you as he   55
Will piece up in himself.

PAULINA   Indeed, my lord,
If I had thought the sight of my poor image
Would thus have wrought you—for the stone is
    mine—
I'd not have showed it.

LEONTES   Do not draw the curtain.

PAULINA No longer shall you gaze on 't, lest your fancy   60
May think anon it moves.

LEONTES   Let be, let be!
Would I were dead, but that methinks already—
What was he that did make it? See, my lord,
Would you not deem it breathed? And that those
    veins
Did verily bear blood?

POLIXENES   Masterly done!   65
The very life seems warm upon her lip.

LEONTES The fixure of her eye has motion in 't,
As we are mocked with art.

PAULINA   I'll draw the curtain;
My lord's almost so far transported that
He'll think anon it lives.

LEONTES   O sweet Paulina,   70
Make me to think so twenty years together!
No settled senses of the world can match
The pleasure of that madness. Let 't alone.

56 **piece up** make his own   62 **Would . . . already** May I die if I do not think it
moves already (Staunton)   67 **fixure** (early form of "fixture")   72 **settled** sane

PAULINA I am sorry, sir, I have thus far stirred you;
    but
I could afflict you farther.

75 LEONTES   Do, Paulina;
For this affliction has a taste as sweet
As any cordial comfort. Still, methinks,
There is an air comes from her. What fine chisel
Could ever yet cut breath? Let no man mock me,
For I will kiss her.

80 PAULINA   Good my lord, forbear!
The ruddiness upon her lip is wet;
You'll mar it if you kiss it; stain your own
With oily painting. Shall I draw the curtain?

LEONTES No, not these twenty years.

PERDITA   So long could I
Stand by, a looker-on.

85 PAULINA   Either forbear,
Quit presently the chapel, or resolve you
For more amazement. If you can behold it,
I'll make the statue move indeed, descend,
And take you by the hand—but then you'll think,
90 Which I protest against, I am assisted
By wicked powers.

LEONTES   What you can make her do,
I am content to look on; what to speak,
I am content to hear; for 'tis as easy
To make her speak, as move.

PAULINA   It is required
95 You do awake your faith; then, all stand still.
Or those that think it is unlawful business
I am about, let them depart.

LEONTES   Proceed.
No foot shall stir.

PAULINA   Music, awake her: strike.
'Tis time; descend; be stone no more; approach;

77 **cordial** heart-warming

Strike all that look upon with marvel; come;   100
I'll fill your grave up. Stir; nay, come away;
Bequeath to death your numbness, for from him
Dear life redeems you. You perceive she stirs.

[*Hermione comes down.*]

Start not; her actions shall be holy as
You hear my spell is lawful. Do not shun her   105
Until you see her die again, for then
You kill her double. Nay, present your hand.
When she was young, you wooed her; now, in age,
Is she become the suitor?

LEONTES   Oh, she's warm!
If this be magic, let it be an art   110
Lawful as eating.

POLIXENES   She embraces him.

CAMILLO She hangs about his neck;
If she pertain to life, let her speak too.

POLIXENES Ay, and make it manifest where she has
    lived,
Or how stol'n from the dead.

PAULINA   That she is living,   115
Were it but told you, should be hooted at
Like an old tale; but it appears she lives,
Though yet she speak not. Mark a little while:
Please you to interpose, fair madam; kneel,
And pray your mother's blessing; turn, good lady,   120
Our Perdita is found.

HERMIONE   You gods look down,
And from your sacred vials pour your graces
Upon my daughter's head! Tell me, mine own,
Where hast thou been preserved? Where lived? How
    found
Thy father's court? For thou shalt hear that I,   125
Knowing by Paulina that the oracle
Gave hope thou wast in being, have preserved
Myself to see the issue.

127 in being alive

PAULINA   There's time enough for that,
Lest they desire upon this push to trouble
130 Your joys with like relation. Go together,
You precious winners all; your exultation
Partake to every one. I an old turtle,
Will wing me to some withered bough, and there
My mate, that's never to be found again,
Lament till I am lost.

135 LEONTES   O peace, Paulina!
Thou shouldst a husband take by my consent,
As I by thine a wife. This is a match,
And made between 's by vows. Thou hast found
    mine,
But how, is to be questioned; for I saw her,
140 As I thought, dead; and have in vain said many
A prayer upon her grave. I'll not seek farre,
For him, I partly know his mind, to find thee
An honorable husband. Come, Camillo,
And take her by the hand, whose worth and
    honesty
145 Is richly noted, and here justified
By us, a pair of kings. Let's from this place.
What! Look upon my brother. Both your pardons,
That e'er I put between your holy looks
My ill suspicion. This your son-in-law,
150 And son unto the King, whom, heavens directing,
Is troth-plight to your daughter. Good Paulina,
Lead us from hence, where we may leisurely
Each one demand and answer to his part
Performed in this wide gap of time since first
155 We were dissevered. Hastily lead away.   *Exeunt*.

FINIS

129 **upon this push** at this exciting moment 132 **Partake** communicate, share
141 **farre** farther 144 **whose worth and honesty** i.e., Camillo's 147 **Look
upon my brother** (Hermione has presumably shown some natural embarrassment
about greeting Polixenes)

Textual Note

The Winter's Tale was placed at the end of the section of Comedies in the Folio of 1623. There was no earlier edition, and so all subsequent editions derive from the Folio text. Bibliographical evidence shows that the play was added to the Folio late, when a number of the History plays had already been printed. Possibly no copy was available until then. The copy that eventually reached the printing house was almost certainly a transcript of the play made by Ralph Crane, whose hand is now well known to scholars. Crane did a good deal for Shakespeare's company, the King's Men, and the Folio texts of *The Tempest*, *The Two Gentlemen of Verona*— and possibly other plays too—are attributable to him. Certain of his characteristics—notably his fondness for brackets and his habit of placing all the entries at the head of the scene, whether or no they are repeated when the character actually comes in—are abundantly in evidence in the Folio text of *The Winter's Tale*.

The text is very deficient in stage directions, and Crane's copy was evidently not made for use in the playhouse. But he was an intelligent scribe, and doubtless gave the compositor clean copy. In fact, this is one of the cleanest of Shakespeare's texts, despite the difficulty of some of the verse. The present edition deletes the superfluous entries at heads of scenes and places them at the appropriate positions, modernizes spelling and punctuation, and translates from Latin into English the Folio's act and scene divisions. The list of characters, here prefixed to the play, in the Folio follows the play. Other material departures from the Folio text are listed below in bold type, followed by the Folio's reading (F) in roman; only in three or four places is there any real difficulty involved.

I.i.28 **have** hath

I.ii.104 **And** A   158 **do** does   208 **you, they say you say**   276 **hobby-horse**

373

TEXTUAL NOTE

Holy-horse 327–28 sully/The purity Sully the puritie 446–47 thereon,/ His execution sworn Thereon his Execution sworne

II.i.25–26 I have one/Of I have one of

II.ii.6 whom who 52 let 't le't

II.iii.38 What Who 52 profess professes 176 its it

III.ii.1 session Sessions 10 Silence [F italicizes, as if s.d.] 32 Who Whom 107 for no

III.iii.18 awaking a waking 119 made mad

IV.iii.10 with heigh, with heigh With heigh 57 offends offend

IV.iv.2 do Do's 12 Digest it with Digest with 13 swoon sworne 98 your you 160 out on't 365 who whom 423 acknowledged acknowledge 427 who whom 432 shalt see shalt neuer see 443 hoop hope 471 your my 494 hide hides 503 whom who 553 asks thee, the son, forgiveness asks thee there Sonne forgiuenesse 709 know not know 739 or toaze at toaze 849 Exit Exeunt

V.i.12 True, too true [F places the first "true" at the end of Leontes' previous speech] 61 just cause just such cause 75 I have done [F gives to Cleomenes]

V.ii.36 Hermione Hermiones

V.iii.18 Lonely Louely 96 Or on

374

WILLIAM SHAKESPEARE

THE TEMPEST

Edited by Robert Langbaum

Names of the Actors

ALONSO, King of Naples
SEBASTIAN, his brother
PROSPERO, the right Duke of Milan
ANTONIO, his brother, the usurping Duke of Milan
FERDINAND, son to the King of Naples
GONZALO, an honest old councilor
ADRIAN and FRANCISCO, lords
CALIBAN, a savage and deformed slave
TRINCULO, a jester
STEPHANO, a drunken butler
MASTER OF A SHIP
BOATSWAIN
MARINERS
MIRANDA, daughter to Prospero
ARIEL, an airy spirit
IRIS
CERES
JUNO ⎬ [presented by] spirits
NYMPHS
REAPERS
[OTHER SPIRITS ATTENDING ON PROSPERO]

The Scene: An uninhabited island.

THE TEMPEST

ACT I

Scene I. [*On a ship at sea.*]

*A tempestuous noise of thunder and lightning
heard. Enter a Shipmaster and a Boatswain.*

MASTER Boatswain!

BOATSWAIN Here, master. What cheer?

MASTER Good, speak to th' mariners! Fall to't yarely,
or we run ourselves aground. Bestir, bestir!

Exit.

Enter Mariners.

BOATSWAIN Heigh, my hearts! Cheerly, cheerly, my   5
hearts! Yare, yare! Take in the topsail! Tend to th'
master's whistle! Blow till thou burst thy wind, if
room enough!

*Enter Alonso, Sebastian, Antonio, Ferdinand,
Gonzalo, and others.*

ALONSO Good boatswain, have care. Where's the
master? Play the men.   10

BOATSWAIN I pray now, keep below.

Text references are printed in **boldface** type; the annotation follows in roman
type.
I.i.3 **Good** good fellow   3 **yarely** briskly   7–8 **Blow till ... room enough** the
storm can blow and split itself as long as there is open sea without rocks to
maneuver in   10 **Play the men** act like men

377

ANTONIO Where is the master, bos'n?

BOATSWAIN Do you not hear him? You mar our labor.
Keep your cabins; you do assist the storm.

15 GONZALO Nay, good, be patient.

BOATSWAIN When the sea is. Hence! What cares these
roarers for the name of king? To cabin! Silence!
Trouble us not!

GONZALO Good, yet remember whom thou hast
20 aboard.

BOATSWAIN None that I more love than myself. You
are a councilor; if you can command these elements
to silence and work the peace of the present, we
will not hand a rope more. Use your authority.
25 If you cannot, give thanks you have lived so long,
and make yourself ready in your cabin for the mischance of the hour, if it so hap. Cheerly, good
hearts! Out of our way, I say.   *Exit*.

GONZALO I have great comfort from this fellow. Me-
30 thinks he hath no drowning mark upon him; his
complexion is perfect gallows. Stand fast, good
Fate, to his hanging! Make the rope of his destiny
our cable, for our own doth little advantage. If he
be not born to be hanged, our case is miserable.
                                    Exit [with the rest].

                    Enter Boatswain.

35 BOATSWAIN Down with the topmast! Yare! Lower,
lower! Bring her to try with main course! (*A cry
within.*) A plague upon this howling! They are
louder than the weather or our office.

---

23 **work the peace of the present** restore the present to peace (since as a councilor his job is to quell disorder)   24 **hand** handle   30-31 **no drowning mark ... gallows** (alluding to the proverb, "He that's born to be hanged need fear no drowning")   33 **doth little advantage** gives us little advantage   36 **Bring her to try with main course** heave to, under the mainsail   37-38 **They are louder ... office** these passengers make more noise than the tempest or than we do at our work

Enter Sebastian, Antonio, and Gonzalo.

Yet again? What do you here? Shall we give o'er
and drown? Have you a mind to sink?   40

SEBASTIAN A pox o' your throat, you bawling, blas-
phemous, incharitable dog!

BOATSWAIN Work you, then.

ANTONIO Hang, cur! Hang, you whoreson, insolent
noisemaker! We are less afraid to be drowned than   45
thou art.

GONZALO I'll warrant him for drowning, though the
ship were no stronger than a nutshell and as leaky
as an unstanched wench.

BOATSWAIN Lay her ahold, ahold! Set her two   50
courses! Off to sea again! Lay her off!

Enter Mariners wet.

MARINERS All lost! To prayers, to prayers! All lost!
                                        [*Exeunt.*]

BOATSWAIN What, must our mouths be cold?

GONZALO The King and Prince at prayers! Let's assist
them,
For our case is as theirs.

SEBASTIAN   I am out of patience.   55

ANTONIO We are merely cheated of our lives by
drunkards.
This wide-chopped rascal—would thou mightst lie
drowning
The washing of ten tides!

39 **give o'er** give up trying to run the ship   47 **warrant him for** guarantee him
against   49 **unstanched** wide-open   50–51 **Lay her ahold ... courses** (the ship
is still being blown dangerously to shore, so the boatswain orders that the foresail
be set in addition to the mainsail; but the ship still moves toward shore)
51 **Lay her off** i.e., away from the shore   56 **merely** completely   57 **wide-
chopped** big-mouthed   58 **ten tides** (pirates were hanged on the shore and left
there until three tides had washed over them)

GONZALO   He'll be hanged yet,
Though every drop of water swear against it
And gape at wid'st to glut him.

60   *A confused noise within:* "Mercy on us!"
"We split, we split!" "Farewell, my wife and chil-
    dren!"
"Farewell, brother! "We split, we split, we split!"
                              [*Exit Boatswain.*]

ANTONIO Let's all sink wi' th' King.

SEBASTIAN   Let's take leave of him.
                              Exit [*with Antonio*].

GONZALO Now would I give a thousand furlongs of
65   sea for an acre of barren ground—long heath,
brown furze, anything. The wills above be done,
but I would fain die a dry death.   *Exit.*

Scene II. [*The island. In front of Prospero's cell.*]

Enter Prospero and Miranda.

MIRANDA If by your art, my dearest father, you have
Put the wild waters in this roar, allay them.
The sky, it seems, would pour down stinking pitch
But that the sea, mounting to th' welkin's cheek,
5   Dashes the fire out. O, I have suffered
With those that I saw suffer! A brave vessel
(Who had no doubt some noble creature in her)
Dashed all to pieces! O, the cry did knock

---

65 **heath** heather   I.ii.4 **welkin's cheek** face of the sky   6 **brave** fine, gallant
(the word often has this meaning in the play)

Against my very heart! Poor souls, they perished!
Had I been any god of power, I would   10
Have sunk the sea within the earth or ere
It should the good ship so have swallowed and
The fraughting souls within her.

PROSPERO   Be collected.
No more amazement. Tell your piteous heart
There's no harm done.

MIRANDA   O, woe the day!

PROSPERO   No harm.   15
I have done nothing but in care of thee,
Of thee my dear one, thee my daughter, who
Art ignorant of what thou art, naught knowing
Of whence I am, nor that I am more better
Than Prospero, master of a full poor cell,   20
And thy no greater father.

MIRANDA   More to know
Did never meddle with my thoughts.

PROSPERO   'Tis time
I should inform thee farther. Lend thy hand
And pluck my magic garment from me. So.

                       [*Lays down his robe.*]

Lie there, my art. Wipe thou thine eyes; have
   comfort.   25
The direful spectacle of the wrack, which touched
The very virtue of compassion in thee,
I have with such provision in mine art
So safely ordered that there is no soul—
No, not so much perdition as an hair   30
Betid to any creature in the vessel
Which thou heard'st cry, which thou saw'st sink.
   Sit down;
For thou must now know farther.

13 **fraughting** forming her freight   14 **amazement** consternation   21 **thy no greater father** i.e., thy father, no greater than the Prospero just described   22 **meddle** mingle   27 **virtue** essence   28 **provision** foresight   30 **perdition** loss   31 **Betid** happened

MIRANDA   You have often
Begun to tell me what I am; but stopped
35   And left me to a bootless inquisition,
Concluding, "Stay; not yet."

PROSPERO   The hour's now come;
The very minute bids thee ope thine ear.
Obey, and be attentive. Canst thou remember
A time before we came unto this cell?
40   I do not think thou canst, for then thou wast not
Out three years old.

MIRANDA   Certainly, sir, I can.

PROSPERO By what? By any other house or person?
Of anything the image tell me that
Hath kept with thy remembrance.

MIRANDA   'Tis far off,
45   And rather like a dream than an assurance
That my remembrance warrants. Had I not
Four or five women once that tended me?

PROSPERO Thou hadst, and more, Miranda. But how
is it
That this lives in thy mind? What seest thou else
50   In the dark backward and abysm of time?
If thou rememb'rest aught ere thou cam'st here,
How thou cam'st here thou mayst.

MIRANDA   But that I do not.

PROSPERO Twelve year since, Miranda, twelve year
since,
Thy father was the Duke of Milan and
A prince of power.

55   MIRANDA   Sir, are not you my father?

PROSPERO Thy mother was a piece of virtue, and
She said thou wast my daughter; and thy father
Was Duke of Milan; and his only heir

41 **Out** fully   46 **remembrance warrants** memory guarantees   54 **Milan**
(pronounced "Mílan")   56 **piece** masterpiece

And princess, no worse issued.

MIRANDA   O the heavens!
What foul play had we that we came from thence?   60
Or blessèd was't we did?

PROSPERO   Both, both, my girl!
By foul play, as thou say'st, were we heaved thence,
But blessedly holp hither.

MIRANDA   O, my heart bleeds
To think o' th' teen that I have turned you to,
Which is from my remembrance! Please you,
    farther.   65

PROSPERO My brother and thy uncle, called
    Antonio—
I pray thee mark me—that a brother should
Be so perfidious!—he whom next thyself
Of all the world I loved, and to him put
The manage of my state, as at that time   70
Through all the signories it was the first,
And Prospero the prime duke, being so reputed
In dignity, and for the liberal arts
Without a parallel. Those being all my study,
The government I cast upon my brother   75
And to my state grew stranger, being transported
And rapt in secret studies. Thy false uncle—
Dost thou attend me?

MIRANDA   Sir, most heedfully.

PROSPERO Being once perfected how to grant suits,
How to deny them, who t' advance, and who   80

59 **no worse issued** of no meaner lineage than he   63 **holp** helped   64 **teen that
I have turned you to** sorrow I have caused you to remember   65 **from** out
of   70 **manage of my state** management of my domain   71 **signories** lordships
(of Italy)   79 **perfected** grown skillful   81 **trash for overtopping** (1) check the
speed of (as of hounds) (2) cut down to size (as of overall trees) the aspirants for
political favor who are growing too bold

To trash for overtopping, new-created
The creatures that were mine, I say—or changed 'em,
Or else new-formed 'em—having both the key
Of officer and office, set all hearts i' th' state
85   To what tune pleased his ear, that now he was
The ivy which had hid my princely trunk
And sucked my verdure out on't. Thou attend'st not?

MIRANDA O, good sir, I do.

PROSPERO   I pray thee mark me.
I thus neglecting worldly ends, all dedicated
90   To closeness and the bettering of my mind—
With that which, but by being so retired,
O'erprized all popular rate, in my false brother
Awaked an evil nature, and my trust,
Like a good parent, did beget of him
95   A falsehood in its contrary as great
As my trust was, which had indeed no limit,
A confidence sans bound. He being thus lorded—
Not only with what my revenue yielded
But what my power might else exact, like one
100   Who having into truth—by telling of it,
Made such a sinner of his memory
To credit his own lie, he did believe
He was indeed the Duke, out o' th' substitution
And executing th' outward face of royalty
With all prerogative. Hence his ambition
105   growing—
Dost thou hear?

81–83 new-created/The creatures … new-formed 'em i.e., he re-created my
following—either exchanging my adherents for his own, or else transforming my
adherents into different people 83 key (a pun leading to the musical
metaphor) 90 closeness seclusion 91–93 With that … evil nature i.e., with
that dedication to the mind which, were it not that it kept me from exercising the
duties of my office would surpass in value all ordinary estimate, I awakened evil in
my brother's nature 94 good parent (alluding to the proverb cited by Miranda
in line 120) 98 revenue (pronounced "revènue") 99–100 like one/Who having … of it i.e., like one who really had these things—by repeatedly saying he had
them (into = unto) 102 To as to 103–5 out o' th' substitution … all
prerogative i.e., as a result of his acting as my substitute and performing the
outward functions of royalty with all its prerogatives

MIRANDA   Your tale, sir, would cure deafness.

PROSPERO To have no screen between this part he
      played
  And him he played it for, he needs will be
  Absolute Milan. Me (poor man) my library
  Was dukedom large enough. Of temporal royalties   110
  He thinks me now incapable; confederates
  (So dry he was for sway) wi' th' King of Naples
  To give him annual tribute, do him homage,
  Subject his coronet to his crown, and bend
  The dukedom, yet unbowed (alas, poor Milan!),   115
  To most ignoble stooping.

MIRANDA   O the heavens!

PROSPERO Mark his condition, and th' event; then
      tell me
  If this might be a brother.

MIRANDA   I should sin
  To think but nobly of my grandmother.
  Good wombs have borne bad sons.

PROSPERO   Now the condition.   120
  This King of Naples, being an enemy
  To me inveterate, hearkens my brother's suit;
  Which was, that he, in lieu o' th' premises
  Of homage and I know not how much tribute,
  Should presently extirpate me and mine   125
  Out of the dukedom and confer fair Milan,
  With all the honors, on my brother. Whereon,
  A treacherous army levied, one midnight
  Fated to th' purpose, did Antonio open
  The gates of Milan; and, i' th' dead of darkness,   130
  The ministers for th' purpose hurried thence
  Me and thy crying self.

MIRANDA   Alack, for pity!

109 **Absolute Milan** Duke of Milan in fact   112 **dry** thirsty   117 **condition**
terms of his pact with Naples   117 **event** outcome   123 **in lieu o' th' premises**
in return for the guarantees   131 **ministers** agents

I, not rememb'ring how I cried out then,
Will cry it o'er again; it is a hint
That wrings mine eyes to't.

135 PROSPERO   Hear a little further,
And then I'll bring thee to the present business
Which now's upon's; without the which this story
Were most impertinent.

MIRANDA   Wherefore did they not
That hour destroy us?

PROSPERO   Well demanded, wench.
My tale provokes that question. Dear, they durst
140   not,
So dear the love my people bore me; nor set
A mark so bloody on the business; but,
With colors fairer, painted their foul ends.
In few, they hurried us aboard a bark;
145 Bore us some leagues to sea, where they prepared
A rotten carcass of a butt, not rigged,
Nor tackle, sail, nor mast; the very rats
Instinctively have quit it. There they hoist us,
To cry to th' sea that roared to us; to sigh
150 To th' winds, whose pity, sighing back again,
Did us but loving wrong.

MIRANDA   Alack, what trouble
Was I then to you!

PROSPERO   O, a cherubin
Thou wast that did preserve me! Thou didst smile,
Infusèd with a fortitude from heaven,
155 When I have decked the sea with drops full salt,
Under my burden groaned; which raised in me
An undergoing stomach, to bear up
Against what should ensue.

MIRANDA   How came we ashore?

134 **hint** occasion 138 **impertinent** inappropriate 144 **few** few words
146 **butt** tub 155 **decked** covered (wept salt tears into the sea) 156 **which** i.e.,
Miranda's smile 157 **undergoing stomach** spirit of endurance

PROSPERO By providence divine.
  Some food we had, and some fresh water, that   160
  A noble Neapolitan, Gonzalo,
  Out of his charity, who being then appointed
  Master of this design, did give us, with
  Rich garments, linens, stuffs, and necessaries
  Which since have steaded much. So, of his
     gentleness,   165
  Knowing I loved my books, he furnished me
  From mine own library with volumes that
  I prize above my dukedom.

MIRANDA   Would I might
  But ever see that man!

PROSPERO   Now I arise.
  Sit still, and hear the last of our sea sorrow.   170
  Here in this island we arrived; and here
  Have I, thy schoolmaster, made thee more profit
  Than other princess' can, that have more time
  For vainer hours, and tutors not so careful.

MIRANDA Heavens thank you for't! And now I pray
     you, sir—   175
  For still 'tis beating in my mind—your reason
  For raising this sea storm?

PROSPERO   Know thus far forth.
  By accident most strange, bountiful Fortune
  (Now my dear lady) hath mine enemies
  Brought to this shore; and by my prescience   180
  I find my zenith doth depend upon
  A most auspicious star, whose influence
  If now I court not, but omit, my fortunes
  Will ever after droop. Here cease more questions.
  Thou art inclined to sleep. 'Tis a good dullness,   185
  And give it way. I know thou canst not choose.
                      [*Miranda sleeps.*]

---

165 **steaded** been of use   173 **princess' can** princesses can have   179 **Now my
dear lady** i.e., formerly my foe, now my patroness   181 **zenith** apex of fortune
183 **omit** neglect

Come away, servant, come! I am ready now.
Approach, my Ariel! Come!

Enter Ariel.

ARIEL All hail, great master! Grave sir, hail! I come
190 To answer thy best pleasure; be't to fly,
To swim, to dive into the fire, to ride
On the curled clouds. To thy strong bidding task
Ariel and all his quality.

PROSPERO   Hast thou, spirit,
Performed, to point, the tempest that I bade thee?

195 ARIEL To every article.
I boarded the King's ship. Now on the beak,
Now in the waist, the deck, in every cabin,
I flamed amazement. Sometime I'd divide
And burn in many places; on the topmast,
200 The yards, and boresprit would I flame distinctly,
Then meet and join. Jove's lightnings, the precursors
O' th' dreadful thunderclaps, more momentary
And sight-outrunning were not. The fire and cracks
Of sulfurous roaring the most mighty Neptune
205 Seem to besiege, and make his bold waves tremble;
Yea, his dread trident shake.

PROSPERO   My brave spirit!
Who was so firm, so constant, that this coil
Would not infect his reason?

ARIEL   Not a soul
But felt a fever of the mad and played
210 Some tricks of desperation. All but mariners
Plunged in the foaming brine and quit the vessel,
Then all afire with me. The King's son Ferdinand,

---

187 **Come away** i.e., come from where you are; come here   192 **task** tax to the
utmost   193 **quality** cohorts (Ariel is leader of a band of spirits)   194 **to point** in
every detail   196 **beak** prow   197 **waist** amidships   197 **deck** poop   198 **flamed
amazement** struck terror by appearing as (St. Elmo's) fire   200 **boresprit**
bowsprit   200 **distinctly** in different places   207 **coil** uproar

With hair up-staring (then like reeds, not hair),
Was the first man that leapt; cried "Hell is empty,
And all the devils are here!"

PROSPERO   Why, that's my spirit!   215
But was not this nigh shore?

ARIEL   Close by, my master.

PROSPERO But are they, Ariel, safe?

ARIEL   Not a hair perished.
On their sustaining garments not a blemish,
But fresher than before; and as thou bad'st me,
In troops I have dispersed them 'bout the isle.   220
The King's son have I landed by himself,
Whom I left cooling of the air with sighs
In an odd angle of the isle, and sitting,
His arms in this sad knot.
                           [*Illustrates with a gesture.*]

PROSPERO   Of the King's ship,
The mariners, say how thou hast disposed,   225
And all the rest o' th' fleet.

ARIEL   Safely in harbor
Is the King's ship; in the deep nook where once
Thou call'dst me up at midnight to fetch dew
From the still-vexed Bermoothes, there she's hid;
The mariners all under hatches stowed,   230
Who, with a charm joined to their suff'red labor,
I have left asleep. And for the rest o' th' fleet,
Which I dispersed, they all have met again,
And are upon the Mediterranean flote
Bound sadly home for Naples,   235
Supposing that they saw the King's ship wracked
And his great person perish.

PROSPERO   Ariel, thy charge
Exactly is performed; but there's more work.

213 up-staring standing on end   218 sustaining buoying them up   229 Bermoothes Bermudas   231 suff'red undergone   234 flote sea

What is the time o' th' day?

ARIEL   Past the mid season.

PROSPERO At least two glasses. The time 'twixt six
240   and now
          Must by us both be spent most preciously.

ARIEL Is there more toil? Since thou dost give me
          pains,
          Let me remember thee what thou hast promised,
          Which is not yet performed me.

PROSPERO   How now? Moody?
          What is't thou canst demand?

245 ARIEL   My liberty.

PROSPERO Before the time be out? No more!

ARIEL   I prithee,
          Remember I have done thee worthy service,
          Told thee no lies, made thee no mistakings, served
          Without or grudge or grumblings. Thou did
              promise
          To bate me a full year.

250 PROSPERO   Dost thou forget
          From what a torment I did free thee?

ARIEL   No.

PROSPERO Thou dost; and think'st it much to tread
              the ooze
          Of the salt deep,
          To run upon the sharp wind of the North,
255   To do me business in the veins o' th' earth
          When it is baked with frost.

ARIEL   I do not, sir.

PROSPERO Thou liest, malignant thing! Hast thou
              forgot

239 mid season noon   240 two glasses two o'clock   242 pains hard tasks
243 remember remind   250 bate me reduce my term of service   255 veins
streams   256 baked caked

390

The foul witch Sycorax, who with age and envy
Was grown into a hoop? Hast thou forgot her?

ARIEL No, sir.

PROSPERO   Thou hast. Where was she born? Speak!
   Tell me!   260

ARIEL Sir, in Argier.

PROSPERO   O, was she so? I must
   Once in a month recount what thou hast been,
   Which thou forget'st. This damned witch Sycorax,
   For mischiefs manifold, and sorceries terrible
   To enter human hearing, from Argier,   265
   Thou know'st, was banished. For one thing she did
   They would not take her life. Is not this true?

ARIEL Ay, sir.

PROSPERO This blue-eyed hag was hither brought
   with child
   And here was left by th' sailors. Thou, my slave,   270
   As thou report'st thyself, wast then her servant.
   And, for thou wast a spirit too delicate
   To act her earthy and abhorred commands,
   Refusing her grand hests, she did confine thee,
   By help of her more potent ministers,   275
   And in her most unmitigable rage,
   Into a cloven pine; within which rift
   Imprisoned thou didst painfully remain
   A dozen years; within which space she died
   And left thee there, where thou didst vent thy
     groans   280
   As fast as millwheels strike. Then was this island
   (Save for the son that she did litter here,
   A freckled whelp, hagborn) not honored with
   A human shape.

258 Sycorax (name not found elsewhere; probably derived from Greek *sys*, "sow,"
and *korax*, which means both "raven"—see line 322—and "hook"—hence perhaps
"hoop")   258 envy malice   261 Argier Algiers   269 blue-eyed (referring to the
livid color of the eyelid, a sign of pregnancy)   274 hests commands   275 her
more potent ministers her agents, spirits more powerful than thou

ARIEL   Yes, Caliban her son.

285 PROSPERO Dull thing, I say so! He, that Caliban
         Whom now I keep in service. Thou best know'st
         What torment I did find thee in; thy groans
         Did make wolves howl and penetrate the breasts
         Of ever-angry bears. It was a torment
290   To lay upon the damned, which Sycorax
         Could not again undo. It was mine art,
         When I arrived and heard thee, that made gape
         The pine, and let thee out.

ARIEL   I thank thee, master.

PROSPERO If thou more murmur'st, I will rend an oak
295   And peg thee in his knotty entrails till
         Thou hast howled away twelve winters.

ARIEL   Pardon, master.
         I will be correspondent to command
         And do my spriting gently.

PROSPERO   Do so; and after two days
         I will discharge thee.

ARIEL   That's my noble master!
300   What shall I do? Say what? What shall I do?

PROSPERO Go make thyself like a nymph o' th' sea. Be
           subject
         To no sight but thine and mine, invisible
         To every eyeball else. Go take this shape
         And hither come in't. Go! Hence with diligence!
                                        Exit [Ariel].
305   Awake, dear heart, awake! Thou hast slept well.
         Awake!

MIRANDA The strangeness of your story put
         Heaviness in me.

---

295 **his** its   297 **correspondent** obedient   298 **do my spriting gently** render
graciously my services as a spirit   302–3 **invisible/To every eyeball else** (Ariel
is invisible to everyone in the play except Prospero; Henslowe's *Diary*, an
Elizabethan stage account, lists "a robe for to go invisible")

PROSPERO   Shake it off. Come on.
We'll visit Caliban, my slave, who never
Yields us kind answer.

MIRANDA   'Tis a villain, sir,
I do not love to look on.

PROSPERO   But as 'tis,   310
We cannot miss him. He does make our fire,
Fetch in our wood, and serves in offices
That profit us. What, ho! Slave! Caliban!
Thou earth, thou! Speak!

CALIBAN (*Within*)   There's wood enough within.

PROSPERO Come forth, I say! There's other business   315
    for thee.
Come, thou tortoise! When?

          Enter Ariel like a water nymph.

Fine apparition! My quaint Ariel,
Hark in thine ear.   [*Whispers.*]

ARIEL   My lord, it shall be done.   *Exit.*

PROSPERO Thou poisonous slave, got by the devil
    himself
Upon thy wicked dam, come forth!   320

               Enter Caliban.

CALIBAN As wicked dew as e'er my mother brushed
With raven's feather from unwholesome fen
Drop on you both! A southwest blow on ye
And blister you all o'er!

PROSPERO For this, be sure, tonight thou shalt have
    cramps,   325
Side-stitches that shall pen thy breath up. Urchins
Shall, for that vast of night that they may work,

311 **miss** do without   316 **When** (expression of impatience)   317 **quaint**
ingenious   326 **Urchins** goblins in the shape of hedgehogs   327 **vast of night**
... **work** (the long, empty stretch of night during which malignant spirits are
allowed to be active)

All exercise on thee; thou shalt be pinched
As thick as honeycomb, each pinch more stinging
Than bees that made 'em.

330 CALIBAN   I must eat my dinner.
This island's mine by Sycorax my mother,
Which thou tak'st from me. When thou cam'st first,
Thou strok'st me and made much of me; wouldst
      give me
Water with berries in't; and teach me how
335 To name the bigger light, and how the less,
That burn by day and night. And then I loved thee
And showed thee all the qualities o' th' isle,
The fresh springs, brine pits, barren place and
      fertile.
Cursed be I that did so! All the charms
340 Of Sycorax—toads, beetles, bats, light on you!
For I am all the subjects that you have,
Which first was mine own king; and here you sty
      me
In this hard rock, whiles you do keep from me
The rest o' th' island.

PROSPERO   Thou most lying slave,
Whom stripes may move, not kindness! I have
345   used thee
(Filth as thou art) with humane care, and lodged
      thee
In mine own cell till thou didst seek to violate
The honor of my child.

CALIBAN O ho, O ho! Would't had been done!
350 Thou didst prevent me; I had peopled else
This isle with Calibans.

MIRANDA   Abhorrèd slave,
Which any print of goodness wilt not take,
Being capable of all ill! I pitied thee,

345 **stripes** lashes   351–71 (many editors transfer this speech to Prospero as
inappropriate to Miranda)   353 **capable of all ill** susceptible only to evil
impressions

Took pains to make thee speak, taught thee each
  hour
One thing or other. When thou didst not, savage,   355
Know thine own meaning, but wouldst gabble like
A thing most brutish, I endowed thy purposes
With words that made them known. But thy vile
  race,
Though thou didst learn, had that in't which good
  natures
Could not abide to be with. Therefore wast thou   360
Deservedly confined into this rock, who hadst
Deserved more than a prison.

CALIBAN You taught me language, and my profit on't
Is, I know how to curse. The red plague rid you
For learning me your language!

PROSPERO   Hagseed, hence!   365
Fetch us in fuel. And be quick, thou'rt best,
To answer other business. Shrug'st thou, malice?
If thou neglect'st or dost unwillingly
What I command, I'll rack thee with old cramps,
Fill all thy bones with aches, make thee roar   370
That beasts shall tremble at thy din.

CALIBAN   No, pray thee.
[Aside] I must obey. His art is of such pow'r
It would control my dam's god, Setebos,
And make a vassal of him.

PROSPERO   So, slave; hence!   Exit Caliban.

    Enter Ferdinand; and Ariel (invisible), playing
                  and singing.

              Ariel's song.

    Come unto these yellow sands,   375

364 rid destroy 366 thou'rt best you'd better 369 old plenty of (with an
additional suggestion, "such as old people have") 370 aches (pronounced
"aitches")

> And then take hands.
> Curtsied when you have and kissed
> The wild waves whist,
> Foot it featly here and there;
380 And, sweet sprites, the burden bear.
> Hark! hark!
> > *Burden, dispersedly*. Bow, wow!
> The watchdogs bark.
> > [*Burden, dispersedly*.] Bow, wow!
385 Hark, hark! I hear
> The strain of strutting chanticleer
> Cry cock-a-diddle-dow.

FERDINAND Where should this music be? I' th' air or
th' earth?
> It sounds no more; and sure it waits upon
390 Some god o' th' island. Sitting on a bank,
> Weeping again the King my father's wrack,
> This music crept by me upon the waters,
> Allaying both their fury and my passion
> With its sweet air. Thence I have followed it,
395 Or it hath drawn me rather; but 'tis gone.
> No, it begins again.

Ariel's song.

> Full fathom five thy father lies;
> > Of his bones are coral made;
> Those are pearls that were his eyes;
400 Nothing of him that doth fade
> But doth suffer a sea change
> Into something rich and strange.
> Sea nymphs hourly ring his knell:
> > > > *Burden*. Ding-dong.
405 Hark! Now I hear them—ding-dong bell.

377–78 **kissed/The wild waves whist** i.e., when you have, through the harmony
of kissing in the dance, kissed the wild waves into silence (?); when you have kissed
in the dance, the wild waves being silenced (?)   379 **featly** nimbly   382 **Burden,
dispersedly** (an undersong, coming from all parts of the stage; it imitates the
barking of dogs and perhaps in the end the crowing of a cock)   393 **passion** grief

FERDINAND The ditty does remember my drowned
    father.
  This is no mortal business, nor no sound
  That the earth owes. I hear it now above me.

PROSPERO The fringèd curtains of thine eye advance
  And say what thou seest yond.

MIRANDA   What is't? A spirit?   410
  Lord, how it looks about! Believe me, sir,
  It carries a brave form. But 'tis a spirit.

PROSPERO No, wench; it eats, and sleeps, and hath
    such senses
  As we have, such. This gallant which thou seest
  Was in the wrack; and, but he's something stained   415
  With grief (that's beauty's canker), thou mightst
    call him
  A goodly person. He hath lost his fellows
  And strays about to find 'em.

MIRANDA   I might call him
  A thing divine; for nothing natural
  I ever saw so noble.

PROSPERO   [*Aside*] It goes on, I see,   420
  As my soul prompts it. Spirit, fine spirit, I'll free
    thee
  Within two days for this.

FERDINAND   Most sure, the goddess
  On whom these airs attend! Vouchsafe my prayer
  May know if you remain upon this island,
  And that you will some good instruction give   425
  How I may bear me here. My prime request,
  Which I do last pronounce, is (O you wonder!)
  If you be maid or no?

MIRANDA   No wonder, sir,
  But certainly a maid.

408 owes owns   409 advance raise   423–24 Vouchsafe my prayer ... remain
may my prayer induce you to inform me whether you dwell   426 bear me
conduct myself

FERDINAND   My language? Heavens!
430   I am the best of them that speak this speech,
       Were I but where 'tis spoken.

PROSPERO   How? The best?
       What wert thou if the King of Naples heard thee?

FERDINAND A single thing, as I am now, that
           wonders
       To hear thee speak of Naples. He does hear me;
435   And that he does I weep. Myself am Naples,
       Who with mine eyes, never since at ebb, beheld
       The King my father wracked.

MIRANDA   Alack, for mercy!

FERDINAND Yes, faith, and all his lords, the Duke of
           Milan
       And his brave son being twain.

PROSPERO   [*Aside*] The Duke of Milan
440   And his more braver daughter could control thee,
       If now 'twere fit to do't. At the first sight
       They have changed eyes. Delicate Ariel,
       I'll set thee free for this. [*To Ferdinand*] A word,
           good sir.
       I fear you have done yourself some wrong. A
           word!

445   MIRANDA Why speaks my father so ungently? This
       Is the third man that e'er I saw; the first
       That e'er I sighed for. Pity move my father
       To be inclined my way!

FERDINAND   O, if a virgin,
       And your affection not gone forth, I'll make you
       The Queen of Naples.

450   PROSPERO   Soft, sir! One word more.
       [*Aside*] They are both in either's pow'rs. But this
           swift business

433 **single** (1) solitary (2) helpless   439 **son** (the only time Antonio's son is
mentioned)   439 **twain** two (of these lords)   440 **control** refute   442 **changed
eyes** i.e., fallen in love   444 **done yourself some wrong** said what is not so

I must uneasy make, lest too light winning
Make the prize light. [*To Ferdinand*] One word
    more! I charge thee
That thou attend me. Thou dost here usurp
The name thou ow'st not, and hast put thyself   455
Upon this island as a spy, to win it
From me, the lord on't.

FERDINAND   No, as I am a man!

MIRANDA There's nothing ill can dwell in such a
    temple.
If the ill spirit have so fair a house,
Good things will strive to dwell with't.

PROSPERO   Follow me.   460
    [*To Miranda*] Speak not you for him; he's a traitor.
    [*To Ferdinand*] Come!
I'll manacle thy neck and feet together;
Sea water shalt thou drink; thy food shall be
The fresh-brook mussels, withered roots, and husks
Wherein the acorn cradled. Follow!

FERDINAND   No.   465
I will resist such entertainment till
Mine enemy has more pow'r.
                    He draws, and is charmed from moving.

MIRANDA   O dear father,
Make not too rash a trial of him, for
He's gentle and not fearful.

PROSPERO   What, I say,
My foot my tutor? [*To Ferdinand*] Put thy sword
    up, traitor—   470
Who mak'st a show but dar'st not strike, thy
    conscience
Is so possessed with guilt! Come, from thy ward!
For I can here disarm thee with this stick
And make thy weapon drop.

455 **ow'st** ownest   469 **gentle and not fearful** of noble birth and no coward
470 **My foot my tutor** am I to be instructed by my inferior   472 **ward** fighting
posture   473 **stick** i.e., his wand

MIRANDA   Beseech you, father!

PROSPERO Hence! Hang not on my garments.

475 MIRANDA   Sir, have pity.
I'll be his surety.

PROSPERO   Silence! One word more
Shall make me chide thee, if not hate thee. What,
An advocate for an impostor? Hush!
Thou think'st there is no more such shapes as he,
480 Having seen but him and Caliban. Foolish wench!
To th' most of men this is a Caliban,
And they to him are angels.

MIRANDA   My affections
Are then most humble. I have no ambition
To see a goodlier man.

PROSPERO [To Ferdinand] Come on, obey!
485 Thy nerves are in their infancy again
And have no vigor in them.

FERDINAND   So they are.
My spirits, as in a dream, are all bound up.
My father's loss, the weakness which I feel,
The wrack of all my friends, nor this man's threats
490 To whom I am subdued, are but light to me,
Might I but through my prison once a day
Behold this maid. All corners else o' th' earth
Let liberty make use of. Space enough
Have I in such a prison.

PROSPERO [Aside] It works. [To Ferdinand] Come on.
[To Ariel] Thou hast done well, fine Ariel! [To
495   Ferdinand] Follow me.
[To Ariel] Hark what thou else shalt do me.

MIRANDA   Be of comfort.
My father's of a better nature, sir,
Than he appears by speech. This is unwonted
Which now came from him.

485 nerves sinews

400

PROSPERO   Thou shalt be as free
  As mountain winds; but then exactly do   500
  All points of my command.

ARIEL   To th' syllable.

PROSPERO [*To Ferdinand*] Come, follow. [*To Miranda*]
  Speak not for him.   *Exeunt*.

ACT II

Scene I. [*Another part of the island.*]

Enter Alonso, Sebastian, Antonio, Gonzalo,
Adrian, Francisco, and others.

GONZALO Beseech you, sir, be merry. You have cause
  (So have we all) of joy; for our escape
  Is much beyond our loss. Our hint of woe
  Is common; every day some sailor's wife,
  The master of some merchant, and the merchant,   5
  Have just our theme of woe. But for the miracle,
  I mean our preservation, few in millions
  Can speak like us. Then wisely, good sir, weigh
  Our sorrow with our comfort.

ALONSO   Prithee, peace.

SEBASTIAN [*Aside to Antonio*] He receives comfort   10
  like cold porridge.

ANTONIO [*Aside to Sebastian*] The visitor will not
  give him o'er so.

SEBASTIAN Look, he's winding up the watch of his
  wit; by and by it will strike.   15

500 **then** till then II.i.3 **hint** of occasion for 5 **master of some merchant**
captain of some merchant ship 9 **with** against 10–11 **He receives comfort**
like cold porridge ("He" is Alonso; pun on "peace," since porridge contained
peas) 12 **visitor** spiritual comforter 13 **give him o'er so** release him so easily

GONZALO Sir—

SEBASTIAN [*Aside to Antonio*] One. Tell.

GONZALO When every grief is entertained, that's offered
Comes to th' entertainer—

20 SEBASTIAN A dollar.

GONZALO Dolor comes to him, indeed. You have
spoken truer than you purposed.

SEBASTIAN You have taken it wiselier than I meant
you should.

25 GONZALO Therefore, my lord—

ANTONIO Fie, what a spendthrift is he of his tongue!

ALONSO I prithee, spare.

GONZALO Well, I have done. But yet—

SEBASTIAN He will be talking.

30 ANTONIO Which, of he or Adrian, for a good wager,
first begins to crow?

SEBASTIAN The old cock.

ANTONIO The cock'rel.

SEBASTIAN Done! The wager?

35 ANTONIO A laughter.

SEBASTIAN A match!

ADRIAN Though this island seem to be desert—

ANTONIO Ha, ha, ha!

SEBASTIAN So, you're paid.

---

17 **One. Tell** he has struck one; keep count   18 **that's** that which is   23 **wiselier**
i.e., understood my pun   27 **spare** spare your words   30–31 **Which, of he or
Adrian ... first** let's wager which of the two, Gonzalo or Adrian, will first
32 **old cock** i.e., Gonzalo   33 **cock'rel** young cock; i.e., Adrian   35 **laughter**
the winner will have the laugh on the loser

ADRIAN Uninhabitable and almost inaccessible— 40

SEBASTIAN Yet—

ADRIAN Yet—

ANTONIO He could not miss't.

ADRIAN It must needs be of subtle, tender, and delicate
temperance. 45

ANTONIO Temperance was a delicate wench.

SEBASTIAN Ay, and a subtle, as he most learnedly
delivered.

ADRIAN The air breathes upon us here most sweetly.

SEBASTIAN As if it had lungs, and rotten ones. 50

ANTONIO Or as 'twere perfumed by a fen.

GONZALO Here is everything advantageous to life.

ANTONIO True; save means to live.

SEBASTIAN Of that there's none, or little.

GONZALO How lush and lusty the grass looks! How 55
green!

ANTONIO The ground indeed is tawny.

SEBASTIAN With an eye of green in't.

ANTONIO He misses not much.

SEBASTIAN No; he doth but mistake the truth totally. 60

GONZALO But the rarity of it is—which is indeed
almost beyond credit—

SEBASTIAN As many vouched rarities are.

GONZALO That our garments, being, as they were,
drenched in the sea, hold, notwithstanding, their 65
freshness and glosses, being rather new-dyed than
stained with salt water.

45 temperance climate (in the next line, a girl's name) 58 eye spot (also
perhaps Gonzalo's eye)

ANTONIO If but one of his pockets could speak, would it not say he lies?

70 SEBASTIAN Ay, or very falsely pocket up his report.

GONZALO Methinks our garments are now as fresh as when we put them on first in Afric, at the marriage of the King's fair daughter Claribel to the King of Tunis.

75 SEBASTIAN 'Twas a sweet marriage, and we prosper well in our return.

ADRIAN Tunis was never graced before with such a paragon to their queen.

GONZALO Not since widow Dido's time.

80 ANTONIO Widow? A pox o' that! How came that "widow" in? Widow Dido!

SEBASTIAN What if he had said "widower Aeneas" too? Good Lord, how you take it!

ADRIAN "Widow Dido" said you? You make me
85 study of that. She was of Carthage, not of Tunis.

GONZALO This Tunis, sir, was Carthage.

ADRIAN Carthage?

GONZALO I assure you, Carthage.

ANTONIO His word is more than the miraculous
90 harp.

SEBASTIAN He hath raised the wall and houses too.

ANTONIO What impossible matter will he make easy next?

68–69 If but ... he lies i.e., the inside of Gonzalo's pockets are stained 70 Ay, or ... his report unless the pocket were, like a false knave, to receive without resentment the imputation that it is unstained 78 to for 81–82 Widow Dido ... "widower Aeneas" (the point of the joke is that Dido was a widow, but one doesn't ordinarily think of her that way; and the same with Aeneas) 89–90 miraculous harp (of Amphion, which only raised the *walls* of Thebes; whereas Gonzalo has rebuilt the whole ancient city of Carthage by identifying it mistakenly with contemporary Tunis)

SEBASTIAN I think he will carry this island home in his
pocket and give it his son for an apple. 95

ANTONIO And, sowing the kernels of it in the sea,
bring forth more islands.

GONZALO Ay!

ANTONIO Why, in good time.

GONZALO [*To Alonso*] Sir, we were talking that our 100
garments seem now as fresh as when we were at
Tunis at the marriage of your daughter, who is now
Queen.

ANTONIO And the rarest that e'er came there.

SEBASTIAN Bate, I beseech you, widow Dido. 105

ANTONIO O, widow Dido? Ay, widow Dido!

GONZALO Is not, sir, my doublet as fresh as the first
day I wore it? I mean, in a sort.

ANTONIO That "sort" was well fished for.

GONZALO When I wore it at your daughter's marriage. 110

ALONSO You cram these words into mine ears against
The stomach of my sense. Would I had never
Married my daughter there! For, coming thence,
My son is lost; and, in my rate, she too,
Who is so far from Italy removed 115
I ne'er again shall see her. O thou mine heir
Of Naples and of Milan, what strange fish
Hath made his meal on thee?

FRANCISCO   Sir, he may live.
I saw him beat the surges under him
And ride upon their backs. He trod the water, 120
Whose enmity he flung aside, and breasted

99 **Why, in good time** (hearing Gonzalo reaffirm his false statement about Tunis
and Carthage, Antonio suggests that Gonzalo will indeed, at the first opportunity,
carry this island home in his pocket) 105 **Bate** except 108 **in a sort** so to
speak 111–12 **against/The stomach of my sense** i.e., though my mind (or
feelings) have no appetite for them 114 **rate** opinion

The surge most swol'n that met him. His bold head
'Bove the contentious waves he kept, and oared
Himself with his good arms in lusty stroke
To th' shore, that o'er his wave-worn basis
125   bowed,
As stooping to relieve him. I not doubt
He came alive to land.

ALONSO   No, no, he's gone.

SEBASTIAN [*To Alonso*] Sir, you may thank yourself for
     this great loss,
That would not bless our Europe with your
     daughter,
130   But rather loose her to an African,
Where she, at least, is banished from your eye
Who hath cause to wet the grief on't.

ALONSO   Prithee, peace.

SEBASTIAN You were kneeled to and importuned
     otherwise
By all of us; and the fair soul herself
135   Weighed, between loathness and obedience, at
Which end o' th' beam should bow. We have lost
     your son,
I fear, forever. Milan and Naples have
Moe widows in them of this business' making
Than we bring men to comfort them.
The fault's your own.

140   ALONSO   So is the dear'st o' th' loss.

GONZALO My Lord Sebastian,
The truth you speak doth lack some gentleness,
And time to speak it in. You rub the sore
When you should bring the plaster.

SEBASTIAN   Very well.

125 **his** its   125 **wave-worn basis bowed** (the image is of a guardian cliff on the
shore)   135–36 **Weighed, between ... should bow** (Claribel's unwillingness to
marry was outweighed by her obedience to her father)   138 **Moe** more
140 **dear'st** (intensifies the meaning of the noun)

ANTONIO And most chirurgeonly.   145

GONZALO [*To Alonso*] It is foul weather in us all, good
    sir,
When you are cloudy.

SEBASTIAN [*Aside to Antonio*] Foul weather?

ANTONIO [*Aside to Sebastian*]   Very foul.

GONZALO Had I plantation of this isle, my lord—

ANTONIO He'd sow't with nettle seed.

SEBASTIAN   Or docks, or mallows.

GONZALO And were the king on't, what would I do?   150

SEBASTIAN Scape being drunk for want of wine.

GONZALO I' th' commonwealth I would by contraries
    Execute all things. For no kind of traffic
    Would I admit; no name of magistrate;
    Letters should not be known; riches, poverty,   155
    And use of service, none; contract, succession,
    Bourn, bound of land, tilth, vineyard, none;
    No use of metal, corn, or wine, or oil;
    No occupation; all men idle, all;
    And women too, but innocent and pure;   160
    No sovereignty.

SEBASTIAN   Yet he would be king on't.

ANTONIO The latter end of his commonwealth forgets
    the beginning.

GONZALO All things in common nature should
    produce
    Without sweat or endeavor. Treason, felony,   165
    Sword, pike, knife, gun, or need of any engine
    Would I not have; but nature should bring forth,
    Of it own kind, all foison, all abundance,

145 **chirurgeonly** like a surgeon 148 **plantation** colonization (Antonio then
puns by taking the word in its other sense) 152 **contraries** in contrast to the
usual customs 153 **traffic** trade 155 **Letters** learning 156 **service** servants
156 **succession** inheritance 157 **Bourn** boundary 157 **tilth** agriculture
166 **engine** weapon 168 **it** its 168 **foison** abundance

To feed my innocent people.

170   SEBASTIAN No marrying 'mong his subjects?

ANTONIO None, man, all idle—whores and knaves.

GONZALO I would with such perfection govern, sir,
    T' excel the Golden Age.

SEBASTIAN [*Loudly*]   Save his Majesty!

ANTONIO [*Loudly*] Long live Gonzalo!

GONZALO   And—do you mark me, sir?

ALONSO Prithee, no more. Thou dost talk nothing to
175   me.

GONZALO I do well believe your Highness; and did
    it to minister occasion to these gentlemen, who
    are of such sensible and nimble lungs that they
    always use to laugh at nothing.

180   ANTONIO 'Twas you we laughed at.

GONZALO Who in this kind of merry fooling am noth-
    ing to you; so you may continue, and laugh at
    nothing still.

ANTONIO What a blow was there given!

185   SEBASTIAN And it had not fall'n flatlong.

GONZALO You are gentlemen of brave mettle; you
    would lift the moon out of her sphere if she would
    continue in it five weeks without changing.

Enter Ariel [invisible] playing solemn music.

SEBASTIAN We would so, and then go a-batfowling.

190   ANTONIO Nay, good my lord, be not angry.

---

177 **minister occasion** afford opportunity   178 **sensible** sensitive   185 **And if**
185 **flatlong** with the flat of the sword   189 **We would so, and then go a-**
batfowling we would use the moon for a lantern in order to hunt birds at night by
attracting them with a light and beating them down with bats; i.e., in order to gull
simpletons like you (?)

GONZALO No, I warrant you; I will not adventure my
    discretion so weakly. Will you laugh me asleep?
    For I am very heavy.

ANTONIO Go sleep, and hear us.
    [All sleep except Alonso, Sebastian, and Antonio.]

ALONSO What, all so soon asleep? I wish mine eyes   195
    Would, with themselves, shut up my thoughts. I
      find
    They are inclined to do so.

SEBASTIAN   Please you, sir,
    Do not omit the heavy offer of it.
    It seldom visits sorrow; when it doth,
    It is a comforter.

ANTONIO   We two, my lord,   200
    Will guard your person while you take your rest,
    And watch your safety.

ALONSO   Thank you. Wondrous heavy.
    [Alonso sleeps. Exit Ariel.]

SEBASTIAN What a strange drowsiness possesses them!

ANTONIO It is the quality o' th' climate.

SEBASTIAN   Why
    Doth it not then our eyelids sink? I find not   205
    Myself disposed to sleep.

ANTONIO   Nor I: my spirits are nimble.
    They fell together all, as by consent.
    They dropped as by a thunderstroke. What might,
    Worthy Sebastian—O, what might?—No more!
    And yet methinks I see it in thy face,   210
    What thou shouldst be. Th' occasion speaks thee,
      and
    My strong imagination sees a crown
    Dropping upon thy head.

191–92 **adventure my discretion so weakly** risk my reputation for good sense
because of your weak wit   198 **omit** neglect   211 **speaks** speaks to

SEBASTIAN   What? Art thou waking?

ANTONIO Do you not hear me speak?

SEBASTIAN   I do; and surely
215 It is a sleepy language, and thou speak'st
Out of thy sleep. What is it thou didst say?
This is a strange repose, to be asleep
With eyes wide open; standing, speaking, moving,
And yet so fast asleep.

ANTONIO   Noble Sebastian,
220 Thou let'st thy fortune sleep—die, rather; wink'st
Whiles thou art waking.

SEBASTIAN   Thou dost snore distinctly;
There's meaning in thy snores.

ANTONIO I am more serious than my custom. You
Must be so too, if heed me; which to do
Trebles thee o'er.

225 SEBASTIAN   Well, I am standing water.

ANTONIO I'll teach you how to flow.

SEBASTIAN   Do so. To ebb
Hereditary sloth instructs me.

ANTONIO   O,
If you but knew how you the purpose cherish
Whiles thus you mock it; how, in stripping it,
230 You more invest it! Ebbing men, indeed,
Most often do so near the bottom run
By their own fear or sloth.

SEBASTIAN   Prithee, say on.
The setting of thine eye and cheek proclaim
A matter from thee; and a birth, indeed,
Which throes thee much to yield.

235 ANTONIO   Thus, sir:

220 **wink'st** dost shut thine eyes   224 **if heed** if you heed   225 **Trebles thee o'er** makes thee three times what thou now art   229–30 **in stripping ... invest it** in stripping the purpose off you, you clothe yourself with it all the more   234 **matter** matter of importance   235 **throes thee much** costs thee much pain

Although this lord of weak remembrance, this
Who shall be of as little memory
When he is earthed, hath here almost persuaded
(For he's a spirit of persuasion, only
Professes to persuade) the King his son's alive,   240
'Tis as impossible that he's undrowned
As he that sleeps here swims.

SEBASTIAN   I have no hope
That he's undrowned.

ANTONIO   O, out of that no hope
What great hope have you! No hope that way is
Another way so high a hope that even   245
Ambition cannot pierce a wink beyond,
But doubt discovery there. Will you grant with me
That Ferdinand is drowned?

SEBASTIAN   He's gone.

ANTONIO   Then tell me,
Who's the next heir of Naples?

SEBASTIAN   Claribel.

ANTONIO She that is Queen of Tunis; she that dwells   250
Ten leagues beyond man's life; she that from
  Naples
Can have no note—unless the sun were post;
The man i' th' moon's too slow—till newborn chins
Be rough and razorable; she that from whom
We all were sea-swallowed, though some cast
  again,   255

236 **remembrance** memory   237 **of as little memory** as little remembered
238 **earthed** buried   239–40 **only/Professes to persuade** his only profession is
to persuade   246–47 **Ambition cannot ... discovery there** the eye of ambition
can reach no farther, but must even doubt the reality of what it discerns thus
far   251 **ten leagues beyond man's life** it would take a lifetime to get within ten
leagues of the place   252 **post** messenger   253–54 **till newborn chins/Be rough
and razorable** till babies just born be ready to shave   254–55 **she that ... were
sea-swallowed** she who is separated from Naples by so dangerous a sea that we
were ourselves swallowed up by it   255 **cast** cast upon the shore (with a
suggestion of its theatrical meaning that leads to the next metaphor)

And, by that destiny, to perform an act
Whereof what's past is prologue, what to come,
In yours and my discharge.

SEBASTIAN   What stuff is this? How say you?
'Tis true my brother's daughter's Queen of Tunis;
260 So is she heir of Naples; 'twixt which regions
There is some space.

ANTONIO   A space whose ev'ry cubit
Seems to cry out "How shall that Claribel
Measure us back to Naples? Keep in Tunis,
And let Sebastian wake!" Say this were death
That now hath seized them, why, they were no
265   worse
Than now they are. There be that can rule Naples
As well as he that sleeps; lords that can prate
As amply and unnecessarily
As this Gonzalo; I myself could make
270 A chough of as deep chat. O, that you bore
The mind that I do! What a sleep were this
For your advancement! Do you understand me?

SEBASTIAN Methinks I do.

ANTONIO   And how does your content
Tender your own good fortune?

SEBASTIAN   I remember
You did supplant your brother Prospero.

275 ANTONIO   True.
And look how well my garments sit upon me,
Much feater than before. My brother's servants
Were then my fellows; now they are my men.

SEBASTIAN But, for your conscience—

280 ANTONIO Ay, sir, where lies that? If 'twere a kibe,
'Twould put me to my slipper; but I feel not
This deity in my bosom. Twenty consciences

270 **chough** jackdaw (a bird that can be taught to speak a few words)
274 **Tender** regard (i.e., do you like your good fortune) 277 **feater** more
becomingly 280 **kibe** chilblain on the heel

That stand 'twixt me and Milan, candied be they
And melt, ere they molest! Here lies your brother,
No better than the earth he lies upon—   285
If he were that which now he's like, that's dead—
Whom I with this obedient steel (three inches
    of it)
Can lay to bed forever; whiles you, doing thus,
To the perpetual wink for aye might put
This ancient morsel, this Sir Prudence, who   290
Should not upbraid our course. For all the rest,
They'll take suggestion as a cat laps milk;
They'll tell the clock to any business that
We say befits the hour.

SEBASTIAN   Thy case, dear friend,
Shall be my precedent. As thou got'st Milan,   295
I'll come by Naples. Draw thy sword. One stroke
Shall free thee from the tribute which thou payest,
And I the King shall love thee.

ANTONIO   Draw together;
And when I rear my hand, do you the like,
To fall it on Gonzalo.   [*They draw.*]

SEBASTIAN   O, but one word!   300

          Enter Ariel [invisible] with music and song.

ARIEL My master through his art foresees the danger
    That you, his friend, are in, and sends me forth
    (For else his project dies) to keep them living.
                              Sings in Gonzalo's ear.

              While you here do snoring lie,
              Open-eyed conspiracy   305
                  His time doth take.
              If of life you keep a care,
              Shake off slumber and beware.
                  Awake, awake!

286 **that's dead** that is, if he were dead   289 **wink** eye-shut   293 **tell the clock**
say yes

ANTONIO Then let us both be sudden.

310 GONINGALO [*Wakes*]   Now good angels
     Preserve the King!   [*The others wake.*]

ALONSO Why, how now? Ho, awake! Why are you
     drawn?
     Wherefore this ghastly looking?

GONZALO   What's the matter?

SEBASTIAN Whiles we stood here securing your repose,
315   Even now, we heard a hollow burst of bellowing
     Like bulls, or rather lions. Did't not wake you?
     It struck mine ear most terribly.

ALONSO   I heard nothing.

ANTONIO O, 'twas a din to fright a monster's ear,
     To make an earthquake! Sure it was the roar
     Of a whole herd of lions.

320 ALONSO   Heard you this, Gonzalo?

GONZALO Upon mine honor, sir, I heard a humming,
     And that a strange one too, which did awake me.
     I shaked you, sir, and cried. As mine eyes opened,
     I saw their weapons drawn. There was a noise,
325   That's verily. 'Tis best we stand upon our guard,
     Or that we quit this place. Let's draw our weapons.

ALONSO Lead off this ground, and let's make further
     search
     For my poor son.

GONZALO   Heavens keep him from these beasts!
     For he is, sure, i' th' island.

ALONSO   Lead away.

330 ARIEL Prospero my lord shall know what I have done.
     So, King, go safely on to seek thy son.   *Exeunt*.

325 **verily** the truth

Scene II. [*Another part of the island.*]

Enter Caliban with a burden of wood. A noise of
thunder heard.

CALIBAN All the infections that the sun sucks up
From bogs, fens, flats, on Prosper fall, and make
   him
By inchmeal a disease! His spirits hear me,
And yet I needs must curse. But they'll nor pinch,
Fright me with urchin shows, pitch me i' th' mire,   5
Nor lead me, like a firebrand, in the dark
Out of my way, unless he bid 'em. But
For every trifle are they set upon me;
Sometime like apes that mow and chatter at me,
And after bite me; then like hedgehogs which   10
Lie tumbling in my barefoot way and mount
Their pricks at my footfall; sometime am I
All wound with adders, who with cloven tongues
Do hiss me into madness.

Enter Trinculo.

                    Lo, now, lo!
Here comes a spirit of his, and to torment me   15
For bringing wood in slowly. I'll fall flat.
Perchance he will not mind me.   [*Lies down.*]

TRINCULO Here's neither bush nor shrub to bear off
any weather at all, and another storm brewing; I
hear it sing i' th' wind. Yond same black cloud,   20
yond huge one, looks like a foul bombard that
would shed his liquor. If it should thunder as it

II.ii.3 **By inchmeal** inch by inch   5 **urchin shows** impish apparitions   6 **like a
firebrand** in the form of a will-o'-the-wisp   9 **mow** make faces   18 **bear off**
ward off   21 **bombard** large leather jug

did before, I know not where to hide my head.
Yond same cloud cannot choose but fall by pail-
25   fuls. What have we here? A man or a fish? Dead
or alive? A fish! He smells like a fish; a very ancient and fishlike smell; a kind of not of the new-
est Poor John. A strange fish! Were I in England
now, as once I was, and had but this fish painted,
30   not a holiday fool there but would give a piece of
silver. There would this monster make a man; any
strange beast there makes a man. When they will
not give a doit to relieve a lame beggar, they will
lay out ten to see a dead Indian. Legged like a man!
35   And his fins like arms! Warm, o' my troth! I do
now let loose my opinion, hold it no longer. This
is no fish, but an islander, that hath lately suffered
by a thunderbolt. [*Thunder.*] Alas, the storm is
come again! My best way is to creep under his
40   gaberdine; there is no other shelter hereabout. Misery acquaints a man with strange bedfellows. I will
here shroud till the dregs of the storm be past.

                    [*Creeps under Caliban's garment.*]

        Enter Stephano, singing, [a bottle in his hand.]

STEPHANO   I shall no more to sea, to sea;
                    Here shall I die ashore.

45   This is a very scurvy tune to sing at a man's funeral. Well, here's my comfort.   *Drinks.*

            The master, the swabber, the boatswain, and I,
                    The gunner, and his mate,
            Loved Mall, Meg, and Marian, and Margery,
50   But none of us cared for Kate.
            For she had a tongue with a tang,
            Would cry to a sailor "Go hang!"
            She loved not the savor of tar nor of pitch;

28 **Poor John** dried hake   29 **painted** i.e., as a sign hung outside a booth at a fair
31 **make a man** (pun: make a man's fortune)   33 **doit** smallest coin

Yet a tailor might scratch her where'er she did itch.
    Then to sea, boys, and let her go hang! 55

This is a scurvy tune too; but here's my comfort.

Drinks.

CALIBAN Do not torment me! O!

STEPHANO What's the matter? Have we devils here? Do you put tricks upon 's with savages and men of Inde, ha? I have not scaped drowning to be 60 afeard now of your four legs. For it hath been said, "As proper a man as ever went on four legs cannot make him give ground;" and it shall be said so again, while Stephano breathes at' nostrils.

CALIBAN The spirit torments me. O! 65

STEPHANO This is some monster of the isle, with four legs, who hath got, as I take it, an ague. Where the devil should he learn our language? I will give him some relief, if it be but for that. If I can recover him, and keep him tame, and get to Naples with 70 him, he's a present for any emperor that ever trod on neat's leather.

CALIBAN Do not torment me, prithee; I'll bring my wood home faster.

STEPHANO He's in his fit now and does not talk after 75 the wisest. He shall taste of my bottle; if he have never drunk wine afore, it will go near to remove his fit. If I can recover him and keep him tame, I will not take too much for him. He shall pay for him that hath him, and that soundly. 80

CALIBAN Thou dost me yet but little hurt. Thou wilt anon; I know it by thy trembling. Now Prosper works upon thee.

STEPHANO Come on your ways, open your mouth;

64 **at' nostrils** at the nostrils   69 **recover** cure   72 **neat's leather** cowhide
79 **not take too much** too much will not be enough   82 **anon** soon   82 **trembling**
(Trinculo is shaking with fear)

85   here is that which will give language to you, cat.
      Open your mouth. This will shake your shaking, I
      can tell you, and that soundly. [*Gives Caliban
      drink.*] You cannot tell who's your friend. Open
      your chaps again.

90   TRINCULO I should know that voice. It should be—
      but he is drowned; and these are devils. O, defend
      me!

      STEPHANO Four legs and two voices—a most delicate
      monster! His forward voice now is to speak well
95   of his friend; his backward voice is to utter foul
      speeches and to detract. If all the wine in my bottle
      will recover him, I will help his ague. Come! [*Gives
      drink.*] Amen! I will pour some in thy other
      mouth.

100   TRINCULO Stephano!

      STEPHANO Doth thy other mouth call me? Mercy,
      mercy! This is a devil, and no monster. I will leave
      him; I have no long spoon.

      TRINCULO Stephano! If thou beest Stephano, touch me
105   and speak to me; for I am Trinculo—be not afeard
      —thy good friend Trinculo.

      STEPHANO If thou beest Trinculo, come forth. I'll pull
      thee by the lesser legs. If any be Trinculo's legs,
      these are they. [*Draws him out from under Cali-
110   ban's garment.*] Thou art very Trinculo indeed!
      How cam'st thou to be the siege of this moon-
      calf? Can he vent Trinculos?

      TRINCULO I took him to be killed with a thunder-
      stroke. But art thou not drowned, Stephano? I
115   hope now thou art not drowned. Is the storm over-
      blown? I hid me under the dead mooncalf's gaber-
      dine for fear of the storm. And art thou living,

85 **cat** (alluding to the proverb "Liquor will make a cat talk")   89 **chaps** jaws
103 **long spoon** (alluding to the proverb "He who sups with [i.e., from the same
dish as] the devil must have a long spoon")   111 **siege** excrement   111–12 **mooncalf** monstrosity

Stephano? O Stephano, two Neapolitans scaped!

STEPHANO Prithee do not turn me about; my stomach
is not constant.   120

CALIBAN [*Aside*] These be fine things, and if they be
   not sprites.
That's a brave god and bears celestial liquor.
I will kneel to him.

STEPHANO How didst thou scape? How cam'st thou
hither? Swear by this bottle how thou cam'st   125
hither. I escaped upon a butt of sack which the
sailors heaved o'erboard—by this bottle which I
made of the bark of a tree with mine own hands
since I was cast ashore.

CALIBAN I'll swear upon that bottle to be thy true   130
subject, for the liquor is not earthly.

STEPHANO Here! Swear then how thou escap'dst.

TRINCULO Swum ashore, man, like a duck. I can swim
like a duck, I'll be sworn.

STEPHANO Here, kiss the book. [*Gives him drink*.]   135
Though thou canst swim like a duck, thou art made
like a goose.

TRINCULO O Stephano, hast any more of this?

STEPHANO The whole butt, man. My cellar is in a
rock by th' seaside, where my wine is hid. How   140
now, mooncalf? How does thine ague?

CALIBAN Hast thou not dropped from heaven?

STEPHANO Out o' th' moon, I do assure thee. I was the
Man i' th' Moon when time was.

CALIBAN I have seen thee in her, and I do adore thee.   145
My mistress showed me thee, and thy dog, and
thy bush.

121 and if if 144 when time was once upon a time 146–47 thee, and thy
dog, and thy bush (the Man in the Moon was banished there, according to
legend, for gathering brushwood with his dog on Sunday)

STEPHANO Come, swear to that; kiss the book. [*Gives him drink*.] I will furnish it anon with new con-
150   tents. Swear. [*Caliban drinks*.]

TRINCULO By this good light, this is a very shallow monster! I afeard of him? A very weak monster! The Man i' th' Moon? A most poor credulous monster! Well drawn, monster, in good sooth!

155 CALIBAN I'll show thee every fertile inch o' th' island; and I will kiss thy foot. I prithee, be my god.

TRINCULO By this light, a most perfidious and drunken monster! When's god's asleep, he'll rob his bottle.

CALIBAN I'll kiss thy foot. I'll swear myself thy sub-
160   ject.

STEPHANO Come on then. Down, and swear!

TRINCULO I shall laugh myself to death at this puppy-headed monster. A most scurvy monster! I could find in my heart to beat him—

165 STEPHANO Come, kiss.

TRINCULO But that the poor monster's in drink. An abominable monster!

CALIBAN I'll show thee the best springs; I'll pluck thee berries;
    I'll fish for thee, and get thee wood enough.
170 A plague upon the tyrant that I serve!
    I'll bear him no more sticks, but follow thee,
    Thou wondrous man.

TRINCULO A most ridiculous monster, to make a won-der of a poor drunkard!

CALIBAN I prithee let me bring thee where crabs
175   grow;
    And I with my long nails will dig thee pignuts,
    Show thee a jay's nest, and instruct thee how

154 **Well drawn** a good pull at the bottle   175 **crabs** crab apples   176 **pignuts** earthnuts

420

To snare the nimble marmoset. I'll bring thee
To clust'ring filberts, and sometimes I'll get thee
Young scamels from the rock. Wilt thou go with
    me?   180

STEPHANO I prithee now, lead the way without any
more talking. Trinculo, the King and all our company else being drowned, we will inherit here. Here,
bear my bottle. Fellow Trinculo, we'll fill him by and
by again.   185

                        Caliban sings drunkenly.

CALIBAN Farewell, master; farewell, farewell!

TRINCULO A howling monster! A drunken monster!

CALIBAN

    No more dams I'll make for fish,
      Nor fetch in firing
      At requiring,   190
    Nor scrape trenchering, nor wash dish.
      'Ban, 'Ban, Ca—Caliban
    Has a new master. Get a new man!

Freedom, high day! High day, freedom! Freedom,
high day, freedom!   195

STEPHANO O brave monster! Lead the way.   *Exeunt*.

ACT III

Scene I. [*In front of Prospero's cell.*]

Enter Ferdinand, bearing a log.

FERDINAND There be some sports are painful, and
    their labor
Delight in them sets off; some kinds of baseness

180 **scamels** (perhaps a misprint for "seamels" or "seamews," a kind of sea bird)
188 **dams** (to catch fish and keep them)   191 **trenchering** trenchers, wooden
plates   III.i.2 **sets off** cancels

Are nobly undergone, and most poor matters
Point to rich ends. This my mean task
5   Would be as heavy to me as odious, but
The mistress which I serve quickens what's dead
And makes my labors pleasures. O, she is
Ten times more gentle than her father's crabbed;
And he's composed of harshness. I must remove
10   Some thousands of these logs and pile them up,
Upon a sore injunction. My sweet mistress
Weeps when she sees me work, and says such
     baseness
Had never like executor. I forget;
But these sweet thoughts do even refresh my
     labors
Most busiest when I do it.

Enter Miranda; and Prospero [behind, unseen].

15   MIRANDA   Alas, now pray you,
Work not so hard! I would the lightning had
Burnt up those logs that you are enjoined to pile!
Pray set it down and rest you. When this burns,
'Twill weep for having wearied you. My father
20   Is hard at study; pray now rest yourself;
He's safe for these three hours.

FERDINAND   O most dear mistress,
The sun will set before I shall discharge
What I must strive to do.

MIRANDA   If you'll sit down,
I'll bear your logs the while. Pray give me that;
I'll carry it to the pile.

25   FERDINAND   No, precious creature,
I had rather crack my sinews, break my back,
Than you should such dishonor undergo
While I sit lazy by.

6 **quickens** brings to life   11 **sore injunction** severe command   13 **forget** i.e.,
my task   15 **Most busiest when I do it** i.e., my thoughts are busiest when I am
(the Folio's **busie lest** has been variously emended; it may refer to "task," line 4,
the understood object in line 13)   19 **weep** i.e., exude resin

MIRANDA   It would become me
As well as it does you; and I should do it
With much more ease; for my good will is to it,   30
And yours it is against.

PROSPERO [*Aside*]   Poor worm, thou art infected!
This visitation shows it.

MIRANDA   You look wearily.

FERDINAND No, noble mistress, 'tis fresh morning with
     me
When you are by at night. I do beseech you,
Chiefly that I might set it in my prayers,   35
What is your name?

MIRANDA   Miranda. O my father,
I have broke your hest to say so!

FERDINAND   Admired Miranda!
Indeed the top of admiration, worth
What's dearest to the world! Full many a lady
I have eyed with best regard, and many a time   40
Th' harmony of their tongues hath into bondage
Brought my too diligent ear. For several virtues
Have I liked several women; never any
With so full soul but some defect in her
Did quarrel with the noblest grace she owed,   45
And put it to the foil. But you, O you,
So perfect and so peerless, are created
Of every creature's best.

MIRANDA   I do not know
One of my sex; no woman's face remember,
Save, from my glass, mine own. Nor have I seen   50
More that I may call men than you, good friend,
And my dear father. How features are abroad
I am skilless of; but, by my modesty

32 **visitation** (1) visit (2) attack of plague (referring to metaphor of "infected")
34 **at night** i.e., even at night when I am very tired   37 **hest** command
37 **Admired Miranda** ("admired" means "to be wondered at"; the Latin
"Miranda" means "wonderful")   45 **owed** owned   46 **put it to the foil** defeated
it   53 **skilless** ignorant

(The jewel in my dower), I would not wish
55   Any companion in the world but you;
Nor can imagination form a shape,
Besides yourself, to like of. But I prattle
Something too wildly, and my father's precepts
I therein do forget.

FERDINAND   I am, in my condition,
60   A prince, Miranda; I do think, a king
(I would not so), and would no more endure
This wooden slavery than to suffer
The fleshfly blow my mouth. Hear my soul speak!
The very instant that I saw you, did
65   My heart fly to your service; there resides,
To make me slave to it; and for your sake
Am I this patient log-man.

MIRANDA   Do you love me?

FERDINAND O heaven, O earth, bear witness to this
                sound,
And crown what I profess with kind event
70   If I speak true! If hollowly, invert
What best is boded me to mischief! I,
Beyond all limit of what else i' th' world,
Do love, prize, honor you.

MIRANDA   I am a fool
To weep at what I am glad of.

PROSPERO   [Aside] Fair encounter
75   Of two most rare affections! Heavens rain grace
On that which breeds between 'em!

FERDINAND   Wherefore weep you?

MIRANDA At mine unworthiness, that dare not offer
What I desire to give, and much less take
What I shall die to want. But this is trifling;
80   And all the more it seeks to hide itself,

57 **like of** like   69 **event** outcome   71 **What best is boded me** whatever good
fortune fate has in store for me   79 **to want** if I lack   79 **trifling** i.e., to speak in
riddles like this

424

The bigger bulk it shows. Hence, bashful cunning,
And prompt me, plain and holy innocence!
I am your wife, if you will marry me;
If not, I'll die your maid. To be your fellow
You may deny me; but I'll be your servant,   85
Whether you will or no.

FERDINAND   My mistress, dearest,
And I thus humble ever.

MIRANDA   My husband then?

FERDINAND Ay, with a heart as willing
As bondage e'er of freedom. Here's my hand.

MIRANDA And mine, with my heart in't; and now
  farewell   90
Till half an hour hence.

FERDINAND   A thousand thousand!
                    Exeunt [Ferdinand and Miranda
                        in different directions].

PROSPERO So glad of this as they I cannot be,
Who are surprised withal; but my rejoicing
At nothing can be more. I'll to my book;
For yet ere suppertime must I perform   95
Much business appertaining.   *Exit.*

Scene II. [*Another part of the island.*]

Enter Caliban, Stephano, and Trinculo.

STEPHANO Tell not me! When the butt is out, we will
  drink water; not a drop before. Therefore bear up
  and board 'em! Servant monster, drink to me.

TRINCULO Servant monster? The folly of this island!

84 **fellow** equal 89 **of freedom** i.e., to win freedom 93 **withal** by it
96 **appertaining** i.e., to my plan III.ii.2–3 **bear up and board 'em** i.e., drink
up

5　　They say there's but five upon this isle; we are three
　　　of them. If th' other two be brained like us, the
　　　state totters.

STEPHANO Drink, servant monster, when I bid thee;
　　　thy eyes are almost set in thy head.

10 TRINCULO Where should they be set else? He were a
　　　brave monster indeed if they were set in his tail.

STEPHANO My man-monster hath drowned his tongue
　　　in sack. For my part, the sea cannot drown me. I
　　　swam, ere I could recover the shore, five-and-thirty
15　　leagues off and on, by this light. Thou shalt be my
　　　lieutenant, monster, or my standard.

TRINCULO Your lieutenant, if you list; he's no stan-
　　　dard.

STEPHANO We'll not run, Monsieur Monster.

20 TRINCULO Nor go neither; but you'll lie like dogs,
　　　and yet say nothing neither.

STEPHANO Mooncalf, speak once in thy life, if thou
　　　beest a good mooncalf.

CALIBAN How does thy honor? Let me lick thy shoe.
25　　I'll not serve him; he is not valiant.

TRINCULO Thou liest, most ignorant monster; I am in
　　　case to justle a constable. Why, thou deboshed
　　　fish thou, was there ever man a coward that hath
　　　drunk so much sack as I today? Wilt thou tell a
30　　monstrous lie, being but half a fish and half a
　　　monster?

CALIBAN Lo, how he mocks me! Wilt thou let him,
　　　my lord?

---

16 **standard** standard-bearer, ensign (pun since Caliban is so drunk he cannot
stand)　17 **if you list** if it please you (with pun on "list" as pertaining to a ship
that leans over to one side)　19–20 **run, lie** (with puns on secondary meanings:
"make water," "excrete")　20 **go** walk　27 **case** fit condition　27 **justle** jostle
27 **deboshed** debauched

TRINCULO "Lord" quoth he? That a monster should
  be such a natural!   35

CALIBAN Lo, lo, again! Bite him to death, I prithee.

STEPHANO Trinculo, keep a good tongue in your head.
  If you prove a mutineer—the next tree! The poor
  monster's my subject, and he shall not suffer in-
  dignity.   40

CALIBAN I thank my noble lord. Wilt thou be pleased
  to hearken once again to the suit I made to thee?

STEPHANO Marry, will I. Kneel and repeat it; I will
  stand, and so shall Trinculo.

Enter Ariel, invisible.

CALIBAN As I told thee before, I am subject to a
    tyrant,   45
  A sorcerer, that by his cunning hath
  Cheated me of the island.

ARIEL Thou liest.

CALIBAN   Thou liest, thou jesting monkey
    thou!
  I would my valiant master would destroy thee.
  I do not lie.   50

STEPHANO Trinculo, if you trouble him any more in's
  tale, by this hand, I will supplant some of your
  teeth.

TRINCULO Why, I said nothing.

STEPHANO Mum then, and no more. Proceed.   55

CALIBAN I say by sorcery he got this isle;
  From me he got it. If thy greatness will
  Revenge it on him—for I know thou dar'st,
  But this thing dare not—

---

35 **natural** idiot   38 **the next tree** i.e., you will be hanged   43 **Marry** (an
expletive, from "By the Virgin Mary")   59 **this thing** i.e., Trinculo

60   STEPHANO That's most certain.

CALIBAN Thou shalt be lord of it, and I'll serve thee.

STEPHANO How now shall this be compassed?
Canst thou bring me to the party?

CALIBAN Yea, yea, my lord! I'll yield him thee asleep,
65   Where thou mayst knock a nail into his head.

ARIEL Thou liest; thou canst not.

CALIBAN What a pied ninny's this! Thou scurvy
patch!
I do beseech thy greatness, give him blows
And take his bottle from him. When that's gone,
He shall drink naught but brine, for I'll not show
70   him
Where the quick freshes are.

STEPHANO Trinculo, run into no further danger! Interrupt the monster one word further and, by this
hand, I'll turn my mercy out o' doors and make a
75   stockfish of thee.

TRINCULO Why, what did I? I did nothing. I'll go farther off.

STEPHANO Didst thou not say he lied?

ARIEL Thou liest.

80   STEPHANO Do I so? Take thou that! [*Strikes Trinculo.*] As you like this, give me the lie another time.

TRINCULO I did not give the lie. Out o' your wits, and
hearing too? A pox o' your bottle! This can sack
and drinking do. A murrain on your monster, and
85   the devil take your fingers!

CALIBAN Ha, ha, ha!

STEPHANO Now forward with your tale. [*To Trinculo.*]
Prithee, stand further off.

---

67 **pied** (referring to Trinculo's parti-colored jester's costume)   67 **patch** clown
71 **quick freshes** springs of fresh water   75 **stockfish** dried cod, softened by
beating   84 **murrain** plague (that infects cattle)

CALIBAN Beat him enough. After a little time
　I'll beat him too.

STEPHANO　　　　　Stand farther. Come, proceed.　　　90

CALIBAN Why, as I told thee, 'tis a custom with him
　I' th' afternoon to sleep. There thou mayst brain
　　him,
　Having first seized his books, or with a log
　Batter his skull, or paunch him with a stake,
　Or cut his wezand with thy knife. Remember　　95
　First to possess his books; for without them
　He's but a sot, as I am, nor hath not
　One spirit to command. They all do hate him
　As rootedly as I. Burn but his books.
　He has brave utensils (for so he calls them)　　100
　Which, when he has a house, he'll deck withal.
　And that most deeply to consider is
　The beauty of his daughter. He himself
　Calls her a nonpareil. I never saw a woman
　But only Sycorax my dam and she;　　　105
　But she as far surpasseth Sycorax
　As great'st does least.

STEPHANO　　　　　Is it so brave a lass?

CALIBAN Ay, lord. She will become thy bed, I
　　warrant,
　And bring thee forth brave brood.

STEPHANO Monster, I will kill this man. His daughter　110
　and I will be King and Queen—save our Graces!—
　and Trinculo and thyself shall be viceroys. Dost
　thou like the plot, Trinculo?

TRINCULO Excellent.

STEPHANO Give me thy hand. I am sorry I beat thee;　115
　but while thou liv'st, keep a good tongue in thy
　head.

94 **paunch** stab in the belly　95 **wezand** windpipe　97 **sot** fool　100 **brave
utensils** fine furnishings (pronounced "útensils")

CALIBAN Within this half hour will he be asleep.
Wilt thou destroy him then?

STEPHANO   Ay, on mine honor.

120 ARIEL This will I tell my master.

CALIBAN Thou mak'st me merry; I am full of pleasure.
Let us be jocund. Will you troll the catch
You taught me but whilere?

STEPHANO At thy request, monster, I will do reason,
125 any reason. Come on, Trinculo, let us sing.   *Sings.*

Flout 'em and scout 'em
And scout 'em and flout 'em!
Thought is free.

CALIBAN That's not the tune.
Ariel plays the tune on a tabor and pipe.

130 STEPHANO What is this same?

TRINCULO This is the tune of our catch, played by the
picture of Nobody.

STEPHANO If thou beest a man, show thyself in thy
likeness. If thou beest a devil, take't as thou list.

135 TRINCULO O, forgive me my sins!

STEPHANO He that dies pays all debts. I defy thee.
Mercy upon us!

CALIBAN Art thou afeard?

STEPHANO No, monster, not I.

140 CALIBAN Be not afeard; the isle is full of noises,
Sounds and sweet airs that give delight and hurt
not.

122 **troll the catch** sing the round   123 **but whilere** just now   124–25 **reason,
any reason** i.e., anything within reason   126 **scout** jeer at   129 s.d. **tabor** small
drum worn at the side   132 **Nobody** (alluding to the picture of No-body—a man
all head, legs, and arms, but without trunk—on the title page of the anonymous
comedy *No-body and Some-body*)

Sometimes a thousand twangling instruments
Will hum about mine ears; and sometime voices
That, if I then had waked after long sleep,
Will make me sleep again; and then, in dreaming,   145
The clouds methought would open and show riches
Ready to drop upon me, that, when I waked,
I cried to dream again.

STEPHANO This will prove a brave kingdom to me,
where I shall have my music for nothing.   150

CALIBAN When Prospero is destroyed.

STEPHANO That shall be by and by; I remember the
story.

TRINCULO The sound is going away; let's follow it, and
after do our work.   155

STEPHANO Lead, monster; we'll follow. I would I could
see this taborer; he lays it on.

TRINCULO [To Caliban] Wilt come? I'll follow Stephano
                                                    Exeunt.

Scene III. [Another part of the island.]

Enter Alonso, Sebastian, Antonio, Gonzalo,
Adrian, Francisco, etc.

GONZALO By'r Lakin, I can go no further, sir;
My old bones aches. Here's a maze trod indeed
Through forthrights and meanders. By your
      patience,
I needs must rest me.

ALONSO   Old lord, I cannot blame thee,
Who am myself attached with weariness   5

158 wilt come (Caliban lingers because the other two are being distracted from
his purpose by the music) III.iii.1 By'r Lakin by Our Lady 3 forthrights
and meanders straight and winding paths 5 attached seized

To th' dulling of my spirits. Sit down and rest.
Even here I will put off my hope, and keep it
No longer for my flatterer. He is drowned
Whom thus we stray to find; and the sea mocks
10   Our frustrate search on land. Well, let him go.

ANTONIO [*Aside to Sebastian*] I am right glad that
     he's so out of hope.
Do not for one repulse forgo the purpose
That you resolved t' effect.

SEBASTIAN [*Aside to Antonio*] The next advantage
Will we take throughly.

ANTONIO [*Aside to Sebastian*] Let it be tonight;
15   For, now they are oppressed with travel, they
Will not nor cannot use such vigilance
As when they are fresh.

SEBASTIAN [*Aside to Antonio*] I say tonight. No more.

*Solemn and strange music; and Prosper on the top
(invisible). Enter several strange Shapes, bringing in a
banquet; and dance about it with gentle actions of
salutations; and, inviting the King etc. to eat, they
depart.*

ALONSO What harmony is this? My good friends,
     hark!

GONZALO Marvelous sweet music!

ALONSO Give us kind keepers, heavens! What were
20   these?

SEBASTIAN A living drollery. Now I will believe
That there are unicorns; that in Arabia

---

14 **throughly** thoroughly   17s.d. **the top** upper stage (or perhaps a playing area
above it)   20 **kind keepers** guardian angels   21 **drollery** puppet show

There is one tree, the phoenix' throne; one phoenix
At this hour reigning there.

ANTONIO   I'll believe both;
And what does else want credit, come to me,   25
And I'll be sworn 'tis true. Travelers ne'er did lie,
Though fools at home condemn 'em.

GONZALO   If in Naples
I should report this now, would they believe me
If I should say I saw such islanders?
(For certes these are people of the island)   30
Who, though they are of monstrous shape, yet note,
Their manners are more gentle, kind, than of
Our human generation you shall find
Many—nay, almost any.

PROSPERO   [*Aside*] Honest lord,
Thou hast said well; for some of you there present   35
Are worse than devils.

ALONSO   I cannot too much muse
Such shapes, such gesture, and such sound,
    expressing
(Although they want the use of tongue) a kind
Of excellent dumb discourse.

PROSPERO   [*Aside*] Praise in departing.

FRANCISCO They vanished strangely.

SEBASTIAN   No matter, since   40
They have left their viands behind; for we have
    stomachs.
Will't please you taste of what is here?

ALONSO   Not I.

GONZALO Faith, sir, you need not fear. When we were
    boys,
Who would believe that there were mountaineers

25 credit believing   36 muse wonder at   39 **Praise in departing** save your
praise for the end

433

Dewlapped like bulls, whose throats had hanging
45   at 'em
Wallets of flesh? Or that there were such men
Whose heads stood in their breasts? Which now
          we find
Each putter-out of five for one will bring us
Good warrant of.

ALONSO   I will stand to, and feed;
50   Although my last, no matter, since I feel
The best is past. Brother, my lord the Duke,
Stand to, and do as we.

Thunder and lightning. Enter Ariel, like a harpy; claps his
wings upon the table; and with a quaint device the
banquet vanishes.

ARIEL You are three men of sin, whom destiny—
That hath to instrument this lower world
55   And what is in't—the never-surfeited sea
Hath caused to belch up you and on this island,
Where man doth not inhabit, you 'mongst men
Being most unfit to live. I have made you mad;
And even with suchlike valor men hang and
          drown
Their proper selves.
                    [*Alonso, Sebastian, etc. draw their swords.*]
60   You fools! I and my fellows
Are ministers of Fate. The elements,
Of whom your swords are tempered, may as well
Wound the loud winds, or with bemocked-at stabs
Kill the still-closing waters, as diminish
One dowle that's in my plume. My fellow
65   ministers

45 **Dewlapped** with skin hanging from the neck (like mountaineers with goiter)
48 **putter-out of five for one** traveler who insures himself by depositing a sum of
money to be repaid fivefold if he returns safely (i.e., any ordinary traveler will
confirm nowadays those reports we used to think fanciful)   52 s.d. **quaint device**
ingenious device (of stage mechanism)   54 **to instrument** as its instrument
59 **suchlike valor** i.e., the courage that comes of madness   62 **tempered**
composed   64 **still-closing** ever closing again (as soon as wounded)   65 **dowle**
bit of down   65 **plume** plumage

Are like invulnerable. If you could hurt,
Your swords are now too massy for your strengths
And will not be uplifted. But remember
(For that's my business to you) that you three
From Milan did supplant good Prospero;   70
Exposed unto the sea, which hath requit it,
Him and his innocent child; for which foul deed
The pow'rs, delaying, not forgetting, have
Incensed the seas and shores, yea, all the creatures,
Against your peace. Thee of thy son, Alonso,   75
They have bereft; and do pronounce by me
Ling'ring perdition (worse than any death
Can be at once) shall step by step attend
You and your ways; whose wraths to guard you
      from,
Which here, in this most desolate isle, else falls   80
Upon your heads, is nothing but heart's sorrow
And a clear life ensuing.

He vanishes in thunder; then, to soft music, enter the Shapes
again, and dance with mocks and mows, and carrying out
the table.

PROSPERO Bravely the figure of this harpy hast thou
      Performed, my Ariel; a grace it had, devouring.
      Of my instruction hast thou nothing bated   85
      In what thou hadst to say. So, with good life
      And observation strange, my meaner ministers
      Their several kinds have done. My high charms
            work,
      And these, mine enemies, are all knit up
      In their distractions. They now are in my pow'r;   90
      And in these fits I leave them, while I visit

66 **If you could hurt** even if you could hurt us 67 **massy** heavy 71 **requit it**
avenged that crime 81 **nothing but heart's sorrow** only repentance (will
protect you from the wrath of these powers) 82 **s.d. mocks and mows** mocking
gestures and grimaces 84 **devouring** i.e., in making the banquet disappear
85 **bated** omitted 86 **good life** good lifelike acting 87 **observation strange**
remarkable attention to my wishes 87 **meaner ministers** i.e., inferior to
Ariel 88 **Their several kinds have done** have acted the parts their natures
suited them for

Young Ferdinand, whom they suppose is drowned,
And his and mine loved darling.   [*Exit above.*]

GONZALO I' th' name of something holy, sir, why
      stand you
    In this strange stare?

95 ALONSO   O, it is monstrous, monstrous!
Methought the billows spoke and told me of it;
The winds did sing it to me; and the thunder,
That deep and dreadful organ pipe, pronounced
The name of Prosper; it did bass my trespass.
100 Therefore my son i' th' ooze is bedded; and
I'll seek him deeper than e'er plummet sounded
And with him there lie mudded.   *Exit.*

SEBASTIAN   But one fiend at a time,
I'll fight their legions o'er!

ANTONIO   I'll be thy second.
          Exeunt [*Sebastian and Antonio*].

GONZALO All three of them are desperate; their great
      guilt,
105 Like poison given to work a great time after,
Now 'gins to bite the spirits. I do beseech you,
That are of suppler joints, follow them swiftly
And hinder them from what this ecstasy
May now provoke them to.

ADRIAN   Follow, I pray you.
          Exeunt omnes.

---

99 **bass my trespass** i.e., made me understand my trespass by turning it into
music for which the thunder provided the bass part   103 **o'er** one after another to
the last   108 **ecstasy** madness

ACT IV

Scene I. [*In front of Prospero's cell.*]

Enter Prospero, Ferdinand, and Miranda.

PROSPERO If I have too austerely punished you,
Your compensation makes amends; for I
Have given you here a third of mine own life,
Or that for which I live; who once again
I tender to thy hand. All thy vexations   5
Were but my trials of thy love, and thou
Hast strangely stood the test. Here, afore heaven,
I ratify this my rich gift. O Ferdinand,
Do not smile at me that I boast her off,
For thou shalt find she will outstrip all praise   10
And make it halt behind her.

FERDINAND   I do believe it
Against an oracle.

PROSPERO Then, as my gift, and thine own acquisition
Worthily purchased, take my daughter. But
If thou dost break her virgin-knot before   15
All sanctimonious ceremonies may
With full and holy rite be minist'red,

IV.i.7 **strangely** wonderfully   9 **boast her off** (includes perhaps idea of showing
her off)   11 **halt** limp   12 **Against an oracle** though an oracle should declare
otherwise   16 **sanctimonious** holy

No sweet aspersion shall the heavens let fall
To make this contract grow; but barren hate,
20   Sour-eyed disdain, and discord shall bestrew
The union of your bed with weeds so loathly
That you shall hate it both. Therefore take heed,
As Hymen's lamps shall light you.

FERDINAND   As I hope
For quiet days, fair issue, and long life,
25   With such love as 'tis now, the murkiest den,
The most opportune place, the strong'st
          suggestion
Our worser genius can, shall never melt
Mine honor into lust, to take away
The edge of that day's celebration
When I shall think or Phoebus' steeds are foun-
30   dered
Or Night kept chained below.

PROSPERO   Fairly spoke.
Sit then and talk with her; she is thine own.
What, Ariel! My industrious servant, Ariel!

Enter Ariel.

ARIEL What would my potent master? Here I am.

PROSPERO Thou and thy meaner fellows your last
35   service
Did worthily perform; and I must use you
In such another trick. Go bring the rabble,
O'er whom I give thee pow'r, here to this place.
Incite them to quick motion; for I must

---

18 **aspersion** blessing (like rain on crops)   19 **grow** become fruitful   23 **As
Hymen's lamps shall light you** i.e., as earnestly as you pray that the torch of
the god of marriage shall burn without smoke (a good omen for wedded happiness)
26 **opportune** (pronounced "oppórtune")   27 **Our worser genius can** our evil
spirit can offer   29 **edge** keen enjoyment   30 **foundered** lamed   30–31 **or
Phoebus' steeds ... below** i.e., that either day will never end or night will never
come   33 **What, Ariel** (summoning Ariel)   37 **rabble** "thy meaner fellows"

Bestow upon the eyes of this young couple 40
Some vanity of mine art. It is my promise,
And they expect it from me.

ARIEL   Presently?

PROSPERO Ay, with a twink.

ARIEL Before you can say "Come" and "Go,"
And breathe twice and cry, "So, so," 45
Each one, tripping on his toe,
Will be here with mop and mow.
Do you love me, master? No?

PROSPERO Dearly, my delicate Ariel. Do not approach
Till thou dost hear me call.

ARIEL   Well; I conceive. *Exit.* 50

PROSPERO Look thou be true. Do not give dalliance
Too much the rein; the strongest oaths are straw
To th' fire i' th' blood. Be more abstemious,
Or else good night your vow!

FERDINAND   I warrant you, sir.
The white cold virgin snow upon my heart 55
Abates the ardor of my liver.

PROSPERO   Well.
Now come, my Ariel; bring a corollary
Rather than want a spirit. Appear, and pertly!
No tongue! All eyes! Be silent.   *Soft music.*

Enter Iris.

IRIS Ceres, most bounteous lady, thy rich leas 60
Of wheat, rye, barley, fetches, oats, and peas;

---

41 **vanity of** illusion conjured up by   47 **mop and mow** gestures and
grimaces   50 **conceive** understand   51 **be true** (Prospero appears to have caught
the lovers in an embrace)   55 **The white cold ... heart** her pure white breast on
mine (?)   56 **liver** (supposed seat of sexual passion)   57 **corollary** surplus (of
spirits)   59 s.d. **Iris** goddess of the rainbow and Juno's messenger
60 **leas** meadows   61 **fetches** vetch (a kind of forage)

Thy turfy mountains, where live nibbling sheep,
And flat meads thatched with stover, them to
     keep;
Thy banks with pionèd and twillèd brims,
65   Which spongy April at thy hest betrims
To make cold nymphs chaste crowns; and thy
     broom groves,
Whose shadow the dismissèd bachelor loves,
Being lasslorn; thy pole-clipt vineyard;
And thy sea-marge, sterile and rocky-hard,
Where thou thyself dost air—the queen o' th'
70   sky,
Whose wat'ry arch and messenger am I,
Bids thee leave these, and with her sovereign grace,

Juno descends.

Here on this grass plot, in this very place,
To come and sport; her peacocks fly amain.
75   Approach, rich Ceres, her to entertain.

Enter Ceres.

CERES Hail, many-colored messenger, that ne'er
Dost disobey the wife of Jupiter,
Who, with thy saffron wings, upon my flow'rs
Diffusest honey drops, refreshing show'rs,
80   And with each end of thy blue bow dost crown
My bosky acres and my unshrubbed down,
Rich scarf to my proud earth. Why hath thy queen
Summoned me hither to this short-grassed green?

IRIS A contract of true love to celebrate

63 **meads thatched with stover** (meadows covered with a kind of grass used for
winter fodder) 64 **pionèd and twillèd brims** (obscure; may refer to the
trenched and ridged edges of banks that have been repaired after the erosions of
winter) 68 **pole-clipt vineyard** i.e., vineyard whose vines grow neatly around
(embrace) poles (through possibly the word is "poll-clipped," i.e., pruned)
70 **air** take the air 70 **queen o' th' sky** Juno 72 s.d. (this direction seems to
come too soon, but the machine may have lowered her very slowly) 74 **amain**
swiftly (peacocks, sacred to Juno, drew her chariot) 81 **bosky** shrubbed

And some donation freely to estate   85
On the blessed lovers.

CERES   Tell me, heavenly bow,
If Venus or her son, as thou dost know,
Do now attend the Queen? Since they did plot
The means that dusky Dis my daughter got,
Her and her blind boy's scandaled company   90
I have forsworn.

IRIS   Of her society
Be not afraid; I met her Deity
Cutting the clouds towards Paphos, and her son
Dove-drawn with her. Here thought they to have
    done
Some wanton charm upon this man and maid,   95
Whose vows are, that no bed-right shall be paid
Till Hymen's torch be lighted. But in vain;
Mars's hot minion is returned again;
Her waspish-headed son has broke his arrows,
Swears he will shoot no more, but play with
    sparrows   100
And be a boy right out.

                    [*Juno alights.*]

CERES   Highest queen of state,
Great Juno, comes; I know her by her gait.

JUNO How does my bounteous sister? Go with me
To bless this twain, that they may prosperous be
And honored in their issue.   105

                    They sing.

JUNO   Honor, riches, marriage blessing,

85 estate bestow   89 dusky Dis my daughter got (alluding to the abduction of
Proserpine by Pluto [Dis], god of the underworld)   90 scandaled scandalous
93 Paphos (in Cyprus, center of Venus' cult)   98 Mars's hot minion is
returned again i.e., Mars' lustful mistress (Venus) is on her way back to Paphos
99 waspish-headed son (Cupid is irritable and stings with his arrows)   101 a
boy right out an ordinary boy

                    Long continuance, and increasing,
                    Hourly joys be still upon you!
                    Juno sings her blessings on you.
110   [CERES]   Earth's increase, foison plenty,
                    Barns and garners never empty,
                    Vines with clust'ring bunches growing,
                    Plants with goodly burden bowing;
                    Spring come to you at the farthest
115   In the very end of harvest.
                    Scarcity and want shall shun you,
                    Ceres' blessing so is on you.

       FERDINAND This is a most majestic vision, and
                    Harmonious charmingly. May I be bold
                    To think these spirits?

120   PROSPERO   Spirits, which by mine art
                    I have from their confines called to enact
                    My present fancies.

       FERDINAND   Let me live here ever!
                    So rare a wond'red father and a wise
                    Makes this place Paradise.

       Juno and Ceres whisper, and send Iris on employment.

       PROSPERO   Sweet now, silence!
125   Juno and Ceres whisper seriously.
                    There's something else to do. Hush and be mute,
                    Or else our spell is marred.

       IRIS You nymphs, called Naiades, of the windring
                    brooks,
                    With your sedged crowns and ever-harmless looks,
130   Leave your crisp channels, and on this green land
                    Answer your summons; Juno does command.
                    Come, temperate nymphs, and help to celebrate
                    A contract of true love; be not too late.

       108 still ever   110 foison abundance   114-15 Spring come to you ... harvest
       i.e., may there be no winter in your lives   123 wond'red possessed of wonders;
       i.e., both wonderful and wonder-working, and therefore to be wondered at
       128 windring winding and wandering (?)   130 crisp rippling

Enter certain Nymphs.

You sunburned sicklemen, of August weary,
Come hither from the furrow and be merry.   135
Make holiday; your rye-straw hats put on,
And these fresh nymphs encounter everyone
In country footing.

*Enter certain Reapers, properly habited. They join with
the Nymphs in a graceful dance; towards the end whereof
Prospero starts suddenly and speaks; after which, to a
strange, hollow, and confused noise, they heavily vanish.*

PROSPERO [*Aside*] I had forgot that foul conspiracy
Of the beast Caliban and his confederates   140
Against my life. The minute of their plot
Is almost come. [*To the Spirits*] Well done!
Avoid! No more!

FERDINAND This is strange. Your father's in some
passion
That works him strongly.

MIRANDA   Never till this day
Saw I him touched with anger so distempered.   145

PROSPERO You do look, my son, in a movèd sort,
As if you were dismayed; be cheerful, sir.
Our revels now are ended. These our actors,
As I foretold you, were all spirits and
Are melted into air, into thin air;   150
And, like the baseless fabric of this vision,
The cloud-capped towers, the gorgeous palaces,
The solemn temples, the great globe itself,
Yea, all which it inherit, shall dissolve,

138 footing dance   138 s.d. speaks (breaking the spell, which depends on silence)
138 s.d. heavily reluctantly   142 Avoid begone   145 distempered violent
146 movèd sort troubled state   154 it inherit occupy it

155 And, like this insubstantial pageant faded,
Leave not a rack behind. We are such stuff
As dreams are made on, and our little life
Is rounded with a sleep. Sir, I am vexed.
Bear with my weakness; my old brain is troubled.
160 Be not disturbed with my infirmity.
If you be pleased, retire into my cell
And there repose. A turn or two I'll walk
To still my beating mind.

FERDINAND, MIRANDA   We wish your peace.
                    Exit [Ferdinand with Miranda].

PROSPERO Come with a thought! I thank thee, Ariel.
    Come.

Enter Ariel.

ARIEL Thy thoughts I cleave to. What's thy pleasure?

165 PROSPERO   Spirit,
    We must prepare to meet with Caliban.

ARIEL Ay, my commander. When I presented Ceres,
    I thought to have told thee of it, but I feared
    Lest I might anger thee.

PROSPERO Say again, where didst thou leave these
170   varlets?

ARIEL I told you, sir, they were red-hot with drinking;
    So full of valor that they smote the air
    For breathing in their faces, beat the ground
    For kissing of their feet; yet always bending
175 Towards their project. Then I beat my tabor;
    At which like unbacked colts they pricked their
        ears,
    Advanced their eyelids, lifted up their noses
    As they smelt music. So I charmed their ears

156 **rack** wisp of cloud   164 **I thank thee, Ariel** (for the masque?)   167 **presented** acted the part of (?) introduced (?)   170 **varlets** ruffians   174 **bending** directing their steps   176 **unbacked** unbroken   177 **Advanced** lifted up

That calflike they my lowing followed through
Toothed briers, sharp furzes, pricking goss, and
   thorns,   180
Which ent'red their frail shins. At last I left them
I' th' filthy mantled pool beyond your cell,
There dancing up to th' chins, that the foul lake
O'erstunk their feet.

PROSPERO   This was well done, my bird.
Thy shape invisible retain thou still.   185
The trumpery in my house, go bring it hither
For stale to catch these thieves.

ARIEL   I go, I go.   *Exit*.

PROSPERO A devil, a born devil, on whose nature
Nurture can never stick; on whom my pains,
Humanely taken, all, all lost, quite lost!   190
And as with age his body uglier grows,
So his mind cankers. I will plague them all,
Even to roaring.

    Enter Ariel, loaden with glistering apparel, etc.

       Come, hang them on this line.

    [*Prospero and Ariel remain, invisible.*] *Enter*
    Caliban, Stephano, and Trinculo, all wet.

CALIBAN Pray you tread softly, that the blind mole
   may not
Hear a foot fall. We now are near his cell.   195

STEPHANO Monster, your fairy, which you say is a
harmless fairy, has done little better than played
the Jack with us.

TRINCULO Monster, I do smell all horse piss, at which
my nose is in great indignation.   200

180 **goss** gorse 182 **filthy mantled** covered with filthy scum 186 **trumpery**
(the "glistering apparel" mentioned in the next stage direction) 187 **stale** decoy
193 **line** lime tree (linden) 198 **Jack** (1) knave (2) jack-o'-lantern,
will-o'-the-wisp

STEPHANO So is mine. Do you hear, monster? If I
should take a displeasure against you, look you—

TRINCULO Thou wert but a lost monster.

CALIBAN Good my lord, give me thy favor still.
205   Be patient, for the prize I'll bring thee to
Shall hoodwink this mischance. Therefore speak
        softly.
All's hushed as midnight yet.

TRINCULO Ay, but to lose our bottles in the pool—

STEPHANO There is not only disgrace and dishonor in
210   that, monster, but an infinite loss.

TRINCULO That's more to me than my wetting. Yet this
is your harmless fairy, monster.

STEPHANO I will fetch off my bottle, though I be o'er
ears for my labor.

215 CALIBAN Prithee, my king, be quiet. Seest thou here?
This is the mouth o' th' cell. No noise, and enter.
Do that good mischief which may make this island
Thine own forever, and I, thy Caliban,
For aye thy footlicker.

220 STEPHANO Give me thy hand. I do begin to have
bloody thoughts.

TRINCULO O King Stephano! O peer! O worthy
Stephano, look what a wardrobe here is for thee!

CALIBAN Let it alone, thou fool! It is but trash.

225 TRINCULO O, ho, monster! We know what belongs to
a frippery. O King Stephano!

STEPHANO Put off that gown, Trinculo! By this hand,
I'll have that gown!

206 **hoodwink** put out of sight 213–14 **o'er ears** i.e., over my ears in water
222 **peer** (alluding to the song "King Stephen was and a worthy peer;/His
breeches cost him but a crown," quoted in *Othello* II.iii.) 226 **frippery** old-
clothes shop; i.e., we are good judges of castoff clothes

TRINCULO Thy Grace shall have it.

CALIBAN The dropsy drown this fool! What do you   230
    mean
  To dote thus on such luggage? Let't alone,
  And do the murder first. If he awake,
  From toe to crown he'll fill our skins with pinches,
  Make us strange stuff.

STEPHANO Be you quiet, monster. Mistress line, is not   235
  this my jerkin? [*Takes it down.*] Now is the jerkin
  under the line. Now, jerkin, you are like to lose
  your hair and prove a bald jerkin.

TRINCULO Do, do! We steal by line and level, and't
  like your Grace.   240

STEPHANO I thank thee for that jest. Here's a garment
  for't. Wit shall not go unrewarded while I am king
  of this country. "Steal by line and level" is an excellent pass of pate. There's another garment for't.

TRINCULO Monster, come put some lime upon your   245
  fingers, and away with the rest.

CALIBAN I will have none on't. We shall lose our time
  And all be turned to barnacles, or to apes
  With foreheads villainous low.

STEPHANO Monster, lay-to your fingers; help to bear   250
  this away where my hogshead of wine is, or I'll turn
  you out of my kingdom. Go to, carry this.

TRINCULO And this.

STEPHANO Ay, and this.

231 **luggage** useless encumbrances   236 **jerkin** kind of jacket   237 **under the line** pun: (1) under the lime tree (2) under the equator   238 **bald jerkin** (sailors proverbially lost their hair from fevers contracted while crossing the equator)   239 **Do, do** fine, fine   239 **by line and level** by plumb line and carpenter's level; i.e., according to rule (with pun on "line")   239–40 **and't like** if it please   244 **pass of pate** sally of wit   245 **lime** birdlime (which is sticky; thieves have sticky fingers)   248 **barnacles** kind of geese supposed to have developed from shellfish

A noise of hunters heard. Enter divers Spirits in shape of
dogs and hounds, hunting them about; Prospero and
Ariel setting them on.

255 PROSPERO Hey, Mountain, hey!

ARIEL Silver! There it goes, Silver!

PROSPERO Fury, Fury! There, Tyrant, there! Hark,
hark!

[*Caliban, Stephano, and Trinculo are driven out.*]

Go, charge my goblins that they grind their joints
With dry convulsions, shorten up their sinews
With agèd cramps, and more pinch-spotted make
260   them
Than pard or cat o' mountain.

ARIEL   Hark, they roar!

PROSPERO Let them be hunted soundly. At this hour
Lies at my mercy all mine enemies.
Shortly shall all my labors end, and thou
265 Shalt have the air at freedom. For a little,
Follow, and do me service.   *Exeunt.*

---

259 **dry convulsions** (such as come when the joints are dry from old age)
260 **agèd** i.e., such as old people have   261 **pard or cat o' mountain** leopard or
catamount

ACT V

Scene I. [*In front of Prospero's cell.*]

Enter Prospero in his magic robes, and Ariel.

PROSPERO Now does my project gather to a head.
My charms crack not, my spirits obey, and time
Goes upright with his carriage. How's the day?

ARIEL On the sixth hour, at which time, my lord,
You said our work should cease.

PROSPERO   I did say so   5
When first I raised the tempest. Say, my spirit,
How fares the King and 's followers?

ARIEL   Confined together
In the same fashion as you gave in charge,
Just as you left them—all prisoners, sir,
In the line grove which weather-fends your cell.   10
They cannot budge till your release. The King,
His brother, and yours abide all three distracted,
And the remainder mourning over them,
Brimful of sorrow and dismay; but chiefly
Him that you termed, sir, the good old Lord
     Gonzalo.   15
His tears runs down his beard like winter's drops
From eaves of reeds. Your charm so strongly
     works 'em,
That if you now beheld them, your affections

V.i.2–3 time/Goes upright with his carriage time does not stoop under his
burden (because there is so little left to do)   10 weather-fends protects from the
weather   11 till your release until released by you   17 eaves of reeds i.e., a
thatched roof

449

    Would become tender.

PROSPERO   Dost thou think so, spirit?

ARIEL Mine would, sir, were I human.

20 PROSPERO   And mine shall.
    Hast thou, which art but air, a touch, a feeling
    Of their afflictions, and shall not myself,
    One of their kind, that relish all as sharply,
    Passion as they, be kindlier moved than thou art?
    Though with their high wrongs I am struck to th'
25   quick,
    Yet with my nobler reason 'gainst my fury
    Do I take part. The rarer action is
    In virtue than in vengeance. They being penitent,
    The sole drift of my purpose doth extend
30   Not a frown further. Go, release them, Ariel.
    My charms I'll break, their senses I'll restore,
    And they shall be themselves.

ARIEL   I'll fetch them, sir.
                         Exit.

PROSPERO Ye elves of hills, brooks, standing lakes,
      and groves,
    And ye that on the sands with printless foot
35   Do chase the ebbing Neptune, and do fly him
    When he comes back; you demi-puppets that
    By moonshine do the green sour ringlets make,
    Whereof the ewe not bites; and you whose pastime
    Is to make midnight mushrumps, that rejoice
40   To hear the solemn curfew; by whose aid
    (Weak masters though ye be) I have bedimmed
    The noontide sun, called forth the mutinous winds,
    And 'twixt the green sea and the azured vault
    Set roaring war; to the dread rattling thunder

24 **Passion** (verb) 35 **fly him** fly with him 37 **green sour ringlets** ("fairy rings," little circles of rank grass supposed to be formed by the dancing of fairies) 39 **mushrumps** mushrooms 41 **masters** masters of supernatural power

Have I given fire and rifted Jove's stout oak   45
With his own bolt; the strong-based promontory
Have I made shake and by the spurs plucked up
The pine and cedar; graves at my command
Have waked their sleepers, oped, and let 'em forth
By my so potent art. But this rough magic   50
I here abjure; and when I have required
Some heavenly music (which even now I do)
To work mine end upon their senses that
This airy charm is for, I'll break my staff,
Bury it certain fathoms in the earth,   55
And deeper than did ever plummet sound
I'll drown my book.   *Solemn music.*

*Here enters Ariel before; then Alonso, with a frantic
     gesture, attended by Gonzalo; Sebastian and Antonio in
     like manner, attended by Adrian and Francisco. They all
     enter the circle which Prospero had made, and there stand
     charmed; which Prospero observing, speaks.*

A solemn air, and the best comforter
To an unsettled fancy, cure thy brains,
Now useless, boiled within thy skull! There stand,   60
For you are spell-stopped.
Holy Gonzalo, honorable man,
Mine eyes, ev'n sociable to the show of thine,
Fall fellowly drops. The charm dissolves apace;
And as the morning steals upon the night,   65
Melting the darkness, so their rising senses
Begin to chase the ignorant fumes that mantle
Their clearer reason. O good Gonzalo,
My true preserver, and a loyal sir
To him thou follow'st, I will pay thy graces   70
Home both in word and deed. Most cruelly
Didst thou, Alonso, use me and my daughter.

47 **spurs** roots   51 **required** asked for   53 **their senses that** the senses of those
whom   58 **and** which is   63–64 **sociable to the show ... drops** associating
themselves with the (tearful) appearance of your eyes, shed tears in
sympathy   70–71 **pay thy graces/ Home** repay thy favors thoroughly

Thy brother was a furtherer in the act.
Thou art pinched for't now, Sebastian. Flesh and
    blood,
75   You, brother mine, that entertained ambition,
Expelled remorse and nature; whom, with
    Sebastian
(Whose inward pinches therefore are most strong),
Would here have killed your king, I do forgive thee,
Unnatural though thou art. Their understanding
80   Begins to swell, and the approaching tide
Will shortly fill the reasonable shore,
That now lies foul and muddy. Not one of them
That yet looks on me or would know me. Ariel,
Fetch me the hat and rapier in my cell.
85   I will discase me, and myself present
As I was sometime Milan. Quickly, spirit!
Thou shalt ere long be free.
                    [*Exit Ariel and returns immediately.*]

Ariel sings and helps to attire him.

Where the bee sucks, there suck I;
In a cowslip's bell I lie;
90   There I couch when owls do cry.
On the bat's back I do fly
After summer merrily.
Merrily, merrily shall I live now
Under the blossom that hangs on the bough.

PROSPERO Why, that's my dainty Ariel! I shall miss
95   thee,
But yet thou shalt have freedom; so, so, so.
To the King's ship, invisible as thou art!
There shalt thou find the mariners asleep
Under the hatches. The master and the boatswain
100   Being awake, enforce them to this place,
And presently, I prithee.

76 **remorse** pity 76 **nature** natural feeling 85 **discase** disrobe 101 **pre-**
sently immediately

ARIEL I drink the air before me, and return
　　Or ere your pulse twice beat.　　　　*Exit*.

GONZALO All torment, trouble, wonder, and amaze-
　　　ment
　　Inhabits here. Some heavenly power guide us　　105
　　Out of this fearful country!

PROSPERO　　　　　　　　Behold, sir King,
　　The wrongèd Duke of Milan, Prospero.
　　For more assurance that a living prince
　　Does now speak to thee, I embrace thy body,
　　And to thee and thy company I bid　　　　110
　　A hearty welcome.

ALONSO　　　　　　Whe'r thou be'st he or no,
　　Or some enchanted trifle to abuse me,
　　As late I have been, I not know. Thy pulse
　　Beats, as of flesh and blood; and, since I saw thee,
　　Th' affliction of my mind amends, with which,　　115
　　I fear, a madness held me. This must crave
　　(And if this be at all) a most strange story.
　　Thy dukedom I resign and do entreat
　　Thou pardon me my wrongs. But how should
　　　Prospero
　　Be living and be here?

PROSPERO　　　　　　　First, noble friend,　　120
　　Let me embrace thine age, whose honor cannot
　　Be measured or confined.

GONZALO　　　　　　　Whether this be
　　Or be not, I'll not swear.

PROSPERO　　　　　　　You do yet taste
　　Some subtleties o' th' isle, that will not let you
　　Believe things certain. Welcome, my friends all.　　125
　　[*Aside to Sebastian and Antonio*] But you, my
　　　brace of lords, were I so minded,

111 Whe'r whether 112 trifle apparition 116 crave require (to account for it) 117 And if this be at all if this is really happening 124 subtleties deceptions (referring to pastries made to look like something else—e.g., castles made out of sugar)

453

I here could pluck his Highness' frown upon you,
And justify you traitors. At this time
I will tell no tales.

SEBASTIAN [*Aside*] The devil speaks in him.

PROSPERO   No.
130 For you, most wicked sir, whom to call brother
Would even infect my mouth, I do forgive
Thy rankest fault—all of them; and require
My dukedom of thee, which perforce I know
Thou must restore.

ALONSO   If thou beest Prospero,
135 Give us particulars of thy preservation;
How thou hast met us here, whom three hours
    since
Were wracked upon this shore; where I have lost
(How sharp the point of this remembrance is!)
My dear son Ferdinand.

PROSPERO   I am woe for't, sir.

140 ALONSO Irreparable is the loss, and patience
Says it is past her cure.

PROSPERO   I rather think
You have not sought her help, of whose soft grace
For the like loss I have her sovereign aid
And rest myself content.

ALONSO   You the like loss?

145 PROSPERO As great to me, as late, and supportable
To make the dear loss, have I means much weaker
Than you may call to comfort you; for I
Have lost my daughter.

ALONSO   A daughter?
O heavens, that they were living both in Naples,

---

128 **justify** prove   139 **woe** sorry   145 **As great to me, as late** as great to me
as your loss, and as recent   145 **supportable** (pronounced "súpportable")
146 **dear** (intensifies the meaning of the noun)

The King and Queen there! That they were, I wish   150
Myself were mudded in that oozy bed
Where my son lies. When did you lose your
    daughter?

PROSPERO In this last tempest. I perceive these lords
  At this encounter do so much admire
  That they devour their reason, and scarce think   155
  Their eyes do offices of truth, their words
  Are natural breath. But, howsoev'r you have
  Been justled from your senses, know for certain
  That I am Prospero, and that very duke
  Which was thrust forth of Milan, who most strangely   160
  Upon this shore, where you were wracked, was
    landed
  To be the lord on't. No more yet of this;
  For 'tis a chronicle of day by day,
  Not a relation for a breakfast, nor
  Befitting this first meeting. Welcome, sir;   165
  This cell's my court. Here have I few attendants,
  And subjects none abroad. Pray you look in.
  My dukedom since you have given me again,
  I will requite you with as good a thing,
  At least bring forth a wonder to content ye   170
  As much as me my dukedom.

Here Prospero discovers Ferdinand and
Miranda playing at chess.

MIRANDA Sweet lord, you play me false.

FERDINAND   No, my dearest love,
  I would not for the world.

MIRANDA Yes, for a score of kingdoms you should
    wrangle,
  And I would call it fair play.

154 **admire** wonder   156 **do offices** perform services   167 **abroad** i.e., on the
island   171 s.d. **discovers** reveals (by opening a curtain at the back of the
stage)   174–75 **for a score of kingdoms … play** i.e., if we were playing for
stakes just short of the world, you would protest as now; but then, the issue being
important, I would call it fair play so much do I love you (?)

175 ALONSO   If this prove
    A vision of the island, one dear son
    Shall I twice lose.

    SEBASTIAN   A most high miracle!

    FERDINAND Though the seas threaten, they are merciful.
    I have cursed them without cause.   [*Kneels.*]

    ALONSO   Now all the blessings
180 Of a glad father compass thee about!
    Arise, and say how thou cam'st here.

    MIRANDA   O, wonder!
    How many goodly creatures are there here!
    How beauteous mankind is! O brave new world
    That has such people in't!

    PROSPERO   'Tis new to thee.

    ALONSO What is this maid with whom thou wast at
185   play?
    Your eld'st acquaintance cannot be three hours.
    Is she the goddess that hath severed us
    And brought us thus together?

    FERDINAND   Sir, she is mortal;
    But by immortal providence she's mine.
190 I chose her when I could not ask my father
    For his advice, nor thought I had one. She
    Is daughter to this famous Duke of Milan,
    Of whom so often I have heard renown
    But never saw before; of whom I have
195 Received a second life; and second father
    This lady makes him to me.

    ALONSO   I am hers.
    But, O, how oddly will it sound that I
    Must ask my child forgiveness!

    PROSPERO   There, sir, stop.
    Let us not burden our remembrance with
    A heaviness that's gone.

186 **eld'st** longest

GONZALO   I have inly wept,   200
  Or should have spoke ere this. Look down, you gods,
  And on this couple drop a blessèd crown!
  For it is you that have chalked forth the way
  Which brought us hither.

ALONSO   I say amen, Gonzalo.

GONZALO Was Milan thrust from Milan that his issue   205
  Should become kings of Naples? O, rejoice
  Beyond a common joy, and set it down
  With gold on lasting pillars. In one voyage
  Did Claribel her husband find at Tunis,
  And Ferdinand her brother found a wife   210
  Where he himself was lost; Prospero his dukedom
  In a poor isle; and all of us ourselves
  When no man was his own.

ALONSO [*To Ferdinand and Miranda*] Give me your
      hands.
  Let grief and sorrow still embrace his heart
  That doth not wish you joy.

GONZALO   Be it so! Amen!   215

      Enter Ariel, with the Master and Boatswain
                amazedly following.

  O, look, sir; look, sir! Here is more of us!
  I prophesied if a gallows were on land,
  This fellow could not drown. Now, blasphemy,
  That swear'st grace o'erboard, not an oath on shore?
  Hast thou no mouth by land? What is the news?   220

BOATSWAIN The best news is that we have safely found
  Our king and company; the next, our ship,
  Which, but three glasses since, we gave out split,
  Is tight and yare and bravely rigged as when
  We first put out to sea.

214 **still** forever   219 **That swear'st grace o'erboard** that (at sea) swearest
enough to cause grace to be withdrawn from the ship   223 **glasses** hours
224 **yare** shipshape

225 ARIEL   [*Aside to Prospero*] Sir, all this service
        Have I done since I went.

    PROSPERO   [*Aside to Ariel*] My tricksy spirit!

    ALONSO These are not natural events; they strengthen
        From strange to stranger. Say, how came you hither?

    BOATSWAIN If I did think, sir, I were well awake,
230   I'd strive to tell you. We were dead of sleep
        And (how we know not) all clapped under hatches;
        Where, but even now, with strange and several
            noises
        Of roaring, striking, howling, jingling chains,
        And moe diversity of sounds, all horrible,
235   We were awaked; straightway at liberty;
        Where we, in all our trim, freshly beheld
        Our royal, good, and gallant ship, our master
        Cap'ring to eye her. On a trice, so please you,
        Even in a dream, were we divided from them
        And were brought moping hither.

240 ARIEL [*Aside to Prospero*]   Was't well done?

    PROSPERO [*Aside to Ariel*] Bravely, my diligence.
        Thou shalt be free.

    ALONSO This is as strange a maze as e'er men trod,
        And there is in this business more than nature
        Was ever conduct of. Some oracle
        Must rectify our knowledge.

245 PROSPERO   Sir, my liege,
        Do not infest your mind with beating on
        The strangeness of this business. At picked leisure,
        Which shall be shortly, single I'll resolve you
        (Which to you shall seem probable) of every
250   These happened accidents; till when, be cheerful
        And think of each thing well. [*Aside to Ariel*]

232 **several** various   234 **moe** more   238 **Cap'ring to eye** dancing to see
240 **moping** in a daze   244 **conduct** conductor   248–50 **single I'll resolve ...
accidents** I myself will solve the problems (and my story will make sense to you)
concerning each and every incident that has happened

Come hither, spirit.
Set Caliban and his companions free.
Untie the spell. [*Exit Ariel.*] How fares my gracious
  sir?
There are yet missing of your company
Some few odd lads that you remember not.   255

Enter Ariel, driving in Caliban, Stephano, and
Trinculo, in their stolen apparel.

STEPHANO Every man shift for all the rest, and let no
  man take care for himself; for all is but fortune.
  Coragio, bully-monster, *coragio!*

TRINCULO If these be true spies which I wear in my
  head, here's a goodly sight.   260

CALIBAN O Setebos, these be brave spirits indeed!
  How fine my master is! I am afraid
  He will chastise me.

SEBASTIAN   Ha, ha!
What things are these, my Lord Antonio?
Will money buy 'em?

ANTONIO   Very like. One of them   265
Is a plain fish and no doubt marketable.

PROSPERO Mark but the badges of these men, my lords,
Then say if they be true. This misshapen knave,
His mother was a witch, and one so strong
That could control the moon, make flows and ebbs,   270
And deal in her command without her power.
These three have robbed me, and this demi-devil
(For he's a bastard one) had plotted with them
To take my life. Two of these fellows you
Must know and own; this thing of darkness I   275
Acknowledge mine.

258 **Coragio** courage (Italian)   261 **Setebos** the god of Caliban's mother   267
badges (worn by servants to indicate to whose service they belong; in this case, the
stolen clothes are badges of their rascality)   268 **true** honest   271 **deal in her**
command without her power i.e., dabble in the moon's realm without the
moon's legitimate authority

CALIBAN   I shall be pinched to death.

ALONSO Is not this Stephano, my drunken butler?

SEBASTIAN He is drunk now. Where had he wine?

ALONSO And Trinculo is reeling ripe. Where should
        they
280   Find this grand liquor that hath gilded 'em?
        How cam'st thou in this pickle?

TRINCULO I have been in such a pickle, since I saw
        you last, that I fear me will never out of my bones.
        I shall not fear flyblowing.

285 SEBASTIAN Why, how now, Stephano?

STEPHANO O, touch me not! I am not Stephano, but
        a cramp.

PROSPERO You'd be king o' the isle, sirrah?

STEPHANO I should have been a sore one then.

290 ALONSO This is a strange thing as e'er I looked on.

PROSPERO He is as disproportioned in his manners
        As in his shape. Go, sirrah, to my cell;
        Take with you your companions. As you look
        To have my pardon, trim it handsomely.

295 CALIBAN Ay, that I will; and I'll be wise hereafter,
        And seek for grace. What a thrice-double ass
        Was I to take this drunkard for a god
        And worship this dull fool!

PROSPERO   Go to! Away!

ALONSO Hence, and bestow your luggage where you
        found it.

300 SEBASTIAN Or stole it rather.
                        [Exeunt Caliban, Stephano, and Trinculo.]

284 **flyblowing** (pickling preserves meat from flies)   289 **sore** (1) tyrannical (2)
aching

460

PROSPERO Sir, I invite your Highness and your train
　　To my poor cell, where you shall take your rest
　　For this one night; which, part of it, I'll waste
　　With such discourse as, I not doubt, shall make it
　　Go quick away—the story of my life,   305
　　And the particular accidents gone by
　　Since I came to this isle. And in the morn
　　I'll bring you to your ship, and so to Naples,
　　Where I have hope to see the nuptial
　　Of these our dear-beloved solemnizèd;   310
　　And thence retire me to my Milan, where
　　Every third thought shall be my grave.

ALONSO   I long
　　To hear the story of your life, which must
　　Take the ear strangely.

PROSPERO   I'll deliver all;
　　And promise you calm seas, auspicious gales,   315
　　And sail so expeditious that shall catch
　　Your royal fleet far off. [*Aside to Ariel*] My Ariel,
　　　chick,
　　That is thy charge. Then to the elements
　　Be free, and fare thou well! [*To the others*] Please
　　　you, draw near.   *Exeunt omnes.*

EPILOGUE

Spoken by Prospero

　　Now my charms are all o'erthrown,
　　And what strength I have's mine own,
　　Which is most faint. Now 'tis true
　　I must be here confined by you,
　　Or sent to Naples. Let me not,   5
　　Since I have my dukedom got
　　And pardoned the deceiver, dwell

---

303 **waste** spend 306 **accidents** incidents 310 **solemnizèd** (pronounced
(solémnizèd") 314 **Take** captivate 314 **deliver** tell 316 **catch** catch up with

In this bare island by your spell;
But release me from my bands
10   With the help of your good hands.
Gentle breath of yours my sails
Must fill, or else my project fails,
Which was to please. Now I want
Spirits to enforce, art to enchant;
15   And my ending is despair
Unless I be relieved by prayer,
Which pierces so that it assaults
Mercy itself and frees all faults.
As you from crimes would pardoned be,
20   Let your indulgence set me free.   *Exit*.

FINIS

Epi. 9 **bands** bonds   10 **hands** i.e., applause to break the spell   11 **Gentle
breath** i.e., favorable comment   13 **want** lack   16 **prayer** i.e., this petition

TEXTUAL NOTE

The Tempest was first printed in the Folio of 1623, the First Folio. The Folio text has been carefully edited and punctuated, and it has unusually complete stage directions that are probably Shakespeare's own. *The Tempest* is perhaps the finest text in the Folio, which may be why the Folio editors placed it first in the volume.

The present division into acts and scenes is that of the Folio. The present edition silently modernizes spelling and punctuation, regularizes speech prefixes, translates into English the Folio's Latin designations of act and scene, and makes certain changes in lineation in the interest either of meter, meaning, or a consistent format. Other departures from the Folio are listed below, including changes in lineation that bear upon the meaning. The reading of the present text is given first, in bold, and then the reading of the Folio (F) in roman.

The Scene: an uninhabited island ... Names of the Actors [appears at end of play in F]

I.i.38 s.d. **Enter Sebastian, Antonio, and Gonzalo** [in F occurs after "plague," line 37]

I.ii.173 **princess'** Princesse   201 **lightnings** Lightning   271 **wast** was   282 **she** he   380 **the burden bear** beare/ the burthen

II.i.5 **master** Masters   38-39 **Antonio ... Sebastian** [speakers reversed in F]

III.i.2 **sets** set   15 **busiest** busie lest   93 **withal** with all

III.ii.126 **scout** cout

III.iii.17 **Sebastian: I say tonight. No more** [appears in F after stage direction]   29 **islanders** Islands

IV.i.9 **off** of   13 **gift** guest   124 s.d. **Juno and ... employment** [follows line 127 in F]   193 **them on** on them   231 **Let's** let's

V.i.60 **boiled** boile   72 **Didst** Did   75 **entertained** entertaine   82 **lies** ly   199 **remembrance** remembrances

463

THE EVERYMAN SIGNET SHAKESPEARE

THE SONNETS AND NARRATIVE POEMS

TRAGEDIES
Volume 1

Hamlet
Othello
King Lear
Macbeth

TRAGEDIES
Volume 2

Titus Andronicus
Troilus and Cressida
Julius Caesar
Antony and Cleopatra
Timon of Athens
Coriolanus

HISTORIES
Volume 1

King John
Henry VI Parts 1–3
Richard III

HISTORIES
Volume 2

Richard II
Henry IV Parts 1 and 2
Henry V
Henry VIII

COMEDIES
Volume 1

The Comedy of Errors
The Taming of the Shrew
The Two Gentlemen of Verona
Love's Labor's Lost
Romeo and Juliet
A Midsummer Night's Dream

COMEDIES
Volume 2

The Merchant of Venice
The Merry Wives of Windsor
Much Ado About Nothing
As You Like It
Twelfth Night
All's Well That Ends Well
Measure for Measure

ROMANCES

Pericles
Cymbeline
The Winter's Tale
The Tempest

This book is set in EHRHARDT. The precise origin
of the typeface is unclear. Most of the founts were
probably cut by the Hungarian punch-cutter
Nicholas Kis for the Ehrhardt foundry
in Leipzig, where they were left
for sale in 1689. In 1938 the
Monotype foundry pro-
duced the modern
version.